SOCIAL SCIENCE AND SOCIAL PATHOLOGY

by the same author

THE SOCIAL FOUNDATIONS OF WAGE POLICY
TESTAMENT FOR SOCIAL SCIENCE
FREEDOM UNDER PLANNING

out of print

LAMENT FOR ECONOMICS
PLAN OR NO PLAN

BARBARA WOOTTON

ASSISTED BY

VERA G. SEAL AND ROSALIND CHAMBERS

Social Science and Social Pathology

GREENWOOD PRESS, PUBLISHERS
WESTPORT, CONNECTICUT

Library of Congress Cataloging in Publication Data

Wootton, Barbara, Baroness Wooton of Abinger, 1897-
Social science and social pathology.

Reprint of the ed. published by Allen & Unwin, London.
Bibliography: p.
Includes index.
1. Delinquents--Great Britain. 2. Great Britain--Social conditions. I. Seal, Vera G., joint author. II. Chambers, Rosalind, joint author. III. Title.
[HV6944.W84 1978] 364.2'0942 78-3616
ISBN 0-313-20339-3

Reprinted in 1978 by Greenwood Press, Inc.
51 Riverside Avenue, Westport, CT. 06880

Printed in the United States of America

10 9 8 7 6 5 4 3 2 1

PREFACE

MY original interest in the subject matter of this book (and the same is true of most of the others that I have written) sprang more from practical experience than from academic study. On the one hand it was the unanswerable questions which forced themselves upon my attention as a magistrate, serving in both adult and juvenile courts in London, which first set me thinking about what is really known on the subject of criminality, its nature, its causes and the ways in which it can best be handled; while, on the other hand, eight years' experience as Head of a University Department training students for social work provoked much reflection both about socially unacceptable behaviour in general, and about the changing attitudes of the community towards the 'deviants' who indulge in this.

This interest would, however, have remained sterile had it not been for the generosity of the Nuffield Foundation in making it possible for me to prepare this book. No conventional expression of gratitude can do justice to my sense of indebtedness to that generosity, to which, indeed, I owe what has proved to be one of the most intellectually exciting episodes of my life.

Second only to my indebtedness to the Nuffield Foundation, is my obligation to the University of Birmingham and the Rationalist Press Association for an invitation to deliver the Josiah Mason Lectures in 1955. This enabled me to expose a considerable part of the work, at an early stage, to the criticism of an informed and lively audience. The late Josiah Mason, who was never blessed with children of his own, expressed the hope that he would leave behind him, in the students of the college which he founded, an 'intelligent, earnest, industrious, and truth-loving and truth-seeking progeny for generations to come'—students who are 'willing not only to learn all that can be taught, but in their turn to communicate their knowledge to others, and to apply it to useful purposes for the benefit of the community'.[1] From my experience as Josiah Mason lecturer, I can testify that this hope, nearly a century later, is abundantly fulfilled in the university which has grown out of Mason's college.

The actual text of the book (with the exception of the Appendix II) has been put together entirely by myself, though I have sometimes borrowed whole sentences, with or without modification, from drafts prepared by my colleagues Rosalind Chambers and Vera G. Seal. Both these colleagues would, I think, dissent from some of my emphases and conclusions. But if the writing and the sole responsibility for what is said are mine, chief credit for the solid work upon which my conclusions, right or wrong, are founded is due to the zeal, the insight and the accuracy with which they have pursued their researches. I have incorporated much of their original work; and I am deeply grateful to their watchfulness for the elimination of many errors which would otherwise have found their way into the texts. Miss Seal, in particular, upon whom the heaviest load has fallen, has carried that load throughout with such skill and devotion as to create the illusion that no burden existed. That she

[1] Bunce (1890), pp. 5–6.

has both herself conducted extensive and exacting researches, and, in addition, discharged the dreary task of deciphering a long succession of my illegible drafts demonstrates a combination of qualities that is rare indeed.

All the time that this book has been in the making I have sought, and been freely given, so much help in so many quarters that here I can only mention the few upon whose expertize and goodwill I have drawn particularly heavily. To the Family Welfare Association and many other social agencies I am indebted for allowing my colleagues or myself to draw upon their experience, and to consume the valuable time of their officers. In several cases, research workers have been generous enough to let me see their material in advance of publication: Mr Douglas Woodhouse, in particular, went to considerable trouble to let me have early drafts of the report of his inquiry into problem families, as well as a large number of the case histories collected by himself and his colleagues. The list of references has been largely put into shape by Barbara Kyle and Christine Kennedy in the course of their work on *Social Sciences Documentation*: their ever ready skill quickly disposed of endless questions of tiresome detail, but any anomalies or deficiencies that remain must be ascribed to my failure to follow their guidance. To Dr F. G. Pincus I am indebted for a review of criminological research in Germany. Dr Pincus spent some weeks examining material both in this country and on the continent, and it is in no way his responsibility if not very much emerged which could usefully be included in these pages.

Passages in Chapters I, II, VII, X, and XI have already appeared in *The Twentieth Century* for November 1955, May 1956, and August 1957, and passages in Chapter XI in *The Highway* for March 1956. Chapter X contains extracts from my Presidential Addresses to Aslib in 1953 and 1954, published in *Aslib Proceedings* for November of those years. I am grateful to the editors and publishers of these journals for permission to republish this material here.

Finally, I am glad to acknowledge my debts to the University of London and to Dr D. N. Gibbs and Dr R. G. Andry for permission to quote from unpublished doctoral theses; to the Council of Bedford College for providing me with an academic home in which to work; to the College Librarians for their inexhaustible patience in dealing with interminable requests, and for their skill in mobilizing material from all over this country and occasionally also from overseas; and to Mrs Garrood for the speed, accuracy, and skill with which she typed and re-typed successive versions of the text.

This book is not, in the ordinary sense, a work of research, so much as an assessment of the results of researches already undertaken by others; and I have written, therefore, primarily for the interested layman, who must, in these matters, be the final court of appeal on the expert's work. Inevitably, such an assessment will be coloured by its author's subjective judgments. Yet academic research, and particularly research in the field of human affairs, is likely to be all the better if we are not afraid, from time to time, to stop and ask ourselves where we are going and why. At least it is in that belief that this study has been undertaken; and if, as is to be hoped, one assessment provokes another, one subjectivity may likewise be corrected by another.

It has been well said that the social sciences are not so much sciences in their own right as a 'licence to trespass' over existing academic boundaries. In this book I have undoubtedly used that licence boldly, if not indeed rashly, at the risk of incurring the charge of having explored territory which I have no professional title to enter. I can only say that this has been a deliberately calculated risk. By way of defence, perhaps, I might add that, whilst everyone is now agreed that the solution of practical social problems is nearly always an interdisciplinary matter, it is a no less definite, if sorrowful, fact of experience that the occasions when the spokesmen of different disciplines are both able and willing actively to work together upon a common project are still few. There may, therefore, be something to be said for trying to put scattered pieces of knowledge together inside one mind instead of leaving them distributed amongst many. That, at any rate, is the theory upon which I have acted.

The plan of the book is as follows. Part I, after a rapid survey of the nature and extent of social pathology in contemporary Britain, reviews the findings of a number of studies, and attempts both to assess the evidence relating to several of the currently most popular hypotheses and to estimate the success of some experiments in prediction. Most of the material in this section, it will be noted, is drawn from criminological studies—for the reason that this is the only field of social pathology which has as yet been at all thoroughly cultivated. Part I is, I think, the most objective section of the book: but I fear also the least readable.

Part II deals with changing contemporary attitudes towards unwelcome deviants, and in particular with the tremendous revolution, both in the world at large and amongst professional social workers in particular, which is due to the rise of psychiatry. The basic facts here are reasonably well-known, and what matters is their interpretation. It is, therefore, in Part II that the reader will find the text most strongly coloured by the author's personal judgments; but in this section as much as in the rest of the book I have done my best to set out as fairly as possible the evidence upon which those judgments are based.

In Part III, I have tried to draw conclusions relevant, not only to research in social pathology, but to the social sciences generally. Indeed throughout the whole study three purposes have been kept concurrently in mind, and it has been my object to conduct the whole discussion, as it were, simultaneously upon three distinct planes. On the first, the aim is to assess the contributions which the social sciences have made towards the understanding, and thereby also towards the prevention and cure, of the social problems associated with unacceptable forms of deviant behaviour: on the second, to consider—or perhaps I should rather say to speculate upon—the impact of this new knowledge upon traditional attitudes and institutions; and, on the third, to deduce what is to be learned from experience in this field about the potentialities and the limitations of social research, and about the methods that are likely to serve the social scientist well.

It will be noticed that throughout I have concentrated chiefly upon English and American material. This is for reasons of economy and accessibility. At the same time I have tried to keep a weather eye open to what is going on elsewhere: references to work in other areas, where this seemed particularly significant, will be found scattered through these pages. World-wide coverage, had this been possible, would obviously have been preferable. But in a survey which is primarily interested in significant findings, I am hopeful that not much will have been lost by unavoidable geographical limitation. In the social sciences striking discoveries are still unhappily rare; and communications are now so good that those that are made are likely to have left their mark in all the main centres of research.

It remains to clarify two points of detail. First, the list of references contains only titles which are quoted in the text. Footnote references have been given only in brief, and in a form which will, it is hoped, make for easy reference to the fuller information in this list. Secondly, I have in general followed the practice now common in scientific literature of referring to authors by their plain surnames, without initials, titles or distinction of sex. In a work that necessarily depends so much upon quotations, this practice involves a considerable economy of both words and labour. I have, however, deliberately not followed it quite consistently: where considerations of euphony seemed to demand 'Mr', 'Mrs', or 'Professor' before a name, I have yielded to their claims.

BARBARA WOOTTON

ABINGER COMMON
October 1958

CONTENTS

PART III

CONCLUSIONS

INTRODUCTION

ANTI-SOCIAL behaviour, however defined, causes much unhappiness; and sizeable proportions of both public and private resources are consumed in efforts to deal with it. But to the student of the social sciences the rather sordid topics here discussed have certain attractions; for, in the case of these topics at least, the primary requirements of all useful research—the need to begin by asking sensible questions—can be satisfied with relative ease. In the field of social pathology there can be no dispute as to the questions to which the social scientist is asked to address himself. We wish that people did not behave in ways that are socially troublesome, and we would like to know why they do and what can best be done to stop them. These are commonsense questions which it is plainly worth trying to answer; and enquiry into them should, therefore, at least be innocent of one reproach sometimes directed (and not, perhaps, always unjustly) against contemporary projects of social research. That is the reproach that these projects lack any clear terms of reference, or that they are engaged in the collection of facts for facts' sake, undirected by any intelligible standard of significance—that, in short, in the words of Gunnar Myrdal, 'more and more effort is devoted to less and less important problems'.[1]

At the same time, if the questions to be answered are tolerably clear, it has to be admitted that the mere asking of them begs many others. No one can embark on a discussion of anti-social behaviour without making assumptions as to the criterion by which any specific actions are defined as such; and these assumptions are bound to reflect, not only the norms of a particular culture, but in some degree also, the subjective preferences of the person who makes them. What is understood to be socially unacceptable behaviour varies from place to place and from time to time; and even where standards are much the same, actual manifestations will vary. In criminal behaviour, for example, the vagaries of fashion have an obvious influence; nor are the problems in, say, Burma, or even in France, ever quite the same as they are in Britain. Indeed, to illustrate the individual peculiarities found even in cultures which are otherwise much alike, one need only quote the chapter headings of the section on *Deviation and Deviants* in a standard American work on *Social Pathology*, published in 1951.[2] These read consecutively as follows: *Blindness and the Blind*; *Speech Defects and the Speech Defective*; *Radicalism and Radicals*; *Prostitution and the Prostitute*; *Crime and the Criminal*; *Drunkenness and the Chronic Alcoholic*; *Mental Disorders*. Even if we allow for the cultural gulf represented by the Atlantic ocean, this assortment certainly strikes the British reader as curious. And no less curious is the choice of the eminent German criminologist, who included among criminals a category of 'fanatic psychopaths' described as 'offenders from political conviction' prepared to sacrifice the lives and property of their fellow men if their own ideas demand it, together with 'incurably litigious persons' and those who refuse military service.[3]

[1] Myrdal (1953), p. 237. [2] Lemert (1951). [3] Exner (1949), p. 188.

In the present work the social pathology of contemporary Britain is used as a case-study, and the discussion has, to that extent, a domestic standard of reference. That does not, however, imply a domestic scope. It is true that in social pathology (as indeed is usual in many fields of social investigation) any generalizations that can be made are limited both temporally and geographically. What happens in one street may conform to a different pattern from what happens in another; and, in consequence, theories which look good in one place, far from having world-wide validity, may yet collapse when one turns a corner. Nevertheless, similarities of experience, at least as between one industrial community and another, are such that workers in one area have much to learn from research and from events elsewhere: suggestive hypotheses and thought-provoking parallels are distributed without regard to national or other frontiers. In short, if the questions (though often duplicated elsewhere) are primarily British, the answers may come from anywhere.

In some respects, at least, the norms of this contemporary British culture are clear enough. Plainly ours is a society which believes (or believes that it believes) in hard work, sobriety, ambition, cleanliness, order and social advancement; which sets a high value upon property, and upon the conquest of the material environment; and which, if not strictly monogamous, at least professes a deep concern for the integrity of the biological family. These are, moreover, values which we share with much of the Western industrial world, and which seem to be increasingly admired in many 'underdeveloped' but 'developing' areas both in the East and in Africa; and they are values which are reflected on both sides of the iron curtain. A definition of social pathology, therefore, which sees this as failure to conform to these standards has at least the merit of being widely understood.

There remains, however, the problem of locating the point at which non-conformity ranks as truly pathological. Here public expenditure may serve as a rough and ready criterion, social pathology being, for practical purposes, defined to include all those actions on the prevention of which public money is spent, or the doers of which are punished or otherwise dealt with at the public expense. Such a definition, though far from precise and necessarily inclusive of overlapping categories, would cover, in mid-twentieth century Britain, all forms of crime and delinquency, as well as marital separation, divorce, illegitimacy, failure to maintain oneself or one's family and those habits characteristic of so-called 'problem families' which the public authorities are at pains to discourage. Generously interpreted it could be extended to include also prostitution and intemperance, along with what the National Assistance Act so delicately describes as a lack of a 'settled way of living'.

Even this list, however, will evoke very different reactions in different people. We do not all agree with the way in which public money is spent, and some of us regard as certainly innocent, or at least as purely private matters, some of the actions which are officially and expensively discountenanced. Items in the criminal calendar itself will be differently evaluated by different individuals; nor is it certain that the grading of various crimes which is implied by the scale of penalties attaching to them would commend itself to the majority, let alone to everyone. Many citizens whose personal behaviour could hardly be challenged on social grounds, prefer to look on adult homosexuality as a matter of private taste rather than of public morality; while evasion of customs duties (which incidentally carries very heavy penalties) seldom seems to be regarded as seriously anti-social conduct. Even within the sphere precisely defined by the law, therefore, subjective judgments cannot be shut out. And beyond the limits of that sphere, the meaning of such phrases as 'recognized social norms' becomes more and more elusive, especially where, as in our culture, people have wide freedom to live their lives in whatever way happens to please them.

In matters relating to marriage and the family in particular, the limits of social pathology are to-day imfperectly defined. Here, on the one hand, the law provides that a marriage may be dissolved on the initiative of one of the parties (though not of both acting in concert) in prescribed circumstances; and from this it might fairly be argued that there is nothing inherently pathological or socially deplorable in the use of these facilities, and that a divorce is neither good nor bad in itself, but to be judged, like a decision to resign a job, solely in the light of the circumstances of the particular case, some marriages being better continued and some better ended. Divorced persons are no longer precluded from occupying the highest official positions, in spite of difficulties with the Churches or in Royal circles: indeed, they have been well represented in recent Governments. Yet on the other hand, the prevailing climate of opinion cannot be said to take a neutral view of divorce as such. Fluctuations in the divorce-rate are not generally treated as though they were as much matters of social indifference as changes in feminine hairstyles: the normal presumption in public comment is that upward movements of the rate are to be deplored, and reductions welcomed. And, by the suggested criterion of public expenditure, divorces must be counted as one of the manifestations of social pathology; for considerable sums of public money are spent (as in grants to marriage guidance councils, and in the marital conciliation work of publicly-supported probation officers) in attempts to minimize recourse to the facilities for dissolution of marriage which are legally available. The principle that the maintenance of monogamous marriages is desirable for its own sake must thus be accepted as one of the recognized norms of our society, though not one that ranks so high as in all circumstances to override all other considerations. In the report of the recent Royal Commission on Marriage and Divorce, this principle was in fact implicitly or explicitly accepted by all the Commissioners through all the many permutations and combinations of opinions to which they jointly or severally subscribed. Nevertheless, many responsible persons hold that the institution of marriage has no virtue outside the happiness and welfare of the individual partners involved and their offspring, or of other persons directly affected in any particular instance; and, clearly, anyone who takes this view is bound to feel resistance to any definition of social pathology which automatically includes all cases of voluntary termination of marriage—even though from the same standpoint, the desertion of a dependent partner or the neglect of children may be unhesitatingly classified as anti-social actions.

In the bird's eye view of social pathology in contemporary Britain which occupies most of the following chapter, I have, therefore, included a few basic facts about the trend and distribution of divorces as well as of other forms of marital breakdown; but little is said later about the light thrown by social research upon this particular problem—partly for the reasons already given, and partly on account of another, purely practical consideration. The shape of social research, as of other things, is noticeably influenced by tradition, by accident and by fashion, with the result that some topics have been much more fully explored than have others. The fact, for instance, that criminology is well established as an academic discipline abroad, especially in the United States (and also, though more shakily, in this country) accounts for a preponderance of criminological studies as compared with those which deal with forms of behaviour, such as illegitimacy or prostitution, which are socially unacceptable without ranking as criminal. Again, within the field of criminality, fashion has favoured the study of young offenders rather than of their elders; and fashion also (and in this case a peculiarly British fashion at that) has concentrated attention upon, and encouraged a spate of reports on, what are known as 'problem families'. By contrast, the sociological study of divorce, apart from a few American investigations, has remained comparatively unfashionable; and the same is true of both prostitution and illegitimacy—at least as compared with actual criminality. Traditionally, the problems associated with marital breakdowns are presented in a legal, ethical or religious rather than in a sociological or even a psychological setting; and this is a tradition which the recent Royal Commission on the subject showed no wish to defy. Preferring apparently their own unsupported assumptions, the members of this Commission betrayed hardly a flicker of interest in the sociological aspects of their problem or in the light that might have been thrown upon it by scientifically conducted social research.[1]

Along with fashion, changeable currents of social and political opinion must also be reckoned with as liable to sway the direction of social research. Thus in post-war Britain the myth of the 'welfare state' has turned the minds of investigators away from the study of material want and towards some particular aspects of social policy. Much is written about the social services, practically nothing about poverty. Again, a lively interest in social stratification has lately become very noticeable; yet, in the impressive output of studies on this subject, hardly any attention has been given to the association of class or economic status with socially unwelcome behaviour.

The space accorded to any given topic in the discussion that follows must therefore be seen as a measure, not so much of its true importance in the whole picture, as of the strength of its appeal to social investigators or to public opinion. Any apparently haphazard selection or lop-sided treatment of the

[1] For detailed criticism of the Commission's methods, see McGregor (1957), a work which has done much to make good the deplorable inadequacy of the Commissioners' own work.

various elements in social pathology is to be explained, partly by subjective elements in the definition of what constitutes socially unacceptable behaviour (nothing is said in what follows about Radicals or conscientious objectors); and partly by the necessity of dealing only with what actually exists, limited as this is by fashion, tradition and other social influences.

One further restriction of scope needs also to be observed. This book is intended as a sociological, not as a medical, study: for its author to assume the doctor's rôle would indeed be most improper. Yet, in this health-conscious century, the boundary between the medical and the social becomes daily more and more uncertain. Over large areas the psychiatrist, along with his psychiatrically-orientated satellites, has now usurped the place once occupied by the social reformer and the administrator, if not indeed the judge. Any sociologist, therefore, who sets out to study anti-social behaviour is apt to-day to be nervously hesitant as to how far he is entitled to go. Even within what he still believes to be his own province, psychiatric ways of thought have penetrated deeply, as is shown by recent trends in language. In the vocabulary of the social sciences such terms as 'diagnosis', 'treatment' and 'therapy' have already displaced the ethical formulae of an earlier age; and, here as elsewhere, linguistic trends reflect changes in underlying attitudes, philosophies or unspoken assumptions.

In principle, however, this distinction between the medical and the sociological aspects of anti-social behaviour stands; and in principle this study is concerned with what happens on the sociological, or at least on the non-medical, side of the line. But the practical application of this principle proves a tricky business, for, in the midst of present uncertainties, opinions are bound to differ as to just how much ground should be reserved for medical expertize. Echoes of the controversy which has long raged over the McNaghten Rules can be heard grumbling throughout the territory through which the present investigation has to travel: indeed, the issues—practical and philosophical and moral—raised by the rapid growth of psychiatric empires, and by the hazy definition of their frontiers, is the main theme of Part II of this book. But, where boundaries are so ill-defined, one party alone can hardly claim to settle where they should run. Without explorations from both the lay and the medical sides, the limits within which social pathology is exclusively a doctor's problem can hardly be correctly defined.

PART I

A REVIEW OF THE CONTEMPORARY SITUATION AND OF RESEARCH FINDINGS

CHAPTER I

The Social Pathology of England and Wales

A CASE STUDY

I

THE following figures give some idea of the known frequency of the main types of social pathology in contemporary England and Wales:

(1) Lawbreaking	With 735,288 persons found guilty in the criminal courts in 1955.[1] Of these convictions, 107,446 involving 101,359 separate individuals were for indictable offences.
(2) Illegitimacy	With 31,145 illegitimate live births occurring in 1955.
(3) Divorce	With 26,816 marriages terminated (including those annulled) in 1955.
(4) Marital separations other than divorces	With 13,019 maintenance or separation orders made in magistrates' courts in 1955.
(5) Children, other than offenders, committed to the care of 'fit persons', or placed under supervision or sent to approved schools as being in need of care or protection, or beyond their parents' control, or failing to attend school	With 5,069 orders made in the juvenile courts in 1955.
(6) Persons without a settled way of living	With a monthly average population in reception centres ranging from 1,422 to 1,859 during 1955 in Great Britain.[2]

[1] Statistics appear at varying intervals after the events which they record; and the writing of this book has perforce been spread over rather a long period. In consequence later information is available on some topics than on others. On balance, however, the claims of uniformity and comparability seemed to prevail over those of up-to-dateness; and I have, therefore, drawn a line at 1955. All figures quoted relate to that date, except where for special reasons the use of later ones is indicated, or earlier ones alone are available.

[2] The figures relating to items (1), (4) and (5) are taken from the official *Criminal Statistics*; those relating to items (2) and (3) from the Registrar-General's returns. Both these categories relate to England and Wales only. The figures in item (6) are taken from the annual report of the National Assistance Board and cover Scotland also.

By contrast with these figures the number of the resolutely idle is remarkably small. The National Assistance Board reports only forty-nine convictions in Great Britain in 1955 of persons who were said to have persistently failed, by their refusal to work, to maintain themselves or their dependants.

The comprehensiveness of these figures varies greatly. Statistics of criminal convictions, in particular, cannot be taken as anything like accurate measures of actual criminality. The dangers of inference from these statistics are indeed notorious: such inferences continue to be made only because we neither have, nor in the nature of the case can hope to have, much better material to draw upon. Conviction obviously depends both upon the zest with which the offender is pursued, and upon his own skill in escaping detection; while minor changes in the law can also produce startling revolutions in the records of criminality. Every motorist knows that the police undertake periodical drives against illicit parking in particular areas; and the figures for other offences are liable to fluctuate for similar reasons. To quote only one example: in 1955 convictions for the offence of Sunday trading stood at 10·8 per million of population as compared with an annual average for 1930–9 of more than 600 per million. No one believes that this dramatic change is proof of a corresponding decline in the frequency of this offence, or of increasing respect for Sabbatarian principles.

Nor can it be assumed that the record of crimes known to the police, including those for which no conviction is secured, fully compensates for the unreliability of convictions as an index of criminality. What comes to the knowledge of the police is only one degree less chancy than what is actually proved in court. Most people probably call in the police if they are burgled, or (provided that they survive) if they are the victims of unprovoked assault; but, even in cases of dishonesty, it is by no means uncommon for the injured party to refrain from instigating a prosecution; and breaches of the law against homosexual practices, at least in cases where only consenting adults are concerned, are most unlikely to be voluntarily disclosed. Many a drunken motorist, also, must have wobbled unchallenged to his destination.

Methods of police recording or of police action, moreover, are not necessarily uniform throughout the country: what gets into the statistics at one place at one time might have failed to find its way there, had it happened at another place or another time. Nor are magisterial judgments reliably standardized. The variations in local criminal statistics are, in fact, quite astonishing; and since it is from these local particulars that the national figures are compiled, a study of the former induces a most healthy scepticism in the use of criminal statistics as indications of the scale of criminal behaviour. To quote only a few examples,[1] it appears that in 1953 the number of adults found guilty[2] at magistrates' courts varied from 8 per 10,000 of population in the county of Cambridgeshire to 39 in Tynemouth (including the police

[1] The number of persons found guilty is, of course, accurately known; but the population in the relevant age groups, being enumerated only at decennial censuses, must be estimated. The figures quoted in the text must therefore be regarded as only approximate. I regret that it has not been possible to make even this approximation for a later date.

[2] Indictable offences only.

district of the River Tyne, which, however, contains no population); while the cities of Birmingham, Newcastle, St Helens, Warrington and Leeds occupied a middle position with figures lying between 24 and 26 per 10,000. Nor are these variations easily explained by differences in economic and social conditions. Bedfordshire, for example, returned a rate of 15 per 10,000—nearly double that of the neighbouring, and more or less comparably rural, county of Cambridgeshire. The City of Exeter recorded 21, against Reading's 15; for the two Yorkshire towns of Leeds and Sheffield with approximately the same population, the rates were 25 and 14 respectively. Alumni of our older universities may like to note, with satisfaction or dismay as the case may be, that scores of both the county (8) and the city (16) of Cambridge make a slightly better showing than the corresponding figures of 12 and 18 recorded by the county and the city of the sister university of Oxford. But strangest of all, perhaps, is the fact that the Metropolitan Police District and City of London (even allowing for the considerable slice of the Home Counties which this includes) ranked below the peaceful county of Shropshire—with figures of 20 and 24 respectively.

If the statistics for juveniles are set against those for adults, the plot is still further thickened. While it is true that the areas in which the conviction-rate for adults runs high are generally also those with a heavy incidence of juvenile offences, the correspondence is by no means close: the juvenile rate (in proportion to the population at risk) ranges, in fact, from less than double to more than nine times the adult figure for the same area. It is as though in some counties the authorities spent all their energies in relentless pursuit of the young delinquent, regarding the crimes of his elders with comparative indifference, whereas in others no pains were spared to bring the adult offender to justice, while the erring young were allowed to proceed undisturbed upon their wicked ways.

Finally, to complete the confusion, the local variations in the figures, not of actual convictions but of crimes known to the police, in which policy might reasonably be supposed to play at least a smaller part, are hardly less remarkable. In the highest ranking district the number of crimes recorded per 10,000 of population is more than six times that for the area which stands at the bottom of the table.

So far as juveniles are concerned, Grünhut has attempted in a recent study to make sense of these bewildering variations. With many reservations he reaches the conclusions that 'The characteristic pattern of a high-delinquency area is a big industrial town with the typical social structure of an industrial population, not a place where poverty is prevalent, but where there is a high proportion of small incomes, where there is considerable infant mortality, though not necessarily with the highest infant mortality rates'; that 'high-delinquency areas are often places with a significant criminality in general'; and that 'contrary to what one would expect, high-delinquency areas are districts where there is, over a considerable number of years, a consistency in high-delinquency rates within a stable population'.[1] Nevertheless, many

[1] Grünhut (1956), pp. 45–6.

striking anomalies remain unexplained which one can hardly believe to be a true reflection of corresponding differences in the respect for law prevailing in different parts of this tight little island. One can but suppose that they are the result of the divergent attitudes of both police and magistrates; and that the key to the riddle is on the lines of that offered by the Chief Constable of Berwick, who explained an apparently alarming figure of a 48 per cent increase in crimes in his district in one year as mainly due to a new system of reporting, designed to ensure that incidents are recorded quickly and accurately.[1]

In view of these uncertainties we probably ought to refrain from the tempting and common practice of quoting movements in the criminal statistics as evidence of the ups and downs of criminal behaviour. In the case of long-term comparisons the unreliability of the evidence is now generally recognized. Every step backwards in time is seen to aggravate the risks due to changes in the classification of offences, in legislation or in police activity—even though the Home Office, while deprecating attempts to peep into earlier history, continues to play the part of tempter by publishing in the official statistics, decennial averages that go back as much as twenty-five years. Short-term movements, on the other hand, are still much more widely used as indices of the volume of crime; and for this purpose the figures most commonly quoted are the total convictions for indictable crimes, or the number of such crimes 'known to the police'. The choice of these figures may be unavoidable but their use can be very misleading: for the distinction between indictable and non-indictable offences is both legal and arbitrary—a monument to British tradition or to historical accident, rather than a reasonable device for distinguishing 'real' crimes from technical or minor offences. The boy who removes a pump from a schoolfellow's bicycle and is unable to establish his intention to put this back figures among the indictable offenders; yet the brothel keeper and the dangerous driver are omitted. In some instances, moreover, the category to which a particular offence is assigned may itself be governed more by the vagaries of policy or of convention than by the actual nature of the offence. Assaults, for example, may figure in either the indictable or the non-indictable class; and the lines between non-indictable assault, malicious wounding and grievous bodily harm (like the line between careless and dangerous driving) are not at any time easy to draw. For this reason, a rise in convictions in the graver category does not necessarily imply a deterioration in public behaviour. In fact, the correct inference may, paradoxically, be just the opposite: growing public sensitivity to acts of violence may have encouraged resort to the more serious charge whenever there seems even a modest chance that a conviction would result.

Actually the picture of the trend of crime given by the figures for indictable offences is quite different from that shown by movements of the total of indictable and non-indictable offences together. The number of persons found guilty of offences in the indictable class rose from a figure of 78,463 in 1938 to a post-war peak of 132,817 in 1951. Thereafter a drop of 20 per cent to

[1] Berwick, Chief Constable's Report for 1954, p. 3.

106,371 in 1954 was followed by a slight rise to 107,446 in 1955, this last figure being still 37 per cent above that of 1938. Similarly, the number of indictable offences known to the police rose from 283,220 in 1938 to a peak of 524,506 in 1951, falling thereafter to 434,327 in 1954, with, again, a slight rise to 438,085 in 1955. It is on these facts that the pessimist feeds. Yet in regard to offences of all kinds, the story is much more cheerful. In 1938 this total stood at 787,482: in 1952, the highest post-war year, at only 753,012, and in 1955 at 735,288, a decline of nearly 7 per cent as compared with the year before the war—an apparent contradiction of the myth that much regulation has bred a nation of lawbreakers.

What is true of the whole is also, generally speaking, true of the part. Within each category of offences there is room for great heterogeneity. Cases of theft alone, even though they are sub-divided into a dozen different types, ranging from larceny of horses and cattle to larceny from automatic machines, necessarily cover an immense variety of iniquities. The participants in planned shoplifting excursions and those who steal in desperation to meet some cruel emergency necessarily all march under the same banner, in company with the professional pickpockets and the victims of sudden temptation. Nor are variations in the figures for particular crimes generally any more to be trusted as indices of the frequency with which those offences are committed, than are movements in the totals for crime as a whole. No one knows whether the much-publicized increase in sexual offences (which rose with hardly a break from 2,321 in 1938 to 5,408 in 1955) is, or is not, due to a change in sexual morality; and no one can say whether the (so far less publicized but none the less striking) recovery in the number of convictions for drunkenness from the very low figures of the war and immediate post-war period to about the pre-war level threatens the distinguished position which this country occupies at the bottom of the World Health Organization's table of alcoholism, or whether it is merely the consequence of more vigorous police action, inspired perhaps by growing public distaste for manifest inebriation.

That we should reject the official criminal statistics as evidence of criminal trends is hard doctrine, because it means that we must be content to confess ourselves quite ignorant as to whether our population is becoming more, or less, addicted to crime. Nevertheless, such ignorance has to be admitted. The most that can be said is that the figures show two or three features which are so marked and so persistent as to give reasonable grounds for regarding them as likely indications of the relative frequency of different kinds of crime and different types of criminal.

The first of these features is the overwhelming predominance of the offences committed by motorists. In half a century the invention of the internal combustion engine has completely revolutionalized the business of our criminal courts.

The typical criminal of to-day is certainly not the thief, nor the thug who hits an old lady on the head in order to possess himself of her handbag or to ransack her house: the typical criminal of to-day is the motorist. Out of the grand total of 735,288 persons found guilty of criminal offences in England

and Wales in 1955, no less than 354,506 were convicted in magistrates' courts of 'offences relating to motor vehicles',[1] in addition to a small number found guilty at higher courts. Motorists thus constitute over 48 per cent of all those convicted of any criminal charge in any court. Yet this revolution is generally ignored alike by the public and by the professional sociologist—to a degree that really queers all criminological discussion. Apparently on the Marxian principle that the law is made and operated in the interests of the well-to-do, motoring offences generally, and infringements of speed limits in particular, are not ordinarily thought to 'count' as crimes at all. Research into various aspects of criminology, such, for example, as ecological studies of the areas in which offenders live or in which offences are committed, habitually omits motoring crimes. Even a spokesman of the Howard League, in a review of criminal statistics, ignores motoring offences to reach his conclusion that 'the great majority of crimes are offences against property'.[2] In some courts, again, special days are set aside for hearing motoring cases—a practice which may be administratively convenient, but certainly has the regrettable effect of putting motoring offences into a class apart from other crime; and traffic offences are commonly treated as a separate category when the previous convictions of an offender are listed, so that if a motorist guilty of dangerous driving has already a conviction for dishonesty, this is unlikely to be quoted in his record and *vice versa*.

Undoubtedly some motoring offences, like some of the crimes in nearly all other categories, are trivial: and some are not. Any attempt to sort out the figures for the more serious cases is complicated by the fact that all the relevant statistics are not tabulated in exactly the same way. Some refer to number of *convictions*, others to number of *persons* convicted;[3] and these are by no means interchangeable since a defendant often acquires several convictions simultaneously—as when a motorist is found guilty both of careless driving and of failure to conform to a traffic sign, or when a burglar has broken into more than one house.

A few useful facts can, however, be extracted. Taking first the figures for the number of persons convicted, we find that in 1955 no fewer than 41,187 persons are shown as having been found guilty of the offences included under the heading summarized in the *Criminal Statistics* as 'driving dangerously, etc.' Most of these were convicted by the magistrates, but a few were dealt with in higher courts. Obviously, however, the category of 'driving dangerously, etc.' covers a large miscellany of offences of varying gravity. In order to break it down, we have to turn from figures of persons convicted to those relating to convictions. From these it appears that, in 1955, 3,311 convictions were recorded for the offence of motoring whilst drunk or drugged,

[1] Offences Relating to Motor Vehicles for 1955 (1956).

[2] Rees and Usill, eds. (1955), p. 187.

[3] And others again to 'separate' persons. In the *Criminal Statistics* a person (as distinct from a 'separate' person) counts as two if he is convicted twice in a year—but still only as two, however many offences he may run up on each occasion. In the text a 'person' means a person in this sense—not a 'separate' person, who is counted only as one, no matter how many times he may be convicted in a year

including both cases dealt with by the magistrates and the much smaller number tried in the higher courts. For reckless or dangerous (as distinct from merely careless) driving, the number of convictions was 4,770; while the number of cases of motorists who were so indifferent to the havoc that they had caused as to be guilty of failure to report, or to stop after, an accident numbered 6,360. These three categories together, therefore—the drunks, the reckless or dangerous and those who disregarded accidents—account for a total of 14,441 convictions for what are surely very serious offences indeed. And if to these are added the cases of careless driving, numbering 35,063 in 1955, the total of motoring convictions in the categories listed rises to 49,504; while by adding to that figure, again, the 89,714 convictions for disregard of speed limits we reach a total of 139,218 convictions for these motoring offences—which do not, of course, include parking offences, or any of the thirty-odd others officially recorded, except those which I have specifically listed here.

It may be of interest to compare these figures with those for what is always the largest category of 'ordinary' as distinct from motoring crimes—namely, offences against property. In 1955, thieves accounted for 9·3 per cent, and house- or shop-breakers for 2·2 per cent, of the total of persons convicted for any kind of offence—proportions which look modest enough beside the 48 per cent scored by motorists. In the same year, 68,438 persons were found guilty of larceny and 16,411 of 'breaking and entering'. If these are set against the total of 41,187 motorists convicted of 'driving dangerously etc.' we have seven convicted thieves for every four motorists found guilty of dangerous driving or similar offences, but between two and three times as many such motorists as house- or shop-breakers.

These figures, moreover, relate to persons of all ages. Since, however, no-one may legally drive a car until he is seventeen, or a motorcycle until he is sixteen, the great majority of motoring offenders must be over seventeen years of age; and a more appropriate comparison, therefore, would be that between motorists and other criminals over the age of seventeen. Among the motoring offenders none of the reckless or dangerous drivers convicted in the higher courts was under seventeen; and of the 41,187 found guilty by the magistrates of 'driving dangerously, etc.' all but 168 were over that age. A large proportion of offences against property, on the other hand, is committed by youngsters: no less than 52 per cent of those found guilty of breaking and entering, and 34 per cent of those guilty of larceny, were less than seventeen years old. Exclusion of those under seventeen from the total of persons convicted of larceny thus reduces their total from 68,438 to 45,101; and, for adults only, the ratio of motorists in the 'dangerous, etc.' class thus works out at approximately 9 thieves to 8 motorists. Again, among the 16,411 found guilty of breaking and entering, only 7,881 were over seventeen. The 41,019 motorists aged seventeen and upwards convicted of 'driving dangerously, etc.' are therefore more than five times as numerous as the house- and shop-breakers of similar age.

Turning from persons convicted to totals of convictions, we find that the total number of convictions recorded for all offences of dishonesty with or without violence (including house-breaking, burglary, all forms of theft, violent robbery and every kind of fraud) amounted to 123,847 in 1955. If this figure is compared with the 49,504 cases of drunk, dangerous, or careless driving or of failure to report or to stop after accidents, we have a ratio of five convictions for one or other type of dishonesty to every two convictions for bad driving or indifference to accidents; but, if to these motoring offences are added the convictions for disregard of speed limits, it will be seen that the motoring convictions actually exceed those for all property offences by about 12 per cent.

Once again, these figures include those under seventeen. In the case of convictions, as distinct from persons, however, exact adjustments to exclude juveniles cannot be made, as the returns for the higher courts do not give the ages of persons convicted along with the number of their convictions; not do we know how many convictions may have been earned by motorists under seventeen. In each case, however, we do know that the total number of young persons involved was very small. Only 436 out of 11,501 persons convicted of dishonesty in the higher courts were in this age group; while among motorists only 168 juveniles were included among those found guilty in any court of 'driving dangerously, etc.' Where the number of young *persons* involved is so small, we may fairly assume that the contribution of juveniles to the number of *convictions* is also insignificant.

In the case of the magistrates' courts, however, more information about certain classes of crime is available; and from this we know that the elimination of juveniles convicted in these courts reduces the figure of convictions for offences against property from 123,847 to 79,881. If, therefore, the convictions of drunk, drugged, dangerous or careless drivers or of those who have disregarded accidents (but excluding all cases of speeding and other offences) are set against those of persons aged over seventeen found guilty of any or all forms of dishonesty with or without violence, the ratio of property crimes to these motoring offences stands at 8 to 5; but if the infringements of speed limits are also counted against the motorists, their offences exceed all adult convictions for crimes of dishonesty and crimes against the person by approximately 50 per cent.

A long, long way behind the motorists, and a long way also behind the thieves and house-breakers, come those who are convicted of indictable sexual offences. These numbered 5,408 in 1955; though, if the non-indictable offences of prostitutes and male importuners were included, this figure would be raised approximately to the level of the total convicted of breaking and entering. Smaller still, again, is the number of those who are found guilty of crimes of violence. Violent crime looms large in the press; but whether or no it is (as is widely believed) becoming more frequent, it is still happily rare.[1] The number of convictions for all indictable offences of violence against the person (a figure which, however, excludes certain assaults as being non-indictable) stood at 4,958 in 1955, that is less than one for every

[1] That is, if the violence of the reckless motorist is excluded.

thirteen thieves, less than one for every eight drivers convicted of 'driving dangerously, etc.' and between a quarter and a third of the number convicted of breaking and entering. And the number of crimes known to the police, as distinct from the number of cases in which an offender was successfully brought to justice, tells the same story. In a population of some 44 million, 133 persons are known to have been deliberately murdered by their fellows in 1955; and the number of known murders works out at 3·4 per million of population. For attempted or threatened murders, the number known to the police was 5·5 per million for 1955: for manslaughter and for infanticide, 3·7 per million; and for indictable offences of wounding, 177·6. While each of these occurrences represents a tragic incident, it is significant that the figures have to be calculated not per 1,000, or even per 100,000, but per million of population. To anyone familiar with the intensity of the hatreds which lie smouldering in many a family circle (as revealed for instance in matrimonial or similar proceedings in the courts), it is the absence of physical violence, rather than its occasional happening, which remains a standing miracle.

In spite of considerable fluctuations from year to year in the figures of convictions for particular offences (which may or may not be indications of corresponding fluctuations in the number of those offences actually committed) convictions for the main categories of crime have kept their relative positions with fair consistency since before the war, with the motorists leading, the thieves, followed by the house-breakers and smaller classes of offenders against property such as receivers and false pretenders, occupying the next place, and the sexual offenders and the deliberately violent bringing up the rear.

Two other features of the criminal population are equally persistent, and are also widely recognized—namely, the age and the sex distribution of known offenders. Judged by the figures of convictions, if motoring and other non-indictable offences are omitted, law-breaking remains conspicuously a pre-occupation of the young, and of the male young in particular; 'an episode rather than a symptom' as a German criminologist has put it. Amongst men and boys, the group that scores the highest figure of indictable offences in proportion to its numbers is the fourteen- to seventeen-year-old class, with a total in 1955 of 1,603 offenders for every 100,000 in the corresponding population; while boys between the ages of eight and fourteen have a rate of 924 per 100,000, the highest rate of all being that for age fourteen, which stood at 2,068 in 1955. In the seventeen- to twenty-one-year-old group convictions fall to 1,042 per 100,000, while among those aged from twenty-one to thirty the rate drops to 787; and after thirty it stands at a mere 243. The proportion of criminals, as thus defined, amongst those over thirty is thus not much more than a quarter of that found in the eight- to fourteen-year-old group, and less than a sixth of the figures for those between fourteen and seventeen. This rapid decline with advancing years remains, moreover, remarkably constant: the only change in the relative positions of the age-groups since before the war is that since 1954 the seventeen to twenty-one-year-olds have changed place with the eight to fourteens as the second most criminal age group.

Year after year the most criminal epoch in the life of males occurs in the later school and early working years.

This preponderance of young offenders appears even more vividly in the figures that show the proportion of all findings of guilt which are contributed by the younger age groups. In 1955, almost exactly one in three of all offenders (of either sex) found guilty of an indictable offence was under the age of seventeen; and this proportion also has shown little variation for a number of years. Of those found guilty of breaking and entering more than half were under seventeen, while only about one in eight was over thirty. Thieving is rather more evenly distributed through life: those found guilty of larceny are accounted for in approximately equal proportions by the three age classes 8–17; 17–30; and over 30. The characteristic crimes of maturity are frauds and false pretences (with 69 per cent of convicted offenders over the age of thirty in 1955); sexual offences (with 50 per cent over thirty); and receiving (with 48 per cent above that age). These crimes, however, account for only a modest share of the total convictions, even if motoring and other non-indictable offenders are excluded: the thieves and the house-breakers are more than six times as numerous as all the receivers, false pretenders and sexual offenders put together.

What is true of youth is no less true of masculinity. At every age females contribute far less to the criminal statistics than do males. Whereas at all ages 502 males per 100,000 of population were found guilty in 1955 of some indictable offence, the corresponding figure for females was only sixty-nine. Women and girls, however, as well as men and boys, seem to be specially disposed towards criminality in their earlier years, though the picture is not quite the same for the two sexes: the female population appears in the courts a little later, and withdraws a little more slowly, than does its male counterpart. For indictable offences by females the peak age in 1955 was seventeen, at which point the rate reached 179 per 100,000, as against the male peak at age fourteen with a rate of 2,068. In the case of both sexes, the 14–17 year-old class takes the lead, with the 17–21 group running second. In these groups the 1955 rates for women were 172 and 161 respectively, against the corresponding male figures of 1,603 and 1,042. Among women the group that ranks third is the 21–30 age class, with a figure of ninety-three per 100,000, whereas for the opposite sex it is the small boys between eight and fourteen years old who, with a proportion of 924 per 100,000, rank next after the 17–21 class, the 21–30 group coming fourth with a figure of 787. Both sexes alike, however, show the same dramatic drop in convictions after the age of thirty, the female figure falling to fifty per 100,000 and the male to 243.

In short, taking all ages together, men have more than seven times as high a rate of convictions as women; while at the peak age the male figure is more than eleven times as high as the figure for women at their age of maximum criminality, and for boys in the youngest class the rate is over twelve times that of girls of the same age. These differences seem, however, now to be narrowing: women show signs of beginning their criminal careers at a slightly earlier age and are catching up a little on their male contemporaries. In 1938 the male rate at all ages was almost eight times that for females (393 to 51 per 100,000); and at the peak age, which was then thirteen, males had over twelve times as many convictions in proportion to population as had females at the age of nineteen, which was then the year of their maximum score. Though the differences are still very large, the age-distribution of female convictions seems thus to be moving—though only slightly—in the direction of the example set by males.

A more detailed analysis would show that the difference between the rates of conviction of the two sexes is very unequally spread as between different types of offence. For example, whereas in respect of the vast majority of offences far more males than females are found guilty, the number of adult women convicted in the magistrates' courts of larceny from shops or stalls stood in 1955 at 3,666, as against only 1,967 for men. The thieving propensities of men apparently express themselves in other ways as, for example, in larceny in a house (1,276 men to 428 women) or larceny from unattended vehicles—a thoroughly masculine speciality, with 1,208 adult male convictions against only twenty-eight for the opposite sex. I have myself also observed that among the juveniles appearing in the court which I know best the proportion of girls to boys seems to be much higher in the case of railway frauds than in that of any other offence: during periods of just over twenty-four months between March 1951 and June 1956, when I was sitting in this court, 215 boys and 171 girls were found guilty of defrauding or attempting to defraud the railways. The sex distribution of particular types of offence varies, however, noticeably with age. The predominance of females in thefts from shops and stalls, for example, does not appear under the age of seventeen. Up to that age it is boys who engage in this, just as much as in other, forms of thieving.

As will appear later,[1] the frequency of offences—particularly amongst the young—has been made the basis of theories which seek to discover the reasons for criminality. This phenomenon often gives rise also to lamentations on the part of pessimistic moralists, who see in the age-distribution of offenders evidence of the depravity of the young. Those who voice these dirges, however, should remind themselves that the persistence of this distribution is at least proof that their own generation must in its day have been equally blameworthy. Actually, the slight changes that have occurred have been in the direction of reducing the proportion of crimes for which the young are responsible. In 1938 the percentage of all offenders guilty of indictable crimes who were under seventeen stood at nearly 36, as against 33 per cent in 1955. But in any case the steady decline of criminality with advancing years has its optimistic, no less than its pessimistic, aspect: at least it means that for the great majority of offenders the future is hopeful.

The relative rarity of women offenders, on the other hand (like the prevalence of motoring crimes), has for the most part been tacitly ignored by students of criminology, any clues suggested by this sex difference being

[1] See pp. 161 ff.

generally neglected. Apart from the work of a few students who have interested themselves particularly in the offences committed by women,[1] the habitual reaction of sociologists and criminologists to the sex difference in crime has been to eliminate the female subjects from their studies, on the ground that the number of available cases is too small to allow of any valid inferences being made. Yet if men behaved like women, the courts would be idle and the prisons empty.

Of these outstanding and persistent features of British experience, three at least seem to have been very generally shared throughout the European continent. First, most countries of Europe ended the war with significantly higher rates of criminality than they had when it began. Few indeed could venture to rival Professor Andenaes' claim for Norway that by 1949–50 crime which had 'increased heavily' during the war, was 'actually a little below the pre-war level';[2] and few could listen without envy at the meeting of the Criminologists Association in Finland in 1952 to Professor Verkko's reference to his country's 'reversion to peacetime conditions with regard to criminality'.[3] Second, subject to the variations in the age of criminal responsibility mentioned in the next paragraph, the age-distribution follows everywhere the same course: certainly the decline after the age of thirty seems to be the general rule, Third, the variation in the frequency of detected criminal behaviour as between the sexes is equally well established over a wide area; and, although the scale of this difference varies, the tendency for the gap between male and female convictions to narrow constantly recurs.

Unfortunately, more detailed international comparisons, though tempting, are even more dangerous than studies of domestic trends. Indeed, the authors of an enquiry into comparative criminal trends from 1937 onwards, initiated by the Economic and Social Council of the United Nations, had to confess that the chief value of their work lay, not so much in discoveries about comparative criminality, as in the light which it threw upon the difficulties of making any such comparisons at all. Every investigation is bedevilled by differences alike in the classification of offences (which complicates comparisons even between England and Scotland), in age-groupings and in the minimum age prescribed for full criminality: in Sweden, for example, where criminal proceedings cannot be taken against anyone under the age of fifteen, figures of juvenile crime must read very differently from those for England and Wales, where eight-year-olds are charged with indictable crimes.

II

As measured by the statistics, recorded domestic casualties rank well below criminal convictions in the whole reckoning of social failures. The annual total of divorces, of maintenance and separation orders and of illegitimate

[1] As, for example, Pollak (1950). [2] Andenaes (1954), pp. 21–2.
[3] Verkko (1951–52), p. XLIX.

births all put together does not reach the total of persons found guilty each year even of indictable crimes alone, and is indeed less than one-tenth of the figure of those convicted of law-breaking in the widest sense.

In a purely formal sense, the records of domestic breakdowns are complete as no criminal statistics can ever hope to be. Undetected criminals are common enough, whereas an undetected divorce is a manifest impossibility. Similarly, records of illegitimacy, apart from a margin of cases of children of married women by men other than their husbands, may be accepted as reasonably comprehensive. The only unknown factor remaining is the number of domestic casualties which for one reason or another have not resulted in legal action—the discordant families that still hold together, and the voluntary separations of married couples with or without formal financial agreements.

The war and immediate post-war increase in divorces, like the rise in crime figures, has been well publicized: the subsequent decline, not so well. From a figure of 6,092 in 1938, the number of marriages ended by divorce (excluding those annulled) in England and Wales rose to a peak of 58,444 in 1947. By 1951, the annual total had fallen to 28,265. The following year saw a further rise to 33,274 generally attributed, in part at least, to the introduction (in the autumn of 1950) of the Legal Aid scheme which made financial assistance available in the High Court for litigants of small means. If allowance is made for the law's delays, eighteen months to two years must have been needed to work off the backlog of cases accounted for by this scheme. By 1953 the number of divorces had dropped back to 29,736, and it has continued since to fall, reaching a figure of 26,262 in 1955—less than 45 per cent of that recorded at the high point of 1947.

These facts hardly support the evidence given on behalf of the Church of England to the Royal Commission on Marriage and Divorce.[1] The statement that 'there seems little sign of any substantial decrease in the latest figures' seems an unjustifiably pessimistic inference from a drop of over 55 per cent in eight years; while the confident forecast that, as a result of legal aid, the figures are likely to 'soar away up in the next few years' appears to be at the least premature, in view of the fact that, already in the third year after the introduction of legal aid, the figures were 13 per cent lower than in the last year before the scheme became operative, and more than 10 per cent below the total of the immediately preceding year. Indeed, although the facilities for legal aid are now well-established and well-known, the figure is lower than at any time since the end of the war.

Too much attention should not, however, be paid, as the Registrar-General is at pains to point out, to variations as between one year and the next in the number of marriages actually dissolved; since this may be affected by procedural changes (as, for instance, a reduction in the time required for the decree *nisi* to become absolute), or by changes in the rate at which arrears are worked off. The Registrar-General's own valuable study included in his 1946–50 Review is accordingly based mainly upon the numbers of petitions actually filed, as being a more reliable index of trends.

[1] Minutes, Sixth day, pp. 142 and 151.

This analysis, supplemented at some points by later figures, greatly helps to put the whole picture in perspective—the more so, since 'the spectacular rise in the incidence of divorce in the last forty years from 1,000 petitions per year to 30,000 may lead to exaggerated ideas as to the proportion of marriages which ultimately are broken by divorce'.[1] Before the first world war it seems that about half of 1 per cent of all marriages ended in divorce, while between the wars the proportion rose to 1¾ per cent, and by 1950 had reached only about 7 per cent. Later history, moreover, gives but feeble support to the popular view that high divorce figures are chiefly caused by young people who rush light-heartedly into matrimony and out again. Of the 26,816 marriages that were broken by divorce (or annulment) in 1955, 15,430 (over 57 per cent) had lasted more than ten years and 9,718 or 36 per cent were of fifteen or more years' duration. Only 2,861 had lasted less than five years. Marriages, in fact, are more often broken after, than before, they are ten years old. And even these figures need to be read against the background of other demographic changes—notably the diminished risks of mortality in the prime of life. Thanks to these changes, what has been called the 'period of exposure to matrimonial risk' has been significantly lengthened in the present century: many of the marriages now ultimately broken by divorce would, in a physically more precarious age, have been ended by the death of one of the partners. Indeed, even in the United States, in spite of divorce figures very much higher than our own, Professor Kingsley Davis has estimated that, owing to this increased longevity, the proportion of all marriages broken each year from any cause, whether death or divorce, has actually declined since the beginning of the present century.[2]

Under the present English law no distinction is made in the permitted grounds of divorce between those marriages in which there are, and those in which there are not, dependent children; and it is perhaps remarkable that only four witnesses (Mr Claud Mullins, Dr D. H. Geffen, Mr W. J. C. Heyting, and Mrs Moya Woodside) spoke in support of such discrimination before the recent Royal Commission. Apart from these four exceptions, all the witnesses who wished to liberalize the present divorce laws framed their proposals without making any distinction between fertile and childless unions. Since, however, the danger to children that results from broken homes, or from the divisions of their loyalty and affection between disunited parents, is a recurring theme in discussions of marital breakdown, it may be pertinent to add that a substantial proportion (about a third in 1955) of the marriages that are dissolved are, in fact, childless.

Nor do current divorce figures indicate any general distaste for the institution of matrimony in itself. On the contrary, marriage seems to be more popular than ever. Not only is the proportion of married people in the whole population higher now than it has been for at least a century, but, even of those who have failed once, a high proportion, it seems, are disposed to try again. Of the total number of divorced persons the Registrar-General

[1] The Registrar-General's Statistical Review, 1946–50, Text, Civil, p. 61.

[2] Davis, Kingsley (1950) p. 19.

calculates that something between two-thirds and three-quarters may be expected to marry again; indeed, 'at all ages a much higher rate of marriage is shown for divorced men and women than for the other marital conditions'.[1] Once bitten, in fact, twice not at all shy.

Marriages that are not legally dissolved may be formally suspended by the maintenance and separation orders issued in domestic proceedings in the magistrates' courts. So long as divorce proceedings were both expensive and centralized, while facilities for legal aid to the poor remained negligible, these orders were the normal working-class substitute for divorce. The general trend of these proceedings has moved in much the same way as has the record of divorces since 1938, though the peak figure for maintenance orders[2] came a year before divorces reached their maximum, the total rising from 11,177 in 1938 to 25,400 in 1946, and subsequently falling to 12,644 in 1955. While the absolute number of such orders is thus still somewhat greater than it was, it will be seen that whereas, before the war, approximately two maintenance orders were issued in the magistrates' courts for every one case of divorce, to-day the divorces are twice as numerous as the orders made in domestic proceedings. From these facts it is reasonable to infer that some part of the post-war rise in divorces may be attributed to couples who formerly would have had recourse only to the magistrates' courts, since they would have found divorce proceedings prohibitively expensive; and that some of to-day's divorces are merely putting the *de jure* finish to unions, the *de facto* collapse of which would, in any case, have been legally recognized.

Unfortunately, maintenance orders are not well observed. Every year upwards of four thousand men actually go to prison (4,333 in 1955) for failure to observe them; and a much larger number might find their way there if they could be traced. What the National Assistance Board has called the problem of the 'disappearing husband' has indeed to be reckoned amongst one of the major social problems of the time; and the ranks of the contemporary poor get substantial recruitment from deserted wives and children. From a sample enquiry, conducted by the Board in 1953, we learn that, amongst 57,700 separated wives who had been receiving assistance 2½ years earlier, the husbands of 24,000 could not be traced; whilst another 2,750 were known to have left the country—though 4,000 did turn up later. Often also, even when the husband has been located, it is found impossible to compel him to discharge his marital obligations, since he has in fact set up a new establishment with, and fathered the children of, another woman; and, although 'respect for the marriage tie' would suggest that it is the legal wife, rather than the paramour, whose maintenance ought to be the prior charge on the husband's income, nevertheless 'extracting money from husbands to maintain wives from whom they are separated is at best an uncertain business; it is easier to enforce the maintenance of those with whom the man is living than of those from whom he is parted, and the man is more likely to exert

[1] The Registrar-General's Statistical Review, 1946–50, Text, Civil, p. 72.

[2] Separation orders without provision for maintenance are a trifling addition to this total: 375 in 1955.

himself to maintain the former'. Faced, therefore, with this 'delicate problem', the National Assistance Board has been forced to allow principle to give way to those 'important practical considerations' which lead 'inescapably to the other view'—not least of which is the need to avoid unnecessary expenditure of public monies.[1]

In somewhat similar plight are those unmarried mothers who are receiving insufficient financial help (or none at all) from the fathers of their children. In 1955, the National Assistance Board was supporting some 16,000 women in this position. If, therefore, to the 24,000 women whose husbands had vanished we add these 16,000 inadequately supported unmarried mothers, we get a total of some 40,000 women whose dependence upon public funds is wholly due to the neglect by their partners of marital or paternal obligations.

The unmarried mothers supported by the National Assistance Board represent, of course, only a fraction of the number of women in this category. Every year about one in twenty (4·7 per cent in 1955) of all births is registered as illegitimate. The annual total of babies born outside marriage (31,145 in 1955) thus exceeds by about 18 per cent the number of marriages that are dissolved each year by divorce; and is nearly six times as large as the number of persons convicted of sexual offences in a year (5,408 in 1955), though the latter figure seems to excite more public interest. The number of illegitimate maternities would, moreover, be more than two and a half times as great as it is, if it were not for the large number of cases in which the mother marries between the conception and the birth. If to the figure for illegitimate maternities is added that for legitimate maternities occurring within the first eight months of marriage, the total number of babies[2] who must be presumed to have been, so to speak, illegitimately conceived amounted to 81,783 in 1955, a figure which is equivalent to approximately one in three of all legitimate first births.

For a long period before the second world war the figures for illegitimacy showed remarkable steadiness. In the first three decades of this century the proportion of births registered as illegitimate fluctuated consistently between about 4 per cent and 5 per cent of the total, and in the nineteen-thirties the variation ranged only from 4·1 per cent to 4·4 per cent. During the second war there was, as might have been expected, a sharp rise, the annual percentage reaching a maximum of 9·3 per cent. This increase was, however, counterbalanced by a corresponding decline in the number of pre-marital conceptions of children born to married couples. If the illegitimate births and the pre-marital conceptions together are expressed as a percentage of total maternities, the figures read 14·6 per cent for 1938: 14·9 per cent in the peak year 1945: and 12·8 per cent in 1950. It would thus seem that the rise in illegitimacy during the war years was due, not so much to increased immorality, as to the practical difficulties which wartime conditions put in the way of 'forced marriages'—constituting what has been described as an 'inadvertent transfer from the legitimate to the illegitimate class'.[3]

[1] National Assistance Board Report for 1953, pp. 18–21.

[2] This figure counts each maternity as one and so does not take account of multiple births.

[3] The Registrar-General's Statistical Review, 1946–50, Text, Civil, p. 91.

That the stereotype of the single woman struggling to bring up her child alone represents the typical unmarried mother is by no means certain. In a number of cases illegitimate children are born into homes in which their two parents are living together in conditions not noticeably different from those of married people—notably in cases where a previous marriage of one or other of the partners has broken up, but no divorce has followed. Among the more prosperous classes the irregularity of such apparently stable unions is frequently concealed by the use of deed poll procedure, which enables the woman to take her consort's name. Among the working classes such legal facilities are more unusual, and women in this position come instead, by custom, to be known by the name of the man with whom they live. And in a (probably small) number of other cases illegitimate children are born to married women who are normally living with their husbands—as when a wife becomes pregnant by a man other than her husband, while the latter is in prison or abroad, or even while he is at home: though some of this last group are no doubt likely to be, incorrectly, registered as legitimate.

Socially, there is a world of difference between the child of the 'deed poll' or similarly stable union and the child who is conceived in the course of some passing affair by a man and a woman who do not have, and have no prospect or intention of having, a common home, and the day-to-day responsibility for whose care devolves upon the woman alone, with or without financial help from the father. Obviously, however, the Registrar-General's records cannot differentiate between these types of illegitimacy: the child of a 'deed poll' union is as much illegitimate as is the unexpected offspring of a casual liaison in a doorway. Nor have the few local surveys of the fortunes of illegitimate children that have been made in this country been able to make clear distinctions along these lines. Some of their findings do however suggest that the offspring of these 'quasi-married' couples account for a sizeable proportion of the total of illegitimates. The frequency of illegitimate babies who are not first births, for example, may be accounted for in this way. In their 1947 investigation into a sample of a thousand families in Newcastle (one of the very few studies which have, even incidentally, traced the fate of illegitimate children in this country) the late Sir James Spence and his collaborators expressed surprise at finding that rather less than half the illegitimates in their sample were first births, though the total rate of illegitimacy corresponded closely to that for the country as a whole. By way of explanation, these investigators suggested that 'many of the second and third infants were born to parents who were living in established, if unofficial, families'.[1] In Leicester also, where the illegitimate children born in 1949 were followed up five years later, it was found that sixty-eight out of the 199 mothers for whom information was available (many of whom had had previous children either legitimately or illegitimately) had borne a further illegitimate child by the end of 1954, but 'in the great majority of cases' the father of this child was also father of the one born in 1949. Out of every 100 mothers, only 'around two' of those who were single at the time of the 1949 conception, and

[1] Spence and others (1954), p. 143.

who had retained their babies, were neither married nor cohabitating and had also had a further illegitimate child.[1] Likewise in Aberdeen an investigation covering all illegitimate maternities in the period 1949-52 revealed a similar picture. Among 282 women who had previously borne children, over three-quarters of those (eighty-two in all) who had their confinements at home were known to be cohabiting with the child's father, though in the case of hospital patients the corresponding figure was less than 50 per cent. Many of those who were thus cohabiting 'presented themselves for medical care as married women and the fact of illegitimacy was not always known to the almoners antenatally'.[2]

Even of those illegitimates who were not actually born into 'established, if unofficial, families', it seems that, in the experience at least of these local investigations, the great majority were not deprived of family life. In Newcastle most of these, it is said, entered what amounted to 'a family circle'—most commonly that of the actual parents, or, failing this, the mother's family, or that of adopting parents; though it should be added that many of these families offered what the investigators reckoned to be an exceptionally unstable and unsatisfactory environment.[3] In Leicester, out of every 100 mothers of illegitimate children who were investigated five years later, seventy were married (either to the child's father or to someone else) or were cohabiting; and practically all of these had kept their illegitimate children—who were said, in general, to 'settle happily'. Of the remaining thirty, half had parted with their children 'mainly by adoption', while the other half were found to be generally living with the child's grandparents or other relations, and in the majority of these cases also the child appeared to be 'settled well in a reasonably secure and happy home'.[4] Neither the Leicester nor the Newcastle investigation mentions how many of the children whose mothers were found to have married had subsequently been legally adopted by the mother and her new husband; but I can myself testify from personal experience that the typical Adoption Order made in the London juvenile courts relates not (as is often supposed) to infertile couples seeking to acquire a family, but to cases in which a married couple jointly adopt the child born to the woman before her marriage; and in these cases more often than not the man is not the putative father of the child.

If what happens in Newcastle, Leicester, or Aberdeen is at all typical, it seems, therefore, that the Registrar-General's statistics of illegitimacy must include a large proportion of cases in which an illegitimate child's experience of family life is not noticeably different from that of his legitimate contemporaries; and that the case of the unmarried mother struggling along to bring up her child single-handed is quite exceptional. But where these cases occur, the results, of course, for both mother and child may be quite disastrous.

In yet other cases the integrity or independence of the 'normal' family

[1] Macdonald, E. K. (1956), pp. 361–5. [2] Thompson, B. (1956), pp. 83 and 76.
[3] Spence and others (1954), pp. 143–5. [4] Macdonald, E. K. (1956), p. 364.

is disrupted by proceedings in which the children are the principal figures. The chief categories here are children brought before the juvenile courts as being either beyond the control of their parents, or in need of care or protection, together with a (probably not very large) proportion of those who are received into care by local authorities without court proceedings. Such cases cannot be computed in the same way as the number of divorces or separations, since such figures as are available relate to individual children, not to families; and the troubles of one family may lead to six or more children passing into the guardianship of a Local Authority; nor is there any certain way of eliminating such of these cases as are consequential upon one or other of the catastrophes already enumerated, as, for example, where a mother finds her son beyond her control after the father's desertion of the home, or where a child runs away from home and is found wandering by the police after his or her parents have quarrelled and separated. It would seem, however, that the residual number in these categories after deduction of those attributable to other forms of domestic breakdown cannot be large: the total number of children removed from their homes for reasons other than their own offences by orders of the juvenile courts in 1955 was only 2,534;[1] and, though no exact statistics are available, it is the experience of those well acquainted with the work of the juvenile courts that a considerable proportion of these relate to children whose parents are divorced or separated or who are themselves illegitimate.

To complete the tale of domestic irregularity, something ought to be added as to the practice of professional prostitution. Here, however, no estimates of scale or of trends are possible. Official records of convictions are no guide, since the practice of prostitution is not itself an offence, and the risk of prosecution for such offences as soliciting in public places incurred by any given prostitute is quite incalculable. The Wolfenden Committee, who examined the figures of arrests of prostitutes in 1953 in the West End Central London police division, found that the 6,829 arrests made involved 808 prostitutes. Of these, 181 were arrested on one occasion only, while, at the other end of the scale, one was arrested twenty-seven times. In any case, the modern call-girl whose clients make their contacts by telephone, can dispense with public street-walking altogether. Many social changes can be adduced to support the view that 'lady with friends'[2] is not as common as she was: among such, for instance, must be included the increasing opportunities for 'respectable' employment open to women, or the supposed change in sexual morality which is said to encourage extra-marital relations on a purely

[1] In addition to these, a small number of children come into the care of local authorities for similar reasons but without the intervention of any court: but to keep the picture in perspective, it should be remembered that the great majority of children who are looked after by Local Authorities (24,000 out of the total of 38,000 who came into care in the year ending March 31, 1956) are in that position because of the infirmity or temporary illness of their parent or guardian, and not on account of domestic breakdown in the ordinary sense.

[2] It is remarkable to find this elegant euphemism in use as late as 1922—when a murdered prostitute was so described in evidence by one of her friends. See Carswell, ed. (1950), p. 54.

amateur basis.[1] At the same time, many social workers and others familiar with the more sordid districts of our cities believe that prostitution has lately been increasing again, and that it is encouraged by the influx of male immigrants from overseas who come to a wholly strange environment, often, at least at first, without any feminine belongings. Nevertheless, all that the Wolfenden Committee could say was that, so far as London was concerned, they had 'no reliable evidence whether the number of prostitutes plying their trade in the streets' had 'changed significantly in recent years'.[2]

III

Most of the social problems so far mentioned give at least as much trouble as they did before the war: some give very much more. More cheerfully, we may conclude this review by reference to one or two matters on which a little self-congratulation is permissible. The first is truancy from school. Here again exact estimates are not possible, since the statistics compiled by Local Authorities do not usually distinguish between legitimate absences (as for illness) and actual truancy; nor is it satisfactory to use the figures of prosecutions of parents for their children's failure to attend school as a reliable index of truancy. All Local Authorities are reluctant to prosecute, and the question whether they do or do not do so turns, as a rule, on the detailed circumstances of individual cases. Administrative changes also make comparisons with the pre-war situation unreliable, if not actually impossible. But it does seem to be the firm opinion of those who should know that to-day the children no longer go unwillingly to school. Although the Home Office and the Board of Education, in their Joint Memorandum on Juvenile Offences,[3] expressed the view in 1941 that 'the disturbance of home conditions caused by the war' had produced a new crop of truants, Dr W. P. Alexander, as Secretary of the Association of Education Committees, has given it as his opinion[4] that, in spite of 'the hard core of persistent truancy which is associated with those families who are very well known to other branches of the social services', the incidence of truancy is much less than before the war; and he quotes, in support, figures of absences from all causes, and of prosecutions for non-attendance, in 1937–8, 1952–3, and 1953–4, by seven Local Authorities drawn from both urban and rural areas. All show a material decline in the percentage of absences from all causes as between 1937–8 and 1953–4, though in three cases there has been a rise in the actual number of prosecutions. Dr Alexander comments, moreover, on the insignificance of the problem in the whole educational picture. In one large county authority with a school population of 54,000 there were only seven prosecutions for truancy in 1952–3. Some of Dr Alexander's colleagues are said also to

[1] For a wider discussion of possibly relevant social changes (not all of which necessarily point in the same direction), see the League of Nations reports on the Rehabilitation of Prostitutes (1938–39).

[2] Wolfenden Report (1957), p. 82. [3] Juvenile Offences (1941).

[4] Personal communication, November 1954.

have expressed the view that truancy is not an increasing problem; and he himself finds more significance in their general remarks to this effect than in the somewhat dubious statistics which alone are available. Independent enquiries in Birmingham (where it was estimated that there were perhaps 200–250 truants in 1954, in a total school population of 180,000), and in Manchester (where in the year ending July 31, 1954, some 990 children were recorded as having truanted out of a school population of 112,247, as against twice as many in 1947–8 out of a smaller population), confirm the prevailing optimism. Finally, the official records show that for England and Wales as a whole, the number of children who were removed from their parents and committed either to approved schools or to the care of a 'fit person' (which usually means a local authority) because of their failure to attend school was only 177 in 1955; while another 753 were placed, for the same reason, under the supervision of a probation officer or other responsible person.

A second subject for self-congratulation is the collapse of the spectre of an incurably idle proletariat which has so long haunted the secure and the comfortable. The history of social legislation is littered with devices—the workhouse test, the family means test, the definitions of 'genuinely seeking work'—born of the fear that the conduct of the 'working classes' would belie their name. Now, at long last, over fifteen years of near-full employment have demonstrated that the work-shy constitute only a minute fraction of the whole population of tolerably able-bodied and able-minded men and women. The price per head of getting some people into employment and keeping them there may be heavy; some of us are not, perhaps, very efficient; and some, unable easily to adapt ourselves to the harsh requirements of industrial society, drift restlessly from one employment to another. But if jobs are available, most of us have demonstrated our readiness to try them. If the obvious medical casualties are excluded, the number of the near-unemployable is negligible; and, in this community at least, idleness has been proved to be far more a matter of faulty social organization than of personal shortcoming. A sample enquiry conducted by the National Assistance Board in 1951 revealed that, out of 60,000 persons dependent upon the Board's allowances and required to register for employment as being presumably fit and available for work, there were not more than about 7,000 (5,500 men and 1,500 women) of whom the Board's officers were prepared to say firmly that they 'could be working if they really wanted to work'.[1] Yet at the same date our actual working population amounted to about 23½ millions.

The truly recalcitrant fraction appears to be very much smaller still. In a community where the workers are counted in millions, the determined idlers (others than those who are blessed with private means) must be reckoned in tens. In the last resort, those who persistently refuse to maintain themselves or their dependants render themselves liable to criminal proceedings. On these grounds forty-nine persons (including one woman) were actually convicted in 1955, and of these forty were sent to prison.[2] Not all, however,

[1] National Assistance Board Report for 1951, p. 8.
[2] National Assistance Board Report for 1955, p. 30.

even of this tiny band of obstinate loafers, proved to be incorrigible. The woman sentenced in 1955, for instance, was placed in employment shortly after her release, and was reported as having worked almost continuously ever since; and the Board's annual reports are regularly enlivened with picturesque details of other belated conversions to a more conventional way of life.

The National Assistance Board, by virtue of its constitution, is under obligation to keep to its own side of the elusive line which divides the sick from the merely tiresome. It is the Board's duty both to relieve the indigent and at the same time to protect public funds from the depredations of incorrigible idlers; but it is itself precluded from providing any form of medical care. The rehabilitation of those whose inability to support themselves is diagnosed as due to physical or mental handicap becomes the responsibility of the Ministry of Labour, which has to deal in these categories with numbers much larger than the total of those whose idleness is classified as wilful. Here again, however, the records are encouraging. Up to 1955 some 60,000 persons had been admitted to the Ministry's Industrial Rehabilitation Centres; and a sample enquiry based on 7,000 of these showed that 3,698 had been placed in employment at the conclusion of their course, while another 900 had been admitted to ordinary training courses.[1] Six months later 3,058 of the former and 814 of the latter groups were successfully followed up: the remainder were dead, failed to reply to enquiries, could not be traced or were still in training. Of the 3,058 placed in employment, 79½ per cent, and of the 814 admitted to training courses, 81 per cent, were reckoned as successes, in the sense that they were found after a six months' interval to be in satisfactory employment, or to have satisfactorily finished their training. Most of those men and women suffered from obvious physical disabilities or illnesses, such as amputations, respiratory diseases or rheumatism, which put them too far across the line between the medical and the social problem to be considered here. But it is remarkable that of 387 cases diagnosed as 'psychoneurotic' for whom jobs had been found, no less than 78 per cent were among the successes, whilst the comparable percentage for those who had undergone further training stood at 79 per cent. Even those diagnosed as psychotics could claim a 75½ per cent success rate amongst those placed in employment, and 71 per cent amongst the trainees; whilst 70 per cent of the mental defectives for whom work had been found were still satisfactorily employed.

To-day it is not perhaps so much idleness as restlessness which is industry's problem. The number of able-bodied potential workers who receive assistance from public funds is made up less of the chronically idle than of those who are in temporary difficulties. Every year the National Assistance Board deals with something like a million applications for single payments to meet a passing emergency; and an analysis of such payments made during the first week of December, 1953, revealed that about half the total of these grants went to able-bodied unemployed persons. Among the recipients of such temporary

[1] Ministry of Labour Gazette (April, 1955), pp. 121–2.

relief are included some who are returning to work after a spell of sickness, some whose jobs have come to an end for no fault of their own, but who are unable to last out the three days that must elapse before the insurance benefit for which they have contributed becomes payable, and some who have forfeited their right to this benefit by discharging themselves from their previous employment. Amongst the last-named there are undoubtedly some whose extreme mobility at least verges upon anti-social behaviour, since they are continually throwing up jobs for reasons which—at least to other people—appear to be quite trivial. At all events the incidence of job mobility seems to be very unequally distributed as between individuals. In one local enquiry, for instance, which covered adult male workers in a London Metropolitan Borough and in a suburban area, it was found that, if the most mobile 15 per cent in the population sampled had changed their jobs no more often than the remaining 85 per cent, the total volume of movement between employers would have been halved.[1] Although both to the community and to the individual mobility is as much a virtue in moderation as it can be a vice in excess, incessant job-changing should, perhaps, be listed as, in the most literal sense of the word, a symptom of maladjustment.

The more picturesque forms of restlessness are, however, themselves on the decline. The once familiar figure of the tramp has almost disappeared from our highways; few indeed are those who have not now, at least ostensibly, come to terms with the 'settled way of life'. Of those few most are now to be found in the National Assistance Board's Reception Centres—the nearest (but not very near) equivalent of the pre-war casual wards; and the statistics of these centres record a truly remarkable social change. In 1955 their approximate average nightly population was 1,700 for the whole of Great Britain—less than a quarter of the number in the casual wards of England and Wales alone immediately before the 1939 war, and only about one-tenth of the 16,911 counted there at the depth of the depression on May 27, 1932.

This little company of individuals, so persistently resistant (whether by design or by misfortune) to assimilation into our culture, seems however to exercise a real fascination over the authorities responsible for their welfare: in the National Assistance Board's Reports its members enjoy publicity out of all proportion to their numbers. Most of them are said to be young enough and fit enough to work. Some have abandoned a settled life through inability to get on with their wives: some have quarrelled with their parents or step-parents; and a few claim to have been turned out of their homes for drunkenness, trouble with the police, incontinence or other personal problems. 'The picture one gets, however indefinite the outlines, is thus of a body of men of whom few are tramps of the traditional kind and most are young enough and fit enough to be maintaining themselves in employment; of an unhappy or unwise upbringing or misfortunes earlier in the man's career which may have been the cause of an unsettled life in some cases but not in all; and of weakness or indiscipline of character which, again in some cases but not in all, could perhaps be traced back to circumstances earlier in the man's life.'[2]

[1] Jeffreys (1954), p. viii. [2] National Assistance Board, Reception Centres (1952), p. 7.

Such then, in broadest outline, is the picture in mid-century Britain, and such is the order of magnitude of the various elements of which it is composed. In the presentation of this picture details have been deliberately omitted, except where they serve to correct what appear to be general misapprehensions, or where they suggest important clues for research, since the object is to show the problems as the layman, rather than the specialist, sees them. These are the problems which the layman has a right to ask the specialist to solve.

CHAPTER II

Social Pathology and the Social Hierarchy

IN a hierarchical society it is natural to expect that the distribution of socially unacceptable behaviour should conform to, or at least be shaped by, the pattern of the hierarchy. Exploration of the nature and degree of this conformity is, however, still extraordinarily confused. It is confused partly by looseness of thought and definition, but even more by the tenacity of the—often unspoken—hierarchial assumptions of a hierarchial society: the prevalence of criminality among the lower classes[1] is, for instance, easily demonstrated by the use of definitions which automatically exclude those crimes to which the upper classes are most likely to be addicted; and the existence of a 'social problem group' amongst the very poor is no less readily established, if the fact of being extremely poor is held of itself to be a qualification for 'problem status'. So strong indeed is the imprint of the contemporary social hierarchy that much of the research reviewed in this chapter has become the classical example of the difficulty of extricating the social investigator from the shackles imposed by the assumptions and prejudices of his time.

The assumption that the distribution of the multiple forms of social pathology tends to conform to the shape of the socio-economic pyramid is the more easily made in that the upper social classes can be shown to differ, in so many respects, from their social inferiors—generally to the disadvantage of the latter. Thus it has repeatedly been shown that children of the lower social classes are less tall and weigh less than those of the same age in a better social

[1] The discussion in this chapter involves a tiresome question of language. To refer simply to the 'upper' or the 'lower' classes is no longer permitted by the prevailing canons of good taste, presumably because these terms might be read to imply generalized or inherent superiority or inferiority. Some clumsy circumlocution, therefore, has to be found to describe a hierarchy which, for all our delicate sensibilities, demonstrably does exist: it is, for instance, apparently still permissible to refer to 'the lower social classes,' or to the 'lower income groups'. Nevertheless, in any prolonged discussion, the perpetual recurrence of superfluous adjectives becomes very wearisome, the more so when they serve only the cause of hypocrisy. I have, therefore, at times boldly reverted to the practice of calling spades 'spades,' upper classes 'upper' and lower classes 'lower'—in the hope that the text will be good enough testimony that the terms 'upper' or 'lower' in this context simply refer to positions in the undeniable prestige-hierarchy of contemporary British society; and that absolutely no judgment as to other forms of inferiority or superiority is implied.

position; that the prospect of survival improves significantly as one moves up the social scale; and that this difference is of long standing. In the period 1949–53 infant mortality in the lowest social classes was 2·2 times that prevailing in the highest; and indeed there has been 'little change in the slope of the social class gradient' in infant mortality during the past thirty years.[1] From the survey sponsored by the Population Investigation Committee of all the babies born in Great Britain in a single week of March, 1946, the same picture emerges. If the mortality of all social classes were reduced to the level prevailing in the salaried and professional classes, there would be an annual saving of some 4,000 babies who do not live beyond the first month of life, and of over 6,000 others who die before they are one year old.[2] Similarly, in adult life, in 'all the major [morbid] conditions from which adult men in social class V had a higher death-rate in 1930–32 than social class I, the gap was as big in 1950 as twenty years before—and if anything slightly wider'.[3] Only in the last years of life are there now some tentative signs of a change in this relative expectation of life enjoyed by different social classes: from the age of sixty-five onwards lower class men in the Registrar-General's 1949–53 sample had as good prospects of survival as had their contemporaries of superior social standing. Presumably any of the underprivileged who succeed in reaching this age at all must be exceptionally tough.

This differential mortality is itself the outcome of a differential susceptibility to particular diseases. While upper class men succumb to coronary disease or to diabetes, and are more prone to commit suicide than are those less well-endowed with worldly goods, their social inferiors are far more vulnerable to respiratory disorders: male deaths from bronchitis in the twenty to sixty-four age group are about five times greater in the lowest than they are in the top social class.[4] Nor are these class differences confined to such illnesses as are actually fatal. The same story appears in the statistics of hospital patients. The upper classes occupy a disproportionate share of hospital beds with cases of depression and even (somewhat surprisingly) of disorders of character, behaviour and intelligence, while their social inferiors fill the hospitals as well as the cemeteries with cases of bronchitis, rheumatic fever and pneumonia.[5] Perhaps, however, this last discrepancy is explained by the fact that the behaviour disorders of the lower classes are dealt within a different kind of institution.

As with physique, so also with intelligence, or, to be exact, with the ability to perform intelligence tests. In the unusually comprehensive Scottish survey of 1947 it was found that 'The distribution of average height and weight among the occupational classes is very similar to the distribution of mean intelligence

[1] The Registrar-General's Decennial Supplement, 1951, Occupational Mortality, Part 2, Vol. i, p. 155.

[2] Douglas (1951), p. 44. [3] Morris and Heady (1955), p. 557.

[4] The Registrar-General's Decennial Supplement, 1951, Occupational Mortality, Part 2, Vol. i, pp. 46, 42, 68, and 52.

[5] The Registrar-General's Supplement on Hospital In-patient Statistics for 1949, Table H.3.

test score';[1] and numerous other investigations on similar lines that have been made south of the border indicate that in this respect the Scots are not unlike their neighbours.

In face of these well-established and familiar facts, it is easy enough to slip into the assumption that the distribution of unacceptable behaviour must follow a similar pattern. Yet in fact remarkably little is known as to the true shape of the distribution.

In the case of criminal offenders, although everyone who appears in court to answer to a criminal charge is asked to state his occupation, no official classification is attempted, except that the Prison Commissioners collect (though they do not always publish) particulars of the apparent occupations of those who are sent to prison. In a community which carefully classifies the social class of patients admitted to hospital, giving separate figures for every disease, this is surely a curious omission. The following figures, however, which show the social class distribution of all occupied males in England and Wales may be taken as indicating the 'expected' contributions which each social class would make to the criminal population, if the size of the criminal fraction in every social class was the same.

Total (male) Population of England and Wales, occupied and retired: 1951 Census (thousands)

Occupations	*No.*	*Per cent*
Class I professional, etc.	510·3	3·3
Class II intermediate	2,243·0	14·5
Class III skilled	8,160·8	52·9
Class IV partly skilled	2,490·0	16·2
Class V unskilled	2,024·5	13·1
	15,428·6	100

These figures may be set against Rose's finding in his Borstal investigations that 10 per cent of his subjects were the sons of business or professional men, 23 per cent sons of skilled, 27 per cent of semi-skilled, and 40 per cent of unskilled, workers.[2] In this case, therefore, the unskilled workers appear to have contributed considerably more offenders than the percentage to be expected on the basis of their proportionate weight in the total working population; but, at the same time, the contribution of the business and professional classes is fully up to their 'expected' numbers. Rose's figures were, however, based only upon information given by his subjects themselves on committal; nor do his categories necessarily correspond exactly with those of the Census classification. Ferguson, again, in his Glasgow enquiry, found that much the same proportion of his 'ordinary' (i.e. those not physically or mentally handicapped) boys at risk had been found guilty by the Courts in the non-manual, the skilled and the semi-skilled classes: the figures ranged only from 9·3 per cent to 11·3 per cent, though the proportion coming from

[1] Scottish Council for Research in Education, Social Implications of the 1947 Scottish Mental Survey (1953), p. 87. [2] Rose, A. G. (1954), pp. 56, 57.

the class of unskilled workers stood appreciably higher at 14·9 per cent.[1] Case studies also often show a surprisingly high proportion of persistent offenders who come from what would generally be regarded as socially 'good' homes: for example, over 25 per cent of the subjects of Sir Leo Page's *Young Lag* could be so classified.[2] Certainly in my own necessarily limited experience in the courts (adult and juvenile), the procession of those who are found guilty of criminal offences (even excluding motorists) seems to be by no means exclusively composed of the lowest social classes. A formidable file of newspaper cuttings reinforces this impression.

Meanwhile we are completely in the dark as to the contribution which particular social classes make to particular categories of crime. If motoring offences come mainly from the upper social levels, one imagines that thieves and burglars are more likely to be recruited from those below; but this is only guesswork. In the United States, evidence has been found that boys who steal motor cars tend to be socially a cut above the run of delinquents generally;[3] but we do not know if this is also true in this country (or indeed in other American cities beside Detroit where the investigation was made). And what, one may ask, is the social distribution of homosexuality, or of convictions for frauds or for false pretences? Or of shoplifters? The Wolfenden Committee on Homosexual Offences and Prostitution declared that, 'in spite of widely held belief to the contrary', homosexuality is not 'peculiar to members of particular professions or social classes; nor, as is sometimes supposed, is it peculiar to the *intelligentsia*. Our evidence shows that it exists among all callings and at all levels of society; and that among homosexuals will be found not only those possessing a high degree of intelligence, but also the dullest oafs'.[4] Nor do we know how recidivism in the more serious forms of crime is spread over the various ranks of the social hierarchy. All these questions are still unexplored.

Among persons committed to prison, on the other hand, there is undoubtedly a very heavy predominance of the lower ranks. The classification used by the Prison Commissioners (which, it is understood, is shortly to be revised) does not precisely correspond with that of the Registrar-General, so that exact comparison of the actual with the 'expected' proportion of each social class which finds its way to prison is not possible; and it must be borne in mind also that the record of a prisoner's occupation is generally derived from his own statement. Whether, on balance, prisoners are likely to exalt or to debase their occupational level is anybody's guess, but, either way, some elements of imagination probably enter into the records. For these reasons the Commissioners' classification is not available for publication. Nevertheless, it can confidently be said that the upper social classes are much under-represented in prison. But whether this is the result of the nature or the gravity of their offences, or whether it is merely a reflection of the tendency of judges and magistrates to regard prison as a more suitable environment for the lower than for the upper classes, no-one can tell. Undoubtedly the proportion

[1] Ferguson (1952), p. 23. [2] Page (1950), Part 2.
[3] Wattenberg and Balistrieri (1952), p. 578. [4] Wolfenden Report (1957), para. 36.

of offenders sent to prison varies enormously from one offence to another. Thus in 1955, out of 219 persons convicted at quarter sessions or assizes of driving under the influence of drink or drugs, twenty-seven or under 13 per cent were sent to prison; while the proportion of the 126 reckless or dangerous drivers convicted in the same courts who were imprisoned was thirty-nine, that is, 31 per cent. But out of 2,882 persons convicted (also in the higher courts) of crimes against property without violence (mostly thefts of one sort or another), the number imprisoned was 1,941 (67 per cent); and of the 8,619 guilty of crimes against property with violence (which include violence directed only against objects as distinct from persons, as, for example, in housebreaking) 3,888 or 45 per cent were sent to prison. Similarly, in the magistrates' courts in the case of 3,068 convictions for 'driving under the influence' or 'drunk in charge', the number of sentences of imprisonment without the option of a fine was only 182, while in 4,584 cases of reckless or dangerous driving this sentence was imposed in a mere 116;[1] but out of 590 adults convicted of begging, 236 were sent to prison, as were also as many as eighty-eight out of 232 who were found guilty of larceny from the person.

Divorces also, like crimes, are not officially allocated according to the social class of the petitioners and respondents; and there is still little reliable information, official or unofficial, as to their social distribution. It is indeed astonishing that the Royal Commission on Marriage and Divorce which reported in 1956 apparently undertook no investigation into this important aspect of the matter. It may be presumed that until recently most of the marriages that were legally dissolved must have been those of the more prosperous classes, since legal aid was not readily available for this costly form of litigation. Since the introduction of legal aid, however, it has been remarked by those who are familiar with the social problems of the lower ranks of our class hierarchy that divorce appears to be creeping down the social scale. This impression is, moreover, confirmed by an important investigation by Rowntree and Carrier which reached the tentative conclusion that in 1951 (admittedly, an exceptional year) 'couples in each of our broad occupational groups appear to be filing divorce petitions to very much the same extent'. Indeed, manual workers, who comprised 17 per cent of the 1871 divorce population accounted for as much as 59 per cent of the total in 1951; while petitions filed by 'the gentry', professional men and managers and farmers and shopkeepers, or their wives, fell correspondingly from 54 per cent to 18 per cent.[2] Meanwhile in the United States a number of sample investigations have suggested that divorces may be actually more frequent in the lower than in the

[1] It is fair to add that some of these may have been cases in which multiple convictions were recorded, and sentences of imprisonment may have been imposed on one of the other charges involved. But since only 1,186 motorists were sent to prison out of a total of 354,506 convicted by the magistrates, the number of these cases can hardly have been considerable.

[2] Rowntree and Carrier (1958), pp. 224, 222. The authors add, however, that, for several reasons, figures quoted may not represent the long-term trend with complete accuracy.

upper social classes.[1] In one of the most recent American studies of the distribution of divorce by occupational levels, relating to the State of Iowa, the author concluded that 'divorce is much more characteristic to-day of the lower social-economic groups in our society, and much less prevalent than the average in the upper occupational levels'; and he adds that 'in the light of his marital and other frustrations, the idyllic [*sic*] portrayals of the labouring man's home need reappraisal'.[2] From the same journal again, comes evidence from a Finnish investigation that in Helsinki, where divorces are more frequent than in other Finnish cities, the rate was much greater at the beginning of the century, and that 'nowadays there is practically no difference between social classes'.[3] The honour of the upper classes is, however, nevertheless defended by the author's conclusion that members of the lower classes who apply for divorce are, more often than their social superiors, persons who have already shown signs of personal maladjustment as evidenced by participation in crimes, misuse of intoxicants, vagrancy, etc.

Equal reticence prevails on the subject of illegitimacy. Only in Scotland do official records of illegitimate births give an indication of class; and private enquiries are scanty. From the Scottish Registrar-General's report for 1955, we learn that in Social Class I only three illegitimate births were recorded out of a total of 3,542; in Class II the number was 144 out of 9,825 or 1·5 per cent: in Class III, 932 out of 50,215 or 1·9 per cent: in Class IV, 968 out of 14,997 or 6·5 per cent; and in Class V 355 out of 12,368 or 2·9 per cent. Commenting on similar figures for the previous year, Greenland has remarked on the exceptionally heavy incidence of illegitimacy among the partly skilled workers who comprise Class IV, and on its comparative rarity in Class V, 'where most of the problem families would be grouped'.[4] It should, however, be borne in mind that in some 40 per cent of the illegitimate births, social class was not known. From Thompson's survey of illegitimacy in Aberdeen we learn that in that city the incidence of illegitimacy in the case of women bearing their first child 'rises from 2 per cent in the professional and technical group to 19 per cent among the catering and cleaning workers';[5] and it may be hoped that in due course more exact and comprehensive information will be forthcoming from other local areas in which similar investigations are understood to be in progress at the time of writing.

Meanwhile the London Diocesan Moral Welfare Council has from time to time made analyses of the occupations of women applying to them for help in illegitimate pregnancies. In 1952,[6] out of a total of 6,640 applicants whose occupations were recorded, 1,526 came from factory jobs, 1,207 from domestic employments, 960 were clerical workers, 582 were shop assistants or cashiers and 427 had been in the hotel or catering trade. Housewives contributed 349 cases, the nursing profession (including children's nurses) 317, the women's services 129, tailoring and dressmaking 116, schoolgirls 105, landworkers 104,

[1] Goode (1956), pp. 44-8, and Kephart (1955), p. 459. [2] Monahan (1955), p. 324.
[3] Allardt (1955), p. 327. [4] Greenland (1957), p. 150.
[5] Thompson, B. (1956), p. 77. [6] Figures supplied by courtesy of the Council.

the entertainment industry 84, laundry workers 83, telephonists 81, transport 68, hairdressing 42, students 32 and teachers 26. The remainder were either spread in small numbers over several miscellaneous occupations or were described as unemployed. Again, one may guess that girls in the higher ranks of society are better equipped than their social inferiors to avoid unmarried motherhood, and less likely to apply for help to a Moral Welfare Agency when they are overtaken by this catastrophe. As an American writer has pointed out, sampling from agencies produces a 'picture of the unwed mother as being an extremely young, poor, uneducated or psychologically disturbed female';[1] and this may well be misleading. Certainly the Agency figures must be presumed to exclude the children registered as illegitimate who are born to couples living together in stable households, but precluded by present divorce laws from marrying, the number of whom in the light of the evidence already given appears to be considerable.[2] Indeed, when allowance is made for these factors, the proportion of applicants to the Moral Welfare Council who come from occupations that rank in the second, third or fourth, rather than in the lowest, of the Registrar-General's social classes, is perhaps surprising.

II

Over the past half-century the assumption that there is a heavy concentration of the symptoms of social pathology at the bottom of the socio-economic scale has been the starting-point of numerous researches; but these, it must be confessed, are of interest less for their actual findings than for the limitations of their technique, and for the way in which they illustrate the influence of a changing social atmosphere upon the methodology and the hypotheses of social investigation.

Thus, the founders of the Charity Organization Society could take for granted, in their day, that the poorest classes constituted a veritable cesspool of anti-social habits;[3] and, it may be added, that it was the deplorable failure of the more affluent classes to inhibit their charitable impulses which was chiefly responsible for this. Concrete evidence was not at that date thought necessary to prove either the association of poverty with multiple social evils, or the link between unbridled charity on the one hand and general depravity on the other. Shortly after the COS was well on its feet, however, theories about the 'social problem group' took a decidedly eugenic turn: innate inferiority began to supplant indiscriminate charity as the villain of the piece. In 1929, the Wood Committee on Mental Deficiency, in what has

[1] In an attempt to correct this bias, a questionnaire was addressed to doctors whose names appeared in the 1952 medical directory in Alameda County, California, asking about illegitimate maternities in their private practice. Of those approached 71 per cent replied and of these 31·8 per cent said that they had attended such confinements. These included 137 cases in which the mothers were girls who had never been married, and of these over 60 per cent were employed in 'professional or white collar jobs or were college students'. See Vincent (1954). Incidentally, in England at least one home for unmarried mothers is known to cater primarily for the professional classes.

[2] See p. 37. [3] See pp. 268 ff.

become a classic statement, roundly proclaimed that if all the families containing mental defectives of the 'primary amentia type' were segregated, these would constitute 'a most interesting social group. It would include, as everyone who has extensive practical experience of social service would readily admit, a much larger proportion of insane persons, epileptics, paupers, criminals (especially recidivists), unemployables, habitual slum dwellers, prostitutes, inebriates and other social inefficients than would a group of families not containing mental defectives. The overwhelming majority of the families thus collected will belong to that section of the community, which we propose to term the "social problem" or "subnormal" group. This group comprises approximately the lowest 10 per cent in the social scale of most communities.'[1] Again, a few years later, the Brock Committee on Sterilization expressed a similar view, not only as their own, but also on behalf of 'sociologists generally' who, they thought, 'would accept the view that there is a concentration in the lowest social stratum of the physically and mentally defective, the chronic unemployables, the habitual recipients of relief, and a delinquent element of a mentally sub-normal type'.[2] The members of this Committee were, however, of the opinion that their predecessors had exaggerated the size of this sub-normal group.

Meanwhile unofficial investigations were also afoot, from which similar conclusions were to be drawn. The authors of the Merseyside Survey, published in 1934, found that 'the majority of our social maladies—not merely poverty and overcrowding—are conspicuously centred in certain classes, the members of which are handicapped in one way or another from the very beginning or quite early in life, and they consequently fall behind their fellows in the race. Some are born blind or deaf, epileptic, mentally deficient, physically deformed. Others—it may be due to their initial endowment or their early environment—are persistently addicted to drink, crime, immorality. Others again are chronic sufferers from ill-health or unemployment, or they are constantly coming to the Public Assistance Authority or some charitable agency for relief. Many are not born with these defects or disabilities, but in some way or other they acquire them. In all such cases there is some lack of physical, mental, or moral balance, or some failure of social and economic adjustment, which makes them a burden upon the community'.[3] At about the same date also, Mr E. J. Lidbetter published the first results of his investigation into *Heredity and the Social Problem Group*[4] undertaken under the auspices of the Eugenics Society. These consisted mainly of genealogical tables purporting to show the recurrence over several generations of multiple forms of defect in a group of presumably 'substandard' families, the implication being that these defects were evidence of some generalized inferiority, biological or cultural.

The two last-named investigations were particularly concerned to demonstrate the co-existence of multiple forms of inadequacy as evidence of the generalized inferiority of a particular group of families at the bottom of the

[1] Wood Report (1931 Reprint), Pt. III, p. 80. [2] Brock Report (1934), p. 54.
[3] Jones, D. Caradog, ed. (1934), Vol. 3, p. 344. [4] Lidbetter (1933).

social scale. The Merseyside investigators were able to show that an unusually high proportion of mental defectives suffered also from some physical defect such as blindness or deafness—a finding which has been confirmed by many subsequent demonstrations of the physical inferiority of the mentally deficient. In addition it appeared that, apart from any question of mental inadequacy, those who suffered from one congenital defect, such as blindness, were more than averagely likely to suffer also from another, such as deafness; while the mentally deficient, the epileptic, the congenitally deaf or the congenitally blind had an exceptionally large proportion of relatives who were similarly afflicted or who suffered from other physical ills such as tuberculosis.

On the other hand, evidence in support of the hypothesis that physical defect was associated with anti-social behaviour, proved to be much less striking. Attempts to explain how far the physically defective or mentally deficient were addicted to alcoholism, immorality or crime yielded some curiosities but not much more. The blind were found to have exceptionally blameless records; they did not drink to excess; nor (perhaps because their handicap would make success too improbable) did they take to crime; nor, again, could they be convicted of immorality. Among mental defectives, on the other hand, criminal offences were relatively frequent, while the deaf were noticeably inclined to take to the bottle—possibly on account of the prevailing social attitude towards them, which is apt to be impatient and harsh, in contrast with the kindly tolerance generally shown to the blind. Among the families of each group, also, the same order was maintained, the mentally deficient and the deaf having less virtuous relatives than the blind; though some of this may be due to the fact that the information available in the case of the blind was not as full as for the other groups.

In the Lidbetter enquiry heroic attempts were made to carry somewhat similar investigations backwards through at least two or three generations of the lives of families living in the poorer districts of London. One cannot help wondering how reliable the information obtainable can have been; but the author of this investigation was able at least to convince himself that it was adequate to establish the conclusion that 'The pedigrees reveal that there is in existence a definite race of sub-normal people, closely related by marriage or parenthood, not to any extent recruited from the normal population, nor sensibly diminished by the agencies for social or individual improvement'.[1]

Unfortunately, all these early attempts to get at the facts of the 'social problem group' are vitiated by an extremely crude, but at the same time highly pervasive, fallacy—namely, failure to distinguish between personal inadequacy and simple economic misfortune. Several chapters of the Merseyside Survey are devoted to investigations into what are described as 'Sub-Normal Types'; and under this head are included, not only the physically deficient such as the blind, the deaf and the chronically sick; not only the mentally deficient; not only the destitute, the alcoholic, the immoral and the criminal; but also the chronically unemployed (at a time when jobs on Merseyside were scarce

[1] Lidbetter (1932), p. 53.

indeed), together with poverty-stricken widows and deserted wives. Yet, astonishingly, the inclusion of these categories seems to have passed without protest. By the same logic also, in Lidbetter's tables black marks are set, not only against those found to be mentally defective or insane, but also against any who had been brought up in Poor Law Schools, or who had been dependent, either intermittently or for longer periods, upon the rates—and this at a time when no system of national insurance provided protection against loss of earning power through age, sickness or economic depression. Even as late as the nineteen-thirties, therefore, anybody who, for whatever reason, might be unable to support himself or herself, or to maintain a family by his (or her) own legitimate efforts was liable to be labelled 'sub-normal'. By these standards, clearly, every economic depression is bound to inflate the number of these 'sub-normal types'. 'Sub-normality' becomes absurdly dependent upon social policy; and all that is needed to reduce the dimensions of the sub-normal group is a successful policy of full employment, or a welfare state which provides adequate protection against normal economic hazards otherwise than through the Poor Law.

To-day it would not be possible to write in such terms. Women can no longer be described as 'sub-normal' because their husbands have died or taken themselves off. Those whom fate has robbed of their breadwinners or of their jobs are no longer classified along with mental and physical defectives. These earlier concepts are, however, worth reviving because they show how strong was the determination, even up to quite recent times, to identify social or economic inferiority with personal inadequacy, and to assume that, whatever its immediate ostensible cause, it is the quality of the poor which explains their poverty.

Meanwhile research into 'that lowest stratum of the population which is such a headache to our social reformers'[1] has continued. In a comprehensive review of the literature, which appeared in 1957, Philp and Timms[2] have listed 154 publications bearing on what are now called 'problem families,' most of them published in this country, and nearly all of them of post-war date. Among the best known of these are the five local enquiries edited by Dr Blacker[3] for the Eugenics Society; and the vividly descriptive publication *Problem Families*[4] produced by Tom Stephens on behalf of what were formerly known as the Pacifist Service Units; but in addition there have been numerous other local surveys. At the time of writing a five-year investigation of problem families under the direction of Mr Douglas Woodhouse is still in progress, while another intensive study of about thirty-five families over a similar period has been completed by a voluntary organization, though the results have not as yet been published.

How much, then, it may be asked, and how much, in particular, that is of practical value, has yet emerged from this considerable body of research? In a positive sense not, it must be confessed, very much. There have been changes of nomenclature: it is now usual to speak of the 'Problem Family',

[1] Edelston (1952), p. 133. [2] Philp and Timms (1957).
[3] Blacker, ed. (1952). [4] Stephens, ed. (1945).

or, in the more exact American idiom, the 'Multi-problem Family', rather than of the 'Social Problem Group'—a trivial change, which may, however, be symptomatic of the waning influence of eugenic assumptions. Most of what has been written has not, however, advanced beyond the descriptive stage, establishing the recurrences of recognisable syndromes of problem behaviour. Problem families have, in fact, been shown to behave in problem ways. That a certain proportion of contemporary families exhibits an exceptionally high incidence of varied forms of socially unacceptable behaviour is beyond question; and anyone who is not familiar at first-hand with the squalid and disorderly homes of these families, or with their unblushing disregard of the normal rules of housekeeping and of conventional family life, will find in the literature portraits vivid enough to satisfy even the most morbid curiosity. Social workers, in particular, are thoroughly familiar with the varied, not to say picturesque, peculiarities of problem family behaviour, since it is upon them that devolves the task of luring these families into a more conventional way of life. Indeed, a problem family might well be defined as one whose consumption of social workers' time greatly exceeds the average of the local community. Nor do the vagaries of problem family behaviour respect the boundaries between the now highly specialized branches of professional social work. On the contrary, such is the variety of problems in a problem family that in an extreme case no less than five social workers[1] have been found simultaneously visiting a single household, while four others turned up later in the same week.

It was indeed just this multiplicity of their social irregularities which first evoked the interest of the eugenists in these families, prompting the hypothesis that they constitute the biological dregs of our population. To-day, however, even in researches sponsored by the Eugenics Society, explicit eugenic hypotheses are much less conspicuous than they were twenty years ago: to-day we are more apt to think in terms of cultural than of biological dregs. The actual syndromes described, moreover, appear to reflect not only the objective facts of problem family life, but also in equal measure the subjective interests of the investigators concerned. Indeed, it is remarkable how the concept of the problem family has changed with changing times and changing fashions. To the early investigators, as we have seen, continued dependence, for whatever reason, upon public funds, was a qualification for problem status. To the Pacifist Service Units, which were originally founded and staffed by conscientious objectors who substituted social work for military service, it was the physical squalor of the home which distinguished the problem family. Their remedy, accordingly, was to demonstrate the possibility of a more seemly way of life by themselves scrubbing, cooking and shopping for the families which they took under their wing. In the Family Service Units, however, which are descended from these pacifist forerunners, zeal for physical domestic chores seems to be receding in favour of faith in psychiatry, and the problem family is now accordingly conceived more in

[1] Donnison (1954), p. 74.

terms of personal relationships or of mental ill-health than as a failure to maintain reasonable standards of housekeeping. In the eyes of the Medical Officer of Health, again—and more than one of these officials has had much to say on the subject—it is still the squalor and the disregard of the elementary rules of hygiene which are the hallmarks of the problem family; while to other Local Authority departments the problem family is the one which fails to pay the rent, gets itself evicted and must then be housed in Local Authority accommodation. Finally, to the National Society for the Prevention of Cruelty to Children the problem family is, naturally, the one in which the children are neglected; and to the probation officer the one whose members are perpetually turning up in courts.

It follows that, although by nearly every definition the problem family exhibits more problems than one, no standard pattern can be expected; and in practice many permutations and combinations are actually found. In the table opposite Rosalind Chambers has tabulated the characteristics in twenty of these families as listed by the investigators concerned in one of the unpublished studies referred to on page 54.

About the only common characteristics of these families, it seems, are the financial ones. All but two of them were classified as unable to manage their money, while sixteen out of the twenty certainly, and two others possibly, were handicapped by having only a very small income—whether as the result, or as the cause of their other deficiencies no one has been able to say. Apart from this, the various problem characteristics appear to be distributed in most haphazard fashion. The fact cannot, however, be ignored that, as Miss Chambers remarks after careful study of the material, all the investigations that have been made are 'much coloured by the predispositions of the workers, arising partly from their backgrounds and partly from the current fashions in social thought'. Certainly those who are interested in 'loose morals' are apt to be quite unconcerned about 'emotional disturbance': and the NSPCC could hardly accept as typical problem families a group in which only two out of twenty ranked as bad cases of child neglect, with another two classified as doubtfully in this category. The result is, to quote Miss Chambers again, that in the case histories of problem families 'extending over a number of years and consisting of the reports and observations of a long series of people—students, voluntary workers, area secretaries, Care Committee workers, Health Visitors, NSPCC inspectors, etc. and finally the problem family investigators themselves—the careful reader notes the varying emphasis on particular points, the slight mistakes and inconsistencies in reporting which are accepted in later visits and interviews as correct'.

Perhaps the most that can be said is that the various investigations have not succeeded in demonstrating that intense concentration of social problems at the bottom of the social scale which the pioneers of the Wood and Brock Committees envisaged. In particular, references to serious crime in problem families are remarkably infrequent. In the Merseyside enquiry, the proportion of cases in which some physical or mental defect was also associated with criminality ranged from nil in the case of the congenitally blind to thirty-six

Characteristics of twenty 'problem families' in one London borough which were the subject of an investigation in 1951–56

	Family																				*Conclusions*
	A	B	C	D	E	F	G	H	I	J	K	L	M	N	O	P	Q	R	S	T	
1. Neglect or maltreatment of children	—	—	+	+	—	—	—	—	—	—	—	—	—	—	—	—	×	×	—	—	2 bad cases, 2 doubtful cases
2. Marked degree of squalor and dirt	+	—	×	×	—	—	—	×	—	—	—	+	+	+	+	—	×	—	+	—	4 bad cases, 6 less bad cases
3. Bad marital relations	—	—	—	+	×	×	+	×	—	—	+	+	+	+	—	—	+	×	?	—	4 definite cases, 7 doubtful cases
4. Reluctance to work	—	—	×	×	×	×	+	—	+	—	×	—	—	—	—	—	—	—	×	—	6 definite cases, 2 less certain cases
5. Inability to manage money	×	×	×	×	×	×	×	×	×	×	×	×	—	—	×	×	×	×	×	×	18 cases
6. Failure to co-operate with social services	—	—	+	—	—	—	—	—	—	—	—	—	—	—	—	—	—	—	—	—	1 possible case
7. Bad housing conditions	+	—	×	—	—	+	×	+	+	—	+	×	×	×	×	×	—	—	+	—	7 bad cases, 6 less bad cases
8. Large number of children	×	×	—	—	+	+	+	—	—	—	—	—	—	—	×	+	—	—	×	—	8 cases
9. Very small income	×	×	×	×	×	×	×	+	—	×	+	×	×	×	×	×	—	×	×	×	16 cases, 2 borderline cases
10. Bad health	—	×	×	×	×	+	×	+	—	—	—	—	—	×	×	×	×	×	—	—	10 cases, 2 borderline cases
11. Loose morals	+	—	—	+	×	×	—	—	—	?	—	×	×	×	—	—	—	—	—	×	6 established cases, 2 doubtful cases
12. History of delinquency	—	—	×	—	×	—	—	×	×	×	—	×	+	+	—	—	—	×	×	—	8 cases, 2 doubtful cases
13. Mental defect or very low intelligence	—	×	×	×	—	+	—	×	×	×	×	+	—	—	+	—	—	×	×	—	9 established cases, 3 doubtful cases
14. Emotional disturbance	×	—	—	—	—	—	—	×	×	×	—	—	—	—	—	—	×	—	×	—	6 cases
15. Tendency to drink	—	—	—	—	—	—	—	—	—	—	—	—	—	—	—	—	—	—	—	—	No cases
16. Failure to keep jobs	×	—	×	×	×	×	×	×	×	—	×	×	×	×	—	×	+	+	×	—	14 definite cases, 2 doubtful cases

× = clear signs

+ = some indications but not strongly marked

per 1,000 in the case of the mentally deficient.[1] The Lidbetter tables covered a total of over 3,000 names, only five of which carry the symbol assigned to 'criminality'. In the five enquiries summarized by Blacker for the Eugenics Society,[2] forty-nine male heads of households and nineteen housewives were said to have been convicted, or in prison, out of a group of 379 households comprising 2,513 members: no particulars are, however, given of the criminal records of any of the other members of these families. Among the thirty-six[3] families for whom fuller particulars are given, however, there are five convictions for child neglect (a definite problem family characteristic according to some contemporary definitions) and five other cases of parents with criminal records. Dr Hilda Lewis found two mothers and five fathers with criminal records in the sixty-six problem families whose children were included among the subjects of her investigation;[4] and, to judge from the sample that I have seen, it does not look as if criminality would bulk large among the families who are the concern of the Woodhouse investigation. Among published studies it is only in a Southampton Survey that an appreciably larger proportion of criminal records has been reported. There it was found that one of the parents had a prison, probation or court record in thirty-nine out of a total of 109 problem families, while in twelve families there were cases of juvenile delinquency.[5] In Cardiff, also, an unpublished study shows a fairly high incidence of juvenile delinquency among families classified as the 'problem' class.[6]

This negative finding has perhaps some significance. Doubtless none of these investigations succeeded in getting full records; but there seems little reason why they should have been much less successful in tracking down criminal convictions, which after all are objective facts, than in their search for the other, less precisely defined, manifestations of social inadequacy in which they were interested. At least these findings create a presumption that 'that lowest stratum of the population which is such a headache to our social reformers' is not a major source of serious criminality; and that criminal behaviour is something in a class apart from the miscellaneous lapses characteristic of this group. At the same time even this conclusion may be affected by the particular methods of selection favoured by the various investigators. Obviously a very different picture would result from the index of approximately 20,000 'multi-problem families' which, it has been announced, is to be compiled in New York, and consists of those which have 'been identified by the Youth Board as accounting for 75 per cent of its juvenile delinquency'.[7]

Apart from their inability to manage money, the only positive characteristic common to all the families investigated seems to be the fact that they

[1] Jones, D. Caradog, ed. (1943), Vol. 3, p. 471.

[2] Blacker, ed. (1952), pp. 61, 67, and 51.

[3] On p. 92 of this study the total number of families included is given as thirty-five: but actually particulars are given for thirty-six.

[4] Lewis, Hilda (1954), pp. 82 and 79. [5] Ford and others (1955), p. 22.

[6] Wilson, H. (1957). [7] Youth Board News (June, 1957), p. 7.

are generally large ones—with many young children and few supplementary earners. Those covered by the Eugenics Society's five enquiries boasted 1,693 children in 376 households (exclusive of any grand-children of the heads of the household) or 4·5 per household, the figures varying from 4·0 in Luton to 5·0 in North Kensington.[1] The Bristol investigators recorded that their problem families were 'reproducing at a rate at least twice as high as the rest of the population';[2] and Dr Blacker points out that even the high figures for the five enquiries summarized by him (of which the Bristol survey is one) do 'not express the completed fertilities of these families'.[3] In passing, it may be remarked that this means that the parents of these large families are faced with quite exceptionally difficult problems, failure to cope adequately with which might well be a sign, not so much of their own sub-normality, as of their lack of the supra-normal qualities which the situation demands. Family allowances notwithstanding, the household with several young children dependent solely on parental earnings constitutes to-day one of the economically most hard pressed sections of our community: one man's wage is not enough, and the mother of a large family has too much to do at home to be able to supplement this effectively. It may thus well be true that problem families are the victims as much of their economic circumstances as of their own personal shortcomings, and that these shortcomings are themselves, at least in part, the reaction of despair to impossible demands. When problem parents are described as of 'poor intelligence', or as 'emotionally immature', it should be appreciated that only men and women of quite exceptional intelligence, maturity and indeed physical and mental stamina of every kind would be equal to the tasks imposed upon them.

In the eugenist's mind, however, the many children of the problem family foster the fear that undesirable strains in the population will increase and multiply disproportionately fast; for the belief that problem families tend to reproduce their way of life, generation after generation, either by biological or by cultural transmission, is widely taken for granted. In a circular to local authorities, the Minister of Health has categorically stated that 'children in the "problem families", where one or both parents are often handicapped by physical ill-health or are of low intelligence or suffering from mental instability, are peculiarly exposed to physical neglect and risk of mental illness such as psychological disturbance and retarded mental development'; and that 'problem families thus tend to reproduce themselves in the next generation and cost the community an expense out of all proportion to their numbers'.[4] Dr Wofinden, who was responsible for the Eugenics Society's enquiry in Rotherham, has suggested that 'in the majority of cases . . . the problem family is handed down from generation to generation partly by inherited characteristics and partly, in the words of Dr Stallybrass, by an atrocious upbringing of the children'.[5] Lidbetter's conclusion to much the

[1] Blacker, ed. (1952), p. 69. [2] Wofinden (1950), p. 17. [3] Blacker, ed. (1952), p. 69.

[4] Ministry of Health circular 27/54 (1954), *National Health Service: Health of Children: Prevention of break-up of families.*

[5] Wofinden (1946), p. 131.

same effect has already been quoted.[1] Dr Leslie Housden of the NSPCC, writing of 'The Hopeless Home', finds it not surprising that 'the children of these homes find, in later life, that prison is not too bad a place after all'. Parents who are 'inheritors of evil traditions',[2] he predicts, will continue these for their own children. Again, 'the problem family begets the problem family', writes Mr W. A. Hallas, Principal Probation Officer in Bradford,[3] while Dr H. C. M. Williams has declared that 'With the multiplication of problem families it [*sic*] makes it necessary to safeguard the future of the race by providing adequate measures to deal with this social menace';[4] and Dr Catherine Wright, Assistant Medical Officer of Health for the City of Sheffield, has roundly declared that 'as further investigations have been made, and families observed into the second generation, the far-reaching effects on children and adults of an upbringing in a problem family home have come to be understood'; and that, whatever may be the cause of the condition of problem families, this 'acts on the children of these families and is irreversible'.[5]

Such perpetuation does indeed seem likely; though the fact, which has struck more than one investigator, that the children of problem families are often both happy and obviously loved, might create a presumption to the contrary. Dr Hilda Lewis has, for example, observed that, although an unusually high proportion of her problem family children were of poor intelligence, 'their personality and behaviour . . . were in pleasing contrast' to this.[6] Yet none of these authors, except Lidbetter,[7] has produced any evidence for their statements: the self-perpetuating quality of the problem family still remains to be proved or disproved. Doubtless the practical difficulties in the way of pursuing these families to the second or third generation sufficiently explains the omission; but, distorted though its findings may have been by contemporary social prejudice, the Lidbetter investigation deserves the credit of its as yet unrivalled methodological pioneering.

Far indeed from pursuing the social problem group into succeeding generations, most of our investigators have confined their attention to a single phase in the lifetime of any given family. The picture with which we are presented is a singularly static one. This 'lowest stratum of the population', this 'parasitic section of the community',[8] these 'derelict' or sub-normal families, are discovered at the age at which they have young children at home. Yet for all the thousands of pounds that have been spent on problem family research, we are still quite unable to say whether problem status persists through life, or is merely an incident in an otherwise tolerably respectable existence. None of these investigations has disclosed either what happens to these apparently feckless and incompetent parents[9] when their children are

[1] See page 53. [2] Housden (1955), pp. 183 and 249. [3] Hallas (1953), p. 104.

[4] Williams (1953), p. 1137. [5] Wright (1955), p. 381. [6] Lewis, Hilda (1954), p. 80.

[7] Since the above was written further valuable material has been published by Wright, giving particulars of 'second generation problem families' in one large industrial city. See *Eugenics Review*, April, 1958.

[8] Williams (1953), p. 1059.

[9] Except for the occasional follow-ups of re-housed populations. See pp. 72 ff.

grown up, or what their record was like before they became responsible for a family. For light on this we have to turn to the practical efforts of Local Authorities and private social agencies to cope with difficult families, rather than to the activities of research workers. And from these quarters we have at least limited evidence of the possibility of rehabilitation in certain cases; though this of course tells us nothing of what happens in the many cases where no such efforts are made. The London County Council has, for example, experimented with the provision of special housing units for difficult families, where instruction and advice are laid on, and has found that this pays dividends at any rate in the short run. The numbers involved are small, and the experiment has so far only been continued over about four years; but between a third and a half of those admitted seem to have either re-established themselves or to be on the way to doing so. Other authorities have reported similar experiences. In Holland, where more ambitious experiments in this field have been attempted, Dr Querido seems to have established that the individual members of these difficult families adopt more normal standards when they are separated from one another.[1]

For the rest, without in any way belittling the value of the descriptive material collected by these various investigations (which have indeed done signal service in calling attention to tiresome social problems and in stimulating remedial experiments such as those just mentioned), we have to recognize that science cannot make use of concepts so vague and so subjective as those mentioned on page 57. In due course, with the development of more precise techniques and definitions, it may be possible to chart more accurately than has yet been done the degree of concentration at particular points in the social hierarchy of particular varieties of unacceptable social habits, and the degrees of permanence of any such concentration. Pending such improvements, however, we should resist the temptation to present an appearance of greater precision than is in fact justified.

The widely disparate findings of the many estimates of the intelligence of the heads of problem families well illustrate the importance of this caution. According to the Deputy Medical Officer of Health for Bradford (who, however, quotes no figures) 'the bulk of the problem families have parents who were dull and backward at school but not sufficiently so to obtain special educational facilities'.[2] In the five local surveys summarized by Blacker for the Eugenics Society, the proportion of the male heads of problem families estimated to be of less than normal intelligence ranged from 65 per cent in Bristol to 29 per cent in the West Riding; while the corresponding figures for the housewife's intelligence ranged from 84 per cent in North Kensington to 41 per cent in the West Riding. These assessments were, however, derived, not from formal intelligence tests, but from the judgments of investigators who 'while experienced and doubtless shrewd observers' were not 'psychologists versed in testing methods'.[3] It is to be feared that they tell us more about the varying standards of the observers (does the strong local patriotism

[1] Irvine (1954), p. 28. See also Sheridan (1955 and 1956).

[2] McDonagh (1953), p. 95. [3] Blacker, ed. (1952), pp. 59, 65, and 58.

of the West Riding colour even their view of social problems?) than about the true intellectual capacity of the subjects under investigation. Formal intelligence tests are fallible enough, but subjective assessments which are no more than the 'personal impression derived from conversations during the field visits'[1] must be dismissed as of no scientific value whatever—most of all when they are made by different field workers in different areas. That they should be endowed with a spurious air of accuracy by presentation in statistical tables is much to be deprecated.

The use of more reliable measurements would certainly improve the accuracy of our descriptions; but, before we can hope to go beyond description to explanation, certain fundamental semantic difficulties must be dealt with: for failure to appreciate these has reduced many of the 'explanations' of what are classified as problem family characteristics to virtual tautologies. Thus there is today, as shown at length in Part II of this book, a strong trend towards defining poor mental capacity in terms of social inadequacy. But if the heads of problem families are by definition socially inadequate, and if social inadequacy is itself the proof of deficient mental capacity, the discovery that problem parents are of poor intelligence amounts to no more than the discovery that they are, in fact, problem parents. And the same is true of some of the attempts that have been made to explain problem behaviour in psychological or psychiatric terms. Rankin, for example, has diagnosed the emergence of problem families as the result of weak parents 'overloading themselves', the significant weaknesses in this context being listed as 'psychopathic personality, low intelligence and poor health'. Of these Rankin holds the first to be much the most important; and in support of this he describes the 'immature' behaviour of problem parents, observing that, like children, they have no foresight and no regard for household order and so forth.[2]

Thus we reach the near-tautological conclusion that the proof of the psychopathic personality or emotional immaturity of a problem family is to be found in part at least in the characteristic behaviour which merits its inclusion in this class. Yet none of these labels—low intelligence, emotional immaturity or psychopathic personality—can have any meaning except in terms of criteria which are themselves independent oı the behaviour which they are invoked to explain.

III

As an alternative to the difficult and expensive business of chasing particular families over long periods, some investigators have chosen to fix attention upon the history of particular areas. In Liverpool this ecological method has been used to determine how far the 'problem areas' of the city as defined in the Merseyside survey of 1934 were still characterized, twenty years later, by exceptionally heavy incidence of equally varied social problems; and also to test a particular hypothesis as to the development of cities which has been much discussed in the USA. According to this hypothesis, the growth of a

[1] Wofinden (1950), p. 24. [2] Rankin (1956), p. 95.

city involves a continual invasion of residential neighbourhoods by business and industry; and the worst slum areas with the highest delinquency rates tend to be found in the 'transitional' zones near the city centre, in which industrial is gradually supplanting residential use of land. It is, in short, more the process of deterioration than long-established squalor which is to blame for the indifference of the inhabitants of these areas to conventional norms.

The choice of problems to be studied in the later Liverpool investigation clearly reveals the shift in opinion that has occurred over twenty years. Dependence upon public funds is no longer regarded as in itself a qualification for inclusion in the social problem group. In the later study, the defects selected for investigation 'were those which, it was thought, were most likely to precipitate family breakdown and to impose a heavy burden on the social services',[1] such as the frequency of mental defect and of mental illness, or the number of children received into the care of the Children's Department or, alternatively, placed on probation by the Juvenile Courts. But even if the problems were different, their location, it appeared, was still the same: the authors found that 'Liverpool still had a problem area and that the site of the greatest incidence of social ills [as redefined] had not moved noticeably during the past twenty years'.[2] In their opinion 'the subsequent development of social legislation has merely changed the apparent defects and provided care for those who become affected by them, but it has not succeeded in eliminating the problem'.[3] The distribution of these defects, moreover, appeared to give some confirmation of the American hypothesis mentioned in the preceding paragraph. In the Merseyside survey, every ward but one in the inner city area showed an incidence of 'mental defect and epilepsy' above the average for the city as a whole, the figures ranging from 24 to 30 per 10,000 of population as against the city average of 20; while every ward in this area without exception recorded figures for 'immorality, crime and alcoholism' in excess of the city average, the figures in this case ranging from 4·8 to 11·0 against the whole city's figure of 4·4. In the later study it was these same areas which were distinguished by exceptionally heavy incidence of mental defect, of juveniles on probation and of illegitimacy. Against city figures of 35 per 10,000 of population for mental defect, of 104 per 10,000 population of relevant ages for probation cases, and of 5·4 illegitimate births per 100 live births, the wards in the inner area had figures ranging from 38 to 54 for mental defect; from 104 to 376 for probation cases; and from 4·0 to 16·0 for illegitimacy. In addition, the incidence of mental illness, and even of suicides, appears, though less markedly, to have shown the same preponderance in the decaying inner zone of the city. Indeed, one particular ward enjoyed the unenviable distinction of scoring the highest figure for every one of the defects listed in the later study, with the sole and somewhat surprising exception of infant mortality; and this was the very ward which had taken top place for 'immorality, crime and alcoholism' twenty years earlier. This 'inner residential

[1] Castle and Gittus (1957), p. 51. [2] Simey (1955), p. A.3.
[3] Castle and Gittus (1957), p. 57.

ward where the former homes of wealthy merchants have fallen into disrepair and are now occupied by immigrant groups . . . might be regarded as the most extreme point of this central "problem area"'.[1]

This Liverpool investigation is exceptional in the range of its interests. Most of the investigators who have interested themselves in the ecological aspects of social pathology have concentrated their attention more upon actual law-breaking, than upon the generalized social inadequacy associated with problem families: and most of them also have been Americans, studying American conditions, the classic example being the Shaw and McKay studies of the distribution of juvenile delinquency in Chicago and a number of other cities. The work of the last-mentioned authors has been so often described that it is perhaps unnecessary to give more than the briefest summary. In all the cities which they examined (and these were scattered North, South, East and West across the American continent) the findings were both 'astonishingly uniform'[2] and in close conformity with the same hypothesis. In Chicago, Cleveland, Philadelphia, Denver, Seattle and half a dozen other cities delinquency rates ran high in the inner and low in the outer zones, declining almost everywhere in a smooth and regular progression from city centre to outer suburb, and with little regard to topography, industrial development or railway facilities. Only in Baltimore[3] do events appear to have taken a rather different turn. There slums were not concentrated near the city centre, and the invasion of residential districts by industrial enterprise was found to have occurred sporadically in the outskirts as well as in the heart of the city.

In this country sociologists have, at least until recently, not shown great eagerness to map the geography of delinquency. Apart from the Liverpool enquiry already mentioned, and an ambitious project at Bristol, the results of which are not available at the time of writing, there is little to record except an unpublished survey undertaken in an urban area close to Nottingham under the direction of Professor W. J. H. Sprott[4] and a study of the borough of Croydon by Dr T. P. Morris.[5] From the former of these it would seem that the unequal incidence of problem behaviour which was so noticeable in Liverpool is sometimes repeated in the characteristics of particular streets—even in those that lie within a few minutes' walk of one another: the standards of behaviour in Dyke Street are not, apparently, those of Gladstone Road; and, what is more, this is very well recognized by the inhabitants of both. Elsewhere, however, even within the limits of a town of 23,000 inhabitants, this street-by-street concentration was not observed: households which earned a black mark were much more spottily distributed over larger areas; though still not so evenly as to obliterate the contrast between black and white districts. In Morris' investigation, likewise, offenders were found to be heavily concentrated in 'deteriorating areas', the incidence being even more marked in the case of juvenile than in that of adult crime; and, although the smooth progression from city centre to outer suburb, which impressed Shaw and

[1] Castle and Gittus (1957), p. 53. [2] Shaw and McKay (1942), p. ix. [3] Lander (1954).
[4] Sprott (1954). [5] Morris, T. P. (1958).

McKay as characteristic of so many American cities, did not reappear, nevertheless in Croydon as in the USA the homes of offenders tended to be located in the slums.[1]

Though some variety of patterns thus appears possible, no one has found anything that looks like a random distribution of pathological features. Professor E. W. Burgess, whose name is generally associated with the 'concentric zone' theory of city growth, has himself expressed some surprise at the regularity of the progression from centre to suburb which the Shaw and McKay investigation revealed. Yet even the most unprejudiced sociological eyebrows will hardly be raised at the discovery that delinquency tends to be concentrated in particular areas, and that in general those are the slummy ones. Sociologists themselves are constantly collecting material to show that life in the back streets is very different from what it is in the high-class residential neighbourhoods, and constantly trying to introduce those who live in the latter to the habits and modes of life which prevail in the former. Dr Zweig,[2] for instance, has described how the domestic life, the pub habits and the attitude to work of the British working man struck an observant foreigner. Mr Mays[3] has lately produced a picture of the codes, conduct and interests of the members of a Liverpool Youth Club. Dr Spinley,[4] approaching the subject from a more distinctively psychological standpoint, has painted a vivid contrast between what she regards as the 'basic personality type' characteristic of the privileged and the underprivileged classes respectively; and the unpublished Nottingham survey,[5] already referred to, has reported examples of proletarian language with a degree of fidelity which, one imagines, may well make publication difficult. Dr Pearl Jephcott,[6] also, along with her colleagues who are active in youth organizations, has given many vivid pen portraits of the young men and women who have already been at work for three or four years by the age at which the undergraduate enters upon his university career; while a commission appointed by the Church of Scotland has examined on the basis of a questionnaire the leisure occupations, the political interests, the sexual codes and the attitude to the churches of a small sample of Scottish youth from predominantly urban areas.[7]

All these investigators would agree that differing attitudes towards criminal conduct, or, more accurately, towards certain forms of such conduct, are simply illustrations of the differences in what it is now fashionable to call 'culture patterns', in which these attitudes are but one element. The delinquent from the black areas who spends his working hours drifting from one unskilled job to another and his leisure alternately in cinema and dance hall has his own standards of dress, language, sportsmanship, honesty and sexual conduct: and these are emphatically not those professed by his middle-class contemporary. Many of the subjects of Mays' investigation would see nothing wrong in stealing from large shops or stores because they were not taking anything which belonged to the assistants personally, and because in any

[1] Morris, T. P. (1958), Chap. VII. [2] Zweig (1952). [3] Mays (1954).
[4] Spinley (1953). [5] Sprott (1954). [6] Jephcott (1954).
[7] Church of Scotland Youth Committee (1956).

case a 'vast commercial organization could very well afford to sustain a trifling loss';[1] but they were generally more dubious about stealing from known individuals, unless these happened to be their employers. Indeed, it might be added that at no point, perhaps, is the contrast in class attitudes more marked than on this question of stealing from an employer. To the privileged classes this offence is peculiarly heinous as being an abuse of a position of trust; whereas to the unprivileged it is peculiarly venial, as being a fair enough answer to exploitation. Among Mays' subjects shoplifting was looked upon 'as a normal method of acquiring additional pocket money'; and more than three-quarters of his whole group admitted privately that they had at some time or other committed offences for which they could have been prosecuted;[2] Dr Trenaman, also, by an ingenious calculation from official and other sources, came to the conclusion that, in bad areas, one in three of the male members of large families will not only commit, but actually be found guilty of, an offence in the course of his lifetime.[3]

Those who live in these areas are thus exposed not to one but to two sets of norms which are not easily reconciled. For even in districts where certain kinds of crime are taken for granted and evoke no guilt, no one can be unaware of the conventional standards which the police, the schools and the courts exist to uphold. This conflict is, however, easily overlooked in circles where the iniquity of stealing and of similar unlawful actions is treated as axiomatic. In such circles it is all too easy to assume the universal acceptance of one's own implicit code; and it is the merit of these descriptive studies that, with varying degrees of vividness, they expose the false nature of this assumption. It has indeed even been suggested that information as to group norms ought to be made available to the courts; and that the time will come when in criminal cases use will be made not merely of prediction tables[4] or of intelligence and personality tests, but even of 'Tables of Group Values and Group Attitudes', as evidence of say the standards prevailing in the factory in which an offender is employed, or of corresponding information about 'a greengrocer in this or that village or a company director in this or that city'.[5]

For the conflict of norms can indeed be sharp. While the white areas bask under the protection of a friendly 'bobby', to the inhabitants of the neighbouring black spots 'All coppers are bastards and the only good copper is a dead copper'. To the child growing up to find his way about the world it must often be more than a little puzzling. The 'social worker, the teacher, and the employer are . . . baffled in their dealings with the slum child' because 'there is no common language of morality and communication is a crucial problem';[6] and the difficulties raised by the divergences of codes and the obstruction of communication may even be still further aggravated by differences in the basic personality of the 'privileged' and the 'deprived'. As the result of her investigations into widely contrasted social groups, Spinley has concluded that the typical slum dweller 'shows a marked absence of a

[1] Mays (1954), p. 116. [2] ibid., pp. 118 and 81. [3] Trenaman (1952), pp. 204–9.
[4] For a discussion of these see Chap. VI. [5] Mannheim (1955), p. 16.
[6] Spinley (1953), p. 83.

strict and efficient conscience, an unwillingness and inability to deal with disturbing or unpleasant situations'. He is 'unable to postpone satisfactions', while 'his attitude towards authority is one of hostility and rebellion'; whereas the typical public school product 'has a strict, effective conscience'; he 'faces disturbing situations and attempts to deal adequately with them'; he postpones present satisfactions 'for the sake of greater ones in the future'; and in most situations he accepts authority, though he may 'discard rules and commands if they conflict with the standards of his own social group'.[1]

Psychiatrically orientated theories tend to assume that there is something abnormal in stealing; as indeed, from the standpoint of the respectable professional circles in which one must assume that psychiatrists generally move, but from that standpoint only, there is.[2] But to the sociologist this postulate of abnormality, as applied to districts with a heavy incidence of delinquency, is beside the mark. It is conformity rather than deviance which explains the anti-social behaviour prevalent in these areas. Nor, conformity notwithstanding, is there anything to wonder at in the fact that even in the blackest areas criminal behaviour is never universal. For, on the one hand, every culture has its own deviants; while, on the other hand, districts of high delinquency, as has been said, boast not one but two mutually inconsistent codes of morality. Between these two the individual makes his choice, often perhaps vacillating inconsistently from one to the other; and that choice is as likely to be determined by casual contacts or chance happenings, as by the presence or absence of some grave psychological trauma, constitutional weakness or mental abnormality. A medical analogy may be appropriate here. When people fall ill of a contagious disease, previous contact with a source of infection is generally accepted as a sufficient explanation. No doubt careful research could establish variations in individual susceptibility which would also help to determine why some people succumb and others escape; but for practical purposes it is on the search for contacts that attention is generally focused. We certainly do not think it a mark of abnormality if a child in whose school there is an epidemic of measles develops the disease himself; and there is no reason to think differently about those who commit offences in crime-infested areas.

The significance of what can only be called casual contacts or suggestions occurring in a fertile environment certainly deserves more attention than it usually gets. Little support has been forthcoming from other criminologists for the late Professor Sutherland's hypothesis that 'criminality is learned', and that it is due to 'association with other criminals'. Sutherland's own chief interest happened to be centred upon white collar crimes, defined as those committed by the upper social classes in the course of their business activities; and as an explanation of these he suggested that men who have begun life in a good environment may take to crime because they 'get into particular

[1] Spinley (1953), pp. 129–130.

[2] Though in view of the losses sustained by clubs and libraries, even this should perhaps be subject to some reservations.

business situations in which criminality is practically a folkway';[1] but he claimed also that a similar differential association theory would cover all classes of crime. Certainly, from my own experience in the juvenile courts, I have been impressed by the part that casual occurrences appear to play in determining who does and who does not step over the line in districts in which court appearances are not at all unusual. The arrival of a particular family in a particular street may have devastating consequences for the children of neighbours with hitherto blameless records; and so also may the necessity of moving to a new district or a new school where new types of companion are encountered. And if to all this the ruthlessly deterministic psychologist makes the reply that we all choose our friends to suit our basic personalities, one can only comment that a theory which denies to external events any influence on our lives requires a lot of proving.

A simple parallel may be appropriate here. Just as some people in areas of high criminality do, and some do not, commit offences, so, on any given day, some members of the public are, and some are not, walking in the West End of London. Both are largely 'chance' collections; and to invoke psychological abnormalities in order to account for the presence of a particular individual in a shopping crowd might well be no more absurd than to try to account in similar terms for the appearance of another in the dock. In the case of the shoppers, as in that of the criminals, it could, no doubt, in theory at least, be established by sufficiently detailed psychological investigation just why any individual happens on any given occasion to be included in their ranks. Differences in psychological make-up might be shown to play their part in determining the composition of the West End crowds—the window-shoppers including perhaps more than their share of the abnormally acquisitive. But it is not primarily to psychiatry that we should look to explain the congested state of London's West End; nor would a psychiatric explanation generally be invoked to account for an increase in this congestion in the weeks immediately before Christmas. The social custom of Christmas present-giving would be accepted as a more appropriate explanation. Yet what shopping is to some areas, shop-lifting may well be to others: the one is as much taken for granted as the other, and each in its own sphere may be affected by (and indeed a means of meeting) the customary demands of Christmas.

The divergence of norms may itself, moreover, be aggravated by the very processes by which the community seeks to convince the offender of the error of his ways. To be convicted of a crime (other than that which is condoned by the prevailing mores) is to acquire a special experience; and shared experience is the basis of a common culture. Graduation from a period of probation to residence in an approved school, and thereafter to detention centre, Borstal or prison is itself as much a way of life as is graduation from Eton to Oxford and thence into one of the professions. And more is involved in this shared experience than contamination in the sense of exposure to explicit suggestions for future criminal activities from offenders of greater experience. It is the unspoken assumptions that matter—the assumptions that law-breaking is all

[1] Sutherland (1940), p. 11.

in the day's work, and that a period in prison, like a period of national service, is a disagreeable, but by no means an extraordinary, experience. We have, indeed, to face the disagreeable paradox that experience of what are intended to be reformative institutions actually increases the probability of future lapses into criminality: it has, for example, been shown that a previous residence in an approved school is one of the best predictors of recidivism among Borstal boys. The effects of such exposure have, however, been relatively little studied in criminological investigations: indeed, they tend to be discounted. Partly perhaps this neglect is due to the firm hold of the doctrine that anti-social acts are the expression of inherent traits of a person's personality, which are relatively unaffected by the incidents of his life experience—that there is, as Reiss has put it, a 'supposed fixity of the "character structure"' which permits one to decide who, at the age of six, will develop into a delinquent, and which dismisses the social environment of the child from age six to sixteen as a 'negligible circumstance in his life-history'.[1] Partly also recognition of the co-existence of a 'sub-culture' based on familiarity with criminal proceedings and penal institutions may carry implications that are too distressing to contemplate. For even if we do not draw the melancholy inference that our methods of treating offenders actually have deleterious effects in themselves, these methods clearly do evoke, so to speak, their own resistances, not only in the cruder sense that they may from time to time stimulate rebellion, but also, more subtly, in that they are bound to create a fellowship of shared experiences and shared values.

Sociologists have thought it worth while to coin a special term—'anomie'—to describe the unorthodox social values, norms and attitudes to which 'underprivileged' children may be conditioned. In a culture where status and success depend chiefly upon the possession of material goods, the underprivileged, it is argued, are virtually deprived of legal opportunities for acquiring these desiderata: so they make illegal ones instead, thus creating what is known as a state of 'anomie'. A career in delinquency 'offers the promise of economic gain, prestige, and companionship'; and 'crime, in this situation, may be regarded as one of the means employed by people to acquire, or to attempt to acquire, the economic and social values generally idealized in our culture, which persons in other circumstances acquire by conventional means'.[2]

Many of these interpretations have, however, a suspiciously tautological ring, and may be thought to amount to little more than statements that 'delinquency is due to a breakdown or lack of respect for law and order'—a conclusion hardly worthy of the high-powered social research on which it is founded. The sceptic may well ask what is gained by labelling familiar differences in social habits 'sub-cultures', or whether 'anomie' is more than a high-sounding name for the attempts of the poor to get rich quick in the only ways that may be open to them. For after all there is nothing to wonder at in the fact that a light-hearted attitude prevails in certain areas towards breaches of some of our criminal laws. Every class excuses, or perhaps one

[1] Reiss (1951), p. 117. [2] Shaw and McKay (1942), pp. 436 and 439.

should say, sees no need to excuse, the crimes to which it is particularly prone. What is true of the black is true also of the white areas: the tolerated crimes are different, that is all. Indeed, this very impression of whiteness is only obtained *by omitting from the record of convictions in the criminal courts* those that are most likely to be popular in those areas—an omission in which students of the ecology of crime seem as yet to find nothing incongruous. I have already commented upon the significance in this context of the prevailing indifference to convictions for even serious motoring offences. To-day, it seems, even the wife of an MP and former Minister of the Crown can openly sit in the passenger seat while her boy of fourteen drives a tractor on the highway, thus aiding and abetting him in driving under age and without insurance.[1] Nor is it generally thought particularly reprehensible to make free with public property. Mays has described how 'University students remove books from libraries, clerks take stationery from their offices, craftsmen take wood and nails and paint to carry out private jobs and the occupants of railway carriages purloin lavatory paper, lamps, leather straps, ash trays, and other fittings'.[2] In the United States over 42 per cent of a sample of 200 male students admitted to having played truant from school, 69 per cent to having stolen fruit, 14 per cent to having carried concealed weapons, 20 per cent to having possessed stolen goods, 10 per cent to shoplifting and 23 per cent to miscellaneous petty stealing. For these and other offences, however, the number who had been charged in court, 'outside of receiving traffic tickets', was negligible.[3]

The proposition that the residents in some areas, or the members of some social groups, are more disposed to criminality than are their differently placed neighbours ought therefore to be revised. The truth is that the antisocial behaviour of one social circle takes one form, while the members of other circles both behave and misbehave differently. Thus revised, this proposition hardly calls for any recondite explanation of why the residents in what are traditionally regarded as black areas behave as they do. Their light-hearted disregard of the laws of property is in no way more remarkable han the equally cheerful indifference to the provisions of the Road Traffic Acts exhibited by their more prosperous neighbours—to which indeed it is closely analogous. The outward expression differs, but the inward and spiritual lack of grace is the same.

In general, therefore, it may be said that ecological studies have succeeded in establishing that things are very much what one would expect them to be: birds of a feather flock, or at any rate are found, together. But it is the interpretation of these findings which is the critical issue; and this remains a matter for speculation. If it is true that criminality, or, more precisely, some types of criminality, are highly concentrated in particular areas, or associated with slum conditions, then three crucial questions arise. First, is this concentration due to the fact that the slums are tenanted by the dregs of the population who would perpetuate their deplorable habits wherever they lived?

[1] *East Anglian Daily Times* (September 19, 1957). [2] Mays (1954), p. 117.
[3] Porterfield (1946), pp. 41 and 43.

Second, if this is the case, is the transmission biological or merely cultural? Or, third, are slum habits the direct products of the corruption of slum life, destined to disappear in a more favourable environment?

From the angle of policy, it clearly makes a great difference which of these hypotheses is nearest the truth. If sordid areas are tenanted by families whose biological inheritance must be reckoned, in terms of current social values, as at the least unfortunate, then the advocates of sterilization can raise their voices. But if, on the other hand, the perpetuation of unacceptable ways of life in these areas is a cultural rather than a biological process, then the outlook for children who are removed to a more favourable environment (as the children of criminal or exceptionally difficult parents not infrequently are) should be about as good as for anybody else. And if the localized incidence of certain forms of criminality is due merely to the direct impact of slum conditions upon slum-dwellers, then the obvious course is to pull down the slums; and that should be the end of the trouble.

A determined attack upon the social disorganization and sordid physical features of slum areas, besides being highly desirable in itself, would certainly provide a practical test of the relative strength of some at least of these hypotheses. But pending some such holocaust, social investigation has little to offer that would make discrimination between them possible. Varying opinions have been expressed by students of the ecology of crime. Morris, for instance, rejects the thesis that 'the physical deterioration of a neighbourhood is somehow vitally related to . . . delinquency and crime', believing rather that low rentals attract the lowest income group wherein the majority of offenders are found. 'Low status and low rentals are normally found together in urban areas and physical deterioration, where it helps to depress both status and rentals, can be said to be a feature likely to attract those individuals who may be loosely described as the core of the "social problem group".'[1] Spencer, also, has commented upon the 'constant process of self-selection' which takes place in areas that acquire the stigma of 'roughness'. In Bristol, where high delinquency rates tend to be concentrated in housing estates situated on the circumference of the city, rather than in any deteriorating centre district, he noted a high level of residential mobility as characteristic of these estates. Tenants who do not like the neighbourhood move off as fast as they can, and even within the estates 'a corresponding process of segregation takes place in which particular streets or groups of streets acquire a preponderance of delinquent families'[2]—a process which perhaps helps to explain the extremely narrow localization of delinquent families observed by Sprott in Nottingham.[3] Shaw and McKay, on the other hand, incline to favour the view that the slum corrupts its inhabitants, rather than that the corrupt gravitate towards the slummy environment. The unchanging localization of delinquency, they find, overshadows the established correlations with other variables, such as poverty, bad housing, tuberculosis, mental disorder or the proportion of Negroes or of foreign-born inhabitants in an American city; and they infer from this the presence of some 'general basic factor', described as 'social disorganiza-

[1] Morris, T. P. (1958), Ch. VII. [2] Spencer (July 1954), p. 7. [3] See page 64.

tion or the lack of organized community effort to deal with'[1] slum conditions. In their view, in short, slums breed delinquents because nobody bothers about the welfare of slum-dwellers—who, in turn, do not bother about other people's standards of behaviour.

This conclusion is, however, in its turn challenged by Lander. Relying upon more sophisticated statistical methods, he finds 'no evidence to suggest that the delinquency rate is a function of the "invasion" of industry or commerce' into residential areas, or that 'locale per se is an independent or causal factor in the predictions or understanding of delinquency'.[2] In his view 'anomie' operates as a factor of social instability independently of the 'general disorganization' manifested in poverty, bad housing and tuberculosis; and this factor is reflected, for example, in an inverse correlation between home-ownership and delinquency. Whatever their physical environment, people who struggle to buy their own homes tend to be the sort who will eschew crime. To the operation of the same factor also are attributed the differing records of different ethnic groups: the Chinese and the Jews in Baltimore, where Lander's investigations were made, were found to be much less disposed towards delinquency than were the Negroes; and this is explained as the result, not of any inherent criminal propensities in the Negro race, but of the fact that much of the Negro population was living in areas of great racial heterogeneity which do not have common, well-established standards: in those districts in which the Negro population was more concentrated, delinquency was noticeably less marked.

None of these interpretations, however, is very solidly based. For the answers to our critical questions, we must still await the results of long term enquiries; and these, for obvious practical reasons, are not easily undertaken.

The Liverpool investigation already quoted has established, at least for that city, the persistence of social problems in a particular geographical area; but the authors of this did not attempt to ascertain how far the residents in that area are the biological descendants of the 'social problem group' located there by the survey of twenty years before. In Glasgow, however, the subsequent histories of certain slum families have been recorded after they had been rehoused for periods varying from ten to twenty-seven years; and attempts have been made to compare their way of life with that of others who have been left behind in the slums. These families, it is true, were not exclusively or even predominantly drawn from those responsible for the black spots on maps of delinquency or anti-social conduct: their experience is therefore valuable only in so far as it reveals the persistence of patterns of behaviour in general, and not merely of such habits as are socially unacceptable. Valid comparison is, moreover, made difficult by the fact that families who had been rehoused ten or more years ago must now be relatively elderly. But for what it is worth the evidence from this investigation does suggest that 'the eradication of slum sickness does not come with the mere erection of new houses', and that some at least of the characteristic habits of the slum dwellers die hard. 'The feeding habits of the rehoused families showed no improvement

[1] Shaw and McKay (1942), p. xi. [2] Lander (1954), pp. 85 and 87.

on those of the slum families in that the proportion . . . who sat down to meals with some semblance of reasonable order was no higher'. Amongst adolescents in these families the incidence of delinquency was much in excess of that found by Ferguson among Glasgow boys who had left school at the earliest permitted age, and was, indeed, 'very similar to that experienced among young people still living in slums'.[1] Nor was there much difference in the condition of the homes (as assessed by the standards of an experienced Health Visitor) of those who had had over twenty years in which to get used to their new surroundings, as compared with those whose slum experience was only ten to fourteen years behind them.

Apart from this Glasgow enquiry, we have very little evidence as to how far patterns of behaviour (good or bad) persist over long periods in spite of significant changes of environment. Bagot's investigation suggested that, in Liverpool, a heavy incidence of delinquency in families who had been transferred from slums to housing estates was traceable chiefly to the older age groups who had had experience of the bad old conditions; and that otherwise 'the effect of removing families from overcrowded areas to new housing estates is to reduce the amount of delinquency among the juveniles concerned'.[2] But Mannheim, in his English Middletown investigation, took a more pessimistic view, finding that three well-kept housing estates, peopled by those who were previously homeless or had come from the slums, contributed 'more than their due share in juvenile delinquency'.[3] No exact figures are, however, given, either as to the scale of this excess, or as to the period that had elapsed since these families were rehoused.

Ecological studies have thus shown a social and geographical distribution of offenders which conforms to expectations: hardly any surprising facts have emerged. They can, however, throw light upon the mechanisms by which an anti-social culture is absorbed and communicated. And their value is enormously enhanced if they can be prolonged over a considerable period. It is indeed only to long-term studies, extending over more than one generation, and particularly to those which record the history both of an area and of its population, that we must look for answers to the really vital questions as to the concentration of antisocial attitudes at the bottom of the social scale. Indeed, until extensive investigations have been undertaken on these lines, we cannot even say whether in any continuing sense the 'social problem group' about which so much has been written is a myth or a reality.

IV

In a general sense, areas of social disorganization may be said to be areas in which incomes tend to be low: the well-to-do do not live in the slums. To that extent the discovery that certain types of criminal or other anti-social behaviour tend to be concentrated among those who live in such areas con-

[1] Ferguson and Pettigrew (1954), pp. 201, 197–98, 188, 192.
[2] Bagot (1941), pp. 70–71. [3] Mannheim (1948), p. 32.

firms the assumption, common enough a generation or so ago, that poverty and criminality march hand in hand. Even within the poorer neighbourhoods, however, there are large variations in economic status. Any precise study of the association of poverty with criminality, or with other forms of social pathology, would therefore need to take account of the circumstances, both of particular families within these neighbourhoods, and of particular individuals within these families.

Such studies are not in the current fashion. For this a major reason appears to be the astonishing spread of the myth that poverty has been eliminated. The doctrine that 'The Welfare State has feverishly increased its responsibilities until no one is ill-clad or hungry, and no one experiences real want or poverty'[1] or that (in the words of a correspondent in *The Times*) 'necessitous poverty' has been 'banished'[2]—appears to-day to have acquired the status of an axiom; with the result that any investigation into the extent and nature of contemporary poverty, or into the degree of its association with other social evils, is rare indeed. One may search in vain through recent issues of the *Register of Economic and Social Research* for examples of such projects; nor have supplementary enquiries at the main centres of research proved more fruitful.

Even quite superficial acquaintance with the facts, however, is enough to prove that this complacent optimism is quite unjustified. Undoubtedly the past twenty years have seen a significant improvement in the standards of working-class living. In this, however, in contradiction, again, to what is widely believed, the part played by welfare legislation and social service benefits has been a relatively minor one. Far and away the most important factor in the improved economic position of the working class has been the reduction of unemployment. How far this reduction has been itself the conscious result of social policies deliberately framed to embody the philosophy of a 'welfare state', and how far it has been merely the product of lucky accidents, is a matter which cannot be argued here: certainly more than one opinion on the subject is tenable. But the fact that it is full employment, and not social legislation, which, both directly by diminishing the numbers who are deprived of all earning power, and indirectly by putting teeth into wage claims, is responsible for the incomes of the 'lower income groups' being not so low—that fact is established beyond all argument. It was, no doubt, the intention both of the Beveridge Report, and of the Government responsible for the social legislation which followed this, that the social services should be generous enough to do away with poverty, as measured by such standards as those of the late Mr Rowntree's well-known investigations; but that intention, thanks to the persistent erosion of social service payments by inflation, has consistently failed to be realized. Even as early as three years after the 1946 National Insurance Act came into effect, Titmuss had to point out that in 1911, the amount of sickness benefit paid to an individual

[1] MacCalman, in Soddy, ed. (1955), Vol. I, p. 57.
[2] *The Times* (November 5, 1954), p. 5.

worker was 'worth more in purchasing power and, taken by itself, was altogether more generous than the amount paid to-day'.[1]

This means of course that anyone who is unable to enter the labour market has little cause to be anything but highly sceptical of the reality of a welfare state. The very considerable population which is dependent upon allowances provided by the National Assistance Board has constantly, in recent years, dropped below the 'poverty line'. At the time of their York enquiry in 1950, Rowntree and Lavers[2] calculated that an income of 56s 2d a week, after payment of rent, was required for a man and wife to maintain the minimum subsistence income as defined in his well-known poverty line; while for a man, wife and three children the figure was 99s 2d. Yet, up to September 1951, the National Assistance Board was paying only 43s 6d to a married couple and 79s 6d to a family with three children of school age, even if these were all in the 11–15 age group for which the Board's scale reaches its maximum: on Rowntree's own calculations, therefore, assistance families were at this date living well below his poverty line. In September 1951, and again in June 1952, the Board's scales were raised, reaching at the latter date 59s for a married couple and 107s for a couple with three children of the most expensive age. In the meantime, however, the cost of living had increased; and, if the Ministry of Labour's retail price index is used as a measure of this increase, the NAB rates were still below the poverty line. Between October 1950 and June 1952 this index rose by 20 per cent (from 115 to 138), so that the Rowntree minima, if correspondingly adjusted, would have become 67s 5d for a couple on their own and 119s for a family of five. Thereafter prices continued to rise, but not till early in 1955 were the NAB rates raised again, and then not sufficiently to overtake the rising cost of living. Indeed, calculated on this basis, it was not till June 1956 that the NAB rates at last caught up, by which time they were raised to 67s for a married couple and 121s for a family with three children over eleven.

It can of course be argued that the retail price index is not a good measure of changes in the cost of living of families living on national assistance, inasmuch as this index includes all manner of commodities which are at any time far beyond the reach of such families. Undoubtedly, if no account is taken of the prices of any articles other than the absolutely essential foods which compose the Rowntree minimum subsistence diet, and of the Rowntree minimum outlay on fuel, the position of people living on assistance can be made to appear slightly less grim—at least since 1953; but it is still pretty miserable. Schulz,[3] who has made calculations for such basic essentials only, finds that, at that date, after paying for houseroom, minimum subsistence diet and minimum fuel requirements, a family of two persons living on assistance would have had 17s 4d per week left (8s 8d each), while a family of three would have had 20s 8d left between them. Out of this they would have had to provide *everything* except the bare minima of food and fuel—clothes, cleaning materials, newspapers, the occasional bus fare, stamp or postcard, not to mention supplements to the meagre food allowance and chilly standard

[1] Titmuss (1951), p. 191. [2] Rowntree and Lavers (1951). [3] Schulz (1955), p. 225.

of heating. Nor would they have had even this much over, if they had failed to lay out their expenditure on food and fuel in accordance with the extremely economical and judicious budget postulated by Schulz and Rowntree. On this basis Schulz is certainly able to show that those who are dependent on assistance for their living noticeably improved their position after about 1944: but down to 1941 the larger families could not have reached even the Rowntree poverty standard for food and fuel, even if they never spent anything else at all. While this may justify her conclusion that 'poverty, in the sense in which the term was understood before the war, has been abolished'[1] for such families, the evidence hardly justifies the complacent belief that poverty in any more contemporary sense is now unknown.

The number of people who are thus left below what has long been regarded as a very severe poverty line varies a good deal from time to time, but is always considerable. At the end of 1955 the total of persons in receipt of regular allowances from the NAB (excluding blind and tubercular persons who receive special rates) amounted to 1,527,000 persons; and this is indeed the lowest figure recorded for four years. Even this figure, however, related only to the actual recipients of allowances and takes no account of their dependants. If these dependants are also included, together with the blind and the tubercular, the total number of individuals whose standard of living is set by the Board's scales is naturally very much larger:[2] in 1955 more than half a million more would be added to the total. The Board has indeed itself pointed out that in 1949 no less than one person in every thirty in the whole population was in receipt of assistance allowances; and that this was actually a larger proportion of the population (as well as, of course, a much larger absolute number) than that which fifty years ago was dependent, in whole or in part, upon outdoor relief.

Since the NAB allowances are based upon a means test, those who receive them cannot supplement their incomes from other sources: if they do, their allowances will be proportionately reduced. It is true that certain exceptions to this rule are allowed: these include sick pay from a Friendly Society or trade union, and various forms of disablement and superannuation pensions, but only up to very small amounts; and no one can have an income of more than 20*s* a week from all these 'disregarded' resources put together. The difference which permitted income from these sources make to the economic position of the Board's clients is trifling. In 1955 the gross resources in the 'disregarded' category amounted to £236,000 per week, of which £96,000 was taken into account as being in excess of the permitted maxima. The total sum, therefore, which recipients of NAB allowances might have enjoyed in excess of the Board's scales could not have been more than £140,000. At that date, the number of persons, including dependants, who were drawing allowances from the Board amounted to 2,216,000. At the most, therefore, disregarded resources may have added just over 1s 3d per week to these people's income. As we do not know in what way disregarded resources are distributed, we cannot say in how many cases they will have been sufficient

[1] Schulz (1955), p. 232. [2] 604,000 dependants.

to bring their owners above the poverty line; but there can hardly have been many such; and, in any case, the gap between the NAB's scales and the Rowntree poverty line as revised by the Ministry's retail price index has constantly amounted to much more than a mere 1s 3d per week.

The recipients of NAB allowances are largely made up of old age pensioners, widows, deserted wives and the chronic sick and their dependants. It is these classes, today, who constitute the bulk of the army of the New Poor. Their number, as we have seen, is far from negligible; and to them must be added one or two other groups. These include, first, those working-class families in which the breadwinner does not earn exceptionally high wages, and in which there are several young children and no supplementary earners. Children's allowances notwithstanding, families in this position have a very hard struggle. In a second category are those whose incomes are for one reason or another interrupted. Because social service payments have lagged so far behind wages, the gap between normal working incomes and the level to which people are reduced in sickness, retirement or other periods of stringency is constantly increasing, and is now appreciably greater than it was before the war. In consequence, the stresses, when they come, are more acutely felt—both psychologically and economically. The psychological point is obvious: a big drop hurts more than a little one, even if the actual level reached is the same in both cases. Economically, also, interruption of earning power becomes increasingly disastrous as a higher normal standard of living is reflected in higher commitments such as rent or hire-purchase payments; for it is quite unrealistic, as well as inhuman, to expect that in periods of stringency arising from the ordinary hazards of life, durable household goods bought on the instalment system will be the first casualties; and equally unrealistic to refuse to classify as 'poor' those whose consumption of food and other necessaries falls below the poverty line because they are not prepared to face the consequences of defaulting on such commitments. The censorious may look on this as ground for condemning hire-purchase altogether; but moral judgments notwithstanding, the poverty is real.

Similarly, those classes whose normal real incomes, actual or expected, have fallen drastically are naturally also tempted to starve themselves of necessities in order to maintain conventional standards. This is the plight of those sections of the middle class whose incomes have not kept pace with the general rise. For their struggle to keep up appearances at the expense of necessities these classes are far less often criticized than are their working-class neighbours who give a comparable priority to hire-purchase commitments; but the quality of their poverty (though not necessarily the degree) is of the same order.

The New Poor, it will be appreciated, are a scattered, unorganized company. Unlike the unemployed of the Clyde, the Merseyside or the mining districts in the thirties, the Poor of to-day are not geographically concentrated in areas of stagnant industry. Many of them have known more spacious days, and others may reasonably hope that times will not always be so bad: extreme poverty is unlikely, to-day, to continue throughout life. All these facts no doubt help to explain why their existence is so generally overlooked, if not explicitly denied. Some idea of what their lives are like may, however, be gleaned from occasional enquiries undertaken into the welfare of special classes, such as the old or the young; though these have generally been concerned less with the actual poverty, than with the social or medical conditions of their subjects. Vivid illustrations, for example, may be found in Shaw's investigation of a sample of Bristol families whose earnings had been interrupted for six months or more by illness or injury in 1956. In these families the children go without pocket money, the enterprising housewife sells rags and jam jars to make a few coppers, there are no new clothes, cosmetics or hair-do's, the men give up their pipes and even their newspapers, the fire can only be lighted for a few hours each day, and the family goes to bed to keep warm.[1]

Other investigators have drawn much the same picture. An enquiry by the National Council of Social Service in 1953[2] into the living conditions of 100 men and women over seventy living in one London borough revealed that few could afford enough coal to keep really warm without at times going short of food; while a study by two doctors showed that in 1951-2, one in every thirty-six non-selected admissions to two medical blocks of a general hospital (which dealt mainly with the older age groups) suffered from malnutrition. Out of thirty-nine such cases, thirty-three were over sixty years of age, and in twenty-nine cases the lack of proper food was ascribed to poverty. 'Some seriously ill patients in advanced states of semi-starvation presented a typical appearance, identical with that seen among prisoners at the Belsen camp.'[3] Again in Sheffield a study of over 400 old people of all social classes, the results of which were published in 1955, found that as many as 20 per cent were in a state of poor nutrition, and that 'a substantial minority of the elderly were unable to pay for the necessities of life on a subsistence basis at the time of the survey'.[4]

At the other end of life, also, hints of distress are not unknown. The Ministry of Food Survey has noted more than once the tendency for nutritional deficiencies to appear in the diet of households where there are more than three or four children. And in spite of all improvements in the standards of living, about twice as many children as before the war are seen to-day at the London County Council's nutritional clinics. While some of this increase is no doubt due to better detection of the undernourished child, and some of the children who find their way to these clinics are the victims, not of economic circumstances, but of their parents' stupidity or neglect, or of their own faddishness, this does not seem to be quite the whole story. At any rate, three investigators, who reviewed 100 cases from three of these clinics in 1952, and who started their enquiry with the hypothesis that 'the poor appetite,

[1] Shaw (1958), pp. 247–251: and Bowerbank (1958), pp. 283–288. Both articles should be read in full as a commentary upon the myth that 'there is no more poverty'.

[2] National Old People's Welfare Committee (1954), pp. 80–1.

[3] Fuld and Robinson (1953), pp. 860 and 862.

[4] Hobson and Pemberton (1955), pp. 118–19.

fatigue and nervousness of some of the children might be due to the same psychological factors as produced behaviour difficulties in child guidance patients, bedwetting in children attending Enuresis Clinics and growing pains in the non-rheumatic children attending Rheumatism Supervisory Clinics',[1] came to the conclusion that this hypothesis 'oversimplified the problem' and underestimated the effects of poor material environment.

Pending researches which would examine more closely the relation between poverty and various forms of social pathology, these highly accessible facts point to one or two conclusions which are relevant here. They show, in particular, that although certain types of anti-social attitudes may be concentrated in particular social groups, the relation of these attitudes to actual poverty is neither simple nor direct. Shaw comments that 'with two or three exceptions' the families described in her investigation 'showed none of the characteristics associated with "problem" families'.[2] Again, the obvious temptation of the poor is to steal; but poverty in the crude physical sense cannot have much to do with criminality—not even with crimes against property, for such poverty is found chiefly amongst the old, the sick, the widowed and the deserted wives; and, as the facts set out in the previous chapter abundantly demonstrate, the classes which contribute least to the statistics of crimes against property are just those which are most deficient in the world's goods. Generally speaking, women are poorer than men; yet there is one female convicted thief for every five males, and one woman housebreaker for every thirty-five men. Gentlewomen in reduced circumstances, though occasionally (like others not so reduced) caught shop-lifting, do not commonly steal. The old are poorer than the young, yet offences against property are chiefly committed by youths: indeed it could almost be said that thieving is most common at an age when the thief has more money at his disposal than he is likely ever to have again. If by poverty we mean sheer lack of worldly wealth, then poverty seems to be positively correlated with honesty. And the fact that the desperately poor are so often struggling to maintain the higher standards that they have previously experienced makes this relationship even more remarkable. One might well have imagined that it would be the collapse of accustomed standards even more than habitual insufficiency which would make temptation irresistible.

Nor is there evidence that it is poverty in this sense which drives women to prostitution. On the contrary, representatives of the Church of England Moral Welfare Council, as well as the social worker whose researches provided the evidence for a recent first-hand investigation, have, in conversation, given it as their opinion that, while the majority of prostitutes could not command a very high wage level—nothing like what they can earn by prostitution—there is no indication that they are poor in the sense of being below the 'poverty line'. Occasionally a girl who finds herself destitute as the result of running away from home or of some similar crisis may try soliciting as her only immediate means of getting any money; and, in consequence of this experience she may be attracted to professional prostitution, as offering

[1] Bell and others (1956), p. 167. [2] Shaw (1958), p. 249.

far greater material rewards than she could hope to obtain in any other way. I have known such cases myself. But the normal alternatives to-day are not prostitution or near-starvation.

That grinding poverty has not much to do with crime (even if we follow the common practice of defining this so as to omit the crimes committed chiefly by the well-to-do) is obvious enough to anyone with even a superficial acquaintance with the facts. Yet it is a conclusion which would, I think, have surprised our grandfathers. The converse was implicit—and sometimes explicit—in the thought of not so many generations ago; as it is implicit also in the thought of those who express disappointment that the coming of a 'welfare state', which they believe (though mistakenly) to have banished poverty, has not also greatly reduced the criminal statistics. At the same time, it would be a mistake to underrate the economic element in crimes against property. Convictions for dishonesty, as we have seen, are more frequent in the poorer than in the richer quarters of our cities; and, even apart from the fact that it is also in the poorer quarters that suspects tend to first be looked for, there is no doubt that this differential reflects important differences in attitude. But over and above all this, poverty is itself a slippery concept. The Rowntree and other similar standards define poverty in terms of the minimum sums upon which other people ought to be able to live. These standards are framed always by members of one social class for the benefit of another; and those who frame them are very unlikely to have had personal experience of life at the levels for which they are prescribed. Poverty, in the sense of inability to achieve one's own material goals, as distinct from those prescribed by others, goes far above any objectively determined poverty line; and it is fed by envy. The common excuse for theft, 'I was short of money', may mean exactly what it says at any level; and, if it is the richer members of the poorer classes who chiefly practise thieving, that may well be because, in an acquisitive society in which wealth is most unequally distributed, it is this group which is peculiarly sensitive to shortage of money. One must not assume that the horizons of the poorer classes are bounded by the social environment in which they find themselves.

CHAPTER III

Twelve Criminological Hypotheses

EVIDENCE FROM TWENTY-ONE STUDIES[1]

IN this chapter an attempt is made to examine the evidence relating to some of the more popular current hypotheses about the causes or the characteristic features of crime and delinquency,[2] by an analysis of the findings of twenty-one studies, selected in accordance with the requirements that each should deal with at least 200 subjects; should contain data on not less than half, or nearly half, the hypotheses under review; and should be sufficiently substantial to include accounts both of the findings and of the methods used. Contributions to journals were generally ruled out, since in most of these the methodological particulars were inadequate. In the end eleven British, nine American and one Swedish study were selected as most adequately fulfilling the required conditions; and I need perhaps hardly add that these represented, as far as could be judged, methodologically the best pieces of work available and those most likely to yield reliable evidence. A few of the better-known studies of delinquency had to be omitted on one or more of the following grounds: because they produced insufficient relevant material; because their statistical findings could not be divorced from the text or were presented in a form which defied comparative use; or because the samples used were inadequate. Thus Shaw and McKay's famous ecological study[3] and Lander's Baltimore investigation[4] were excluded on the first ground, Stott's work on *Delinquency and Human Nature*[5] on the second and Bowlby's celebrated study of affectionless thieves[6] on the third. The final list of those included reads as follows:

(1) W. Healy's *The Individual Delinquent*, 1915;[7] 1,000 repeated offenders, boys and girls, seen at the Juvenile Psychopathic Institute, Chicago, about whom sufficient data were available. A special effort was made to see the more intractable offenders.

(2) M. R. Fernald, M. H. S. Hayes and A. Dawley's[8] *Study of Women Delinquents in New York State*, 1920; a cross-section consisting of

[1] Practically all the research required for this chapter and much of that in the two immediately following has been undertaken by Vera G. Seal.

[2] These terms are to be regarded throughout as interchangeable, though I have generally followed the prevailing custom of using 'criminal and criminality' to refer to adults, and 'delinquent' and 'delinquency' to refer to children and young persons.

[3] Shaw and McKay (1942). [4] Lander (1954). [5] Stott (1950). [6] Bowlby (1946).

[7] Subsequent references in this chapter to this study refer to the 1929 edition.

[8] Referred to in this chapter as 'Fernald'.

587 women convicted of offences, taken from five institutions, with the addition of a group of women placed on probation. Just over half of the total had been convicted of offences 'against chastity'.

(3) C. Burt's *The Young Delinquent*, 1925;[1] 197 boys and girls (for whom sufficient data existed) referred for psychological investigation or seen at remand homes or industrial schools, as well as a small number from an educational survey, and 400 non-delinquent schoolchildren used as controls. Although the majority had not been charged, most of the children had committed breaches of the law which, in an adult, would have been punishable by imprisonment.

(4) J. Slawson's *The Delinquent Boy*, 1926; approximately half (over 1,600) of the delinquent boys institutionalized in New York State. These boys came from four institutions.

(5) T. E. Sullenger's *Social Determinants in Juvenile Delinquency*, 1929. 1,220 boys and girls who appeared in court in Omaha and Columbia.

(6) S. and E. T. Glueck's *500 Criminal Careers*, 1930; approximately 500 young men released from Massachusetts Reformatory, and studied after a five-year 'post-parole' period.

(7) S. and E. T. Glueck's *Five Hundred Delinquent Women*, 1934; 500 women released from Massachusetts Reformatory, of whom half had been committed for sex offences.

(8) S. and E. T. Glueck's *One Thousand Juvenile Delinquents*, 1934; 1,000 boys referred by Boston Juvenile Court for pyschological examination.

(9) W. Healy and A. F. Bronner's *New Light on Delinquency and its Treatment*, 1936; 105 repeatedly delinquent boys and girls who had appeared in court, at Boston, New Haven or Detroit, and 105 non-delinquent siblings.

(10) J. H. Bagot's *Juvenile Delinquency*, 1941; every case (3,221 in all) in which a child of either sex was found guilty in Liverpool of an indictable offence in 1934 and 1936. The children are divided into two groups of 1,358 and 1,863 respectively.

(11) A. M. Carr-Saunders, H. Mannheim and E. C. Rhodes'[2] *Young Offenders*, 1942; 1,953 boys found guilty of offences in London and the provinces, and 1,970 controls.

(12) W. Norwood East's *The Adolescent Criminal*, 1942; 4,000 boys committed to Borstal, who lived in or around London.

(13) J. H. Bagot's *Punitive Detention*, 1944; 539 out of a total of 559 boys and girls sentenced in Liverpool during 1940–2 to be detained at a remand home. As only fifteen of these were girls, most of Bagot's findings are confined to boys.

(14) E. Otterström's *Delinquency and Children from Bad Homes*, 1946; 2,346 boys and girls dealt with by the Malmö Child-Welfare Board, Sweden, during 1903–1940. These comprise four groups—those taken in charge because of (1) bad homes; (2) bad homes and delinquency too slight for legal action; (3) those 'so delinquent that special educational measures were required'; and (4) juvenile court clientele. Otterström's data are given separately for the two periods 1903–25 and 1926–40.

[1] Subsequent references in this chapter to this study refer to the 1952 edition.

[2] Referred to in this chapter as 'Carr-Saunders'.

(15) H. Mannheim's *Juvenile Delinquency in an English Middletown*, 1948; 109 pre-war and 123 war-time cases of boys on probation or under supervision in Cambridge, mostly—but not all—boys found guilty of an offence.

(16) S. and E. T. Glueck's *Unraveling Juvenile Delinquency*, 1950;[1] 500 (mostly persistent) delinquent boys from two correctional schools in Massachusetts, and 500 non-delinquent boys from public schools.

(17) T. Ferguson's *The Young Delinquent in his Social Setting*, 1952; 2,139 Glasgow boys; these comprise three groups—489 physically handicapped, 301 mentally handicapped and 1,349 'ordinary' boys, who left school at the earliest permitted date. Approved school boys were excluded.

(18) J. Trenaman's *Out of Step*, 1952; 203 young soldiers who had been delinquent during their Army service, and 200 controls mostly from the Army, supported by a larger sample of 700.

(19) A. G. Rose's *Five Hundred Borstal Boys*, 1954; 472 boys a few years after discharge from Borstal institutions.

(20) H. Mannheim and L. T. Wilkins' *Prediction Methods in Relation to Borstal Training*, 1955; 720 youths committed to Borstal training, studied a few years after release.

(21) D. N. Gibbs' *Some Differentiating Characteristics of Delinquent and Non-Delinquent National Servicemen in the British Army*, 1955; 150 National Servicemen with at least one previous sentence of detention undergoing court martial sentences of detention; and 150 National Servicemen without records of military delinquency, after completion of at least fifteen months' service.

This is a regrettably miscellaneous list, spread over a period of forty years. The subjects investigated cover both sexes and a wide range of ages; and no less variable are the definitions of criminality which are responsible for their inclusion. Some of the studies deal with adult males who have served prison sentences; others with adult females in like case; others again with young men sentenced to Borstal; yet others with children appearing before the juvenile courts, whatever their offence and whatever their sentence, or, alternatively, with those dealt with by these courts in a particular way. Old and young, thieves, sex offenders, persons guilty of crimes of violence, recidivists and first offenders are all represented. Such variety seriously diminishes the chance of getting definite answers. But the fact is that, unless the net is widely cast, the haul will be too scanty to be worth having: the number of investigations which deal with closely similar material is still very small.

Actually, although the results of this review are strikingly negative, in the sense that they hardly enable us to prove or to disprove any of the currently fashionable theories, the whole exercise has not, I think, been altogether unprofitable. For on the one hand, it induces a wholesome scepticism; and on the other hand it shows up many of the major technical weaknesses in the work so far undertaken in this field; and, since such work is still hardly out of the pioneering stage, concentrated attention on technical improvement can be a most constructive operation. It is, however, undeniable that to master

[1] References throughout are to the 1951 edition.

the details provided by these studies is a tedious business. The reader who prefers his conclusions ready made is invited to turn to page 134.

The twelve factors on whose possible association with criminality or delinquency light is sought from these studies are as follows:

(1) the size of the delinquent's family
(2) the presence of other criminals in the family
(3) club membership
(4) church attendance
(5) employment record
(6) social status
(7) poverty
(8) mother's employment outside the home
(9) school truancy
(10) broken home
(11) health
(12) educational attainment.

It must be admitted that this selection looks about as arbitrary as the list of investigations just given. Here again, however, choice is limited by what there is to choose from. This miscellaneous list is the result of trying to cover, on the one hand, those hypotheses which underlie currently popular explanations and, on the other hand, those which happen actually to have attracted the interest of investigators: it necessarily, therefore, reflects the influence of fashion in social research. Clearly, also, the various factors listed are of very variable significance. In a later chapter[1] I shall discuss how far it is even legitimate to speak of causative factors in crime or delinquency; but here it may be noted that some of the factors which have been most regularly examined obviously cannot, in the ordinary sense of the word, be regarded as causative. The size of a delinquent's family, for instance, seems to have interested nearly all investigators; but it would hardly be argued that this was a direct cause of delinquency. Its significance (if it has any), must lie in its association with other factors such as social status, intelligence or overcrowding. Again, other possible causes of criminality have necessarily been excluded from the list merely because they have been so little explored by investigators that it would be futile to include them. Thus not one of our twenty-one studies has made any serious attempt to examine the late Professor Sutherland's differential association hypothesis—the theory that the question of whether you go straight or crooked depends mainly upon the company that you happen to be thrown with.

We now turn to consider the findings, and their limitations.[2]

[1] See pp. 323 ff.

[2] None of the twelve factors (except the broken home) has been examined by every one of the twenty-one investigations. The absence of any reference to the findings of any one of the twenty-one studies on a particular hypothesis or factor in the survey that follows in the text means that that study contributed no evidence, positive or negative, on this hypothesis or factor.

In many cases the individual findings of these studies are based on a proportion only

1. *Size of Family*

Even in so apparently simple a matter as the size of a delinquent's family, problems of definition can be troublesome. Some authors state whether deceased, half- or step-siblings are included, or whether the delinquent himself is counted in the total of family members. Others give no indication of what exactly is covered by such terms as 'siblings' or 'children in the family', though on this one can sometimes make what seem to be reasonable assumptions. One investigation refers to the size of 'family at home', another to the size of family 'alive'. In their 1934 study of juveniles the Gluecks took account of siblings living; but, in their study of delinquent women published at the same date, the siblings included were all those born alive.

The British studies on the whole give a fairly definite finding of from some 4⅓ to 6⅓ children in delinquents' families, the non-delinquent figures offered for comparison being generally in the region of three children to a family. Of the British material, ten studies give data, one quoting figures in a form which cannot be extracted for comparison with the rest. If this last-mentioned study is excluded, five of the other nine offer control or comparative figures.

Trenaman, who uses a control group, found that his young soldiers' families had an average of 6·3 children, as against only 3·6 among the controls; but he suspects that the 6·3 may be an inflated figure, since men who came from broken homes may well have included in their families any siblings who had gone away with the absconding parent; and it may be that step- and half-sibs have also been counted. (One must presume from this that he has reason to believe that his control figure is not similarly inflated). Bagot (1944) found a similar gap between the size of delinquents' and non-delinquents' families, his Liverpool delinquents averaging 5·76 children per family, as against the 2·97 average shown by the Merseyside survey for a working-class family. Norwood East closed the gap a trifle, his delinquents at age fourteen coming from families with an average of 5·0 children. This he regarded as considerably larger than the normal figure, which (on the basis of the 1921 Census) he suggested would not be more than three, even when the families were completed. Carr-Saunders, using controls, gives figures of a lower order, relating, however, to an undefined 'family at home'; but these figures refer only to his group of 'normal' families (that is to say, those that were normally constituted and had a 'normal' home atmosphere) who accounted for about 40 per cent of the delinquents and about 70 per cent of the controls in this investigation for whom particulars were available.[1] On this basis, in London and selected provincial cities, the average size of delinquents' families ranged from 3·6 to 5·3 members, the comparable limits

(and sometimes a very small proportion) of all the subjects studied, usually because data were not available for the total sample. In order to reduce the complexity of the figures in this chapter, I have not always indicated where samples fall short in this way. For comment on the considerable bias that may arise from loss of part of a sample, see p. 309.

[1] Many, if not most, of Carr-Saunders' findings are restricted to this limited section, subsequently referred to in the text as the 'normal' group. See Carr-Saunders, pp. 59, 70 and 85.

for the controls standing at 3·0 and 4·4. Among Gibbs' military delinquents 'youths from families of 5–7 children' were said to be most prone to offend, and military delinquents were 'more likely than controls to come from families with four or more children'.[1]

Turning to those studies which include no control figures, we find that, in Mannheim's groups of war-time and pre-war cases of boys on probation or under supervision, the average number of children in the family was 4·38 and 4·35 respectively. Rose's figure is a little higher, his Borstal boys on commitment having an average of 5·2 children in the family. Bagot (1941) found figures for his two Liverpool groups which were very near to his 1944 figure—viz: averages of 5·18 and 5·28. Ferguson, approaching the subject from a different angle, stressed the link between the three factors of family size, overcrowding and delinquency. In general, in the case of both 'ordinary' and mentally handicapped boys, the larger the family or the number of people living in the house, the higher the incidence of delinquency and the greater the frequency of convictions. But, amongst the 'ordinary' boys, 'in both large and small families the proportion of boys convicted was higher where overcrowding was severe, though the influence of overcrowding was worse in the group of larger families. Where there was no overcrowding the conviction-rates, even in large families, were below those for the study as a whole'.[2] Mannheim and Wilkins, using data which had to be found amongst 'unsystematic narrative reports of various kinds' found that, 'whilst there was some slight association between the number of siblings and the likelihood of success [after discharge from Borstal], this association was not so large as that reported in some American studies'.[3]

We thus conclude, for what it is worth, that in England delinquents, at the various dates of these investigations and in terms of their various definitions, were found, with some consistency, to come from families that were larger than the average.

The American evidence on the whole points the same way. The Gluecks in their 1934 study of juvenile delinquents found the average number of *children* in their delinquents' families to be 4·98, which they contrasted with a figure of 4·5 *persons* per family, derived from the 1920 census. On this basis they conclude that the delinquents come from families 'appreciably larger' than the average Massachusetts family. Similarly, their 1930 study of reformatory men gave an average of 5·3 children per family, contrasted with the 1910 census figure of 4·6 *persons*; while, in their parallel investigation into reformatory women, the figures were 6·43 children in the offenders' families and 4·4 *persons* in the average Massachusetts family. Fernald, also, again using the 1910 census figure of 4·5 *persons* per family, gave a figure of 5·76 children in the families of offenders.

On the other hand the Gluecks' 1950 enquiry found 6·8 children in their delinquents' and 5·9 in their controls' families, and concluded that the difference was not significant. Slawson, also, concluded in 1926 that the larger

[1] pp. 269 and 421. [2] p. 21. [3] p. 88.

families 'contribute only slightly to juvenile delinquency',[1] since in three of his four institutions, the delinquents' families averaged 5·2 children against the norms of 4·49, 4·69 and 4·73 which he derived from Burdge's (1918) study of 16–18-year-old working boys in various cities. Indeed, it is perhaps worth noting that the average for the *control group* of the 1950 Glueck enquiry is actually larger than that for the families of *offenders* in either their 1930 or their 1934 (juveniles) enquiry, and larger also than the figures for offenders' families given by both the Fernald and the Slawson investigations. Among Sullenger's delinquent subjects the average family in the proportion of cases for which particulars were available in the urban group had 5, and in the rural group 3·4 children; but in the absence of controls or of more precise definitions these figures do not mean much.

Otterström's subjects were more various than those studied by most of our other investigators. In general, her data did not make it possible for her to give accurate information about the number of sibs; but she reports that, in the second of the two periods into which her study was divided, it appeared that Groups III and IV (the two delinquent categories) were drawn from families with more children than the general population average.

2. *Criminality in the Family*

The majority of the studies include enquiries into the extent to which criminality is found amongst other members of the delinquent subjects' families. Here again precise comparison is made difficult by vagaries of definition. One author will distinguish offending mothers, fathers and siblings; another is content with such categories as offending 'relatives' or 'offenders in the family'. Occasionally totals are aggregated in such a way that it is not possible to ascertain just how many delinquents come from families with, or without, other convicted members. The fact that x per cent of the delinquents had, say, convicted parents and that y per cent had convicted sibs has plainly quite different significance according as these auxiliary offenders are concentrated in a small group of thoroughly criminal families, or more or less evenly spread over the whole company. Occasionally comparison is precluded because data as to criminality in the legal sense are combined with evidence of an undefined 'immorality'.

Of the eleven British studies nine give material on this point. From Ferguson's figures it appears that, of the delinquent 'ordinary' (i.e. not mentally or physically handicapped) boys, over 41 per cent came from families in which another member had been convicted: whilst only amongst 15 per cent of the non-delinquents was there another member of the family with a 'record'. Amongst the physically handicapped the comparable percentages were 46 per cent and 18 per cent, while amongst the mentally handicapped the figures for other offenders in the family were over 45 per cent for the delinquents, and 26 per cent for the non-delinquents. Ferguson himself comments, with reference to the 'ordinary' boys, that 'the influence of another convicted member of the family in the home is at least as great as that of any

[1] p. 418.

of the other adverse factors that have been studied', adding that, throughout the whole study, 'to a remarkable extent the convictions of the boys and of other members of their families ran parallel'. 'A much higher proportion of the boys . . . had been convicted when another member of the family had been convicted as well. The more frequently the boy included in the study had been convicted, the larger the number of other members of the family convicted.'[1]

The findings of the remaining eight British studies are as follows. Burt, in an article of 1923[2] published in advance of *The Young Delinquent*, found that altogether 10·6 per cent of his delinquents had relatives (parents, siblings and others) who had been sentenced for crime. Bagot (1941), who divided his two groups into recidivists and first offenders, records that 39 per cent of the recidivists and 29·9 per cent of the first offenders in his 1934 group had at least one other juvenile delinquent in the family, whilst, of the 1936 group, 43·2 per cent and 29·4 per cent had delinquent siblings. In his 1944 study of delinquents who had been sentenced to punitive detention, 47·6 per cent of the subjects were found to have come from families with at least one other delinquent. Norwood East records that fifty-two per 1,000 of his boys had a 'family history of crime', and that about thirty-eight per 1,000 had criminal siblings. Mannheim found that thirty-nine of the families in his study of 232 boys had one or more other delinquent children; and he comments that there was a 'fairly strong concentration of delinquency within a small group of people',[3] evidenced by nineteen families with forty children on probation. In the Carr-Saunders investigation it appears that, among the London cases, 4·7 per cent came from families with one or more other delinquents (adult and juvenile) as against 0·8 per cent among the controls; while, among the provincial cases, the corresponding figures were 9·0 per cent and 0·3 per cent. The authors warn us, however, that 'it is not known how complete this information is', and they themselves give reasons for regarding their material with scepticism.[4] Gibbs reports that of his delinquents 16 per cent had delinquent fathers, 3 per cent delinquent mothers, 39 per cent delinquent sibs and that 46 per cent had at least one conviction in the family, whereas for the controls the figures were 9 per cent, 0 per cent, 15 per cent, and 21 per cent respectively. This information was, however, derived from the subjects themselves; and the author adds that 'because of the delicacy of this subject, one must expect considerable unreliability of reply, and it is probable that the controls have been more reluctant to give the facts'.[5] Mannheim and Wilkins discovered 'other crime in the family' in 131 of their 720 cases, but could get no details in sixty-four of these.

Thus, while there is general agreement that the presence of one offender in a family increases the probability of the appearance of another, the variation in the frequency with which this familial concentration is found by different investigations is enormous—ranging, in fact, from 4 per cent to 47 per cent of the cases examined.

Amongst the American studies, all except two give data that can be extracted. The Gluecks' latest work on juveniles finds the families of delinquents

[1] pp. 67 and 151. [2] Burt (1923), p. 14. [3] p. 25. [4] pp. 97–8. [5] p. 271.

fully twice as delinquent, judged by the number of offenders that they include, as those of the controls. The figures, which exclude trivial offences, are as follows:

65·2 per cent of the delinquents and 25·8 per cent of the controls had criminal sibs
44·8 per cent of the delinquents and 15 per cent of the controls had criminal mothers
66·2 per cent of the delinquents and 32 per cent of the controls had criminal fathers.[1]

The results of the other Glueck investigations give much the same picture. In their earlier study of juveniles, 57·9 per cent of the subjects were found to have offending parents or sibs or both, whilst 45·5 per cent of their reformatory women had parents or sibs who had at least been arrested. Amongst the reformatory men the comparable figure for 'court records' in the family was 51·5 per cent.

Other American investigators, however, do not give such high figures. Healy and Bronner found that 20 per cent of the parents of their delinquents had a court record. (Any figure for delinquent sibs is necessarily excluded in this case, as this study is based on a comparison of delinquents with their non-delinquent sibs.) Of the women covered by the Fernald enquiry 15·9 per cent came from homes in which some member of the family had a conviction. Although this is the lowest figure produced by the American studies, the authors comment that 'though we have no way of measuring the percentage of families in the general population in which there has been a conviction, this percentage would seem to be so high as to be of great significance in affecting home conditions'.[2] Sullenger's figures must be treated with caution as he apparently does not allow for both the parents and the sibs of a particular delinquent having criminal records. By adding together the cases with delinquent parents and those with delinquent sibs, however, he arrives at the conclusion that 32 per cent of his Columbia cases and nearly 40 per cent of those from Omaha came from families in which there were other offenders: but this last figure related to only 125 of his total of 1,145 cases.

Otterström's findings from Sweden point also in the same direction. She concludes that 'the children of criminal parents themselves become criminals somewhat more frequently than other children'. For all her four groups together, in those cases in which information was forthcoming (a large majority of the whole), 21·4 per cent had offending fathers, whereas the proportion of the male general population in the same area who had been convicted up to the age of fifty was only 9·3 per cent. Offending mothers were found in 7·4 per cent of these cases (about five times the estimated total for the general population). These figures relate, moreover, only to cases in which parents were sentenced for the 'more serious' offences. In the first of her two strictly delinquent groups, 23·5 per cent had, in the first period of nvestigation, 'one or more sibs who had been in contact with the Child-

[1] pp. 101–2. [2] pp. 241–2.

Welfare Board or the Court of Justice'.[1] Not all of these children, however, were necessarily delinquent in the technical sense of having been formally found guilty by a court.

The sense of the American and Swedish is thus consistent with the British findings; and the quantitative variation in the figures produced by the various studies from other countries is no less conspicuous than that found by the British investigators.

3. *Club Membership*

The belief that membership of a 'social club or organization for the constructive use of leisure'[2] militates against delinquency, especially amongst young people, is widely held. But the evidence supplied by these twenty-one studies is far too inconclusive to permit of firm support for any such generalization.

Apart from all the other difficulties, the term 'club' may have very different meanings. Trenaman's young soldiers enquiry, for instance, included billiard and snooker clubs, which would certainly not have fallen within Bagot's much narrower definition. The Gluecks in their studies of adults include under this general head 'studying music', or the pursuit of 'vocational courses', and even extend the word club to cover 'labour unions or other occupational associations' as well as political clubs.

Again, 'membership' is an equally vague conception. It can, for instance, be used to cover membership 'at some time or other', as by Trenaman; whilst those who seek a more precise definition can take their choice of a variety of alternatives. Thus Ferguson distinguished membership throughout the period of the survey, and membership or non-membership at age fourteen. Bagot (1941) specifies membership at the time of the offence, Healy and Bronner membership 'at some time prior' to the study. Carr-Saunders, more ambitiously, subdivides club membership into four categories; regular, nominal, previous and none. Unfortunately, however, the value of this attempt at refinement is somewhat lessened by the fact that the data again refer only to the proportion of his total cases that was included in his 'normal' group. Bagot, again (1941), raises the possibility that any data on this subject may be biassed by juvenile offenders finding their delinquency an obstacle to joining a club. Finally, it must be borne in mind that at least two of the studies relate to war-time periods; and that the various districts covered by the various investigations may well have differed in the extent to which club facilities were then available. Bagot (1944), in particular, speaks of the war-time dearth of local club facilities.

Of the British studies eight attempt to give data. Five of these furnish controls or comparisons, though even in these the evidence is somewhat sketchy. Among his 'ordinary' boys Ferguson found a lower incidence of delinquency amongst members of clubs or similar organizations, 10 per cent of club members being delinquent as against 13·7 per cent of non-members, in both cases

[1] pp. 317–8 and 170. [2] Glueck, S. and E. T. (1930), p. 128.

at the age of fourteen. Bagot (1941) found that, in his 1934 group, 12 per cent of the recidivists and 17 per cent of the first offenders were members of a club, as were 11 per cent and 15 per cent respectively of the 1936 group, as against local membership figures for the eligible population of 23 per cent and 24 per cent. Carr-Saunders, on the other hand (again confining himself to his 'normal' boys), came to the conclusion that we can make no inference as to the effect of club membership in discriminating between the offenders and the apparently virtuous. He found that, amongst London delinquents, 29 per cent were regular members and 53 per cent non-members of clubs, as compared with the controls' figures of 35 per cent and 51 per cent respectively. In the provincial towns, 28 per cent of the delinquents were regular club members and 58 per cent non-attenders, as against 30 per cent and 54 per cent among the controls. Trenaman, who speaks of the evidence of earlier surveys as being 'wildly contradictory', considers that, although 49 per cent of his young soldiers claimed to have belonged to a social organization at some time or another, it is doubtful whether at age fifteen more than 25 per cent belonged to a club, 'and those who did would not have been members for long'.[1] He adds that 'the corresponding estimated figure for the general youth population is 44 per cent'; but his source for this figure is not given.

Gibbs dealt with club membership in some detail. He gives data regarding kind of club, longest membership, membership during schooldays and during post-schooldays; and concludes that 51 per cent of his delinquents and 76 per cent of the controls could claim to be, or to have been, members of clubs at some time for at least three months; and he adds that 'even when they do belong to clubs or similar groups, potential military recidivists are likely to maintain membership for shorter periods than other youths'. Gibbs also found a marked tendency for 'fewer delinquents to belong to clubs at all during their schooldays'. 'The control group as a whole shows a higher club or other organization pre-service membership rate, and the individuals within that group show greater stability in membership than the delinquents. This is probably due in part to the Court action taken against the potential military delinquents during those periods'. All these conclusions have, however, to be qualified by the usual caution. 'Every research', the author writes, 'has been confronted with the usual problems of obtaining accurate information, and most investigators have been forced to state that their material is in this respect unreliable. The present study is no exception.'[2]

Of the remaining studies, Bagot (1944) gives 3·8 per cent as members of youth organizations; but this relates to war-time when there were few clubs available in Liverpool. Mannheim mentions sixteen and six respectively out of his two groups of 109 and 123 subjects as being club members.

Mannheim and Wilkins include a table of participants in 'Club, organized group activities'; but this has, in their own words, 'little value'. Indeed, their remarks on this subject are valuable chiefly for their uncompromising exposure of the difficulty of getting reliable information. 'Well over half the

[1] pp. 155 6. [2] pp. 273–7.

cases', they write, 'were lost when we attempted to obtain data relating to leisure activities. No systematic attempts had been made to obtain information and the sources of data where these were available were varied. In some cases the police report included this item and in others the visitors' report.'[1]

In the British material, therefore, such evidence as we have of a tendency for club members to be less delinquent than non-members is so slight as to be insignificant. But, as is indeed to be expected in view of the divergence of area and date covered by these studies, the proportion of delinquents found to be club members varies enormously from one enquiry to another: the percentages recorded by our various investigators read 3·8, 5, 11, 12, 14, 15, 17, 28, 29, 49, and 51. Meaningful conclusions are, moreover, inhibited by the inadequacy of the available evidence as to club membership amongst controls, as well as by uncertainty both as to the duration of membership and as to the extent to which any estimates of this relate to comparable social classes.

The American authors have paid even less attention than the British to this subject, and their findings are even more inconclusive. Five of the nine give data. Healy and Bronner are alone in finding that more of their delinquents than of their controls had had 'prior club connections', the respective figures being forty-seven as against twenty-eight out of the two groups of 105 each. 'It is not surprising', the authors comment, 'that more of the delinquents had registered club connections, in view of the fact that they on the whole were more outgoing and active.' Indeed, Healy and Bronner find that similar differences occurred also in Scout membership, athletic skill, marked sports activity or interest, frequent cinema attendance and fondness for reading. 'But', they continue, 'then we discovered that in many instances clubs had not represented a long continued interest; attendance was irregular or the activities soon ceased to be attractive.'[2] On the regularity of attendance of the controls they make no comment. The Gluecks, in their earlier study of delinquents, found that, among those of their subjects about whom the facts were known, 75·2 per cent had never belonged to supervised clubs such as the 'Y.M.C.A., Boy Scouts, school centres, settlements, church clubs, or attended vocational classes'; and, just prior to the study, only 10·6 per cent so belonged. In their study of women offenders, these authors collected data as to the extent to which their subjects had engaged in 'constructive recreations and interests', defined as the 'purposeful use of leisure time for self-development, as vocational courses, studying music', or as 'a member of a well-supervised club, etc.'[3] Only 0·8 per cent, it appeared, were known to have had such constructive recreations and interests within a year of their commitment; though at some earlier time of their lives 19·7 per cent of those for whom particulars were available (just over four-fifths of the total) had engaged in some such activities. In the case of the Gluecks' reformatory men, again, only 15·8 per cent were recorded as having 'belonged to any social club or organization for the constructive use of leisure'. The authors add that,

[1] pp. 101–2. [2] pp. 71 and 77. [3] p. 386.

although local comparative figures are not available, 'it is reasonable to assume that the situation is not generally so bad as that existing among our young ex-prisoners'.[1]

The findings of the Gluecks' latest study of delinquents are best described in their own words. 'In view of the high degree of organization of club activities for boys in the Boston area in recent years', they write, 'it is perhaps not surprising to find that almost all the delinquents as well as the non-delinquents had had some contact with boys' clubs, settlement houses, and similar supervised recreational services at one time or another. It does not follow, however, that their participation in such activities was necessarily more than casual. The fact is that of the 343 delinquents and 334 non-delinquents from whom the psychiatrist was able to elicit information concerning the regularity of their use of organized recreational facilities, 59·5 per cent of the delinquents attended clubs twice or more a week, as compared with 72·7 per cent of the non-delinquents; while a far greater proportion of the delinquents (24·8 per cent: 9·6 per cent) attended on special occasions only, such as the showing of a movie, an athletic contest, or some other event in which they had especial interest.' On enquiring into the reasons for the boys' attendance, the Gluecks were led to conclude 'that more than half (56·7 per cent) the delinquents were directed to organized recreational activities by adults in authority over them (probation and parole officers, parents, teachers, and so on), and that most of the non-delinquents (70 per cent) participated of their own volition or upon the urgence of companions or brothers and sisters'[2]—a fact which in itself immediately makes suspect any attempt to read any causal significance into figures of club membership amongst delinquents and non-delinquents. If, however, account is taken only of those in 'attendance at present', the difference between the figure for delinquents and that for controls narrows; for we find that 55·2 per cent of the former are in club membership, as against 61 per cent of the latter. Thus the Gluecks' investigation, no less than that of Carr-Saunders in this country, illustrates the need to distinguish the quality or levels of club attendance in any attempt to assess the significance of club membership in delinquency.

Once again the American findings are quantitatively as variable as the British, the percentages of delinquents claiming to be or to have been club members in the various studies reading as follows: 10·6, 15·8, 19·7, 24·8, 44·7 and 55·2. In the two cases which quote controls the figures for these are 26·6 per cent and 61 per cent.

4. *Church Attendance*

Few opinions on the subject of delinquency have enjoyed more publicity than has the view that delinquent behaviour is the result of the decline of religious belief or at least of religious observance; and few rest upon more flimsy evidence, though what little can be extracted from these studies does on the whole favour the popular view. Several of our investigators ignored

[1] pp. 128–9. [2] pp. 164–6.

the subject, perhaps because they shared the view of Sir Norwood East that 'whilst recognizing the fact that religious principles affect the conduct of life of many, regard was given to the fact that religious values cannot be tested or verified with exactness . . .'[1] Indeed, to illustrate the catastrophic effects of mere changes in the methods of recording, we may quote the experience of Mannheim's enquiry in our series. In this investigation it was found that only one out of ninety-two of the pre-war delinquents was 'registered as belonging to no religious community'; whereas, of the war-time delinquents, fifty-five out of 122 were so listed. It appears, however, that at the later date the probation officer had adopted the practice of listing 'all those whose membership had to be regarded as merely nominal as belonging to no religious community, even if they had described themselves as "C of E"'[2]—a fact which suggests a very obvious interpretation of this difference.

The findings of the five British studies that do contain data (each of which, however, defines church attendance differently from the others) are as follows. Carr-Saunders, attempting to differentiate between 'a merely formal profession and an active participation', distinguished, as in the case of club membership, three levels of attendance—'regular', 'nominal' and 'previous', with 'none' as a fourth category. His conclusion (which once again relates only to his group of 'normal' subjects) is that 'generally . . . there is a difference between the delinquents and controls', more of the controls being regular attenders and fewer being non-attenders. In London the figures for *regular* attendance show 29 per cent of the delinquents and 39 per cent of the controls as church-goers, those for the provincial towns standing at 41 per cent and 51 per cent respectively. Ferguson, who also distinguishes three categories (those attending throughout the survey, those attending at age fourteen, and non-attenders at age fourteen) comments that, among such of his 'ordinary' boys as were church attenders, 'delinquency-rates were low, both during and after school years; so was the proportion of boys with more than one conviction'.[3] Of his 'attenders throughout survey' only 8·9 per cent were delinquent, as compared with a figure of 12·2 per cent of 'ordinary' boys who became delinquent. Of the non-attenders at age fourteen, the delinquent proportion was 14·9 per cent. Mannheim, perhaps sceptical of the value of such data, merely quotes figures for membership of 'church choir or Sunday school', in which category 17 per cent of his pre-war cases and 16 per cent of his war-time group were included. Trenaman simply says that 'nearly half (42 per cent)' of his delinquent subjects 'went to church'. Gibbs gives a figure of 56 per cent of delinquents as at least occasional church-goers as against 74 per cent of controls. That is all we have for Britain.

Less than half the American studies give data, and, of the two which use controls, one concludes that considerably more of the controls than of the delinquents are regular attenders, whilst in the other the difference is found to be less marked; but the latter is based on too small numbers to be of much significance. The first finding is that of the Gluecks' most recent study of

[1] p. viii. [2] pp. 27–8 [3] p. 38.

delinquents, in which the percentages relating to church attendance are as follows:

Church attendance	*Delinquents* *Per cent*	*Controls* *Per cent*
Regular	39·3	67·1
Occasional	54·2	28·7
None	6·5	4·2

The second piece of evidence comes from Healy and Bronner. Of their 105 pairs of siblings, forty-six delinquents and sixty-four controls were regular attenders at church or Sunday school.

The two remaining American investigations which touch on the subject are the Gluecks' reformatory studies. Amongst the men, the Gluecks comment that 'infrequent church attendance characterizes the group', but they add that comparison cannot be made with the general population because of lack of data. Their figures show 8·5 per cent in regular attendance, 88·5 per cent as irregular and 3 per cent as non-attenders. In the case of the women, an attempt was made to enquire a little more deeply, the results for those for whom information was available being as follows:

Church attendance	*During childhood* *Per cent*	*During adolescence* *Per cent*	*Within one year of commitment* *Per cent*
Regular	55·4	24·1	13·5
Irregular	38·7	62·8	50·0
None	5·9	13·1	36·5

The very scanty evidence that we have, therefore, supports the view that regular church attendance or church membership is uncommon amongst offenders; and the few studies that attempt comparison with controls find that the latter are more likely to be church-goers.

5. *Employment Record*

Most of our investigators have interested themselves in one or other aspect of the employment record of their subjects; but the explicit or implicit hypotheses which may have evoked this interest, the angles from which the subject may be thought to have significance and the methods by which it is treated are all highly variable. The two aspects on which data have most commonly been collected are the extent of unemployment amongst delinquents, and the frequency with which they change their jobs. As regards the first of these, however, it is obvious that the measure in which delinquents experience unemployment must largely depend upon how much unemployment there is for anybody to experience: the results of any enquiry conducted in the nineteen-thirties can hardly be compared with those of the fifties. Again, experience of unemployment may be measured in various ways. One investigator will concentrate on the fact of unemployment at the time that an offence is committed, while another is more concerned with the total period during which his subjects have been out of work.

Amongst the British studies the actual findings are as follows. Burt, in

1925, confining his calculations 'strictly to those of an employable age' found that 16 per cent of the delinquent boys and 6 per cent of the delinquent girls were unemployed (apparently at the time of his enquiry); and he gave it as his opinion that lack of suitable employment or of employment of any kind are 'two points of capital importance in considering adolescent crime'.[1] Carr-Saunders reports that 'for each age, the proportion of unemployed amongst delinquent cases is higher than the corresponding proportion amongst control cases'; but his figures show considerable variations as between different age groups. In London the proportion unemployed at the time of the investigation was 6·1 per cent of the delinquents and 1·3 per cent of the controls at age fourteen; 19·5 per cent and 0·7 per cent at fifteen; and 31·2 per cent and 0·7 per cent at sixteen; while in the provincial towns the corresponding figures were 14·3 per cent and 6·4 per cent at fourteen; 21·6 per cent and 3·0 per cent at fifteen; and 28·3 per cent and 3·8 per cent at sixteen.[2]

Bagot, writing in 1944, found 66 per cent of his boys at age fourteen to sixteen unemployed at the time of the offence, despite the fact that his enquiry related to a period of near-full employment; and, in his 1941 study, his comment on the employment figures for delinquents on the one hand, and for nearly comparable youths in the local population on the other, is that 'it is evident when these proportions are contrasted that we have here the most outstanding difference between delinquent and non-delinquent that has yet been discovered in this enquiry'.[3] Of his 1934 group of delinquent boys aged fourteen to sixteen, 69 per cent were unemployed, and of the 1936 group, 58 per cent. Ranging these figures against the most nearly comparable group, namely insured juveniles in Liverpool aged sixteen and seventeen, Bagot found that the percentages unemployed among the latter at the same date were 9·8 per cent and 12·4 per cent respectively. In the opinion of the Superintendent of the Juvenile Employment Bureau, however, unemployment was 'somewhat lower' amongst the fourteen–fifteen-year-olds than in the higher age-groups, so this estimate is likely to overstate the amount of unemployment in the juvenile population as a whole.

Ferguson, again, who gives varying data for his three groups, found that amongst 'ordinary' boys, the incidence of crime increased with the total time lost from all causes, whether incapacity, unemployment or any other reason, the percentage found guilty rising from 9·4 per cent for those who had lost no time to 18 per cent for those who had lost three months or more. Among the physically handicapped, three years after leaving school the proportion found guilty of an offence (18·5 per cent) was higher amongst the unemployed than it was amongst the skilled or semi-skilled workers in employment (7·7 per cent) or amongst unskilled workers (13·5 per cent) or in the non-manual group (3·4 per cent). Mannheim remarks that 'unemployment, already

[1] pp. 177–8.

[2] It is not clear whether these figures relate to all of the employed boys or only to the 'normal' group to which many of the findings refer.

[3] p. 56.

low in the pre-war group, seems to have been absent during the war. However, in a large number of cases this important item was not clearly brought out in the records':[1] for this reason, his figures are not quoted here. Norwood East approached the subject from a slightly different angle. 'The general inference from the figures', he concludes, 'seems to be that although the convicted lads had not experienced appreciably more than the average amount of unemployment, they were much more prone to commit an offence during periods of unemployment than at other times.'[2]

The hypothesis that delinquency is associated with mobility of employment or frequency of job-changing (as distinct from the fact of unemployment at the time of offending) has been examined by several of our investigators. Ferguson found that amongst his 'ordinary' boys 'high delinquency-rates were associated with frequent change of employer'; and 'even during school years these young people who later flitted from employer to employer had conviction-rates well above the average'.[3] He also observed 'a similar tendency for delinquency-rates to increase with the number of jobs held', the percentage of offenders rising from 5·3 per cent for those with only one job, to 27·9 per cent for those who had tried five or more over a period of three years. Among the physically handicapped likewise 'the more frequent the change of job, the greater the incidence of delinquency',[4] the percentage rising from 6·5 per cent for those with one job to 25 per cent for those with five or more.

Trenaman likewise reckoned that great mobility was a bad sign. The average number of jobs for his delinquents was 4·5 as against 2·3 for his controls; though it must be remembered that his information came largely from the delinquents themselves. In the Carr-Saunders investigation the same picture is repeated: London delinquents at ages fourteen, fifteen and sixteen had held on the average 2·0, 2·6, and 3·8 jobs respectively, the corresponding figures for the controls being 1·2, 1·8 and 2·0. In the provinces the delinquents, at the same ages, had held an average of 1·9, 2·9 and 3·1 jobs respectively, against 1·3, 1·6 and 2·1 for the controls. Mannheim also found that, at the same ages, his pre-war delinquents had held on the average 2·0, 2·5 and 3·2 jobs, the figures for the war-time group being 2·2, 2·4 and 4·7—a surprisingly small difference in view of the change in the employment situation. Bagot (1941) merely records that 'a high proportion of the delinquents change their jobs frequently'.[5]

Rose makes the same comment about his Borstal boys. 'The usual picture', he writes, 'is the boy with the long string of jobs of short duration and of an unskilled character'.[6] In this connection he uses a threefold classification of work habits, which rank as 'good' if changes of employment have been infrequent and if there has been little or no unemployment; 'fair' if a previous record of steady and regular employment has subsequently dropped off

[1] pp. 37–8.

[2] pp. 156–7. Incidentally, Norval Morris (1951, p. 347) found that at a time of full employment over 72 per cent of his 270 'confirmed recidivists' were unemployed the last time they recommenced their criminal activities.

[3] p. 35. [4] p. 82. [5] p. 57. [6] p. 154.

considerably, or if there have been occasional discharges from steady work on account of misconduct; and 'bad' if there is a record of continual job changes, frequent discharges and much unemployment, for reasons other than ill-health and so forth. Of his subjects, 23 per cent qualified on this basis as good, 16 per cent as fair and 61 per cent as bad. Comparing these results with those of other studies, the author remarks that 'it seems clear enough that work habits are a significant factor'.[1] Although Mannheim and Wilkins finally select unstable work records as one of the best predictors of recidivism among ex-Borstal boys, their study did not yield much information on the subject which can be simply reproduced here. Information covering 448 of their subjects showed that the average duration of a job was eight months or more in 171 cases, between four and seven months in 162, and from one month to four months in 101, while fourteen had had no employment at all since leaving school. In view of the fact that many youths are known to have a habit of changing their jobs every few weeks, these figures can hardly be said to suggest extreme instability. Gibbs, on the other hand, gives unusually full material on this subject. At one end of the scale, 7 per cent of his delinquents and 44 per cent of his controls had only had one job; while at the other extreme, 46 per cent of the delinquents, as against 8 per cent of the controls, had been in five or more situations between leaving school and call-up. Amongst his delinquents 23 per cent had remained for twenty-five months or longer in one job, whereas the same was true of no less than 64 per cent of the controls. Gibbs concludes that 'the delinquents show much greater job instability than non-delinquents'; but at the same time 'it is important to note . . . that some delinquents evidently have quite as stable job records as non-delinquents'.[2]

As a rule, the only American studies which refer to employment records are those which relate to adults, perhaps because the relatively high minimum age of employment in many American states makes the subject unrealistic in the case of juveniles. Among such investigations, that of the Gluecks on reformatory men included a classification of the work habits of 378 of the total of 500 subjects examined. Under this, a 'poor' worker is defined as one who, 'in the long run, constitutes a liability to the employer' for various reasons; whilst one who has previously held regular employment but has recently deteriorated, or is a potentially regular worker who interrupts his work for various unacceptable reasons, is classified as 'fair'; and the 'reliable, steady, industrious' worker qualifies as 'good'. On this basis the distribution of the reformatory population was as follows: poor, 52·5 per cent; fair, 27·7 per cent; good, 19·8 per cent. In view of the fact that the 'data as to the work habits of youths of the general population are not available for comparison',[3] and that 54·1 per cent of the Gluecks' sample were customarily engaged in unskilled work, which may have been specially vulnerable to the economic vagaries of the time, not much can be made of these results. Nevertheless, the authors append the somewhat light-hearted comment that

[1] pp. 71–2. [2] pp. 417 and 258. [3] p. 135.

'the chances are that of the youths employed [in the general population] more than 20 per cent are good workers, or they would not be retained'.[1]

Fresh difficulties arise in the case of the Gluecks' parallel enquiry into the employment records of reformatory women. Half these women were known to have lived as prostitutes prior to commitment; and their employment records were further confused by the fact that many were married, though only in a few cases could the marriages be said to be functioning. On the other hand, such information as could be obtained seems in this instance to have been handled with unusual care: 'All the cases', the investigators observe, 'contained data uniform in detail and in the method of gathering and verifying it'.[2] The results, for what they are worth, show 71·6 per cent of these women as 'idle' (i.e. presumably not gainfully employed, unless as prostitutes) at the time of the arrest resulting in commitment. An additional 4·8 per cent were doing their own housework, while the remainder, 23·6 per cent, were gainfully employed. This was at a period 'when there was no markedly high unemployment'; but again no data are offered which would facilitate comparison with women in the general population. Looking back over the work history of these women, the Gluecks found that, of the 97 per cent who entered gainful employment, 7·5 per cent were regular workers (working almost continuously, with not more than an average of two months' unemployment in a year), 32·8 per cent fairly regular and 59·7 per cent irregular (with frequent or long periods of unemployment and no periods of sustained work). The quality of their work habits was correspondingly classified as 16·2 per cent good, 55·4 per cent fair and 28·4 per cent poor. The women thus show somewhat better records than the men.

Fernald, although she devotes a seventy-five-page chapter to 'occupational history and economic efficiency', is also limited—indeed to an even greater extent—by the fact that as many as 66·2 per cent of her women were prostitutes, even if the 17·8 per cent described as 'sexually irregular, though not for money' are excluded. Nevertheless she shares the opinion of the authors of several of the other studies, that 'one of the most striking facts . . . is to find how large a part of the women were idle at the time they committed the offenses which led to both their first and present convictions'[3] (59·9 per cent and 54·3 per cent respectively); and that 'on the whole, the records show, for the most part, poor ability, great irregularity, and a low wage, though probably no lower wage than the bulk of unskilled workers in the same occupations outside are earning'. She and her colleagues are, however, cautious in their inferences. 'For the most part, however, we believe that the elements of occupational influences and low wages are not the direct and immediate causes of the delinquency, though indirectly their influence is great.'[4] And, 'we cannot draw as definite conclusions as we should like because of the difficulty of obtaining comparative data . . .'[5]

The Fernald enquiry also 'aimed to show how much of the time in a woman's work history she was actually working when she had no other legitimate means of support'.[6] The 486 women who had done any work at all

[1] p. 135. [2] p. 337. [3] p. 378. [4] p. 379. [5] p. 377. [6] p. 361.

between their first job and the time of the enquiry were divided into five classes according to the regularity of their work record (periods of marriage, of keeping house or of residence in institutions being excluded from 'idle time'). In the upshot it appeared that only 3·5 per cent had worked nearly as long as they could; 35·6 per cent had worked about three-quarters, 28·4 per cent about one-half and 23·9 per cent about one-quarter of the maximum possible period, while 8·6 per cent had worked hardly any of the time. To these figures the investigators added a 'total estimate of the efficiency of the work history'. According to this estimate, 12·7 per cent of the women ranked as very poor workers and 37·1 per cent as poor (i.e. not able to be self-supporting), 36·5 per cent were graded as fair (i.e. women who with 'great care' and no ill fortune could live on their earnings); while 12·3 per cent had a good, and 1·7 per cent a very good, work record.[1]

Of the American investigations dealing with juveniles, the Gluecks' earlier study alone probes into work records. Details were obtained for 625 of the 1,000 boys examined, and of these 19·8 per cent were regarded as regular workers, defined as having maintained 'continuity of employment, with periods of unemployment no longer than a month except for such reasons as are beyond the control of the worker'; while 80·2 per cent were classified as irregular workers—because of their 'frequent changes of jobs without any effort on the boy's part to advance himself vocationally'. The authors comment that 'the extent to which habits of irregularity of employment are carried over into adult life can hardly be demonstrated as yet; it can only be inferred from the fact that many adult offenders are found to have been delinquent in childhood and are unsteady workers in adulthood'.[2]

A rough comparison of the data contributed by the four American studies concerned thus shows that in every case about three-quarters of the subjects for whom information is available were poor or only fair workers; and all the investigators, British or American, who have explored the subject are agreed that their subjects tend to be characterized by poor work records.

6. *Social Status*

Social status is a vague enough concept at the best of times, and it is not, therefore, surprising that such material as is forthcoming on this subject is almost too diverse and sketchy to allow of any conclusions being reached. Relatively few of the British studies have tackled the subject, and the findings of several of those that have done so relate to only a few of their subjects. In most cases status is defined by the occupational rank of the delinquent or his father, but only, as a rule, in quite general terms, by reference to degree of skill. Although some studies give fuller occupational descriptions, these are seldom mutually comparable. In other cases, social position has to be inferred from the use of such terms as 'working-class' or 'poor', or from references to overcrowding, or to the type of district from which a delinquent comes, or to the fact that a case is known to some social agency, such as the National

[1] Much fuller details and definitions will be found in Fernald (1920), pp. 364–9.
[2] p. 90.

Society for the Prevention of Cruelty to Children. Such material has, necessarily, no more than purely descriptive value and cannot be used as a basis for comparisons.

The fullest evidence is that of Ferguson. He found that amongst his 'ordinary' boys delinquency was 'relatively infrequent among the children of skilled workers' and 'more frequent among the children of unskilled workers . . . and especially where there was a bad parental history of unemployment'. The figures for delinquency rise from 9·3 per cent among the children of skilled manual workers to 14·9 per cent for the families of unskilled manual workers and 11·3 per cent in the non-manual group. If the fathers had a good record of regular employment, the proportion of children who were delinquent was 11 per cent; but if not, the figure rose to 15·5 per cent. Among Ferguson's physically handicapped boys, 'the sons of unemployed and, to a lesser extent, unskilled fathers had a high incidence of delinquency . . .' Delinquency rates, in this group, were approximately 20 per cent for the boys of unemployed fathers, 10 per cent for the skilled manual and 15 per cent for the unskilled; while among the mentally handicapped, 'delinquency-rates were much higher among the sons of unskilled workers than among the sons of those engaged in skilled or semi-skilled work'.[1] The figures in this group ranged from 31·2 per cent for the sons of unskilled manual fathers to 16·6 per cent for the sons of skilled and semi-skilled manual workers, the figure for children of the unemployed being, somewhat surprisingly, at 24·4 per cent lower than that for the unskilled.

Rose, relying on his subjects' own information, obtained what he calls a 'rough indication of the socio-economic groups represented' as judged by the paternal occupation in 281 cases out of a potential 471, though he adds that in some instances the occupation listed may not have been the father's normal calling. On this basis 40 per cent of his fathers were classified as unskilled, 27 per cent as semi-skilled, 23 per cent as skilled and 10 per cent as belonging to the professional or business class. Comparing these results with the corresponding figures of 12 per cent unskilled and 16 per cent semi-skilled for England and Wales, and of 24 per cent and 14 per cent for Liverpool, shown by the 1951 Census 1 Per Cent Sample, Rose infers that there is a disproportionate representation of the lower social groups amongst his Borstal population; and he adds that the Merseyside Survey gives figures almost identical to his own, though not based on heads of households. Other investigators give similar findings. Thus Bagot (1944) comments that 'no sons of professional people are in the group studied, no sons of independent shopkeepers'. In 337 of his 524 cases, in which information was available, thirty-one were sons of 'skilled tradesmen', sixty-nine of semi-skilled and 224 unskilled workers. Bagot also notes the extent of unemployment amongst his boys' fathers, 16·6 per cent being out of work at a time of near-full national employment. Trenaman gives percentages for a dozen categories of the paternal occupations of his young soldiers, showing that none of these delinquents had fathers in clerical, professional or administrative work—a fact which he

[1] pp. 23, 80 and 90.

contrasts with a total of 8·5 per cent in such occupations shown by the 1931 Census. Mannheim lists five groups of employment for the fathers of 166 of his total group of 232 Cambridge boys who, he said, belonged 'mainly to the labourer and artisan class'; but his data do not make it possible to extract figures as to degrees of skill. Mannheim and Wilkins could only give the occupation of the head of the household in just over 100 of their cases, and on this they comment that 'it seemed that those who came from homes where the head of the household was in a supervisory grade or a clerical or distributive occupation, the lad afforded a better risk than all others. On the present data this cannot be stated with any certainty, and there seems no point in producing the tabulation of these results'.[1]

Several of our investigators also assess social status by the occupations of the delinquents themselves, as distinct from those of their fathers. Ferguson found that at the age of seventeen, as against a delinquent rate of 12·2 per cent for the whole group of 'ordinary' boys, the figure for skilled workers or apprentices stood at 7·2 per cent, that for semi-skilled at 19·3 per cent and for unskilled at 22·6 per cent. Amongst those engaged in non-manual work, the rate was 5·2 per cent for the 'higher', and 10·6 per cent for the 'lower', group—both figures, it will be noticed, being below that for the group as a whole. Ferguson also noticed that the incidence of delinquency was high amongst 'stop-gap' employees, for whom the rate was 21·6 per cent, as against 9 per cent for those in 'permanent 'work. Similar data are given for physically handicapped boys three years after leaving school. In this group as a whole the percentage of proved offenders stood at 10·6 per cent. Boys in non-manual work were again below the average with 3·4 per cent delinquent; and the same was true of those in skilled or semi-skilled manual work, among whom the percentage found to be delinquent was 7·7 per cent; whilst the figure for the unskilled worker stood at 13·5 per cent and for the unemployed at 18·5 per cent.

Rose gives figures for the various kinds of jobs which his boys held longest or most commonly. It appears that 'no less than 25 per cent (112) were engaged in completely dead-end jobs such as messenger boys, van boys, tea boys and the like'.[2] Mannheim, too, comments that 'the great majority of the boys had to work in blind-alley jobs. Only four of them had obtained apprenticeships'.[3] Mannheim assigned ninety-six (particulars for the rest being unknown) of the 122 boys from both of his groups who had left school to various occupational categories; of these seventy-two were described as 'errand boy' or 'roundsman, porter, labourer, office boy, garage hand, etc.'

Using the same grouping as for parental occupations, Trenaman gives one set of figures for his soldiers' occupations and another for the frequency of each employment in the various jobs listed, since 'each man had held a number of jobs'. He comments that 'the groupings suggest functions but they convey only an imperfect impression of actual occupations. The majority were employed at menial or unskilled work because of their youth and backwardness. Even apprentices to a skilled trade were relatively few (14 per cent).

[1] p. 88. [2] p. 70. [3] p. 37.

The total number claiming some sort of apprenticeship or skilled training was 36 per cent compared with 57 per cent in the control groups. For "transport worker" one could therefore generally read "driver's mate"; for "clerical", "office boy",' and so on. But, 'the degree of social standing of the offenders' families is not a factor that can be gauged from the present records with any exactness'.[1]

Similar data are given by Bagot (1941). He found that, whereas the Liverpool Juvenile Employment Committee's figures for 1936 recorded 16·8 per cent of the boys with whom they dealt as having been placed in clerical or commercial posts or in trade apprenticeships, and 83·2 per cent in '"various occupations" which included very many who were classed as shop and errand boys', the employed delinquents 'were almost all in jobs of this last type'.[2] Gibbs classified his delinquents and controls according to the degree of their skills, the proportions in each category being as follows:[3]

	Delinquents *Per cent*	*Non-delinquents* *Per cent*
Unskilled manual	62	37
Semi-skilled	30	26
Skilled manual	7	25
White collar	1	12

Mannheim and Wilkins give brief details of occupation on committal to Borstal for 366 of their 720 boys. Of these, 292 were employed in labouring and other unskilled jobs such as errand boy or lorry driver's mate, whilst thirty-seven were in skilled grades: the remainder were either in the Forces or in other occupations, or had not worked since leaving school. The authors, however, add the pertinent comment that 'there is little point in showing that Borstal boys do not often have "good jobs", since employers will seldom be prepared to accept for a "good job" the youth who has a record', and, 'since the great majority of Borstal boys have a crime record before entry to Borstal, the inter-association between crime and opportunity of employment will already have begun to operate'.[4]

Finally, we have a number of descriptive comments which can be regarded as in a limited degree indications of social class. Among Ferguson's 'ordinary' boys, the percentage of delinquents rose from 6·9 per cent in the 'good working class' districts to 22·3 per cent in the 'slum' areas. A similar rise was associated with the degree of overcrowding in the home. Bagot (1941) found that juvenile delinquency was 'concentrated in one section of the population, the very poor'[5] and was rarely found in the 'comfortable families'. Trenaman remarks that most of his young soldiers 'came from working-class families of which a large proportion were in the lower income groups';[6] and Carr-Saunders likewise says that 'the occupation of the father of the case was described in the records. Most were descriptions of working-class jobs',[7] but this term is hardly exact enough to allow comparison with other studies. On the other hand, two of Norwood East's references to social class findings

[1] pp. 136 and 139–40. [2] p. 57. [3] p. 257. [4] p. 125. [5] pp. 85–6. [6] p. 52. [7] p. 83.

appear to be at variance with those of the majority of our investigators, unless the conflict is to be explained as due to differences of definition. He found that 32 per cent of his lads 'appear . . . to have lived only in poor class areas and 64 per cent only in artisan or superior districts';[1] these terms are not, however, defined.

In the American studies also social status is generally identified with occupational classifications. All but one of the studies provide some material—and there is a fair amount that is broadly comparable.

Dealing first with paternal occupations, we find that Slawson comments on a 'preponderance of unskilled workers among fathers of delinquent boys as compared with those among the unselected population', though he regards his finding as 'only an indication of a rough association between inferior occupational status of father and delinquency of son'.[2] He reports that his delinquents, with the possible exclusion of those from a school for Jewish boys, were markedly inferior in social status to the unselected population. Thus, among non-Jewish boys in his various institutions, proportions ranging from 26·5 per cent to 29·1 per cent had fathers who were classed as 'day laborers, etc.', as against a figure of 7·5 per cent in the local general population. Similarly, whereas 7·5 per cent of the general population were engaged in professional occupations, for the fathers of the delinquents the figures ranged from 0·6 per cent to 2·8 per cent, with 3·3 per cent for the Jewish group.[3]

The Gluecks' observations on 392 of their 500 reformatory men showed that 'an appreciably greater percentage of the general male population than of the fathers of our men are engaged in the professions. Not a single parent of our group earned his living in clerical service as compared with 5·6 per cent of the general population so engaged'.[4] Figures are given for eight groups of occupations, with comparisons; and 36·6 per cent of the delinquents' fathers are classified as belonging to the skilled occupational group, 23·4 per cent to the semi-skilled and 40 per cent to the unskilled.

From their parallel study of delinquent women (for whom particulars were obtained in all but twenty-eight cases) the Gluecks conclude that 'clearly . . . the occupational status of the fathers of our girls is far below that of the general population'.[5] Comparing certain categories of parental population (prior to the daughters' commitment) with those of the general male population of Massachusetts in 1920, they found that 1·1 per cent of the delinquents had professional fathers, as against 4·6 per cent of the general population; whilst 1·7 per cent of the delinquents' fathers, as against 20·1 per cent of the general population, were engaged in clerical occupations. From these and other details of family background, the authors infer that 'it is not necessary to commit ourselves to any special theory of crime-causation in order to conclude from the foregoing analysis that our women offenders were most unfortunate in their biologic, social, and economic background'.[6]

[1] p. 110. [2] pp. 392–3. [3] pp. 121–4. [4] p. 115. [5] p. 66. [6] p. 73.

In their 1934 study of juvenile delinquents the Gluecks again conclude that they are dealing 'with parents and homes that in many respects must be characterized as unwholesome or under-privileged'.[1] While figures are given for various occupations in which the fathers were engaged when the boys in the study were examined, comparisons are not available; but it is noteworthy that only 1 per cent had fathers in the professional category.

The Gluecks' latest study of juvenile delinquents shows less difference between delinquents and controls in respect of paternal occupation than do the studies so far considered. Giving data for those fathers who are making their homes with the families of the boys and who are also employed, the Gluecks comment that 'in respect to occupational skill, the fathers of the delinquents make a poorer showing than those of the non-delinquents, although the difference between the two is not as striking as in other respects'.[2] 'About equal proportions' of the two groups are found to be engaged in skilled or semi-skilled trades, or in factories, or working as teamsters, truck drivers or chauffeurs; but lower proportions of the delinquents' fathers were in business for themselves (3·5 per cent against 8·5 per cent), or employed as clerks, salesmen, insurance brokers, lawyers, bondsmen 'and the like' (2·4 per cent against 4·5 per cent). On the other hand a higher proportion (39·7 per cent against 30·5 per cent) is described as unskilled.

Healy and Bronner devote relatively little space to social status. In a list of 'general statistics' for their 133 families, they simply note that 47 per cent of their children have fathers who are skilled workers, 40 per cent unskilled and 13 per cent professional or 'white collar'. Fernald does not attempt to discuss social class, but, in giving various data for certain early home conditions, she concludes that 'very few attempts have been made to use uniform schemes for estimates or for grading homes, and up to this time the descriptive method has been felt to be of more value. Because of this trend, there is little available data for comparison, and we are able to say little more regarding the home conditions of our group than that these women come from the poorer classes, to a very large extent . . . '[3] Sullenger gives data in only 110 Omaha cases, and in these the occupational distribution of the delinquents' fathers compares with that of the general population as follows:

	Delinquents	*Omaha male population over 24 years*
	Per cent	*Per cent*
Skilled (5 occupations)	7·3	7·5
Semi-skilled (6 occupations)	7·3	36·6
Unskilled (7 occupations)	85·4	55·9

In Sweden Otterström reports that 'The parents of the children in this material more often come from the lower classes of society than in the normal popula-

[1] p. 80. [2] p. 88. [3] p. 244.

tion'[1]; and in support of this generalization she gives the following figures for her 1926–40 cases:

Social Class	*Fathers of children investigated*	*Men entitled to vote 1921–40*
	Per cent	*Per cent*
I	0·8	9·3
II	14·3	28·2
III–IV	84·9	62·5

The above figures, however, relate to the total of all four of Otterström's groups, including those not known to have committed criminal offences. If attention is concentrated solely on the delinquent and criminal groups, the results become:

Social Class	*Men entitled to vote*	*Fathers of*	
		Group III	*Group IV*
	Per cent	*Per cent*	*Per cent*
I	9·3	1·5	0·6
II	28·2	13·1	17·9
III–IV	62·5	85·4	81·5

On the subject of the occupational status of the delinquents themselves, as distinct from their fathers, less material is forthcoming from the American studies. Of the Gluecks' reformatory men, just over half (54·1 per cent) were customarily employed in unskilled work, whilst 32·1 per cent were semi-skilled and 13·8 per cent skilled. The categories quoted do not include professional or clerical, though 6·1 per cent are said to have been employed as salesmen and store-clerks. No comparative material is given.

It will be remembered that in the Gluecks' study of reformatory women, nearly three-quarters were 'idle' at the time of the arrest that resulted in commitment. The respective figures for the first and last job before commitment showed, however, that 53·4 per cent and 44·4 per cent had worked in factories, 31·4 per cent and 29·7 per cent in domestic service and day work, 4·4 per cent and 14·2 per cent in hotels or restaurants, 4·9 per cent and 3·4 per cent as shopgirls, etc., 2·9 per cent and 2·1 per cent in clerical and 1·5 per cent and 4·6 per cent in other occupations. Without comparative figures it is difficult to base, on this material, any inferences about social status; but it is encouraging to note that this classification was deliberately devised so as to facilitate comparison with Fernald's work. Fernald's own conclusion is that 'it is difficult to classify accurately kinds of work done by women of varying ages for different periods of time'. Questions regarding the kind of work done 'were asked very carefully with a view to finding out what was meant by "factory work", "office girl", "nurse", etc.' and the results, 'codified by the main divisions of the Census Index to Occupations' were later 'regrouped into eleven classes which seemed to fit the needs of a selected group of women better than did the entire census scheme which was made up from returns of occupations for all wage-earners in the country, both male and female'. Fernald's final comment is that 'with the exception of vaudeville performers

[1] p. 152.

who work under especially bad conditions, the delinquents have larger representation than we should expect among the occupations which are comparatively unskilled, principally domestic service and, to a lesser degree, factory work while they have a smaller percentage than the general population in occupations which require special training, such as clerical work and professional service'.[1] Actually, the percentage of her delinquents in domestic service was 42 per cent as against the Census figure of 23·7 per cent for the general female working population, while vaudeville workers had 'eight times their proportional representation in the general population'. Clerical workers, on the other hand, accounted for 3·1 per cent of the delinquents—'less than one-quarter of their quota in the general population', and workers in professional services, with 0·8 per cent, furnished 'less than one-ninth of what we might expect'.[2] At the same time the authors draw attention to the fact that the Census figures, unlike those for the delinquents, all refer to a given point of time, and that these comparisons consequently cannot be regarded as exact.

So far as juveniles are concerned, the Gluecks remark that any classification by degrees of skill is 'obviously beside the point . . . because we are dealing with very young boys the vast majority of whom could not possibly have been yet engaged in occupations requiring any degree of skill'.[3] They do, however, regard with concern the fact that 58·1 per cent of their boys were engaged in street trades as newsboys, bootblacks, errand boys or messengers, occupations which they consider to be both conducive to anti-social behaviour and little affected by socializing influences.

We thus reach the unsurprising conclusion that, on the definitions used by these investigators, those who find themselves in trouble with the criminal law on either side of the Atlantic are predominantly drawn from the lower social classes; but even so we are not able to say whether, or how far, this predominance exceeds that to be expected from the proportion which these classes contribute to the non-criminal population.

7. *Poverty*

Most of our investigators have interested themselves in the economic position of their subjects. The standards used tend, however, to be descriptive rather than precisely quantitative and, as one would expect, common measures are altogether lacking. 'To be poor' means all sorts of things to all sorts of people, and indeed, even to the same people the expression has different meanings in different circumstances. Some investigators have gone so far as to try to assess the significance of poverty as a factor in, or a cause of, delinquent behaviour; but such attempts run into fresh difficulties. Most of the crimes covered by these studies are offences against property. Stealing and other unlawful methods of attaining property are forms of acquisition: some people steal, just as others buy, the things without which they feel impoverished. In a sense, therefore, it could be argued that all crimes against property are due

[1] pp. 311 and 322. [2] pp. 320–2.
[3] Glueck, S. and E. T., *One Thousand Juvenile Delinquents* (1934), p. 89.

to economic need if not to actual poverty. In extreme cases, as when frauds are committed by a very rich man, such a conclusion may sound absurd, but in the absence of any agreement as to where poverty ends and economic affluence begins, a sense of impoverishment cannot be ruled out as a factor in quite a considerable range of cases.[1] The whole topic is, moreover, still further complicated by the existence of divergent ideas about how much should be spent on what. In the view of some investigators 'poverty' may be caused by what they regard as unwise spending. Burt, for instance, found that 56 per cent of his delinquents came from poor or very poor homes—the highest of whose family's 'small, but constant' earnings did not 'suffice to maintain a constant level of physical health, because, though theoretically above the minimal standard for necessities, much of it is absorbed by other expenditure, useful, needless, or unintelligent'.[2] He was not, however, much impressed by poverty as a causal factor. 'Since of the total inhabitants of London no more than 30 per cent belong to the lowest social strata . . . the amount of delinquency coming from those lowest social strata is, beyond question, disproportionate; nevertheless, in the higher and more prosperous ranks, its frequency is still unexpectedly large. And, when nearly half the offenders come from homes that are far from destitute, poverty can hardly be the sole or the most influential cause.'[3] In the opinion of this investigator 'only in 3 per cent of the male delinquents, and in not one of the female, could the effects of poverty be called the prime contributory factor'. He continues: 'our general conclusion, therefore, on the influence of poverty must be this. If the majority of delinquents are needy, the majority of the needy do not become delinquents'.[4] Indeed, in Burt's view, it is more remarkable that 42 per cent come from those classes 'designated by Booth as "comfortable"'. He adds, 'this figure will probably surprise those familiar with none but the industrial school type. The explanation is clear. In the better kind of home, the parents and interested friends more often desire—and more successfully attempt—to debar their children's petty misdemeanours from becoming a subject of official inquiry and action; the official agency in its turn, when apprised of all the facts, is more reluctant to banish a child from a good home to an industrial school'.[5] Only a minority of Burt's 'delinquents', it will be remembered, had appeared in a juvenile court.

Trenaman's evidence on this topic is more descriptive than statistical. In his conclusions he lists poverty as one of the factors 'strongly associated with delinquency',[6] and comments that his soldiers came 'almost without exception, from poor, sometimes the poorest homes (the men from middle-class homes number between 1 and 2 per cent)'.[7] In a discussion of under-nourishment, Trenaman notes further that 'altogether, gross poverty was traced in the early lives of some 15 per cent of the cases, and the true figure may well have been a good deal higher'. Among the offenders 14 per cent (as against 10 per cent in the control groups) said on a questionnaire that they went 'short of food through (their) mother finding it difficult to make both ends meet'.[8] In a considerable number of cases also (40 per cent of the total)

[1] See p. 80. [2] pp. 68–9. [3] p. 70. [4] p. 92. [5] p. 69. [6] pp. 198–9. [7] p. 141. [8] p. 51.

the father was an invalid or dead or separated, and in 16 per cent frequently unemployed; and this, it is suggested, might be another factor which 'would tend to add to the relative poverty of their homes'. Of the picture as a whole Trenaman observed that it is 'probably no exaggeration to say that a majority of the offenders' families were living near the poverty line . . .'[1]

In Bagot's 1941 enquiry, poverty was regarded as a 'vital factor among the causes of juvenile delinquency in Liverpool'.[2] Bagot is fortunate in being able to use for comparative purposes information contained in the Merseyside Survey, which relates to the same area and to a period (1929–32) which is fairly near to that of his 1934 and 1936 studies; but his figures are unfortunately based on only two-thirds of his total group. Since in a number of the omitted cases the parents had definitely refused to disclose their income, and since in Bagot's view income in such cases is usually good or adequate, his selection may be unavoidably biassed. Subject to this limitation, he reports that 'more than 50 per cent' of the delinquents' families were below the Merseyside poverty line, the corresponding figure for the Merseyside families generally being 16 per cent; while, if, alternatively, comparison had been made with Rowntree Human Needs standard (which runs materially above that used in the Merseyside survey), no less than 85·7 per cent of the delinquents' families would have been below standard, as against 30 per cent of all Merseyside families.[3]

The remaining studies give less adequate data. Bagot's 1944 work contains no factual data on the extent of poverty, nor was he able to give any figures of comparison with the population at large. He has, however, recorded the number of adults (or equivalents) who were in receipt of certain net sums. Here his information is based on 434 out of a potential 524 cases, where the information was said to be 'reasonably accurate', though the figures are 'probably lower than they should be'.[4] Mannheim's data concerning the economic position are, 'largely limited to the occupation and wages of the father and the number of rooms and the rent paid . . .' No comparative figures are available. Since Mannheim can give the father's earnings in only ninety-nine out of a potential 232 cases, his evidence does not amount to much; and he himself considers it 'unsafe to draw any sweeping conclusions'.[5]

Although Ferguson gives considerable data regarding overcrowding, unemployment and other factors which provide general indications of economic position, he does not deal with poverty as such. In any case, he might well be limited by the fact that his 'ordinary' boys were 'probably in the main the lads drawn from homes in which the pressure of economic factors was most severe', since they were those who left school at the earliest possible moment; while the general social background of his handicapped boys was even less favourable.[6] Carr-Saunders, similarly, gives no data regarding economic status, but he does find differences— even if 'not great' ones—between delinquents and controls in overcrowding, condition of home and regularity of fathers' employment. 'It may be suggested', Carr-Saunders says, 'that these several inferiorities are linked with and, in a sense, are

[1] p. 143. [2] p. 62. [3] pp. 61-2. [4] p. 43. [5] pp. 28–29. [6] pp. 15 and 108.

manifestations of economic inferiority'; but at the same time 'any attempt to argue that low economic status, of a kind attributable wholly to heavy burdens and external misfortune, is the main cause of delinquency, is defeated by the facts that most poor families are not delinquent and that much delinquency occurs in relatively well-off families'.[1]

The rest of the British evidence does not, therefore, wholly support Bagot's 1941 comment that 'agreement is fairly general that poverty is one of the strongest forces to be reckoned with in any attempt to reduce the number of delinquents'.[2]

Although the American material is presented in a considerably more consistent fashion than is the British, it is less, rather than more, conclusive. Healy, like Burt, listed the cases in which he considered various conditions to be a main or minor causal factor. Poverty was noted as a major factor in only four, and as a minor one in fifty-nine of 823 cases. Healy comments that 'my observations would lead me to believe, for instance, that vastly more delinquency could be attributed to poverty in London than in Chicago . . . A word about our not finding poverty to be a very large causative factor is here in order. Local conditions of relative financial welfare in Chicago constitute part of the explanation—in clinical and court experience here one rarely indeed sees the physical evidences of poverty which simply abound in some European cities.[3] Then, on the other hand, in contravention of the first impulse to attribute much to poverty, one finds either other members of the same poor family living righteously, or that the poverty itself arose from an anterior factor, such as alcoholism or mental defect, which often is the progenitor of both poverty and delinquency.'[4] Healy is not alone, as we have already seen, in this approach, which he follows up later with 'poverty, and crowded housing and so on, by themselves alone are not productive of criminalism. It is only when these conditions in turn produce suggestions, and bad habits of mind, and mental imagery of low order, that the trouble in conduct ensues.'[5]

The economic circumstances of the families of the Gluecks' reformatory men were classified in the three following categories: (1) dependent, i.e. receiving aid continuously from public or other funds; (2) marginal, i.e. living on daily earnings and accumulating little or nothing, with perhaps occasional aid; and (3) comfortable, i.e. having sufficient resources to maintain the family for at least four months during a financial crisis. In 447 families out of the total of 500, 14·8 per cent were in the dependent group, 56·4 per cent in the marginal and 28·8 per cent in the comfortable. 'These three terms', it is explained, 'represent a summary of the economic status of the family from the time of the boy's birth to the time of his sentence to the Reformatory'. The Gluecks remark that it would be illuminating to compare

[1] pp. 95–6. [2] p. 60.

[3] I cannot refrain from remarking that this is an astonishing statement to anyone with even a superficial acquaintance with the Chicago slums. Perhaps, however, we each see only the beams in our neighbours' eyes.—B. W.

[4] pp. 129–30. [5] p. 284.

these figures with the general population of Massachusetts, but find that this cannot be done. They do, however, go so far as to say that, if such material could be available, 'it may safely be stated . . . that . . . it would probably not disclose as high a degree of dependency and marginality . . .'[1] Classified on the same basis, the economic status of the families of the Gluecks' reformatory women, during childhood and adolescence, is recorded as 13·3 per cent dependent, 78 per cent marginal and 8·7 per cent comfortable.

In the Gluecks' 1934 study of juveniles, particulars are given for 925 of the total of 1,000 subjects. Of these 8·1 per cent came from the families who were economically dependent, while the families of 68·2 per cent were in marginal, and those of 23·7 per cent in comfortable, circumstances. Once again, although comparable data for the general population of Massachusetts are not available, the authors are confident that the facts 'would hardly disclose so high a degree of dependency and marginality during a normal period of employment'.[2]

While the Gluecks' most recent study of juveniles has the merit of including a control group, its contribution to the evidence on the subject of poverty is necessarily limited by the fact that the controls and the delinquents were matched for residence in 'underprivileged' areas. Even so the authors found 'slightly better economic conditions in the families of the non-delinquents', the proportions at the time of the study being as follows: dependent[3]—delinquents 28·6 per cent, non-delinquents 12 per cent; marginal—delinquents 66·4 per cent, non-delinquents 76 per cent; comfortable—delinquents 5 per cent, non-delinquents 12 per cent.[4] Accordingly they conclude that: 'as for the economic status of the two groups of families, a finding has emerged which is particularly significant in view of the fact that the boys were matched at the outset on the basis of residence in underprivileged areas, namely, that sporadic or chronic dependency has been markedly more prevalent among the families of the delinquents. This is attributable, at least in part, to the far poorer work habits of the fathers, and in part also to less planful management of the family income. These differences between the families of the delinquents and the families of the non-delinquents do not so much pertain to the obvious issue of the relationship of dependency or poverty to crime . . . they are important, rather, as reflecting the differences in the quality of the adults in the families and therefore the variance in influence on the children.'[5]

The Gluecks also interested themselves in the extent to which their two groups of families had made use of various social agencies. It appears that the proportion of the delinquents' families who were receiving financial assistance from public or private agencies was nearly twice as great (21·2 per cent as against 11·6 per cent) as the corresponding figure for the controls;

[1] p. 113. [2] p. 69.

[3] Defined as 'dependent on relief agencies or relatives for support', a definition which does not include the word 'continuous' as did the previous Glueck studies.

[4] Some allowance was made in certain cases where, on account of the war, wages were out of proportion to normal earnings, the more usual figures being used (p. 85).

[5] p. 280.

and that, whereas similar proportions (43·4 per cent and 42·8 per cent respectively) of the two groups were 'sporadically dependent', 36·2 per cent of the delinquents', as against only 14·6 per cent of the non-delinquents', families were 'usually dependent'. Enquiring further into the reasons for economic dependency, the Gluecks comment, that apart from those families who required aid on account of illness, the numbers of which were equal in the two groups, 'inadequacy of income stemming from economic depression and seasonal unemployment was the major reason for supplemental support in the majority of the families of the non-delinquents (59·1 per cent) needing aid, as compared with 38·9 per cent of the families of the delinquents. By contrast, unwillingness of the bread-winner to assume his responsibilities was the chief reason for resort to outside aid among the families of the delinquents (45·5 per cent: 25·1 per cent)'.[1]

Healy and Bronner's investigation was conducted during the acute depression of the 1930's, which 'the economic conditions of our families naturally reflect'.[2] It is, therefore, surprising to find that their figures show a higher proportion of 'comfortable' incomes than does any of the other American studies, although only one of these others gives a higher figure for the proportion in a state of 'dependency'. As many as 33 per cent of Healy and Bronner's families were living on a 'comfortable income or better', while 51 per cent existed on marginal incomes and 16 per cent were dependent on aid at the time that the child concerned was seen. Fernald, after excluding one institutional group of just over 100 women (together with some others) on account of inadequate or unreliable data, classified the remaining 420 as follows: very poor (dependent all or a large part of the time)—5·7 per cent; poor (managing with difficulty, with occasional aid)—35·7 per cent; fair (normally self-supporting but without surplus)—45 per cent; good (with money saved or its equivalent)—13·1 per cent; while 0·5 per cent were reported to have considerable means.[3] Of the earnings of those of the women who had been in employment, Fernald concludes that 'on the whole, the records show, for the most part . . . a low wage, though probably no lower wage than the bulk of unskilled workers in the same occupations outside are earning'.[4] Finally, Sullenger reports that, in a random selection of 500 of his Omaha cases, 45 per cent were 'registered for having received some kind of aid from public and private relief agencies', while the corresponding proportion for sixty-nine Columbia cases was 40·5 per cent.[5]

American investigators thus find some tendency for delinquency to be associated with poverty or dependence on public funds; but, since most of the studies either give no comparative material or use controls deliberately drawn from the 'underprivileged', not much can be made of this result.

Otterström's data from Sweden likewise emphasize the poverty of the homes from which the children in all her four categories were drawn. 'Nearly all these homes', she writes, 'are also very poor'.[6] 'Naturally, no exact data are

[1] p. 105. [2] p. 27.
[3] These figures refer to the time of childhood and adolescence.
[4] p. 379. [5] p. 41. [6] p. 160.

available as to the family breadwinner's income, how many he is obliged to support, etc. All we have to go on are the direct statements by the inspectors as to the existence of poverty, and the official registers as to whether the respective families have been in receipt of poor relief . . . however, an attempt has been made to estimate the degree of poverty of the various homes . . . according to their descriptions by the inspectors. This estimation is based on expressions such as 'the children starve and are in a bad way' or 'the children are ragged and dirty' or 'the dwelling consisted of a "rickety shack" or "a partition in a municipal barrack" . . .'[1] On this basis the percentages of the children in the two delinquent categories who came from what the author describes as 'poor homes' were as follows:

	Per cent
Group (III) boys 1st period	32·8
Group (III) boys 2nd period	27·8
Group (III) girls 1st period	34·5
Group (III) girls 2nd period	36·3
Group (IV) boys 1st period	35·5
Group (IV) boys 2nd period	16·0
Group (IV) girls 1st period	36·7
Group (IV) girls 2nd period	26·1

8. *Mother's Employment outside the Home*

'Mothers who go to work and are not home in time to greet their children returning from school in the evening', my colleague Mr John Watson is reported to have said, 'are a major cause of juvenile crime'[2]. Mr Watson is an experienced magistrate and his pronouncements carry weight; and without doubt, the opinion here expressed is widely held. How far, then, does the evidence of our twenty-one studies support this generalization?

At the outset, there are the usual difficulties of imprecision to be faced. Presumably the effect upon home life of a mother's going out to work will greatly depend upon how long she works and at what hours. Mr Watson's reported observation refers, it will be noticed, to what are sometimes described as the 'latch key' children—those whose mothers are not home at the time of their return from school. Most of our investigators, however, treat employment outside the home as a single category, without further refinement; though the Gluecks do distinguish between regular, occasional and sporadic work. Ferguson found that 230 out of 1,234 of his 'ordinary' boys had working mothers. Of these boys, 10·4 per cent were delinquent; but a slightly larger proportion (12·4 per cent) of the boys whose mothers did not go out to work were delinquent. He concluded that this factor 'had not been found to be of any great importance in relation to delinquency'. For the mentally handicapped group the findings were similar (none are given for the physically handicapped), the figures being 24·1 per cent for the small group of twenty-nine whose mothers worked, as against 23·3 per cent of the 233 boys whose mothers were not employed. Again, Ferguson considered that this factor

[1] p. 165. [2] *Evening Standard*, November 3, 1955.

'did not appear to be of any importance'.[1] The Carr-Saunders investigation, in which a control group was available, gives particulars only for the 'normal' families. Amongst these, 15·9 per cent of the London delinquents had mothers who went out to work, as against 9 per cent of the controls; whilst in the provincial towns 9·1 per cent of delinquents' mothers were at work, as compared with the control figure of 7·4 per cent. Where the mother was the sole head of the household, 67·5 per cent of the delinquents and 52·5 per cent of the controls had working mothers in London, whereas the corresponding figures for the provincial towns were 31·6 per cent of the delinquents and 31·4 per cent of the controls. The authors comment that 'we might be able to argue that the delinquency of these cases in London is related to the fact that the boy is not controlled as much as he would be if his mother were at home doing housework, but we certainly cannot build up any such argument from the evidence of the figures for the provincial towns'.[2]

The remaining British studies simply give percentages, without comparison or comment. Mannheim found that the mother was employed in forty-one of his 232 cases: Bagot (1941) noted 'mother employed' in the case of 5·9 per cent of the boys and of 13·8 per cent of the girls in his 1934 group, the comparable figures for his 1936 group being 4·6 per cent and 7·8 per cent. In his 1944 study the percentage of delinquents with working mothers is given as 6·7 per cent. Finally, in a schedule of questions answered by Trenaman's subjects, 32 per cent of the delinquents and 33 per cent of the controls answered affirmatively the question: 'Has your mother gone out to work?'

Thus the British figures (which incidentally include some wartime studies when the number of working mothers might be expected to be abnormally high) show proportions of delinquents whose mothers were employed[3] ranging from 4·6 per cent to 32 per cent, whilst the only available control figures stand at 7·4 per cent, 9 per cent and 33 per cent. Clearly, although all these six investigators have tried to get evidence on the subject, the results give no factual support to generalizations such as that attributed to Mr Watson; but their very inconclusiveness leaves the door wide open for purely subjective opinions.

Of the American studies giving data on the point, one does not make it clear whether the mother worked inside or outside the home; the rest either specifically mention outside work, or give details of the mothers' occupations from which it is possible to estimate roughly what proportion worked inside the home. Slawson dismissed the very slight connection between maternal employment and delinquency revealed by his study because, when social status was held constant, the mothers of the controls were found to be out at work more frequently than were those of the delinquents. Thus amongst 1,306 of his delinquents for whom information was available, 23·1 per cent of the delinquents' mothers went to work, as against 18·2 per cent of the mothers of 3,005 ordinary school-children. When, however, differences in social status were eliminated, the positions were reversed, 34·3 per cent

[1] pp. 24 and 91–2. [2] p. 108.

[3] Excluding Carr-Saunders' families with only one head.

of the controls as against only 23·1 per cent of the delinquents coming from families in which the mother was gainfully employed. In Healy's investigation only 165 mothers of 1,000 cases were said to go out to work; and in a group of 823 in which the evidence was regarded as sufficiently good 'to be used for satisfactory comparison of causative factors', the mother's work was reckoned as a major causal factor in the child's delinquency in twenty-one cases, and a minor one in thirty-two.

In the earlier Glueck studies a considerable difference appears between the frequency of employment amongst the delinquents' mothers and amongst married women in the general population of Massachusetts with whom comparison is made; but if allowance were made for differences of social status, these results might well be subject to the same modification as Slawson's. Moreover, the general population figures used by the Gluecks apparently include married women without dependent children, in which case the comparison is misleading, since married women without children are presumably more likely to take outside employment than are those with children at home. In the case of the Gluecks' reformatory men, all that can be said is that information was available in 456 cases, and of these 28 per cent recorded mothers working outside the home either on a full- or a part-time basis. In the case of the reformatory women somewhat more data are available. Enquiring into the extent to which family income had been supplemented by the mother's employment during the childhood and adolescence of their subjects, the Gluecks found that 55·7 per cent of these mothers had been employed, a figure which they set (as already noted, somewhat dubiously) against the 11·6 per cent of all married women found to be at work in Massachusetts in 1910. Of these, about half had worked almost continuously, a quarter fairly regularly and another quarter sporadically. The general Massachusetts figure (which incidentally related to a date some twenty years earlier than that of the Gluecks' enquiry) is not, however, given in such detail: clearly, if 'sporadic' workers are not included in the census figure, the difference would be materially diminished. Similarly in the earlier Glueck study of juveniles, out of 937 delinquents 41·5 per cent had mothers who were gainfully employed in various ways which are described; and this figure, again, is set against the 1920 census return of 9·9 per cent of married women (with or without dependent children) in gainful employment.

In the latest Glueck study, in which, it will be remembered, the controls as well as the subjects came from underprivileged areas, fuller information is given. More of the delinquents' than of the non-delinquents' mothers (47 per cent against 33 per cent) worked 'outside the home', a phrase which, however, includes some such work as running a lodging house, which was not strictly outside employment. When, however, the totals were broken down so as to distinguish between regular and occasional work, it appeared that 20·4 per cent of the delinquents' and 18·3 per cent of the non-delinquents' mothers were regular workers; and that the major difference related to cases in which the mothers were only occasional workers. In this group were found 26·6 per cent of the delinquents, but only 14·7 per cent of the controls.

From this evidence the Gluecks somewhat surprisingly leap to the conclusion that 'whether the matter is approached from the psychoanalytic point of view of the deleterious effect upon the development of personality and character, or simply from ordinary observation and common experience, maternal neglect and careless oversight of children are accepted as major sources of maladjustment and delinquency; and, clearly, the mothers of the delinquent boys, as a group, were much more remiss in the care of their children than the mothers of the non-delinquents'.[1]

The American studies generally therefore, can only be said to show results at least as diverse and as inconclusive as their British counterparts.

9. *Truancy from School*

Truancy is generally classified in these studies as 'persistent', or 'occasional' or, without qualification, merely as 'truancy'. In their latest investigation, the Gluecks have distinguished between those who truant 'very occasionally' and those who do so 'persistently'. Although only a few of the studies indicate the origin of their information, the chief source in most cases must be school records; but this cannot be true in every case, for Mannheim used probation and other records, and he has remarked that 'it is not unlikely that many cases of occasional truancy among probationers were not brought to the notice of the Probation Officer'.[2]

Among those of the British studies which give data, the most striking results come from Ferguson. He found that amongst 'ordinary' boys 'delinquency increased with irregularity of school-attendance, especially in the small group where the irregularity was due to truancy'.[3] Of 1,348 boys, delinquent and non-delinquent, 362 were irregular attenders at school, the reasons being ill-health (165 cases), domestic causes (149 cases) and truancy (46 cases); but it will be noticed that the known truants did not constitute a large proportion of the total population. In these three groups the percentages of proved delinquents were 12·7 per cent, 16·1 per cent and 39·1 per cent respectively; and the proportion of boys found guilty of more than one offence rose from 2·4 per cent in the first group to 23·9 per cent in the third. Ferguson gives no data for his physically handicapped group, but amongst the mentally handicapped the incidence of delinquency was also found to be higher where school attendance was irregular. In this group the percentage of delinquents stood at 19·3 per cent amongst those in regular attendance (a total of 208 boys) and 30·8 per cent for the irregulars (numbering sixty-five boys); but the reasons for irregularity are not broken down as in the case of the 'ordinary' boys into ill-health, domestic causes and truancy.

Burt also took a serious view of truancy from school or home, describing this as 'usually the first step on the downward stair to crime'.[4] Persistent truancy from school is included in his classification of offences, and the proportions of truants recorded were 17·1 per cent of his boys and 4·1 per cent of the girls. 'The typical truant of to-day', Burt himself comments, 'is the small child of seven or eight . . . '[5] Trenaman, again, on information

[1] pp. 112–3. [2] p. 47. [3] p. 29. [4] p. 455. [5] p. 498.

provided by the delinquents themselves, records truanting by as many as 57 per cent of his young soldiers, as against 15 per cent of his controls; and he adds that 81 per cent of the 'job-changers' (those with four or more jobs, representing about 44 per cent of the total) admitted to truancy, as against 38 per cent of the others. Norwood East has noted, amongst those of his boys who had only elementary education, 'a history of truancy' in 5·8 per cent of the cases. He, like Ferguson, noted that 'absence from school, especially truancy, was associated with multiple convictions to a significant degree'.[1] Gibbs likewise remarks that the association between truancy and subsequent military delinquency is 'very high indeed'. Among his delinquents 54 per cent are said to have truanted 'often'; 23 per cent 'sometimes'; 23 per cent 'never'; whereas among the controls the corresponding figures were 11 per cent, 37 per cent and 52 per cent. Mannheim and Wilkins asked no specific questions about truancy, and were only able to get school reports in less than half their cases, while such reports as were available were said to be 'in large measure unguided and unsystematic'. In these circumstances, their finding of some 'evidence of truancy' in sixty-two cases cannot have much significance. Finally, by way of contrast we have Mannheim's report that 'there is not much evidence of truancy' among his subjects; but this conclusion must be read in the light of his own comment on the inadequacy of his material.

Amongst the American studies the most striking is the Gluecks' latest work. Two-thirds of the subjects of their study had truanted persistently, no less than 94·8 per cent having done so 'at one time or another during their school careers, while only 10·8 per cent of the non-delinquents had truanted, and then only occasionally'.[2] The delinquent truants, moreover, were found to have begun to evade school at the average age of ten, two and a half years earlier than the controls. Similar results come also from the Gluecks' earlier study of young delinquents, in which the authors record that, although 'complete data on all types of youthful misbehavior were unobtainable, the case-histories reveal that 630 (64·1 per cent) of the boys had truanted'.[3] Healy and Bronner have likewise stressed the importance of truancy, remarking that the question 'why in the same family is one child delinquent and another not delinquent'? might well be paraphrased to read, 'why, coming from the same family, is one child truant and another not? If adequate attempts were made to answer this specific query, what an opportunity there would be for school people to detect and check impending serious delinquent tendencies!' Using school records, these investigators found that 'almost all the non-attendance of the controls was occasioned by illness or changing residence. But about 60 per cent of the delinquents were out-and-out truants, with evasions of attendance running as high as one year in one case'.[4] In a schedule of offences committed by Healy's 1,000 repeated delinquents ('not only as charged in court, but as obtained from the story of parents and others'), 'truancy' is mentioned in connection with 225 of the 694 boys and with twenty-three out of the 306 girls. These, moreover, were 'only marked cases', absence from school for 'a day or two infrequently' not being regarded as truancy for

[1] p. 140. [2] p. 148. [3] p. 95. [4] pp. 61–2.

this purpose. Fernald classified her subjects' school attendance as 'very poor', 'poor', 'fair' and 'very good', but for various reasons did not regard the findings as of much value. Sullenger goes as far as to say that in Omaha truancy was 'at the basis of at least 90 per cent' of the cases, while in Columbia two-thirds of the delinquents handled by the court had been in trouble on account of truancy.

There is thus fairly general agreement amongst those of our investigators who have explored the subject that truants are more than averagely likely to be also delinquents; although, as with other factors, there are the widest variations in the degree of association found to obtain between truancy and delinquency. At the same time, if the prevailing optimism of the educational authorities as to the extent of contemporary truancy in Britain is justified, the great majority of delinquents cannot also be truants.

10. *The Broken Home*

Of all the hypotheses as to the origins of maladjustment or delinquency, perhaps the most generally accepted is that which associates such social failure with the 'broken home'. All our investigators have looked for evidence on this subject. Attempts fairly to assess the significance of their findings are, however, thwarted, first, by the absence of precise definition of what constitutes the 'breaking' of a home, and, second, by lack of any information as to the frequency of the 'broken home' amongst the population in general. The material on this most popular hypothesis is, in fact, quite exceptionally difficult to sort out.

All the British studies have something to report. Carr-Saunders concludes that about 28 per cent of his delinquents and about 16 per cent of his controls come from families which are abnormal in the sense, either that they have two heads other than the parents living as husband and wife, or that they have only one head. On this basis it appears that the percentages of broken homes are 'markedly higher for delinquents than for the controls' in every area except that of one London Court. Of the London delinquents, 25·6 per cent came from broken homes, as against 13 per cent of the controls; while for the provinces the figures were 31·5 per cent of the delinquents, as against 18·6 per cent of the controls. In addition, out of forty-seven homes 'where the heads, not being parents of the case, were cohabiting, forty-three had cases of delinquency'. Nevertheless, the authors' comment is cautious. 'We can only point out that the broken home may have some influence on delinquency, though since we get control cases coming from broken homes, we cannot assert that there is a direct link between this factor and delinquency'.[1]

The other British studies which attempted to establish some standard of comparison between the frequency of broken homes in delinquent and non-delinquent populations are those of Trenaman, Gibbs, and Mannheim and Wilkins. Of Trenaman's young soldiers, 57 per cent came from broken homes, as against only 12 per cent of the controls; while 71 per cent, as against 19 per cent of the controls, 'were either homeless, or came from broken homes,

[1] pp. 62 and 149.

or their parents were chronic invalids, or their parents had been away from home for long periods'.[1] Gibbs, whose definition includes cases in which the home was broken by death, separation, desertion or divorce, or in which either a parent had been permanently institutionalized or the child concerned had been sent to live with relatives or in an institution, also classified his cases according to the child's age at the time when the break occurred—an aspect which has been generally ignored by other investigators, but one which, it might well be supposed, could be of considerable importance. Using this criterion he found that 13 per cent of his delinquents and 6 per cent of his controls came from homes which had been first broken when the children concerned were not more than five years old; that 14 per cent of the delinquents and 8 per cent of the controls had experienced such a break between the ages of six and ten, and that a break between the ages of eleven and fifteen had befallen 26 per cent of the delinquents and 11 per cent of the controls. It appears, however, that these figures were much affected by the author's rather unusual definition which, as we have seen, included cases in which the child itself was removed, for whatever reason, to an institution. On this Gibbs himself comments as follows: 'The analysis has shown that "homes broken" from all causes is, in this study, associated with military delinquency.' Nevertheless, 'evidence of homes broken by death, divorce, separation, etc., did not appear with greater frequency in delinquent histories than in the backgrounds of non-delinquents. Removal of the delinquents as children to institutions (usually as a result of court convictions) did result in more frequent disruption of their family circumstances than was experienced by the controls'.[2] Apart from a 'very small correlation due, as far as could be ascertained, to familial factors' in the 0–5 year level, by far the main difference between delinquents and non-delinquents in the 6–10 and 11–15 year groups lies in the category of 'child institutionalized'; and, since these cases all resulted from Court action, 'delinquency, rather than domestic disturbances, would account for these zero-order correlations'.[3] In other words, more often than not it was the delinquency which disrupted the child's home life, not the disruption of the home which provoked the delinquency.

The Mannheim and Wilkins study is distinguished for its attempt to establish a comparative standard of the incidence of broken homes among the general population. On the basis of a sample investigation, these authors estimated that the proportion of adolescents who might be expected to come from homes which lacked father or mother or both would be 14 per cent; whereas for the Borstal boys who were the subjects of this enquiry the corresponding figure was found to be 22 per cent in those cases (about four-fifths of the total) for which information was available.

Burt gives a coefficient of association between delinquency and 'defective family relationships', in which broken homes are included, of 0·33.[4] Unfortunately, however, much of his abundant material is presented in a form that does not lend itself to comparison with other studies. In Bagot's definition the chief peculiarities are the inclusion among broken homes first of those in

[1] pp. 174 and 191. [2] pp. 268 and 420–1. [3] p. 267. [4] p. 53.

which the father was 'unemployable'; second, of those in which the child concerned was illegitimate; and, third, of those in which the mother was 'out working'. In the figures that follow, the first and third of these categories have been eliminated, but the second has been included on the assumption that illegitimate children would be covered by most definitions of broken homes, even though they may not be explicitly mentioned. On this basis Bagot is able to give particulars for 2,917 of the 3,221 children in his 1941 enquiry. These show that, in 1934, 54·9 per cent of his girls and 37·7 per cent of his boys came from broken homes, the corresponding figures for 1936 being 44 per cent and 36·2 per cent. In his 1944 study the percentage (for boys only) was 42·3 per cent. Mannheim, using the same definition of a broken home as Carr-Saunders, found that 34 per cent of his pre-war and 30·3 per cent of his war-time cases (or 39·4 per cent if homes with fathers in H.M. forces are treated as 'broken') came from broken homes; and he goes so far as to add the comment that 'it may be regarded as a well-established fact', that, 'on the average, about one-third of all juvenile delinquents in English towns come from broken homes as this term is defined above'.[1] Among Rose's 500 boys, information was available in 471 cases, and of these 'almost exactly half came from families which were, at sentence, broken by death, desertion or separation'.[2] Norwood East's material is hardly comparable, but it may be just worth recording that 44·4 per cent of his subjects were living with both parents at ages five and fourteen and immediately prior to conviction.

Ferguson's results, like those of Gibbs, are in decided contrast with the findings of the majority of British investigators. He concludes that 'the fact that a home was "broken" has not, in itself, constituted a major factor in the production of delinquency'.[3] Using the absence or the death of one or both parents as the criterion of a broken home, Ferguson arrived at the following figures: out of 1,078 'ordinary' boys with both parents alive and in the home, 11·7 per cent had been found guilty at least once between the ages of eight and eighteen years; whilst, among 271 boys with one or both parents absent, the comparable figure was 13·2 per cent. In the light of more detailed figures Ferguson adds that 'in this study families from which a parent was absent were found to produce slightly more than their share of delinquency, but this was true only at post-school ages, not during school-days. If both parents were absent the rate was higher, but still only above average at post-school ages. Delinquency-rates were worse, both during and after school years, when family disruption was due to causes other than death.'[4] Amongst the physically handicapped, sixteen or 11·1 per cent of the 144 who came from broken homes were delinquent, as against thirty-four or 9·9 per cent of the 344 whose homes were intact. Amongst the mentally handicapped, out of 104 children from broken homes, 28·8 per cent were delinquent, as against 21·4 per cent of those whose homes were intact.

All the American studies also give data. Only the Gluecks' latest investigation, however, provides any control figures. In this it appeared that consider-

[1] p. 21. [2] p. 55. [3] p. 145. [4] pp. 22–23.

ably more of the delinquents (60·4 per cent) came from homes broken by separation, divorce or death or by the prolonged absence of a parent than was the case with the controls, for whom the corresponding figure was only 34·2 per cent. Moreover, 'in every type of family break, the delinquent group exceeded the non-delinquent in incidence'.[1] In a few other studies attempts have been made to compare the incidence of broken homes amongst delinquents with that prevailing amongst the population at large. Thus, in their earlier study of juveniles, the Gluecks found that their delinquents 'come largely from homes which were for one reason or another broken or distorted', whereas 'the probability that non-delinquents have so high an incidence of inadequate homes is remote'.[2] In support of this conclusion, they refer to an analysis of unpublished census data of Chicago families showing that 'slightly fewer than one-seventh of such families were broken by death, desertion, separation, or divorce'[3]—a far lower proportion than that found amongst their delinquents, which stood at 45·5 per cent, or 48 per cent if the definition is extended to include prolonged parental absence. Again, using the same standard of comparison in their investigation of reformatory women, the Gluecks found that 'the proportion of broken homes is much higher in our group of families than in the general population':[4] in all 58·4 per cent of the women had suffered parental death, desertion, separation or divorce before they had reached the age of twenty-one, while another 4 per cent had experienced 'prolonged absence of one or both parents because of illness or imprisonment'.[5] In the case of the reformatory men, no comparison with the general population was attempted, but 60 per cent were found to have come from homes broken by parental death, divorce, separation, desertion or prolonged absence at some time before the men reached the age of twenty-five. Even this figure, however, was thought to be an understatement, 'since it was difficult to take account of brief, sporadic desertions'. The authors conclude that 'the precise weight of this factor [broken homes], in a complex, partly imponderable, social-economic situation cannot be given . . . But the number of "broken homes" . . . is so large in our group as to render it probably safe to assume that it is far greater than the incidence of this disintegrative factor of family life in the American population in general.'[6]

In the remaining studies, the evidence is less full. Healy gives figures for parental death, separation or desertion, and records that 498 of his 1,000 young offenders had suffered one or other of these experiences; though 234 of these had acquired foster-parents or step-parents. In the 823 cases which he considered to have been studied sufficiently well for an analysis of causal factors to be made, he reckoned that 'family broken up' was a major causal factor of delinquency in twenty instances, and a minor one in thirty-five others. In Healy and Bronner's study the proportion of delinquents coming from broken homes appears to be 34·5 per cent; whilst over 50 per cent of Sullenger's Omaha delinquents, and 52 per cent of those from Columbia, came from one or other of several categories of 'broken home'. Slawson found that 'a boy coming from a disintegrated home is much more apt to become delin-

[1] p. 123. [2] p. 76. [3] p. 77. [4] p. 71. [5] p. 454. [6] pp. 116–17.

quent';[1] but he admits that slightly different results might have been obtained, had his delinquents not been older than the boys used for comparison. Using the criterion of death, separation or divorce (but not prolonged absence), Slawson found that, of 1,649 of his delinquents, 45·2 per cent came from broken homes: of 3,198 ordinary schoolchildren, 19·3 per cent came from such homes. It is, however, noteworthy that the percentages of broken homes varied very widely in the different institutions from which his boys came, the figures ranging from 39 per cent to 71·9 per cent. Finally, Fernald's conclusions are conspicuously guarded. Details showing 'the exact status of homes regarding the parents who are separated, dead, imprisoned, etc.', would, she argues, be inappropriate in the case of a group of women 'of varying ages, many of them so old that we should naturally expect their parents to be dead'.[2] Enquiry into the percentage of these women who were very young when either parent died again revealed marked differences between the different institutions covered by the investigation, the figures for cases in which the father had died before the child was five years old ranging, for example, from 8·3 per cent to 21·4 per cent. In Sweden Otterström found that her delinquent boys (Group III) came from broken homes 'in a little over one-third of the possible cases in the earlier period, and in one-half of the possible cases in the later period', but among the seriously criminal boys (Group IV), the number from broken homes was smaller.[3]

The majority of our twenty-one investigations are thus in agreement in showing high rates of 'broken homes' amongst delinquents: various British studies place anything from 22 per cent to 57 per cent of their delinquents in this category, whereas control figures, when available, range only from 11 per cent to 18 per cent. In the American studies the proportion of delinquents found to come from broken homes varies from 34 per cent to 62 per cent, while the comparative figures used as norms range only from 14 per cent to 34 per cent. The validity of these norms is, however, more than a little dubious. In the USA, at any rate, remarkable differences have been found in the frequency of broken homes amongst different nationalities. Messrs Shaw and Mckay,[4] for instance, after collecting data on over 7,000 Chicago schoolboys, found that the average broken home rate for eight nationality groups (computed so as to allow for a slight variation in age), ranged from 19·8 per cent for the Jewish to 48·7 per cent for the Negro groups; while the rate for boys attending different schools varied from 16 per cent to 53 per cent. Similarly, the age at which the investigation is undertaken must materially affect the proportion of homes that are no longer complete: the Shaw and McKay enquiry showed that the average (computed) broken home rate for the total group according to age ranged from 25·5 per cent for the ten-year-old boys to 36·2 per cent for those of seventeen. It is perhaps pertinent to add that these authors, having thus tried to establish specific norms, found that in a group of some 1,600 boy delinquents, the broken home rate was 42·5 per cent against 36·1 per cent among a similarly constituted group of controls.

[1] p. 446. [2] p. 232. [3] pp. 145–7.

[4] National Commission on Law Observance and Enforcement (1931), pp. 265–283.

They comment that 'it would be difficult to ascertain whether this difference between the rate of broken homes in the delinquent and control groups is a significant factor in delinquency, or whether it indicates a greater likelihood of a boy from a broken home being brought to court. Surely, the latter is a probability'; and, from a further study described in the same volume, it appears that the broken home rate for a group of ninety-three 'largely serious gang offenders' (juveniles) is very slightly lower (25·8 per cent) than the rate (26·4 per cent) for the total population of 1,167 from which these offenders were drawn: and that, with nationality held constant, the difference is accentuated.

The evidence of our twenty-one studies thus suggests that a fairly large proportion of the highly miscellaneous collection of offenders covered does not come from homes in which two parents are living together in respectable matrimony. Even so, the few investigators who have attempted comparisons with the population at large are still not unanimous in finding that this proportion exceeds that to be expected. The evidence is, moreover, extremely imprecise, based as it is on a great variety of definitions of the 'broken home' and on offenders of many (and often unstated) ages. Inasmuch as everyone's home is eventually broken, the lack of data as to age is a particularly unfortunate omission.

11. *Physical Health*

Material on the physical health of delinquents is exceptionally difficult to organize; for there are no norms by which comparative judgments can be made; and assessments that are not based on careful medical examination are of little value. For what it is worth the evidence from the twenty-one studies may be summarized as follows.

Of the British investigations the majority give some material, though this is generally scanty. Mannheim comments that his data must be regarded with the utmost reserve, because medical reports were available for only about half of his group and, even when obtainable, were 'frequently several years old'.[1] In the case of 101 of his 232 children, for whom reports were available, health was said to be 'normal', while eleven suffered from various defects: the condition of the rest was unknown. Bagot encountered similar difficulties and commented that, because of the paucity of the material, it was 'not possible to draw very definite conclusions'. In his 1941 study medical reports were available for only 2,253 out of 3,221 cases, and these again were often out of date. He concludes that on the whole 'this inquiry has not shown that inferior health is an important factor in causing delinquency', but he adds that more adequate information might change this picture. As compared with the general Liverpool school population, his delinquents were found to have a 'slightly higher' proportion with various defects, the most significant difference being a 'considerably greater amount of subnormal nutrition among the delinquents'. In his 1944 study medical reports were available in about 66 per cent of the cases: of these 54 per cent were said to be in 'normal

[1] p. 50.

health'. Most of the defects reported were minor ones; but, again, poor nourishment was noted in a quarter of the cases. Bagot adds that the proportion of such cases in his 1936 group amounted to 14·1 per cent, while for the non-delinquent population the figure stood at 10·6 per cent.

Burt attached more weight to poor physical condition as a factor associated with delinquency. He comments as follows: 'the frequency among juvenile delinquents of bodily weakness and ill-health has been remarked by almost every recent writer. In my own series of cases nearly 70 per cent were suffering from such defects; and nearly 50 per cent were in urgent need of medical treatment. It is to be remembered, however, that children coming from those districts and those social classes in which delinquents are preponderantly found are far more subject to disease and deformity than children from healthier areas and superior homes. A comparable control-group is again essential as a check. In London I find that defective physical conditions are, roughly speaking, one and a quarter times as frequent among delinquent children as they are among non-delinquent children from the same schools and streets . . . In about 10 per cent of the boys I have examined, and 7 per cent of the girls, some illness or bodily infirmity seemed the principal source of the child's faults. These percentages are not high . . . The actual conditions observed are, for the most part, mild physical weaknesses and irritations—anaemia, chronic catarrh, swollen glands, tonsils and adenoids, headache from diverse causes, and malnutrition of every degree. The few major or precipitating factors are, as a rule, either diseases and disorders involving the nervous system—as chorea, epilepsy, and the after-effects of encephalitis—or defects of the special senses—as partial deafness and imperfect vision'.[1]

Trenaman also concludes that 'as a group the offenders were inferior in almost every physical respect'.[2] Although the proportions of both delinquents and controls graded as A1 were much the same (86·3 per cent and 89·0 per cent respectively), it should be noted that, in its military sense, this category merely indicates 'the absence of any disability likely to impair efficiency in battle'. Had the Army used the term A1 in its popular sense, 'very few men would have gone into battle'. Trenaman concludes that 'physical fitness, in the sense of complete absence of any disease or disorder is apparently rare even in males. According to the findings of the Peckham Health Centre, where 3,911 persons of varied social groups were medically examined, only about 14 per cent were found to be in a state of health, about 30 per cent were diseased, and the remaining 66 per cent had some recognizable disorder that needed attention. Judged by such standards the majority of these offenders would have been found far from healthy. With so wide a disparity of standards and without any special medical examination, it is difficult to say how near they were to a state of positive health. One can only speak relatively, and judging by their medical categories and the large numbers who reported having diseases in early life, it would appear that they were less healthy than the general run of young soldiers'. Additional evidence obtained from questionnaires showed three 'significant differences' between the offenders and

[1] pp. 249 and 251. [2] p. 54.

the controls: first, the offenders had experienced more ill-health in early life (the proportion being 25 per cent as against 18 per cent); second, they suffered more from defects of hearing, sight and speech (33 per cent against 15 per cent); third, they revealed more anxieties about their health (39 per cent against 25 per cent). As to poor nutrition, it has already been noted that 14 per cent of the delinquents and 10 per cent of the controls remarked that they had gone 'short of food through (their) mother finding it difficult to make both ends meet'.[1]

Ferguson observed that, amongst his 'ordinary' boys the 'presence of the ordinary physical defects commonly encountered at routine school medical inspection did not greatly affect delinquency-rates', although 'the rates tended to rise as general physical level . . . deteriorated'.[2] His figures showed 9·7 per cent of those in good physical condition as delinquent, as against 12·2 per cent of those with fair, and 15·5 per cent of those with bad, physique. Unfortunately, however, it is not clear whether, in this context, physical assessment includes health as well as physique in the narrower sense of bodily size and structure. Ferguson's own conclusion is that 'the extent of variation between good and bad physique is not so wide as for many of the other social and environmental factors studied, but it is sufficient to warrant further investigation'.[3] Mannheim and Wilkins noted the presence of physical defects in 105, and their absence in 286, of their cases; but this leaves over 300 for whom no information was available. Gibbs took the view that it was not worth while examining medical documents, since 'there is little evidence from other researches that medical history is a very important factor in the development of delinquent behaviour. Furthermore, men with a history of chronic physical malfunction are unlikely to be accepted for service'. Actually 'eighteen forms of disease were identified in the histories of these two samples. Their incidence was very evenly distributed between the groups, neither exceeding the other in any instance by more than three cases'. The delinquents, however, tended to 'have had more injuries during childhood than non-delinquents. The actual differences between groups in respect to particular kinds of accidents' were, however, 'small'.[4]

The American material, if studied chronologically, shows a steady development in refinement of method. Healy's work, first published in 1915, well illustrates the difficulty of making any worthwhile assessment of physical condition. In his table of causative factors 'abnormal physical conditions, including excessive development' was regarded as a main causal factor in forty, and a minor factor, in 233 of his 823 cases. His data are, however, so complex that it is not possible to get any clear answer to the question how many of his delinquents suffered from ill-health.

The Fernald enquiry of 1920 made no comprehensive attempt to report on the health of its subjects, except in regard to a few specific conditions such as tuberculosis, epilepsy and venereal disease: available records were compiled in too many diverse ways. Slawson in 1926 obviated some of the difficulties by confining himself to the study of five defects which lent themselves to com-

[1] pp. 43–51. [2] pp. 28–29. [3] pp. 115–16. [4] pp. 263 and 265.

parative treatment. He found that just over a fifth of his delinquents suffered from defective vision, as against only about 8 per cent of each of two control groups of ordinary school-children; defective hearing was found in 4 per cent of the delinquents, but only in 1·1 per cent and 0·4 per cent of the two groups of controls; and defective tonsils occurred among 25·7 per cent of the delinquents, as against 15·3 per cent and 26·4 per cent of the controls. It must, however, be borne in mind that Slawson's control groups contained more younger children than were included amongst his delinquent boys, and that they were also drawn from both sexes—differences which may well have distorted his comparisons.

The Gluecks, in their study of reformatory men published in 1930, confine themselves to broad general categories, without definition. Thus, on admission, 'of the 444 men concerning whom such information was available', sixty-three (14·2 per cent) were found to be in good, 349 (78·6 per cent) in fair and thirty-two (7·2 per cent) in poor physical condition.[1] Individual figures are given[2] for one or two specific conditions, and in two cases an attempt is made to establish comparisons with other norms: in one of these (organic heart diseases) schoolchildren are used as controls, as they were 'the nearest comparable material at hand'. Under the heading of 'mental make-up', it is mentioned also that out of 384 cases where psychiatric information was available, a total of 6·8 per cent of the reformatory cases were suffering from alcoholic deterioration, drug deterioration, epilepsy or congenital syphilis. Presumably these conditions are taken into account in the figures for general physical condition, but this point is not made clear.

In their 1934 volume on women offenders, the Gluecks again had the advantage that their subjects had been medically examined on admission; only in forty-three cases were particulars not obtainable. They found that 44·9 per cent of the women were in good physical condition ('no physical disorder (except for uncomplicated venereal disease)'); 43·1 per cent were in fair condition ('mild physical disorder as anaemia, gonorrhoea, or acute secondary syphilis with pelvic pain, sore throat and lesions, etc.'); and 12 per cent were in poor condition ('serious physical disorder, as heart trouble complicated by other conditions').[3] The proportion suffering from epilepsy, alcoholic deterioration, congenital syphilis or drug addiction is recorded as 9·2 per cent.[4] As in the earlier study of male offenders, these figures are given separately from those relating to general physical health, in which one must suppose them to be included. Finally, particulars are added as to 'chronic physical conditions or such handicaps as partially or totally incapacitate the individual for normal recreational outlets during childhood or adolescence and which might therefore be contributory to a personality maladjustment'. Out of some 400 cases, 35 per cent were found to have suffered some such 'serious handicap' during their earlier years.[5]

In their 1934 study of juveniles, the Gluecks reported that, out of 967 of their total of 1,000 boys, 56·7 per cent were in 'sound physical condition' ('general development good or fair, even if goiter, carious teeth, tremor,

[1] p. 153. [2] p. 154. [3] pp. 464 and 391. [4] p. 465. [5] pp. 387 and 425.

premature or delayed puberty, overdevelopment of sex characteristics, or slight nose and throat ailments'); 30·2 per cent were in 'fair health' ('poor general development but no serious disease or handicaps'); while 13·1 per cent were in poor condition ('serious disease or handicaps'). In this investigation those suffering from such conditions as epilepsy, syphilis or partial paralysis are expressly stated to have been included in the 'poor' group.

In none of these three studies by the Gluecks is any comparative material to be found. This aspect of the matter was first tackled by Healy and Bronner, who, however, found little difference between the delinquents and their more law-abiding sibs. 'Half or more of both proved to be in good physical condition and marked physical assets were shown by ten delinquents and sixteen controls.'[1] In a total of 210 delinquents and sibling controls they note the 'absence of anything except perhaps very slight pathological conditions' in fifty-two delinquents and sixty-eight controls.[2] As regards specific defects, the delinquents had more cases of defective vision, whilst the controls were more defective in hearing: the delinquents were more often troubled by their tonsils or their teeth or by endocrine disorder; but all the figures are necessarily small.[3] Only in 'developmental history' do Healy and Bronner find 'remarkable contrasts', listing 170 'developmental deviations' for the delinquents as compared with seventy-four for the controls. The typical delinquent picture is said to be, broadly, one of a difficult, sickly and worrying pregnancy for the mother, followed by a similar babyhood and childhood for the infant.[4] Summing up, these authors ascribe a history of 'distinctly good health' to forty-four delinquents as compared with seventy-five controls.[5] They comment, however, that 'the physical status of the delinquent at the time of the study could only be shown to have meaning for the production of delinquency in rare cases, and then usually very indirectly. For any given individual the meaning of the *physical deviations* given at the end of this chapter are not clear as related to the causation of conduct trends, except as they may be related to emotional and social life—producing inferiority situations and dissatisfactions, for instance.'[6]

The Gluecks' latest work points to an equally negative conclusion. 'We see', they write, 'that the view that delinquents are in poorer health than non-delinquents receives no support. Very little, if any, difference exists between the physical condition of the two groups as a whole'. Indeed they found 15·0 per cent of their delinquents and 14·7 per cent of the controls to be in 'excellent' health, while the proportions of those whose health was classified as 'good' were 77·1 per cent and 73·3 per cent respectively, the comparable figures for 'fair' health standing at 6·9 per cent and 11·0 per cent, and for 'poor' health at 1·0 per cent for both groups.[7] Unlike Healy and Bronner, the Gluecks found no significant differences even in developmental history or in pre-natal conditions, though a higher proportion of delinquents than of controls (14·6 per cent as against 9·6 per cent) were said to have been sickly as babies.[8] Individual conditions are dealt with in detail, and, in view of Healy and Bronner's findings, it may be mentioned that no significant

[1] p. 56. [2] p. 73. [3] p. 74. [4] p. 57. [5] p. 74. [6] p. 40. [7] p. 181. [8] p. 170.

differences were found regarding teeth, tonsils, glands, vision and hearing.

Sullenger gives information on the health of only 105 of his Omaha families, of whom he reports that 19·0 per cent were in 'good', 42·9 per cent in 'fair' and 38·1 per cent in 'poor' condition; but his gradings are not defined[1]. Otterström observes that 'data as to the state of health of the children and juveniles is defective in several respects'.[2] Available material related only to 63·2 per cent of the boys and 68·7 per cent of the girls, nor could the delinquent groups be separated from the others. Nevertheless she expresses the opinion that 'it can be said of the children in this material that their physical equipment was, on the whole, the same as that of children in general; if anything, the percentage of sickly subjects was low, though this of course may be mainly due to the somewhat inadequate data'.[3]

The evidence of these studies thus does not support the view that delinquents are characterized by their poor health. Any suggestion to the contrary seems to be the result of the relatively crude methods of investigation formerly employed. In more recent work, as definitions have become more precise, and comparisons are made with appropriately selected control groups, differences between the health records of delinquents and non-delinquents have tended to disappear.

12. *Educational Achievement*

Differences in educational achievement may reflect differences in native intellectual endowment, or in educational opportunities or in the use made of such opportunities; and the assessment of such achievement may be based either on subjective ratings made by teachers, or on some such test as examination results. Although most of our investigators have interested themselves in this topic, not all have consistently maintained a clear distinction between ability and achievement; and their methods of assessment are exceedingly various. Educational achievement, in the present context, cannot, therefore, be taken to mean more than 'school record taken at its face value'.

All the British studies give some data, the most definite voices being those of Ferguson, Trenaman and Burt. Ferguson, who throughout uses the expression 'scholastic ability' (as assessed by head teachers), found that a 'low level of scholastic ability' among his 'ordinary' boys was 'probably the most powerful single factor associated with high incidence of delinquency: it operated with almost equal force during and after school-days'.[4] After investigating various combinations of 'unpromising circumstances', he adds that 'the combination of low scholastic ability and any other adverse social factor is very likely to produce a high incidence of juvenile crime'.[5] Among 1,349 'ordinary' boys, graded in five scholastic groups, it was found that the percentage of delinquents rose group by group from 6·1 per cent in the top two grades, to 26·5 per cent in the fifth[6]. On the other hand, although the general level of scholastic ability at school-leaving was lower among the physically handicapped than among the 'ordinary' boys, Ferguson's physically handicapped group showed 'no very great difference' in the incidence of

[1] p. 42. [2] p. 194. [3] p. 198. [4] p. 55. [5] p. 50. [6] p. 29.

delinquency among those who had, and those who had not, passed the appropriate school examination—the figures being 9 per cent and 10·9 per cent respectively.[1] Within the mentally handicapped group, no data as to relative attainment are available; but it may be noted that, in the whole of this group, the proportion of delinquents was 23·9 per cent as against 12·2 per cent among the 'ordinary' boys. Moreover, the higher the IQ of these handicapped children, the higher the proportion found guilty of an offence, and the greater the frequency of repeated offences. In contrast, Norwood East found that those of his boys who attended schools for the defective or retarded had very slightly *lower* average conviction rates than those who had attended ordinary elementary schools only.[2]

Trenaman also found a marked inferiority in his offenders' educational achievement, and was convinced that many of these had the capacity to do a great deal better than they did. Devoting a considerable part of his book to this aspect of his offenders, Trenaman comments that 'the most striking feature about the mental state of these offenders was their educational backwardness',[3] although the average level of their native intelligence appeared to be nearly normal, as compared with that of men of similar background. Comparing his offenders' results in the Matrix Intelligence Test with norms for the Army intake of the same age during the corresponding period of recruitment, he found that 'even if it were true that the delinquent is rather duller than his normal neighbour—though these figures suggest that he is not greatly so—the fact remains that a large number of offenders are more intelligent than the normal'. Amongst the offenders 47 per cent, as compared with the control norm of 56·7 per cent, 'were above the mid-point of average intelligence'.[4] The contrasts in educational achievement were, however, of an altogether different order. Thus whereas 85 per cent of the offenders were below mid-point in the Arithmetic Tests, the corresponding Army control figure was 55 per cent: in the Verbal Tests, the figures were 78 per cent and 51 per cent respectively. 'Reading from the original scores', comments Trenaman, '50 per cent of the offenders show an educational attainments lag of at least one whole group' (in five groups ranged in a scale from 'very good' to 'dull'), while 'over 20 per cent have a lag of at least two groups'. Even this result was thought to be an underestimate, since the scale employed was not fine enough to show degrees of illiteracy at the bottom. In round figures Trenaman estimated that 44 per cent of the offenders had a standard of education 'very much below' the elementary school leaving standard, as compared with a figure of 26 per cent for the Army as a whole, according to a 1947 statement of the Secretary of State for War.[5]

Burt gives extensive data, from which it appears that, whereas 35·5 per cent of his delinquents appear dull and backward or defective in intelligence, the proportion in these categories is much higher (59·9 per cent) if the criterion used is not intelligence, but educational attainment. Nine out of every ten of Burt's delinquents fell 'below the middle line of average educational attainment; and three out of every five are so far below it as to be classifiable

[1] pp. 76 and 121. [2] p. 143. [3] p. 64. [4] p. 60. [5] pp. 64–66.

as technically "backward"[1] in school work'. This result is contrasted with a figure of roughly 10 per cent of backward children in the whole London population, as estimated by a London County Council Report of 1917.[2] Among Burt's non-delinquents, the proportion of backward children (15·7 per cent) was appreciably higher than this LCC figure, but we are reminded that these children, 'being selected from the same schools and social classes as the delinquents, form an inferior sample in point of culture and attainments'. Burt concludes that 'the majority of criminal children, though not to be branded as defective or subnormal, are nevertheless indubitably backward. The educational ratio of the average juvenile delinquent is only 81 per cent... At every stage he is far more behind in knowledge than in capacity; and tends, all through his school career, to be a year or more beneath even the low standard of scholastic work, to which, with his intelligence, he should at least attain.'[3]

The remaining British studies give less detail. In the Carr-Saunders enquiry, data are given only for the 'normal group', of whom we are told that 'the inference is that the aggregate of the delinquents is not on a par with the aggregate of the controls for scholastic prowess'. Actually, 69·0 per cent of the London delinquents and 82·0 per cent of the controls reached a normal standard; and the figures for the provincial group were similar.[4]

Mannheim, whose work was restricted by the fact that in seventy-three of his 232 cases no school report was available, laments the dearth of assessments of the intelligence of juvenile delinquents, both in general and in relation to his own subjects. He comments that his groups classified as 'below normal' school attainment are considerably larger than those of Carr-Saunders, the figures being 48 per cent for his pre-war, and 49 per cent for his wartime, cases.[5] Bagot (1944), after criticizing the lack of precision and other inadequacies of the school reports (which were available in 438 out of his 524 cases), found that 34·7 per cent of his Liverpool delinquents had been assessed by headmasters as 'below average' in 'mental ability', with a further 11·4 per cent classified as 'very much below average'. This backwardness is, he considers, 'much greater than a random sample might be expected to show'. Earlier, in his 1941 enquiry, Bagot had attempted, although cautiously, to make some comparison between the attainments of delinquents and of other children, by asking each delinquent's headmaster to assess his mental ability under one of four headings—above average, average, below average and very much below average. Although such a classification is admittedly 'of limited value' and 'liable to error', nevertheless Bagot regarded it as 'likely on the whole to reflect fairly soundly the general position'. Meanwhile, a 'sample from the non-delinquent male school population was obtained for comparative purposes by asking the headteachers of most Liverpool schools to make a similar estimate of the mental ability of a random group of non-delinquent boys selected in a specified

[1] Burt defines 'technical backwardness' as 'a retardation to the extent of more than 15 per cent, but less than 30 per cent of the chronological age' (p. 336).

[2] p. 336. [3] pp. 336–7. [4] p. 86. [5] p. 46.

manner'.[1] The upshot of this was that, whereas 75·1 per cent of the non-delinquents were placed in the 'above average' and 'average' groups, only 54·9 per cent of Bagot's 1936 group and 51·1 per cent of his 1934 group were so placed. Again, 21·3 per cent of the non-delinquents were ranked as below average, whereas the corresponding figures for the two delinquent groups were 36·6 per cent and 35·3 per cent; while the 'very much below average' proportion among the non-delinquents stood at 3.6 per cent, against 8·4 per cent and 13·6 per cent for the two groups of delinquents. Whilst regarding it as unwise, in the absence of a special examination, 'to attempt detailed quantitative conclusions about the mental ability of the delinquents', Bagot draws the inference that 'making all necessary allowances for possibilities of error, it must be concluded that backwardness is strongly associated with delinquency'.[2] Gibbs likewise found that 'the educational standard of the delinquent group was, on the whole, lower at Army entry than that of non-delinquents' and that this group had 'on the whole, lower intelligence than non-delinquents'.[3] Using educational tests, he graded 53 per cent of his delinquents and 39 per cent of the controls as ranking among the lowest 30 per cent of the population; whilst 1 per cent of the delinquents and 19 per cent of the non-delinquents had either been educated beyond the compulsory minimum age, or were ranked among the top 30 per cent of the population. In respect of intelligence (as distinct from attainment), 6 per cent of the delinquents and 17 per cent of the non-delinquents were classified as above average, 35 per cent of the delinquents and 26 per cent of the controls as below average, and 23 per cent of the delinquents and 15 per cent of the controls as 'dull'.[4]

In Rose's study, out of 243 of the 500 Borstal boys for whom school reports were available, 48 per cent were 'stated to be distinctly below average';[5] but these reports do not discriminate between intelligence on the one hand and attainment or position in the eyes of the school authorities on the other. In the light of intelligence tests, however, the author concludes that 'the influence of intelligence upon the factors in this study does not seem very great'.[6] In Norwood East's investigation, which includes a short chapter on school factors, the only relevant finding is that, among the 3,087 of his subjects who attended only an elementary school, 17·7 per cent failed to reach standard VI, while 27·9 per cent achieved this but failed to reach standard VII and the remaining 54·4 per cent succeeded in reaching standard VII.[7] Mannheim and Wilkins have no information on 657 of their subjects and are thus only able to give slender data: they simply note that the educational standard was good in nine, fair in thirty-one and bad in twenty-three cases.

Although the evidence of the American studies seems to be less definite than that of the British, on the whole it appears to support the finding of educational inferiority. The value of the earlier Glueck studies is limited not only by the absence of control figures, but also by the fact that the reformatory men and women appeared to have had an excess of the lower intelligence

[1] pp. 50–51. [2] pp. 50–51. [3] pp. 415–6. [4] pp. 246, viii and 248. [5] pp. 69–70.
[6] p. 145. [7] p. 138.

grades. Although the reliability of intelligence tests has increased since the time when these adults were tested, the Gluecks hold that 'making ample allowance for this fact, the high incidence of defective intelligence still remains'.[1] Of the reformatory women it is said that, with an average of only 6·34 years of schooling, they progressed 'relatively little through the grades or in high school and college'. The proportion who failed to pass beyond fifth grade amounted to 35·8 per cent of the group, while 60·5 per cent were rated by their teachers as 'poor students', as compared with a figure of 10·3 per cent of Boston schoolgirls generally; as many as 89·6 per cent were said to be one or more years retarded in school, as compared with 8·7 per cent of Massachusetts schoolgirls generally.[2] As to intelligence, although the group was 'burdened with feeblemindedness', the Gluecks considered that the 'correlation between the school retardation of our group and their intelligence level suggests that, while mental deficiency partly explains it, retardation is partially due to other causes. For instance, while 43 per cent of the girls retarded two or more years were feeble-minded, 15·5 per cent were of normal intelligence'.[3] They conclude that in educational achievement their reformatory women 'fell considerably below the average, as to both length of schooling and competence as students'.[4]

Their conclusions relating to the reformatory men were much the same. 'In the matter of age of withdrawal' from school, they write, 'as well as in educational achievement and in school retardation, our Reformatory group does not compare favourably with the general population'.[5] Among these men there was 'a greater degree of retardation . . . than among the comparable general population'. 'A considerable number . . . were educationally retarded one or more years.' Out of a total of 454 only 4·6 per cent continued throughout the ninth grade and only 55 per cent the sixth or any higher grade, whereas as many as 53 per cent of Boston schoolchildren in general, in 1910, had attained the ninth grade.[6]

In their earlier study of juveniles, the Gluecks refer to the 'meager educational equipment' of their subjects, adding that, in the case of the 397 who had already left school, 'it is clear that their schooling is greatly below that of Boston school boys in general'.[7] Among 935 of the delinquents for whom data were available 84·5 per cent were at least one year behind grade in their school work, and just over half were two or more years retarded. By way of comparison, figures are quoted showing that 37·8 per cent of Boston public schoolboys were reported as educationally retarded in 1925, and that 12 per cent of Massachusetts boys were similarly reported in 1927; but the degree of backwardness in these cases is not stated. Nor does the Glueck investigation make it clear how far the educational inferiority of their subjects is due to native incapacity, though on the subject of intelligence they remark that 'the difference in the intelligence of our delinquents and that of children of the general population is so marked that it can hardly be attributed largely to' the fact that they 'doubtless come of a lower social and economic status'.[8]

[1] p. 192 (*Five Hundred Delinquent Women*). [2] pp. 79–80. [3] p. 80.
[4] p. 300. [5] p. 134. [6] pp. 132–3. [7] pp. 86–7. [8] p. 102.

In their latest enquiry, the Gluecks were particularly emphatic about the evidence of retardation. 'Despite the original matching of the boys in age and general intelligence and despite the similarity of the two groups in the age at which they entered the first grade, the delinquents were definitely more retarded educationally than were the non-delinquents.'[1] On first meeting their subjects they found that 'twice as many delinquents (36·4 per cent: 17·2 per cent) had not yet gone beyond the sixth grade in school; and that an excessive number (24·2 per cent: 9.8 per cent) were still below the sixth-grade level or had been placed in special classes. On the other hand, only about half as many delinquents (22·2 per cent: 38·2 per cent) had completed work beyond the eighth grade, that is, were in junior high school or high school . . . The delinquents were, as a group, a year behind the non-delinquents in educational achievement'. This difference in grade, it is added, is 'only partly' explained by the fact that the delinquents 'may have had to repeat grades now and then' on account of placement in foster homes or committal to correctional schools. Whereas 68·6 per cent of the delinquents were retarded by one or more years, this was true of only 44·2 per cent of the controls. Twice as many delinquents as non-delinquents (41 per cent: 21·2 per cent) were two or more years behind the grade proper for their age, and 'considering only those boys who were markedly retarded (three years or more), there is an even more striking difference between the delinquents and non-delinquents (22·6 per cent: 8·2 per cent)'.[2] According to their school reports, '41·4 per cent of the delinquent boys, compared with but 8·2 per cent of the non-delinquents, were very poor students, as reflected by marks of D and E in most or all of their subjects'; and, 'while the bulk of the non-delinquents (90·8 per cent) were average pupils (the B and C group), only 57·6 per cent of the delinquents attained this status'.[3] Sullenger also found his 'average delinquent' to be 'retarded nearly two years', though his data are inadequate for more precise comparisons.

Healy and Bronner on the other hand find the educational inferiority of their subjects less striking. After calling attention to the 'very careful psychological testing' that was undertaken, 'not only for the purpose of ascertaining intelligence levels, but also for the sake of knowing educational qualifications and special capacities or disabilities',[4] they conclude that 'physical status and intellectual level do not in general distinguish the delinquent from his non-delinquent sibling, though they may have importance as factors in the individual case'.[5] Similarly in the case of their 105 pairs of delinquent and non-delinquent sibs they observe that 'somewhat to our surprise . . . the mental age-levels of the two groups prove to be only slightly contrasting. Skilful psychological testing shows that well within the limits of normal mental ability, according to standard age-level tests, there were 98 of the delinquents and 94 controls. Superior ability was demonstrated by 14 delinquents as compared to 18 controls'.[6] On the relation of capacity to achievement, these authors note that the scholarship record of the delinquents 'correlates fairly well with their intelligence levels except as they were retarded on account of

[1] p. 153. [2] pp. 135–8. [3] p. 140. [4] p. 18. [5] p. 203. [6] p. 60.

frequent change of residence or many absences';[1] while in the light of evidence from school records 'definitely poor scholarship was registered for only 34 per cent of the delinquents, as against 18 per cent of the controls . . . Partly to check up on this we gave school achievement tests and found considerably below the standards for grade or age only 20 per cent of the delinquents—and 5 per cent of the controls'.[2]

Fernald, who devotes one whole chapter to educational background and three to 'mental capacity', reaches no less cautious conclusions. 'With reference to educational background', she writes 'without reliable standards for the general population, we have no way of knowing how far the delinquent group lags behind the general population in this respect. We have found, however, that the delinquent group falls decidedly behind the requirements of present opinion regarding the minimum amount of schooling which should be accepted as furnishing the rudiments of preparation for meeting the demands of adult life. This is especially true as regards school *attainment*'. But, 'we saw reason for believing that this was to some extent a secondary effect of the somewhat inferior intelligence of the group'. 'All indications are that the group of delinquent women is somewhat inferior to the general population, though the difference is slight and the overlapping large'[3].

Finally, Otterström makes the prudent observation that 'Probably the most uncertain indicators of intellect are the school reports';[4] but her material, which is based partly upon such reports and partly upon intelligence tests, does not permit of a clear distinction being drawn between intelligence and educational attainment.

It thus appears that there is fairly good agreement on both sides of the Atlantic that those who are found guilty of offences tend to have poor school records. Much of this evidence, however, is based upon the assessments of schoolmasters, which can hardly be regarded as objective, or as reasonably certain to be free of bias. Delinquent children are likely to be unpopular with their teachers; and our investigators are not generally explicit on the vital point of whether the assessments quoted were made with, or without, knowledge that the subject was in trouble with the law.

All in all, therefore, this collection of studies, although chosen for its comparative methodological merit, produces only the most meagre, and dubiously supported, generalizations. On the whole, it seems that offenders come from relatively large families. Not infrequently (according to some investigators very frequently) other members of the delinquents' (variously defined) families have also been in trouble with the law. Offenders are unlikely to be regular churchgoers, but the evidence as to whether club membership discourages delinquency is 'wildly contradictory'. If they are of age to be employed, they are likely to be classified as 'poor' rather than as 'good' workers. Most of them come from the lower social classes, but again the evidence as to the extent to which they can be described as exceptionally poor is conflicting; nor is there any clear indication that their delinquency is associated with the employment of their mothers outside the home. Their

[1] p. 48. [2] p. 61. [3] pp. 525–7. [4] p. 201.

health is probably no worse than that of other people, but many of them have earned poor reputations at school, though these may well be prejudiced by their teachers' knowledge of their delinquencies. In their schooldays they are quite likely to have truanted from school, and perhaps an unusually large proportion of them come from homes in which at some (frequently unspecified) time both parents were not, for whatever reason, living together; yet even on these points, the findings of some enquiries are negative. And beyond this we cannot go.

CHAPTER IV

Theories of the Effects of Maternal Separation or Deprivation

IT is now widely held that a child's personality is damaged by separation from its mother in infancy, or by rejection by her or by loss of her affection (all of which are by no means the same thing), and that these experiences inhibit his ability to make affectionate relationships with other people, or predispose him towards anti-soçial or delinquent conduct (which again are not at all the same thing). Both on account of its practical influence and because it affords an outstanding illustration of the inexact nature of the concepts with which social scientists have to deal, the evidence for this hypothesis deserves to be examined in detail.

The theory itself is sometimes expressed in remarkably sweeping terms, as is illustrated by the following examples. Reporting on her researches in France Jenny Aubry concludes with the observation that 'Quel que soit l'âge d'un enfant la séparation définitive d'avec le milieu familial et la carence de soins maternels ont des répercussions fâcheuses sur son intégration sociale. La *carence* est d'autant plus grave que l'enfant est plus jeune et moins autonome. Avant 1 an la carence atteint profondément la structure psychique d'un enfant et les lésions risquent d'être irréversibles. Entre 1 an et 4 ans elle provoque encore des troubles graves et ce n'est qu'a partir de 5,6 ou 7 ans que le développement intellectuel et physique peut se pour-suivre à peu pres normalement; le développement affectif reste perturbé par la carence si celle-ci se produit avant la puberté.'[1] In an article published in 1954, Ainsworth and Bowlby postulate as the 'basic hypothesis' underlying separation research, that 'actual physical separation from the mother in early childhood, to the extent that it involves privation or deprivation of a relationship of dependence with a mother-figure, will have an adverse effect on personality development, particularly with respect to the capacity for forming and maintaining satisfactory object relations'.[2] According to a statement submitted by the World Federation of Mental Health to the First United Nations Congress on the Prevention of Crime and the Treatment of Offenders, although 'babies may stand one change of care without lasting ill-effects, many babies cannot stand two changes, and few can stand more than two without there being permanent damage to their character-formation, unless the quality of maternal care which

[1] Aubry (1955), p. 181. [2] Ainsworth and Bowlby (1954), p. 6.

they ultimately receive is unusually satisfying'.[1] Spitz early suspected that the damage inflicted on children by their being deprived of 'maternal care, maternal stimulation, and maternal love, as well as by their being completely isolated', would be incurable; and, with true analytic fervour, he regards evidence of retardation at less than five years old as a mark of 'irreparable' injury.[2] According to a leading article in the *Manchester Guardian*[3], 'careful studies have shown that a long spell in hospital, and the consequent separation from parents, can do much to make a child permanently unhappy . . .' Roudinesco and Appell open an article with the words 'Les fâcheux effets, sur les jeunes enfants, de la carence de soins maternals et de la vie en collectivité, peuvent actuellement être considérés comme certains, tant les preuves de ces répercussions néfastes sont nombreuses et concordantes'.[4] In a commentary on Mental Health through Public Health Practice, the World Health Organization includes 'the separation of mother and child' among 'certain well-established and accepted concepts' likely to affect mental health.[5] A writer in a 1955 issue of the *British Medical Journal*, in a section devoted to answering correspondents' questions, speaks of neurotic behaviour problems arising 'as an immediate sequel' in a deprived child, adding that 'for this there is reliable evidence';[6] while another investigator even claims to have discovered, as the result of a study of 883 children in fifty-seven village schools, 'a clear association between maladjustment and transport', increasing with the lengths of both bus and walking journeys. He adds that a fatigue hypothesis 'does not fit the data' and that 'the evidence suggests that deprivation symptoms may occur when constant, though intermittent, separation is accompanied by a child's perception of his mother as inaccessible'.[7] And, as a final sign of the times, it may be noted that in some at least of the British juvenile courts it is now standard practice for probation officers to ask in the course of their enquiries whether a delinquent (who may be over sixteen years old) has been separated from his mother for any appreciable period in infancy.

Dr Bowlby, who has done so much to popularize these theories both in this country and elsewhere, is generally more cautious than most of the authors just quoted, in that he is more disposed to say that maternal deprivation 'may' have deleterious effects than that it 'will' do so. The range of the claims which he makes has, however, varied from time to time. In 1946, after reviewing the work of other investigators, he reached the conclusion that 'on the basis of this varied evidence it appears that there is a very strong case indeed for believing that *prolonged separation of a child from his mother* (*or mother-substitute*) *during the first five years of life stands foremost among the causes of delinquent character development and persistent misbehaviour*';[8] and five

[1] Soddy (1955), pp. 126–7. [2] Spitz (1946), p. 115. [3] November 8, 1955.

[4] Roudinesco and Appell (1951), p.106.

[5] World Health Organization, *Chronicle* (September 1955), p. 253.

[6] August 20, 1955, p. 501.

[7] Lee (1957), p. 10. If these findings are correct, shall we not reach the point of regarding school itself no less than the journey to and fro as a traumatic experience?

[8] Bowlby (1946), p. 41.

years[1] later he still held this conclusion so strongly that he was ed to reproduce it in his WHO Monograph.[2] At a conference in 1949, he is reported to have expressed the view that maternal separation and parental rejection 'are believed together to account for a majority of the more intractable cases [of delinquency], including the "constitutional psychopaths" and the "moral defectives"'.[3] In 1951 with the publication of his WHO Monograph we reach what has become the classic statement of the Bowlby hypothesis—expressed in terms of a child's need to experience 'a warm, intimate, and continuous relationship with his mother (or permanent mother-substitute) in which both find satisfaction and enjoyment'. The ill effects of the lack of this experience are said to vary with the degree of deprivation, but its complete absence has 'far-reaching effects on character development and may entirely cripple the capacity to make relationships'.[4] In 1954, in association with Mary Ainsworth, he writes that 'it is our opinion that there is now a sufficient weight of evidence supporting the validity of the general hypothesis that it can be accepted, at least with respect to extreme instances of prolonged separation under institutional conditions'.[5] At the same time, we are reminded that separation is not merely 'a simple homogeneous aetiological factor' but is a term which refers 'to a wide range of events and an intricate complex of associated conditions, which in different constellations may have different effects on the course of development'.[6]

Bowlby has more than once admitted to being puzzled as to why some children succumb to deprivation while others appear to be unaffected. In a paper published in 1955 he withdrew so far as to say that 'we know now that the affectionless character is not the most frequent result of prolonged separation, for only a minority of children who suffer separation develop this particular character'.[7] In his most recent work—a study of some sixty children (matched against a control group of like age and sex), who had been admitted to a sanatorium suffering from uncomplicated pulmonary tuberculosis before the age of four and had been followed up to ages ranging from 6+ to 13+—he and his co-workers emphasize this point still further. 'It is clear', they write, 'that some of the former group of workers [Bender, Goldfarb and Spitz], including the present senior author, in their desire to call attention to dangers which can often be avoided, have on occasion overstated their case. In particular, statements implying that children who are brought up in institutions or who suffer other forms of serious privation and deprivation in early life *commonly* develop psychopathic or affectionless characters (e.g. Bowlby, 1944) are seen to be mistaken. The present investigation confirms the findings of Beres and Obers, and Lewis. Outcome is immensely varied, and of those who are damaged only a small minority

[1] Although Bowlby's Monograph was first published in 1951, all references are to his 1952 edition.
[2] Bowlby (1952), p. 34.
[3] Bowlby, in *Conference on . . . Juvenile Delinquency* (1949), p. 37.
[4] Bowlby (1952), pp. 11–12. [5] Ainsworth and Bowlby (1954), pp. 22–23.
[6] ibid., p. 3. [7] Bowlby, in Soddy, ed. (1955), vol. I, p. 119.

develop those very serious disabilities of personality which first drew attention to the pathogenic nature of the experience. Though we may be relieved that this is so, there are no grounds for complacency'.[1] The same point is, moreover, repeated more than once in this paper in the same language; and we are reminded that 'the outcome of a separation experience is partly dependent on the child's experiences whilst away'.[2] In March, 1958, however, Bowlby thought it wise to reassert in a letter to the *Lancet* that, contrary to what various professional workers, medical and non-medical, were implying, he had not changed his position 'in any material way'.[3] Nor is there anything in his recent pronouncements which conflicts with the view expressed in 1951 to the effect that 'the fact that some children seem to escape is of no consequence. The same is true of the consumption of tubercular-infected milk or exposure to the virus of infantile paralysis. In both these cases a sufficient proportion of children is so severely damaged that no one would dream of intentionally exposing a child to such hazards. Deprivation of maternal care in early childhood falls into the same category of dangers'.[4]

On the permanent or irreversible effects of severe deprivation, Bowlby, like Aubry and Spitz, has committed himself rather far. 'There is', he wrote in 1951, 'abundant evidence that deprivation can have adverse effects on the development of children (*a*) during the period of separation, (*b*) during the period immediately after restoration to maternal care, and (*c*) permanently';[5] and from Goldfarb's work he draws the inference that even good mothering 'is almost useless if delayed until after the age of 2½ years'.[6] Bowlby also shares both with Aubry and with many other investigators the view that early deprivation is in general more damaging than separation at a later age.

Most of the evidence in support of the maternal-deprivation theory which had appeared before 1950 is reviewed in Dr Bowlby's WHO Monograph, and for that reason no similar summary is included here. The commentary that follows is more of an assessment than a summary; but work that has appeared since the publication of the Bowlby Monograph or was not there reviewed is dealt with below in greater detail.

Much of the research in this field—notably the work of Spitz and Goldfarb in the United States and of Roudinesco in France—has relied upon comparisons between the development of children in institutions and in the world outside. In the picture which emerges from these comparisons, the institutionalized children are generally shown as handicapped in several different ways. It is, for instance, suggested that even their physical resistance to disease may be affected. Thus Spitz found that his institutional children succumbed more easily to measles than did those who live in families[7] while Lefort is said to have established that the incidence of, and the death rate from, rhinolaryngitis and infantile diarrhoea are abnormally high even in creches and orphanages where material conditions are good.[8] Other investigators have suggested that physical growth may be retarded by emotional

[1] Bowlby (1956), p. 240. [2] ibid., p. 215. [3] March 1, 1958, p. 480.
[4] Bowlby (1952), p. 47. [5] Bowlby (1952) p. 47. [6] ibid., p. 49. [7] Spitz (1945), p. 59.
[8] Referred to by Wall (1955), p. 33.

difficulties consequent upon the loss of parental care or affection. In other cases again—and these are more typical—the social development or the intelligence of children in institutions has been measured by the use of appropriate psychological tests. Repeatedly these children have been found to lag behind the standards of those who live at home: to have both lower intelligence and lower developmental quotients, and to be, more over, relatively backward in both speech and walking. Goldfarb, who has been one of the most active investigators in this field, records that those who had spent their earliest years in infants' homes were apt to be retarded both in general, and in particular in speech. They were also more destructive and aggressive, more restless and less able to concentrate and more indifferen to privacy rights than other children.[1] They were, in fact, impoverished in all aspects of their personality.[2] Summarizing these results (which, to be fully appreciated, need to be consulted in the original papers), Bowlby observes that 'positive evidence that the causative factor is maternal deprivation comes from innumerable sources';[3] and in support of this observation he notes that in several of the investigations it has been found that the longer the depriva tion, the lower falls the developmental quotient; and that, even where a child remains in the same institution, extra mothering soon gives good results while spectacular improvement has been observed when a child has been transferred from 'the emotionally arid' atmosphere of a hospital to a good home.

Since the publication of the Bowlby Monograph, further research has been undertaken into the possible significance of unhappy domestic experience in the case of children classified as feebleminded. Bourne set out to investigate '(1) whether severe mental defect may result from social and psychological adversity in infancy . . . and (2) to discover the prevalence and clinical features of psychogenic amentia if it really exists'. To this end he examined 154 consecutive admissions to the Fountain (Mental Deficiency) Hospital Of these only sixteen were classified as without 'discernible organic disease' so that any tentative conclusions could only be based on this very small number. Bourne found, however, that twelve of the sixteen cases had suffered either maternal deprivation or 'pathological mothering' in the sense that the child's mother was 'either overtly psychotic, or known to local social agencies as notoriously psychopathic, or a feckless dullard so neglectful as to attract the attention of' the NSPCC. From this he somewhat boldly concludes that the defective child, 'though physically healthy, will present severe backward ness evident from about the second year, with curious behaviour disorder and a history of perverted mothering in infancy. In his first two years he will either have been reared by an extremely disordered person, commonly a psychopath, or else deprived for long and repeated periods of the mother or her substitute; usually he will have suffered both misfortunes'. (Incidentally the alternative possibility that a child may have inherited the mental abnorma lities of his mother is very light-heartedly dismissed.) Although the number of Bourne's cases was small, they are said to have represented some 10 pe

[1] Goldfarb (1943), p. 106. [2] Goldfarb (1945), p. 31. [3] Bowlby (1952), p. 21.

cent of the 'severe aments' in the Fountain Hospital; and from this it is inferred that maternal deprivation in one or other sense may be responsible for filling thousands of beds in mental deficiency hospitals throughout the country.[1]

Among other studies of institutionalized children not included by Bowlby in his survey, is one undertaken by Skeels and others on behalf of the Iowa Child Welfare Research Station as long ago as 1938. These investigators concluded that 'children of dull-normal intelligence may become mentally retarded to such a degree as to be classifiable as feebleminded under the continued adverse influence of a relatively non-stimulating environment'.[2] In another study instituted under the same auspices at about the same date, a comparison was attempted between orphanage children attending a nursery school and a matched control group who lived in the same institution but were not sent to the nursery. The results seem to have surprised the sponsors of the investigation. 'No one', writes the Director of the Research Station concerned, 'could have predicted, much less proved, the steady tendency to deterioriate on the part of children maintained under what had previously been regarded as standard orphanage conditions. With respect to intelligence, vocabulary, general information, social competence, personal adjustment, and motor achievement the whole picture was one of retardation. The effect of from one to three years attendance in a nursery school still far below its own potentialities, was to reverse the tide of regression which, for some, led to feeble-mindedness.'[3]

An alternative line of investigation is to work backwards, examining the early history of neurotic or delinquent adolescents or adults in order to see whether they have a history of maternal deprivation in infancy in this connection. As examples of this method Bowlby quotes his own well-known work on 'affectionless thieves', as well as the experience of the Hawthorne-Cedar Knolls School near New York, an institution which specializes in grave psychiatric disorders, and in which 'the degree of disruption of parent-child relations for the whole group' is said to be illustrated by 'only 25 per cent of them having been brought up by both parents'.[4] Burt's work is also quoted as pointing in the same direction; and reference is made, in addition, to an American study of delinquent girls by Powdermaker and others, in which subsequent failure to respond to psychotherapy was said to have been closely correlated with the breaking of family ties. To these investigations may be added a later study by Dr John Rich dealing with some 200 boys admitted to a London Remand Home, all of whom had been charged with theft and had been remanded for a psychiatric report. Rich reports that he could 'find no clear relation between age at, or length of, separation and type of present offence, but a clear association between early separation and early stealing. There was also a clear association between early separation and stealing from home at any time. In other words, children who are separated early tend to begin their stealing early and tend to steal from home.'[5]

[1] Bourne (1955).

[2] Skeels in *National Society for the Study of Education* (1940), p. 300.

[3] Skeels and others (1938), p. 3. [4] Bowlby (1952), p. 35. [5] Rich, J. (1956), p. 497.

Yet other investigators have set to work to trace the after-history of deprived children in adolescence or adult life. Goldfarb tried a number of psychological tests at ages between ten and fourteen on some thirty children, half of whom had been brought up in foster homes, while half had spent their infancy in institutions. In this as in other cases he found the institution children significantly behind the others in intellectual performance, social maturity and ability to make relationships.[1] Theis, in another and more extensive study, described by Bowlby as being 'in the first rank', has attempted to assess the social adjustment of over 900 people who had been placed in foster homes in early childhood, some of whom had, moreover, been sent to an institution before they were two years old. In this case it was observed that the ninety-five subjects who had spent five or more years of their childhood in institutions 'adjusted significantly less well than those who had remained during their first five years in their own homes'.[2] On this Bowlby comments that 'The fact that no less than one-third of the institution children turned out to be "socially incapable", of which nearly half were troublesome and delinquent, is to be noted'.[3] Lowrey, again, found 'severe personality disturbances' at five years of age or older in a group of twenty-two children who had been admitted to an institution before their first birthday and had remained there until they were transferred to another fostering agency at the age of three or four.[4] Finally, somewhat dubious support is offered by Beres and Obers' study of thirty-eight subjects at ages between sixteen and twenty-six, all of whom had been institutionalized during their first two years of life. Of these, twenty-one were said to suffer from character disorders, seven being of the type often described as affectionless psychopaths, while four were schizophrenics.[5] Since, however, the sample was drawn from cases known to be in need of further care, such results are hardly surprising and do not tell us much.

II

Critics of the maternal deprivation hypothesis can point to a number of other investigations the findings of which are, if not in conflict with the hypothesis, at least not at all persuasive in its favour. Bowlby mentions only three of these, and those only very briefly, expressing the opinion that 'none of them is of high scientific quality or bears comparison with the work either of Goldfarb or of Theis'.[6] First of these three is a study by Orgel, who examined sixteen children from the same institutions as those quoted by Lowrey, and found unfavourable personality features in only two of them. On this Bowlby comments that 'no details are given and there appears to have been no systematic clinical investigation'.[7] Next is an investigation by Fred Brown of Pennsylvania State College who applied the 'Brown Personality Inventory' to 200 children from orphanages and to 100 boys of low socio-economic status, who were said to be representative of 'a social class in which broken homes and

[1] Goldfarb (1943). [2] Bowlby (1952), p. 40. [3] ibid., p. 40. [4] ibid., p. 39.
[5] Beres and Obers (1950). [6] Bowlby (1952), p. 41. [7] ibid., p. 41.

familial discord predominate'.[1] After comparing these two groups with a random selection of 200 children drawn from such of the general population as had completed similar tests, Brown concluded that 'There is no difference between socio-economically inferior boys living in their own homes and institution children': both tended to be more neurotic than the population at large. 'The neuroticism of institution children is not attributable to the institutional environment but is a consequence of the environment from which they originate.'[2] On this Bowlby comments that 'Not only is a personality inventory an unsatisfactory criterion, but no evidence is given regarding the age at which the children entered the institution'.[3] Finally, Bowlby mentions a third critical study by Bodman and others, purporting to show that the maternal deprivation hypothesis may underestimate the force of hereditary factors. These investigators compared fifty-one institutionalized children with fifty-two living at home, and found that, while the former made lower scores on the Vineland Social Maturity Scale, the incidence both of mental illness and of misbehaviour was much higher amongst the relatives of the institution children than amongst those of the controls—*none* of whose relatives, it is boldly said, had been guilty of anti-social conduct.[4] After expressing scepticism as to the appropriateness of the Vineland Scale, Bowlby dismissed these findings, by no means unjustly, on the ground that they are 'ill-judged and certainly cannot by sustained by the evidence presented'.[5]

Since the appearance of the Bowlby Monograph, fresh doubts have been raised by Dr Hilda Lewis' study of 500 children admitted to a Reception Centre. Lewis found that 'Unless separation of child from mother had occurred before the age of two years and had been lasting, it bore no statistically significant relation to the normality or otherwise of the child's mental state at the time of admission. No clear connexion was evident between separation from the mother and a particular pattern of disturbed behaviour. Neither delinquency nor incapacity for affectionate relationships was significantly more frequent in the separated children'.[6] It was, moreover, the mildly, rather than the violently, disturbed children who accounted for the statistical significance even of lasting separation from the mother; whereas according to the Bowlby hypothesis 'the cases of most serious harm should be found among those children who had been separated from their mothers for long periods or permanently before the age of two years'.[7] As judged by the criteria used by Lewis, at any rate, early or lasting separation appears to have had no such disastrous consequences as are predicted by the Bowlby school—an observation which does not surprise its author in view of the fact that the mere physical presence or absence of the child's own mother is no true index of the quality of mothering which it may have enjoyed. 'Unduly dogmatic statements about ill-effects of maternal deprivation', she comments, 'often leave out of account the emotional hazards and harms children may suffer from bad mothers and indifferent mother-substitutes, or the variety of sources (in-

[1] Brown, F. (1937), p. 379. [2] ibid., pp. 382–3. [3] Bowlby (1952), p. 42.
[4] Bodman and others (1950). [5] Bowlby (1952), p. 42. [6] Lewis, H. (1954), p. 83.
[7] ibid., p. 106.

cluding the father) from whom children may draw the love and support necessary for their happiness.'[1] Although separation from the mother before the age of five years was found to be 'a prognostically adverse feature', yet 'nearly a third of the children who were separated from their mothers' were 'in a satisfactory condition at the end of the follow-up period' (i.e. from two to three and a half years after admission to the Centre); 'and permanent separation before the age of two had not been the prelude to a particularly unsatisfactory condition of the child at the end of the period'.[2]

It will be seen that Lewis hints that fathers matter as well as mothers. Other investigators also claim to have found evidence that points the same way. Thus Holman, after studying 200 children at a Child Guidance Clinic, half of whom had, while half had not, been 'ascertained' as maladjusted, concluded that 'What seems to emerge from the material studied here is that there is no one type of misfortune which, judged by the reactions of the child, is in itself significantly worse than another; what is damaging is a series of misfortunes. Many of the misfortunes are, however, of the sort that engender other misfortunes. Permanent separation from the parents is of this sort . . . It is clear from the studies quoted by Bowlby that this is the case and that he would be far from denying it.'[3] But at the same time a 'point of apparent inconsistency between the results of this study and of Bowlby's is that permanent early separation from the father is here shown to be no less adverse in its results than permanent early separation from the mother'.[4] Commenting upon the family circumstances of Borstal inmates, Norwood East also found fathers to be important. Amongst 3,277 offenders against property or the person examined by him 'the most noteworthy excess of offences' was 'shown by the 114 lads who had both parents at the age of five, but neither parent at fourteen or after . . . ' whereas the only group showing no excess was that 'with no mother throughout but with a father at certain ages'. Further, in at least one sub-group of his subjects, 'lads who had lived with other relatives or with foster parents showed only a slight excess of convictions over the number expected, whilst the group of 153 lads who had spent some time in care institutions showed no excess'.[5]

Such indications of the importance of a father in a child's upbringing are, of course, susceptible of more than one interpretation. Adherents of a more old-fashioned school than that of the psychoanalytic theorists who have been chiefly responsible for popularizing the maternal deprivation hypothesis might, for instance, be disposed to see in them evidence of the value of paternal discipline. But so long as study of the role of the father continues to be so much neglected as compared with that of the mother, no opinion on the subject can be regarded as more than purely speculative.

Even more vulnerable is the contention that maternal deprivation not only damages the personality, but does so in a way that is likely to be irreversible. Hardly any evidence is in fact available to support this far-reaching conclusion—unless indeed we are to accept as axiomatic the view that nobody's

[1] Lewis, H. (1954), p. 75. [2] ibid., p. 122. [3] Holman (1953), p. 685. [4] ibid., p. 685.
[5] East (1942), pp. 94, 96 and 123.

personality can change after, at latest, adolescence or early adult life. On any other assumption there can be no justification whatever for speaking of 'permanent', 'irreparable' or 'irreversible' damage unless and until the victims of maternal deprivation have been followed right through life. Yet, as is shown by the quotations already given,[1] these words have been freely bandied about by enthusiastic adherents of the maternal deprivation hypothesis. Actually, few investigations have succeeded in tracing the fortunes of the maternally deprived after adolescence: instances of follow-up beyond marriage are quite exceptional. Even in the Beres and Obers follow-up, none of the subjects was over twenty-six, and Theis, who kept track of some of her subjects up to the age of forty, stands practically alone. Rarely, therefore, has it yet been possible to test the—on the face of it not unreasonable—possibility that the injuries of those who may have suffered from infantile deprivation might in later life be healed by a happy choice of spouse. Indeed, we can still congratulate ourselves that no evidence at all has yet been produced that comes near to justifying the depressing claim that to be sent to an institution in infancy is tantamount to being wrecked for life. Happily, however, even the psychoanalytically inclined are beginning to allow a rather less rigid, and therefore less dismal, attitude. 'Our results indicate', write Beres and Obers, that the 'psychic structure is not immutably fixed'; and they quote other authorities to the effect that 'The potentialities for the formation of personality throughout latency and adolescence have for some time been underrated in psychoanalytic writings'.[2]

Even before the appearance of the Bowlby Monograph, a forceful attack upon the supposedly exaggerated importance attached by the Freudian school to infantile experiences in fixing subsequent character came from Dr Orlansky of the Department of Anthropology at Yale. Most of this paper (which is not mentioned by Bowlby) is devoted to a critical review of the evidence upon which the psychoanalytic view of child-rearing practices (swaddling, sphincter-training and so forth) is based; but in a final section the author deals with the more general problem of the overall importance of what happens in infancy in the shaping of personality. In this he concludes that 'Analysis of the neonate state has been too much colored by a naïve reading-in of adult emotions into the infant which is comparable to the anthropomorphizing views of insect behavior once current among an earlier generation of biologists'.[3] 'The rigidity of character structuring during the first year or two of life has been exaggerated by many authorities, and . . . the events of childhood and later years are of great importance in reinforcing or changing the character structure tentatively formed during infancy.'[4] In fact, 'The picture of the infant obtained from many psychoanalytic accounts has much in common with the medieval notion of the infant as a homunculus or miniature adult'.[5] In adopting this more sceptical view, Orlansky seems to have been influenced more by deficiencies in the evidence produced by those who claim to have demon-

[1] See pp. 136, 139. [2] Beres and Obers (1950), p. 232. [3] Orlansky (1949), p. 30.
[4] ibid., p. 38. [5] ibid., p. 36.

strated the indelible quality of infantile experience, than by any more positive indications that point to a different conclusion; though he draws also upon anthropological investigations and upon experiments in animal behaviour, adducing examples of the various and unexpected types of personality that emerge from particular systems of child-rearing.

Advocates of the maternal deprivation hypothesis are criticized also for the degree to which they have relied upon the experience of children in institutions, and in arbitrarily selected institutions at that, and for their disregard of the many variables introduced by this procedure. In order to establish that the damaging factor in a child's experience is his separation from home rather than the régime of the particular institution in which he finds himself, it would be necessary to study the development, not only of a sufficient sample of children, but also of children who have lived in a sufficiently representative sample of institutions. An institution is not a standard unit; and there can be good institutions as well as bad ones. Generally speaking the information given by investigators (notably Goldfarb, Spitz, Roudinesco) about the way in which their institutionalized children lived is far from full. One is, however, left with the impression that these children were not as a rule very intelligently or even always very kindly treated. Nor has sufficient weight generally been given to the possibility that communal homes for children may differ from families in other respects beside the opportunity which they offer for intimate affectionate relationships. How, one would like to know, were the institutionalized children fed? Could their backwardness have been due, in any degree, to dietary deficiencies? Little seems to have been done to control such important variables as these. Again, in many cases evidence was drawn from children who had spent considerable periods in hospital. But a hospital is a frightening place (and the illness which gets you there can be a frightening experience too), quite apart from the fact that being in hospital means being away from home and mother. Sweeping condemnations of institutional life in general cannot fairly be based upon the anxieties and depression manifested by children in hospitals—even if, as some investigators have shown, sick children cheer up considerably when they are allowed to keep contact with their mothers.[1]

Nor has adequate information been produced about the reasons which led to the children studied being uprooted from their homes; or about the conditions in which they had lived before this happened. One can hardly assume that the boys and girls found in a Children's Home constitute a fair sample of the child population generally: something unusual either in themselves or in their environment must have happened to account for their being deprived of ordinary family life. Here again factors that may well be important have too often been neglected; and even where these have been recognized, they have in some cases been treated with a levity that is altogether astonishing. Thus Bowlby, commenting on a comparative study by Theis, boldly observes that 'so far as could be determined the heredity of the two groups was similar . . . Since heredity is, so far as possible, held constant

[1] Bowlby (1952), p. 22.

for these two groups, the difference cannot be explained in this way'.[1] Even with the qualification 'so far as could be determined' such a light-hearted dismissal of the influence of differential inherited factors is incredibly naïve, especially when it comes from a scientifically trained medical man who must be aware of the complexity of the subject. Yet Roudinesco and Appell are equally sweeping in their assertion that the children from a populous Paris suburb whom they used as controls in their study of the inmates of a Paris public assistance institution were 'analogues au groupe étudié quant aux conditions de vie sociale et aux facteurs héréditaires'.[2] In his own study of *Forty-four Juvenile Thieves* Bowlby has himself stated that the main criterion by which the presence of defective hereditary factors was diagnosed was the 'presence of neurosis, psychosis, or serious psychopathy in parents or grandparents'[3]—a criterion which implies a degree of confidence both as to the diagnoses of two generations earlier and as to the conditions governing the inheritance of morbid mental conditions which can hardly be justified by the evidence on the subject. By contrast, Shields' careful study of *Personality Differences and Neurotic Traits in Normal Twin Schoolchildren*[4] puts these facile assumptions in a very different light; although, it must be admitted that the attitude of those whose work points to different conclusions from those of the Bowlby school is by no means always more scrupulous in its methods. It will be remembered that Bodman, for example, went so far as to assert that none of his controls had relatives guilty of anti-social behaviour —a statement which it must surely be quite impossible to substantiate.

The maternal deprivation theory is, moreover, generally so loosely expressed as to embrace a number of quite different hypotheses, many of which point to mutually contradictory practical conclusions. The concepts involved are indeed both vague and various; and occasionally also, it must be added, the devices employed to establish their validity are clearly questionable. The exact nature of the damaging factor is, for instance, not consistently defined by different authors or indeed even always by the same one. Thus Bowlby's classic (1952) statement that what is believed to be 'essential for mental health is that the infant and young child should experience a warm, intimate, and continuous relationship with his mother (or permanent mother-substitute) in which both find satisfaction and enjoyment'[5] reappears two years later in the form that 'actual physical separation from the mother in early childhood, to the extent that it involves privation or deprivation of a relationship of dependence with a mother-figure, will have an adverse effect on personality development, particularly with respect to the capacity for forming and maintaining satisfactory object relations':[6] the 'warm, intimate and continuous relationship' has thus become a matter of 'dependence' on 'a mother-figure'. While this particular change has perhaps little significance, except as an illustration of the difficulty of conducting accurate scientific investigations without a recognized scientific vocabulary, in other cases differences in formulation do seem to reflect real differences in meaning. Thus the supposedly

[1] Bowlby (1952), p. 40. [2] Roudinesco and Appell (1951), p. 107. [3] Bowlby (1952), p. 34.
[4] Shields (1954). [5] Bowlby (1952), p. 11. [6] Ainsworth and Bowlby (1954), p. 6.

damaging factor is sometimes defined in a way which puts the emphasis on physical separation: in the passage just quoted Bowlby seems to be chiefly concerned with this. Other investigators, however, lay much more stress upon the dangers of emotional rejection which may befall children who continue to live with their families equally with those who are uprooted. Thus the author of a recent study of adolescent delinquent girls, some three-quarters of whom were in trouble for stealing, found that 'a specific association was shown between thieving and separation or rejection',[1] since these factors occurred much more frequently in the histories of thieving than of non-thieving delinquents.

Clearly, since any child who is physically separated from his mother is liable to feel, unless steps are taken to demonstrate the contrary, that he has been abandoned by her, evidence that emotional rejection has damaging effects creates a presumption that physical separation will, in many cases, produce similar results. But the rejection hypothesis and the separation hypothesis are not one and the same. Certainly, the practical implications are different, according as we believe that what matters is that a child should live with his mother, or that he should be loved either by her or by someone who can take her place. If the second is the correct hypothesis, this actually strengthens the case for the break-up of families in which warm continuous affection is not forthcoming. Moreover, the rejection hypothesis—the theory that it is the loss of the mother's love rather than of her physical presence which is dangerous—is itself susceptible of various interpretations. Rich, for instance, has suggested that 'the history of early separation may be associated with present [anti-social] behaviour because it is also associated with present rejection'.[2] In other words, early separation is not so much to be feared for its own sake, as because it may be the first sign of a breakdown which only becomes serious if and when it is prolonged into later years; and the maternal deprivation hypothesis should be revised to read 'maternal rejection has an adverse effect on personality growth; and maternal separation is often one way of spotting a rejecting mother'.

Even more elusive than the damaging factor is the actual damage which this is said to produce. On the contribution of maternal separation or deprivation to subsequent delinquency in the sense of formal law-breaking, the evidence, as indeed might be expected, is extremely scanty. True, it was the study of a particular type of delinquent that seems to have first aroused Bowlby's interest in a possible connection between maternal deprivation and anti-social behaviour. But the famous thieves who were the subject of this investigation, it should not be forgotten, numbered only forty-four. Out of this total seventeen were found to have suffered early or prolonged separation from their mothers or mother-figures during the first five years of their lives, as against only two of the forty-four controls who were drawn from other children attending the same Child Guidance Clinic; while of the fourteen thieves who were specifically labelled affectionless, twelve had been separated, as against five of the remaining thirty. In this group the affectionless children

[1] O'Kelly (1955), p. 65. [2] Rich, J. (1956), p. 497.

were found to be 'significantly more delinquent than the other thieves'; and they constituted 'more than half of the more serious and chronic offenders';[1] and, as additional support of his own conclusions, Bowlby adds that in 'the late 1930s, at least six independent workers were struck by the frequency with which children who committed numerous delinquencies, who seemed to have no feelings for anyone and were very difficult to treat, were found to have had grossly disturbed relationships with their mothers in their early years'.[2]

The stereotype is indeed familiar enough—in the nineteen-fifties quite as much as in the thirties. Certainly anyone familiar with the juvenile court clientèle can recall more than one case of a child or adolescent in whom general indifference to the standards of behaviour normally expected is associated with a history of being pushed around from one home or institution to another, with little chance to experience ordinary family life. Yet, contrary to what seems to be widely believed, we have practically no hard evidence as to the strength of this association between deprivation either of family life in general or of mother-love in particular and subsequent criminality. Even a first-hand perusal of all the independent studies referred to above by Bowlby[3] has failed to reveal any support other than the impressions of the investigators concerned for the existence of a link between maternal deprivation and delinquency. Actual delinquency is in fact very rarely mentioned in these investigations. What they do purport to show is that deprived babies or children may grow up difficult, retarded or unhappy; but even so it should be remembered that in none of these studies had the subjects reached the age of nineteen.

In addition to his own forty-four thieves, Bowlby quotes both Burt's and the Gluecks' investigations.[4] It should, however, be noted[5] that, when the subjects of the latter were followed up, the question whether they had enjoyed 'the affectionate regard of their mothers'[6] turned out to have nothing to do with the persistence of their delinquent behaviour. Clearly this finding (to which no reference is made in the Bowlby Monograph) is in direct conflict with Bowlby's own conclusion that the two factors which are especially common among *persistent* delinquents, and which distinguish them from 'children suffering from other forms of maladjustment', are separation for six months or more from the mother or mother-figure in the first five years, during which the child is with strangers, and 'being more or less unwanted by parents who are themselves unstable and unhappy people and whose attitudes towards him are, on balance, hostile, critical and punishing'.[7] In other quarters also the absence of any clear link between separation and delinquency has been noted. Thus Edelston reports that he is led by his study of the effects upon children of the 'hospitalization trauma' to believe that 'the proportion of delinquent reactions is not very large'.[8] Andry again concluded from his examination of eighty delinquents and eighty controls

[1] Bowlby (1946), p. 54. [2] Bowlby (1952), pp. 30–2. [3] ibid., pp. 30–2.
[4] ibid., p. 34. [5] See p. 307. [6] Glueck, S. and E. T. (1940), p. 108.
[7] Bowlby in *Conference on the Scientific Study of Juvenile Delinquency* (1949), p. 36.
[8] Edelston (1952), p. 131.

that 'separations between a child and one or other or both parents . . . do not seem to be primary factors in the etiology of delinquency'.[1] Lewis found that 'neither delinquency nor incapacity for affectionate relationships was significantly more frequent in the separated children'.[2] From Goldfarb's studies no evidence is forthcoming; and, although his institution children often failed to make affectionate relationships, they did not apparently make up for this by stealing.

For additional evidence of delinquent tendencies amongst the maternally deprived Bowlby has to fall back upon the experience of the Hawthorne-Cedar Knolls School and upon Armstrong's study of runaway boys.[3] These, however, can hardly throw much light on the relation between delinquency, as ordinarily understood, and maternal separation or deprivation. For the Hawthorne-Cedar Knolls School, as Bowlby has himself stated, deals primarily with 'grave psychiatric disorders'; and its population is, therefore, hardly typical of the delinquent world in general; while runaways, though sometimes delinquent, cannot be identified with those guilty of stealing or other criminal acts. After all, there is nothing very remarkable, or indeed very helpful as a general explanation of anti-social conduct, in the discovery that children tend to run away from homes where they are not loved.

Since the appearance of Bowlby's Monograph it has not been easy to find much additional evidence on the relation between maternal deprivation and anti-social behaviour. The chief relevant study is the latest work of the Gluecks; and in this the findings are equivocal. This investigation has, on the one hand, produced considerable concrete detail showing that the delinquents' home and family life was generally less satisfactory than that of the controls; yet at the same time 'a considerable likeness' was observed 'between the delinquents and non-delinquents in respect to the time at which the physical cohesion of their families first suffered a blow'.[4] In the broken families, 56·3 per cent delinquents and 46·7 per cent controls were under the age of five when the break occurred; while 28·1 per cent and 31·0 per cent respectively were between five and nine years old at the time of the break. It follows that the break in the families of 84·4 per cent of the delinquents and 77·7 per cent controls occurred before the children concerned were ten years old. The differences are thus not very large. Elsewhere,[5] however, the Gluecks have suggested that the delinquents enjoyed a smaller ration of love and affection than did those whose conduct was less troublesome; though again it was also found that substantially more of the delinquents than of the controls were said to have 'overprotective' mothers.

The possibility of a link between maternal deprivation and forms of psychological damage which do not necessarily express themselves in delinquent behaviour is much more prominent in the literature. As we have seen, those who have studied children who live in institutions have stressed their intellectual and emotional retardation and their exaggerated demands for affection. In addition there figure among the consequences attributed to maternal

[1] Andry (1955), p. 357. [2] Lewis, H. (1954), p. 83. [3] Bowlby (1952), pp. 35 and 161.
[4] Glueck, S. and E. T. (1951), p. 122. [5] ibid., p. 125.

deprivation such defects as selfishness, enuresis, 'social incompetence', excessive craving for affection or the development of an affectionless character. The prominence of these traits is, however, to some extent explained by the fact that the starting-point of many of the retrospective studies has been the experience of child guidance or psychiatric clinics. Naturally those who are found in these clinics tend to suffer from psychological troubles; and if, on investigation, it turns out that a fair proportion of such cases have a history of maternal deprivation or separation, this history readily becomes suspect as a possible 'aetiological factor'. Yet in order to evaluate that suspicion we obviously need to know the incidence in the population at large of comparable infantile experiences.

It is, therefore, much to be regretted that Dr Bowlby has apparently decided to give up as hopeless any attempt to get light on this essential quantitative aspect of his problem. In a paper on *Research Strategy in the Study of Mother-Child Separation* he writes, 'Mention should be made of the "population survey" which has frequently been suggested to us as desirable by those with whom we have discussed research into mother-child separation. Such a survey implies studying a representative sample of a general population to ascertain both the incidence of separation experiences and the extent to which they seem linked to the severe effects which have been attributed to them as a result of studies such as those of Goldfarb and Bowlby. A population survey conceived in this way involves (*a*) a comparison of the personalities of the total separated group and of the total non-separated group, (*b*) the classification of separation experiences in terms of some criterion of severity and (*c*) the comparison of sub-groups of separated children so classified. Although perhaps attractive at first sight, an examination shows such a project to be fraught with great difficulties. For instance, collection of the data would present the same problems as are met with in the follow-up approach, multiplied many times because of the larger scope of the project. Furthermore, such a survey, if done carefully with thorough clinical appraisals of personality, would be an undertaking of such magnitude as to lie outside the limit of feasibility. Whether it would be worth undertaking on a more superficial basis is doubtful . . . On the other hand, starting with the assumption that separation has already been shown to be a pathogenic factor, it might fruitfully be used to answer certain sociological questions: where in the population does separation occur most frequently and in connection with what problems?'[1]

This is certainly a counsel of despair as well as a grave breakdown in logic. The assumption that separation is a pathogenic factor cannot be substantiated unless and until it is demonstrated that the pathological symptoms appear more frequently amongst the separated than amongst the non-separated. No matter how intensively we may study the experience of those among the separated who are known to suffer from such symptoms, we can never assess the pathogenic nature of that experience so long as we have no idea how often others with similar histories manage to make out at least as well as the rest of

[1] Ainsworth and Bowlby (1954), pp. 21–2.

us. To attempt such an assessment in the absence of this vital information is on a par with trying to calculate the insurance premiums to be charged for fire risks by reference only to those houses which have actually caught fire.

Fortunately, however, other investigations have begun to tackle this problem. Reference has already been made[1] to the 1946 survey of women in Great Britain who gave birth to babies during a single week in March. By following up a sample of these babies at later dates, investigators have been able to throw light upon other problems beside those which inspired the original investigation. Thus Rowntree reports that by the time they were four years old, 6 per cent of the (legitimate) babies in the original sample were living in households in which one parent was no longer present, being dead, divorced, estranged or temporarily absent. After matching each child so deprived with another from 'a stable and united family' for sex, birth order and certain family circumstances, she arrived at a total of 277 pairs for whom 'complete information on social background, child health and development' was available. Rowntree comments that the amount of information obtainable on behaviour difficulties in these two groups of children was 'inevitably limited by the nature of the National Survey. In 1950 questions were asked only on eating difficulties and on enuresis, and in 1952, the latter query was repeated, along with several extra questions on certain nervous habits . . . and on night-terrors'.[2] However, in the upshot, the children of broken homes 'were not exceptionally prone to the grosser forms of emotional disturbance, apart from a rather higher incidence of bed wetting at four years old, which affected only the better-off families'.[3] So far as could be estimated, 'the great majority of children in broken homes were as well and as normal in behaviour as those living in more stable circumstances'.[4]

Equally non-committal are the findings of Douglas and Blomfield. In a survey of 4,668 legitimate children they found that 52 per cent were separated between birth and the age of six. Those separated for more than four weeks were matched with others not separated in similar types of family and the same locality. The authors conclude that 'there was no suggestion that separation affected children adversely in any way if they remained at home. Among the children sent away from home more nightmares and bad habits, such as thumb sucking' were reported for the separated as against controls. 'Rather more of the former also attended Child Guidance and Speech Therapy clinics later. But these differences were relatively small.'[5] At the same time it is cautiously added that, without individual contact with the separated children, reliable judgments of their emotional stability cannot be formed. 'Although so far we have no records of serious disturbances, and most of the mothers themselves do not appear to be worried, we do not in any way regard this as a final conclusion.'[6]

Investigations such as these promise valuable new checks upon theories about the effects of separation; but, for the time being, the fact must be recognized that we still have no serious quantitative assessment of the signifi-

[1] See p. 46. [2] Rowntree (1955), p. 260. [3] ibid., p. 263. [4] ibid., p. 262.
[5] Douglas and Blomfield (1958), p. 149. [6] ibid., p. 116.

cance of maternal separation or deprivation in the whole picture of anti-social behaviour. Such studies as have been made are descriptive or clinical rather than statistical. Moreover, even where statistical techniques have been used, the methods employed are not always impeccable, nor is the work either of those who support the deprivation hypothesis or of those who incline to different conclusions always free from lapses from the standards proper to scientific enquiry. Spitz's researches in particular, which have been much quoted as evidence of the dangers of maternal separation, have been subjected to well-founded, if exceptionally ferocious, criticism by Pinneau. Among the major deficiencies exposed is the fact that the findings of Spitz's follow-up of children in a Foundling Home are based on only twenty-one of his original group of ninety-one; while records of declining developmental quotients quoted as evidence of the 'spectacular' deterioration of his foundlings appear to have been drawn, not from the same children at different ages, but actually from different children at different dates. Again, Spitz seems to be extraordinarily careless in his statements as to the number of children in the Nursery with whose inmates his foundlings were compared. In his first article, as Pinneau has observed, Spitz 'reports that the total number in the Nursery sample was sixty-nine, in the second article 122, in a third 123, and in a fourth 196'.[1] Nor are his inconsistencies confined only to numerical statements: his assessment of the personality of the mothers of his cases seems to have been varied quite shamelessly to suit the needs of the various stages of his argument. Thus at one point these women are said to be 'mostly delinquent minors as a result of social maladjustment or feeble-mindedness, or because they are psychically defective, psychopathic, or criminal. Psychic normalcy and adequate social adjustment is almost excluded';[2] yet later we are told that 'in a large percentage of the cases' their 'failure in social adaptation' was 'not severe, consisting mainly in sexual indiscretion at the wrong age'.[3] In another instance, a group of children is described in one article as having an 'unusually high level of health',[4] whilst in another 37 per cent of the same group were said to show 'a great susceptibility to inter current sickness'.[5]

Spitz's reply to these strictures (which was followed by a further counter-attack from Pinneau) hardly restores confidence in the reliability of the methods employed in his much-quoted studies. Nor is it upon Spitz alone that suspicion falls. As time goes on, Bowlby's assessment of the statistical significance of his own work seems to have become increasingly rosy. Thus when his *Forty-four Juvenile Thieves* first appeared in 1946, we were warned by the author that 'the constitution of the sample' was 'chancy, the recording of data unsystematic, the amount of data on different cases uneven';[6] but by 1952 this work had become a 'systematic clinical and statistical study;'[7] and reference has already been made to the light-hearted attitude of more than one investigator to the risk that hereditary factors may have affected comparisons between various groups of children.

Nor is it only in relation to these statistical aspects of their work that

[1] Pinneau (1955), p. 434. [2] Spitz (1945), p. 60. [3] ibid., p. 98.
[4] Spitz (1946), p. 117. [5] ibid., p. 320. [6] Bowlby (1946), p. 2. [7] Bowlby (1952), p. 32.

supporters of the maternal deprivation hypothesis have at times allowed their enthusiasm to run away with them. As we have seen, the nature of the damage inflicted by deprivation is not always clearly conceived. Except in those studies which are specifically concerned with delinquents, some such formula as 'social competence' is the test usually employed. Theis, for example, defined as socially incapable a subject 'who is unable or unwilling to support himself adequately, who is shiftless, or who has defied accepted standards of morality or order of his community';[1] and she found that over one-third of those of her cases who had spent their childhood in institutions were 'incapable' by this test. As Bowlby has observed, the fact that the other two-thirds turned out to be socially capable may be reckoned as 'so far as it goes . . . satisfactory', but sheer wishful thinking must have dictated his subsequent comment that 'as no psychiatric examination was carried out, neurotic and psychosomatic troubles not leading to social incompetence were not recorded. It is virtually certain that the incidence of psychiatric disturbance was much above the 34·5 per cent of overt social incapacity'.[2] Plainly we must either adhere to the test of overt social incapacity, or substitute some other criterion: the device of shifting from one formula to another, if the results given by the first prove disappointing, cannot possibly be justified. In practice, psychiatric examination of children brought up in their own families is not habitually carried out: if it were, who knows what the incidence of neurotic and psychosomatic troubles among them might not prove to be?

III

After all this, what can we be said to know? Bowlby's own confidence rests on the belief that 'what each individual piece of work lacks in thoroughness, scientific reliability, or precision is largely made good by the concordance of the whole. Nothing in scientific method carries more weight than this'.[3] This seems decidedly dangerous doctrine, inasmuch as it comes near to an assertion that it does not greatly matter if all the work is slipshod, so long as all the answers are much the same. A more prudent course would surely be not to go beyond Bowlby's alternative statement that 'relatively few studies taken by themselves are more than suggestive'.[4]

But suggestive of what? Of the fact that a child needs 'a warm continuous relationship with a mother or mother-substitute' or, in still simpler terms, of the fact that children (like their elders) need to be dependably loved, and that without such dependable love, they are likely to become frightened, unhappy or mentally retarded? It is indeed a melancholy conclusion that it should have been thought necessary to employ so much costly research, with so pretentious a scientific façade, in order to demonstrate these homely truths: one might have hoped, or even have assumed, that these were axioms to humane and kindly people long before social research was ever heard of. Naturally, the degree to which any particular child does in fact enjoy this love depends upon an infinitely complex and variable set of experiences, which

[1] Theis (1924), p. 199. [2] Bowlby (1952), p. 40. [3] ibid., p. 15. [4] ibid., p. 46.

cannot be simply differentiated according to whether he happens to live in his own family, in a foster home or in some kind of institution. Moreover, most of these experiences are still immeasurable, and cannot be made the subject of statistically valid research. That there can be deprived children in families, and emotionally satisfied children in institutions, is admitted by all; and it is equally plain that some children are tough, and that their toughness enables them to endure much without noticeable damage. Certainly, 'there is no such statistically reliable correlation between neurosis, for example, and some syndrome of childhood experiences as there is between syphilis and the paresis that sometimes follows it, the paresis never existing without the pre-existing syphilis'.[1]

What the maternal deprivation investigators can claim to have demonstrated (assuming their observations to be well founded) is that, as things are at present, children have a better chance of finding dependable love in families than in institutions. This, however, is a social, rather than a psychological, fact; it is a commentary upon the way in which many institutions are or have been run. In so far as communal life has failed to give many institutionalized children a 'warm continuous relationship with a mother-substitute', the fact of these children's backwardness may be due to that failure, rather than to any inherent superiority of family over institutional life as such. There are, indeed, practical quite as much as psychological conclusions to be drawn: as much good may be done by running the institutions better as by leaving the children in their homes. This, it is fair to add, is explicitly appreciated by the more careful investigators; but the point does not always get through to the popular versions of the separation hypothesis which too often deal in crude comparisons between homes and institutions, and which deprecate separation as such, without regard to the quality either of the family life from which the child is taken or of the communal régime to which it is transferred.

The imperfections of children's homes or hospitals are unlikely to be widely known except to the minority who have had firsthand contact with them. On the assumption, therefore, that their observations are correct, social research workers can justly take credit for having discovered and publicized these imperfections. But to parade as a novelty the familiar psychological principle which gives this discovery its practical importance is at best futile, and at worst seriously misleading. When Elizabeth Fry exposed the insanitary conditions that obtained in nineteenth-century prisons, no one applauded her for the discovery that good sanitary conditions were to be desired: the merit of her work was its demonstration that such conditions were not to be found in prisons. The parallel holds. By a curious misplacement of emphasis, even the best work on maternal deprivation seems to have obscured its own genuine discoveries by highlighting what are little more than platitudes.

Among the unfortunate consequences of this development is the risk, as Edelston puts it, of '"mother separation" becoming an all-embracing cliché every bit as much as the "broken home"'.[2] While the more careful workers

[1] Lemkau and others (1953), p. 437. [2] Edelston (1952), p. 137.

recognize that ' "separation" is not a simple homogeneous aetiological factor and that the term refers to a wide range of events and an intricate complex of associated conditions, which in different constellations may have different effects on the course of development',[1] the fact remains that the physical event of separation lends itself to study in a way that 'an intricate complex of associations' does not. It is no doubt for this entirely practical reason that the more recent research plans of Bowlby and his associates seem to be directed towards separation rather than towards deprivation. Yet the fact that a child has been physically separated from his mother cannot, obviously, be taken as more than a rough guide to the degree in which he has been deprived of the affection and security that he needs. Investigators are only driven to concentrate their attention upon this fact by the extreme difficulty of finding measurable external events which will serve as tolerably reliable indicators of those subtle complexities which alone are significant, but which themselves elude precise measurement— a difficulty, it may be added, that is all too familiar in many fields of social investigation.

Up to the present, therefore, research into the effects of maternal deprivation is to be valued chiefly for its incidental exposure of the prevalence of deplorable patterns of institutional upbringing, and of the crass indifference of certain hospitals to childish sensitivities. Without doubt this research has already had excellent practical effects in stimulating many of the authorities responsible for children's homes and hospitals to change their ways for the better. Meanwhile, it is clear that, where the old bad methods survive, the children, as one would expect, suffer according to their temperaments and circumstances in various ways and in various degrees. Now and again their deprivation seems to express itself in a well-marked pattern of indifference to everybody except themselves, of which one of the expressions is repeated stealing. More than this, however, we cannot say. That the damage is lifelong or irreversible, that maternal deprivation is a major factor in criminal behaviour, or that the younger the child the greater the risk, all these must be regarded as quite unproven hypotheses.

[1] Ainsworth and Bowlby (1954), p. 3.

CHAPTER V

Criminological Theories Based on the Age of the Offender

I

THE striking predominance of the younger age groups in the criminal statistics of all the countries for which we have particulars has encouraged the growth of theories which suggests that the age of an offender or the age of his first criminality is significantly related to the pattern of his criminal career. In the present chapter an attempt is made to analyse the better known of these theories and to assess the state of knowledge on this subject.[1]

If crime is predominantly a pursuit of youth, it follows that the great majority of young offenders (who have not died or emigrated) must have reformed before they reach the age of thirty, or else have learned either to escape detection or to content themselves with committing only non-indictable or motoring offences. Indeed, for all the official statistics tell us, *all* our young offenders may have changed their habits in one or other of these ways, since the figures do not reveal how far the individuals convicted in any given age group are or are not identical with those convicted in a younger age group at an earlier date. At the least, since it is known that some people acquire their first conviction relatively late in life, we can be sure that the number of those who drop out of the ranks of young offenders as they grow up must exceed even the substantial difference between the totals in the older and the younger age groups. The difference between the proportion of the population over the age of thirty and of those between twenty and thirty who get convicted would be even greater than it is, if there were not some offenders who start their (recorded) criminal careers after they are thirty.

Special investigations are thus necessary in order to ascertain the extent to which the adult criminal population is recruited from its juvenile predecessors. In order to get a full picture we need to know both the percentage of young offenders who graduate as adult criminals, and the proportion of the latter who have themselves been in trouble as juveniles. For obvious reasons information on the second of these points is more easily come by than on the first. A life-long follow-up is necessary before it can be confidently said that anyone has finally given up the practice of law-breaking; whereas the juvenile records of adult offenders are at least a matter of past history,

[1] Much of the material reviewed in this chapter is subject to the important limitation mentioned in the footnote on page 84.

and not still in the lap of the future. Even these records, however, are not always wholly reliable, especially in countries such as the USA where there is substantial immigration. Immigrants are not likely to publicize in the country of their adoption any criminal offences that they may have committed in their country of origin.

Such follow-ups as have been undertaken have generally extended only over relatively short periods. There are, however, a few exceptions to be mentioned. Outstanding amongst these is Otterström's investigation in Sweden[1] of which particulars have been given in Chapter III. Otterström traced the history down to January 1, 1944, of more than 2,000 young persons who had been the subject of official action in the municipality of Malmö during the period 1903–40; though many of these, it will be remembered, were not actually delinquent, but only came to the notice of the authorities on account of their bad home conditions. Another Swedish investigator— Ahnsjö—has also studied the records of female reformatory inmates in that country from 1903 to 1937.[2] The Gluecks kept track of their male reformatory cases and of their earlier group of juvenile delinquents for fifteen years.[3] Shaw and McKay, using official records, followed right up to 1938 the 'subsequent careers of a one-third sample of all Chicago boys brought into the Juvenile Court of Cook County on a delinquency petition during 1920'.[4] Another American study on somewhat unusual lines, by Dunham and Knauer, recorded the later history of a random selection of 100 juvenile first offenders in the first year of each five-year period from 1920–40;[5] while Rumney and Murphy studied the subsequent careers over an eleven-year period of subjects placed on probation in 1937 at ages ranging from ten to seventy-three.[6] In other cases contact was lost after a period varying from one to five years; but there is perhaps reason to hope that a five-year crime-free spell is a fair indication that the criminal phase is over; although inevitably the evidence of investigations that cover only brief periods of time must remain inconclusive.

Bovet, after reviewing much of the material, concluded that 'of the numbers of young delinquents brought before a court, a small percentage only (about 10 per cent to 20 per cent) tends to prolong delinquency into adult years. That means that about 80 to 90 per cent of the juvenile delinquents brought before a court will not offend again, or at least will not retain their delinquent tendencies beyond the crisis of their juvenile adaptation'.[7] These figures cannot be regarded as more than a rough averaging of widely different findings. Even so, Bovet's estimate seems somewhat optimistic. In several of the more prolonged investigations it has been found that the proportion of juvenile delinquents who continue their offences at least into early manhood exceeds 20 per cent and may be much higher. The Gluecks record that out of 318 of their ex-delinquents who were known to have reformed within a fifteen year period, 210 had done so before reaching the age of twenty-one,

[1] Otterström (1946). [2] Ahnsjö (1941). [3] Glueck, S. and E. T. (1945).
[4] Shaw and McKay (1942), pp. 127–8. [5] Dunham and Knauer (1954).
[6] Rumney and Murphy (1952). [7] Bovet (1951), p. 44.

and 138 before they were eighteen.[1] Shaw and McKay found that 60 per cent of their Chicago boys subsequently appeared as adult offenders;[2] whereas Dunham and Knauer, who were interested primarily in the efficiency with which the juvenile court dealt with young offenders, reported that the proportion registered as adult offenders in each of the five-year periods covered by their enquiry varied between 24 per cent and 37 per cent.[3] In the Rumney and Murphy investigation the proportion of subjects who still had a clear record after eleven years stood at 22 per cent of those aged 10–12 at the time of their original offence, at 39 per cent of those in the 13–15 year age group and at 30 per cent of those aged 16–18.[4]

Even if Bovet's estimate does not exaggerate the frequency of early reformation, it could still be true that the majority of older offenders had begun their criminal careers in early youth, since the number of juvenile offenders is so much larger than the figure for later age groups. As many as 80 per cent or 90 per cent of offenders who had a court record before they were sixteen might have reformed before their seventeenth birthday, and still the remaining 10 per cent or 20 per cent might be sufficiently numerous to comprise at least half the convictions scored by their age group as they grew older.

Actually such evidence as we have suggests that the proportion of late starters is not negligible. Dr W. F. Roper, Principal Medical Officer of Wakefield Prison, found that out of 1,100 prisoners whose records he investigated, only 24 per cent had been convicted before the age of seventeen and 32 per cent before the age of twenty-one.[5] If the facts are complete, this would mean that three-quarters of that prison population had not graduated through the juvenile court. Even among more hardened recidivists at Dartmoor the same investigator found that less than half had begun as juvenile or adolescent offenders.[6] Spencer, who also studied a group of Dartmoor prisoners, records that about two-thirds had, and one-third had not, convictions dating back to before they were eighteen; whereas at Maidstone prison, where the population was less hardened than that at Dartmoor, the proportions of late and early starters were roughly reversed, thirty-eight per cent having acquired records under the age of eighteen.[7] Benson, in yet another study of Dartmoor and Parkhurst convicts, comments on the relatively mature age at which these offenders began their careers, 42 per cent of the Dartmoor and 34 per cent of the Parkhurst group having adult first convictions;[8] and he refers to similar findings by Norval Morris, who records that 39 per cent of the habitual offenders in his study had no record of conviction as juveniles—a circumstance which, as Morris has elsewhere himself suggested, casts doubt 'on the oft-suggested criminal precocity of habitual criminals'.[9] Benson, however, reminds us that 'one explanation is undoubtedly that fifty years ago country police forces were very haphazard in reporting juvenile offences'. Nevertheless he does not think it likely that

[1] Glueck, S. and E. T. (1940), pp. 89 and 304. [2] Shaw and McKay (1942), p. 128.
[3] Dunham and Knauer (1954), p. 295. [4] Rumney and Murphy (1952), p. 162.
[5] Roper (1951), pp. 246–8. [6] Roper (1950), p. 17. [7] Spencer (1954), pp. 112 and 142.
[8] Benson (1953), p. 201. [9] Morris, N. (1951), p. 301.

this fact alone explains the high proportion of late starters, but inclines rather to the conclusion that 'a considerable proportion of habitual criminality starts at a comparatively late age'.[1] Mannheim also, if unexpectedly, found similar evidence in a survey of men and women recidivists convicted in London between 1915 and 1935, and adds the comment that 'it is surprising that amongst the men who commenced their criminal activities after the age of forty there are comparatively many who at that late stage have become habituals with twenty or more convictions for stealing, etc.'[2] Ferguson in the latest follow-up of his 'ordinary' Glasgow boys undertaken after they had completed their National Service, records that, out of a total of 568, the number who had a court record amounted to eighty-nine. Of these, fifty-eight had been found guilty between their eighth and eighteenth birthday, but not subsequently; nineteen had been convicted for the first time after reaching the age of eighteen; while in only twelve cases was there a record extending both before and after the eighteenth birthday.[3] The sample was small, and the period in which adult convictions could have been acquired was short; but, so far as it goes, this experience suggests a considerable discontinuity between the juvenile and the adult population of offenders.

Sellin, who, in 1940, reviewed a number of studies, both American and European, mentions that several of these showed that by no means all offenders learn the business in their childhood: in Amsterdam, for instance, 'almost all those under eighteen were first offenders, while of those eighteen or nineteen years of age only 16 per cent had previous convictions'.[4] In the USA a warden of Sing Sing prison is said to have reported that, of 1,000 consecutive admissions to that prison in 1934–5, 'only 25 per cent had official records before the age of sixteen, an additional 24 per cent between the ages of seventeen and twenty, and 51 per cent at twenty-one or later'; and that 'there is evidence also, that after about age twenty-five the percentage of criminals who are first offenders increases with increasing age'.[5] Fernald, again, in her study of convicted women found that only 6·8 per cent of her group had convictions recorded below sixteen years of age, while less than half had acquired their first conviction before the age of twenty-four. Commenting on this result, she suggests that 'the chief insistence on the extensiveness and importance of juvenile convictions in connection with the problem of recidivism has come from persons concerned primarily with men delinquents or with boy offenders. It is entirely possible that the situation is quite different as it affects women delinquents.'[6]

In spite of the enormous drop in recorded criminality in the higher age groups, it thus appears that the late starters cannot be dismissed as negligible. Their histories might indeed prove to be a profitable field of study. Unless we are to suppose that their apparently blameless youth is due to skill in evading detection, it seems as if they would be missed by the Gluecks' social prediction[7] scale: at least it is hard to believe that, if their anti-social behaviour is

[1] Benson (1953), p. 201. [2] Mannheim (1940), p. 359.
[3] Ferguson and Cunnison (1956), pp. 73 and 76. [4] Sellin (1940), p. 110.
[5] Sutherland (1955), p. 110. [6] Fernald and others (1920), p. 144. [7] See p. 179.

primarily traceable to the domestic circumstances of their childhood, it would not have manifested itself before they were grown up. One would certainly like to know whether some catastrophe occurred in their lives which was responsible for their deferred criminality—as is perhaps suggested by Norval Morris' observation that, of thirteen men first convicted between the ages of thirty and forty-two, 'four committed their first crimes during their first protracted period of unemployment', and five did so after serious disturbances in their marital relationships by death, desertion, etc.[1]

For the most part, however, criminologists have interested themselves more in the heavy incidence of crime upon the young than in the relatively atypical late entrants. To Dr Roper there is nothing to be surprised at in the tendency to outgrow criminal habits. 'Crime', he writes, 'is essentially the solution of personal problems at a childish level of conduct either because basic attitudes have never developed beyond that level or because there has been regression to childish attitudes as a result of frustration. It is natural for a young child to lie, to strike others, to intrude, to be indecent (if judged by adult standards) and to take the belongings of others . . . But some children are not properly trained; they do not abandon their early attitudes and they do not develop self-control. Some proceed directly into juvenile delinquency; others manage some kind of makeshift self-control which may give way in later life when they are faced with that particular stress or temptation to which their early training, or lack of it, has left them vulnerable. Generally speaking, the older one grows the less this vulnerability and it is not surprising that crime is predominantly a weakness of the young'. 'Criminality is essentially the persistence of immature attitudes' and it 'therefore declines with age unless fixed by other factors such as aggregation to criminal groups'.[2]

If the relation of criminality to immaturity seems commonsensical enough to Dr Roper, the Gluecks, on their side, have constructed from their extensive investigations what purports to be an elaborate theory on the relation of criminality to the process of 'maturation'. In the light of the ten-year follow-up of the subjects of one of their earlier studies, they reached the conclusion that ageing had 'played a significant role in the process of improvement with the passage of the years'; and that, 'if reformation has not occurred by the thirty-sixth year, it is less likely to occur thereafter than it would have been previously'. At the same time, they warned us that this does not mean that 'thirty-one to thirty-five years is *absolutely* the most likely age of reformation'. On the contrary 'a combination of influences' is involved, and these influences include both the age of the offender and the stage that he has reached in his criminal career. It is in fact necessary to 'go more deeply into what might be denominated the *content* of age'.[3] Many of their offenders, it seems, both adult and juvenile, did not reform until they were 'well along in adulthood as well as in criminalism'; and from this it was 'tentatively concluded that the factor of *maturation* must play a pervasive role in the process of recidivism and reform', and that 'it was not achievement of any particular

[1] Morris, N. (1951), p. 340. [2] Roper (1950), pp. 18 and 27.
[3] Glueck, S. and E. T. (1945), pp. 78–9.

age, but rather the achievement of adequate maturation regardless of the chronologic age at which it occurred that was the significant influence in the behavior changes of our criminals'.[1]

Later investigations by the Gluecks also suggested that 'the tendency to settle down or become less aggressive in anti-social behavior is not attributable to arrival at any particular chronological age-span'.[2] No close resemblances were found between the behaviour of offenders of like ages. On the contrary, it was the mere lapse of time which was important: in a given five-year period there would be general improvement in the records of each group of subjects, irrespective of the particular age which they had reached. Furthermore, in the case of those offenders who, even after the lapse of some years, had not wholly abandoned criminal practices, a decline in the seriousness of the offences committed was generally apparent; and this again was related rather to the lapse of time than to the age of the actual offender. From this the Gluecks have drawn what they describe as 'the highly important conclusion' that 'not age, per se, but rather the acquisition of a certain degree of maturation regardless of the age at which this is achieved among different offenders, is significantly related to changes in criminalistic behavior once embarked upon . . . On the whole, if the acts of delinquency begin very early in life, they are abandoned at a relatively early stage of manhood, provided various mental abnormalities do not counteract the natural tendency toward maturation which gradually brings with it greater powers of reflection, inhibition, postponement of immediate desires for more legitimate later ones, the capacity of learning from experience, and like constituents of what is generally recognized as a mature, self-managing, and successfully adapting personality. If, on the other hand, the acts of delinquency begin in adolescence, the delinquent tendency seems to run its course into a later stage of adulthood, again, however, provided the natural process of maturation is not interfered with.'[3] In the light of their experience, both of juvenile offenders and of adult reformatory inmates, therefore, the Gluecks postulate that delinquency, 'regardless of age at the time it begins . . . runs a fairly steady and predictable course',[4] and that 'it is lack of adequate maturity . . . that seems to underlie persistence in recidivism'.[5]

Of this theory it must be said that either it means something or it does not. If it has a meaning, this can presumably be summarized as follows. Delinquency is a symptom of immaturity; and, since some people grow up more slowly than others, some people pass through the delinquent phase later than others. In general nearly everybody grows out of it, if not by a certain age, at least after a lapse of a certain period from the beginning of a criminal career—those who begin late prolonging their criminality to a later age than those who took to it earlier in life.

If this could be shown to be true, it would be of some importance, the more so as the theory runs directly counter to the more commonly held view

Glueck, S. and E. T. (1945), pp. 79–81. [2] Glueck, S. and E. T. (1940), p. 93.
Glueck, S. and E. T. (1945), p. 84. [4] Glueck, S. and E. T. (1940), p. 264.
Glueck, S. and E. T. (1945), p. 85.

(which, incidentally, is supported by the Gluecks in another context[1]) that it is those who begin their criminal careers early who turn into the obdurate recidivists. It is, however, very doubtful if the notion of a criminal phase of more or less constant duration can be established from the data on which the Gluecks rely. After reviewing their experience of both adult reformatory inmates and juvenile delinquents, these authors were, it seems, struck by the fact that 'the conduct of the two groups of offenders, who were drawn from different places, at different times, at different levels in society's official apparatus for coping with criminality (i.e. juvenile court and young-adult reformatory), and who were studied entirely independently one of the other, was so much alike at a time in their lives when the two groups were found to be approximately the same average distance away from the onset of their criminal careers'.[2] The significance of this similarity, however, obviously depends upon all the subjects having been first offenders at the time of the original investigation, in which case alone could the younger subjects fairly be classified as having begun their delinquencies at an earlier age. But in point of fact, reference to this investigation shows that over 63 per cent of these boys had been arrested, sometimes more than once, before the date at which they became the subjects of the Gluecks' enquiry and from which the period of follow-up was measured. Some of those, therefore, who were among the first to reach the 16–20 year age group because they were already comparatively old when the Gluecks got to work on them, may in fact have had just as long histories of delinquency as their juniors.

In any case the theory that offenders tend to work their criminality out of their system after the lapse of a roughly constant period is not pressed too hard by the Gluecks themselves; for they are equally impressed by the significant minority of exceptions, in whose case this desirable process of maturation fails to occur; and the theory itself has no way of accounting for these. If, however, the maturation theory does not imply a roughly constant process of maturation which is irrespective of the offender's chronological age, what meaning can it be said to have at all? The discovery that ageing 'turned out to have played a significant role in the process of improvement with the passage of the years'[3] then becomes merely a rather pompous way of saying that with the passage of the years the subjects both grew older and behaved better. This, however, we knew already: indeed, the fact that people tend to reform as they grow older is just what we are out to explain. And as for the 'highly important conclusion that *not age, per se, but rather the acquisition of a certain degree of maturation regardless of the age at which this is achieved among different offenders, is significantly related to changes in criminalistic behavior once embarked upon*'[4]—this is reduced to nothing better than a circular argument. The majority of criminals (again, as we already know) cease to get convicted as they grow older, or as the beginning of their criminal careers recedes into history; and the explanation of this, we are told, lies in their '*acquisition of a certain degree of maturation*'. But the

[1] See p. 165. [2] Glueck, S. and E. T. (1940), p. 97.
[3] Glueck, S. and E. T. (1945), p. 78. [4] ibid., p. 84.

only evidence offered in support of their having acquired this maturity is the fact that they have outgrown their criminal habits; while, conversely, the minority who have not outgrown these are recognized as still immature by the very fact that they have not done so. This circularity is indeed explicitly admitted by the Gluecks themselves when they observe that 'under such a theory, the average age at which delinquency begins is significant as fixing the point at which the symptoms of abnormal functioning of the maturation process first manifest themselves in the form of delinquent conduct of a kind, serious and consistent enough, to come to the attention of the authorities'.[1]

The maturation theory of criminality is thus reduced to nothing more than a high falutin' way of saying what has all along been obvious—viz: that a minority of young criminals become recidivists, while the majority do not. It is in fact one of the—unhappily not infrequent—occasions on which a label has been mistaken for an explanation.[2]

Nevertheless, the Gluecks have proceeded to develop their own theory as to the factors conducive to 'maturation' from other evidence as to the differences between the reformed and the unreformed young offender. The reformed, they found, were less disposed to misconduct (including truancy) at school, less often diagnosed as suffering from mental disease, distortion and instability, better disciplined by their parents, more often the children of Protestant or Hebrew than of Catholic parents, and more often also children of Slavic rather than of Irish parents.[3] In these respects at least the recidivists and the reformed were found to be markedly different, while several slighter differences were also recorded. From this the authors conclude that 'there are certain superior qualities of Nature, as well as of Nurture, which distinguish the offenders who reformed within a fifteen-year span following their control by the Juvenile Court from those who continued to commit crimes. In the former, the natural maturation process was facilitated, or at least not blocked, with the passing of the years; in the latter, ageing did not bring with it that development and integration of forces which are translated into social adaptability and law-abiding conduct'.[4] Offenders, in fact, are of two kinds: those whose behaviour is 'due more to adverse environmental and educational influences than to any deep-seated organismal weaknesses', and those 'whose inability to conform to the demands of a complex society is more nearly related to innate (and, partly, early-conditioned) abnormalities' of the kind that set limits to the degree of maturation that may be reached, and who may 'never achieve a stage of maturity requisite to lawful adaptation in our society.'[5] In other words, those who were either suitably endowed by nature or blessed by nurture mended their ways, while others with different endowments and different experiences continued to recidivate. Such a conclusion is certainly unexceptionable, even if it is expressed in terms which are too general to be very helpful: but the introduction of a concept of maturation adds nothing to it.

[1] Glueck S. and E. T. (1945), p. 90. [2] See p. 317.
[3] Glueck, S. and E. T. (1940), pp. 111–14. [4] ibid., p. 115. [5] Glueck, S. and E. T. (1945), p. 86.

Indeed, in the course of enunciating the differences between the reformed and the unreformed, the Gluecks have themselves presented evidence which conflicts with the only intelligible meaning of the maturation theory. Thus they repeat that 'almost twice the proportion of youths who reformed as of the persistent offenders did not begin their delinquencies until reaching the higher age groups',[1] though in this case early 'delinquencies' are so defined as to include misbehaviour other than that which was the subject of legal action. Clearly, this finding directly negatives the hypothesis that criminality is due to immaturity, and that maturation is a process which continues for a more or less constant period after the beginning of a criminal career. In the end, therefore, what the maturation theory boils down to seems to be this. In the case of those offenders whose criminal careers start early and end late, the youthful beginning is a sign that maturation never will be achieved; whereas in the case of those who both begin and finish early it is a sign that, thanks to the normal processes of maturation, an early finish was to be predicted. Clearly there are no facts, however mutually contradictory, which a theory thus constructed cannot accommodate.

II

The hypothesis that among those whose offences first appear in adolescence 'the delinquent tendency seems to run its course into a later stage of adulthood'[2] than is usual in the case of those who begin early is not the prevailing view among criminologists. More general support, as Mannheim has lately remarked, is given to the opposite hypothesis that 'those who are early starters in delinquency are more likely to develop criminal habits than those who start later'.[3] Thus Roper holds that if 'crime is the result of a failure to solve difficulties in childhood', it is to be expected that 'the more intractable the criminal the earlier, as a rule, he will begin his operations';[4] though the logic behind this inference is by no means clear. In Ferguson's view 'young people who take to crime early tend to be persistent offenders'.[5] The distinguished Swiss criminologist Frey is emphatic that those with a history of early delinquency (the 'frühkriminellen') are apt to show a considerably higher 'intensity' of criminal behaviour than do those whose criminal careers began at a later age.[6] In a highly selective study, the Liverpool City Police have commented that 'it is a significant fact, easily shown [*sic*] by statistics, that it is the young who are most prone to drift into criminal habits and become recidivists, and that older persons do not so easily become habitual criminals'.[7] Morris categorically declares that 'persistent adult criminality is almost invariably the successor to a history of juvenile crime'.[8] Healy, without quoting any statistical evidence, goes so far as to say that 'practically all confirmed criminals

[1] Glueck, S. and E. T. (1940), p. 114. [2] Glueck, S. and E. T. (1945), p. 84.
[3] Mannheim (1955), p. 124. [4] Roper (1950), p. 21. [5] Ferguson (1952), p. 17.
[6] Frey (1951), pp. 77 ff. [7] Liverpool City Police (1956), p. 2.
[8] Morris, T. P. (1958), p. 190.

begin their careers in childhood or early youth';[1] though in his joint work with Bronner he expresses the opposite view that 'on the whole, then, there seems no ground for stating that the chances for reformation for our Chicago group . . . were to any great degree affected by the age of first court appearance';[2] Mannheim and Wilkins found that, 'since the younger the youth began crime the more likely he was to be a failure', there was 'a positive correlation between success and age of commencing crime',[3] while Hurwitz has categorically declared that 'through many investigations it has been ascertained that persistent criminals start on their criminal career at a very early age'.[4]

On the face of it the hypothesis appears simple enough: the younger you start, the worse you become, or the longer you go on. But the simplicity is deceptive; and its deceptiveness is a vivid illustration of the pitfalls which beset even the most apparently straightforward social investigation. For analysis of the evidence upon which these opinions are based reveals that the various investigators who have interested themselves in this matter are not all dealing with the same questions, but often with quite different ones which may well have different answers.

Of all those who are impressed by the significance of criminality at an early age, Frey has made the most elaborate investigations. Frey sought to establish an index of criminal intensity and to show that this was associated with the early onset of criminal activity (Frühkriminalität). After following the subsequent careers of groups of delinquent boys in the city of Basle over a considerable number of years, Frey concluded that the 'frühkriminelle' must be judged worse risks than the 'nichtfrühkriminelle' by any one of several tests. Thus of the 'frühkriminelle' 60·7 per cent became recidivists, against only 22·6 per cent of the 'nichtfrühkriminelle'; and among those who were reconvicted 29·3 per cent of the 'frühkriminelle' scored only one additional conviction, against 54·1 per cent of the nichtfrühkriminelle; while at the other end of the scale 13 per cent of the frühkriminelle were reconvicted more than ten times, whereas none of the other group were known to have committed more than nine further offences, most of them having much shorter records. From this and many similar observations on the same group of subjects Frey concludes that 'Frühkriminalität und Rückfallskriminalität scheinen miteinander in einem gesetmässigen Zusammenhang zu stehen'. It is, however, fair to say that Frey's figures are based upon rather small samples: there were in fact only thirty-seven in the 'nichtfrühkriminellen' category to whom the above figures relate.[5] His findings have also been criticized by Mannheim, on the ground that his figures do not always support the inferences that he draws from them.[6]

Mannheim and Wilkins were concerned to estimate the chances that an ex-Borstal boy (who necessarily falls within a narrow age-span) would be reconvicted of any crime within three to four years of his discharge; but

[1] Healy (1929), p. 10. [2] Healy and Bronner (1926), p. 95.
[3] Mannheim and Wilkins (1955), pp. 75–6. [4] Hurwitz (1952), p. 263.
[5] Frey (1951), pp. 78–89. [6] Mannheim (1952), p. 134.

they have not, as yet, made it their business to enquire what happens to him twenty or thirty years later. They report that success in avoiding reconviction for this period was achieved by 35 per cent of those whose criminal record began at the age of eleven or less, but 54 per cent of those first found guilty between the ages of sixteen and twenty-one.[1] Rose, who also dealt with Borstal boys, followed the careers of his subjects for a minimum of five years, distinguishing three categories—occasional offenders, habitual offenders and non-offenders, from which last group, however, 'minor traffic offences', assaults and drunks were excluded. The evidence that his study can contribute is, however, somewhat equivocal. The proportion of his subjects who were subsequently classified as non-offenders varied between 40·5 per cent for those first found guilty between the ages of eight and ten, and 55·0 per cent for those whose first offence occurred when they were between seventeen and twenty-two; while the proportion of occasional offenders varied very little as between those convicted in all the younger age groups (21·4 per cent for those who began their criminal careers between eight and ten, 22·4 per cent for those beginning between eleven and thirteen, and 20·3 per cent for the fourteen to sixteen-year-old group) but dropped sharply (to 8·6 per cent) for those whose first conviction did not occur till somewhere between seventeen and twenty-two. But in the case of those classified as habitual offenders the differences were much less, ranging only from 35·5 per cent for those beginning in the eleven to thirteen and fourteen to sixteen age groups to 38·1 per cent for those with first convictions between the ages of eight and ten.[2]

When the Gluecks followed up their 1,000 delinquent boys, they used as their bench-mark the 'first known misbehavior' in preference to the first occasion of being dealt with by the courts. On this basis they found that, of the youths who had reformed in the course of a fifteen-year period, 33·8 per cent were known to have 'misbehaved' themselves before the age of nine, while 43·5 per cent had a record of 'first known misbehavior' between the ages of nine and twelve and 22·7 per cent between the ages of thirteen and sixteen. The corresponding proportions of those who had still not reformed after the lapse of fifteen years were 37·4 per cent, 49·8 per cent and 12·8 per cent[3]—figures which seem to give about as much support to the alternative theory of a definite period of maturation as to the hypothesis that the younger you begin, the longer you continue. In their study of ex-reformatory men, however, the Gluecks found that, while '20 per cent were successful in avoiding the commission of crime', 'those who began their criminal activities under the age of eleven and those who were first delinquent between eleven and thirteen contribute appreciably smaller proportions of their respective totals to the successes (9·5 per cent and 13·3 per cent). Those who began their criminal careers between fourteen and sixteen or at seventeen or over, on the other hand, have a higher percentage of successes than the 20 per cent noted above'. This general indication that, the earlier the first delinquencies, the

[1] Mannheim and Wilkins (1955), p. 65. [2] Rose, A. G. (1954), p. 67.
[3] Glueck, S. and E. T. (1940), p. 114.

smaller the percentage of post-parole success is, however, said to be 'not so clear in the case of those who were only partial failures'.[1] In Sweden, Ahnsjö, who studied only females admitted to Swedish detention homes and reformatories, and whose investigation had the merit, along with that of Otterström,[2] of having covered a very long period, concluded that 'Generally speaking, a certain tendency towards a higher frequency of failures may be said to occur as regards cases entered at a lower as against a higher age'.[3] It is, however, possible that, although the age of admission to a penal institution is not at all the same as the age of first criminality, this finding is to be explained by the likelihood that those who find their way to such institutions at unusually tender ages are particularly difficult cases. And it is also possible, unfortunately, that a long period of institutional life may have a corrupting effect.

Ferguson's opinion appears to be based on the fact that among his 'ordinary' Glasgow boys the 'ratio of convictions to boys convicted was higher between the ages of eight and eleven . . . than at ages over eleven'.[4] Roper's two investigations dealt, it will be recalled, with various types of prisoner, among whom the first and less hardened Wakefield group had a lower percentage (27 per cent) of convictions before the age of twenty-one than had the (tougher) subjects of his later investigation at the same prison, while the latter, with 32 per cent convicted under twenty-one, in turn ranked below the Dartmoor convicts, of whom 41 per cent had had convictions before they were twenty-one.[5] Among the Wakefield prisoners, moreover, 66 per cent of those with a previous prison record, and 50 per cent of those previously convicted but not confined, were under twenty-one at first conviction. On the basis of this somewhat slender information, together with his own (not subsequently validated) clinical assessment, Roper reached the conclusion that 'the differences are marked, and show that the likely recidivist tends to start young'.[6] If, however, seventeen instead of twenty-one is used as the limit for 'starting young', rather stronger support for this generalization is forthcoming, since out of 1,100 Wakefield prisoners 24 per cent had been convicted before this age, while as many as 47 per cent of the eighty-six Wakefield corrective trainees and 48 per cent of the Dartmoor recidivists were so convicted. Spencer's comparison of Dartmoor convicts with the presumably less hardened inmates of Maidstone prison likewise showed a higher proportion of convictions under the age of eighteen among the former;[7] but Benson, who also investigated hardened types at Dartmoor and Parkhurst, found that 'A late first conviction seems to have very little correlation with failure or success', the proportions with adult first convictions being 42 per cent for Dartmoor and 34 per cent for Parkhurst. In the Parkhurst group (who, however, numbered only fifty) 'the success rate of those with convictions below the age of twenty was 60 per cent, while those with adult first convictions showed a rate of 72 per cent'.[8] In Dartmoor an overall success rate of

[1] Glueck, S. and E. T. (1930), p. 248. [2] Otterström (1946). [3] Ahnsjö (1941), p. 290.
[4] Ferguson (1952), p. 17. [5] Roper (1950), p. 17. [6] Roper (1951), p. 246.
[7] Spencer (1954), pp. 112 and 142. [8] Benson (1953), p. 201.

60 per cent 'applied equally to early and late convictions'. But Benson himself emphasizes the danger of drawing deductions from his sparse material. We should, perhaps, be content with the cheerful inference that it is, apparently, never too late to mend.

Equally scanty and miscellaneous is the evidence produced by those investigators who are disposed to doubt the precociousness of determined criminals. Healy and Bronner report that the heaviest rate of failure amongst their group of 420 boys was among those first convicted between ten and fourteen years of age (66 per cent); while for their 255 girls, those first convicted at fifteen had the highest rate of failure (56 per cent), and for both groups the lowest rates (42 per cent for boys and 40 per cent for girls) were achieved by those whose first court record was acquired at the age of sixteen.[1] Norval Morris offers little evidence, and indeed the material in his main study gives no clue as to whether his early starters had particularly bad records. Fernald, whose study, it will be recalled, dealt only with women, found that only 6·8 per cent of her 587 subjects had been convicted before they were sixteen, while more than half (52·8 per cent) had had a clear record up to the age of twenty-four. On the strength of this she observed that 'for the most part, there is no proof that the most serious female delinquents have begun their criminal careers in childhood or early youth'.[2]

Finally Otterström's investigation suggests that, as so often, what looked like promising generalizations threaten to fall to pieces as material becomes more abundant and discrimination grows sharper. It will be recalled that this investigation covered other categories beside those known to be delinquent. Neither amongst the delinquent nor amongst those removed from their homes for 'prophylactic reasons' was there any clear sign that those who became the subjects of official action at a particularly early age were specially bad risks. Of the latter, she wrote, 'It cannot be shown . . . that the fact of having been taken in charge before or after seven years of age has any significance for the prognosis in respect of criminality'. As for those who had been taken into care 'on account of slight or severe delinquency', the total risk in their case was found to be 'higher for those who came into contact with the authorities at a later age than for those who were in this situation at an earlier age. Thus there is no indication that delinquency arising at an early age gives a worse prognosis'.

Although it appears that both for non-delinquent children and for those actually sentenced by the court, 'symptoms of delinquency of any sort are a serious omen which foreshadow the future development . . .', the author concludes that 'no information is given by this material as to whether the fact of such symptoms first arising at an early or a late age gives any indication as to the final prognosis. It is quite possible that a larger material showing more pronounced age-differences would have given results in one direction or the other'.[3]

[1] Healy and Bronner (1926), p. 256. [2] Fernald and others (1920), p. 144.
[3] Otterström (1946), pp. 309–10.

III

Perhaps it would be absurdly optimistic to hope that any proposition about the significance of early criminal behaviour as a predictor of subsequent criminality could emerge from this welter of studies of offenders of both sexes and different ages, and of inmates of different types of institutions, in different countries, with different histories, kept under observation over different periods—especially when the bulk of even this material refers, not to offenders in general, but almost exclusively to those who have been deprived of their liberty. About the after careers of those not deprived of their liberty, 'absolutely nothing', as Radzinowicz[1] has reminded us, is generally known. Clearly, even if we accept all the available evidence at its face value (and, as has already been indicated, there are risks in that), the prevailing opinion amongst criminologists as to the ominous significance of early criminality must still be regarded as only a hypothesis in need of much more rigorous testing than has yet been possible. Indeed, there has been little significant advance since Sellin, after an extensive review of relevant material, came despondently to the conclusion nearly twenty years ago that 'the research student who in the pursuit of an answer to the question of the relationship of age to crime consults the reports just mentioned, is doomed to disappointment'.[2]

This disappointment is regrettably typical of contemporary social research; and the no less typical reasons for it are not far to seek, and have already been mentioned in other contexts. Foremost among them is the devastating lack of precision in the terms employed. Even the concept of 'first delinquency' itself is defined in widely differing terms by different authors. Most commonly the 'age of first delinquency' is taken to be the age at which the subject was first found guilty by a court—an interpretation which, though certainly arbitrary, is at least unambiguous; but occasionally (as for instance at least once in the work of the Gluecks) the notion of 'first appearance of delinquent behaviour' is substituted—a definition which, incidentally, is calculated to yield a most alarming prognosis in the event of the hypothesis that early starters become hardened offenders proving to be true; for there can be few indeed whose symptoms of what, in old-fashioned language, would have been called 'naughtiness' do not date from a very tender age. Yet even the Gluecks themselves have admitted that 'when the child first begins to display aberrancies of conduct it is very difficult to say whether these are the true danger signals of future persistent delinquency or merely transient manifestations of a healthy trying of his wings. Bits of identical behavior may, at this early stage, be symptomatic of two divergent roads of development'. Actually, 'a fourth of the 500 non-delinquents in this research showed danger signals that might easily have been misinterpreted'.[3]

More elusive still are the other terms in the equation. The 'confirmed criminality' which an early start purports to augur could be a matter of the

[1] Radzinowicz, in Davies and others (1945), p. 160. [2] Sellin (1940), p. 13.
[3] Glueck, S. and E. T. (1951), pp. 257 and 288.

duration of a criminal history, or of the number of convictions, or of the frequency of convictions or of the gravity of the later offences. These are all different dimensions. A criminal career which begins with a theft of sweets at the age of eight, and continues to accumulate further convictions for minor dishonesties every few months for the best part of half a century, is not at all the same as one which, with a similar beginning, later extends to steadily more and more ambitious schemes of burglary, accompanied perhaps with violence for, say, twenty-five years, and then suddenly ceases. Human motivation being as complex as it is, we can hardly hope to establish any relationship between the age of inception of a criminal career and its subsequent course, if we are not prepared to break down loose generalizations about 'hardened' or 'habitual' recidivists into much more precise categories. At the very least we need to treat duration of criminality, frequency of conviction and gravity of offences as distinct quantities.

Nor is there any consistency in the choice of age groups. Largely no doubt on account of the need to make do with whatever information happens to be available, the groupings used by different investigators, as well as their conceptions of what is meant by 'early', are thoroughly miscellaneous. Some discriminate between eight-year-olds and ten-year-olds, while others make no subdivisions under the age of twenty-one. The youth who is first convicted at the age of eighteen would rank as an early starter to some investigators and a late one to others. Indeed, in more than twenty studies which have provided material for this analysis, there are no two which have used categories sufficiently homogeneous to make their findings comparable. In consequence it remains impossible for any one piece of research to be used to corroborate or to correct another.

Still other complications also have to be reckoned with. The material available for judging the significance of the age of first delinquency among those serving the same type of sentence—as for example corrective trainees in a particular prison—is generally far too scanty to count for much. Yet, if this material is supplemented by comparisons between groups undergoing different types of penal treatment, these are liable to be distorted by the fact that a history of early criminality may itself influence the sentence imposed. The chance of a Borstal sentence, for example, is certainly increased for those who already have a considerable record of offences; and since only young men and women are eligible for Borstal, a long record in this case almost inevitably means one that begins early; and the discovery that Borstal inmates tend to have embarked early on their criminal careers may be due only to the fact that those who began young are particularly likely to be selected for Borstal treatment.

Again, much depends upon the length of the follow-up period and upon the ages of the subjects at the time that investigations are made. Thus Otterström found that the annual risk of failures in the case of boys in her Group II (the mildly delinquent with bad homes) 'aged between fifteen and twenty years is higher for those who came into contact with the authorities before the age of eleven years than for those who came into contact later'. But, 'if the total risks by the age of thirty-five years are compared it is found that the risk is higher for those who came into contact with the authorities later'.[1] Those whose criminality has begun early have, by definition, a relatively long period of exposure to the risk of recidivism; but, if they are still young when their records are investigated, their full subsequent history will not have had time to manifest itself. To quote Sellin again, 'since (1) the likelihood of a person's becoming a second offender is many times greater than that of his becoming a first offender; (2) the probability of a person's committing a subsequent crime increases with each new conviction . . . there is every reason to assume that a person who begins his delinquency in youth or who continues his career as juvenile delinquent into the youth period, is much more exposed to the hazard of recidivism than are those who begin their criminal careers later in life'.[2]

On the question of the significance of an early start in criminal behaviour, we are thus left with a mass of confused and contradictory evidence. On the one hand the theory that criminality is a symptom of 'immaturity' seems to amount to little more than a repetition in somewhat grandiose terms of well-known facts about the age-distribution of offenders; while, on the other hand, the hypothesis that those who begin early are likely to go on is certainly not proven, and cannot even claim to be supported by a preponderance of the available evidence. Perhaps the most that can be said is that Frey's 'frühkriminelle' do correspond to a definite and recurring type of recidivist, even while we are unable to give even an approximate indication of the part which this type plays in the whole picture of recidivism; or of the extent to which in other cases early criminality may turn out to be a false alarm.

[1] Otterström (1946), pp. 307–8. [2] Sellin (1940), p. 116.

CHAPTER VI

Studies in Criminological Prediction

I

MOST of the authors whose work has been reviewed so far have not made it altogether clear whether their work is primarily intended to uncover the causes of delinquency or to predict its occurrence: they take for granted, so to speak, that you can only foretell that something is going to happen if you know the reasons why it should. Thus the Gluecks, more than one of whose researches have culminated in the construction of a prediction table, also claim to have 'unraveled and laid out the separate strands of the tangled skein of causation';[1] and such expressions as 'probable causal factors' or 'aetiology' are freely used in their concluding chapters. In marked contrast is the attitude of Mannheim and Wilkins, who roundly declare that 'there is no way of knowing whether the word "cause" may or may not be reasonably applied to any of our factors. We shall make no claim to unravel causes of recidivism and we would not claim that even those factors which we find to be most highly associated with failure are in any part a cause of such failure. If we show that truancy is associated with recidivism the remedy would not be likely to be found in making truancy impossible. Truancy and recidivism may reflect a common element of some other factor or factors which so far we may have been unable to isolate, describe or measure.'[2] These authors, in short, do not look upon prediction experiments as anything more than experiments in prediction; and they are, accordingly, careful to emphasize their scepticism by consistently printing the word 'cause' in inverted commas.

Philosophically speaking, it is indeed doubtful whether any rigid distinction between the causative and the 'merely' predictive will stay put, thanks to the slippery meaning of causation as applied to social phenomena. Statistical predictions are always based on observed associations between phenomena; they take the form of statements, that, where A is present, experience teaches that B is likely to follow. In those cases, however, in which we do not, as we say, 'know why' this should be so, such associations are said to be 'merely' empirical or predictive. In medical practice, for example, some treatments, such as shock therapy for mental depression, are said to be empirical because they are not based on knowledge of the 'causes' of the disease for which they are prescribed. In the last resort, however, this distinction between 'causal' understanding and observed associations that have no rational explanation seems to be merely a matter of the length of the chain of association involved.

[1] Glueck, S. and E. T. (1951), p. 272. [2] Mannheim and Wilkins (1955), pp. 43–4.

As I have said elsewhere, 'the search for causal connections between associated phenomena simply resolves itself in turn into a long process of "explaining" one association in terms of another. If a person becomes ill with what are known as diabetic symptoms, we measure the sugar-content of his blood. If this is higher than that found in people not exhibiting such symptoms, we say that the high sugar-content is the *cause* of the illness; which is only another way of saying that the two are linked by a law of association previously established. If we go further and ask why the diabetic has so much sugar in his blood, this in turn is said to be "explained" by a failure of the pancreas to function normally, that is to say, by an observed association between a certain condition of the pancreas and the sugar-content of the blood. And so on, with one law of association following another, until we are at last stuck with something which we have not yet been able to associate consistently with anything else.'[1] The longer the chain, the more satisfying is its supposed capacity as an explanation; and yet each of its links, individually, is nothing more than an 'empirically observed' association.

Philosophical subtleties apart, however, in practice the distinction between 'diagnostic' and 'predictive' researches in the field of social phenomena is plain enough, as is well illustrated by the passage just quoted from Mannheim and Wilkins; and it is from their success in prediction, more than from anything else that the social sciences derive their title to rank as genuinely scientific, and their right to the name which they carry.

Actually, predictive techniques, most of which embody the same basic statistical design, have been used to forecast social or personal behaviour in a number of fields. Some of these remain more or less academic exercises. It is for instance unlikely that the work of Dr Burgess and his collaborators[2] on the prediction of adjustment in marriage carries much weight when it comes to making, accepting or rejecting a real-life offer of marriage. On the other hand, extensive practical use has been made of similar techniques in vocational guidance or selection; and these also, inasmuch as they are in essence devices for forecasting who is likely to be successful at what, deserve to be classified as instruments of prediction. In the field of social pathology, delinquent behaviour has been the chief subject in relation to which predictive exercises have been attempted, and in which the results of such exercises have actually influenced practical decisions; though in the United States tables have also been worked out to predict at an early stage which mothers of illegitimate children would be likely to keep and which to part with their babies.[3]

The technical methods involved in statistical prediction have been so fully described elsewhere that detailed description seems unnecessary here. The reader who seeks further information cannot do better than consult the admirable exposition with which Mannheim and Wilkins[4] have prefaced their own predictive study, in which will also be found a review of all important

[1] Wootton (1950), p. 18. [2] Burgess and Cottrell (1939).

[3] Meyer and others (1956).

[4] Mannheim and Wilkins (1955), especially chapters I and IV.

work on criminological prediction previously published. In brief, the essential procedure is to derive from case records factors which can be shown to be consistently associated with the 'criterion' which it is desired to forecast. In the case of criminological predictions, this means, of course, factors associated with subsequent delinquent acts by the subjects studied. In so far as experience shows the presence of these factors to have increased the probability of delinquency in the past, it is presumed that in similar circumstances the same will be true also in the future. The factors in question are, therefore, combined, in accordance with one or other of various statistical techniques, in the hope that they will serve as reliable predictors of such behaviour on future occasions.

A few examples may help to illustrate the more striking variations that have been evolved in criminological investigations on this main theme, as well as the problems that emerge and the contribution which this type of exercise has made, or might make, to the real-life business of dealing with anti-social behaviour. The earlier studies, as might be expected, were more concerned with the prediction of recidivism than with the more difficult task of detecting future criminals in a population with a hitherto clean record; and, again as might be expected, predictive experiments in the sphere of criminality have appealed particularly to the authorities responsible for deciding, under the system of indeterminate sentences which obtains in many countries, the date at which a convict should be released on parole. Among the earlier investigations on these lines is that of Vold, who worked out the correlation of thirty-four factors with the subsequent conduct of prisoners paroled from the Minnesota State Prison and State Reformatory from 1922-27. The results were as shown below:

Number of cases	*Correlation obtained*	*Pre-parole Categories compared with 'Outcome on Parole'*
1,192	·283	Previous criminal record.
1,192	·241	Marital status at time of offence.
1,192	·237	County from which received.
1,187	·227	Prison punishment record.
1,186	·214	Social type of inmate (six place classification).
1,185	·208	Work habits prior to conviction.
1,191	·208	Occupation at or before conviction (six place scale).
1,192	·204	Nature of crime of which convicted.
1,192	·200	Size and type of community in which offence was committed.
1,180	·183	Size and type of community in which inmate was brought up.
1,175	·179	Habits and character: whether ambitious or lazy.
1,175	·173	Habits and character: whether honest or dishonest.
1,175	·149	Habits and character: use of drugs.
1,179	·145	Institute of Child Welfare classification of occupation.[1]
1,175	·145	Habits and character: use of liquor.

[1] The 'Institute of Child Welfare classification of occupation' represents merely the application of another schedule of classifications to the category 'Occupation at or before conviction'. The table, therefore, really represents only 33 different pre-parole factors.

Number of cases	*Correlation obtained*	*Pre-parole Categories compared with 'Outcome on Parole'*
1,189	·142	Mobility of inmate before conviction.
917	·139	Estimate of inmate's mentality (by prison officials).
1,093	·103	Home condition (whether parents are living, dead, separated).
1,192	·092	Length of maximum sentence imposed.
722	·088	Mental age (from mental tests).
1,192	·088	Number of associates in offence for which convicted.
1,175	·088	Habits and character: sex immorality.
973	·086	Weight (in pounds).
1,188	·083	Education of inmate before conviction.
1,184	·083	State or country where born.
766	·081	Number of siblings in inmate's family.
1,192	·079	Months in prison before parole was granted.
654	·079	Whether trial judge favoured clemency for inmate.
665	·077	Intelligence Quotient (from tests).
1,192	·074	Whether inmate pleaded guilty or not guilty.
618	·074	Whether county attorney favoured clemency for inmate.
983	·069	Height (in inches).
1,184	·068	Judgment of prison conduct (made by prison officials).
1,192	·060	Age at conviction.

Vold (1931), p. 84

Similarly, at a later date (1951), Lloyd E. Ohlin has described prediction tables designed to assist in the making of parole decisions in the Illinois State Penitentiary system. These were based on the following twelve predictive factors:[1] (1) the type of offence, (2) the nature of the subject's sentence, (3) the type of offender (e.g. whether a first offender, or whether the offence could be classed as purely 'technical'), (4) the status of his home, (5) the degree of his family's interest in him (as shown by such things as letters or visits received while in prison), (6) his social type (e.g. whether an 'erring' or socially inadequate citizen, or a drunkard), (7) his work record, (8) his community (e.g. whether urban or rural), (9) his prospective job on parole, (10) the number of his associates in crime, (11) his personality (e.g. whether 'unstable' or 'egocentric') and (12) a psychiatric prognosis. The score of each convict paroled was then calculated under each of these headings in accordance with a prescribed system of marking, and the results correlated with his subsequent record. By applying this scale Ohlin found[2] that in the period 1940–45 of those who had between five and ten favourable points 3 per cent had violated their parole, while 75 per cent of those with five or six unfavourable marks had done so. In the light of this experience it was suggested that the factors listed might well be used as predictors to guide future decisions as to who should and who should not be paroled.

In their *Criminal Careers in Retrospect*, the Gluecks sought to construct a prediction table from experience of the after-careers of the 510 reformatory graduates, originally investigated in their earlier work on 500 *Criminal Careers*, during a fifteen-year span after release. The factors which they found

[1] Ohlin (1951) p. 52.
[2] ibid., p. 58.

to be predictive of subsequent criminality, and the percentage of cases in which these were associated with actual failure, were as follows:[1]

Prediction factors and sub-categories	*Percentage incidence of criminality*
Number of children in family	
Seven or more children	26·7
Two to six children	33·2
One child	48·1
Economic status of parents	
Dependent or marginal	27·5
Comfortable	39·8
Skill of father	
Unskilled	23·3
Semi-skilled or skilled	36·1
Intelligence of offender	
Not feebleminded	30·5
Feebleminded	40·8
Age at first delinquency	
Fourteen and older	24·7
Under fourteen	36·3[2]

By assigning points in accordance with the figures in this table, and then classifying their subjects into those who remained serious offenders, those who committed only minor offences, those who reformed completely and those who had a temporary lapse after a period of reform, the Gluecks concluded that 'if an offender scores under 150 he has two chances in ten (22 out of 100) of continuing to be a serious offender during a fifteen-year period following expiration of a reformatory sentence, almost three chances in ten of becoming a minor offender; four in ten of reforming entirely and less than one in ten of relapsing into criminality after a long period of good behavior'. 'But if an offender scores 180 or more he has almost seven chances in ten of remaining a serious offender, less than two in ten of becoming a minor offender or of reforming entirely.'[3]

In Switzerland in 1951, Frey published a predictive system based on the following ten groups of factors: (1) hereditary disease, (2) personality type, (3) 'family milieu', (4) 'leisure milieu', (5) educational difficulties, (6) attitude to the offence, (7) early criminality and (8) nature of the offence, (9) behaviour during sentence and (10) behaviour after licence.[4] For this he claims that 84 per cent of correct predictions could have been made in the seventy-five cases from which it was derived.

[1] It should be noted that the number of cases from which these percentages are derived is not constant, and ranges in fact from 27 to 311. This fact perhaps explains some of the oddities apparent in this table, notably the high percentage incidence of recidivism in the small family.

[2] Glueck, S. and E. T. (1943), p. 224.

[3] ibid., p. 225.

[4] Frey (1951), pp. 326–8.

In this country the credit of pioneering research in criminological prediction belongs to Mannheim and Wilkins for their work in calculating the chances that male Borstal inmates will transgress again after they are released. The 'predictive equations' reached by these investigators read as follows:[1]

	Score
If evidence of drunkenness	24
If any prior offence(s) resulted in fine	9
If any prior offence(s) resulted in committal to prison or to Approved School	8
If any prior offence(s) resulted in a term on probation	4
If *not* living with parent or parents	7·5
If home is in industrial area*	8
If longest period in any one job was:	
Less than one month	11·7
Over 4 weeks up to 6 weeks	10·4
Over 6 weeks up to 8 weeks	9·1
Over 2 months up to 3 months	7·8
Over 3 months up to 4 months	6·5
Over 4 months up to 6 months	5·2
Over 6 months up to 9 months	3·9
Over 9 months up to 12 months	2·6
Over 1 year up to 18 months	1·3
Over 18 months	0

* Any town where the ratio of the rateable value of industrial to total hereditaments exceeded 0·009.

In the 385 cases in which all this information was available it was found that 87 per cent of those who scored from 0–9·9 points were 'successful', in the sense that they were not reconvicted for at least an average of 3½ years after discharge: while, for those with scores of between 10·0 and 14·9 points, the proportion of successes was 67 per cent: for scores between 15·0 and 23·9, 60 per cent: between 24·0 and 39·9, 34 per cent; and for those scoring 40·0 and upwards, 13 per cent. The proportion of successes in the group as a whole stood at 57 per cent.[2]

All the foregoing examples (which are only a selection from a very much larger volume of studies) are concerned with the prediction of recidivism in the case of persons already convicted of offences. In their latest work on juvenile delinquency, however, the Gluecks have attempted to go further, and to derive from data relating both to presumably innocent controls and to known delinquents an instrument by which prospective offenders might be identified before they have actually graduated as such. Three alternative tables have been evolved by the Gluecks for this purpose, one based on 'social' factors, one on Rorschach tests and one on psychiatric assessments. The factors included in the 'social' table and the weights assigned

[1] Mannheim and Wilkins (1955), p. 145.

[2] ibid., p. 146.

to them, which are derived from the frequency of their occurrence amongst the delinquents, read as follows:[1]

	Score
1. Discipline of boy by father—	
Overstrict or erratic	72·5
Lax	59·8
Firm, but kindly	9·3
2. Supervision of boy by mother—	
Unsuitable	83·2
Fair	57·5
Suitable	9·9
3. Affection of father for boy—	
Indifferent or hostile	75·9
Warm (including over-protective)	33·8
4. Affection of mother for boy—	
Indifferent or hostile	86·2
Warm (including over-protective)	43·1
5. Cohesiveness of family—	
Unintegrated	96·9
Some elements of cohesion	61·3
Cohesive	20·6

From these ratings the authors calculate that the chance of a boy becoming delinquent ranges from 2·9 per cent for those with scores of under 150 up to 98·1 per cent for those with scores of 400 and over.

In the second table, based on character traits as determined in the Rorschach personality test, the scoring is as shown below:[2]

	Score
1. Social Assertion—	
Marked	75·9
Slight or suggestive	63·8
Absent	39·7
2. Defiance—	
Marked	91·0
Slight or suggestive	76·7
Absent	34·9
3. Suspicion—	
Marked	67·3
Slight or suggestive	47·3
Absent	37·5
4. Destructiveness—	
Marked	77·7
Slight or suggestive	69·9
Absent	35·7
5. Emotional lability—	
Marked	75·2
Slight or suggestive	65·0
Absent	40·0

For this table it is claimed that those with scores of less than 205 have a 14·7 per cent chance of delinquency, as against a risk of 91·7 per cent for those

[1] Glueck, S. and E. T. (1951), p. 261.
[2] ibid., p. 263.

with scores of from 355–379. In this case the chance does not, however, appear to increase smoothly as the score rises. Those scoring 305–329 points have a higher risk of delinquency (97·0 per cent) than those with scores of 355–379, for whom the figure is 91·7 per cent.

Finally, in the third table,[1] in which personality traits as determined in a psychiatric interview are used as predictors, we have the following method of scoring:

	Score
1. Adventurous—	
Present in marked degree	75·3
Not prominent or noticeably lacking	35·4
2. Extroverted in action—	
Present in marked degree	66·5
Not prominent or noticeably lacking	37·8
3. Suggestible—	
Present in marked degree	69·4
Not prominent or noticeably lacking	35·5
4. Stubborn—	
Present in marked degree	83·4
Not prominent or noticeably lacking	39·0
5. Emotionally unstable—	
Present in marked degree	62·0
Nor prominent or noticeably lacking	26·5

Judged by this standard, the chances of delinquency rise from 4·5 per cent for those with scores of less than 195 to a maximum of 94·0 per cent for those with 295–319, dropping back to 91·8 per cent for those with 320–344, and finally rising again to 93·5 per cent for those with 345 or more points.

With three separate predictive instruments, the risk naturally arises that each may give a different answer. In this case, however, the Gluecks find that the discrepancies are small. 'All three tables place a boy in his proper predictive category in 49 per cent of the cases, while in an additional 37·8 per cent, two of the three tables do so, making a total of 86·8 per cent of the 424 boys concerning whom two or all three of the tables are in correct agreement as to the predictive category in which they belong. In 2·4 per cent of the cases all three tables incorrectly identify delinquents and non-delinquents and vice versa, while in an additional 10·8 per cent two of the three tables do so, making a total of only 13·2 per cent in which two or all three of the tables place a boy in the wrong predictive category'.[2] Where any marked divergence between the findings of the various tables does occur, the authors argue that this should be treated as an indication of whether the primary aim of preventive measures should be the improvement of environmental factors or of personal qualities. Thus it may be supposed that a boy for whom a low delinquency potential is shown by the social table, and a high one by the Rorschach or the psychiatric predictors, might be rescued by psychotherapy; while in the reverse case the inference is that efforts should be made to get his family to modify their mutual relations. No mathematical combination of the three modes of prediction has, however, been suggested by these

[1] Glueck, S. and E. T. (1951), p. 264. [2] ibid., pp. 266–7.

authors; and the fact that 'the five factors in the social background can be more easily and widely obtained than the factors of the other two prediction tables, simply because there are many more persons skilled in gathering social data'[1] gives a decided practical advantage to the social table. In subsequent attempts at validation (on which more is said below)[2], it is, no doubt for this practical reason, the social table which has been generally used.

Yet another line of experiment is that devised by Hathaway and Monachesi in the Minnesota Multiphasic Personality Inventory. This, as its formidable name suggests, is 'a psychometric instrument designed ultimately to provide, in a single test, scores on all the more clinically important phases of personality'. It consists of a series of statements (no less than 550 in all) covering a 'wide range of subject matter, from the physical condition of the individual being tested to his morale and social attitude',[3] to each of which the subject is asked to answer 'true', 'false' or 'cannot say'. The results are then marked according to a prescribed scale intended to ensure that any subjective bias on the part of the investigator is eliminated, and that the findings will be the same, no matter who operates the tests. The tests themselves, which are said to 'derive from psychiatric practice', were primarily designed with the object of revealing 'neurotic or psychotic personality syndromes'. Their authors, accordingly, expect them to predict only such cases of delinquency as are analogous to mental illness; and they are not convinced that all delinquents necessarily fall into this category.

After trying out the tests on children of various ages and of both sexes, the authors conclude that certain of the scales 'have an excitatory role in the actuarial numbers predicting the development of asocial behaviour'.[4] Translated into the vernacular, this seems to mean that these scales can be successfully used as predictors of delinquency. When, moreover, additional tests were devised to act as checks on the honesty of the answers given to others, a correlation was found between known delinquency and high scores for dishonest answers.[5] At the same time the scope of this particular predictive device is admitted to be limited by the fact that 'a large proportion of delinquent adolescents do not show definite characteristics as measured by this instrument that would link them to known patterns of illness'.[6]

II

In any attempt to assess the contribution which these and similar experiments make to the understanding and control of anti-social behaviour, the obvious first question to be asked is: what evidence is there that they do in fact predict correctly? The simplicity of this question is, however, deceptive; for it conceals a cluster of other questions which are best tackled in distinct stages. Confusion can arise if attempts are made to combine more than one stage in a single operation, since it then becomes impossible to see at what exact point

[1] Glueck, S. and E. T. (1951), p. 269. [2] See pp. 183 ff.
[3] Hathaway and Monachesi (1953), p. 13. [4] ibid., p. 136.
[5] Hathaway and Monachesi (1952), p. 706. [6] Hathaway and Monachesi (1953), p. 136.

the errors responsible for any inaccuracy in the final results have crept in.

At the first stage, attempts at validation are merely hypothetical. They do no more than show that, *had* certain predictive formulae been applied to a population whose subsequent history is, by definition, known, these formulae (which are themselves derived from the history of that population) *would* have proved to be reliable forecasters. Such hypothetical statements are commonly expressed in terms of the percentages of correct answers that could have been obtained by the use of the relevant formulae, or alternatively in terms of the degree of association of the 'predictors' with the 'predicted' result. But it has to be admitted that in such cases (and they comprise the bulk of so-called predictive studies in criminology) the term 'prediction' is something of a misnomer. No future event has in fact been forecast. Indeed, the claim that a demonstrable association of certain past events with other succeeding past events is 'prediction' is little more than tautological. The so-called 'prediction' is only another way of describing the existence of the association. For, it is self-evident that, if certain features of a given population are significantly correlated with particular elements in the subsequent history of that population, then anyone with fore-knowledge of this association could have predicted that history from these features.

At the same time the demonstration that past events have followed a recognizable pattern raises hopes that history will, in fact, repeat itself, and that, accordingly, this pattern may serve as a true predictor on some future occasion. The existence of a pattern at least demonstrates that the course of events is not always so irrational and inconsistent as to make the very possibility of prediction unthinkable. Even at the hypothetical level, therefore, it is pertinent to ask whether the degree of reliability of demonstrable associations has on past occasions been such that valid predictions could have been made. Yet at the same time it must be recognized that 'validity' is necessarily a relative term: cast-iron certainty, in the sense of associations that are one hundred per cent reliable, is admittedly out of the question. The critical issue, in short, turns on whether predictions based upon statistically demonstrable correlations would, or would not, have proved superior to those made in other ways: that is to say, on whether the reliability of the statistically demonstrable associations on which hypothetical predictions could have been made is better or worse than that of other kinds of guesses or forecasts.

To settle that question some comparative standard is required; and the next step is, therefore, to choose the standard that is most appropriate. Here one possible course is to measure the efficiency of 'predictive' tables against the probabilities indicated by the records of the whole population studied. As long ago as 1949, Messrs Ohlin and Duncan claimed that a 'truly rigorous comparison' of 'relative actual predictive efficiency' of forecasts could be made in this way. To illustrate their suggested procedure, they made an analysis of the histories of 5,624 cases paroled from one of the Illinois State penitentiaries from January 1, 1925, to December 31, 1935, dividing this total into two sub-groups composed, respectively, of those who had, and of of those who had not, violated their parole. The former group, it was found, comprised 40·1 per cent, and the latter 59·9 per cent of all those paroled; and from these figures it was argued that, in the absence of any other information whatsoever, the best guess in any individual case would always be 'non-violator', since, with a slight numerical preponderance of non-violators, the odds were always in favour of parole being kept. Obviously, forecasts on this basis, though more often right than wrong, would still be wrong in 40·1 per cent of cases, so that an error of this degree of frequency becomes a yardstick by which to measure the degree of improvement attained by the use of predictive techniques. On this basis, when the prospects of success on parole for the whole group were forecast in accordance with twenty-seven (unspecified) predictive factors, the proportion of wrong answers was reduced from 40·1 per cent to 32·5 per cent, showing a 'percentage reduction in the error of prediction' relative to the error entailed 'in prediction from knowledge of the over-all violation rate alone' of 19 per cent. When, however, the same authors proceeded to apply this standard to some fifteen other essays in criminological prediction, the results were found to be 'somewhat disappointing'. 'In only two instances do the reductions in error greatly exceed 25 per cent'; and the maximum percentage reduction of error recorded (43·0 per cent) occurred in a 1942 study covering only 226 cases. In a number of other instances, moreover, which were also examined by the same investigators, 'predictability runs even lower. Not a few prediction tables have been published where the reduction of error is exactly zero'!—so that we are led to the depressing conclusion that the 'routine application of these techniques to the types of data usually secured is in no sense a guarantee of substantial improvements in prediction over the crudest method available—prediction from total rates'.[1] These results, moreover, relate only to 'predictive techniques' which were hypothetical, as already defined, in that they showed the degree of improvement which would have been achieved, had they been applied to a group whose subsequent record is already known and from which they are themselves derived. Still more discouraging, when assessed by the same standard, was the potential efficiency of true predictions, i.e. those based on the application of factors derived from the experience of one group to predict the future of another group in apparently similar circumstances.

Rigorous though it may appear to be, however, the Ohlin-Duncan test is not the standard to which appeal is most likely to be made in real life. Its merits are academic rather than practical. The authorities who have to decide the future of offenders are unlikely, in the absence of any guidance from prediction tables, to make their decisions on the basis of a crude calculation of probabilities derived from the overall record of success or failure of a population similar to that whose fate they are required to determine. Nor is the Ohlin-Duncan criterion itself quite as objective as its inventors would have it appear. As Goodman has pointed out, 'The data available to the sociologist who attempts to construct a predictive instrument is determined by the decision procedure in practice, since he uses experience tables of persons whom the board decided to parole in the past. Hence the population

[1] Ohlin and Duncan (1949).

whose behavior the sociologist attempts to predict is not those persons appearing before the board (which would be the important population if the sociologist were interested in suggesting that the board fully utilize the predictive instrument in making the original decisions), but those persons whom the board has decided to parole. Clearly, after the sociologist has made a thorough study of the experience tables of those persons whom the board has paroled, he is not justified in suggesting that it fully utilize the predictive instrument he has developed in making decisions for all persons appearing before it.'[1] It follows, therefore, that, in the figure of 59·9 per cent successes to 40·1 per cent failures recorded by Ohlin and Duncan for their Illinois subjects, allowance must be made for the fact that this refers, not to the entire prison population which could have been paroled, but only to that fraction of it which actually was released. What the authorities have to decide, however, is what individuals are to be included in that fraction. To infer that because the figure for past successes *in this fraction* has exceeded 50 per cent, therefore success would be the best guess in the future for any individual in the *whole eligible population* is quite unjustifiable. In practice paroling authorities who assumed that, because the majority of their decisions had proved right in previous cases, therefore the odds were in favour of paroling *everybody* would soon find out their mistake! Plainly these odds can relate only to a population whose composition is similar to that of the original group from which they were calculated. The true implication is, not that everybody should be paroled, but that if selections continue to be made on lines similar to those of the past, the odds are in favour of their being successful. 'Similarity' in this sense, however, is far from being an objectively defined—or even definable—concept.

Much more credible as a criterion of predictive success is a comparison of the relative accuracy of forecasts made by persons of 'informed judgment', such as magistrates, probation officers or those who work in penal establishments, with those based on statistical 'prediction' tables. Materials for the application of this standard have, however, hitherto been only rarely available. Even those who are most emphatic as to the superiority of 'intuitive judgments' over 'mechanical calculations' have been somewhat slow to put their theories to the test by recording those judgments in advance of the events which they attempt to forecast, and then matching the results against more objective methods. Here and there, however, there have been exceptions—and amongst them is the Mannheim-Wilkins enquiry into the after-history of Borstal boys. In this case the forecasts based upon 'predictive tables' were matched against others made either by the governors of the institutions in which the subjects were detained, or by professional psychologists; and the results come out very strikingly to the credit of the predictive tables, even though, it must be stressed, the authors of these tables had never made the acquaintance of any of the subjects whose careers they were forecasting, whereas the Borstal governors had lived with the boys concerned for periods that usually exceeded a year. Actually the statistical procedures were a

[1] Goodman (1953), pp. 503–4.

least three times as efficient as the subjective judgments of Governors of the Institutions' in which the subjects had been detained, 'and more accurate than a psychologist's prognosis'.[1] And this result is the more remarkable, inasmuch as one of the authors of this investigation had some fifteen years previously recorded the opinion that 'Although it is impossible, without knowing the actual facts of the individual cases, to say whether the recorded opinions of the Governors, Medical Officers and Housemasters concerned give a true picture, it is evident from their reports that these officials are, for the most part, masters in the art of portraying with a few strokes even an apparently complicated individual. And that these pictures are essentially right in diagnosis and prognosis is shown by the fact that the known after-history is largely in harmony with the forecasts'.[2]

In other instances, several of which are quoted by Mannheim and Wilkins themselves, the advantage, though generally on the side of the predictive technique, is not quite so dramatic. Thus in Bavaria a statistical prediction worked out by Schiedt for 500 men discharged from Bavarian prisons in 1931 suggested that in 131 promising cases a failure rate of only 12·2 per cent could have been foretold, whilst at the other end of the scale it would have been possible to predict a 96·3 per cent failure rate for eighty-one incorrigibles, and a rate of 52·9 per cent for 288 'doubtfuls'. By contrast, the forecasts of the prison doctors would have been wrong in 26 per cent of their favourable and 28 per cent of their unfavourable prognoses, even though these only related to those members of the group (in all two-thirds of the total number of discharges) about which they felt able to be tolerably definite. Again, in Switzerland, Frey, though disposed to be critical of elaborate statistical methods, raised the correct proportion of his own intuitive forecasts (in seventy-five cases) from 74·6 per cent to 84 per cent by the use of the prognostic categories described on p. 177, in spite of the fact that these categories contained large subjective elements.

From these and similar examples[3] we may fairly conclude that intuitive forecasts, however they may be determined, are not always the best that can be got; better results might sometimes have been obtained by forgetting 'intuition' and 'intangibles' and relying on certain concrete pointers. These pointers are however, themselves only identifiable in the light of subsequent experience. To put the matter in another way, later history has provided clues which, had they been previously available, would have improved our ability to foretell that very history.

We thus reach the next and more crucial stage in validation, at which the reliability of these pointers must be tested for populations other than that from which they were derived. Here again answers may be given in terms of more than one standard. Judged by the Ohlin-Duncan criterion, the results are again dismal. In the predictive experiments reviewed by these authors, the materials for validation in the Ohlin-Duncan sense were available only in six cases. Of these the most successful showed a reduction in error as the

[1] Mannheim and Wilkins (1955), p. 141. [2] Mannheim (1940), pp. 252–3.
[3] See Mannheim and Wilkins (1955), pp. 19–21.

result of the application of predictive techniques of 25·4 per cent over the probabilities indicated by the record of the group of subjects as a whole. But the next best figure showed an improvement of only 2·4 per cent; and in the remaining four cases a zero figure was recorded in one, while those for the other three were actually negative. From this the authors infer that in at least half the cases actually *better* results would have been obtained by forgetting all about the so-called specifically predictive factors, and simply assuming that the odds in favour of the success or failure of a future group of parolees as a whole would correspond with the overall results shown by their predecessors;[1] but this inference, it must be appreciated, is subject to the important qualification mentioned on p. 184.

Where, alternatively, the criterion of 'informed judgment' has been used as a standard against which to measure the efficacy of actual predictive techniques, the results have been conflicting. In connection with the well-known Cambridge-Somerville Youth Study, initiated in Massachusetts in 1935, Dr Eleanor Glueck was invited to test the Glueck 'social prediction scale' on a sample of 100 boys, against the 'forecasts' of a selection committee consisting of one psychiatrist and two social caseworkers with special training in criminology using only their own judgment, undirected by any formal predictive technique. For this purpose, Mrs Glueck, we are told,[2] was supplied only with information relating to the five predictive factors specified by the Glueck social scale; but it is perhaps pertinent to recall that this information itself necessarily involved highly subjective judgments which must already have been made, not indeed by Mrs Glueck or her associates, but by workers connected with the experiment. The result proved tolerably flattering to the scale, since it appeared that Mrs Glueck's prediction would have proved correct in 91 per cent of the cases, as against a score of from 61·5 per cent to 65·3 per cent of correct forecasts by members of the Committee. In the case of those boys, twenty in all, who did actually become delinquent, there was not much to choose between the Glueck predictions and the Committee's forecasts. Where, however, the latter did fall down was in their undue pessimism over the eighty boys whose subsequent records proved satisfactory: about 50 per cent of these were correctly classified by the Committee as non-delinquent, whereas Mrs Glueck identified over 90 per cent of the non-delinquents.[3]

In several other cases, also, attempts have been made to test the validity of the Glueck social prediction table when operated in circumstances that differ in varying degrees from those of the original experiment. At the Hawthorne-Cedar Knolls School at Hawthorne, New York, this scale, along with the alternative predictive table derived from the Gluecks' earlier enquiry into delinquency, was tried out as a means of forecasting the risk of recidivism among children already receiving special educational and psychiatric treatment. In this instance that risk proved very much less than either the earlier or the later Glueck scale (there was little difference between the two sets of findings) would have indicated; but it is perhaps fair to add that these children

[1] Ohlin and Duncan (1949). [2] Thompson, R. E. (1953), pp. 289–97. [3] ibid., p. 295.

were given intensive and prolonged help with their problems, to the success of which the discrepancy may be in some degree a tribute.[1] Substantial claims have also been made for the capacity of one of the earlier Glueck social prediction scales to detect tendencies to misbehaviour among soldiers.[2] According to Mrs Glueck herself[3], by the use of this scale it should have been possible to spot as likely delinquents 84 per cent of a group of 200 soldiers who were found guilty of offences both in civilian and in military life; but it has not been made clear whether the scale would have been equally successful in picking out those who did not actually prove delinquent.[4] In Illinois, again, where under Dr Ohlin's influence prediction tables have actually made their way into practical use, it has been claimed that they have raised the accuracy of forecasts by as much as 36 per cent. On the other hand an elaborate analysis by the U.S. Department of Justice of the case histories of over 22,000 persons released from Federal penal institutions in 1930–35 led its authors to the conclusion that 'there was no evidence' that the use of prediction tables 'would produce any substantial improvement in the Federal parole practice'.[5] In Wisconsin an attempt, the results of which were published in 1950, has been made to test whether a set of factors found to be tolerably successful as predictors of success or failure for offenders on probation would be equally successful when applied to parolees, and also to assess the constancy of these factors over a period of time. In this case, the conclusion was that, at least on the basis of the data available, 'it is impossible to predict future behavior of the convict in Wisconsin, except for one or two categories, and except for a very short period of time'. The 'prediction tables for probation worked out elsewhere do not apply to Wisconsin parolees'.[6]

In Europe the Schiedt table, to which reference has already been made, has been applied, as reported by Mannheim and Wilkins, to a number of groups of ex-prisoners in various German cities. It can only be said that sometimes the results, as measured against the intuitive guesses of prison, medical, or otherwise experienced staffs, have been gratifying: and that sometimes they have not. When applied by the medical officer of another Bavarian prison to a group of 100 convicts discharged a year later than those from whom Schiedt drew his data, this table, it appears, would only have given 51 per cent of correct forecasts as against the doctor's own score of 71 per cent. On the other hand, when the Crimino-biological Service at Hamburg tried the scale on 200 prisoners examined between 1929 and 1933, it gave wrong answers in only 11·4 per cent of the favourable and 6·1 per cent of the unfavourable prognoses, whereas the corresponding figures for the Service's own guesses were 61·6 per cent and 46·7 per cent.[7] Perhaps, however, the explanation lies not so much in the quality of the scale as in the variability of the standard against which it is measured. The doctor in the first case may have been

[1] Mannheim and Wilkins (1955), p. 18. See also *Journal of Criminal Law, Criminology and Police Science* (November–December, 1953), p. 481.

[2] Schneider and others (1944). [3] Glueck, E. T. (1956), p. 20. [4] See below pp. 191, 192.

[5] Mannheim and Wilkins (1955), pp. 13–15. [6] Gillin (1950), p. 553.

[7] Mannheim and Wilkins (1955), pp. 19–20.

exceptionally skilful, or the members of the Service in the second exceptionally clumsy.

One of the most thorough attempts at validation is contributed by the Mannheim and Wilkins investigation itself. Having derived the data for their predictive table from the experience of one in every three inmates discharged from all Borstal institutions between August 1946 and July 1947, these investigators tested their findings by applying the resultant table to the discharges of those who had been admitted to one such institution in the last half of 1948. At the two ends of the scale, the predictive table scored a very high record of correct forecasts. In the group ranked as the most hopeful the predicted success rate was 87 per cent as against an actual result of 81 per cent; in the next class the figures were 67 per cent predicted, 68 per cent actually realized. At the other end of the scale, the predicted success rate for the class with the most pessimistic rating worked out at 13 per cent against a realized rate of nil; while the figure for the next lowest class stood at 34 per cent against an actual figure of 33 per cent. If the two top classes and the two bottom classes are each combined to form one group of hopefuls and one of incorrigibles, the Mannheim and Wilkins' prediction scale would have scored approximately 100 per cent success.[1] It is, however, fair to add that, in 126 of the 338 cases in the validation sample, no prediction was attempted. In these cases, which composed the middle group whose prospects of success appeared to be neither very bright nor very dim, prediction was not found to be practicable, at any rate not without additional information which was not generally available even in the original sample. The very high score of successful prediction thus relates only to some 60 per cent of the whole group.

Most of the investigations to which reference has up to this point been made are trying to forecast the future behaviour of persons who have already qualified as 'delinquents': these studies are, therefore, concerned with predictions of recidivism rather than with the detection of potential offenders in an undifferentiated population; and in practically every one of these cases also, as has already been said, the predictions are potential rather than actual; indeed, they might even ironically be described as 'retrospective', inasmuch as their authors can claim only to have been wise after the event.

Neither of these limitations applies to the much more venturesome experiment with the Gluecks' social prediction scale now in progress in New York City under the auspices of the City's Youth Board. In this experiment all the boys (223 in all) entering the first grade between September, 1952 and May, 1953, of two schools, each of which serves a district which has a declining population, a large influx of Negro and Puerto Rican population and a low socio-economic status, have been graded by the Glueck scale—the necessary data being obtained from home enquiries by caseworkers, from interviews with teachers by research workers and from social agencies who know the boys' families. From these gradings, which have been made independently by two raters, and submitted to Mrs Glueck for arbitration in case of dis-

[1] Mannheim and Wilkins (1955), p. 163.

agreement, each boy's chance of delinquency, as defined in the latest Glueck study,[1] has been predicted, and an annual follow-up is in progress to watch the outcome.[2] If the Glueck scale is reliable, this group should produce a considerable volume of delinquency, for about one-third of the children concerned have been assigned failure scores of 250 or more, which means a 50 per cent or greater chance of becoming delinquent. It will, however, be five years before the authors will feel able to judge whether the scale has enabled them correctly to identify the future delinquents. In the meantime, it seems a little unfortunate that, in a preliminary report on the project published by the Youth Board's Research Department, these high-score children are already referred to as 'delinquents', even though the authors are careful to point out, and indeed to underline, the fact that '*The designation "delinquent" does not indicate actual delinquent behavior on the part of the children so described.* It refers to boys who are *potentially* delinquent (a 50 per cent or more chance of becoming delinquent) in terms of the social predictive factors described by the Gluecks in *Unraveling Juvenile Delinquency*'[3]. It would have been simple enough, and would certainly have inspired more confidence, if these children had been described by some such term as 'high-score cases' rather than as 'delinquent'; nor is it reassuring to find that whereas in the earlier part of the report the label 'delinquent' is printed always in inverted commas, this precaution is later omitted.

III

Since the techniques employed in criminological prediction were first devised, very considerable efforts have been devoted to their improvement. Mostly these have been concerned with such questions as the number of factors to be included in the construction of a prediction table, or the elimination of overlapping (i.e. of cases in which different factors in effect repeat the same information and do not therefore add anything significant to the final result), or the method by which the various factors are weighted. By improvements in these and similar matters, the statistical efficiency of the whole operation has undoubtedly been very much increased, and much of the credit for the successful record of some of the most recent experiments must certainly be given to this progress in technique.

For practical purposes, however, the vital issue is the extent to which the experience of one population is a safe basis from which to predict the future of other populations in different times, places or social contexts. In the case

[1] 'Delinquency refers to repeated acts of a kind which when committed by persons beyond the statutory juvenile court age of sixteen are punishable as crimes (either felonies or misdemeanors)—except for a few instances of persistent stubbornness, truancy, running away, associating with immoral persons, and the like. Children who once or twice during the period of growing up in an excitingly attractive milieu steal a toy in a ten cent store, sneak into a subway or motion picture theatre, play hooky, and the like, and soon outgrow such peccadillos are not true delinquents even though they have violated the law.' (New York City Youth Board (1953), p. 19.)

[2] Whelan (1954), pp. 432–41. [3] New York City Youth Board (1953), p. 12.

of changes through time, methods have already been evolved for keeping a check upon the validity of a given set of prediction equations, at least in such relatively homogeneous populations as the output from a particular type of penal institution. By continuous sampling of later results, it is possible to detect the point at which a given prediction is beginning to give an increasing proportion of wrong answers.[1] The selection and weighting of the various factors in the prediction table can then be overhauled in the light of later experience, those which prove untrustworthy being discarded in favour of others which are more reliable; in this way, piecemeal revision of the original tables should keep the system running accurately for considerable periods.

Theoretically also it should be possible to use the same devices to modify predictions derived from the experience of one population so as to make them applicable also to others differing in nationality, race, sex, age, place of residence and so forth. But the difficulties here are more formidable; for the range of these social and ethnic differences is much greater than those likely to be found between relatively homogeneous populations at dates not very widely separated. Undoubtedly many of the failures of earlier experiments are accounted for by the light-hearted way in which prediction tables were applied to populations quite differently constituted from those from which they were derived. What is true in Illinois may not hold good for Wisconsin, while the factors that have proved good predictors in the case of boys may turn out to be quite hopeless when applied to girls (for whom, incidentally, fewer experiments in criminological prediction appear yet to have been tried). Commonsense alone would suggest that, when it comes to forecasting the history of one group from the experience of another that was quite differently constituted, expectations should be pitched low. For these reasons the New York Youth Board's testing of the Glueck scales should be very instructive, since these are being tried out on a sample of quite different ethnic composition from that of the population from which the scales were themselves constructed. In the original sample from which the Glueck prediction tables were derived the majority of the subjects were of English, Italian, Irish or Russian extraction. Only 2 per cent were Jewish boys, and no Negroes or Puerto Ricans were included. But in the sample from the New York schools in which the Youth Board's experiment is being conducted, nearly 59 per cent are Negroes, 23 per cent are white (and half of these are Jewish) and 18 per cent are Puerto Ricans.

The objective testing of criminological prediction tables demands, moreover, that those who are responsible for practical decisions about the treatment of actual or potential delinquents should be willing to sit back and let events take their course; and that is not always easy to do. In so far as administrators accept the hypotheses implied in prediction tables, they are bound to feel the urge to modify their own actions accordingly—by refraining, for example, from paroling those whose chances of renewed offences are rated highly, or by giving special help and attention to those designated as likely new recruits to the ranks of delinquency. A forecast that a particular

[1] See Mannheim and Wilkins (1955), pp. 218–20.

child is likely to become delinquent may thus be falsified by the fact that the very making of it provokes counter-measures: teachers, psychiatrists, social workers are mobilized to avert the threatened disaster. Such counter-measures, however, obviously modify the conditions of the original prediction, and so preclude its validation by experience.

Occasionally, however, the claims of science are allowed, in whole, or in part, to prevail over those of practical social welfare. Under the New York Youth Board's experiment in only one of the two selected schools will boys with high scores for prospective failure be given the opportunity of specially planned treatment: equally unpromising risks in the other school are to be left to take their chance of such help as is available in the ordinary way. By this means it is hoped both to prevent the validation of the forecasts from being distorted by therapeutic activities and, at the same time, to provide a check on the effectiveness of current methods of treatment.

Nevertheless it is one thing to forecast the behaviour of a tough American convict released on parole, and quite another to identify which child in a class of six-year-olds will later take to shoplifting or specialize in emptying gas-meters. For more reasons than one the prediction of recidivism is a much less formidable task than is the detection of future delinquents in a mixed population. For, in the first place, the chances of future criminality in a group which already has a record of offences are much greater than in a population not thus selected; and this fact itself obviates one source of error inherent in the use of predictive tables based on comparisons between delinquents and non-delinquent controls to identify the potentially delinquent members of an unselected population. In the latter case the comparative rarity of the phenomenon whose occurrence it is sought to predict may lead to a serious exaggeration of the risks. The fallacy involved is analogous to that which Asher[1] has shown to be consequential upon the use of similar methods to forecast from early symptoms the probability that particular subjects will be the victims of relatively infrequent diseases. Thus, to quote Asher's own illustration, if it is found that of 200 epileptic subjects, 24 per cent have suffered from infantile convulsions, while only 2 per cent of a control group composed of an equal number of 'normals' have been similarly affected, we may be tempted to conclude that any baby which suffers convulsions ought to be treated as a prospective epileptic. Since, however, the incidence of epilepsy in the whole population works out at only about one in 400, it follows that out of 40,000 people, 100 will on the average be epileptic, and that of these twenty-four will have been predictable from their convulsions in infancy. Yet in the same population approximately 800 (2 per cent of 40,000) normals will also have been convulsed. Hence preventive measures based on the prediction of epilepsy from infantile convulsions would result in some 800 subjects being treated, of whom only twenty-four actually become epileptics. In the prediction of delinquency similar miscalculations are likely to result from the use of similar methods; and these will not be shown up by the, so to speak, retrospective validations which are all that we have

[1] Asher (1954), p. 461.

generally had to rely upon up till now. Thus the Glueck predictive scale which, it is claimed, would have detected no less than 85 per cent of those members of a group of soldiers who were subsequently known to have committed offences, might well have also marked as future delinquents a much larger number whose military careers in fact turned out to be quite blameless. If delinquency, like epilepsy, is a relatively rare phenomenon, such a result would indeed by analogy with Dr Asher's figures, be extremely likely. But this error could not, by definition, be revealed by a 'validation' which examined only the records of the actual offenders. True prediction, however, obviously requires that white sheep should be as correctly identified as black ones.

Predictions of recidivism, on the other hand, are much less exposed to this risk of exaggerated pessimism, because those who have offended once are more than averagely likely to do so again: of the male ex-Borstal inmates discharged in 1952, for instance, over 54 per cent had been reconvicted by the end of 1956.[1] In cases such as this, where the bad risks actually outnumber the good ones, or in those where there is only a slight excess of good risks, the fact that a small proportion of the latter may exhibit a factor which is more commonly associated with subsequent failure than with success becomes a much less dangerous source of error.

Secondly, predictions of recidivism not infrequently owe their success to the weight which they give to factors which are by definition unavailable to those who aim to identify as yet undeclared delinquents; in particular to those factors which are connected with the subjects' previous criminal career. As van Bemmelen pointed out in a paper to the Third International Congress on Criminology, in every country in which he has examined the figures, 'the chance that an individual who has already been convicted will commit a new crime is much greater than the chance that one who has not been previously convicted will commit his first offence'. Indeed, on the basis of the English figures he finds that after the fifth conviction the chance that a man will return again to prison is about 85 per cent.[2] These facts (which incidentally throw a rather melancholy light on the effectiveness of current penal methods) greatly facilitate the prediction of recidivism; and it is, accordingly, not surprising to find that they are heavily drawn upon for this purpose. In the Mannheim and Wilkins' Borstal prediction, for instance, previous offences which have resulted in fines or in committal to a penal institution or in a period on probation rank second only to evidence of drunkenness as indicators of future offences. Indeed it has to be recognized that the comparative success of predictive techniques in forecasts of recidivism is largely due to the simple fact that one of the best predictors of future criminality is past criminal experience—a factor which is obviously unavailable in the case of new recruits to the ranks of criminality.

In any case it cannot be taken for granted that the factors which prove to be the best predictors of recidivism are necessarily identical with those

[1] Commissioners of Prisons Report for 1956, p. 99.

[2] van Bemmelen (1955), pp. 5–6, in a paper described by the author as 'an elaborated translation' of the 4th chapter of the 3rd ed. in Dutch (1952) of his textbook.

which indicate the likelihood of delinquency in persons whose records are hitherto blameless. The available evidence on the point is scanty and conflicting. In a paper prepared for the 1955 International Congress on Criminology, Pinatel[1] attempted a comparison of the factors which had been found to be predictive of delinquency in juveniles on the one hand and of recidivism among adult thieves on the other, as shown by the researches of M. Heuyer and Mme Galy. In this case the factors classed as either 'social' or 'biological' were found to be much the same in both groups. The only substantial differences related to school attendances, educational attainment and apprenticeship. The educational level of the recidivists was higher, and their record of school attendance worse, than those of the young offenders; and a smaller proportion of them had served apprenticeships. Since, however, these adults had presumably had their schooling or industrial training some years earlier than the young delinquents with whom they are contrasted, it may well be that these differences are due as much to changes in the educational world generally as to anything specifically connected with a disposition towards criminality. Similar contrasts might well be found between any groups of adults and of young people of the same ages. This possibility is not, however, discussed in Pinatel's paper.

In this context it is of interest that the Mannheim and Wilkins reaearches have indicated that even that reliable standby, the 'broken home', seems to lose its predictive value when it comes to forecasting the after-careers of those who have already come into serious conflict with the law: in these cases later experience seems to have more influence than early family life.[2] Healy and Bronner, also, as well as the Gluecks have reported similar findings.[3]

In any review of the whole range of studies in this field, one conspicuous feature is the variety of factors which have been used as the basis of prediction tables. Both objective facts (such as the length of a sentence) and subjective judgments (such as personality assessments) have been freely drawn upon; in some cases such 'hard' and 'soft' data have been combined in the same table. At one extreme of objectivity stands the Mannheim and Wilkins table. These investigators worked with conspicuous success from purely administrative records, without any personal acquaintance with their subjects. The Gluecks on the other hand have used very different types of factors in their various enquiries. Thus in their 'retrospective prediction' of offenders in the armed forces, the table used was based upon the educational level of the subject's parents, his own intelligence, his age at the time of his first offence, his age on starting work and his industrial skill; and numerous other variants are to be found in their work on *Criminal Careers in Retrospect*. In their latest juvenile delinquency enquiry the Gluecks have concentrated primarily on what they called 'social factors' (which, however, under their definition, are confined solely to relationships within the family), while offering also alternative systems based on psychiatric interviews or on Rorschach tests. All of the

[1] Pinatel (1955), pp. 12 and 17.
[2] Mannheim and Wilkins (1955), p. 87. See also below pp. 307, 308.
[3] See Healy and Bronner (1926), p. 123, and Glueck, S. and E. T. (1940), p. 108.

factors which they used involved large subjective elements: certainly we do not yet have reliable standards of parental discipline or affection, or of family integration.

In Illinois, again, the factors used for parole prediction have included a varied assortment of precise and imprecise data such as the offender's social circumstances (in a much wider sense than that in which the term is used by the Gluecks), his work record and his personality as assessed in psychiatric terms. Of the twelve factors quoted on p. 176, only two (the length of sentence and the number of persons associated in the crime) can be regarded as wholly objective. All the others involve varying elements of subjective judgment; nor is there any place in this table for detailed analysis of family relationships in the Glueck manner. In the Minnesota Multiphasic Personality Inventory social factors are wholly ignored and the data themselves are quite imprecise, though the method by which they are measured is as far as possible standardized. In this case an attempt has been made to get the best of both worlds by devices for the objective measurement of inherently elusive qualities. For whether a person labels a statement submitted to him as 'true' or 'false' is a question of fact about which there cannot be the kind of dispute raised by, for example, the judgment that he is insufficiently disciplined at home or that he shows marked social assertiveness. Treated strictly on their merits, therefore, the results of such tests as the MMPI stand on a par with, say, records of the number of jobs which a subject has held, or the size of his family: both are plain factual statements. Obviously, however, personality tests have only been invented in order to measure aspects of personality. The Minnesota people, along with those who use Rorschachs, would certainly infer that it is the degree of 'interpersonal sensitivity' or of 'social introversion or extraversion' or of other similar personal qualities which is the true predictor of delinquency, the tests themselves being, so to speak, merely the language through which these qualities find external expression. The ultimate data fall, therefore, into the 'soft' category; and the validity of the results turns upon the accuracy with which these are measured by the 'hard' facts of the subject's responses.

The foregoing are but selected examples of a variety which is as extensive as is the range of predictive studies that have been attempted. Although certain patterns (notably family relationships, work-record or, in appropriate cases, previous criminal history) recur fairly often, every investigator makes his own table and every one of these tables differs materially from every other. Some indeed of the variants are highly ingenious—as for instance the expectancy tables for paroled offenders which Ferris F. Laune[1] has based upon the judgments of their fellow prisoners. Wide, however, as is the variety of factors used in different prediction tables, these tables are sometimes criticized on the ground that it should be wider still. Dr Albert Reiss has, for instance, taken the Gluecks severely to task for their 'limited perspective of what are generally called "sociological factors" in delinquency'. As a sociologist, he questions the assumption that delinquency '"must have sprung from individuals whose

[1] See Monachesi (1950), pp. 278–80.

physical and psychologic equipment inclined them to select the anti-social culture as opposed to the conventional, or who found the former more congenial to their biologic tendencies'"; and that 'the primary causal factors are constitution, temperament, attitude and reactive patterns, and family milieu'. In his view, 'the social environment of the child from age six to sixteen is hardly so negligible a circumstance in his life-history'.[1] The force of this criticism lies in its emphasis on the fact that the Glueck type of enquiry is, by its very design, limited to only one aspect of what we have already seen to be a double-sided problem: inasmuch as the Gluecks are concerned only with the discovery of those individuals *within a more or less socially homogeneous group* who are especially likely to become social nuisances. The other half of the problem, which would involve predictions of the incidence of delinquency in contrasted social environments, is by definition excluded. To revert to the analogy already used, the Glueck method is like trying to forecast the incidence of typhoid in a given community solely by tests designed to show the susceptibility of different individuals to the disease, and without any regard to the presence or absence of sources of infection such as tainted food or water. If the object of the exercise is to eliminate the disease (and the object of criminological investigation is certainly to help in the elimination of crime) this would seem to be, at the least, a somewhat short-sighted procedure.

Even in the detection of susceptible individuals, moreover, it is assumed by the Glueck scale that nobody is ever deeply affected by any experience outside the intimacies of the family circle: nothing that happens to a child in school, street or playground apparently affects his chances of becoming delinquent. The many parents who express longings to get their children away from the temptations of bad neighbourhoods must be distressing themselves to no purpose; for, if there is trouble coming, it is the children themselves, or the way in which they are handled at home, not in the neighbourhood, which alone is recognized as the cause of it. Such conclusions are, however, only reached by what Reiss has called the Gluecks' 'cavalier treatment' of any of their own data which point in other directions—such, for instance, as the high degree of correlation between gang membership and delinquent activity.

Other American investigators have voiced criticisms on much the same lines. It has, for example, been suggested that the weakness of some predictions may be due to their failure to distinguish between the 'deviant' delinquent who defies the standards of his family and neighbourhood, and the 'non-deviant' whose anti-social behaviour is normal and acceptable in the circles in which he finds himself; and that the attempt to cover such diverse material within the terms of a single prediction table is like 'trying to use the same set of measures to evaluate the ripeness of oranges and watermelons'.[2] Different prediction tables, according to such critics, must be constructed for use with offenders who have 'different dynamic patterns'.

In the case of the Minnesota Multiphasic Personality Inventory the force of this criticism has been frankly admitted. The inventors of these tests

[1] Reiss, A. J., Jr. (1951), pp. 116–17. [2] Wattenberg and Balistrieri (1950), p. 752.

explicitly recognize that, for the present at least, the 'best prediction figures for actual delinquency would require the combination of two measures obtained from two approaches. The first of these is the measurement of the pertinent personality variables in the individual, and the second is the evaluation of the environmental factors that provide opportunity and stimulus for delinquent acts and that establish the definition of what behavior will be called delinquent.' Nevertheless in the end it is the personality tests which win, and we are left with the conclusion that 'among modern personality evaluation methods there is much more likelihood of finding practicable delinquency indicators by using objective personality tests than by any other approach'.[1]

As applied to such studies as the latest Glueck investigation, the criticism that sociological factors are underestimated has two possible meanings. On the one hand, it may be interpreted to imply that the Gluecks have not given adequate weight to certain of their own findings which have relevance even within the admitted limits of their particular enquiry. If that charge is justified it should be possible to demonstrate that their predictors would have gained in accuracy, had this material not been neglected. This has not, so far as I known, been done. Alternatively, such criticism may be construed as a commentary upon the scope of the investigation, rather than upon its execution. In that case it is fair to repeat that the Gluecks never professed to do more than to predict the differential liability to delinquency of children with a more or less standardized social background. They addressed themselves only to the question why one child succumbs to, while another withstands, the temptations of that environment, and their work is in no way concerned with the problem of what might happen in quite different social conditions. They may have been misguided to impose this limitation on themselves, but, having done so, they cannot fairly be blamed for having used instruments which might have proved defective in fields other than those in which they were employed.

If, however (as is now proposed), scales derived from one social environment are to be used for forecasting the behaviour of children with much more varied background, the risk that predictions may be falsified through neglect of sociological variables may become much more menacing. But here again we can only wait and see what happens. If the Glueck scales turn out to be less accurate when thus more widely applied, their failure to take account of social differences may well be held responsible; but if in fact they prove equally well fitted to detect the pauper and the millionaire delinquent, then complaints of their sociological inadequacies will be beside the mark. Meanwhile, to the charge that the Gluecks are blinkered, it can at least be replied that the blinkers which they wear are fashionable enough. If the belief that criminals are born and not made went out with Lombroso, its place has certainly been taken by the doctrine of early predestination which came in with Freud.

In any case, as compared with the identification of future delinquents in an unselected population, predictions of recidivism are less open to criticism

[1] Hathaway and Monachesi (1953), p. 12.

on the ground that the social background of their subjects is not standardized. Groups of offenders may be predominantly, but they are not as a rule wholly, drawn from one social class; and investigators who hope to forecast the prospects of recidivism in any such group normally take its social composition as they find it. If social origin proves in fact to be significantly associated with recidivism, this will become apparent in any analysis of the experience of a group of mixed social composition; and the results can be included in any prediction table constructed from this experience. Nor, again, are recidivist predictors confined, as are enquiries into juvenile delinquency of the Glueck type, to infantile experiences. With older subjects, happenings that have occurred later in life can also be drawn upon; and, as we have seen, some of the most successful investigations have relied largely upon these.

The extreme diversity of the factors used in prediction tables seems to exceed that which would result from differences in the exercises which the various investigators have set themselves. While, as has already been said, the factors which prognosticate repeated criminality may well differ from those which are predictive of first lapses, and while the predictor that proves efficient in Illinois may be comparatively worthless in Middlesex, one cannot but suspect that the bias of the investigators' own interest has much to do with the actual selection made. Reiss' criticism in particular suggests that there is a marked contrast between those who are biassed towards psychological factors, and those who rely more upon factors that are social in a sense much wider than that in which the Gluecks use this word. Moreover, the habitual concentration by particular investigators on particular kinds of predictive factors—the interest which they show, for example, *either* in emotional relationships within the family, *or* in the external facts of their subjects' careers—suggests that experiments in prediction are liable to be conditioned by theories of causation: that those who are looking for useful predictors are inclined to direct their search towards what they believe also to be probable causes. The Glueck-Reiss controversy, certainly, lends itself to explanation in those terms; and it is only in exceptional cases that the makers of prediction tables distinguish as clearly as do Mannheim and Wilkins in the passage quoted on p. 173 between predictive and causative phenomena, or that they show such thoroughgoing indifference to the possible causative rôle of the factors from which their tables are constructed.

In any case it would seem worth while to explore the relative efficiency, as applied to more or less homogeneous populations for homogeneous purposes, of the multifarious factors that have actually been used in the construction of tolerably successful tables of criminological prediction. If in fact there is little difference between the efficiency of any one and any other of these factors—if, that is to say, a future offender or recidivist can be equally well picked out by any one of a large variety of signs—the important social inference may be drawn that a potential offender differs from other people in a great many ways. But, if, as seems more likely in view of other evidence, such pronounced differences are not usual, and the predictive efficiency of the many types of factors used in the tables is far from equal, then it would seem urgent to investigate further how far the relative success of different predictive experiments is related to the type of factor on which they have relied: to what extent, for example, the encouraging results of the Mannheim and Wilkins investigation are due to the fact that the authors made so much use of objective, external facts, and in particular, of the previous criminal experience of their subjects. By enquiries along these lines it might be possible to avoid waste of energy in the use of relatively unpromising types of data, and so greatly to accelerate progress.

Certainly the best of the work that has already been done in this field has yielded exceptionally promising results, which contrast most favourably with the fruitlessness of investigations into the causes of social phenomena, whether of the pathological or of the wholesome variety. In a later chapter it will be argued that the comparative success of the social sciences in certain types of prediction carries important implications as to the kind of question which may most profitably be put to the social scientist. Questions that begin with 'why' are exceptionally difficult, and generally so far beyond our capacity that they are best left alone. But those that begin with 'which', and offer the choice between a limited range of alternatives, are much more likely to be manageable. By tackling this type of question, the makers of criminological prediction tables have shown that it is possible by accurate observation to calculate probabilities, and so to improve our forecasts of future events or of the results of our own actions. That at least brightens the outlook for rational behaviour.

Or should brighten it; for it has to be admitted that the development of exact statistical techniques sometimes evokes nostalgic sighs of yearning for 'wise judgment' or for due regard for 'imponderables'. According to Roper, 'The virtue of . . . a statistical index lies in avoiding the errors of subjective assessment; the defect is that it perforce leaves a good many imponderables out of account . . . Such an index will have to be treated like a laboratory finding in medicine; that is, as a valuable aid, but not as the full deciding factor'.[1] A member of an Approved School staff goes further with the astonishing lament that 'As knowledge increases in the modern world the power of judgment is declining'.[2] And even the Gluecks themselves are modest in their final assessment of the function of their own predictions. 'It should again be emphasized', they write, 'that these prediction tables should not be used mechanically and as a substitute for clinical judgment'[3]—a statement which taken at its face value would appear to suggest—what surely cannot be intended—that in the end the Gluecks have greater faith in their own intuitive judgment than in the prediction tables which all their elaborate investigations and calculations have produced.

Such doubts are reminders that, as predictive techniques improve, it becomes increasingly important accurately to appraise their function, and not to allow emotional resistance to 'mechanical', as opposed to 'intuitive', methods to distort judgment of their usefulness. In the forecasting of criminal

[1] Roper (1951), p. 253. [2] Quoted by Gittins (1952), p. 20.
[3] Glueck, S. and E. T. (1951), p. 269.

(or other) forms of human behaviour there are, no doubt, ponderables and imponderables to be reckoned with—factors which can be measured and factors which cannot. It is reasonable to hope that as knowledge advances the former may gain upon the latter, with corresponding advantage to the accuracy of any prophecies that are systematically made. What, however, is indefensible is that at any given moment ponderables should be treated as imponderables or *vice versa*. Once it is established that statistical methods applied to a particular type of problem give consistently more valid results than the intuitive judgments of even wise and experienced men (and as we have seen there are occasions when this has happened), then the claim of those men to wisdom can hardly be sustained, if they still insist on the superior merits of their own intuition in relation to that particular problem. Conversely, in those areas where statistical techniques have not demonstrated their greater accuracy, we must continue to rely on the best guesses that can be made without their help. The fact that in no case do statistical methods succeed in measuring all the relevant factors, or give a 100 per cent correct result, does not affect the issue, or justify overriding them in the interests of a sentimental attachment to imponderables in cases where the latter are demonstrably less reliable prognosticators. The sensible course is to use one method or the other, according to which has proved itself the more reliable in any particular case: the mistake is to mix them.

PART II

THE CONTEMPORARY ATTITUDE TO SOCIAL PATHOLOGY:

THE SOCIAL IMPLICATIONS OF PSYCHIATRY

CHAPTER VII

Social Pathology and the Concepts of Mental Health and Mental Illness

I

THE most striking changes in public attitude and public policy towards social deviants which have shown themselves in recent history are those due to the growing influence of medical, and in particular of psychiatric, concepts. Indeed, thanks to this development, it would seem that in the course of a couple of centuries some wheels have nearly come full circle. In the eighteenth century no clear distinction was drawn between the mentally afflicted and the criminal. Lunatics were treated more or less as criminals. In Paris the principal eighteenth-century institutions for the care of the insane—the Bicêtre and the Salpétrière—were indifferently known as hospitals or as prisons. To-day, for quite different reasons, the distinction between the two classes has once more become confused; but, instead of treating lunatics as criminals, we now regard many criminals as lunatics, or at any rate as mentally disordered.

There was a time, however, when lines were much more sharply drawn. The pioneering work of the American Dorothea Dix in the mid-nineteenth century was followed by 'widespread realization of the fact that insanity, feeble-mindedness and criminality are conditions between which it is well to make a clear distinction, and the practical approach to which should be governed by separate and distinct principles. The mere segregation of these three main groups of persons made the problems peculiar to each group stand out in such a way as to demand attention. The treatment of the insane, the mentally defective and the criminal thus each became the subject of special study, with its own experts and its own methods.'[1] In Britain the Criminal Lunatics Act of 1844, provided that 'sundry modifications should be made in the case of prisoners who appeared to be from imbecility of mind unfit for the same discipline as other prisoners'; whilst at about the same date the existence of a category of 'weak-minded' prisoners, additional to the idiots, imbeciles and insane persons specifically designated by the criminal law, was officially recognized. In 1856 we find a well-known 'psychologist' and 'a physician practising in the department of lunacy'[2] called in to deal with two particularly difficult prisoners at Pentonville and Millbank respectively; and in 1879 'the Committee on the Working of Penal Servitude Acts recom-

[1] Flugel (1948), p. 110. [2] East (1936), pp. 127–8 and 133.

mended that weak-minded convicts should be segregated in special prisons and should undergo a special regimen'.[1] But, generally speaking, during the nineteenth century the care of prisoners' mental health was not distinguished from their moral instruction, and was regarded as belonging more to the chaplain's than to the doctor's province.

Early in the twentieth century, however, the Prison Commissioners issued special regulations for various categories of weak-minded prisoners, classified as suffering from 'congenital deficiency with and without epilepsy; imperfectly developed stage of insanity; mental debility after an attack of insanity; senility; alcoholic; and undefined'.[2] By about 1909, Norwood East is himself conducting 'psychotherapeutic interviews' and is 'much impressed by the good results';[3] and in 1919, the Birmingham justices asked the Prison Commissioners for a whole-time medical officer to be appointed to the prison service, and for portions of the hospitals to be adapted for the reception of persons on remand whose mental condition appeared to require investigation. This last venture is said to have aroused great interest.[4] It was soon followed by similar developments elsewhere, until to-day the position has been reached in which all medical officers in the prison service are required to have psychiatric experience; whilst the 'expertise of the senior Medical Officers is so far recognized that some of the leading psychiatric hospitals attach their Registrars to certain prisons for instruction in forensic psychiatry'.[5] Psychotherapeutic treatment, specifically so called, is now practised in a number of prisons; and in addition an undefined amount of what the Prison Commissioners have called 'minor psychotherapy'[6] is undertaken by medical officers in the course of their ordinary duties.

Nor is it only in the case of offenders who are actually committed to prison that a doctor's help is invoked. At the foundation in 1931 of the Institute for the Scientific Treatment of Delinquency (now the Institute for the Study and Treatment of Delinquency) the choice of title was significant: delinquency, it was implied, must be treated, as diseases are—not just punished or made the subject of moral exhortation. By 1932, again, we find the report of a Departmental Committee on Persistent Offenders venturing as far as the opinion that offenders' mental condition merited attention, and that some might be amenable to psychological treatment—although the authors were cautious enough to add that 'no witness was able to give us any precise information concerning the curative value of psychological treatment in any large number of law-breakers', and that the 'practical treatment of psychological disorders by this means is as yet experimental and . . . still uncertain in its results'.[7] Caution did not, however, preclude the Committee from suggesting that a medical psychologist should be attached to one or more penal establishments, that use should be made of Child Guidance Clinics, and

[1] Radzinowicz and Turner, in Craig and others (1944), p. xx.
[2] East and Hubert (1939), pp. 3–4. [3] ibid., pp. 9–10.
[4] Ruggles-Brise (1921), p. 194. [5] Fox (1952), p. 245.
[6] Commissioners of Prisons, Report for 1951, p. 85.
[7] Departmental Committee on Persistent Offenders (1932), p. 45.

that suitable offenders should be tried on probation while attending hospitals or clinics. These recommendations have since all been carried out: indeed, under the Criminal Justice Act of 1948, the obligation to undergo mental treatment can be made a binding condition of a probation order.[1]

Meanwhile, steps have been taken to encourage magistrates to keep up with the times. As long ago as 1889, the Home Office strongly urged them to obtain evidence of the mental condition of trial prisoners in all doubtful cases. In 1934, they were officially advised that recent developments in knowledge relating to methods of mental examination and mental treatment had enlarged the category of cases in which medical information might be useful to courts; that this information should be obtained and considered before sentencing; and that, in certain cases of mental abnormality, dismissal or binding over would be proper.[2] Although we have not yet reached the stage hoped for by Dr Hamblin Smith (himself a former prison medical officer) in which every Court for young offenders would 'sit with an expert medical assessor',[3] it seems that magistrates have not been unwilling to learn their psychological lessons. By 1927 the number of cases remanded to prison for psychiatric examination was estimated by Sir Norwood East at about 2,000;[4] by 1955 it was officially said to have reached over 4,800—exclusive of juveniles for whom psychiatric examinations are arranged either in remand homes or without resort to any form of detention. And in the case of every offender sentenced to Borstal, to corrective training or to preventive detention, medical reports covering mental as well as physical fitness are now invariably obtained.

Meanwhile outside the sphere of criminality altogether, the statutory recognition of new classes of mental defectives, dating from the Mental Deficiency Act of 1913, has created a large category of legally 'subcultural' individuals who are defined as such in medical terms and as the result of medical diagnosis; and the provision of facilities, under the Mental Treatment Act of 1930, for voluntary mental treatment has again greatly enlarged the range of aberrant behaviour which may be brought to the notice of the medical profession.

II

All these developments involve far-reaching consequences. Nevertheless, as often happens with accomplished revolutions, those who are accustomed to, or who have grown up with, the new order sometimes find it difficult to appreciate the magnitude of the change that has occurred. That the psychiatric aroma which now pervades the discussion of problems of anti-social behaviour is no longer felt to be obtrusive is but a sign of its prevalence. At every turn the current vocabulary of social pathology (including that very

[1] Subject, that is, to the offender's consent; although, if he refuses this, he may forfeit the chance of a period on probation altogether, and so lay himself open to the prospect of an alternative, and probably more disagreeable, sentence.

[2] East (1936), p. 423. [3] Smith (1933), p. 166. [4] East (1927), p. 28.

phrase) bears witness to the degree to which concepts of mental health and mental illness or defectiveness now permeate our thinking. Indeed, these concepts have now even invaded our interpretation of animal, as well as of human, behaviour: according to Dr Konrad Lorenz 'mentally healthy dogs' do not usually attack their master's children while 'cats always announce their intention of attacking, and, except in the case of unreliable or mentally deficient psychopaths—which occur in cats just as in dogs—they never bite or scratch without giving previous unmistakable warning to the offender'.[1]

In the analysis that follows, the scientific validity of these contemporary ideas is subjected to somewhat critical discussion. It may be well, therefore, to remind ourselves at the outset that the impact of psychiatric concepts upon the treatment of offenders and of other social deviants has been in overwhelming degree a humanizing influence. The doctor's professional responsibility is for the health, not for the morals, of his patient; and the consulting room has no place for the principles of retribution and revenge which have played so large a part in the evolution of penal codes. Much indeed of the professional ethic of the medical profession is concerned to emphasize the single-minded concentration upon his patient's welfare which the doctor is expected to show. He is, for instance, under obligation to respect the patient's confidences, even in circumstances in which some doctors themselves now argue that the public interest might be better served by their disclosure.[2] It is true that, with the growth of psychiatry, and the consequential increase in the preoccupation of the medical profession with problems of behaviour, the possibility of conflict between medical and social ethics is enhanced; but it remains also true that in psychiatry, no less than in any other branch of medicine, the doctor conceives his first duty to be that which he owes to his patient, and that there is no sign of this traditional medical ethic being abandoned, merely because the patient is referred for medical treatment on account of his deviant behaviour. Nor is it likely that pursuit of the patient's health will lead the doctor to prescribe the more brutal methods favoured by many penal codes; since, on whatever other grounds such methods may be defended, there is no evidence of their effectiveness as ameliorative instruments.

Without question, therefore, in the contemporary attitude towards anti-social behaviour, psychiatry and humanitarianism have marched hand in hand. Just because it is so much in keeping with the mental atmosphere of a scientifically-minded age, the medical treatment of social deviants has been a most powerful, perhaps even the most powerful, reinforcement of humanitarian impulses; for to-day the prestige of humane proposals is immensely enhanced if these are expressed in the idiom of medical science. Indeed we might go so far as to say that, even if the intellectual foundations of current psychiatry were proved to be wholly unsound, and even if psychiatric 'science' was exposed as nothing more than fantasy, we might yet have cause to be grateful for the result of so beneficent a delusion. In all subsequent criticism this is an aspect of the matter never to be lost to view.

[1] Lorenz (1954), pp. 80 and 176. [2] See Dawson (1954), pp. 1474–8.

The intellectual structure underlying the prevailing contemporary views of the role of mental disorder[1] in anti-social behaviour seems to rest upon a series of closely related propositions. First, it is postulated that mental health and its correlative, mental illness, are objective in the sense that they are more than an expression either of the tastes and value-judgments of psychiatrists, or of the cultural norms of a particular society: mental health is to be regarded as closely analogous to, and no less 'real', than its physical counterpart. Second, it is presumed to be possible both in theory, and also (even if not always very precisely) in practice, to diagnose these objective conditions of mental illness or defectiveness by criteria which are independent of any anti-social behaviour on the part of those who suffer from them; so that anti-social persons can be divided into the two classes of those who are mentally disordered, and those who are not thus handicapped. Third, the presence of mental disorder, when established, is held to 'explain' certain socially unacceptable aberrations in the sense that these are deemed to be attributable to that disorder; while, fourthly, the peculiar behaviour of the mentally sick is not only explained, but also in some degree excused, by their sickness. Mental illness is thus held, at least in some circumstances, to diminish, if not wholly to abrogate, moral responsibility; and it is widely argued also that it ought to carry with it a corresponding freedom from legal responsibility. At the same time, since mental illness is not coterminous with, nor to be defined in terms of, manifestations of socially unacceptable behaviour, it follows that it is only the behaviour of some, not that of all, deviants that is explicable or excusable in this way.

All these propositions are evidently logically interdependent, those that follow being contingent upon the first. For if mental health and mental illness are not objective realities, definable otherwise than in terms of social misbehaviour, then, plainly, there can be no criterion by which to divide those who indulge in such behaviour into the sick and the healthy; and, if this division cannot be made, or if the diagnosis of mental disorder is itself based only on the criterion of anti-social conduct, then it is equally plain that no distinction can be drawn between those who are morally or legally guilty and those whose offences are explained or excused by their mental condition.

Taken together, these propositions are an expression of the contemporary desire to assimilate as far as possible attitudes to mental and to physical ill-health; and, in particular, to guarantee that mental illness shall give the same protection against blame as physical illness already does. In the physical sphere, the presumption that illness is unchallengeable as both explanation and excuse of certain shortcomings is already treated as virtually axiomatic. If you are ill, you obviously cannot do what you otherwise ought to do; and, if you are ill enough, you will, without question, be excused for doing what you otherwise ought not to do. In a high fever one is not blamed for saying

[1] In this and the following chapter the terms 'mental illness' and 'mental disorder' are used somewhat loosely, though I have generally followed the practice of the recent Royal Commission in treating mental disorder as covering 'the whole range of abnormal conditions of the mind' including both psychopathic states and mental deficiency.

and doing things which would be held to be inexcusable at a body temperature of 98·4 Fahrenheit. Similarly, in principle at any rate, mental illness is regarded as conferring an equivalent immunity. The idea that a man who is mentally deranged should suffer the penalties prescribed by law for criminal actions is generally accepted as repugnant to civilized feeling. Indeed in all the controversies that have raged around the application of the McNaghten rules, it is remarkable how it has always been taken for granted that, *if* the presence of incapacitating mental illness can be established, then there can be no question of the law taking its course. Dispute turns only on the terms in which mental incapacity should in this context be defined, never on the question whether the sick should be exempted from the penalty imposed upon the healthy. The principle that any illness which causes misconduct also excuses that misconduct is certainly deep-seated in contemporary notions of responsibility, at least as these are applied in practice.

As long ago as 1926, the Royal Commission on Lunacy and Mental Disorder recommended that 'the lunacy code should be recast with a view to securing that the treatment of mental disorder should approximate as nearly to the treatment of physical ailments as is consistent with the special safeguards which are indispensable when the liberty of the subject is infringed'.[1] To-day the wish to carry this policy further is very noticeable in the evidence submitted from many quarters to the Royal Commission on the Law Relating to Mental Illness and Mental Deficiency whose report has recently appeared.[2] Many of the Commission's witnesses advocated modifications in the law relating to certification, with a view to removing the 'stigma' from mental illness, and in the hope that the public would be encouraged to seek medical aid for mental conditions with as little hesitancy or shame as in cases of bodily disease. Thus on behalf of the Association of Municipal Corporations it was submitted that 'it is now agreed that mental ill-health is a medical condition requiring the same amount of care and attention as any other medical condition',[3] and that 'in general, where patients of unsound mind are concerned, the more the kind of procedure governing admissions to and discharge from other hospitals is adopted for mental hospitals the less stigma is attached to treatment there, and the more likely is it to be sought when necessary'.[4] Asked by Mrs Braddock, one of the Commissioners, whether it would not be desirable 'to have very extensive propaganda amongst the public that mental illness is just similar to physical illness and requires treat-

[1] Royal Commission on Lunacy and Mental Disorder, *Report* (1926), p. 157.

[2] In general the Commission's own Report conforms to the view that the distinction between mental and physical illness ought to be obliterated. 'Mental disorders', it affirms, 'are forms of ill-health, and care and treatment are usually based on medical diagnosis and advice' (para. 86). Its authors recommend, accordingly, that special legislation relating to mental health should be abolished, holding that it is 'essential' that mental health services should be an integral part of the present national health and welfare services. At the same time, however, they do recognize that 'mental disorder has special features which sometimes require special measures' (para. 136).

[3] Royal Commission on the Law Relating to Mental Illness and Mental Deficiency, 1954–1957. *Minutes of Evidence*, Fourth Day, p. 118.

[4] ibid., Fourth Day, p. 120.

ment in hospital', the same witnesses expressed their full agreement, reiterating that 'the note we believe we must strike is that people who suffer from mental illness are entitled just as much to sympathy as anyone who suffers from a physical illness'.[1] The Royal College of Physicians opened their evidence with a declaration that 'Certification with judicial order should be reduced to the minimum and the procedure for treatment of the mentally ill should approximate as far as possible to that of the physically ill'.[2] In cross-examination Dr Strauss, representing the College, referred with approval to the so-called neurosis centres in general hospitals, where patients are treated in precisely the same way as in other wards, Professor Lewis adding that 'This is a precedent: we are suggesting it should be extended'.[3] The County Councils Association, though recognizing the need for restraint in certain cases, expressed the view that our aim should be 'so far as is practicable, to model the services for persons suffering from mental affliction of any kind upon those now provided for persons suffering from other forms of illness or physical handicap',[4] and made suggestions for 'accelerating' the 'process of gradually placing the treatment of mental and physical illness on a similar footing'.[5] In cross-examination Mr Adam, one of the Association's witnesses, urged that 'modern thought is trying to suggest that mental illness is no different from any other'.[6] The spokesmen of the Confederation of Health Service Employees gave it as their view that, generally, 'hospital treatment for mental illness or disorder should be available by a similar process as treatment for physical ailments is obtained in other types of hospital';[7] and they proposed accordingly to abolish the magistrate's order for all initial admissions, only allowing unwilling patients to communicate directly with the Board of Control or with a magistrate.[8] Certain members of the Association of Psychiatric Social Workers argued that non-statutory admission to mental hospitals was an advantage 'on the grounds that it brings the treatment of nervous and mental disorders more closely in line with that of physical illness', although other members of the same Association took the view that 'non-statutory admission appears to have a disadvantage in that it may create an unfortunate discrimination between the different categories of patients'.[9] Finally, Dr E. W. Dunkley, after eleven years' experience of a hospital observation unit, welcomed the suggestion that 'patients should be allowed to enter a mental hospital as they do a general hospital without any formalities at all'.[10]

The wish to assimilate the treatment of mental and physical illness is thus widely supported, although it is true that many of those who take this view recognize that there are cases in which mental patients must be detained in hospital against their will, and that in these a special procedure is necessary.

[1] Royal Commission on the Law Relating to Mental Illness and Mental Deficiency. 1954–1957, Fourth Day, p. 135. [2] ibid., Thirteenth Day, p. 491.
[3] ibid., Thirteenth Day, p. 495. [4] ibid., Fourteenth Day, p. 533.
[5] ibid., Fourteenth Day, p. 534. [6] ibid., Fourteenth Day, p. 545.
[7] ibid., Eighteenth Day, p. 654. [8] ibid., Eighteenth Day, p. 655.
[9] ibid., Twenty-fifth Day, p. 1002. [10] ibid., Twenty-ninth Day, p. 1204.

Such cases, however, are always treated as regrettable exceptions to what, it is implied, ought to be a more liberal rule. There can be no doubt in which direction opinion is moving.

The intention to obliterate any distinction between the treatment of mental illness on the one hand and of physical illness on the other necessarily implies the validity of the first of the four propositions listed on p. 207. It assumes that mental health and mental ill-health exist, and often makes this assumption so confidently that further explanation of the meaning of these terms is not considered necessary. The charming young woman who, a few days before these words were written, sought to win a contribution from me towards a London street collection for the promotion of 'Mental Health' certainly felt no obligation explicitly to define the meaning of this term: if pressed to do so, she might well have answered that the prevention of mental illness would keep people out of mental hospitals just as the prevention of poliomyelitis would keep them out of iron lungs. Obviously the very decision to organize a 'Flag Day' for mental health implies a conviction that plenty of ordinary citizens will have a clear enough idea of what is meant to be willing to consider spending their money on it.

Such an assumption seems to pass unchallenged in very diverse circles. In the United States, 'the women's magazines and other mass media', it is said, 'are telling how to "get" mental health and how not to "lose" it as if it were as tangible as a permanent wave';[1] while at more sophisticated levels, as for instance in the enormous volume of representations (including many of a highly expert nature) submitted to the recent Royal Commission, explicit definition of mental illness is the exception rather than the rule; nor is the meaning of these terms defined in the Commission's terms of reference. Questions of terminology did indeed receive a good deal of attention in the Commission's own report; but discussion of these was generally concerned, either with purely legal definitions of various forms of mental disorder, or with the social problems raised by the behaviour of certain categories of persons—notably 'psychopaths'—who were assumed to be mentally afflicted. The Commissioners were wary enough to avoid the type of definition of which numerous examples are given later in this chapter;[2] and that extremely vigorous body, the World Federation for Mental Health, has likewise generally assumed that those who take part in its international congresses and other discussions will know, without being expressly told, what it is that they are supposed to be talking about.

In many contexts, as, for example, in expert medical discussions, it is no doubt proper to make the assumption that the terms 'mental illness' and 'mental health' will call up in the minds of all concerned certain definite empirical phenomena, and that the phenomena suggested to every one of those minds will be nearly enough the same. In such circumstances the words are effective vehicles of communication, and that is all that need be asked of them. In other contexts, however, it matters not only that the words should convey the same meaning to all who use them, but, no less, what that meaning

[1] Pratt (1952), p. 182. [2] See pp. 211 ff.

is. The issues involved are more than semantic, or, at the least, they are semantic with a difference; for, where capital punishment survives, the balance of life and death itself may turn on the precise definitions employed in the criminal law.

It is, therefore, worth examining with some care the terms of such definitions as have been attempted. In the case of mental health, if we exclude those definitions which use a purely statistical criterion, classifying as healthy or normal those whose mental condition does not differ greatly from that of most other people, the following selection seems to be reasonably representative.

Mental health is 'the full and free expression of all our native and acquired potentialities, in harmony with one another by being directed towards a common end or aim of the personality as a whole'.[1]

'A mentally healthy individual has been defined as a person endowed with a good physical and mental constitution, whose personality develops harmoniously, and who becomes so well adjusted both in himself and to the outside world that his emotional and intellectual balance cannot be disturbed by either internal conflicts or the vicissitudes of life.'[2]

'The term normal or healthy can be defined in two ways. Firstly, from the standpoint of functioning society one can call a person normal or healthy if he is able to fulfill the social role he is to take in that given society—if he is able to participate in the reproduction of society. Secondly, from the standpoint of the individual, we look upon health or normalcy as the optimum of growth and happiness of the individual.'[3]

'A mature and mentally healthy person is one who (1) respects and has confidence in himself and because he knows his true worth wastes no time proving it to himself and others; (2) accepts, works with, and to large extent enjoys other people; and (3) carries on his work, play, and his family and social life with confidence and enthusiasm and with a minimum of conflict, fear and hostility.'[4]

'Let us define mental health as the adjustment of human beings to the world and to each other with a maximum of effectiveness and happiness. Not just efficiency, or just contentment—or the grace of obeying the rules of the game cheerfully. It is all of these together. It is the ability to maintain an even temper, an alert intelligence, socially considerate behavior, and a happy disposition. This I think, is a healthy mind.'[5]

'A normal individual is anyone who is free from symptoms, unhampered by mental conflict and who shows satisfactory working capacity', and 'who is able to love someone apart from himself.'[6]

'Mental health consists of the ability to live (1) within the limits imposed by bodily equipment; (2) with other human beings; (3) happily; (4) productively; (5) without being a nuisance.'[7]

[1] Hadfield (1950), p. 14. [2] Leff (1953), p. 213.
[3] Fromm, quoted by Eaton (1957), p. 85.
[4] Rennie and Woodward, quoted by Eaton (1951), p. 85.
[5] Menninger, quoted by Eaton (1951), p. 85.
[6] Glover (1932), p. 154. [7] Preston, quoted by Eaton (1951), p. 85.

'The conception of healthy personality, as we to-day may tentatively state it. is of a person who recognizes the life tasks and problems that living in a social order and in a symbolic cultural world presents to every person, but who meets them with self-confidence, courage, and the ability to conduct his interpersonal relationships with generosity and dignity, responding with feelings that are appropriate to his stage of development.'[1]

'A human being in good mental health is capable of positive emotional, social and intellectual adjustment to his environment and is able to establish harmonious relations with other people. But this adaptation should be a dynamic one and not a static one, and this implies that an individual participates in a positive fashion in the modification of his physical and social environment.'[2]

The mental hygiene programme 'is concerned with effecting harmonious inner adjustment of the individual's different traits, urges, ideals, and motives, to the end that the individual will not be at war with himself . . . The purpose of mental hygiene on the psychological level is the consolidation from the individual's early life of all his lines of development or growth, physical, intellectual, emotional, social, and moral, into co-ordinated and unified habit patterns, so that the end result will be an integrated, harmonious personality, capable of attaining maximum efficiency, satisfaction, and self-realization with the least expenditure of energy and the least strain from interfering and conflicting desires and habits, and maximally free from serious inner strife, maladjustment, or other evidence of mental discord.'[3]

'The well-adjusted personality, which characterizes a happy and efficient man or woman, is a harmonious blending of these varied emotions and character traits, resulting in self-control and habits of conformity.'[4]

'Happiness is, in general, the sign of mental health. But it should be lasting happiness; for of course one can be happy for the moment, like the maniac or the drunkard, without having a mind that is really healthy.'[5]

The healthy personality is one which 'functions more or less perfectly in its cultural milieu'.[6]

'A "mature, healthy person" is extremely difficult to define; indeed, a clear-cut and complete definition is impossible at this time. Suffice it to say that he is one who is able to live at relative peace with himself and with his neighbors; who has the capacity to raise healthy children; and who, when these basic functions are accomplished, still has energy enough left over to make some further contribution to the society in which he lives.'[7]

' . . . we suggest tentatively that a combination of three criteria be used for determining the mental health of an individual: (*a*) active adjustment or attempts at mastery of his environment as distinct both from his inability

[1] Frank (1953), p. 169.

[2] International Federation of Senior Police Officers, quoted in United Nations, *The Prevention of Juvenile Delinquency in Selected European Countries* (1955), p. 84.

[3] Wallin (1949), pp. 116–7.

[4] Thom, quoted by Davis, Kingsley (1938), p. 59.

[5] La Rue, quoted by Davis, Kingsley (1938), p. 59.

[6] Richmond, quoted by Davis, Kingsley (1938), p. 59.

[7] Lemkau (1955), p. 132.

to adjust and from his indiscriminate adjustment through passive acceptance of environmental conditions; (*b*) unity of his personality, the maintenance of a stable, internal integration which remains intact notwithstanding the flexibility of behavior which derives from active adjustment; and (*c*) ability to perceive correctly the world and himself.'[1]

'The criterion of mental health is the ability to adapt oneself to changing conditions without setting up conflicts or causing individuals to suffer pain or to feel discomfort.'[2]

'The structure of mental health is built upon a foundation of values that are understood, accepted, and applied by the individual. If the value-foundation is contradictory, the superstructure will be weak. When the value-foundation is consistent and strong, the structure can withstand great stresses and strains.'[3]

'The mentally healthy person is one who acts according to a consistent inner regulation and is relatively free from conflicts among the three constituent parts of personality (id, ego, and superego)—in other words, an integrated individual. It is perhaps not quite superfluous to add that this does not imply freedom from conflicts with his environment.'[4]

'For the first component of a healthy personality I nominate a sense of *basic trust*, which I think is an attitude toward oneself and the world derived from the experience of the first year of life. By "trust" I mean what is commonly implied in reasonable trustfulness as far as others are concerned and a simple sense of trustworthiness as far as oneself is concerned.'[5]

'Mental health as the committee understands it is influenced by both biological and social factors. It is not a static condition but subject to variations and fluctuations of degree; the committee's conception implies the capacity in an individual to form harmonious relations with others, and to participate in, or contribute constructively to, changes in his social and physical environment. It implies also his ability to achieve a harmonious and balanced satisfaction of his own potentially conflicting instinctive drives—harmonious in that it reaches an integrated synthesis rather than the denial of satisfaction to certain instinctive tendencies as a means of avoiding the thwarting of others. It implies in addition an individual whose personality has developed in a way which enables his potentially conflicting instinctive drives to find harmonious expression in the full realization of his potentialities.'[6]

'A relatively simple, working definition of mental health would be most useful, even if it were not entirely "scientific". In my work in other fields, my co-workers and I have settled for some such simple criteria as these: the ability to hold a job, have a family, keep out of trouble with the law, and enjoy the usual opportunities for pleasure.'[7]

[1] Jahoda, in Rose, A. M., ed. (1955), p. 566. [2] Tómasson (1954), p. xviii.

[3] McSwain and Haskew in National Society for the Study of Education (1955). Part II, p. 346.

[4] Jahoda, in Kotinsky and Witmer, eds. (1955), p. 306.

[5] Erikson, quoted by White (1956), p. 117.

[6] World Health Organization, Expert Committee on Mental Health (1951), p. 4.

[7] Ginsburg, in Kotinsky and Witmer, eds. (1955), p. 7.

'"Mental health", in a very broad sense, might be defined as the goal of our attempts to achieve for each individual the development of his potential capacities so that he will be respected by himself and by the groups of which he is a member.'[1]

'We might go so far as to say . . . that the behaviour of a mentally healthy person is always characterized by the qualities of reasonableness and balance. A person's mental health may be said to be more complete in the measure that he is capable of widening his most personally meaningful perceptions, and is thus able to satisfy in a reasonable and balanced manner all his needs, both the instinctual needs and those which belong to the field of values.'[2]

To this collection may be added two others distinguished for the more specific quality of the terms in which they are expressed.

'Wholesome-minded people are not averse to frank consideration of sex under proper conditions and right motives, but they do not enjoy having it dragged into prominence on every possible pretext and occasion. Dignity and decency are the marks of successful sex adjustment.'[3]

'Industrial unrest to a large degree means bad mental hygiene, and is to be corrected by good mental hygiene. The various anti-social attitudes that lead to crime are problems for the mental hygienist. Dependency, insofar as it is social parasitism not due to mental or physical defect, belongs to mental hygiene. But mental hygiene has a message also for those who consider themselves quite normal, for, by its aims, the man who is fifty per cent efficient can make himself seventy per cent efficient.'[4]

III

The foregoing quotations certainly justify Kingsley Davis' comment that it is difficult 'to get behind the emotionality and loquacity of mental hygiene literature to see the essential logic'. However, 'after all the verbiage has been laboriously sifted', one can at least detect the recurrence of certain themes.[5] Mental health tends to be equated with happiness, preferably of a 'higher' order, with vigour, with the full use of capabilities, with integration in the sense of freedom from conflict within oneself, and with harmonious adjustment to the environment.[6] Certainly, the meaning of these terms is sufficiently objective to call up a reasonably identifiable portrait: we can all recognize the person who is happy, who exerts himself to the full and is not at war either with himself or his neighbours.

At the same time, there are difficulties underneath. For one thing, if such definitions are consistently applied, they are liable in certain social environments to produce violent conflicts between health and morals. If, on the other

[1] Zimmerman, in Soddy, ed. (1955), Vol. 2, p. 215.

[2] Krapf (1955), p. 147.

[3] Howard and Patry, quoted by Davis, Kingsley (1938), p. 59.

[4] Bromberg, quoting a 'prominent spokesman' of the mental hygiene movement, referred to by Davis, Kingsley (1938), p. 55.

[5] Davis, Kingsley (1938), p. 60.

[6] We do not seem to have travelled very far since Carlyle wrote that 'the great law of culture is: let each become all that he is capable of being'.

hand, they are to be read as applicable only in particular social conditions, then the claim of mental health to rank as an objective, natural condition, independent both of the personal tastes or value-judgments of those who frame them, and of the cultural norms of a particular society, falls to the ground. This dilemma is fundamental. In order fully to appreciate its quality, it may be helpful to consider how many of these definitions would allow a wholehearted Nazi to qualify as a mentally healthy person in a Nazi-controlled society. In such a society, our Nazi (provided only that he is happy in his Nazidom) would have to be recognized as mentally healthy according to the criteria proposed, at least by Hadfield, Leff, and Fromm; by Glover (so long as he loves someone), by Thom (if he has any self-control), by La Rue, by Wallin, by Richmond (most emphatically in the appropriate environment), by Jahoda and probably by Ginsburg, by Zimmerman and by Howard and Patry—unless his perception of the world or himself is too distorted, which, if he is a realist, it need not be. On the other hand he would perhaps be excluded by Rennie and Woodward on the ground that, although qualified by his 'confidence' and 'enthusiasm', he is bound to exhibit considerable manifestations of hostility; by Menninger, on account of wha might be judged socially inconsiderate behaviour; by Preston because he is (according to our standards) a nuisance; by Frank because he lacks dignity and generosity; by Erikson because his life is not based on trustfulness; and perhaps by WHO because his contribution to his environment is not 'constructive'. And what goes for the Nazi goes also for many a sadist in our own society,[1] who also could be said to be exercising the 'full and free expression of all his native and acquired potentialities, in harmony with one another by being directed towards a common end or aim of the personality as a whole'.

It must be recognized that from one point of view there is nothing inherently absurd in these results. Indeed, so long as mental health is defined in terms that are independent of moral or social virtue, it is to be anticipated that there will be some persons who enjoy tolerably good mental health, but whose social behaviour leaves much to be desired, just as there are many others in excellent physical health of whom the same can be said. Mental health is, no doubt, in itself a desirable aim, and its promotion a proper goal of social policy. But, so long as it is defined in terms that are independent of socially approved behaviour, it can rank as only one amongst many possible social goals, between which there may at times be conflict. The analogy with physical health, of which exactly the same is true, is conspicuously apt. Physical health remains a proper goal of social policy, even though it might well have been a great social blessing had Hitler and all his associates been lifelong sufferers from some crippling disease; and mental health remains an equally proper goal of social policy, even though it might have been a great social blessing had Hitler and his associates all been incapable imbeciles. So long as we are prepared to face the possibility that, the better some people's mental or physical health, the greater their potentialities for anti-social conduct, we can accept definitions of mental health as an objective neutral

[1] As for instance the late Neville Heath. See Critchley, ed. (1951).

condition that is neither determined by, nor necessarily consistent with, any personal or social standards of what constitutes proper or admirable conduct.

It must, however, be admitted that most of the current definitions of mental health do not easily lend themselves to such an interpretation. Most of them with their visions of 'inner harmonious adjustment', of 'trustfulness' and of 'socially considerate behaviour'—not to mention happy family life, successful sex adjustment, training for citizenship, economic independence and freedom from industrial unrest—most of them are clearly attempts to formulate conceptions of the ideal, under the guise of the healthy, man. They express the personal value-judgments of their authors, rather than scientifically established facts; and for this they have, in fact, been trenchantly criticized by Professor Kingsley Davis, who, after reviewing thirteen volumes on the subject of mental health and collecting numerous definitions (from which a number of those quoted in this chapter have been taken), pronounced the American concept of mental health to be strongly tinctured with the 'Protestant open-class ethic' or the ideals of the American 'free enterprise' society. That ethic he describes as being, in essence, (1) democratic, in that it favours opportunity to rise by merit, not by birth; (2) worldly, in that its goals are the pursuit of a calling, the accumulation of wealth or attainment of status; (3) ascetic in its emphasis on abstinence, sobriety, thrift, industry and prudence; (4) individualistic, in that it holds the individual responsible for his own destiny and stresses personal ambition and self-reliance; (5) rationalistic and empirical in its assumption that the world is discoverable by sensory observation; and (6) utilitarian in that it conceives human welfare in secularized terms, and as attainable by human knowledge and action. All these features, Davis goes on to suggest, are plainly discernible also in the mental hygiene movement. For this movement involves a 'psychologistic' approach to human conduct, in that it seeks to explain behaviour in terms of traits originating within the individual, rather than in society. It tacitly assumes the existence of a 'mobile class structure'; it accepts social advancement as a natural goal, while lack of ambition is felt to represent a 'definite symptom of maladjustment'. So also the existence of a competitive régime is taken for granted, but at the same time competition must be kept within the rules of the game, that is to say by 'empirico-rational ingenuity and ascetic self-discipline. The maladjusted person must learn to face reality, i.e., the competitive facts. He must not achieve victories in fancy only, or flee the memory of his failures. Parents must not coddle their child and thus make him unfit for the competition of adult life'. Enjoyment is not frowned upon, but it must be 'wholesome'. 'Behaviour should manifest prudence, rationality, and foresight, and material possessions should not be dissipated by whimsical extravagance.' The values of individualism, again, are implied in the assumptions that a person is responsible for his own destiny, his will being the object of treatment in the event of neurosis; that individual happiness is the ultimate good; and that human behaviour is understandable in terms of individuals abstracted from their society. Finally, specialization is implicitly accepted in the emphasis laid upon the value of a particular kind of work adapted to one's talents; while utilitarianism appears in the assumption that 'to function, to grow, to do is regarded as the purpose of life . . . Human welfare is seen as attainable by the application of rational science'.

Those who study the full original text of this important paper, of which the foregoing is but a much abbreviated version, will see that its author has no difficulty in supporting his interpretation of what is meant by mental health by reference to numerous explicit definitions in the current literature. Indeed, he has assembled a formidable body of evidence in support of his conclusions that 'Mental hygiene can plunge into evaluation, into fields the social sciences would not touch, because it possesses an implicit ethical system which, since it is that of our society, enables it to pass value judgments, to get public support, and to enjoy an unalloyed optimism. Disguising its valuational system (by means of the psychologistic position) as rational advice based on science, it can conveniently praise and condemn under the aegis of the medico-authoritarian mantle'. At the same time, 'since the fiction of science is maintained, the ethical character of the movement can never be consciously and deliberately stated—hence the goals must be nebulous and obscurantist in character'. Mental hygiene 'hides its adherence behind a scientific façade, but the ethical premises reveal themselves on every hand, partly through a blindness to scientifically relevant facts'.[1]

Naturally, this line of criticism is particularly forceful when directed against such specific definitions as those quoted above from Bromberg and from Howard and Patry. In these the value-judgment is unmistakable. The scientific objectivity of the statement that industrial unrest means bad mental hygiene can hardly escape challenge, unless we are to believe that health consists in accepting without protest that state of life, or of employment, whatever this may be, to which one happens to have been called; while the assumption that a man who is 70 per cent efficient is more mentally healthy than one who is 50 per cent efficient[2] must carry an implicit assumption as to the virtue of whatever he is efficient at. Similarly, the United Nations Report on *The Prevention of Juvenile Delinquency in Selected European Countries* seems to come dangerously near equating health with keeping out of the hands of the police, when it commends the International Federation of Senior Police Officers for insistence that police training should aim 'to impress upon all policemen the importance of that part of their duties which pertain to the protection of mental health'.[3]

In sexual matters, Howard and Patry's definition only too plainly describes the particular type of behaviour which these particular representatives of mid-twentieth century American culture happen to find admirable. Less explicit, but no less real, are the value-judgments inherent in much of the practical work of marriage guidance. One cannot, for example, read accounts of the intimate discussions staged by the Family Discussion Bureau[4] without

[1] Davis, Kingsley (1938) [2] See p. 214.

[3] United Nations, *The Prevention of Juvenile Delinquency in Selected European Countries* (1955), p. 89.

[4] Bannister and others (1955).

becoming aware of the influence of a silent form in the background—the figure of a presumed ideal marital relationship in which there is no 'undue' dependence, passivity, aggression or dominance on the part of either party; though what, in this context, the limits of the 'due' may be is not so clear. Similarly in Slater and Woodside's valuable study[1] of English working-class marriages, an outline of the particular type of personality esteemed by its authors as 'normal', and therefore presumably 'healthy', peeps through the lines of the questionnaire printed at the end of the book for use as a test of the presence of neurosis. Yet, even within the institution of marriage as embodied in the current laws of England and Wales, the subtleties and varieties of human relationship are surely infinite, and bold indeed is he who would presume to pronounce on which of these are right, or even which are 'healthy'; while the range of relationships which might be possible under other laws is greater still. Adjustment to the latter, however, lies outside the current terms of reference of the mental hygienists: mental hygiene does not extend to divorce law reform.

In the literature of mental health generally, this concept of adjustment is particularly prominent. Fine phrases cannot, however, obscure the fact that adjustment means adjustment to a particular culture or to a particular set of institutions; and that to conceive adjustment and maladjustment in medical terms is in effect to identify health with the ability to come to terms with that culture or with those institutions—be they totalitarian methods of government, the dingy culture of an urban slum, the contemporary English law of marriage or what I have elsewhere called the standards of an 'acquisitive, competitive, hierarchical, envious' society.[2]

In the application of their techniques to cultures other than their own, psychiatrists and other experts in mental hygiene often show themselves to be alive to the presence of this slippery element in their own definitions. Thus Moloney describes how the authoritarian mores of the Japanese conflict with the psychoanalytic aim of creating free, adaptable individuals. The aim of therapy in psychiatric (as distinct from psychoanalytic) practice should, he thinks, be frankly to adjust the patient to the demands of his society; but for the psychoanalyst, the answer to the question 'to be or not to be free?' he finds more difficult. 'Should the American and the Japanese psychoanalytic therapist', he asks, 'encourage individualism or should they insist upon insensible and unconscious submissive conformity to the existing culture?' 'The Japanese psychoanalyst, faced with the problem of curing a mentally ill person, must first of all diagnose him as "ill" because he does not adhere to the rigidly prescribed culture patterns I have outlined. The "cure" upon which the analyst then embarks constitutes the opposite of a cure by western standards. Instead of endeavoring, as do occidental psychoanalysts, to free the individual from his inner thongs, the Japanese analyst actually tightens those thongs.'[3] Similarly, Eaton and Weil, posing the question whether the Hutterite sect (whose members live in self-contained communities in Canada

[1] Slater and Woodside (1951). [2] Wootton (January 1956), p. 115.
[3] Moloney (1954), pp. 5 and 213.

and the western United States under a system of 'communism in the classical and non-political sense') can be regarded as a 'healthy' society, are driven to admit that 'the concept of mental health is not a scientific but a value judgment. The Hutterite social system is quite healthy if it is judged by the frequency of anti-social manifestations'.[1]

Signs of uneasiness, and of recognition of the dangers inherent in too close an identification of mental health with adjustment, are apparent also in several of the definitions already quoted as well as in other quarters. Jahoda, for instance, is careful to point out that personal integration does not involve freedom from conflicts with the environment; and the Police Officers' Federation speaks of 'dynamic' adaptation, and of the individual participating 'in a positive fashion in the modification of his physical and social environment'.[2] Sir Geoffrey Vickers has urged rejection of 'the cosy heaven of mutual adjustment',[3] and Lord Adrian writes of 'the danger that too much insistence on mental health will raise a new standard of good or, rather, of uniform behaviour', and exhorts us to 'aim at a stable and contented society but not one without the reformers and critics and eccentrics, the people who will not conform and are a nuisance to their fellows . . . Clearly we want a contented society where people do not become so angry with one another that they will try to settle their differences by fighting, but we must allow them to have differences, to experience strong emotions, not always pleasurable, and to develop new ideas and habits of life which may not commend themselves to the majority'.[4] Hartmann concedes that 'if we are to insist that some connection exists between mental health and adaptation, we are bound to admit . . . that the concept of health may bear inconsistent meanings according to whether we think of it in relation to the individual or to the community . . . adaptation is only capable of definition in relation to something else, with reference to specific environmental settings'.[5] Aubrey Lewis, who has more than once shown a degree of awareness of the problems involved in the definition of mental health that is unusual among his colleagues, observes that, 'although social disapproval has obviously played a large part in deciding what shall be called social maladaptation, and is its main feature in current psychiatric usage, it cannot be accepted as a satisfactory criterion, varying as it does according to the group of people who express the disapproval'.[6] 'Mental health . . . has been described by some as a state in which one's potential capacities are fully realized. But unless some capacities are characterized as morbid and excluded from the generalization, this is absurd. We all have deplorable potentialities as well as desirable ones.'[7] Finally, a recent Government Committee on Maladjusted Children opens its report with a paean in which adjustment and rebellion are alternately praised in strophe and antistrophe. 'A man can develop his powers to the full and lead a happy

[1] Eaton and Weil (1955), pp. 27 and 189.

[2] International Federation of Senior Police Officers, quoted in United Nations, *The Prevention of Juvenile Delinquency in Selected European Countries* (1955), p. 84.

[3] Vickers (1955), p. 524. [4] Adrian (1956), p. 1192. [5] Hartmann (1939), p. 318.

[6] Lewis, Aubrey (June, 1953), p. 116. [7] ibid., p. 113.

life only if he achieves some measure of adjustment or of harmony with those around him and with the circumstances in which he is placed. Not that he need be satisfied with his environment; some environments are so unhealthy that they ought to be altered. Without the characteristically human attitude of discontent with things as they are, there would be no development either of the individual or of the community, but it is possible to combine even a burning determination to right wrongs with mental balance and tranquillity of disposition. Adjustment however can never be complete; continual adjustment and readjustment are necessary throughout life.'[1]

Value-soaked definitions and explanations thus leave the scientific, objective status of the concept of mental health in a decidedly shaky condition; nor is it surprising that, at a meeting of some of the leading American psychiatrists, doctors, sociologists and anthropologists, all of them 'researchers in the field of mental health', the question: What is mental health? was received in silence.[2] The gradual elimination of ethical or social ideals from the discussions of the World Federation for Mental Health, and the growth of a 'more critical attitude about our fundamental knowledge' between the date of the Federation's London Congress in 1948 and the Toronto Congress of 1954, were indeed remarked upon by the Federation's President, Dr Rumke. 'At Toronto we heard nothing about "world citizenship" or about "prevention of war" . . . We have a more critical attitude about our fundamental knowledge than we had in London. Many people confess openly that they do not know what mental health really is.' Yet the acquisition of such knowledge still remains, in Rumke's opinion, 'our nuclear problem', even though 'experience has proved that remarkable results can be achieved, especially in the field of mental hygiene, without knowledge of what mental health really is . . .' 'In the long run neglect of this problem will be ruinous.'[3]

Whether the confusion arises because we do not know what we are talking about, or because we do not know how to talk is anybody's guess. Possibly the trouble lies in the clumsiness of our attempts to describe a mental condition which is at least as objective as is bodily health, and is no more strongly coloured than is its physical counterpart by social or personal value-judgments: possibly it is only poor observation or inefficient use of language that prevents this condition being defined with scientific accuracy. Alternatively, it may be that no such condition exists. But whatever the reason, the fact remains that current definitions of mental health bear a strong cultural stamp.

In an article on *The Concept of Normality in Clinical Psychology*, Dr J. W. Thibaut has made an interesting, but not, I think, wholly successful attempt to resolve this confusion. Thibaut freely admits the unsatisfactory nature of any criterion of normality which implies adjustment to a particular culture, commenting that this makes mental health 'something distinct from "physical health"', and so 'perpetuates the mind-body dichotomy'. The solution which

[1] Ministry of Education, Committee on Maladjusted Children (1955), p. 3.
[2] Eaton (1951), p. 81.
[3] World Federation for Mental Health, Annual Report, 1954, pp. 9–10.

he himself favours (which is itself borrowed from a suggestion of Dr Trigant Burrow), is that psychotherapy should attempt 'not merely to heal the individual but to develop a healthy community basis of behavior that will be effective throughout the organization of man as a phylum'. Thus 'instead of merely "adjusting" a non-conforming individual to any culture he happens to be in, there will be a shift in emphasis to the revision of the culture as a whole'; and although we have to confess that, up to the present, it is 'impossible to present any precise bill of specifications' for a culture conducive to mental health, 'this difficulty . . . is not insuperable, since the norm provides a conceptual orientation which by specific suggested researches can eventually further describe the optimal societal conditions for collective adjustment'.[1]

In the simpler language current on the Eastern side of the Atlantic, this seems to mean that, instead of measuring a man's mental health by his ability to get along in whatever environment he finds himself, we should try to find out what kind of environment is itself conducive to mental health. Undoubtedly it is a step forward that mental hygienists should wake up to the fact that all ways of life are not equally good, and that 'adjustment' cannot be accepted as a criterion of health unless we face the question: Adjustment to what? Nevertheless the fundamental confusion remains. For merely to say that mental health results from adjustment to a wholesome environment, or to 'optimal societal conditions' brings us no nearer to any value-free definition of either 'health' or 'wholesomeness'. Many of us do indeed rejoice that psychotherapists are more often concerned with bringing about the adjustment of murderers and rapists to a gentler way of life, than with the adjustment of deviant liberals to a Nazi or similar regime. Such a preference is, however, derived from ultimate moral judgments or choices. To assert that the psychiatrist's activities are conducive in the one case to mental health, but in the other to its opposite, is suspiciously like an attempt to increase the appeal of a purely ethical judgment by clothing it in the fashionable medical dress favoured by a scientifically-minded age; or in Kingsley Davis' metaphor, to hide ethical preconceptions 'behind a scientific façade'.[2] The psychiatrist, in fact, 'talks the language of the scientific method and has the professional need to consider his social preference as having resulted from scientific observation. He is in danger of replacing the semantics of social morality with that of psychological morality without changing the substance.'[3]

IV

An alternative approach to the whole problem is to begin at the other end and to attempt a definition of mental disorder, rather than of mental health. In principle this approach is often preferred, on the ground perhaps that, in this vale of tears, failure may be easier to identify than success. Thus in the course of an American seminar on *Needed Research in Health and Medical Care* a physiologist is reported to have given it as his opinion that 'the con-

[1] Thibaut (1943). [2] Davis, Kingsley (1938), p. 65.
[3] Freedman, in Hoch and Zubin, eds. (1955), p. 43.

cept of positive health is of no use whatsoever . . . I prefer to work with the concept of disease as an entity that is present or not present'.[1] Explicit definitions of mental disorder seem, however, to have been less often attempted than have their opposites, perhaps because, when people are ill enough, the fact is unmistakable and definitions appear unnecessary. To-day, however, the term 'mental illness' is used to cover a great deal more than real madness; the days are past when the expert in mental medicine was invoked only to deal with violent or deluded patients, or with those who were unmanageably hysterical, depressed to the point of total incapacity or senile to the point of infantilism. The contemporary psychiatrist no longer expects to be solely concerned with such major catastrophes. Even the child guidance clinics and the mental hospitals, let alone the private consulting rooms of psychiatrists, are now occupied by all manner of cases whose troubles would certainly not have been classified, by the more rigorous standards of an earlier age, as due to illness. In the United States in 1948, over 15 per cent of first admissions to all reporting State mental hospitals are not diagnosed as psychotic: in over 10 per cent of admissions 'no mental disorder was reported'.[2] To-day, doctors in clinics, hospitals or private practice are called upon to deal with children who steal or have violent tempers or who wet their beds; with men and women who cannot get on with their spouses or manage their love affairs satisfactorily; with criminals convicted of various offences, as well as with the victims of all manner of irrational fears, anxieties and depressions and sometimes also of quite rational ones. As one group of authors has somewhat despairingly put it, 'The psychiatrist deals with people who are complaining or who are complained about'.[3]

Perhaps the simplest method of defining the limits of these large and vaguely defined areas of social maladjustment which are now regarded as manifestations of mental ill-health would be merely to turn upside down such formulations as those quoted on pp. 211–214, as Bowlby, for instance, does when he finds 'the most concrete concept of mental ill-health' to be 'derangement of the capacity to make co-operative relationships with other human beings'.[4] The mentally sick person would then appear as unhappy, as at war with himself and his environment, inefficient, inconsiderate, lacking in purpose, confidence and enthusiasm, fearful and indifferent to the development of his own potentialities—even if we do not add that he disturbs industrial peace, inclines to crime or to a position of social dependency, or that he either shrinks from discussion of sexual matters or enjoys this to a degree which outrages dignity and decency. Obviously, however, merely to turn our notions of mental health upside down does not have the effect of emptying them of all their ethical content. The validity of the discussion on pp. 216–221 is not affected by its transposition into a negative form; nor are the difficulties avoided if the negative version is adopted from the beginning. As Stycos

[1] Sheps and Taylor (1954), p. 140.
[2] See Eaton and Weil (1955), pp. 232–3.
[3] Lemkau and others (1953), p. 436.
[4] Bowlby, in Soddy, ed. (1955), vol. 1, p. 117.

has found himself compelled to admit, 'the concept "mental disorder"—particularly in relation to the functional psychoses—means little more than deviation from some expected social behavior'.[1] Even upward deviations from the expected standards of charitable behaviour, in the United States at any rate, are to-day regarded as symptoms of mental illness. You are, for instance, liable to be sent to hospital if, on learning from a taxi-driver that what he most wants in life is to own his own cab, you give him 5,000 dollars to enable him to do so:[2] or if you stand on the pavement and toss a wad of dollar bills to the wind;[3] though, in our own somewhat less psychiatrically minded country, similar exhibitions of unusual generosity are apparently more likely to engage the attentions of the police.[4]

Even the test of employability or of working efficiency does not serve to distinguish the sick from the sound. The National Assistance Board, as we have seen,[5] is acutely conscious of the difficulty of distinguishing the culpably workshy from the mentally handicapped; and to complicate the picture still further it appears that some of those who are diagnosed as neurotics are not merely adequate, but even exceptionally good, workers. Investigations conducted a few years ago by the Medical Research Council in which the performance of apparently healthy men and women in the iron and steel industry was contrasted with that of a group of neurotics, showed that 'those who had a poor record of recent mental health combined with low intelligence had as a group an average output, and, in every case but one, were rated by the supervisors as well-adjusted to their job . . . The more intelligent men did not produce more than the dull ones, nor were those who produced least men with rather poor mental health'.[6]

The difficulty of separating moral, from strictly medical, judgments is indeed abundantly illustrated on every hand. As proof of a woman's 'neurotic make-up' Guttmacher and Weihofen calmly quote the fact that she had embarked upon her fourth marriage.[7] In the evidence submitted on behalf of the Institute for the Study and Treatment of Delinquency to the (Wolfenden) Committee on Homosexual Offences and Prostitution, there occurs the statement that 'To the psychiatrist the problem of homosexuality raises no question of criminality unless the sexual deviation is associated with acts of violence, assault or seduction of minors'.[8] That may well be: psychiatrists generally, and the particular group of psychiatrists in whose name this evidence was drawn up, are as much entitled to their personal opinions as anybody else. They may, if they wish, dislike violence or assaults upon minors, while raising no objection to homosexual acts between consenting adults, or

[1] Stycos (1949), p. 302. [2] *The Times* (January 15, 1958).
[3] *News Chronicle* (November 4, 1953). [4] *News Chronicle* (August 9, 1955).
[5] See p. 42.
[6] Markowe (1953), pp. 99–100. Against these findings, however, is to be set a number of studies which point in the opposite direction, summarized by O'Connor and Tizard (1956), pp. 56–7.
[7] Guttmacher and Weihofen (1952), p. 91.
[8] Institute for the Study and Treatment of Delinquency and the Portman Clinic (1955), p. 3.

at least deprecating the prohibition of these by the criminal law; but in what sense such views (which, incidentally, are shared by the present author) can claim to be *medically* established is far from clear.

Most teasing of all, perhaps, in this context is the problem of deciding what attitude should be adopted towards what has hitherto been called 'malingering'. Is the malingerer to be blamed or pitied? punished or given the benefit of therapy? To describe anyone as a malingerer certainly has traditionally implied moral censure; but 'in psychoanalytic writings' malingering is now treated 'as if it were a scientific concept designating a distinct mode of behavior or a psychopathological syndrome'. In the opinion, however, of at least one critical writer 'malingering is not a "diagnosis", in the usual sense of the word'. It 'expresses the physician's moral condemnation of the patient in general, and of a specific pattern of behavior in particular. It thus tells us more about the observer (physician) . . . than it does about the observed (patient)'. Statements that malingering is a disease (along with similar statements about crime) 'are declarations of faith and explicit affirmations of one's mode of approach to a problem. If the method in question possesses much prestige, the very act of adherence to it may appear as a meritorious accomplishment. This is, however, sheer illusion. Thus, to maintain that criminality, malingering, or some aspects of political leadership are matters of "psychopathology" is to indulge ourselves in such an illusion. By so doing, we merely substitute the vague and all-inclusive notion of "mental illness" for all sorts of other problems'.[1]

Mental illness, in short, is no less elusive than mental health—at any rate in its milder manifestations. Stycos concludes that 'one is left with the following: mental disorder is manifested either by a prolonged state of confusion or deterioration in which a person is incapable of assessing life situations; or manifested in a persistent and inflexible mode of assessment which is culturally illogical'.[2] Thorpe and Katz can only define a psychoneurosis as 'a dysfunction of behavior due to emotional stress developed as the result of frustrations, conflicts, deprivation, or great personal insecurity';[3] while Marzolf proposes to abandon the term 'mental disease' altogether.[4]

V

Whichever way, therefore, the problem may be approached, no solid foundation seems to be discoverable on which to establish the propositions formulated on p. 207.

If this is true, important consequences follow. First, the attempt to assimilate mental and physical disorders and to treat both alike breaks down. For in those physical disorders which are accompanied by disregard of social norms, the aberrant behaviour is incidental to, or at least independent of,

[1] Szasz (1956), pp. 442 and 438.
[2] Stycos (1949), p. 302.
[3] Thorpe and Katz (1948), p. 359.
[4] Marzolf (1947), p. 219.

the physical symptoms; it is the fever which calls for treatment, not just the delirious babblings which are its accompaniment. By contrast, many of the symptoms, at least of the milder mental conditions for which psychiatric treatment is now commonly sought, are *essentially* behavioural. As definitions of mental illness become ever vaguer or more deeply entangled in the accepted norms of social conduct, so does it become ever more evident that many of those who are labelled 'mentally sick' acquire this label merely because in one way or another they have failed to manage their lives conformably with the demands of the social environment in which they find themselves. The suspicious, the irritable, the bad-tempered, the aggressive are cajoled or driven by their suffering friends and relatives or by 'the authorities' to seek medical advice—especially, perhaps, if they are of tender years, since the young are generally at the mercy of their elders and must go and do where and what they are told. In such cases it is the anti-social behaviour which is the precipitating factor that leads to mental treatment. But at the same time the fact of the illness is itself inferred from this behaviour: indeed it is almost true to say that the illness *is* the behaviour for which it is also the excuse. But any disease, the morbidity of which is established *only* by the social failure that it involves, must rank as fundamentally different from those of which the symptoms are independent of social norms.

This distinction will, moreover, still remain even if we reach the stage, as we very well may, when every mental process has its known physical accompaniment, and when our present dualistic language, along with the distinction between 'organic' and 'functional' disorders, can be discarded. For even then it will still be true that some abnormalities are deplored because they cause fever or boils, others because they induce a disregard of property rights—even though it may be shown that the latter no less than the former, are associated with happenings in the stomach, the liver or the brain, and can be cured by suitable pills, injections or electric shocks. Even in this case a social judgment is still implied in the decision to rank the thieving tendency together with its bodily concomitants as symptoms of disease or dysfunction; for if it had not been for their social consequences, these physical concomitants would never have been reckoned as abnormal at all. In a sense, therefore, the effect of extending physical 'explanations' to cover all forms of aberrant conduct would be to infuse into certain conceptions of physical health elements of value-judgment comparable to those which already bias the terms in which mental health is defined. Long indeed is the road to be travelled before we can hope to reach a definition of mental-cum-physical health, which is objective, scientific and wholly free of social value-judgments; and before we shall be able, consistently and without qualification, to treat mental and physical disorders on exactly the same footing.

Meanwhile a second and no less important consequence of defining illness as, or inferring its presence from, aberrant behaviour instead of from symptoms that are independent of this behaviour, is that conventional concepts of responsibility are undermined. For if illness excuses bad temper, and if a man is only known to be ill by reason of his temper, the same logic may be used to absolve him of responsibility for other forms of behaviour which are classified as anti-social. The large and complex issues thus raised are the subject of the following chapter.[1]

[1] In anticipation of this discussion, it may be of interest to note that Lord Pakenham, writing as a devout Catholic, has found it necessary in the same context to wrestle with much the same problems, and has apparently reached much the same conclusion as does so thoroughgoing an agnostic as myself. See Part II of his *Causes of Crime* (1958).

CHAPTER VIII

Mental Disorder and the Problem of Moral and Criminal Responsibility

I

IF mental health and ill-health cannot be defined in objective scientific terms that are free of subjective moral judgments, it follows that we have no reliable criterion by which to distinguish the sick from the healthy mind. The road is then wide open for those who wish to classify all forms of anti-social, or at least of criminal, behaviour as symptoms of mental disorder. Among the experts a few are in fact prepared, either explicitly or by implication, to take this road and to obliterate the distinction between criminality and illness altogether. For them the line between the sick and the healthy either does not exist or is irrelevant to problems of social behaviour; and they are prepared accordingly to treat all offenders as 'patients', and to dispense with the concepts of responsibility altogether. Such views are important and are discussed in some detail below. But they are as yet exceptional. Without doubt the preponderance of psychiatric, as well as of both lay and legal, opinion still leans to the view that, for practical purposes, an intelligible division can be made between those deviants who must be regarded as sick, and those whose nuisance-behaviour cannot be explained on grounds of ill-health; and that, even if the expert is at times unable to put into words the distinctive characteristics of the two varieties, nevertheless he may be able in practice to make a distinction between them. Indeed the expert may even go farther and attempt to say how he actually sets about this; for in this as in some other matters, practice, it seems, has outstripped theory.

As an example of unequivocal belief in the reality of the distinction between the healthy and the sick deviant, we may quote the late Sir Norwood East's dictum that 'as the result of more than fifty years practical experience of crime I am unable to regard crime as a disease, although sometimes the result of it'.[1] So also to Dr Desmond Curran it is 'absurd to maintain that an unhappy man is necessarily sick . . . or that a delinquent man is necessarily sick. The decision as to whether a man is sick or not does not purely depend upon unhappiness, inefficiency, or social inadequacy as such'.[2] Professor Aubrey Lewis, again, observes that the psychiatrist 'is nowadays often, and quite properly, asked to investigate and treat disturbances of behaviour in children which can hardly be included within any warranted conception of illness

[1] East, in East, ed. (1954), p. 5. [2] Curran, in East, ed. (1954), p. 29.

(though of course they may be the prelude to illness) . . . It may be that there is no form of social deviation in an individual which psychiatrists will not claim to treat or prevent—the pretensions of some psychiatrists are extreme. That time has not come, fortunately.' But in his opinion 'the criteria of health are not primarily social: it is misconceived to equate ill-health with social deviation or maladjustment'.[1] And even in the United States, where psychiatric influence is even stronger than it is here, some psychiatrists take equally modest views. 'Unfortunately', writes one of them, 'so large a section of our educated population has been persuaded that the way to achieve personal happiness is through psychotherapy that all private practising psychiatrists, including myself, are called upon to "treat" people who for one or another reason are very unhappy but by no means diseased. From this point of view, psychiatry has nowadays spread itself out too far and taken on a bigger piece of human discontent than it can ever handle, to say nothing of eliminate. Unless psychiatrists make a distinction between the common or garden variety of unhappiness encountered in our society and bona fide psychiatric disease, they will be contributing to the current confusion.'[2]

In much the same vein the Director of Medical Services for the Prison Commissioners constantly plays down the role of psychotherapy in the treatment of prisoners. Although an 'elucidative discussion' of their problems is said in some cases to help prisoners in the acceptance of their guilt, nevertheless 'the number of prisoners suitable for major psychotherapy is relatively small', even if 'a different view is not infrequently but erroneously expressed';[3] while the suggestion that 'a vast number of cases—especially those of a violent and sexual nature—have only to be subjected to specialized psychiatric treatment for their anti-social proclivities to be effaced' is described as 'uninformed'.[4] And, in the United States also, caustic comment has been made upon the judge who 'passes the buck' to the psychiatrist and then goes to lunch 'full of rectitude and up-to-dateness'.[5]

Many authorities are thus in agreement both with one another and with the law in holding that, at least in practice, a line can be drawn between those whose offences are explained by illness, and those who cannot legitimately plead ill-health as mitigation of, or excuse for, their conduct, but must shoulder responsibility for their own actions. In the view of these authorities the critical dispute relates, not to any question whether this line should be drawn at all, but to the decision where it should run. And on that question opinion is far from homogeneous.

Of all contemporary attempts to define the limits within which mental incapacity undermines responsibility, the narrowest and most rigid is the famous formula embodied in the McNaghten rules which govern English law in cases other than those now excepted by the Homicide Act of 1957. By this a man is held to be responsible for his actions unless he is 'labouring under such a defect of reason, from disease of the mind, as not to know the

[1] Lewis, Aubrey (June 1953), pp. 120 and 124. [2] Wortis, in Wolff (1956), p. 204.
[3] Commissioners of Prisons, Report for 1954, p. 102.
[4] Commissioners of Prisons, Report for 1953, p. 98. [5] Davidson (1954), p. 19.

nature and quality of the act he was doing, or, if he did know it, that he did not know he was doing what was wrong'.[1] This formula, though usually quoted in connection only with capital cases, applies, in principle, to responsibility for criminal acts of every kind. Indeed even in civil cases the same test is liable to be used. Thus the Court of Appeal[2] has upheld the view that the McNaghten rules are applicable to petitions for divorce on grounds of cruelty. If a defendant in such cases can prove insanity within the terms of the rules (the onus of proof lying on him) this appears to be a good defence; and in that event the marriage (together with, presumably, the cruelty) must go on. The only reason why reference to the McNaghten doctrine generally occurs only in cases of capital murder is that in these cases the court has no choice of sentence. In dealing with other offences a judge or magistrate who has doubts about the mental responsibility of an offender not proved to be insane in the McNaghten sense can usually take account of these by suitable modification of the penalty that he imposes; but in charges of capital murder only sentence of death is permitted.

Whether applied to criminal or civil matters, the McNaghten formula is essentially a test of responsibility; and it must be judged by its merits as an interpretation of the third and fourth of the four propositions outlined on p. 207; for it exists only to determine who are rightly answerable for their acts and who should be absolved on grounds of mental disorder. In this capacity both its strength and its weakness are derived from its distinctively intellectualist nature: *intellectual* understanding of the nature of one's actions, and *intellectual* grasp of the accepted meaning of right and wrong are the McNaghten criteria of responsibility.

The strength of this intellectualism lies, first and foremost, in the fact that, by virtue of its very narrowness, it provides a safe and commonsensical definition of the *minimum* group about whose inclusion in the category of irresponsibles there can be no dispute. It may be, and indeed it is, much criticised as being unduly *ex*clusive: but no-one could suggest that it *in*cludes any who ought to be counted as sane. So long as any concept of responsibility survives at all, the man who literally does not know what he is doing, or who literally does not know what are the everyday moral judgments of his own community—the man, in fact, who would have committed his crime 'with a policeman at his elbow'—such a man must surely have the strongest claim to rank as mad to the point of irresponsibility.

In the second place, the intellectualist quality of the McNaghten formula makes it, at least by comparison with suggested alternatives, such as are discussed below, a model of clarity and precision—in spite of the clouds of legal argument in which its interpretation has from time to time been enveloped. Much of this legal argument has been concerned with attempts to stretch the formula to cover other than purely intellectual disorder. But within, so to speak, its own narrow horizons, there is scope for major controversy only on two points. The first relates to the meaning to be ascribed

[1] Royal Commission on Capital Punishment, 1949–53, Report (1953), p. 79.
[2] *The Times*, Law Report (October 29, 1954).

in this context to the words 'right and wrong'. Since philosophers have entertained themselves with argumentation about these words for almost as long as we have written records, the theoretical possibilities of confusion here are immeasurable; but in a legal sense the matter is capable of being, and apparently has been, definitely settled. For the purpose of determining legal responsibility, the terms 'right' and 'wrong' are now definitely held to mean 'consonant with, or contrary to, the law'—a ruling which, unlike many philosophically more sophisticated alternatives, at least has the virtue of clarity.

The second point of criticism relates to the scope of the expression 'disease of the mind'. In the sense in which this phrase is generally used in medical parlance, it includes only disturbances of minds that have previously been 'normal', but excludes those that have failed ever to develop in the ordinary way. In layman's language, it includes the mad, but not the feeble-minded; and a feeble-minded murderer who might well be qualified as not knowing that what he was doing was wrong, but could only be classified as defective, not as insane, could be executed for his crime. It would, however, be simple enough, without destroying the fundamentally intellectualist basis of the rules, to extend their coverage to cases of mental deficiency, and to free from criminal responsibility mentally defective as well as lunatic offenders, on the ground that the former also either do not know what they are doing or do not know that it is wrong. Such an amendment has in fact now been included in the extension of the rules under the Homicide Act of 1957.

For more reasons than one it is not surprising that the McNaghten formula appeals to lawyers. Partly it appeals to lawyers because the intellectualist conception of the nature of responsibility which it embodies is both deep-seated and widespread in our legal system. The McNaghten rules are, for example, of a piece with the concept of 'mens rea' as applied to children. According to this doctrine, a child below a minimum age (at present fixed at eight years) is incapable of crime because it is too young to *understand* the difference between right and wrong; while for some years even above that age the onus rests upon the prosecution to show, not only that a child committed the illegal act with which he is charged, but also that in so doing he knew that he was doing wrong. Thus the very young child and the madman exempted under the second limb of the McNaghten rules both escape responsibility on exactly similar grounds.

But not less attractive to the legal profession is the very narrowness of the formula and its consequential (comparative) precision. The state of a man's intellect or knowledge is much more easily tested by such court procedures as cross-examination than is, say, the state of his will. A purely intellectual test presumes a general rationality of behaviour, and seeks to prove or disprove normal intellectual capacity by the degree in which such rationality is maintained. Thus, in accordance with this assumption of rationality, the defence that an offender did not know his action to be wrong will not stand up, if he can be shown to have taken precautions against detection. Conversely, if a man can be shown to be incapable of performing the simplest intellectual operations, if there is evidence (independent of the actual offence with which he is charged) that he cannot add two and two together, or that he believes himself to be a second incarnation of the deity, there is at least a *prima facie* case that his judgment is so confused that he may not know right from wrong. It may be true that the risk of intellectual incapacity being falsely assumed cannot be ruled out; but it does certainly require great ingenuity for an intelligent person to maintain a fiction of complete silliness against clever cross-examination. For the same reasons also the McNaghten rules are comparatively well adapted to application by laymen; and it is laymen who, as magistrates or juries, in the vast majority of cases have to decide the question of guilt or innocence, of responsibility or irresponsibility, in the courts.

Most important of all the merits of the McNaghten formula, however, is the fact that a defence of intellectual insufficiency can be tested by criteria external to the actions which it is invoked to excuse. The proof that a man is deluded or lacks understanding lies, not in the fact that he commits a crime, so much as in his behaviour before and afterwards, or even in his capacity to understand things that have nothing to do with his offence. He is deemed to be mad, not because of the crime which he has committed, but because of his inability to appreciate such facts as that he is not the King of Siam and that the trees in his garden are not a horde of parachutists. And, since his insanity is thus inferred from aspects of his behaviour other than his actual offence, there is comparatively little risk of becoming entangled in the circular argument that the offender 'must have been mad to do such a thing'.

For many years now, however, the McNaghten formula has been subjected to a formidable stream of criticism, especially from medical quarters, on the ground of the very intellectualism, which, as we have seen, is, in one sense, its chief virtue. Insanity and irresponsibility, it is said, are at least as much a matter of disordered emotion as of defective reason. Even as far back as the first decade of this century we find a representative of the Royal College of Physicians of London urging upon a Royal Commission the view that 'the conception of insanity as an intellectual disorder solely should be superseded by the understanding that it is inability, by reason of mental (not necessarily intellectual) defect and disorder to manage oneself and one's affairs'.[1] In 1922, a Committee appointed by the Lord Chancellor to consider the law relating to insanity in criminal trials would have recognized a person as 'irresponsible for his act when the act is committed under an impulse which the prisoner was by mental disease in substance deprived of any power to resist'.[2] More recently similar criticism has been revived in great force in the evidence submitted by a number of medical witnesses to the Royal Commission on Capital Punishment. The British Medical Association, for instance, condemned the formula on the ground that it 'takes account only of the cognitive faculties and is therefore based on an antiquated and outworn conception of mental disease, which is now recognized as involving morbid emotional changes and not solely, nor even necessarily, an impairment

[1] Radnor Report (1908), p. 151.

[2] See Royal Commission on Capital Punishment, 1949–53, Report (1953), p. 81.

of intellectual powers'.[1] Instead, the Association wished to substitute a formula which reads as follows: 'To establish a defence on the ground of disease of the mind, the party accused must prove that, at the time of the committing of the act, he was labouring, as a result of disease of the mind, under (1) a defect of reason such that he did not know (*a*) the nature and quality of the act he was doing, or (if he did know this) (*b*) that he was doing what was wrong; or (2) a disorder of emotion such that, while appreciating the nature and quality of the act, and that it was wrong, he did not possess sufficient power to prevent himself from committing it.' In the interpretation of this formula it is moreover specifically provided that 'disease of the mind' should cover 'incomplete mental development as well as grave disturbances of mental health', and that 'wrong' should mean, not 'punishable by law', but morally wrong in the accused person's own opinion.[2]

Until recently the supporters of the McNaghten rules have successfully resisted revision on these lines, pleading that the application of the rules in practice is not always so rigid as a strict interpretation of their terms might suggest. In 1957, however, an important, if limited, extension of the McNaghten formula was introduced into England in the Homicide Act. Section 2 (i) of this Act reads as follows: 'Where a person kills or is party to the killing of another, he shall not be convicted of murder if he was suffering from such abnormality of mind (whether arising from a condition of arrested or retarded development of mind or any inherent causes or induced by disease or injury) as substantially impaired his mental responsibility for his acts and omissions in doing or being a party to the killing.'

Outside England provisions of this kind are by no means uncommon. Even the McNaghten formula itself has not run, or at least has not run with full authority, north of the Tweed, where 'diminished responsibility' has long been admissible as a defence to a criminal charge; while many European codes and many, though by no means all, of the States in the USA also admit, or have at some time admitted, a defence of irresistible impulse or of diminished responsibility. It can at least be said that experience outside England has shown that laws which recognize such concepts as 'irresistible impulse' or 'diminished responsibility' are workable in practice, no matter how vulnerable these concepts may be on theoretical grounds.

Thus both weighty medical opinion and much judicial practice support the view that the McNaghten formula is too rigid a device for discriminating between the wilful and the sick offender, even in capital charges. And in circumstances not involving homicide the same reasoning would no doubt have even greater force. To-day probably no psychiatrist, and no doctor experienced in cases of social maladjustment, would diagnose mental sickness only in those instances in which intellectual faculties were clouded to the degree envisaged by the McNaghten formula; though it is perhaps appropriate to remind ourselves that such an attitude would have been quite natural a hundred years ago, and by no means unusual even at the beginning of this century.

[1] Royal Commission on Capital Punishment, 1949-53, Report (1953), p. 87.

[2] ibid., p. 93.

Definitions of criminal responsibility which attempt to discriminate between the fully responsible, the irresponsible and those whose responsibility is diminished in terms wider than those of the McNaghten rules are, however, fraught with formidable difficulties. The interpretation of the rules themselves, for all their relative simplicity, has proved tricky enough; but the problems thus raised are trivial compared to those which present themselves once the intellectualist definition of mental disorder as the criterion of criminal responsibility is abandoned in favour of one which admits that we may cease to be responsible for our actions, not because we do not appreciate their nature, but because we have lost the power to control them. At once we are in danger of becoming involved in circular argument. As in the analogous problem of defining mental health or mental disorder, the difficulty is to avoid defining the phenomenon in terms of itself. For just as, in the case of an anti-social act that is said to be due to mental illness, the existence of the illness cannot, without circular argument, be inferred solely from the fact that the act was committed, so also it must not be inferred that an impulse was irresistible merely because it was not resisted. If irresistible impulse or diminished responsibility is to be a valid excuse for anti-social actions, some criterion of irresponsibility must be found which is independent of the act itself. But the crux of the matter is: What is that criterion to be? A number of alternatives have been suggested; but, as is argued in what follows, not one of them appears to be logically tenable.

II

To the lay mind perhaps the simplest method, other than the McNaghten formula, of dividing the sick sheep from the healthy but reprehensible goats, and the one which involves the least departure from McNaghten intellectualism, is the concept of 'motiveless behaviour'. Indeed this concept provides a kind of bridge between a purely intellectualist position and one which admits disorders of the will as factors in irresponsibility. The basic presumption of rationality remains: mentally healthy normal men are still presumed to act from rational motives. Judged by this criterion anyone who knows what he is doing and knows it to be wrong, but who has no intelligible motive for his action, must be mentally sick: the sickness lies—and here is the concession to the more modern notions of disorders of the will—in the absence or, alternatively, in the irrationality, of motive.

Though not perhaps much favoured by up-to-date psychiatric opinion, this concept of the 'motiveless' crime or 'motiveless' behaviour has certainly had significant practical influence. Indeed its power may well be due to the smallness of the breach which it makes with traditional intellectualism. The concept of kleptomania, as not merely vulgar stealing but as a symptom of disease, is a case in point. 'Purposeless', 'senseless' stealing, sometimes defined as kleptomania, is the typical motiveless crime; and occasional 'motiveless' killings fall into the same category.

This concept of motiveless behaviour, however, as Cressey has convincingly argued, itself involves a considerable element of social judgment. In his view the concepts of 'compulsive crime are no less "wastebasket categories" than is the "psychopathic personality" concept'. Casual observation indicates, at least, that the application of the "compulsive crime" label is resorted to in cases where neither the subject nor anyone else is able to account for the behaviour in question 'in terms of motives which are current, popular, and sanctioned in a particular culture or among the members of a particular group within a culture'.[1] Applying this reasoning to our own, highly acquisitive, culture, Cressey goes on to suggest that the practice—which sometimes provokes considerable class feeling—of ascribing the thefts of the well-to-do to kleptomania, and those of the poor to criminality, is fundamentally logical. A well-to-do person, who can buy anything that he desires, has no socially recognized motive for stealing, and must therefore be judged to be mentally sick if he is guilty of dishonesty. The stealing of the poor, by contrast, must be criminal just because it is rational, except in cases where the poor also engage in repetitive stealing of 'useless' objects. Even a poor person who endlessly stole, let us say, packets of hairpins would be judged to be mentally peculiar. By way of illustration Cressey himself quotes Alexander and Staub's judgment that a physician was not behaving neurotically when he stole medical books and supplies, but only when he helped himself to porcelain figures which were of no value. Such distinctions, he would argue, are, in fact, merely reflections of the particular motivations acceptable in our particular culture, and most noticeably of its emphasis on the rationality of economic or acquisitive motives.[2]

Cressey concludes that 'the economic status of the observer probably is of great importance in determining whether he thinks a person is not in economic need and is consequently compulsive . . . If all psychiatrists were poverty-stricken the proportion of shoplifters called "kleptomaniacs" probably would be much higher than it is.'[3] And by the same logic what is true of thieving is no less true of other crimes. Fire-raising as such generally ranks as 'motiveless'; but fire-raising in order to defraud an insurance company is a different matter. On this principle, incidentally, fire-raising in England on November 5th poses some nice questions. If the desire for fires for their own sake on this date is held to fall within the range of socially intelligible motives, then indulgence of this desire beyond the limits of what is socially tolerated must rank as criminal rather than as neurotic. But if Guy Fawkes bonfires are judged to be 'motiveless', then anyone responsible for a dangerous or destructive conflagration must be classified as sick rather than sinful.

Actually, if the argument is carried one step further, the line between the 'motivated' and the 'motiveless' action itself becomes blurred; for the range of intelligible motives is itself modified by new knowledge and new attitudes. Thanks to the popularity of psychiatric notions, the urge to steal for stealing's sake begins to find its place among the recognized, if not indeed the 'normal', motives for theft; for our conception of the normal is itself defined by 'linguistic constructs'. With the invention of the term 'kleptomania',

[1] Cressey (1954), p. 35. [2] ibid., p. 37. [3] ibid., p. 36.

a sociological 'rôle' is established for the previously 'motiveless' thief. No longer compelled to plead that he 'doesn't know what made him do it', he can now at least explain his own conduct: 'I did it', he says, 'because I am a kleptomaniac'; and 'I did it', says the poor man, 'because I was hungry'. The analogy is complete.

The classification of behaviour as motivated or motiveless cannot, therefore, claim to rank as 'natural' or as self-evident, or even as being uninfluenced by cultural idiosyncracies: it reduces itself to a division into culturally respectable and culturally surprising or peculiar motives. But it does at least provide a criterion for distinguishing normal from abnormal deviants which avoids circular argument; since the abnormality is inferred from the peculiarity of the motive, not from the fact of the deviant behaviour itself. To that extent it may be said to explain certain forms of misbehaviour which are not otherwise explicable.

Explanation, however, is not necessarily the same as exculpation: the fourth of the propositions on p. 207 is additional to, not identical with, the third. Into the argument about motiveless or strangely motivated conduct a second strand is, in fact, woven, and one which may be traced also in other, more sophisticated, criteria for distinguishing the sick from the healthy. That second strand is the assumption that, if a person exhibits symptoms of mental disorder, this fact by itself diminishes moral or criminal responsibility for his actions. Whatever criterion of mental health is used, that assumption is not necessarily justified. Some mental illnesses may undermine the patient's capacity to restrain himself from wrongful actions; but we have no more right to assume that all mental disorders will have this effect than to assume that, because a man is not held responsible for violent behaviour in a delirium, therefore similar behaviour is equally excusable when he is suffering from whooping-cough. Even if we allow the test of motivated or motiveless to distinguish the normal from the abnormal, we still have no right to leap light-heartedly to the paradoxical conclusion that the urge to actions that rank as 'motiveless' is in fact more powerful than any of the motives which prompt 'rational' behaviour. As Cressey has put it, 'the apparent inability of a person to explain his actions to the police, to a psychiatrist, or even to himself' is not sufficient reason for classifying those actions as 'compulsive'.[1] All that is known of such actions is that they spring from motives that are not socially acceptable; but their supposedly superior strength needs to be demonstrated in its own right: it is by no means self-evident that the physician's yearning for valueless porcelain figures is inevitably stronger, or more nearly irresistible, than the poor man's hunger for a square meal or for a packet of cigarettes.

Not far removed from the notion of motiveless or strangely motivated behaviour is the hypothesis, apparently favoured by the psychoanalytic school, that a distinction should be drawn between conscious and unconscious motivations. If I rightly understand the psychoanalytic teaching on the subject of the role of mental disorder in anti-social behaviour, the

[1] Cressey (1954), p. 38.

essence of this is that actions which are the result of unconscious urges are in a different category from those of which the motives are fully conscious. How far the psychoanalytic school wish to retain any concept of moral responsibility is not altogether clear: possibly many of their adherents would prefer to bypass this in the way described on pages 247 ff. In so far, however, as the psychoanalytic distinction between conscious and unconscious motives has any bearing on the question of moral or criminal responsibility, or on the definition of the medical factors in anti-social conduct, it seems reasonable to infer that we can only be said to be fully responsible for those actions which are consciously motivated.

For two reasons I do not propose to examine this line of thought further. The first reason is the purely practical one that there seems very little prospect that any differentiation between the responsible and the irresponsible in terms of conscious and unconscious motives is likely to be carried into practical effect. Reliable diagnosis of unconscious motives cannot, according to psychoanalytic teaching, be made, except by those who have themselves been psychoanalytically trained. It follows, therefore, that, if this criterion were used, the distinction between those who could, and those who could not, be held responsible for their misdeeds could only be drawn by trained psychoanalysts. In the present climate of opinion there is no sign that psychoanalysts enjoy the public's confidence to a degree which gives any expectation that they might be entrusted with virtually the last word on what may be a matter of life and death. So long as the opinions of every medical man are subject in the courts to lay criticism and in the last resort to lay adjudication, it seems unlikely that one section of the medical profession, and that by no means the most orthodox, will, in the foreseeable future, win the right to speak with unquestioned authority.

The second reason is that, at least in my experience, fruitful discussion of psychoanalytic theories is not at present possible between those who are, and those who are not, convinced of their essential truth. Constructive controversy will continue to be inhibited so long as the psychoanalyst denies the capacity of those who have not been analysed to pass judgment upon his theories, and so long as he is more concerned to identify in his critics unconscious motives which prevent their acceptance of his doctrines, than to consider the merits of any criticisms that they have to offer. Psychoanalysts themselves are quite candid about this. Thus Fenichel observes that 'Those who have not undergone a personal analysis will probably be able to understand intellectually what is presented in this book; but probably many things will seem to them even more incredible and "far-fetched" than psychoanalytic case reports. Persons who "do not believe in psychoanalysis" will not be convinced by reading this book.'[1] Another writer explains the failure of anthropologists 'to interpret completely Freud's concepts in terms of verified field observations' as due to their 'resistance to psychoanalytic hypotheses';[2] while from yet another source we learn that the philosopher's

[1] Fenichel (1945), pp. 8–9.
[2] Muensterberger, in *Psycho-analysis and the Social Sciences* (1955), p. 10.

'determination to adhere to traditional ethical terms' is symptomatic of a 'resistance-phenomenon'. 'Only psychoanalytical method can make explicit the anxiety-inducing property of ethical terms';[1] while empiricist philosophy itself turns out to be founded 'not on logic but upon emotion',[2] the underlying unconscious process being again revealed only to the psychoanalytically qualified. Indeed even amongst the converted, it seems, this belief that those who do not agree with you are the victims of their own unconscious motives is now so well established as to be recognized as a possible source of error. In a singularly frank article Dr Edward Glover has remarked that 'It is scarcely to be expected that a student who has spent some years under the artificial and sometimes hothouse conditions of a training analysis and whose professional career depends on overcoming "resistance" to the satisfaction of his training analyst, can be in a favourable position to defend his scientific integrity against his analyst's theories and practice'; and we are, therefore, in his view, obliged to make the working assumption that 'no system exists whereby the scientific authority of research workers can be distinguished from the prestige of senior analytical practitioners and teachers'.[3]

None of this proves, of course, the rightness or the wrongness of psychoanalytic theories. They may be right: they may be wrong. But it is clearly useless for anyone who is outside the fold, and who by definition lacks the 'prestige of senior analytical practitioners and teachers', to discuss them.

Much more open to rational discussion is the criterion which distinguishes between the sick and the responsible among anti-social persons in accordance with the presence or absence of recognized symptoms of abnormality which are independent of their misbehaviour. This is perhaps the criterion which is most favoured to-day by expert psychiatric opinion. Thus Curran, who, as we have seen, thinks it 'absurd' to maintain that a delinquent is necessarily sick, diagnoses mental illness by the presence of a psychiatric syndrome additional to the anti-social behaviour.[4] Professor Aubrey Lewis, in an exceptionally penetrating discussion of the whole problem, draws what amounts to a similar distinction. To him, the criterion alike of mental and physical ill-health is the presence of specific symptoms, or the 'evident disturbance of part-functions as well as of general efficiency'. 'In physical disease', he adds, 'this needs no demonstration: in mental disorders it is shown by the occurrence of, say, disturbed thinking as in delusions, or disturbed perceptions, as in hallucinations, or disturbed emotional state, as in anxiety neurosis or melancholia. Deviant, maladapted, non-conformist behaviour is pathological if it is accompanied by a manifest disturbance of some such functions. It is true . . . that functions are an artificial construct, and that disorder in any particular function will be commonly accompanied by less conspicuous disorder in many other functions—just as in the body. But, for illness to be inferred, disorder of function must be detectable at a discrete or differentiated level that is hardly conceivable when mental activity as a whole is taken as the irreducible datum. If non-conformity can be detected only in total behaviour,

[1] Feuer (1955), pp. 26 and 24. [2] ibid., p. 66. [3] Glover (1952), pp. 403–4.
[4] Curran, in East, ed. (1954), p. 29.

while all the particular psychological functions seem unimpaired, health will be presumed, not illness.'[1] The deluded, the anxious, the abysmally depressed are, in fact, mentally ill; whereas for the cheerful 'rational' wrongdoer there is no excuse.

This criterion has many virtues. Chief of these is its strength as a defence against the circular argument which explains anti-social behaviour by ill-health, while inferring the ill-health from the behaviour. By the use of this criterion the sick are always to be distinguished from the healthy by the fact that there is *something else* peculiar about them, beside their inability to keep the rules of the social game. It is moreover well-established (though the significance of this fact needs to be critically assessed) that deviants do often exhibit such additional symptoms: many thieves are depressed or anxious, even if some might take a prize for gaiety. Recognized psychiatric syndromes are genuine realities, and the association of anti-social behaviour with anxiety or depression is characteristic of some of them. These disturbances of part-function are, moreover, ranged along a spectrum; and the symptoms which the experienced specialist can diagnose at one end of this scale can be recognized as less severe versions of those associated at the other end with mental derangement to the point even of insanity in the McNaghten sense. This fact alone would explain the attention paid even to mild varieties of such symptoms.

Attractive though it is, this criterion offers, however, no adequate solution either to the theoretical or to the practical difficulties. In the practical sphere it leaves untouched (as indeed must every other criterion that defines illness in terms independent of anti-social behaviour) the problem of the so-called psychopath—the persistent offender who shows no symptom other than his complete resistance to the influence of social norms. The desperate confusion into which the invention of the 'psychopath' as a medical category has thrown the whole question of responsibility is discussed more fully below.[2] Here, however, it must be acknowledged that Lewis himself accepts this limitation unhesitatingly, rejecting the hypothesis that psychopaths suffer from abnormal impulse, or disturbance of the conative part-function. 'Impulse is, psychologically, an imprecise and somewhat old-fashioned term. With the dethronement of Will in modern psychology, it is not easy to specify abnormalities of conative function in terms of impulse, and it is certainly impossible to measure them. It would seem, then, that until the category [of psychopaths] is further defined and shown to be characterized by specified abnormality of psychological functions, it will not be possible to consider those who fall within it to be unhealthy, however deviant their social behaviour.'[3] The legal and moral aspects of this conclusion are not discussed in Professor Lewis' paper; but, logically, it must leave the psychopath with full responsibility for his actions.

Psychopaths apart, the theoretical difficulties of diagnosis by disturbance of part-function are still formidable. For the concept of 'normal functioning' does not necessarily acquire a firm outline, or lose its social content, merely

[1] Lewis, Aubrey (June 1953), p. 118. [2] See pp. 249 ff. [3] Lewis, Aubrey (June 1953), p. 119.

because it is shifted from the whole to the part. As Lewis himself says, 'So far as we cannot designate formal, major functions of the human organism and lack means for judging whether they work efficiently, we are handicapped in recognizing health and illness in a reliable and valid way. The physiological functions can be thus designated and judged far more satisfactorily than the psychological'.[1] In the emotional sphere at least, the concept of 'normal performance' of the part-function is only one degree less elusive than is that of the normal functioning of the organism as a whole. The norms set for the part-function, as much as any others, must be determined in terms either of statistical frequency or of some ideal expectation; and the anxieties and depressions suffered by all of us can only be relegated to the neurotic category on the ground, either that they are in the strict sense of the word uncommonly severe, or that they are more severe than, in some defined sense, they 'ought to be'. In either case the standard reflects the particular expectations, if not of the individual who defines it, at least of the culture in which it is employed.

Again, the presence of a psychiatric syndrome or of a disturbance of part-functions does not, of itself, necessarily explain, still less does it necessarily excuse, disregard of social norms. Even at the level of mere explanation, the link between the two needs to be demonstrated. Many anti-social persons may prove to be suffering from anxieties or depressions, or even from delusions or hallucinations. So long, however, as they remain sane enough to know what they are doing and to know whether this is right or wrong, it is far from self-evident that these mental peculiarities explain their violence or their thieving, their casual attitude to domestic ties or their general social incompetence. Many anti-social persons may equally prove to be suffering from high or low blood pressure, from incipient peptic ulcers or even from malignant tumours; but we do not assume, and we are not entitled to assume without evidence, that these morbid conditions have anything to do with their standards of social behaviour.

At the level of explanation, the missing link can, no doubt, often be supplied. As a rule the most convincing demonstration will be statistical. If it can be shown that particular mental symptoms, such, for example, as depression, are associated with particular forms of anti-social behaviour in a degree which is statistically significant, then these symptoms may be accepted as an explanation (even if we are still too cautious to say 'a cause') of that behaviour. And if, in addition, some intellectually satisfying hypothesis—as, for instance, the theory that a deprived child steals material objects to make up for the human affection that he has missed—is adduced, which in its turn accounts for this empirically demonstrable association, then the link between the mental symptom and the anti-social behaviour becomes more readily acceptable. In practice, of course, much scientific research is directed towards supplying evidence of the existence of such associations.

Once again, however, explanation is not the same as exculpation. Arguments closely analogous to those used by Cressey in relation to 'motiveless' actions again become relevant here. Undoubtedly people who suffer from

[1] Lewis, Aubrey (June 1953), p. 124.

disturbances of mental part-functions have to carry the burden of those disturbances on top of whatever happens to be their share of the ordinary troubles and difficulties of human life. But so also do those who suffer from migraine or weak digestions. How can we be sure that it is legitimate in the one case, but not in the other, to leap to the conclusion that, for those who suffer from these disabilities, the standards of social expectation ought to be lowered? Why is dishonesty excused as well as explained by depression, but not by indigestion? Why should we accept a plea of diminished responsibility for the unlawful revenges of the deluded against their imaginary persecutors, but not for similar actions perpetrated against real enemies by rational persons, if both parties alike recognize what they do is wrong? At what point do the jealousies of the suspicious spouse cross the line that separates the inconsiderate from the crazy? These questions are not easily answered—at least not in any cases in which the mental faculties are not impaired to the point of irresponsibility in the McNaghten sense. While in practice it may be convenient, as it is certainly humane, to make generous assumptions about diminished responsibility, the problem of proving just how far, and in what way, a mild psychiatric syndrome affects the power or the will to maintain expected standards of social behaviour remains unsolved: indeed, if intellectually convincing proof is required, it looks insoluble.

Yet another approach to the problem has been tried by Dr Stafford-Clark through a definition of 'medical crime'. This reads as follows: 'Medical crime is crime in which the individual capacity of the criminal to refrain from committing the act is effectively diminished by factors both recognizable and, at some stage, treatable by medical means. This implies a diminution, in varying degree, in the individual's responsibility; but since these medical factors must be regarded as influencing rather than as finally determining the individual's conduct, the concept of medical crime does not and cannot overthrow or exclude the concept of normal responsibility in the majority of people, as distinct from those who are clinically clearly not responsible because they are deluded, insane, or mentally defective.'[1] Dr Stafford-Clark adds that he thinks that this definition would meet with the approval of 'most' of his colleagues (presumably in the field of psychiatry). In the particular context in which it appears his formula relates only to criminality; but the medical factors in any kind of anti-social behaviour could presumably be defined in similar fashion.

It will be seen that this criterion differs radically from those previously reviewed inasmuch as it is purely pragmatic. Any attempt to establish an independent 'natural' criterion of health or sickness or to list the symptoms which betray mental disorder is abandoned. By this standard illness becomes anything that doctors can recognize and treat. On the face of it such a definition seems to conflict with Lewis's confident pronouncement that 'psychiatrists, and other doctors, look after plenty of people who are not ill'.[2] The two points of view can, however, at least in theory be reconciled, if a distinction

[1] Stafford-Clark, quoted in Pakenham (1958), p. 94.
[2] Lewis, Aubrey (June 1953), p. 120.

is made between 'what doctors treat' and what is treatable by 'medical means', i.e. between what doctors do when they are behaving in the special fashion peculiar to doctors and using the special means peculiar to their profession, and what they do when they drop the Aesculapian mantle and behave as ordinary men and women. Whether or not Dr Stafford-Clark intends such a distinction to be made is not clear; but, since his position seems to make better sense if doctors using 'medical means' in their professional capacity are distinguished from doctors doing, so to speak off-duty, what anyone else might do, it will be assumed in what follows that 'treatable by medical means' implies 'treatable by doctors in their professional capacity'.

As a prescription for action this criterion has obvious merits: indeed it is in its pragmatic quality that the strength of its appeal lies. If an anti-social person can be changed by medical treatment into a well-conducted citizen, it is only common sense that he should be so treated. Considered as a test of responsibility, however, in either the moral or the legal sense, Dr Stafford-Clark's definition runs into formidable difficulties.[1] If treatability is taken as the test of responsibility, it follows that those who cannot or will not be treated must be regarded as liable to punishment. Starkly put, such a conclusion looks more than a little ruthless: as, for instance, when the Committee on Persistent Offenders inferred from the evidence of medical witnesses with experience of psychotherapy that 'even if it is practicable to select from the offenders appearing before the Courts those who appear to be suitable for psychological treatment, the need will still remain for subjecting to punishment those who fail to benefit by such treatment'.[2] It hardly seems just to punish a sick man because his illness fails to yield to any (as yet discovered) treatment—especially when the frontier of actual responsibility (assuming that such exists) and the frontier of known responsibility are unlikely to coincide, owing to the limitations of our knowledge; so that, amongst those for whom, at any given moment, no satisfactory treatment can be devised, there may well be some who, did we but realize it, are no more responsible for their actions than are many of those for whom treatment is practicable. Besides, as research progresses, the frontier of known responsibility is likely to be moved. What doctors can recognize and treat depends upon what doctors know, and knowledge is always growing; and, in consequence, some who have been held to be punishable for their actions may, a year or two later, find that others, in similar cases, are excused on the ground of partial, or even of total, irresponsibility.

Repugnant though these implications may appear to ordinary notions of justice, they are perhaps unavoidable; and it might be argued in mitigation that they are inherent also in what happens now; for, wherever and however the line between responsibility and irresponsibility may be drawn, some of those who are at present held liable to punishment might, with fuller know-

[1] None of the criticisms which follow would be relevant if Dr Stafford-Clark's definition were used merely as a guide in the choice of the treatment of offenders instead of as a criterion of responsibility. See below, pp. 245 ff.

[2] Departmental Committee on Persistent Offenders (1932), p. 46.

ledge, be excused on grounds of mental infirmity. And whenever that line is moved in conformity with the advance of knowledge, some offenders will be transferred from one side of it to the other. Any apparent injustice, it can be said, must be borne as the inevitable price of new insight which in the long run will make for juster treatment; and the fact that, in our ignorance, we may have punished some whom we later recognize as not fully responsible is no reason why we should continue to do so once we know better.

What doctors (in their professional capacity) can recognize and treat, however, depends not only upon what is known. It depends no less upon a choice, within all known means, of those to be designated as 'medical'. In an earlier, and less psychiatrically-minded, age, doctors were primarily interested in the cure of bodily ills, and the means which they employed were chiefly of a physical nature: the bottle of medicine, the surgical operation, the dietary régime are typical examples of traditional 'medical means'. In recent years, however, a double change has been in progress. First, these traditional medical methods have been used in the cure of troubles of which the primary symptoms are not physical at all: such techniques as shock therapy or leucotomy are now employed in the treatment of those who are adjudged to be ill by their mental symptoms alone. Second, doctors are increasingly turning to quite different methods, and spending their professional energies in the solution of quite new types of problem.

In this double change the first element raises no problems that are relevant here. That surgery and shock treatment are medical means is unlikely to be disputed, though in other contexts the ethical issues involved in, say, surgical procedures that change the whole personality are obviously fundamental. But the use of more distinctively psychotherapeutic or purely psychological methods breaks through the established conceptions of what is to be understood by 'medical means'. Again the change is two-sided—affecting both the methods themselves and the area to which they are applied. For in the first place, the new tools resemble in important respects those used by laymen in everyday life, rather than those that have hitherto been typical of medical practice. No matter how esoteric its techniques, the psychiatric interview remains an interview, not a bottle of medicine; and its content, like the content of other interviews, consists of the interchange of verbal symbols with or without emotional or intellectual accompaniments. And, in the second place, the scope of the ills which psychotherapeutic treatment is designed to cure, as well as of any specific advice which may emerge from it, far exceeds what is traditionally associated with the medical profession. The psychotherapist may feel called upon to try to change almost any aspect of the attitudes, feelings or behaviour of those whose lives bring distress to themselves or to their neighbours; and any advice or instructions that he may give in the pursuit of such changes may range over any part of the patient's life or of his relationships with other people.

As so often happens, these developments are well illustrated by changes in contemporary language. In this context, the changing uses of the word 'clinic' and of its derivatives are particularly significant. A 'clinic' means a place where sick people are treated by doctors, and 'clinical judgments' mean the judgments which a doctor makes about his patient's condition. Originally, the word itself, being derived from the Greek for 'bed', carried the implication of sickness in an old-fashioned, pre-psychiatric sense, in which sick people were expected to be ill in bed. To-day clinics have been extended to include places that have no connection at all with beds, as in the child guidance clinic where parents seek advice about the moods or the behaviour of their children, instead of about their illnesses in the traditional sense of that term; and a clinical judgment, in the psychiatric sense, means the judgment that a doctor makes not about the condition of a patient's heart or lungs, but about his character or personality.

We have thus reached the position in which an important branch of medical practice consists simply of talk, even if this is a rather special form of talk. In the therapeutic interview the talk itself is intended to be a therapeutic process; and it may, in addition, include advice to the patient, not only about such traditionally medical matters as his diet, his sleep, his exercise, but also about his emotional and personal relationships. When this stage is reached, however—when the medical profession has enlarged its toolbox to make room for words alongside of its traditional bottles, drugs and forceps—at this stage the definition of 'medical' methods becomes infinitely elastic: and there is no longer any logical reason why the medical treatment of crime should not be interpreted as covering all known methods of dealing with anti-social persons. Moral exhortation by a clergyman and psychotherapeutic sessions with a doctor are both forms of verbal communication, distinguished only by their content; and the doctor who is presumed to be able to assess the influence of marital disharmonies upon an offender's behaviour can hardly long be debarred from claiming equal authority to pronounce upon the effects of, say, a monetary penalty or a period of imprisonment.

Nor is it relevant to the issue that psychiatric treatment cannot (theoretically at least) be compulsorily thrust upon unwilling recipients, whilst other methods can be and are thus enforced. As a purely practical rule for the division of duties between judges and magistrates on the one hand and doctors on the other, a classification into compulsory and non-compulsory is appropriate enough; but as part of a definition fixing the limits of responsibility it is absurd. Doctors may, for their own good reasons, refuse to deal with persons who will not voluntarily accept their ministrations; but their refusal can hardly be held of itself to confer criminal responsibility upon those who do so.

In practice, moreover, the limits of what is recognized as the medical sphere at any given time, are set by what happens to be taught in medical schools, or to have been taught there a few years previously. Not so long ago it would have been considered absurd to consult a doctor professionally about a child who persistently steals; the little knowledge that we had about how to deal with such a problem would have been looked for in moral, rather than in medical, quarters. To-day that knowledge is taught (and, we hope, added to by researches) in medical schools; and it has come to be regarded as medical for no other reason than that doctors have decided to enlarge their empires so as to include territory formerly regarded as belonging to morality rather than to medicine, and so as to make a place for psychiatry in the medical curriculum. And there are no reasons at all why doctors should not, and doubtless some compelling reasons why they should, carry this encroachment further still.

It will be suggested later that these developments are in part at least the expression of important social influences that affect the position of the medical profession in our society.[1] Here, however, their significance lies only in the vividness with which they illustrate the wholly conventional and arbitrary limits of what may be classified as 'medical means'. Obviously, the limits of responsibility (on which it must be repeated the issue of life or death may turn) cannot be set by anything so arbitrary or so temporary as the division of the whole field of knowledge and research between medical and other disciplines—dependent as this is on the fads and fancies of the academic authorities concerned.

To put the matter in another way, the classification of medical crimes as those that doctors can recognize and treat reduces itself in the last resort to a tautology. Medical crimes are those that doctors treat and the crimes that doctors treat are medical crimes. It would seem that the medical world is not afraid of such tautologies: they are, for example, of a piece with the astonishing definition of mental illness recommended for statutory use by the Committee on Psychiatry and Law of the [U.S.] Group for the Advancement of Psychiatry. According to this, '"Mental Illness" shall mean an illness which so lessens the capacity of a person to use (maintain) his judgment, discretion and control in the conduct of his affairs and social relations as to warrant his commitment to a mental institution'. By this formula, it will be observed, committal to an institution is justified by the presence of mental illness, yet this illness is itself defined only in terms of the need for committal.

Objection need not be taken to such circular arguments, if it were not for the risk that they may be used as though they were meaningful statements, and that they may serve as cover for dangerous practical policies. Under the American definition just quoted, wrongful detention in a mental institution becomes impossible, inasmuch as no room is left for any criterion of health and sickness other than the fact of committal. Far from being disturbed by this, however, the Committee which drafted it would like to go even further, and would revise the American criminal codes in such a way that no person could be 'convicted of any criminal charge when at the time he committed the act with which he is charged he was suffering with mental illness' as thus defined, 'and in consequence thereof, he committed the act'.[2] Those who determine fitness for committal by a criterion which makes their judgment infallible would thus consequentially determine (with equal infallibility) the question of moral responsibility. No Pope could ask for more. And Dr Stafford-Clark's formula, though less obviously dangerous, would confer

[1] See pp. 337 ff. [2] Group for the Advancement of Psychiatry (1954), p. 8.

the same infallibility upon those who determine the content of medical curricula, or the boundaries of medical empires.

This position is so absurd that one must suppose that it cannot possibly be what is intended. There are two solutions. The first is to assume that some criterion of moral irresponsibility other than fitness for committal to an institution, or accessibility to medical treatment as defined in contemporary medical curricula, is implicit in these definitions: to assume, that is to say, that those who commit anti-social acts or mismanage their lives for reasons other than sheer superfluity of naughtiness distinguish themselves also by one or other of the signs already discussed: that they exhibit some familiar psychiatric syndrome, or that their actions appear motiveless or strangely motivated, or that they may even be unaware of what they are doing or unable to appreciate ordinary conceptions of right and wrong. On one or other of these assumptions it makes sense to define such cases as 'medical', and to refer to doctors those among them whom experience has shown to be likely to improve under current methods of medical treatment, or to commit to hospitals those whose symptoms are particularly severe. For on such assumptions, but on such assumptions alone, can the illness which diminishes or abolishes moral or criminal responsibility be diagnosed as established in its own right, independently either of the offender's behaviour or of the fact that doctors have been encouraged to take an interest in his peculiarities. As we have seen, however, even these assumptions are open to the objections, first, that they fail to identify the sick offender by criteria which are independent, on the one hand, of cultural or moral judgments and, on the other hand, of his own social delinquencies; and, second, that they are grossly unsatisfactory if not actually absurd when used to fix the limits of moral responsibility.

The alternative solution is to abandon the concept of responsibility altogether. Dr Stafford-Clark himself clearly rejects this course, since he expressly declares that the concept of medical crime 'does not and cannot overthrow or exclude the concept of normal responsibility in the majority of people';[1] and in this he shares the views already quoted of Norwood East, Aubrey Lewis, Curran and many other authorities who hold that crime may be caused by, but must not be identified with, disease, and who have accordingly given thought to possible methods of discriminating between the responsible and the irresponsible. All our difficulties would, however, disappear, if we could but dispense with the whole idea of responsibility altogether. For in that event, the need to discriminate between the sick and the healthy would lose its urgency, since exculpation from guilt (and by consequence from liability to punishment) would no longer be involved. Moreover, once judgments as to moral responsibility are eliminated, the definition of the mentally sick as those whose peculiarities are likely to yield to treatment by persons holding medical degrees becomes nothing more than a useful practical device for settling who is to be dealt with by whom. Stafford-Clark's pragmatic formula demands in fact a pragmatic philosophy, and, only in terms of such a philo-

[1] Stafford-Clark, quoted in Pakenham (1958), p. 94.

sophy does it make sense. Given such a philosophy it becomes a natural bridge between those theories which still associate mental disorder with irresponsibility, and those which adopt the radical course of rejecting, or at least of bypassing, the very idea of responsibility itself.

Most outspoken of those who go the length of out-and-out rejection is Dr Eliot Slater. By his endorsement of the uncompromising doctrine that 'No theory of mental medicine could develop without the working hypothesis of determinism', Slater has effectively disassociated himself from all those whose views we have so far examined. For him the ' "free will", on which both law and religion are based, proves a heuristically sterile idea. If we attempt to inject it into our analysis of causation it only introduces an element of the unknowable.' Statements about the moral responsibility of other people are, moreover, really only statements about the speaker's own state of mind. When we 'give opinions about the responsibility of others we are really reporting on our own states of mind. Perhaps we are doing little more than identifying ourselves with the criminal and asking ourselves whether or not we could have been guilty of his crime. If we then feel that we could have done it only after going mad, we may give one sort of answer; if we feel that we could have done it, but only by suppressing the whole of our better nature, then we shall give another sort of answer. Responsibility, it is worth noting, does have some meaning subjectively, in our judgments on our own actions. It is only when we apply the concept to the actions of others that it breaks down.'[1]

This full-blown determinism, it should be noticed, is presented as an essential hypothesis in the development of *mental medicine* rather than as implicit in any general theory of behaviour. Possibly a distinction is implied between normal behaviour and those abnormalities with which alone medicine is normally associated, only the latter being conceived in deterministic terms. Slater does not, however, pursue this aspect of the matter; nor is it clear from his remarks (or indeed of primary relevance to his thesis) whether he does or does not postulate any condition of mental health which can be objectively distinguished from its opposite, disease, in other than social terms. In his attitude to crime, however, discrimination along these lines certainly seems to play no part; for he defines abnormality in the purely statistical sense which identifies the abnormal with the unusual. By that criterion all crime (and indeed all deviant behaviour) is abnormal; and, in Slater's view, the practical question in criminal cases is whether the abnormality lies in the action or in the person who performs it. Thus, when a man rides a bicycle after dark without a light, it would be 'highly uneconomic, in the application of deterrent measures, to bother oneself about the possible abnormalities in the wrongdoer. He may be adjudged as average, and subjected to the procedure appropriate to the average case'. But if, by contrast, we find 'that X is now being tried for his thirtieth offence of indecently exposing himself, the evidence is overwhelming that it is not the circumstances which are unusual but the man'.[2]

[1] Slater (1954), p. 717. [2] ibid., pp. 717–18.

Explicit determinism is always easy meat for the critics; and on the publication of Slater's lecture correspondents immediately leapt into battle with the orthodox replies. In the words of one of them[1] the 'whole tone and purpose' of the lecture, in its dealing with the application of the McNaghten Rules to a particular case, implied that both the judge in the case and the authors of the McNaghten formula 'ought to, and therefore could, have acted differently'. 'Is, then, the judge', it was asked, 'the sole exception to the rule of determinism, or does free will only occur above a certain intellectual level?' Obviously, on a determinist hypothesis, what is sauce for the goose must be sauce also for the gander, be he judge, juror or even psychiatrist: what anyone thinks or does, he thinks or does because he was made that way, and that is all that there is to be said.

It would be unprofitable to pursue this ancient controversy further here. But it is very much to the point to recognize that such thoroughgoing determinism is not really necessary even to Slater's own position. For the real lynch pin of that position seems to be that it is predictability, rather than determinism, which is essential to any theory of mental medicine; and we know very well from experience that it is perfectly possible to predict behaviour, without passing any judgment on the reality of free will. In the present context this means that the determinist controversy can be bypassed, and the concept of responsibility left in suspense rather than explicitly rejected. What the application of successful 'mental medicine' to the treatment of anti-social persons demands is not determinism, but the ability to predict which persons are likely to be successfully treatable, and to devise methods that will deflect them from their unacceptable ways. For this purpose it is unnecessary to ask whether an offender is, or is not, a free agent, or a responsible person in the sense that he could, if he wished, have done otherwise than he did; any more than one need enquire into the freedom of a motorist's will, in order to predict that he will drive on the left of the road in England and on the right in France. The prediction can be empirically justified without raising any profound philosophical issues.

At times Slater himself seems to come near to accepting this position—as for instance when he dismisses the now famous dictum that 'a thug is a thug because he wants to be a thug; a psychopath cannot help it', with the comment that he cannot see either the force or the usefulness of this distinction. Other authorities, however, are much more definite in their determination to circumvent the conception of responsibility, and consequently more successful in guarding themselves against anti-determinist criticism. Thus Macdonald looks on the 'concepts of responsibility and punishment popular in legal and psychiatric practice' as 'theological and metaphysical anachronisms', best relegated to the 'amusement of the religious and others of that kidney'. To him all that matters in any case of anti-social behaviour is that 'appropriate action may be decided upon. Questions of "mad" or "bad", with their value-judgments and emotional loadings, do not arise. We are confronted with a person who has committed some action that is abnormal,

[1] *British Medical Journal* (October 16, 1954), p. 929.

by its infrequency of occurrence, and that has brought its doer into conflict with his fellows; we have to decide how to obviate or minimize repetition of such conflict, for the good of all concerned'.[1]

On the other side of the Atlantic such views are not uncommon. Thus Dr Board, after commenting on the 'strange turn in history' by which it is the mentally ill who have become exempt from being witches, suggests that the right line is, not to raise the issue of moral responsibility, but to use only the practical test of whether punishment will in fact deter the offender and/or others, and to apply this test in the most humane way possible. For criminal responsibility we thus substitute 'deterrent efficiency and/or efficient punishability', these concepts being respectively defined as 'the degree of effectiveness of the criminal serving as a deterrent example before the law in deterring most others from crime'; and as 'the susceptibility of the criminal to being adequately rehabilitated, as regards social acts, by the method of reasonable punishment'.[2]

Much the same stand has also been taken by Dr Bernard Glueck, the Supervising Psychiatrist of Sing Sing Prison. Glueck flirts with determinism to the extent of suggesting that 'present psychiatric knowledge would seem to indicate' that the basic premise of free-will 'is faulty'. He avoids, however, committing himself further, by arguing that the 'problem would be eased, however, and certainly the question of responsibility would not have to be raised, if the concept of management of the anti-social individual were changed from that of punishment as the main instrument of control, to a concept of the anti-social individual as a sick person, in need of treatment rather than punishment'. With this end in view, he proposes a number of radical changes in legal procedure, an important advantage of which, it is claimed, would be 'the elimination of the question of determining criminal responsibility'.[3]

It will be seen that at this stage the extreme position is reached. The frontier of responsibility, which, under the influence of psychiatric opinion, has been gradually moving forward from the restricted McNaghten position to one or other of the more advanced points favoured by Sir Norwood East, Professor Lewis or Dr Stafford-Clark is now abolished altogether; and it is abolished because the same fate has overtaken the corresponding frontier between the healthy and the sick. Whereas, on the more orthodox view, the line which separates the sick from the healthy offender divides also the responsible from the irresponsible, in the judgment of Dr Glueck and those who think with him no such line is necessary at all for either purpose. Anti-social behaviour is itself indicative of illness, nor is there any need to search for any criterion independent of this. Crime, in fact, in defiance of the strong support for Norwood East's dictum,[4] has become a disease.

It will be seen that two separate propositions are inherent in Dr Glueck's position—first, that questions of responsibility can be bypassed; and second, that criminality is itself a disease. Dr Glueck himself connects these closely,

[1] Macdonald, J. E. (1955), pp. 715–16. [2] Board (1956), pp. 332–36.
[3] Glueck, Bernard (1954), pp. 127 and 130. [4] quoted on p. 227.

in effect deriving the first from the second. Nevertheless they are in fact distinct, and it is, as I hope to show, possible to hold the one without necessarily being committed to the other.

Acceptance of the first of these propositions seems to be the ultimately inevitable outcome of contemporary trends of thought. Admittedly the idea of ignoring all questions of responsibility in the treatment of anti-social persons involves so radical a departure from the basic presumptions of ancient and honoured legal systems that any prospect of its practical acceptance may seem Utopian. Nevertheless the logical drive towards that conclusion is very powerful. For, once we allow any movement away from a rigid intellectual test of responsibility on McNaghten lines, our feet are set upon a slippery slope which offers no real resting-place short of the total abandonment of the whole concept of responsibility. All the intermediate positions, described in the foregoing pages, have shown themselves to be logically quite insecure. Already in many countries, amongst which England must now be included, the first steps down this slope have been taken; and the possibility cannot be dismissed that the relaxation of definitions of responsibility which is already in progress is the beginning of a process which, in the remoter future, is destined to result in the total destruction of the concept itself.

A significant element in this process is the growing prominence contemporary discussion gives to what has come to be called 'the psychopathic personality'. In technical language the condition of 'psychopathy' is defined as 'a mental disease which develops before or during puberty, caused by inherited predisposition, or by acquired personality deviation due to psychic or somatic factors or both, which, in turn, cause super-ego deficiency; it is characterized by stereotyped deviations in the moral, social, sexual and emotional components of the personality without intellectual impairment, psychosis or neurosis, with lack of more than [*sic*] insight or ability to profit by experience, and is of lifelong duration in almost all cases'.[1] In the simpler language of the Royal Medico-Psychological Association, psychopaths are persons whose 'daily behaviour shows a want of social responsibility and of consideration for others, of prudence and foresight and of ability to act in their own best interests. Their persistent anti-social mode of conduct may include inefficiency and lack of interest in any form of occupation; pathological lying, swindling and slandering; alcoholism and drug addiction; sexual offences, and violent actions with little motivation and an entire absence of self-restraint, which may go as far as homicide. Punishment or the threat of punishment influences their behaviour only momentarily, and its more lasting effect is to intensify their vindictiveness and anti-social attitude.'[2] In simpler language still, psychopaths are extremely selfish persons and nobody knows what makes them so.

The modern psychopath is himself the linguistic descendant of the 'moral defective', to whom statutory recognition was given in the Mental Deficiency

[1] Darling (1945), p. 125.

[2] Royal Commission on the Law Relating to Mental Illness and Mental Deficiency, 1954–57. Minutes of Evidence, Eighth day, p. 287.

Act of 1927—a term which was condemned by many of the witnesses before the recent Royal Commission, and is indeed now very unpopular, largely because it has led to anti-social persons of good intelligence being committed to mental deficiency institutions along with cases whose deficiency is chiefly intellectual; and because such persons have been found to be nearly as much of a nuisance inside these institutions as they are outside them. In ordinary language, however, in spite of these objections, 'moral defective' is an excellent shorthand description of the psychopathic type of personality; and Dr W. A. Heaton-Ward, Medical Superintendent of Stoke Park Hospital, even though himself anxious that the term 'defective' should be omitted from any title assigned to the psychopathic group, did in fact admit to the Royal Commission that the anti-social psychopath and the moral defective 'are the same'.[1]

Already in the case of the anti-social psychopath, the problem of responsibility is not, as a rule, explicitly raised, at least not in circles in which he carries this title. Instead, it is normally taken for granted that the psychopath is a 'patient' in need of appropriate 'treatment'; and it is accordingly in medical, or para-medical, quarters that his existence is chiefly recognized and discussed. Before the recent Royal Commission, for example, it was in the evidence given by the Royal Medico-Psychological Association, the Royal College of Physicians, the Institute for the Study and Treatment of Delinquency, the British Medical Association and the National Association for Mental Health, together with that of a number of specially experienced medical men, that the psychopath figured most conspicuously.

The volume of the literature on the subject of psychopaths is rivalled only by the depth of the confusion in which this literature is steeped. But one thing at least is clear—that the psychopath is a critical case for those who would retain a distinction between the responsible and the irresponsible. For, as Professor Lewis himself has admitted, the psychopath makes nonsense of every attempt to distinguish the sick from the healthy delinquent by the presence or absence of a psychiatric syndrome, or by symptoms of mental disorder which are independent of his objectionable behaviour. In his case no such symptoms can be diagnosed because it is just the absence of them which causes him to be classified as psychopathic. He is, in fact, *par excellence*, and without shame or qualification, the model of the circular process by which mental abnormality is inferred from anti-social behaviour while anti-social behaviour is explained by mental abnormality.

That persons who conform to the RMPA's formula quoted on p. 249 exist is indisputable. Anyone with practical experience of offenders will have known some among them who were apparently totally lacking in regard for other people, and at the same time totally unresponsive either to reformative treatment or to such punitive measures as it is nowadays thought proper to impose. Such people used to be thought extremely wicked: to-day they are classified as cases of mental disorder. Paradoxically, this has the effect that, if you are

[1] Royal Commission on the Law Relating to Mental Illness and Mental Deficiency 1954-57, Minutes of Evidence, Thirtieth day, p. 1225.

consistently (in old-fashioned language) wicked enough, you may hope to be excused from responsibility for your misdeeds; but if your wickedness is only moderate, or if you show occasional signs of repentance or reform, then you must expect to take the blame for what you do and perhaps also to be punished for it.

So illogical a position can hardly, one would think, prove tenable for long. Hence the psychopath may well prove to be the thin end of the wedge which will ultimately shatter the whole idea of moral responsibility as a factor in the treatment of anti-social personalities. The distinction between the thug and the psychopath may be given up as hopelessly elusive; and it may even happen that, just as the definition of responsibility has gradually spread far beyond the narrow intellectual boundaries of the McNaghten formula, so will the concept of psychopathy spill over into wider and wider areas of delinquent behaviour, sweeping away in its course any concept of moral or legal responsibility.

In this context it is perhaps not without significance that suggestions are afoot which would restrict the area of responsibility in another quarter also. As has been said, in this country children below the age of eight are not held to be responsible at law, and are not subject to criminal prosecution, on the ground that, like McNaghten lunatics, they cannot be held to know right from wrong. To-day, however, a considerable body of opinion contends that this threshold of criminal responsibility (which in England is much below that prevailing in many other Western European countries) should be fixed at a higher age. The ranks of the fully responsible are thus threatened with the defections at once of the psychopaths, of the victims of emotional disorder and of the very young.

Revolutionary though the prospect of abandoning the concept of responsibility may be, it is clear that we are travelling steadily towards it. Primarily what would be involved, as Dr Bernard Glueck has pointed out, is a shift of emphasis in the treatment of offenders away from considerations of guilt and towards choice of whatever course of action appeared most likely to be effective as a cure in any particular case. The legal process for determining who has in fact committed certain actions would continue as at present; but once the facts had been established, the *only* question to be asked about delinquent persons would be: what is the most hopeful way of preventing such behaviour in future? In criminal procedure the age-old conflict between the claims of punishment and of reformation would thus be finally settled in favour of the latter.

How far such a suspension of the issue of responsibility would mean handing over the treatment of anti-social persons to the medical profession is not so certain. For, when this point is reached, it does not matter in principle whether we say that all offenders are sick or that none of them is; any more than it matters whether we privately believe any or all of them to enjoy the power of responsible choice. The critical step that is involved in by-passing questions of criminal responsibility is the abandonment of the division of offenders into those who are sick and irresponsible, and those who are not. If all offenders are, as Dr Glueck would say, by definition sick persons, their illness being diagnosed from the fact of their misconduct, only questions of politeness will determine which appellation is preferred. The role of the medical profession will then depend upon the relative success of those who hold medical degrees in comparison with others not so qualified in inducing such persons to mend their ways; and this in turn, as is inherent in what has already been said, will depend upon the scope of medical training; and, it must be added, upon the influence enjoyed by the medical profession in the community.[1] In other words, once the concept of responsibility is abandoned, Dr Stafford-Clark's definition comes into its own: medical crime does become what doctors can recognize and treat; and the only remaining distinction between Dr Glueck and Dr Stafford-Clark is that, whereas the one is out for doctors to treat every offender, the other more modestly lays claim only to some of them.

In this and in other matters the only ultimate proof of the pudding must be in the eating; and that proof is essentially a statistical one. Subject only to the over-riding social and moral limitations mentioned below, the rôle of medical or psychiatric, as against educational, or what are now regarded as penal, methods in the treatment of backsliders will depend upon the actual success which each can show in dealing with different types of case. Dr Glueck's concept of the 'anti-social individual as a sick person' must stand or fall, not by the compelling logic of psychiatric theories, but by a simple demonstration of the degree to which doctors are more successful than other people in inducing favourable modifications of deplorable behaviour; and that is a matter that can only be demonstrated in statistical terms. No matter who has the first word, the last is always with the statistician. The task of the social sciences is to mobilize indifferently the results of *every* form of expertize and the evidence on *all* available methods of handling cases of anti-social behaviour; and it is not by deductive argument but only by willingness to submit to the test of experience and by a temper at once 'critical, distrustful of elaborate speculation, sceptical, candid, and tough'[2] that psychiatry or any other science can hope to justify whatever claims it ventures to make.

Even so, proof of the probable effectiveness of particular methods of dealing with an offender is not necessarily a conclusive argument for the use of those methods. That argument is subject to two qualifications. The first is related to the dual objective of prevention and cure towards which the treatment of offenders is directed. In practice the purpose of this treatment is not only to discourage one who has transgressed once from doing so again: it is also to prevent other people from following his example. The deterrent theory of punishment, based on the conventional view of responsibility, light-heartedly assumes that these two objectives can be simultaneously pursued. The psychology implied is simple: it is expected that the unpleasant consequences of wrong-doing will make anyone who has experienced them think twice before exposing himself to them again; and that they will equally

[1] See below pp. 337, 338.

[2] Lewis, Aubrey (December 1953), p. 405, describing Henry Maudsley.

serve as an effective warning to other potential offenders. In fact, however, there is no evidence at all that the treatment which is most effective for the one purpose is also most effective for the other. On the contrary there is some reason to fear that this is not so. Whereas lenient and sympathetic handling may be most efficacious in bringing an offender to see the error of his ways, the effect of this upon other people may well be to foster the belief that they 'can get away with it'. The very serious practical problems that are involved here (which are discussed further in the concluding chapter of this book) seem to attract less attention than they should, at any rate in scientific circles. The courts are well aware of them, but research tends to focus only upon the problem of reforming those who have already gone wrong. In the present context the relevance of this dilemma lies in the limitation which it sets upon the policy of using the test of reformative efficiency (so far as the offender himself is concerned) as the sole criterion in the choice of treatment. It is futile to uproot one blade of grass by methods which encourage the proliferation of others.

The second limitation in the use of this criterion involves questions of morality. Refocusing attention away from culpability and responsibility and towards choice of treatment in no way involves indifference to, or rejection of, moral considerations: that choice itself must be conditioned by moral factors. To take an extreme example, the most effective method of dealing with anti-social conduct would be to inflict capital punishment in every case: this policy alone gives 100 per cent guarantee against recidivism. If the elimination of deviant behaviour were the sole consideration to be taken into account, this treatment would deserve priority over all others. Moreover by the strict logic of Dr Glueck's argument, capital punishment would be equally appropriate or inappropriate to the crimes committed by persons now generally reckoned as mentally deranged, and to those done by persons who are indubitably sane: if the test is the efficiency of the treatment, not the moral responsibility of the offender, it must be recognized that capital punishment is certainly of equal efficacy in both cases. Hence if the use of this method is debarred, it must be debarred on the ground that moral considerations in this context outweigh considerations of efficacy. Nor is it only in such an academically extreme example that these problems arise. In the treatment of anti-social persons (sane or insane, responsible or irresponsible) decisions as to the legitimate exercise of force have to be made every day; and the invention of modern techniques, such, for instance, as brain surgery, have multiplied rather than diminished the gravity and the variety of the critical moral decisions to be made.

Merely to delete the distinction between the tiresome and the sick thus offers no easy escape from the claims of morality. Indeed one of the major difficulties to be found in discarding the concept of responsibility, and selecting treatment solely by reference to its probable efficacy, is that this might lead to the use of what are now generally regarded as penal measures against persons who, as things are, would be exempt from these on grounds of mental disorder. Once the concept of responsibility has been dropped, it could for example be argued that it was, if anything, more reasonable to execute an insane rather than a sane person, since the latter might be the more likely to respond favourably to some alternative treatment. Similarly some mentally defective offenders might be found to respond best to treatment by deprivation, while in the case of others who were better endowed more agreeable methods might prove more effective. Such a reversal of present practice, in which a successful plea of mental incapacity precludes or mitigates punishment, might be thought to do too much violence to existing notions of morality; and in this way the discarded concept of responsibility might yet creep its way in again by the back door.

Be this as it may, with the elimination of the concept of responsibility, the moral problems that arise in the treatment of offenders are only brought into line with those inherent in the use of almost any scientific instrument. So long as the presumption of responsibilty survives, a unique complication is introduced into the treatment of the anti-social: for methods of high effectiveness may be ruled out, not because they are in themselves immoral, but because of the risk of conflict with the requirements of this presumption. Only when this presumption is removed can science pursue unhindered its morally neutral task of designing, in this as in other cases, the method of achieving a prescribed aim that is most likely to be effective; but whether that instrument be hydrogen bomb, hangman's noose or analyst's couch, the demonstration of effectiveness is not, and cannot be, by itself a command to use.

III

Contemporary thought on the relation between mental deficiency and anti-social behaviour has shaped itself to much the same pattern as that which governs the prevailing attitude to mental illness in this connection. The problems that present themselves are much the same in both cases; but there are differences of emphasis.

Mental deficiency, in contrast to mental illness, has been defined, indeed elaborately defined, by statute. As is well-known, four categories of defectives are legally recognized, namely, idiots, imbeciles, feeble-minded persons and moral defectives; and in each case the statutory definition of deficiency requires that it should be due to a condition of 'arrested or incomplete development of mind' existing before the age of eighteen years. In the case of idiots and imbeciles the defect is so gross that no dispute is likely to arise, either as to the reality of the handicap or as to its effect in impairing capacity to conform to expected standards. It is in respect of the feeble-minded and the moral defective (a label which in practice has been sparingly used) that the really controversial issues arise, if only because 'any person who falls within the definition of moral defective also falls within the definition of one of the other classes'.[1] These categories are respectively defined as 'persons

[1] Royal Commission on the Law Relating to Mental Illness and Mental Deficiency, 1954–57. Minutes of Evidence, First day, p. 16.

in whose case there exists mental defectiveness which, though not amounting to imbecility, is yet so pronounced that they require care, supervision, and control for their own protection or for the protection of others or, in the case of children, involves disability of mind of such a nature and extent as to make them, for the purposes of section fifty-seven of the Education Act, 1944, incapable of receiving education at school', and 'persons in whose case there exists mental defectiveness coupled with strongly vicious or criminal propensities and who require care, supervision and control for the protection of others'.

These definitions clearly postulate mental deficiency as an independent condition which may cause failure of social adaptation, rather than as one to be inferred from or identified with such failure. The mental defect is envisaged as existing, so to speak, in its own right, and as *causing* the need for care and control, or as *co-existing* with vicious or criminal propensities. At the same time it is by no means clear how, in the case of adults, the existence of this mental defect is to be established except as it manifests itself in behaviour which calls for 'care, supervision or control'. At no time in the history of mental deficiency legislation has this problem been effectively tackled. The members of the Radnor Commission, which paved the way for the first Mental Deficiency Act, discussed in some detail (with reference to both adults and children) the merits of various criteria of mental defectiveness, including ability to earn a living; and they suggested that feeble-minded persons should be defined as those who, even though they might be able to earn a living under favourable circumstances, were incapable, owing to mental defect, '(*a*): of competing on equal terms with their normal fellows; or (*b*) of managing themselves and their affairs with ordinary prudence'. The decision to retain this criterion, which had been suggested by the Royal College of Physicians of London, was defended on the ground that 'being able to earn a living is often, on the social side at least, the critical question in regard to feeble-minded children'.[1]

As with the McNaghten definition of insanity, so in the case of mental deficiency, circular argument from mental defect to social inadequacy and from social inadequacy to mental defect was avoided, in the first instance, by recourse to an intellectual criterion. Thus the Wood Committee in their exposition of the subject in 1929 laid it down that 'the most important of the general factors [affecting social adaptation] are "general intelligence" and "general emotionality". These general factors of intelligence and emotionality are essential for normal behaviour and any serious lack of such endowments will make it impossible for a person so affected to adapt himself satisfactorily and efficiently to the social environment appropriate to his age and class.' Moreover, 'a wide range of special disabilities is suggestive of a defect of general intelligence. Educational attainments, general knowledge, practical ability, are all acquisitions in part dependent on intellectual capacity, so that failure in these directions is suggestive of the presence of mental defect, the absolute existence of which can only be determined by direct examination'.

[1] Radnor Report (1908), pp. 188–89.

The Committee went on to suggest that 'a person with a mental ratio of between 50 and 70 per cent is probably feebleminded',[1] though to this there might be exceptions.

In thus tentatively linking intelligence quotients with grades of mental defective, the Wood Committee are by no means alone. In the 1946 edition of their *Text-book of Psychiatry* Drs Henderson and Gillespie record that 'an intelligence quotient below seventy corresponds roughly to clinical feeblemindedness (moronity) and below forty to imbecility';[2] and they suggest also levels of intelligence which could be regarded as presumptive evidence of idiocy or imbecility. The Radnor Commission, in wrestling with the problem of the moral imbecile, quoted with approbation Sir James Crichton-Browne's definition of this class of defective as 'a person who by reason of arrested development or disease of the brain dating from birth or early years displays at an early age vicious or criminal propensities which are of an incorrigible or unusual nature, and *are generally associated with some slight limitation of intellect*';[3] although, when it came to the point of offering their own definition, the Commissioners did not include any specific mention of 'limitation of intellect'. Finally, the influence of intellectual conceptions of mental deficiency is apparent also in the current definition of defective children as those unable to receive 'proper benefit from the instruction in ordinary schools'.

The use of an intellectual test to establish mental deficiency has, however, incurred even more criticism than have purely intellectual conceptions of insanity—with the result that more and more emphasis is now laid on the social element in deficiency, and that argument on the subject tends to become more and more frankly circular. Mental defectiveness tends increasingly to be diagnosed *only* by the defective's inability to accommodate himself to the demands of the society in which he finds himself. Indeed, Professor Penrose has remarked that, even in the various intelligence or educational tests now employed, it is just the social element which is chiefly valuable. 'The practical value of the scholastic type of test is mainly due to its use in estimating just those qualities which make adjustment in a highly industrialized civilization easy or difficult. Tests dependent upon special sense discrimination are not used for the diagnosis of defect, though it is possible to imagine a civilization in which the recognition of tunes or colours was as important as, say, arithmetic is to us. Some brilliant scholars are less capable of recognizing common tunes than are most imbeciles. No amount of intelligence can enable a colour-blind person to appreciate colours which he cannot physiologically perceive'.[4] In the opinion of the Joint Committee of the British Medical Association and the Magistrates Association 'it might well be advisable', when the Mental Deficiency Acts come to be rewritten, 'to revise the terminology so as to stress the importance of social adaptation or social efficiency as the criteria to be used in determining

[1] Wood Report (1929), Parts 1 and 2, pp. 8–9 and 12.

[2] Henderson and Gillespie (1946), p. 567.

[3] Radnor Report (1908) p. 189: italics not original.

[4] Penrose (1949), p. 31.

mental deficiency'.[1] Whether or no mental deficiency is in any sense a 'natural' condition, its presence cannot, it is now argued, be reliably detected by any test that is itself independent of social behaviour.

It follows from this that if, as may be supposed, the capacity for social adjustment conforms to a more or less normal pattern of distribution, the cut-off point at which defectiveness is held to be established must depend upon how exacting this demand for adjustment happens to be. This is now frankly recognized by leading authorities. Thus Kanner, arguing in favour of 'intellectual inadequacy' as a term to be preferred to 'mental deficiency', observes that 'apparent deficiency is an ethnologically determined phenomenon relative to the local culture and, even within the culture, relative to educational postulates, vocational ambitions, and family expectations . . . A person with an I.Q. of eighty-five is not fit to occupy the chair of professor of economics but may well be suited to dispense articles in a Five and Ten Cent Store. One with an I.Q. of seventy-five may not even be capable of doing that but may well be trained to usefulness as a cog in the wheel of the industrial Taylor System. And one with an I.Q. of sixty may learn to milk cows and wash dishes satisfactorily.'[2] Similarly, Tredgold, who regards 'the social as not only the most logical and scientific concept of mental deficiency, but as the only criterion which the community can justly impose',[3] defines the 'essential purpose of mind' as 'that of enabling the individual so to adapt himself to his environment as to maintain an independent existence'. In his view, from a biological and social angle, the individual who 'can do this is to be regarded as normal, while the one whose mental development does not admit of this is to be regarded as defective'. He is, however, careful to add that the 'ability to maintain an independent existence must be judged in relation to circumstances which normally obtain, not to those which are grossly exceptional. To constitute abnormality and defect the failure must be due to psychological and not to economic and social causes; and there is usually little difficulty in distinguishing between the two.'[4]

The concluding words of this quotation strike a remarkably optimistic note. Other authorities do not find it so easy to disentangle psychological from economic and social causes. Thus Drs Lyons and Heaton-Ward, while admitting that 'there is some rough correlation between the intelligence quotient and the class of mental defect', hold that 'it is often impossible to classify a patient merely from an assessment of his intelligence quotient', since from a 'practical point of view the criterion of mental deficiency is a social incapacity';[5] while in another context Heaton-Ward has argued strongly against the 'acceptance of the I.Q. as a basis for diagnosing mental defect', adding that it is the identification, in the public's mind, of mental deficiency with low I.Q. which 'underlies the recurring allegations of wrongful certification'.[6] Nor do these authors shrink from the inference that the

[1] Royal Commission on the Law Relating to Mental Illness and Mental Deficiency, 1954–57. Minutes of Evidence, Ninth day, p. 363. [2] Kanner (1948), p. 71.
[3] Tredgold (1952), pp. 4–5. [4] ibid., p. 5. [5] Lyons and Heaton-Ward (1953), pp. 7 and 9.
[6] *British Medical Journal* (May, 11, 1957), p. 1120.

criterion of defectiveness may depend upon such completely adventitious factors as the state of the employment market. 'The opinion', they write, 'is often expressed that mental deficiency is on the increase. It is more probably the case that, owing to the increased tempo of the times, the defective is unable to keep pace with modern stress and consequently falls by the wayside when employment is competitive. In times when suitable employment is easy to find, he manages to keep going and, being occupied, he keeps out of trouble.'[1] So also in Tizard's view, 'what constitutes subnormality is to a very large extent socially determined by the thresholds of community tolerance'; and one cannot 'tell from surveys how many adults who are socially incompetent during periods of heavy unemployment would have been so under conditions of full employment'.[2]

In a less sophisticated age we should have said that one of the merits of full employment was that it made it easier for mental defectives to obtain employment. Now apparently we have to say that it actually reduces the number of such defectives. To appreciate the full significance of this distinction we may imagine what would happen if similar reasoning were applied to the analogous case of some incontestable physical disability, such as the loss of a limb. Full employment certainly makes it easier for legless persons to get jobs, but no one in his senses would take this to mean that under full employment there are fewer persons without legs. Similarly, full employment makes it easier for ex-prisoners to get jobs; but that is not to say that full employment diminishes the number of ex-prisoners, as distinct from the number who are able to get employment. Such statements would be manifestly absurd; but their absurdity well illustrates the difference between a disability which is established by a criterion that is, and one established by a criterion that is not independent of current standards of social competence. And so long as defectives are subject, as they are, to legal and other disabilities, the significance of this difference is much more than semantic. If defectives are deprived of full civic rights and responsibilities, and even in some cases of their personal freedom, and if the number of defectives varies with the state of the employment market, it follows that some people are liable to lose their status as fully responsible citizens or to be deprived of their liberty, merely because employment is bad.

The strength of opinion in favour of a social criterion for the diagnosis of mental defect has lately been shown up by the weight of evidence given in this sense to the Royal Commission on the Law Relating to Mental Illness and Mental Deficiency. Indeed, many of the witnesses who argued in favour of such a criterion also explicitly deprecated reliance, or, at any rate, exclusive reliance upon a test of intellectual capacity. The Ministry of Health and Board of Control expressed the wish to clarify existing statutory definitions so as to remove any 'doubt as to whether some degree of sub-normal intelligence is not a condition precedent to ascertainment as a mental defective

[1] Lyons and Heaton-Ward (1953), p. 8.
[2] Tizard (1953), p. 428.

subject to be dealt with under the Act'[1]—although their representatives themselves regarded the 'present definitions as enabling medical practitioners to certify mentally defective patients on the ground that they have characteristics from early youth which make them anti-social *although their intelligence might be quite normal*'.[2] The same point was reiterated many times in the course of these witnesses' replies to the Commissioners' examination. 'The feeble-minded need not be of low intelligence.'[3] 'Our only point is . . . to make it quite clear that a mentally defective person might be someone of quite normal intelligence who has defects of character, but those defects of character must have appeared, or symptoms of them, at an early age, before the age of eighteen.'[4] Many other witnesses also took up the same standpoint. The Liverpool City Council proposed that the concept of social inefficiency should be incorporated in the definition of mental deficiency by the use of the words 'resulting in an incapacity for successful independent social adaptation'.[5] The spokesmen of the Society of Chief Administrative Mental Health Officers declared themselves unequivocally in favour of a 'new criterion of social inefficiency'.[6] Asked what meaning was to be attached to this, however, in view of the risk that, on such a test all prostitution might be interpreted as evidence of mental deficiency, these witnesses appeared unable to maintain their original position, and suggested only that 'you have to prove the patient to be feeble-minded in the first place if you are going to certify her in addition to her being socially inefficient'.[7] The Royal Medico-Psychological Association submitted that 'mental deficiency is not to be regarded as a disease or group of diseases in the medical sense, but as a term covering a large number of individuals whose common feature is a failure to acquire the ability to meet the minimum requirements of the society in which they live . . . Social inadequacy is . . . the criterion for bringing into operation the special care measures provided by the law, and it is immaterial whether the inadequacy is associated with a lack of "intelligence" or with an emotional or adaptive defect'. The fact that in practice it is often required that a mentally defective patient 'should fall below a certain arbitrary level on one of the recognized "intelligence test scales"' is explained by the Association as possibly due to the circumstance that the 'study and measurement of "intelligence" came earlier in date than that of personality and social maturity'.[8] Once again the same point was reiterated in the examination that followed, and once again the quest for a safe criterion of social inefficiency led into deep waters. Challenged by the Chairman of the Commission to explain the 'very astonishing proposition' that 'socially inadequate' included 'a person who is incapable of benefiting from particular measures taken by the State', the Association's witnesses merely replied that 'these are just slight modifications of the existing definitions'.[9]

[1] Royal Commission on the Law Relating to Mental Illness and Mental Deficiency, 1954–57. Minutes of Evidence, First day, p. 24.
[2] ibid., p. 61. Italics not original. [3] ibid., p. 62. [4] ibid., p. 63.
[5] ibid. Twenty-fourth day, p. 961. [6] ibid., Third day, p. 102. [7] ibid., p. 103.
[8] ibid., Eighth day, p. 281. [9] ibid., p. 327.

The British Medical Association dealt with the matter at some length, arguing that an arrested or incompletely developed mind may manifest itself in a failure of intelligence, but may also be manifested by 'failure to attain normal control of the emotions or to achieve the qualities needed for normal social behaviour'; and they urged accordingly that the condition of arrested mental development should be judged 'mainly by the degree of the patient's social inadequacy'.[1] Dr Heaton-Ward proposed that mental deficiency should be defined as arrested mental development which prevents an individual from 'attaining the degree of social independence normal for his age'.[2] In answer to questions, he elaborated this criterion as follows: 'I think we measure them just by the test of how a person responds to the test of life, as it were, how they manage to maintain a normal degree of social independence without falling down whenever they come up against any difficulties';[3] and he later agreed that social independence meant a 'person's independence in his conduct in the community',[4] and even 'the extent to which he is able to look after himself without any help from social workers and those sort of people'.[5]

Relatively few of those who appeared before this Commission laid much stress on the difficulties and dangers associated with a purely social test of mental defectiveness. But there were a few who did, and several of these expressed themselves very forcibly. Most trenchant of all was the evidence submitted on behalf of the National Council for Civil Liberties. According to this, 'There can be no objective standards of "social efficiency". That which one person may consider socially efficient may appear to another thoroughly undesirable. In consequence, to use "social inefficiency" as a criterion is to set up a series of subjective criteria, varying from individual to individual. There is certainly no evidence that the standards of the local health authorities or the mental deficiency service have any transcendental value. If it suits the fashion of some psychiatrists to classify in one group the intellectually retarded, the maladjusted adolescent, the orphan who cannot be "fitted in", the juvenile delinquent and the woman who joins the trade union, under the general heading of "social inefficiency", that, of course, is their affair. Forty years ago their predecessors, classified together the consumptive, the intellectually retarded and the sufferer from migraine under the general heading of "national degeneracy". Forty years hence, their successors will doubtless have evolved a new classification containing new categories.'[6] The Council did not recall, however, as they might well have done, that the definition of feeble-mindedness favoured by the Radnor Commission even included 'the prodigal and the facile'.

Similar, if more moderately phrased, criticism came from the British Psychological Society, who pointed out the difficulties of interpreting 'incomplete development of mind' so broadly as to include virtually any aberrations of behaviour, irrespective of whether these are due to emotional immaturity

[1] Royal Commission on the Law Relating to Mental Illness and Mental Deficiency, 1954–57, Minutes of Evidence, Twenty-sixth day, p. 1047. [2] ibid., Thirtieth day, p. 1223. [3] ibid., p. 1224. [4] ibid., p. 1225. [5] ibid., p. 1225. [6] ibid., Twenty-second day, p. 842.

or to lack of intelligence. 'It is', they said, 'extremely difficult to determine at what level social incompetence due to emotional immaturity is to lead to treatment as mental defect on the one hand, or to treatment as neurosis on the other. If, however, competent certifying officers also take into account and give weight to the intelligence quotient (or some equivalent assessment) derived from tests or other observations, then the proportionate number of mistakes they are likely to make will be comparatively small; but if they attempt to base their decisions solely on an assessment of general emotionality or social adaptability they will often find themselves giving opposite verdicts about cases that are near the border-line.'[1] On this point the Society's representatives were quite unequivocal in their answers to the Commissioners' questions, giving an unqualified affirmative answer to the suggestion that they 'would like to see mental deficiency defined so as to be limited to intellectual defect'.[2] Somewhat more subtle, if much less logical, was the proposal presented by the National Association of Mental Health that the criterion of defectiveness should be, not simple social inefficiency, but 'social inefficiency due to mental defect'.[3] Elaborating this, Dr Hilliard expressed the belief that 'there are many people in the community to-day who are in fact mentally defective by ordinary accepted standards, mentally or psychologically, but who are doing a job in the community, who are not getting into difficulties, and who are socially efficient, even at a low level',[4] adding later that 'we do want to underline that the inefficiency is due to mental defect'.[5] However, beyond expressing the opinion that 'mental defect in adults should be primarily measured not only by academic intelligence tests but by capacity for making an adequate social adjustment', the Association showed no disposition to wrestle with the thorny problem of how we are to discriminate between the social inefficiency which is, and that which is not, due to mental defect.

In their own report, the Commissioners went a long way towards accepting the view that mental deficiency cannot be defined in purely intellectual terms. Even the present Mental Deficiency Acts, they declared, were correctly interpreted to include 'among the feeble minded and moral defectives, patients whose intelligence is within the normal range but whose mental development is incomplete or abnormal in other respects'.[6] And on the subject in general they observed that 'Although most of those who are at present described as feeble-minded are sub-normal or at least below average in intelligence, what distinguishes them and moral defectives and psychopaths most clearly from normal people is their general social behaviour . . . But it is difficult to describe the characteristics of these . . . groups of patients in terms which distinguish them from the sort of failings which are common to almost all human beings in one degree or another. There is, however, no doubt that there are many persons, at present described as feeble-minded, moral defectives or psychopaths, whose intelligence is not seriously impaired but who have pathological defects or abnormalities of personality

[1] ibid. Seventeenth day, p. 607. [2] ibid., p. 622. [3] ibid., Twelfth day, p. 468.
[4] ibid., p. 481. [5] ibid., p. 481. [6] ibid., Report (1957), para. 162.

which result in behaviour which makes it most necessary, in their own interests or in the interests of society as a whole, to provide them with special forms of help or treatment and in certain circumstances to subject them to special forms of control.'[1]

In practice mental defectives are, without doubt, not diagnosed purely by their intellectual deficiency: even though the average I.Q. in a mental deficiency institution would, equally without doubt, be found to be much lower than that of the population outside. Hilliard and Mundy report that of ten consecutive admissions to the Fountain (Mental Deficiency) Hospital, London, 'the psychometric results show that four had I.Q. levels of 90–108, that is, were of average intelligence according to their Wechsler-Bellevue full-scale I.Q.s: five were intellectually dull but still within the normal range. Only one was a borderline defective. Two might have been regarded as borderline defectives, but their verbal scores were reduced by educational backwardness and they achieved higher matrices results.' These results encouraged further investigation into a 'more statistically reliable sample' of 132 female admissions; and from this it appeared that 54 per cent of the 'so-called high-grade patients' were not 'in fact intellectually defective'. Commenting, in the light of this, upon the 'false impression of the problem of mental deficiency' which results from present classifications, the authors add the significant observation that 'such patients may be socially incompetent, but in many cases institutional life itself has aggravated their emotional difficulties'.[2]

Much the same picture is drawn also by Tizard in a summary of an official 5 per cent sample of some 12,000 defectives who had been institutionalized in London, Surrey and Kent. In this, the average intelligence quotient of young feeble-minded adults was found to be about seventy, while 7 per cent scored over eighty-five; one in every hundred ranked actually above the intelligence level of the general population. In short, 'substantial numbers must be regarded as *normal* in *intelligence*'. Tizard concludes that there seems no reason why most of such feeble-minded adults should not be restored to the community after a period of education and training;[3] and it has in fact been established both at home and abroad that this can be successfully achieved.

If mental deficients are not to be diagnosed by their intellectual deficiencies, some alternative criterion must be employed. The problem of avoiding a circular definition of behaviour in terms of defect and of defect in terms of behaviour seems, however, to have attracted less attention than has been given to the parallel problem of defining mental illness. There are no clear equivalents to the 'motiveless' actions or the psychiatric syndromes used for this purpose in connection with mental illness. Those who reject definitions of mental deficiency in terms of intelligence quotients, generally speaking offer only behavioural tests of social competence as alternatives. Diagnosis by social competence, however, implies acceptance of one or other of two

[1] Royal Commission on the Law Relating to Mental Illness and Mental Deficiency, 1954–57. Report (1957), para 166. [2] Hilliard and Mundy (1954), pp. 645–6.

[3] Tizard (1954), pp. 158 ff, italics not original.

possible logical positions, both of which lead to the same practical result. Either mental deficiency must be regarded as itself merely another name for social incompetence, or we must assume that it is a 'natural' condition (whether inborn or acquired during early life) of an unknown and indefinable nature, which exists independently of, but causes, social incompetence, and which is discernible only by this social manifestation. In practice, the second of these alternatives is no doubt the more acceptable; but one may search in vain for any light on the question how, apart from its social manifestations, the existence of this condition is to be detected.

Social competence itself moreover needs also to be defined. Intellectual capacity is to-day commonly measured by intelligence test performance. No similar instrument, however, is available for the measurement of social competence; and those who would define defectiveness in social terms seldom commit themselves with any precision as to what in this context social 'competence' or adequacy means. One might perhaps say that social competence seems, by implication, generally to be identified with, or at least to involve, economic independence; a mental defective is regarded as socially incompetent (and therefore as defective) if he cannot maintain himself.

Judged by this test, however, many of those who are at some time classified as defectives subsequently acquit themselves remarkably well. Writing in 1954, O'Connor records that 'pre-war surveys generally gave figures showing that between 40 per cent and 60 per cent of cases were self-supporting after some years. In addition an unpublished work in England has shown that "40 to 50 per cent of adult institutional patients might be fully employable" (Gibbens). Some postwar surveys of people of low IQ, in fact of feeble-minded people living in the community have shown very much higher percentage successes.'[1] In the same article an American survey of males with I.Q.s between fifty-five and seventy-five is quoted in which 'significant differences between normals and morons' were found to be few. Similar results were obtained also by O'Connor in his own investigations. On comparing the records of defective boys from Darenth Park Mental Deficiency Institution employed on a construction job with those of a 10 per cent sample of normal labourers working alongside them, O'Connor found that, although the defectives had a heavier load of failures in the early months, 'at the end of the first year there was no difference in the numbers who had failed in each group. The position remained unchanged like this until the job was completed'.[2] Kirman, giving evidence of overlap between defectives and the general population in test performance, observed among the former 'little evidence of gross departure from accepted standards of stability and behaviour'.[3] Tizard quotes an American investigation of 206 adults classified as subnormal of whom, fifteen years later, 83 per cent were self-supporting, 'the range of occupations being from "managerial positions to unskilled labour".'[4] In another American investigation Bobroff records that, among 121 products of special classes or centres for defectives in Detroit, twelve

[1] O'Connor (1954), p. 173. [2] ibid., pp. 175–6. [3] Kirman (1957), p. 1221.
[4] Tizard (1953), p. 435.

years later thirty were in unskilled jobs, thirty-six in semi-skilled and fifteen in skilled, while eight were employed in service occupations, six in clerical and five in managerial and similar posts: only seven were unemployed. A high proportion had, moreover, remained with the same employer for seven years or more, and 65 per cent had had fewer than five different employers. Most, in fact, were 'functioning considerably above minimal levels of acceptability'.[1] Schmidt, who followed up a group of feebleminded, often 'ineducable', children from Chicago schools, for whom a special programme for training in independence had been instituted, found that after eight years a similarly remarkable degree of social competence had been attained. At ages 12–14, this group of 254 children registered I.Q.s of from twenty-seven to sixty-nine, with a median of 53·1. Behaviour problems were not particularly formidable, only 14·9 per cent being socially maladjusted. Five years later, 27 per cent had completed a high school course and 5·1 per cent had carried their education further. Employment records were generally good and, with an average gain of over forty points in I.Q., only 7·2 per cent could be reckoned (presumably by an intellectual criterion) as still feebleminded.[2]

To round off the picture one might perhaps quote a letter of resignation from the Eugenics Society written in 1946 by a member who had worked for six years among defectives, and who, after expressing doubts as to the wisdom of over-stressing the criterion of intelligence, goes on to observe that defectives 'showed such a great variety of other virtues—generosity, goodwill, altruism, sweet temper—that I began to think a world peopled by mental defectives might be an improvement on the present one'.[3]

If social incompetence is the test of deficiency, such findings prove either that defectives are capable of considerable improvement as the years go by, or that the original diagnosis was wrong. The second of these alternatives seems seldom to be considered in the literature. Yet the extraordinary variation in the rate of ascertainment of defectives in different parts of the same country suggests that, at the least, the criteria employed are decidedly erratic. In 1953 the number of defectives reported to the Local Health Authorities per 1000 of estimated population ranged from 8·02 in the County Borough of Walsall to 1·00 in Merionethshire: in London the figure was 4·17; while the proportion institutionalized varied from 2·44 in Walsall to nil in Merionethshire, with London standing at 2·35. In France also a large scale survey recently completed, quoted by Tizard, shows an even greater variation in prevalence rates, the figures ranging from 1½ per cent to 11 per cent among school-children.[4]

In assessing the validity of a social competence test, it is moreover wise to remember the early age at which most defectives are at present ascertained as such. Indeed, in all the various definitions of mental deficiency, the one consistent element seems to be the principle that mental defectives suffer from arrested or incomplete development, and that whatever is wrong with them must have been so from an early age. According to the Ministry of Health,

[1] Bobroff (1956), pp. 525–535. [2] Schmidt (1949).
[3] *Eugenics Review*, October 1946, p. 115. [4] Tizard (1953), p. 430.

in 1952 and 1953 'nearly all defectives ascertained as subject to be dealt with were reported while at school or about the time when they left school'. In 1953, of 7,224 cases reported as 'subject to be dealt with', 5,168 were under sixteen years of age.[1] The opportunities for demonstrating their social competence or incompetence which these children enjoyed must in the nature of the case have been somewhat restricted. Significantly, however, the number institutionalized or placed under guardianship was small. Altogether over 6,000 defectives proved able, if only under statutory supervision, to take some kind of place in the community, even though the social incompetence of five out of every seven of them had been officially established before their sixteenth birthday.

The urge to get away from purely intellectual concepts of mental deficiency, and to substitute the criterion of social competence, has thus left us with a situation which is fantastically complicated—or, perhaps, 'muddled' would be a better word. In the modern usage, a mental defective may be as intelligent as anybody else, and defective only in his social competence. Social competence depends, however, upon the expected levels of competence, and these in turn depend upon such extraneous factors as the state of the employment market; yet at the same time, many defectives, given the chance, prove themselves socially competent. The muddle seems to culminate in such statements as the following from Tizard and O'Connor that 'although perhaps more liable to emotional instability than those of higher intelligence, there is no reason to suppose that the defective is less persistent or more suggestible than other members of the community of comparable socio-economic status. His performances on level of aspiration tests do not distinguish him as a class from the normal. He is apparently no more susceptible to monotony than a normal worker and may even be less so. There is no evidence that he is likely to vary in output more than the normal worker and, unless neurotic, is unlikely to be more prone to injury than his fellows.'[2] Indeed O'Connor's cheerful conclusions that 'the feebleminded are capable of a degree of social competence and independence which we are almost afraid to acknowledge'[3] is rendered meaningless if social incompetence is the mark of mental deficiency; for by that test mental defectives cannot, by definition, be socially competent, and the socially competent cannot be feebleminded.

In the same way, diagnosis of defectiveness by social incompetence makes nonsense of all attempts to estimate the contribution which defectives make to the social problem group, since the two categories become interchangeable. By this standard the incidence of defectiveness is related, both, as already noted, to the capacity of the labour market and to the shape of the economic and social pyramid; and the apparent confusion of economic and non-economic forms of social failure which bedevilled early eugenic investigations[4] proves to have been no confusion at all. There will be more defectives in bad times than in good, but fewer in the upper social levels where economic

[1] Ministry of Health *Report* for 1953, Part 1, p. 263.

[2] Tizard and O'Connor (1950), p. 156. [3] O'Connor (1954), p. 180. [4] See pp. 53 ff.

stress is less severe than in the lower where it is harsher—not because of any differences in genetic constitution or in early experience between different social groups, nor even because poor defectives are more likely to be certified than rich ones—but because defectiveness is itself a function of economic status. The size of the mental deficiency hospital population in any area becomes not so much 'a reflection of the population of its catchment area' as 'a result of the social conditions of that area, and *depends on the policy and opinions of the administrators and others in it*', as, for example, in one 'very rural county' which, we are told, 'sent in feeble-minded girls only if they had illegitimate children'.[1] On this situation remarks made on behalf of the National Council for Civil Liberties before the Royal Commission are highly pertinent, and it may well be asked how far 'social competence' precludes prostitution or illegitimate maternity.

The practical implications are considerable. If deficiency is to be defined by social competence, the National Assistance Board will be relieved of the burden of distinguishing between those whose 'sole handicap is laziness', those who, 'though not malingerers' 'are disposed to accept passively the situation in which they find themselves'[2], and those in whom 'weakness of will seems to be pathological'.[3] And the powers and duties of Local Health Authorities, also, will be similarly affected. Under present law, among the grounds which render a defective 'subject to be dealt with' by his Local Health Authority is the fact that he is without visible means of support, or that he is a habitual drunkard. These provisions clearly imply that it is possible to discriminate between the defective drunkard and the drunkard pure and simple; but if inability to maintain oneself, whether through excessive drinking or any other cause, is itself proof of mental defect, then this distinction also will be obliterated, and all habitual drunkards will become 'subject to be dealt with' as defective.

As in the case of mental illness, the definition of mental deficiency is much more than a semantic matter. Under the Homicide Act, a plea of diminished responsibility is now open to mental defectives as well as to the mentally sick: evidence of mental defect can, therefore, be a life and death matter. In other criminal cases, if a court is satisfied on medical evidence that a convicted person is mentally deficient, it may commit him to an institution for defectives instead of passing any of the sentences prescribed, in the ordinary case, for the offence in question; and persons who are imprisoned or detained in approved schools or remand homes, and who are proved to the satisfaction of the Home Secretary, and on the evidence of two medical practitioners, to be mentally defective, may similarly be transferred to such an institution. Since the period of detention in, and the prospects of discharge from, mental deficiency institutions are very different from those relating to imprisonment or other forms of penal detention, important considerations of personal liberty are involved here. That there are grave risks in allowing these

[1] Letter in the *British Medical Journal* (September 18, 1954), p. 703. Italics not original.
[2] National Assistance Board *Report* for 1954, p. 21.
[3] ibid., *Report* for 1953, p. 14.

very considerable powers to be exercised against persons, the only proof of whose defectiveness is that they are judged to be socially incompetent by the standards of members of the medical profession, will hardly be denied. For the temptation to identify the exceptional or the challenging with the socially incompetent is always present. Under the criteria now authoritatively advocated, the founder of the Christian religion would without doubt have been liable to 'ascertainment' as 'subject to be dealt with' under the Mental Deficiency Acts.

Inevitably, definitions of mental defect in terms of social competence threaten to undermine, in just the same way as do similar definitions of mental illness, the concept of responsibility which is so deep-seated in our social and penal legislation. But here again, as in the parallel case of mental illness, the resulting practical difficulties can be avoided if this concept is bypassed in the manner suggested by Dr Bernard Glueck. Just as Glueck's object in treating criminality as a disease is to concentrate attention, not on the degree of an offender's blameworthiness, but on the practical problem of how best his behaviour may be reorientated, so the primary purpose of classifying socially inadequate persons as defective should be to make available to them whatever help they need. It then becomes unnecessary to distinguish between those whose drunkenness is a symptom of mental defect and those who are 'ordinary' drunkards; or between those whose laziness is pathological and those who are just lazy. And, with the disappearance of these moral distinctions between what might be called capable and defective failures, differentiation between the one and the other will be called for only insofar as it affects the kind of treatment that is likely to be helpful.

CHAPTER IX

Contemporary Attitudes in Social Work

I

ACCORDING to the 1951 Census there are now some 22,000 social workers in England and Wales—that is to say, slightly more than one social worker to every two barmen or barmaids. In the struggle against social pathology it is these social workers who largely constitute the first line of defence (or perhaps one should say of attack); and their attitudes and theories are, accordingly, of crucial importance in the present context.

In the course of the past half-century those attitudes and theories have been remoulded in remarkable fashion, largely under the influence of the developments described in the two preceding Chapters. As is well known, the early professional or semi-professional social work, from which modern 'case-work' is descended, concerned itself chiefly with the relief of poverty. The techniques of 'investigation' invented by the pioneers of the Charity Organization Society were designed to protect the charitable from the impositions of the fraudulent, and to eliminate wasteful duplication—such as would occur if one applicant obtained relief from several sources simultaneously, with or without each being aware of what the others might be doing. In this phase the social worker's function was to distribute alms in such a way, and with such safeguards, as to encourage the virtues of thrift, self-help and independence, acting, it would seem, on what Mr (now Lord) Attlee has called the 'general assumption that all applicants are frauds unless they prove themselves otherwise'.[1] Even hospital almoners, whose ostensible function was 'to secure for the "patients such care, assistance and attention outside the hospital as should enable them to profit to the full by the medical treatment received"' seem, originally, to have acted as 'enquiry agents' to prevent 'the abuse of hospital charity'.[2] By the same logic, the progenitors of the Charity Organization Society resolutely opposed the introduction of old age pensions, school dinners and other similar measures, though they did occasionally raise their voices in support of the few social reforms which they felt to be compatible with the virtues to be inculcated into the lower classes; and the assumption that criminality or indifference to prevailing social standards is peculiarly characteristic of the lower classes was likewise allowed to pass unquestioned, and did not have to be dressed up in any way to suit the susceptibilities of the time; although it was always also recognized that,

[1] quoted in Young and Ashton (1956), p. 111.
[2] ibid., pp. 108–9.

swamped in the mass of 'chronic pauperism, beggary and crime',[1] would be found representatives of the 'deserving poor' whom indeed it was the social worker's function to succour. In her history of social work in London in the last three decades of the nineteeth century, Mrs Bosanquet quotes the view of a London physician that, if one could but contrive to 'handcuff the indiscriminate almsgiver', the result would be 'no destitution, little poverty, lessened poor-rates, prisons emptier, fewer gin-shops, less crowded madhouses'—in short, 'an England worth living in'.[2] In 1868 a paper read by the Rev Henry Solly to the Society of Arts, and described in the same work as 'the trumpet call which summoned the forces [of the would-be organizers of charity] into the field',[3] resulted in the formation of a Society for the Prevention of Pauperism and Crime; while in the United States, in keeping with the same philosophy, the National Conference of Social Work began life as the 'Conference of Charities and Corrections'.[4] The multiple deficiencies which the Wood Committee[5] found in the social problem group in 1929 had fifty years earlier tripped lightly off the tongues of the organizers of charity, as they described the poorer classes of their day.

All this has changed. Indiscriminate almsgiving, though still deprecated, is no longer credited with such magical powers of comprehensive mischief. The contemporary social worker no longer regards the relief of poverty as her primary function: still less does she concentrate upon the detection of fraud or upon discrimination between the 'deserving' and the 'undeserving'. To-day the 'maladjusted', or the social misfits, have taken the place formerly reserved for the poor in the ideology of social work.

In explanation of this change, much prominence has been given to the supposed disappearance of poverty from the list of urgent problems confronting the so-called 'Welfare State'. In a much-used contemporary text-book, for example, Penelope Hall remarks that 'In the past, problems of poverty, of public health, of long hours and unsatisfactory conditions of work were so pressing that to a large extent social reformers concentrated on them'; whereas 'the most urgent problems which confront sociologists, social administrators and workers to-day are such symptoms of a sick society as the increasing number of marriage breakdowns, the spread of juvenile delinquency, and the dissatisfaction and sense of frustration of the worker in spite of improved pay and conditions—that is, problems of psychological maladjustment rather than material need'.[6] In the same way, in the United States, where the switch-over from the economic to the psychological is even more marked than it has been here, the change has been ascribed to the enormous growth of public relief services and of public charity which was made necessary by the Great Depression of the early nineteen-thirties—developments which threatened in fact to put the old-fashioned type of social worker out of a job. 'Almost overnight the voluntary case-work agencies were deprived of their major function, and subsidies from tax funds were discontinued. As a result

[1] Bosanquet (1914), p. 5. [2] ibid., p. 7. [3] ibid., p. 18.
[4] Keith-Lucas (1953), p. 1078. [5] See p. 52. [6] Hall (1952), p. 8.

they turned quite naturally to case-work services that could be developed independently of relief giving.'[1]

How far this loss of faith in the prophecy that we shall always have the poor with us is justified may well be questioned in the light of facts already quoted.[2] Nor is it clear that social work has lost its predominant concern with the 'lower income groups', even if the direct relief of extreme poverty does occupy less of the average social worker's activities than it did. In the United States in 1950 as many as 41 per cent of all social workers were said to be still employed in the administration of public assistance.[3] But whatever the facts, it is certainly true that social workers no longer see themselves as primarily dispensers of charity, and that it is not the poverty of the poor in which they are chiefly interested. Believing themselves, rightly or wrongly, to have been deprived of one function, they have lost no time in inventing another.

Other factors have also pulled in the same direction. For reasons which it would take too long to explore here, the past thirty or forty years have seen remarkable changes in the nature of our susceptibility to guilt. A generation or so ago, the rich assuaged the guilt which they felt for their richness by distributing charity to the poor—or at least to such of the poor as could prove themselves to be 'deserving'. To-day the act of alms-giving enhances rather than diminishes guilt, inasmuch as it calls attention to differences in wealth, which, by the more egalitarian standards now prevailing, might demand justification. The relation of donor and donatee has thus become embarrassing to both partners, and even humiliating to the former. Charitable benefactions to institutions and causes are still possible and indeed even laudable; but hardly anyone to-day is bold enough openly to play the part of Lord or Lady Bountiful to individuals.

Meanwhile, the timely growth of psychiatry, and of psychoanalysis in particular, has provided social workers with just that new interpretation of their function of which they thus found themselves so badly in need. In the United States, as early as 1919 'psychiatry swept the National Conference of Social Work'.[4] Eleven years later Mildred Scoville, in a Presidential Address to the American Association of Psychiatric Social Workers, spoke of the 'realization in the social work field that all social case work has a psychological or mental hygiene aspect'.[5] By 1940, according to one American writer, any deviation from 'Freudian psychology' in the theory of social work 'was looked upon by some with the same horror as a true Stalinist appraising a Trotskyite'.[6] In this country, if the social workers' surrender to Freud has been less unquestioning than has that of their American colleagues, the influence of psychiatry has certainly been sufficient to revolutionize both the language which these workers use and the conception of their rôle which they present alike to themselves and to others. In a very few years practically the whole profession has succeeded in exchanging the garments of charity for a uniform borrowed from the practitioners of psychological medicine.

[1] Miles (1954), p. 107. [2] See pp. 73 ff.
[3] Miles (1954), p. 74. [4] Robinson (1930), p. 32.
[5] Scoville (1931), pp. 147–48. [6] Miles (1954), p. 9.

These changes have been generally welcomed with somewhat uncritical admiration. They have certainly done some good. They have, for instance, provided a way of escape from the inquisitorial methods by which charitably disposed well-to-do persons previously sought protection, both for themselves against fraud, and for the community against that threat to the virtues of industry and thrift which they believed to be inherent in the payment of unearned income to the poor, though not, apparently, to the rich. Admittedly also the past few decades have seen a great improvement in the standard of manners and courtesy which social workers think it proper to observe in their dealings with those whom they now call their 'clients'. But the price of these advances has been the erection of a fantastically pretentious façade, and a tendency to emphasize certain aspects of social work out of all proportion to their real significance, while playing down others that are potentially at least as valuable. Nor is it certain that the substance of what social workers do to-day differs quite as radically as does the form from the parallels of an earlier epoch.

To particularize: modern definitions of 'social casework', if taken at their face value, involve claims to powers which verge upon omniscience and omnipotence: one can only suppose that those who perpetuate these claims in cold print must, for some as yet unexplained reason, have been totally deserted by their sense of humour. Thus Mary Richmond, who is widely regarded as the founder of modern casework, once defined this as 'the art of doing different things for and with different people by co-operating with them to achieve at one and the same time their own and society's betterment'[1]—a formula inclusive enough to cover any and every kind of altruistic activity; while in another context she speaks of social casework as consisting of 'those processes which develop personality through adjustments, effected individual by individual, between men and society'.[2] According to a more recent American writer, whose prestige also stands very high among social workers, casework offers 'help with the personal aspects of ordinary living' (that is to say, presumably, with the problems which have troubled the human race since the beginning of self-consciousness); and casework is 'the only one of the "humanistic" professions wherein practitioners are educated for this function'.[3] To these claims may be added Hollis' description of the caseworker as one who assists 'families and individuals in developing both the capacity and the opportunity to lead personally satisfying and socially useful lives'.[4]

In a paper published in 1949, Swithun Bowers has collected over thirty definitions, the authors of which seem determined to outbid one another in the immensity of their claims. This pretentiousness reaches its peak in Swift's identification of casework with the 'art of assisting the individual in developing and making use of his personal capacity to deal with problems which he faces in his social environment', and in Lee's sublimely comprehensive formula—'the art of changing human attitudes'.[5] Bowers has himself produced

[1] Richmond (1930), p. 374. [2] ibid., p. 477.
[3] Hamilton (1952), p. 24. [4] Hollis (1948), p. 5.
[5] Bowers, in Kasius, ed. (1950), pp. 101 and 103.

a definition which competes with these. To him it is 'an art in which knowledge of the science of human relations and skill in relationship are used to mobilize capacities in the individual and resources in the community appropriate for better adjustment'.[1] Most staggering of all the American definitions, however, is that given by Margaret Rich to the Third International Conference of Social Work in 1936. According to this the 'essential elements of the social case work process' are said to involve '(*a*) an attempt to understand the individual as a "psychobiological organism the functioning of which is determined by its structure and the peculiar development compelled by the interacting stimuli of inner needs and of environmental conditions and demands"; (*b*) sharing this understanding with the individual to the degree that he can accept and use it for further understanding of his difficulties and possibilities as a basis for developing his capacity to make his own social adjustment; (*c*) gauging the ability and tempo of the individual so as to free him from responsibilities too heavy for him to carry and at the same time to leave him with those that he should and can assume; (*d*) helping him to make use of available resources—educational, medical, religious, industrial—in working out his own social programme; (*e*) establishing a relationship with the individual through a willingness to let him "find himself without dictation, condemnation or didactic advice", thus making it possible for him "to work out an individual adjustment consonant with his own essential feelings and founded on his increased ability to utilize his personal and environmental resources" '. After all this, it is not perhaps surprising to be told that the social caseworker who aims so high must be equipped with 'a definite body of knowledge about human behaviour, social relationships, social resources, and with the skills required to relate this knowledge to the individual situation'.[2] He—or more probably she—will need them.

Lest it be thought that these are just examples of an American tendency to overstatement, some European examples may be added. From Yugo-Slavia we learn that social work 'endeavours systematically to understand motivation, to accept people as they are, to estimate and develop their capacities for self-help'.[3] A Norwegian reminds us that a social worker needs to know about 'the multiplicity of social causations and the psychological interplay between a person and his environment';[4] while from an Italian writer we learn that 'social service aims to orientate the individual in reference to his own task in his daily life, his relationships with members of his family or of the community, his health, his home, his work, his leisure time, in order that he may find in himself the elements for alleviation of grievance, and for his own improvement'.[5]

In this country we owe the classic statements to Eileen Younghusband. The modern social worker, she has said, 'will know [*sic*] what kinds of behaviour, what characteristic reactions, to expect from people of different ages and mentalities, in different social and cultural settings, having suffered

[1] Bowers, in Kasius, ed. (1950), p. 127. [2] Rich, M. E. (1938), pp. 476–7.
[3] Pusic, in *New Trends in European Social Work* [1954], p. 84.
[4] Tjensvoll, ibid., p. 102. [5] Corgiat, ibid., p. 73.

from a variety of damaging experiences; and of varying degrees of personal integration or internal conflict'.[1] In a collection of papers which has become a standard English textbook on the subject, we are told by the same authority that 'it is now demanded' of this social worker 'that she shall seek to understand the person in need, not only at that particular moment in time, but also the pattern of personality the major experiences and relationships which make him the person he now is: with conflicts of whose origin he may be unaware; with problems whose solution may lie less in external circumstances that in his own attitudes; with tensions, faulty relationships, inabilities to face reality, hardened into forms which he cannot alter without help. Instead of seeing his situation through her own eyes and producing a ready-made solution, the social worker must be able to understand him and his needs and his relationships as these appear to the person in need himself. She must enter into his problems as he sees them, his relationships as he experiences them, with their frustrations, their deprivations, their satisfactions, and see him, or his different selves, as they appear to him himself. Yet at the same time she must also be clearly aware of the realities of the situation and through her professional skill in relationships enable him to come to a better understanding of himself and others.'[2]

It might well be thought that the social worker's best, indeed perhaps her only, chance of achieving aims at once so intimate and so ambitious would be to marry her client. Miss Younghusband, however, puts her faith in the 'body of knowledge to be learned, skills to be acquired, and wisdom to begin in training and mellow through the years of professional practice' which distinguish the trained caseworker from the 'good, sensible woman (or still more, man) with an all-round experience of life, who has travelled about the world a bit', and who is widely, though not in her view wisely, believed to be 'just as, if not more valuable, than the specialized social worker'.[3]

In the language used to describe the practice of these ambitious arts, the contemporary influence of psychiatry is particularly noticeable. Ever since the publication of Mary Richmond's famous volume on *Social Diagnosis* the literature has been richly strewn with references to 'diagnosis', 'therapy,' 'treatment' and similar medical terms: it is clear that at least a considerable proportion of caseworkers see themselves as a species of social doctors. Where an older generation would have spoken of 'investigation', the modern social worker writes on '*Diagnosing Family Situations*'.[4] Gordon Hamilton,[5] in a textbook which is widely used on both sides of the Atlantic, heads one chapter 'Diagnostic and Evaluation Processes' and another 'Methods of Treatment'; and this model has been followed by scores of writers on casework theory in the United States and by many others also in this country. McDougall and Cormack, writing on *Case-work in Practice*, refer to the definite *stages* (italics original) in the conduct of a 'case', such as 'the first contact, the collection of information, diagnosis and treatment'; and add that, apart from certain 'therapeutic effects', 'treatment might be considered

[1] Younghusband (1952), p. 722. [2] In Morris, C., ed. (1955), p. 199.
[3] ibid., pp. 200 and 205. [4] Stott (July, 1954), p. 940. [5] Hamilton (1952).

as mainly that part of the case-work process which occurs after diagnosis has been made'.[1] Whale, writing of case work as applied to problem families, remarks that 'the crux of the social casework idea is that all problems are psycho-social, deriving from the inner world of the mind and also from the social environment in which the personality finds itself'.[2]

On the Western side of the Atlantic, this psychiatric preoccupation of social workers has taken a distinctively psycho-analytic turn. In a book dedicated to the Pennsylvania School of Social Work and published in 1930, Virginia Robinson has discussed at length the contribution to casework theory made by the 'ego-libido method of case analysis' presented by Kenworthy to the National Conference of Social Work four years earlier in 1926; and she passes the judgment that 'the value of this psychiatry for the case work field in this decade cannot be overestimated'. This 'ego-libido method of analysing a case history', we are told, 'penetrates below the sociological generalities of Miss Richmond's diagnostic summary into concrete psychological fact and necessitates constant refinement of understanding in analysing the relation between experience and its meaning to the individual.' By this method, also, the social worker is enabled to 'pick out on the ego-libido chart the causative factors of undesirable development in destructive experience and to balance these with constructive satisfying experience'.[3]

The suggestion that complex problems of personal unhappiness or of defiance of social standards can be resolved by a young woman with an academic training in social work is difficult to take seriously. Yet from many of the contemporary definitions one would imagine that a casework session was only a few steps away from a full-blown psycho-analysis; though writers on casework are generally careful modestly to deny that they claim so much. Davison, for example, has described the whole business of social work in psycho-analytic terms, referring to the 'giving of insight' and of the 'criteria by which one may attempt to measure [the client's] ego-strength',[4] while Robinson also, in the eulogy of Kenworthy just mentioned, quotes with approval the latter's description of the 'positive transference' which social workers, teachers, ministers and physicians are apparently thought to be liable to encounter in the course of their work.[5] In other cases, again the influence of psychoanalysis upon social work theory shows itself in an unquestioning assumption of the significance, for subsequent social adjustment, of infantile experience. Howarth, for instance, observes categorically that 'the causes of personality maladjustment' are 'most frequently' found to be 'rooted in the events of childhood';[6] while attempts are now made to explain the peculiarities of the parents of 'problem families' in terms of their infantile experiences. In extreme cases, descriptions of social work reach an almost mystical level, notably in the writings of Anita Faatz. According to this writer, when anyone goes to a social work agency with some simple practical problem, such as finding a job or a place to live, or for help in completing naturaliza-

[1] in Morris, C., ed. (1955), pp. 38 and 49. [2] Whale (1954), p. 883.
[3] Robinson (1930), pp. 85, 91, 92 and 90. [4] Davison (1955), pp. 85, 83.
[5] Robinson (1930), pp. 90–1. [6] Howarth (1949), p. 331.

tion papers, or even for being put in touch with a doctor, 'the concrete reality of the helping situation carries the true projection of the deepest conflict of the self', so that 'help upon a practical, tangible life problem affords the potentiality for help which touches the core of the self and sets in motion an authentic process of growth'; and 'out of a helping process there eventuates, in slow growth, an experience in which there is a heightened sense of life; as if here, in this moment of time, has been manifest an expression of movement and change like a veritable piece of life itself'. Even so commonplace a matter as the spacing of interviews between a client and a caseworker carries apparently the same deep spiritual significance. 'When interviews are spaced at weekly intervals, as they very frequently are in the casework service, the hour of engagement between the helper and the one who seeks help can be intense, deeply disturbing, and penetrated by the new sense of life which every human being fears intensely yet craves so deeply. A week is none too long in which to thrash about in one's own aloneness—in confusion, in rebellion, in yielding, in conflict, all gathering toward the moment of return, in new organization, in new discovery of what the self is like by telling it to another whose responses are accurate.'[1]

Symptomatic also of the psychoanalytic influence upon social workers is the emphasis which is laid upon 'the relationship' between the social worker and those who either seek her aid or have this thrust upon them. In the case of psycho-analytic treatment, it is intelligible enough that what happens in the consulting room between patient and analyst is the heart of the matter: the analyst does not indeed normally profess to purvey any service over and beyond this. But a social worker might have been expected to devote much of her activity to mobilizing the various forms of practical assistance that are now available for dealing with certain problems of situation or behaviour, her relationship with her client being merely incidental to this task. Nevertheless, discussion of 'the relationship' (again in an almost mystical sense) has now become a central theme in the literature of social work. In the language of Pray's sweeping definition, 'The core of these processes, methods, and skills of generic social work practice is obviously in the disciplined use of one's self in direct relations with people, both individually and in groups. All else is secondary and incidental and assumes significance only as it eventuates in the more effectual performance of the worker in that direct relationship.'[2] Gordon Hamilton devotes a whole chapter to *The Use of Relationship*, and includes in this some discussion of the extent to which 'transference' is to be expected in what many of her colleagues constantly refer to as 'the casework situation'. According to her, 'At the center of the casework process is the conscious and controlled use of the worker-client relationship to achieve the ends of treatment'.[3] McDougall and Cormack, in the paper already quoted, refer to caseworkers being able to 'use the relationship therapeutically';[4] Charlotte Towle writes of 'new elements in our conduct of the relationship':[5] Robinson devotes three chapters to various

[1] Faatz (1953), pp. 43, 65 and 134. [2] Pray, quoted in Kasius, ed. (1950), p. 123.
[3] Hamilton (1952), p. 22. [4] in Morris, C., ed. (1955), p. 50. [5] Towle (1955), p. 10.

aspects of 'relationship', and is at pains to point out how far the modern social worker has travelled from the days when the relationship between 'client and the worker was accepted' by the latter 'as a matter of simple, natural, human friendliness'.[1] Clearly she would regard it as the height of naïveté to read into Davison's observation that 'the initial phase of a treatment relationship' 'sets the pattern for the whole process',[2] merely the fact that people are more likely to make extended use of a social worker's services if they are courteously received and attentively listened to; and so, for that matter, would Davison herself. Emphasis, indeed, is constantly laid upon the fact that 'the relationship' has both a professional and a highly self-conscious character. 'Professional relationships are not just friendly associations', writes Hamilton. 'The professional relationship differs from most of conventional intercourse largely in the degree to which the aim must be the good of others (whether individual or group), in the amount of self-awareness to be attained by the worker, and in the techniques to be assimilated and consciously utilized . . . The professional self is controlled towards the end one is serving—namely, to understand and meet the psycho-social needs of clients.'[3] According to Howarth, while there may 'continue to be a use for the spontaneous friendlinesss and understanding of the voluntary untrained social worker', 'professional casework has another role to play'.[4] Rapoport observes that 'in understanding the *emotional* needs of the client, we come to know what our mutual goals are, and use the case-work relationship in a conscious manner in order to effect these goals';[5] while Britton, writing of children's problems, sums the whole matter up by defining the professional relationship as 'the technique whereby we provide a limited and enclosed environmental setting which is personal because it contains all that the client has put into it himself, and which is reliable because it is accepting and holding. Through it the natural integrating processes are given a chance.' The relationship is, in fact, 'the basic technique, the one by means of which we relate ourselves to the individual and to the problem'; and 'the professional self', it is good to learn, 'is the most highly organized and integrated part of ourselves. It is the best of ourselves, and includes all our positive and constructive impulses and all our capacity for personal relationships and experiences organized together for a purpose—the professional function which we have chosen.'[6]

To those who are familiar with psychoanalytic ways of thought it will not come as a surprise that the professional case worker shows little hesitation in claiming to understand those with whom she deals better than they understand themselves, discerning subconscious or preconscious motivations of which they are themselves unaware. Thus Hamilton: 'Caseworkers must sometimes bring to the attention of the client ideas and feelings, whether acceptable or not, of which he was previously unaware'. 'The treatment situation is used to release feeling, to support the ego, and to increase the person's

[1] Robinson (1930), p. 128. [2] Davison (1955), p. 82.
[3] Hamilton (1952), pp. 28–29. [4] Howarth (1951), p. 532.
[5] Rapoport (1954), p. 912 (italics original). [6] Britton (1955), pp. 7 and 5.

self-awareness by bringing to his attention his attitudes and patterns of behavior . . .'[1] According to McDougall and Cormack, 'in discussing with the client his troubles and the events which led up to his needing casework help, the client can learn something about himself which can in turn help him to help himself'.[2] Betty Joseph, writing specifically about *Psychoanalysis and Social Casework*, gives numerous examples of 'the way in which clients show us the existence of important unconscious feelings which are activating their behaviour'. In her view, 'this concept of people being motivated by, or else expressing needs and feelings of which they themselves are not conscious, or only partially conscious' is 'one which we use a great deal in our casework, but to which we could usefully become increasingly sensitive', though she does later deprecate the idea that because of their 'awareness' of other people's 'defence mechanisms', social workers should go about, 'as it were, probing for deep-down unconscious feelings'.[3] Finally, Muriel Cunliffe, UN Adviser on Casework Training, is reported to have told the Association of General and Family Caseworkers that 'in gauging whether a client could be helped through the casework method it was important to remember all that he brought to the situation: his natural endowments, established patterns of behaviour, memories of past experiences, ways of forming and using relationships, attitudes to people and life, formal and less formal education, religious beliefs, acquired sets of values and, never to be forgotten, *his unconscious*'.[4]

In consequence of this conviction on the part of the caseworker that she can understand other people better than they understand themselves, a practice has grown up of refusing to accept at their face value the emergencies which cause people to seek the aid of a social work agency. A favourite theme of contemporary casework literature is the social worker's capacity, and indeed her duty, to penetrate below what is called the 'presenting problem' to the 'something deeper' that is supposed to lie underneath. According to Miles, if a woman asks for financial help because she has been recently widowed, or because she cannot manage a difficult son, 'the factual information about the immediate problem can be easily discovered. Experienced case workers, however, recognize that during the period of social study there is movement from surface problems to those that are deeper and more significant';[5] or, as Davison has put it, 'often the worker sees quite soon that the presenting problem is not the only or perhaps the most fundamental one'.[6] While it may be 'best to begin at the point where the client considers help is needed', and, if the request is for material help to grant this whenever funds permit, the merit of this procedure is not that the client gets the money he requires, but that it will enable him to 'move forward from talking about things to talking about feelings'.[7]

In illustration of this technique, Joseph has described a case in which a woman came to a casework agency seeking help to buy a layette for a baby

[1] Hamilton (1952), pp. 73 and 270. [2] in Morris, C., ed. (1955), p. 49.
[3] Joseph (1951), pp. 591–3. [4] Cunliffe (1955), p. 98 (italics not original).
[5] Miles (1954), p. 82. [6] Davison (1955), p. 82. [7] Whale (1954), pp. 885–86.

due in a few weeks' time. Her husband, it appeared, was in the habit of changing his jobs frequently, and was often unemployed, so that money was short. Although financial stringency may have been the ostensible motive for Mrs A's call on the agency, her real needs are found to be quite different: she is in fact dissatisfied with her position, as the wife of a man who does not support her or care for her as a really masculine man might be expected to do. Of this 'area of her difficulties' Mrs A is said to have 'only a glimmering', being 'largely unconscious of her real needs'[1]—although anyone not imbued with the ideology of modern casework might have thought that women who are married to shiftless men are generally only too well aware of the fact. According to the caseworker's diagnosis, however, the immediate practical need for a layette was only a pretext for seeking help with other more fundamental problems. What help was or could be forthcoming in these is not divulged; but Mrs A apparently relieved her feelings by expatiating to a social worker in 'the relationship' upon the shortcomings of her husband—as she very likely also did from time to time in non-professional conversation with her friends and neighbours. Hudson, also, in an article which received special editorial commendation, has described how a Mrs X sought the help of an agency in paying off her arrears of rent—but reluctantly so, because she, too, like Mrs A, resented the fact that her husband did not contribute more to the home. Two interviews between Mrs X and the caseworker are described at length, in the course of which it becomes apparent that, although Mrs Hudson scrupulously avoided asking directly prying questions, her apparently sympathetic interest and leading remarks (such as that Mrs X must doubtless be fond of her husband in some ways since she had stayed with him so long) encouraged Mrs X also to unburden herself to the caseworker on the subject of her relations with her husband.[2] Finally, Robinson quotes the hypothetical case of a man who wants a load of coal to tide over a hard month, or seeks help in getting work during a season of unemployment, and who in consequence finds his private affairs brought under discussion. 'Rapidly he becomes involved, through the case worker's interest and concern for his whole economic situation, his health, his family relationships, in asking and taking help on his fundamental problems, and consequently in a relationship with the caseworker which was *unsought on this level* and therefore not accepted and understood in advance.' 'Records', she says, 'show a steady increase in the *intimacy* and completeness' of case histories, as is illustrated by the 'growth in detail and intimacy in the record of the individual's social history'.[3]

In some cases this emphasis upon the hidden psychological issues that are supposed to be uncovered by what has come to be known as the 'casework process' has gone so far as to lead to almost deliberate disregard of the practical problems which were the immediate occasion of the relationship being established. Thus Robinson quotes McCord on the value of the psychiatric approach for all children's caseworkers to the effect that 'it is the inside, and not the outside, story which we care most about learning'.[4] Such matters

[1] Joseph (1951), pp. 590–91. [2] Hudson (1955), p. 79.
[3] Robinson (1930), pp. 151 and 153 (italics not original). [4] ibid., p. 99.

as the 'treatment services given on the statistical cards used by social case work agencies' are said to be 'merely the bare bones of what is involved in social case treatment. The flesh and blood is in the dynamic relationship between social case worker and client, child, or foster parent; the interplay of personalities through which the individual is assisted to desire and achieve the fullest possible development of his personality'.[1] According to Faatz, the student in training has a natural tendency to pay an 'exaggerated attention to content', which, however, she admits to be 'wholly logical, for, if one is to help with a reality problem, then what is more reasonable than that the helper and the one being helped should focus wholly upon solving this problem?' Nevertheless, this 'bondage to the reality content' is characteristic only of the beginner, who must learn that there are dangers and difficulties which arise when 'the helping person reaches out and touches the concrete problem through some mistaken effort to share with the client the burden of solution of the reality problem'; and the risks, it seems, of this (to the lay mind, admirable) co-operation are particularly great in connection with 'the reality situations of finding a job, or consulting a physician, or finding a place to live'.[2]

Happily, it can be presumed that the lamentable arrogance of the language in which contemporary social workers describe their activities is not generally matched by the work that they actually do: otherwise it is hardly credible that they would not constantly get their faces slapped. Happily, also, the literature of social work is not generally read by those who receive its administrations. Without doubt the majority of those who engage in social work are sensible, practical people, who conduct their business on a reasonably matter-of-fact basis. The pity is that they have to write such nonsense about it: and to present themselves to the world as so deeply tainted with what Virginia Woolf has called 'the peculiar repulsiveness of those who dabble their fingers self approvingly in the stuff of others' souls'. Indeed, the very fact that social workers in general *are* sensible, practical people makes it the more surprising that they should continue unblushingly to perpetrate such fantastic claims; and that they should so blandly ignore the ethical questions raised by practices which suggest that they take advantage of other people's poverty, sickness, unemployment, or homelessness in order to pry into what is not their business. One need not dispute that women who ask for assistance in equipping themselves for a confinement which is only a few weeks off, or families who cannot keep themselves in coal through the winter or who fall behind with the rent, have other problems in their lives (who indeed has not?) which may well be connected with their economic difficulties. But to recognize this is not to admit that those who are invited to deal with one matter are entitled also to explore others, or that it is proper to give professional training in the art of extracting from those who seek help on one problem details of others of a more intimate, personal nature. Nor can one view with anything but repugnance the practice of including in this training hints about little

[1] Robinson (1930), p. 112, quoting the *Report of the Milford Conference*, 1921.

[2] Faatz (1953), pp. 112–13 and 115.

tricks of artificial friendliness—as when it is suggested that where embarrassing questions have been asked 'it is most important, where this has been the case, that in the last five or ten minutes of the interview we dwell upon hopeful and cheerful things, and leave in the mind of the client an impression not only of friendly interest but of a new and energizing force, a clear mind and a willing hand at his service';[1] or when the interviewer is taught to make 'stimulus questions and interpretative comments . . . in the clients' own words'.[2] The virtue of such devices, one suspects, would quickly evaporate if the clients were made aware that these were the result of deliberate teaching.

In spite of all her exalted claims, however, it can at least be said that the modern social worker has divested herself of the censoriousness which was so characteristic of her forebears, substituting for this a lofty 'non-judgemental' tolerance. In all the literature emphasis is laid upon the importance of respecting the client's personality—although it may be questioned whether some of the practices described above are wholly consistent with this proper and necessary principle. Thus, as Cormack and McDougall put it, 'the fundamental basis of all case work is the belief that the individual matters. He matters in himself, and not merely as a unit of cannon-fodder, labour-power or population, not as a vote, not as a useful citizen, not as a potential criminal, an invalid, an anti-social nuisance; but because every man has the right and duty to work out his own salvation, and therefore, within the necessary limits of his society, must also be allowed the chance to do so'.[3] Again, J. H. Nicholson, as reported by Kitchin, declares that 'the social worker must respect, even when he does not share, the other's values, must never criticize or condemn, but always try to build up or restore the power of decision in the bewildered and undecided'.[4] According to Hamilton, 'Social workers desire neither conformity with their opinions nor uniformity in cultural and individual patterns of behavior'; and they 'are trained to avoid "disapproval" of asocial conduct and to acquire understanding, which is neither tolerance nor intolerance'.[5]

In the quasi-technical language of social work this attitude of 'neither tolerance nor intolerance' (which, it must be confessed, appears more than a little elusive to the lay mind) is often described as 'acceptance'. Such acceptance, according to Hollis, is 'quite different from approval' of a client's behaviour, and does not 'necessitate any giving up of one's own personal code of ethics'.[6] In the same vein Robinson has expressed dislike of the term 'participation' (defined by the Milford Social Work Conference as 'the method of giving to a client the fullest possible share in the process of working out an understanding of his difficulty and a desirable plan for meeting it'), since this 'implies a subtle patronage of knowing what is right for the client and permitting him to help in the worker's plan'.[7] The social worker, as

[1] Richmond (1925), p. 131. [2] Hamilton (1952), p. 61.
[3] in Morris, C., ed. (1955), pp. 31–2. [4] Kitchin (1952), p. 697.
[5] Hamilton (1952), pp. 21 and 40. [6] Hollis (1955), p. 42.
[7] Robinson (1930), p. 114.

Younghusband has put it, should be 'chary of doing things "for" people, or of persuading them to do anything at all against their will . . . Therefore she will put people in the way of getting things but leave the final decision and the final steps to their own initiative'.[1] In McDougall and Cormack's version, 'because caseworkers first meet the individual when he is not independent but in need of help, and is, in consequence, particularly liable to be unduly influenced, they have to make a point of working with him with a view to establishing his ultimate independence, rather than of trying to impose their own ideas upon him for the sake of a quick solution of his difficulty which might still leave him without initiative when on his own'.[2] The same point again, if I understand her rightly, is expressed by Faatz in her own inimitable language. 'The final phase of the process requires of the one being helped that he take back into himself the will to do, and the belief that he has the strength to do; and, even more crucially, that he accept the final and ultimate outcome, that he must do it alone'. 'The client's self is left room to move toward ever greater discovery of its own desire, direction, nature, and capacity . . .' Meanwhile, 'the helper accepts his unique role . . . in containing and holding the slower, more rhythmic movement while the client flounders around in indecision or premature decision . . . until at last the precipitation of the ending creates the inescapable moment when he must take over into himself the responsibility for affirming, through word or action or both, that this is the way it will be'.[3] Presumably this means that the caseworker gets on with her knitting until the client makes up his mind.

Inasmuch as social workers are much concerned with difficult people, or with those who fail to conform to currently acceptable standards of behaviour, the 'non-judgmental' attitude clearly raises some awkward problems. For the plain fact is that in these cases social work is only undertaken with the object of changing people's behaviour in a particular direction; and, no matter how conscientiously criticism may be withheld, norms are inevitably implicit in the caseworker's 'goals'. Social workers, as one exponent of contemporary theories puts it, 'are, in a very real sense, the agents of society who are entrusted with one aspect of the preservation and enforcement of the moral code'.[4] There is, therefore, a possible inconsistency, of which some social work theorists are uncomfortably conscious, in 'believing so firmly in the acceptance of the client and in his right to self-direction on the one hand, and our having in our own minds on the other hand treatment goals toward which we are trying to move him, although he may not himself even know what these goals are'.[5] On the theory that 'all that one can do for a client in the professional relationship is to give him emotional support in the direction in which he wishes to go', it does indeed appear to be 'a contradiction to assume that social casework could be used by a person who represented authority, such as a probation officer'.[6]

However, this potential inconsistency is resolved by the age-old device of

[1] Younghusband (1952), p. 723. [2] in Morris, C., ed. (1955), p. 32.
[3] Faatz (1953), pp. 135, 72 and 133–4. [4] Miles (1954), p. 25.
[5] Hollis (1955), p. 45. [6] Bruno (1957), pp. 288–89.

inducing the other party to want what we want him to want. Only if the social worker's treatment goals are 'clearly subordinated' to the condition that 'it is absolutely impossible to *make* a person develop understanding about himself against his will', will there be a 'favourable atmosphere for these goals also to become the client's'. At the same time, as Hollis reminds us, the 'right to self-direction is never an absolute'. The mentally or physically sick and the socially dangerous, as well as in some circumstances at least the very young, cannot be allowed to choose their own goals: the caseworker therefore 'must decide when the principle of self-determination is superseded by the necessity for protection or direction', at the same time being careful not to 'decide too readily that protective care is needed'.[1]

All this is clearly good enough sense—even if the observation just quoted does recall the division of responsibility said to have been agreed by Sidney and Beatrice Webb upon their marriage, under which Sidney was to decide the important questions, and Beatrice the unimportant ones, Beatrice having the right to say what was important and what was not. Actually, of course, casework, like any other purposive activity, must have some definite goal in view. If the object of social work is to induce some change in attitude or behaviour, the direction of this change cannot be a matter of indifference. Nor, obviously, is it possible to estimate the degree of success attained without some definition of what is the objective in view. It is not surprising that a group of investigators who attempted to design a 'movement scale' for estimating the subsequent progress of the subjects of casework services inevitably found themselves driven to define what they were no less inevitably driven to describe as 'the caseworker's goals'; and not surprising that they classified these goals as '(1) changes in adaptive efficiency, (2) changes in disabling habits and conditions, (3) changes in attitude or understanding indicated by the client's verbalizations, and (4) changes in the client's environmental situation (economic, physical, and social)'.[2]

With the general terms of this formulation few would quarrel. What has to be recognized is that its concrete application is a more tricky business. As Donnison has put it: 'It is generally agreed that disease and burst pipes are undesirable. Physicians and plumbers are therefore employed to prevent or cure ills without having to think much about the purpose or social consequences of their prescriptions. They are experts in their fields and laymen are usually in no position to question their prescriptions. The ends to be attained and the areas of competence are both fairly clear. But in social work this is not so. There is no generally understood state of "social health" toward which all people strive; our disagreements on this question form the subject matter of politics the world over.'[3] Assessments of 'changes in attitude or understanding' are, however, highly subjective matters. In the investigation mentioned above, the reading of the 'movement scale' depended upon the judgment of caseworkers (including some who had had no previous contact with the persons concerned) as to how far individual clients had in fact

[1] Hollis (1955), pp. 46 and 44. Italics original.
[2] Hunt and others (1950), p. 8. [3] Donnison (1955), p. 349.

advanced towards the fivefold goals prescribed; and the possibility of reaching any conclusions at all was contingent upon the presence of a considerable consensus of opinion among these judges. Clearly what any such consensus primarily indicates is the prevalence among caseworkers of a common conception of the objects of their endeavours. Clearly also the nature of this conception is crucial. A single example may suffice to make the point clear. Among the cases quoted to illustrate improvement is that of 'a young, pregnant wife of a college student living on his GI scholarship' who 'has been damaging her husband's health, efficiency, and hopes by nagging, complaining about the little money he can give her, and holding their present poverty to be all they can look forward to. After several months of casework, the husband reports that his wife's nagging, complaining, and hopelessness have vanished.'[1] Significantly we are not told whether or not the casework led to the husband allowing his wife more money upon which to run the home. But in this omission a whole universe of moral judgments is contained, though whether the implied norm is 'peace at any price' or 'wives, submit yourselves to your husbands' is not apparent.

In psychiatrically orientated social work, in fact, just as in psychotherapy itself, moral judgments may lie concealed in what appears to be the neutral language of science or medicine. It would seem that here is a neglected field of discussion which the more alert minds among the exponents of social work theory, and in particular those who are concerned to 'put the social back into social work',[2] would do well to explore. For it is idle to pretend that the social worker is concerned only to help people to make their own decisions, in lofty indifference to the question of what those decisions may be. Such a view is wholly unrealistic, nor (as is clear from the evidence already given) are social workers so rash as to go all the way with its implications. But if the purpose of social casework is to encourage in others attitudes and behaviour conformable to particular norms, then the obligation to examine those norms and to make them explicit becomes imperative. Of this, however, in the literature in social work there is as yet little sign.

This need to be frank about norms or goals is the more pressing inasmuch as, in the United States at least, social workers are beginning to take a more 'aggressive' (the word is theirs) view of their own place in society; and, if past experience is anything to go by, what American social workers do today European ones will do tomorrow. In a recent report, the Executive Director of the New York City Youth Board, after expressing the opinion that 'forcing services upon people would defeat our purpose of helping them to re-build the self-reliance and inner strength necessary to conduct one's own affairs in a responsible manner' immediately proceeds to press the opposite view. 'We also recognize', he continues, 'that for the residue of disturbed, deprived and defeated people, we must go further. Such human beings can be found if we would look for them—not only in New York City, but in every other city, town, village and hamlet in the country. They contribute repeatedly far more than their share to dependency, ill-health,

[1] Hunt and Kogan (1952), p. 32. [2] See below p. 287.

delinquency and crime statistics. They represent . . . the "hard core"—the real challenge—that our social, health, education and religious agencies must learn to deal with if they are to reduce the indices of crime, mental illness, alcoholism and other social pathologies. We must locate them and provide services of a kind that they need and in such a manner that they will be able to use them. In casework, this means going out to individual families, refusing to take "no" for an answer, and sticking with the situation on any constructive basis—such as help with health and environmental problems, until there was enough improvement to warrant entry into the more subtle ramifications of the family relationships.' In accordance with these ideas, the Youth Board, it appears, has established a new Service to Families and Children, 'staffed by professionally trained and experienced caseworkers and supervisors who, in addition to their training . . . . have a willingness to work in the "market-place". In this service the usual role of the social worker is reversed. He goes to the clients, instead of the client coming to him'.[1]

These are bold words. It is true that from the tenor of the Director's later remarks, it would appear that the aggressive social work of which he speaks is concerned with the protection of neglected or ill-treated children, and insofar as this is so, the invasion of adult privacy may well be justified. But for a profession defined by its spokesmen as 'the art of changing human attitudes' or of 'untangling and reconstructing the twisted personality'[2] such words are indeed heady wine.

II

From within the social work world, some criticism of contemporary trends is occasionally heard, though this does not yet amount to much more than tentative murmurs. Most noticeable is the clash of doctrine and attitude between the so-called 'functional' and the 'organismic' or 'diagnostic' schools. In theory, at least, the representatives of the functional school, who are most influentially represented at the University of Pennsylvania, though still definitely a minority group, pitch their aims less high than do their 'organismic' colleagues. While both schools agree that the social worker's function is to deal with people who 'are experiencing some breakdown in their capacity to cope unaided with their own affairs', the functionalists hold that the help given should be directly related to the area of this breakdown, and must in fact be limited by the nature of the agency for which the social worker acts. The functional caseworker 'will start with the assumption that the individual faces a social reality in *some part* of his life with which he cannot at the moment cope alone and with which, therefore, he asks help'. This conception, 'which has sometimes been characterized as resting on a "partializing" of experience', is then contrasted with the rival attitude, which stresses 'the importance of the "total personality" as involved in the client's problem and, therefore, at the focus of the caseworker's responsibility',[3] and which con-

[1] Whelan (1956), pp. 5–8. [2] quoted by Bowers in Kasius, ed. (1950), p. 101.
[3] Pray (1949), pp. 248 and 250.

ceives the 'direct result' of casework 'as the total reorganization of the self of the client', in such a way that he achieves 'a complete resolution of his neurotic conflicts, an inner reorganization into an integrated individual who copes both with the problems that he brought and with other inner stresses and outer conflicts in a mature way—in effect, "a character analysis"'. By contrast, the functionalists urge that 'we must create casework criteria, casework goals that derive directly from the service we have to offer, wherein the method of help has certainly been psychiatrically influenced, but the objective of help must be indigenous to casework purpose and method'.[1]

On the face of it this sounds like a wholesome reaction, a self-denying resolution not to be lured into the search for 'something deeper underneath'; and the functionalists do in fact claim that, thanks to their 'partialization' of aim, they are less likely than their rivals to take responsibility which rightly belongs to the client, and to make decisions for others which are better made by the people concerned. Indeed, in order to emphasize this, they prefer to describe their activities as a 'helping process' used by the client, rather than as a treatment process controlled by the social worker. Occasionally, also, representatives of the functional school have even gone so far as to suggest that the arrogant readiness of their rivals to manage other people's lives does violence to the fundamental principles of a democratic society. Thus Keith-Lucas, has charged the 'organismic' writers with limiting the client's alleged right of self-determination to cases in which, in the caseworker's opinion, the exercise of this 'right' would not be '"highly detrimental to himself and others"', the social worker in fact deciding 'whether a citizen may exercise what is in the same sentence described as a right'. Nor does he mince his words on the subject of the irritatingly superior attitude of social work theorists, other than those of his own way of thinking. 'Self-determination', he writes, 'has, in fact, had to retreat before the growing conviction of case-workers that man is irrational. One group after another is declared incapable of making its own decisions': first it is unmarried mothers, then the parents of difficult children. 'The client apparently cannot choose either for what he needs help or how he is to be helped . . . The diagnostic school accepts not only responsibility for the whole client, but whole responsibility for him.' Passages are quoted to illustrate the lack of humility of the organismic school. For all that their authors stress the need to practise this virtue, it is not 'humble to believe that one has within one's grasp a key which may finally solve all problems, including those of the ends as well as the means'. The real danger, in the view of this critic, does not lie so much in the well-intentioned infringements of personal liberty which have already occurred, or in the claims of the 'self-appointed "social physician"' to a paternalistic dictatorship based on superior, scientific knowledge. The real danger lies in the fact that in unscrupulous hands 'positivist science can be perverted to serve bad as well as worthy ends, and since the only appeal is to the science itself or to the human failings of those who administer it, there is no way to check its growth. Particularly might this be so where the "science" in question

[1] Gomberg (1950), p. 362.

is one about which there can be such wide disagreement as there is about modern psychiatry, and which postulates man to be basically irrational'.[1]

Unfortunately, the effect of this plain speaking is somewhat mitigated by the fact that the 'functionalists' do not seem to have emancipated themselves from a mystical view of the 'casework process' and of the 'relationship' any more than have the 'diagnosticians'. Indeed, the exalted language of many of their utterances surpasses that of even the most ecstatic of their rivals—as will be readily appreciated from the fact that both Robinson and Faatz, from whom numerous quotations have already been given, are leading adherents of the functional school. For the functionalists, no less than the diagnostic school, are steeped in the mysteries of Freudianism. As Miles—one of the few writers whose own criticism goes further—has said, 'Both brands of caseworkers believe that the early years of life hold the key to the individual's personality, both believe in the value of lengthy verbal catharsis as the way out for the client, both forms of therapy are client-centered and relationship-dominated, and neither avoids pan-sexualism'.[2]

Meanwhile the contemporary emphasis upon the 'casework process' or upon 'relationship' is open to the further charge that it deflects attention away from the problems created by evil environments. Always plumbing the depths of her client's personality, the social worker all too easily ignores glaring evils on the surrounding surface; and she may even see in these merely an unsatisfied demand for the services of caseworkers—regretfully observing that 'So unwholesome is the environment in which vast numbers of persons live that the case-work method—time-consuming and expensive—is, of necessity, limited to a mere fraction of those in need of treatment'.[3] The notion that social work should be in any way self-liquidating has even been said to 'frustrate the performance of the constructive service which social work in its highest estate is capable of adding to the community's resources for rebuilding and sustaining its own strengths'; while the idea that we have only to create 'a new and different economic order, an adequate educational system, a just legal and political mechanism, and, presto!, individual human beings will inevitably and automatically find the incentives and the capacities for meeting all the problems of daily social living' has been condemned as resting 'upon a rather derogatory estimation of the dignity and worth of individualized service itself. It is the abandonment of professional self-respect, and the denial of any proper claim of professional social work to the respect of others'.[4]

Notwithstanding the curious logic of this last passage, with its implication that the validity of a proposition stands or falls by its effect upon the status of a particular profession, there have lately been welcome signs of sensitivity to the limitations imposed by the social worker's extreme concentration upon personal problems to the exclusion of everything that happens in a wider world. Writing on *The Responsibilities of a Socially Orientated Profession*, Lurie has observed that there is 'not enough understanding of the

[1] Keith-Lucas (1953), pp. 1087–1091. [2] Miles (1954), p. 114.
[3] Brown, E. L. (1942), p. 184. [4] Pray (1949), pp. 30–1.

social agency as an element in our culture and too little grasp of its potentials as a cultural influence'; and that 'social work will begin to lose much of its meaning if social workers do not remain alert to the implications of unsatisfactory mores and social institutions in their own lives and in the lives of clients they serve'.[1] As Miles has more bluntly put it: 'It seems futile to spend professional energy in attempts to adjust people who are living in slums.'[2] Illustrative also of the same trend is the current American demand for 'putting the "social" back into social work'—a slogan which might mean much or little, though I must confess that, until writers on social work substitute more concrete language for their habitually misty vocabularies, I am myself left in some doubt as to what it does mean. A recent paper by Professor Towle,[3] however, gives the impression that to 'put the "social" back into social work' implies first, a relaxation of the hitherto popular attempts to imitate psychoanalysis, and, second, realization of such facts as that families live in streets amongst neighbours, not in a vacuum, that much of most lives is spent in factories or other workplaces, and that people are affected by what happens outside their homes as well as by their domestic relationships.

Some of this criticism may presage a radical change of attitude. It is refreshing, for instance, to find Miles frankly lamenting the fact that 'so many groups in our society feel compelled to elevate their status by using a meaningless mumbo jumbo to frighten the uninitiated'.[4] As yet, however, the façade, at once defensive and pretentious, by which social work seeks to justify its professional existence, has not been seriously shaken. Already we have full-blown professional associations of family caseworkers, medical social workers, psychiatric social workers, moral welfare workers as well as a number of other categories; while the question whether the designation 'social worker' ought not itself to be a protected title has already come under discussion.

The history of this rapid growth of professionalization, and of the splintering of generalized welfare work into numerous highly specialized professions, is an interesting story in itself—and, it may be added, one that is highly characteristic of the present century; it is told in outline by Miss Chambers in Appendix II. But the aspect of this story which is significant here is the continued reiteration by nearly all types of social workers of references to the 'professional' nature of their activity, or to the quality and activities of their 'professional' selves, or to their 'professional' relationships. Indeed, the recurrence of the words 'profession' or 'professional' is so conspicuous a feature of contemporary papers on social work as to suggest that the authors do protest too much; and that this extreme self-consciousness of the social worker on the subject of his professional status indicates a condition of considerable insecurity.

Actually, the pretence that professional casework is of a piece with other more established professions can only be maintained by disregarding some very obvious differences; and it is significant that in a comprehensive study[5]

[1] Lurie, in Kasius, ed. (1954), pp. 45 and 50. [2] Miles (1954), p. 65.
[3] Towle (1955). [4] Miles (1954), p. 128. [5] Carr-Saunders and Wilson (1933).

of the professions, published in 1933, social work is not included, and that the author does not even find it necessary to explain the omission. As Abraham Flexner remarked more than forty years ago to a conference of social workers, 'All the established and recognized professions have definite and specific ends: medicine, law, architecture, engineering—one can draw a clear line of demarcation about their respective fields.' 'Would it not be at least suggestive therefore to view social work as in touch with many professions rather than as a profession in and by itself?' 'To the extent that the social worker mediates the intervention of the particular agent or agency best fitted to deal with the specific emergency which he has encountered, is the social worker himself a professional or is he the intelligence that brings this or that profession or other activity into action? The responsibility for specific action thus rests upon the power he has invoked. The very variety of the situations he encounters compels him to be not a professional agent so much as the mediator invoking this or that professional agency.'[1]

In an ordinary case of professional consultation, interviews with clients are arranged in order that advice may be offered, or action suggested, which can be put into effect outside the interview itself. The doctor prescribes an appropriate course of conduct or of treatment to be followed, the lawyer gets instructions for representing his client in court, the architect discusses plans for a house to be subsequently built. Occasionally, it is true, professional services may be rendered within the interview itself, as when a dentist fills teeth or a doctor lances an abscess in his surgery; but in these cases what the professional expert contributes is a highly specialized service over and above the actual business of interviewing the client. Except in psychotherapy, the interview itself has no special significance. Doubtless all professional practitioners would do well to pay attention to their interviewing habits in such matters as good manners, attentiveness to the client's requirements or economical use of time; and doubtless, also, doctors and lawyers at times use their interviews to give reassurance, or to inform the client of aspects of his situation which are apparent only to the technically qualified. But a dentist does not 'use relationship' in order to cure his client's toothache; and an architect who treated this as a method of designing houses, or an accountant who expected it to solve his client's tax problems, would soon find himself out of business. In the professions generally, 'to maintain a professional relationship' means to give good service (of the kind requested by the client) for a prescribed fee, while treating the client's business as confidential. Hence if casework is to establish a title to professional status in its own right, and not merely as an inferior kind of psychotherapy, its justification must be that the social worker, like the doctor, the lawyer, the accountant or the architect, has some specialized skill and knowledge to put at his client's disposal. As is suggested below,[2] there is indeed no reason why such a claim should not succeed; but before that success can be realized, there must be a great change of emphasis.

This confusion as to the professional status of social work may be illus-

[1] Flexner (1915), pp. 585–86. [2] See pp. 295 ff.

trated further by the contemporary use, among social workers, of the word 'client'. According to Mary Richmond, who, if she did not actually introduce the term, certainly has much responsibility for its general adoption, the expression 'client' can do duty for a variety of alternative names previously used to describe those with whom social caseworkers have to deal—such as 'applicants, inmates, cases, children, families, probationers, patients'. For 'client', she significantly adds, is a word which has itself enjoyed 'advancement from low estate to higher. First it meant "a suitor, a dependant". Later it meant "one who listens to advice", and later still "one who employs professional service of any kind".'[1]

In this, which has become its modern, meaning, 'client' is certainly an odd word to apply to the subjects of social work. Indeed its use in this sense smacks of a deliberate attempt to pretend that things are other than they are, and looks like an illustration of the recurrent human tendency to employ words as instruments of self-deception. One need not dispute that social caseworkers would like, or at the very least that they think that they would like, their 'clients' to be clients in the ordinary sense, and their own position to correspond with that of professionally qualified persons in other spheres. The wish that this were so is no doubt the principal reason for the pretence that it is. But probationers would certainly be surprised to hear themselves described as the clients of their probation officers, and would be unlikely to see themselves as employing the professional services of these officers, in the way that they might hope to employ an accountant or a lawyer; as would also the subjects of the 'aggressive' social work described on p. 283. Nor do applicants for financial aid of any kind dare to behave as though those who dispense this were their professional servants. As for the literature of contemporary casework, that can hardly be said to support the proposition that the relation between the professional social worker to his 'client' is analogous to that obtaining in other professional contacts. Far from suggesting that the caseworker's function is to carry out his client's wishes or to act under his client's instructions, this literature, on the contrary, invariably portrays the caseworker as holding a dominant, if not indeed a positively paternalistic, position in the relation between client and worker. Most of the extracts already quoted would be strange to the point of grotesqueness if offered as descriptions of any normal professional relationship. For the mutual relations of a client with his accountant, architect, lawyer, or his doctor or dentist, have been evolved on the good old principle that he who pays the piper calls the tune. Naturally, the social worker's 'client', never having been in a position to pay any piper, must expect to have to make the best of whatever tune the caseworker chooses to play.

As with 'client', so with 'casework' also. Outside the esoteric world of social work this word also is not understood; nor can one easily imagine any social worker's 'client' saying: 'I must get hold of the services of a caseworker' as he might say: 'I must find a doctor or a solicitor'. In the mind of the uninitiated, the professional label 'caseworker' immediately provokes the

[1] Richmond (1925), p. 38.

question—case of what? Other professions specify the nature of their cases: in medicine, general practitioners deal with cases of illness, specialists with cases of particular diseases: judges and magistrates deal with cases of fraud, burglary, homosexuality or dangerous driving; but the caseworker deals with—cases of what?

It is indeed remarkable how this question is evaded in the literature. To the old-time caseworker the implied answer would certainly have been either 'cases of financial distress' or 'cases of social nuisance associated with lower class status'; and she would not have been ashamed to say so. But the modern caseworker would be deeply ashamed to say anything of the kind. The only answer that she could give would be couched in terms of one of the ultra-comprehensive definitions, of which examples have been quoted on pp. 271, 272. She might, for instance, suggest that 'cases' meant to her 'cases' of sufferers from 'a variety of damaging experiences',[1] or of 'twisted personality' or of inadequate 'ego-development', or of 'difficulty in social relationships', or of 'social or emotional difficulties', or simply of 'trouble' or of 'incapacity to deal with one's problems'[2]—in fact, cases of anything uncomfortable or disagreeable (to oneself or other people) which does not at present rank as an illness suitable for treatment by the medical profession. The 'client', it would seem, could almost be described in the slang use of the word simply as 'a case'. Indeed one writer has gone so far as to assert that it is just this all-round competence which distinguishes the social worker's from any other profession. 'The essential difference', according to Lurie, 'between the newer developing profession of social work and the older professions is that in social work the focus of concern has been the individual as a whole or at least the individual in his social setting, whereas in the other professions the focus has been on concrete aspects of individual health, education, or legal relationships.'[3] One can only comment that, if indeed this claim to universal understanding is justified, it is much to be regretted that social workers do not exercise their functions more widely; since they are masters, apparently, of everything that escaped from Pandora's box. But of course the claim is nonsense.

Meanwhile, fresh point has been given to the conception of the caseworker's 'case' by the recent move towards the establishment of training courses in 'generic' casework. Such courses are already in operation in several British universities. Insofar as they represent a reaction against extreme professionalization, this is a welcome development; for it does indeed seem absurd to provide entirely separate courses of training for those who wish to be child welfare workers, or hospital almoners or probation officers, or to restrict subsequent transfer between these callings on the ground that those who are qualified for one of them are not qualified for any of the others. Each of these professions, it is true, calls for its own body of specialist knowledge: the child welfare worker needs a knowledge of child health, child development and psychology, as well as of relevant legal and administrative procedures: the almoner must have some medical knowledge,

[1] Younghusband (1952), p. 722. [2] Bowers in Kasius, ed. (1950).
[3] Lurie, in Kasius, ed. (1954), p. 36.

and the probation officer some knowledge of the law. A 'generic' course might well have the merit of including opportunity to acquire competence in more than one of these fields. But, with the present trend towards emphasis on 'relationship' or the 'something deeper underneath', the danger is that 'generic' training courses will be designed, not to give a wider range of appropriate specialist knowledge, but to magnify out of all proportion the elements that are supposed to be common to all casework. To those, however, who see 'relationship' or the 'helping process' as ancillary to the practical advice or help that the professional social worker (like the professional lawyer, architect or accountant) can give, these common elements do not amount to much. Good manners, ability and willingness to listen, and efficient methods of record-keeping are the principal elements required. But to the sponsors of generic courses for whom casework is one and indivisible, these are trivialities in comparison with the all pervading mystique of 'the relationship', descriptions of which adorn the social work manuals; and it is the mastery of this mystique, rather than the acquisition of any specialized practical knowledge, that is said to matter. As Donnison has said, summarizing the American attitude, 'To establish a "good relationship" with the client (and supervisor) marks a person as a good social worker. *Providing practical help and advice does not.*'[1]

III

All this amounts to saying that (both in the USA and in Europe) conceptions of what is meant by social work seem to have taken a remarkable—and, in the view of the present writer, a most unfortunate—turn during the past thirty years or so. The root of the trouble seems once again to be traceable to the habit of confusing economic difficulties with personal failure or misconduct. The contemporary caseworker is directly descended from predecessors whose concern was only with the poor; and who cheerfully assumed, without further investigation, that pauperism, crime and other forms of unacceptable behaviour normally all went together. In relieving the necessities of the poor, these predecessors adopted an attitude often of benevolence and sympathy, but equally of unashamed superiority: those who credited the poor with more than their share of idleness, vice and criminality, credited themselves, if less explicitly, with more than their share of wisdom and sense of responsibility.

Ostensibly, the modern social worker wishes to have done with all this; but, like others, she does not find it so easy to shake herself free of the past. Much of the recent literature of casework seems to be inspired by the wish to disown former attitudes, while at the same time retaining them; and much of what strikes one as forced or false in the current ideology is due to old patterns being so clearly discernible underneath the new. The terminology is ultra-modern, but the concept suspiciously reminiscent of older models. As Miles has remarked, the clients who, in the psychotherapeutic epoch, are described as 'unable to benefit from therapy' were known to the sociological

[1] Donnison (1955), p. 346. Italics not original.

era as 'unco-operative',[1] a term which, it may be added, takes us half-way to the still earlier label 'undeserving'; while the modern call for 'aggressive' or 'intrusive' social work has its exact parallel over a hundred years ago in Dr Chalmers' belief in the 'necessity of aggressive movements upon the lowest classes of the population in order to accomplish their moral reformation'.[2] Medical science thus walks in at the door as moral judgment flies out of the window. Even the contemporary emphasis on the function of social casework as helping people to help themselves is not so new as it looks: it has its analogue in the principles devised to suit what on the face of them look like very different sets of values. Under the old order, financial help was only to be given to those whose efforts to provide for themselves satisfied the extremely severe standards of the time; and 'charity organization' meant that charitable aid should be available only for those likely to be most reluctant to accept it. Self-help was the pre-condition of help by others: without it demoralization must inevitably ensue. To-day help by others must be used only as a means to self-help: otherwise the result is undesirable 'dependency'. The interpretations may be poles apart, but the underlying principle in the one case is strikingly reminiscent of the other; and one may well endorse, if not precisely in the sense that the author herself intended, Annette Garrett's observation that 'the attempt to modify the client's attitudes and behaviour —that is, his personality—is not a recent or revolutionary development but is an evolutionary development of aims that were envisaged from the beginning'.[3]

Perhaps the main difference between the social work of to-day and that of yesterday lies less in the nature of its presumptions, than in the degree of their explicitness. Social workers of the unashamedly charitable period had clear enough ideas of the qualities which distinguished the deserving from the undeserving poor: they were out to encourage the self-reliant, industrious, thrifty working-man at the expense of his opposite, and they were not afraid to say so. By contrast, the modern caseworker, under obligation to maintain an attitude of 'neither tolerance not intolerance', and conceiving her function as concerned with 'psychological maladjustment rather than material need', necessarily finds it harder to say clearly what she is driving at. The one explicit and consistent factor in her handling of every kind of social problem is her unwavering dependence upon psychiatric interpretation. Moral and economic problems alike are reduced to common psychiatric denominators and expressed in identical terms. The probation officer and the psychiatric social worker at the child guidance clinic alike 'diagnose' their cases and conduct 'therapeutic' interviews with them; and the family caseworker goes one step further still, by using the same terms to describe his dealings with those who come to his notice for no better reason than that they cannot make ends meet. Before we know where we are, in fact, poverty no less than crime will rank as a form of mental disorder.

This psychiatric approach to social work, in short, makes it possible

[1] Miles (1954), p. 105. [2] Young and Ashton (1956), p. 88.
[3] quoted by Rapoport (1954), p. 910.

simultaneously to disown and to retain the attitude of superior wisdom and insight traditionally adopted by the rich towards the poor: to retain, to quote Virginia Woolf again, the 'easy mastery of the will over the poor', and to preserve class attitudes, while denouncing class consciousness. In an article from which I have already quoted, Howarth gets dangerously near to saying this in so many words. The movement 'away from the idea of social work as a function of the privileged to the under-privileged' has, she believes, been a source of 'anxieties and of apparent loss of confidence. It is, too, a reason for a turning towards psychiatry and psychology for added understanding, for as soon as the individual is identified apart from his social category, it is necessary to come to terms with much in his behaviour which is difficult to understand'. While playing down material dissatisfactions as 'pegs upon which a client hangs his dissatisfactions with himself and with his social relationships',[1] the modern caseworker no longer needs to fear the loss of the position of privilege on which her prestige has been founded. Psychology and psychiatry provide a new kind of authority, and one which, if necessary, can be independent of a client's 'social category'. So we pass out of the frying-pan of charitable condescension into the no less condescending fire—or rather the cool detachment—of superior psychological insight.

Apart from its lamentable arrogance, the danger of this 'social-scientific naïveté' is that, once again, it has 'offered a convenient excuse for some social workers to neglect social action. In the days of the classical economists the individual was poverty stricken through personal fault. In the heyday of Freudianism he got that way because of his early childhood. At neither time did social workers have to become agitated about simple environmental factors such as low wages, inadequate housing, and lack of protective labor legislation'. Even though 'there have always been heroic characters associated with social work', it remains true that 'the old-time charity organization societies and the modern voluntary casework agencies have never been havens for them'.[2]

Actually, the extent to which the modern social worker serves any but the poorer classes cannot be precisely ascertained. Some American writers have been at pains to make the point that the 'clients' of the modern caseworker are by no means only to be found amongst the 'underprivileged'. One of the American follow-up studies which seek to measure the effectiveness of casework quotes figures purporting to undermine the 'widely prevalent' belief 'that those who request help from social agencies are somewhat below the average population in class or status';[3] but the evidence for this observation is based on a sample of only thirty-eight families, of whom twelve were said to belong to the lower and twenty-six to the upper middle, middle or lower middle, classes, the unmistakably upper classes being, however, not represented at all; and even in this small group is seems that economic and

[1] Howarth (1951), p. 531.
[2] Miles (1954), p. 128.
[3] Kogan and others (1953).

employment problems were, apart from illness, the most frequent reasons for which help was sought. If Miles' estimate[1] that over 40 per cent of American social workers are engaged in dealing with applicants for public assistance is correct, it looks as if problems of immediate poverty still bulk large in the social worker's agenda even in the United States. In Britain, Howarth has observed that 'people still go to social caseworkers because they have material and financial need and are likely to go on doing so', adding the rather curious comment that 'this is in keeping with the social convention by which a man in our society is to a considerable extent measured by himself and others by how much he can earn'; and by the same logic she finds it 'easy to understand why an individual more easily asks for help because he is dissatisfied with some material thing which has gone wrong, than because he is unhappy or dissatisfied with his relationships with other people'. However, there are signs that things are changing . . . 'individuals are learning, if gradually, to take their difficulties of social relationships, their personal unhappiness and dissatisfaction, to social caseworkers'; and 'in the process of learning to see the individual more clearly it has been inevitable that there has been a move away from the idea of social work as a function of the privileged to the under-privileged . . .'[2] No evidence as to the actual social distribution of the clients of caseworkers is, however, available in this article, or indeed, as far as I have been able to ascertain, anywhere at all in this country.

One thing at least, however, is certain: the agencies in which students get their basic casework training operate predominantly in the poorer working-class neighbourhoods: these agencies are not ordinarily situated in Mayfair or in the prosperous suburbs of London or of any other city. Whatever may happen to social work trainees afterwards, it is in the poorer districts that they learn their business; and whatever they may subsequently do to change their habits, it is in these districts, one most suppose, that those habits are formed.

IV

If the theory and teaching of social work have taken an unfortunate turning, there is, happily, no reason why they should not turn back again. And they do not have to look far to find a helpful signpost. In refreshing contrast to the caseworker's determination to interpret material dissatisfaction as 'pegs upon which to hang dissatisfactions with oneself or one's social relationships' is the attitude of the National Assistance Board. Far from confusing economic with personal inadequacies, the Board actually goes out of its way to emphasize that 'the people receiving assistance from the Board are . . . in the main competent to manage their affairs and differ from other people only in point of income. There is, for example, no reason to suppose that the 700,000 old people who depend in whole or in part on assistance are less able to manage their affairs than many of the 6,000,000 old

[1] Miles (1954), p. 74.
[2] Howarth (1951), pp. 530–1.

people whose resources make it unnecessary for them to seek assistance. The primary business of the Board is to ensure that people applying to them have a sufficient income, and have it in the majority of cases with as little trouble and inconvenience to themselves as is possible'. What is wanted, therefore, in the Board's view, in dealing with typical cases of economic need, is not any special skill, so much as 'a helpful disposition, common sense, a comprehensive knowledge of the different agencies, official and voluntary, which can be brought to bear on a case, and good relations with their local representatives'. At the same time it is admitted that the recipients of assistance include 'a proportion of people who need a watchful eye kept over them. The fact, however, that a minority need special attention is no reason for departing from the general principle that people who do not need such attention should not have it forced on them'; and this difficult minority, it is recognized, is not found 'only, or even mainly, among the recipients of assistance'.[1]

One could not wish for a clearer statement of the difference between economic and personal difficulties and of the absence of any necessary connection between the two. It is hardly, therefore, surprising that these pronouncements of the Board have been described as a 'significant challenge to casework and its claim to a professional training'.[2] For the Board has clearly appreciated what the exponents of casework theory so assiduously ignore—the essential dichotomy in social work as it is to-day practised. On the one hand, some social workers such as probation officers, or those responsible for the supervision of prisoners on licence, are 'entrusted with the preservation and enforcement of the moral code'. On the other hand, others are concerned with a number of practical emergencies such as might befall anyone, however unexceptionable his conduct may be, as judged by the standards of his community. The distinction remains, even though on occasion the same individual may be involved in both categories, and even though the same social worker may sometimes find himself called upon to straddle this division and to discharge both functions—as when the probation officer helps his (in this context most inappropriately named) 'clients' to obtain National Assistance, or when the child care worker encourages his charges to keep in good odour with the authorities. While, however, enforcement of the moral code may lead on to practical or material assistance, passage in the opposite direction is generally improper. Rather than search for 'something deeper underneath' when her help is sought in external practical emergencies, the social worker would do better to look for something more superficial on top when she is confronted with problems of behaviour. If she uses a request for practical help as an opportunity to intrude into other aspects of her client's life, she does so, or should do so, at her peril.

Nor in thus restricting her activities, and relinquishing her claim to near-omniscience, need the social worker fear that she must surrender her title to

[1] National Assistance Board, Report for 1949, pp. 16–18.
[2] Howarth (1951), p. 528.

professional status. On the contrary an alternative and dignified conception of social work is entirely possible; and a genuine professional status as well as a genuine parallel with other professions becomes actually easier to achieve. Donnison's warning that 'it may be unwise for social workers on either side of the Atlantic to take the older professions as their model'[1] has far less force, once the social worker has climbed down from her position of lofty superiority, and is content to offer a limited practical expertise. For, unquestionably, in the complicated modern world with its ever more complicated system of social services, such expertise becomes more and more valuable. Flexner's doubt as to whether the social worker has a right to a profession of her own, or ranks merely as a middleman mobilising the services of professional colleagues, is already losing its relevance; for this middleman function is itself now so expert a service as to qualify for professional status in its own right. The range of needs for which public or voluntary services now provide, and the complexity of relevant rules and regulations have become so great, that the social worker who has mastered these intricacies and is prepared to place this knowledge at the disposal of the public, and when necessary to initiate appropriate action, has no need to pose as a miniature psychoanalyst or psychiatrist: her professional standing is secured by the value of her own contribution. To-day few ordinary citizens have the time to learn all that needs to be learned about the Health Service, the Education Acts, the allocation of houseroom by local authorities or the facilities offered by local Children's Committees. The service rendered by those who are masters of all this and much more beside, and who can mobilize these facilities intelligently and efficiently to suit the requirements of particular individuals, is both skilled and honourable.

Such service, it is true, will be called for, in the main, by the less 'privileged' section of the community—if only for the reason that those who are more fortunately placed are able to provide from their own resources for many of the contingencies with which social work is equipped to deal. Members of well-to-do households employ high-powered secretaries or domestic workers to make the arrangements that have to be made when they fall ill, suffer domestic bereavement, require surgical belts, add to their families, change their jobs or move house; and, should occasion arise, they may even cope with crippled or defective children, ne'er-do-well sons, or with daughters who become illegitimately pregnant, without recourse to any social worker. The poor, who cannot afford to buy such services for themselves, must necessarily look to professional social workers to provide an acceptable substitute. And the more closely this substitute approximates to the services which the well-to-do normally provide for themselves, the easier will it be for the social worker to establish a professional relationship genuinely analogous to that which obtains in other professional consultations, where a client employs an expert, not to run his life for him, but to do a job which he wants done. The social worker who does for the run of ordinary people

[1] Donnison (1955), p. 350.

what confidential secretaries and assistants do for the favoured few is putting a genuine professional skill at the disposal of those who may properly be called her clients; and she is as essential to the functioning of a 'welfare state' as is lubrication to the running of an engine. Without her the machinery would seize up.

[illegible] the well-to-do [illegible], and those of the poor [illegible] is fundamentally logical. A well-to-do person, who can buy anything that he desires, has no socially recognized motive for stealing, and must therefore be judged to be mentally sick if he is guilty of dishonesty. The stealing of the poor, by contrast, must be criminal just because it is rational, except in cases where the poor also engage in repetitive stealing of 'useless' objects. Even a poor person who endlessly stole, let us say, packets of hairpins would be judged to be mentally peculiar. By way of illustration Cressey himself quotes[a] Alexander and Staub's judgment that a physician was not behaving neurotically when he stole medical books and supplies, but only when he helped himself to porcelain figures which were of no value. Such distinctions, he would argue, are, in fact, merely reflections of the particular motivations acceptable in our particular culture, and most noticeably of its emphasis on the rationality of economic or acquisitive motives.[b]

Cressey concludes that 'the economic status of the observer probably is of great importance in determining whether he thinks a person is not in economic need and is consequently compulsive [illegible] poverty-stricken the proportion of shoplifters called "kleptomaniacs" probably would be much higher than it is.'[c] And by the same logic what is true of thieving is no less true of other crimes. Fire-raising as such generally ranks as 'motiveless'; but fire-raising in order to defraud an insurance company is a different matter. On this principle, incidentally, fire-raising in England on November 5th poses some nice questions. If the desire for fires for their own sake on this date is held to fall within the range of socially intelligible motives, then indulgence of this desire beyond the limits of what is socially tolerated must rank as criminal rather than as neurotic. But if Guy Fawkes bonfires are judged to be 'motiveless', then anyone responsible for a dangerous or destructive conflagration must be classified as sick rather than sinful.

Actually, if the argument is carried one step farther, the line between the 'motivated' and the 'motiveless' action itself becomes blurred; for the range of intelligible motives is itself modified by new knowledge and new attitudes. Thanks to the popularity of psychiatric notions, the urge to steal for stealing's sake begins to find its place among the recognized, if not indeed the 'normal', motives for theft; for our conception of the normal is itself defined by linguistic constructs. With the invention of the term 'kleptomania',

[a] Cressey (1954), p. 35. [b] Ibid., p. 37. [c] Ibid., p. 36.

PART III

CONCLUSIONS

CHAPTER X

Conclusions—Methodological

I

IT is clear from what has been said that few generalizations can be made with confidence about those whose behaviour is socially unacceptable, and that not many are applicable even to any one group of these. For the popular theories about the delinquency of latchkey children, about social failure repeating itself generation after generation, about the beneficial effects of boys' clubs or the disastrous consequences of illegitimacy—for these and similar generalizations we have, as yet at any rate, little solid factual evidence. Perhaps we can go so far as to say that the lack of secure affection in infancy is likely to create difficulties in after-life, and that one possible manifestation of these difficulties is a reluctance to conform to what society expects. But that those who are not loved are likely themselves to hate rather than to love is hardly a discovery for which modern science can take the credit. Man has known this truth in theory for as long as he has disregarded it in practice.

It is clear also that, as observation becomes more precise, generalizations which previously looked promising have a way of collapsing. Nowhere has this been more apparent than in the study of 'criminal personality'. In 1950, Schuessler and Cressey attempted an evaluation of all the material published in the USA in the preceding twenty-five years on the subject of personality differences between criminals and non-criminals, as defined by objective tests of personality. No less than thirty different tests, they found, had been employed, in all 113 times, without yielding any satisfactory evidence that criminals are different from other people; and they leave us with the conclusion that 'when the results are considered chronologically, there is nothing to indicate that the personality components of criminal behavior are being established by this method. On the contrary, as often as not the evidence favored the view that personality traits are distributed in the criminal population in about the same way as in the general population'.[1] Similarly, Metfessel and Lovell, after reviewing the (mainly American) literature published in the decade 1930–40 on the subject of the individual correlates of crime, find that sex and age are the only constants, and that, when everything is checked against everything else, 'no clear-cut picture of a criminal personality can be drawn'. These authors, moreover, make the important point that the theories which last longest are those which deal in relatively vague categories such as 'bad parents'. More concrete, measurable factors

[1] Schuessler and Cressey (1950), p. 483.

which can more easily be put to the test are seen to lose their significance as soon as they are subjected to really vigorous scrutiny.[1]

That in fact is just what has happened in the history of theories about the intelligence of delinquents. Forty years ago, as Woodward observes in her scholarly and comprehensive review, it was generally accepted that 'low intelligence was the most important single cause of delinquency and crime, and that "every feeble-minded person is a potential criminal"';[2] and even to-day many German criminologists seem disposed to agree with Exner's dictum that the general intelligence level of the totality of criminals is lower (though not considerably so) than that of the average of the population, and that recidivists tend to have markedly lower intelligence scores than have first offenders.[3] Yet, as the techniques for more accurate measurement of intelligence have been refined, the foundations of the once widely held belief in the existence of a negative correlation between intelligence and criminality have crumbled away—until now we have to admit that 'low intelligence cannot be regarded as an important causal factor in delinquency', and that it plays no part in delinquency, or at the most that it indirectly plays a minor aggravating role.[4] And what has happened to intelligence has happened also to one supposed peculiarity of offenders after another; even though the Gluecks[5] have recently been accumulating massive evidence in support of the thesis that delinquents differ from non-delinquents in their bodily structure.[6]

The reason for this barrenness and the conditions for the fruitfulness of future researches in this field are many and various. Of central importance is the choice of appropriate fields and the selection of appropriate material for study. In criminological researches, particularly, little attention seems to have been given to these points; and their neglect is in dramatic contrast with the ever-increasing elaboration of the technical methods employed in the investigation of whatever material happens to have been selected. Many of these researches seek to establish the presence of factors which distinguish a mixed delinquent from a non-delinquent population, usually within a given age and sex group. As time goes on and techniques improve, the search for these factors is pursued with greater and greater refinement. In their latest work the Gluecks, for instance, have constructed statistical tables, each of which compares their subjects and their controls in respect of a single trait or circumstance. Altogether over three hundred such traits, ranging from the subjects' genital pathology to the rents payable for their homes, have been investigated.

By contrast, the amount of thought that appears to have been given to the selection of the material to be subjected to such minute examination is surprisingly meagre. The Gluecks are indeed exceptional in the care with

[1] Metfessel and Lovell (1942), pp. 160 and 153. [2] Woodward (1955), p. 3.

[3] Exner (1949), pp. 163, 164. [4] Woodward (1955), p. 22.

[5] Glueck, S. and E. T. (1956).

[6] in much the same way, apparently, as Oxford undergraduates differ from army cadets at Sandhurst! See Tanner (1954), p. 154.

which they have sought to guarantee the homogeneity of the delinquent character of their subjects. In their study, delinquency is defined as 'repeated acts of a kind which when committed by persons beyond the statutory juvenile court age of sixteen are punishable as crimes (either felonies or misdemeanors)—except for a few instances of persistent stubbornness, truancy, running away, associating with immoral persons, and the like'.[1] Yet even this definition is far from precise. Such loose phrases as 'repeated' acts and 'few instances' contrast oddly with the precision of the statistical work that follows; while the nature of the persistently anti-social conduct which caused a boy to be included among the Gluecks' delinquents is itself exceedingly variable. While over 58 per cent of the subjects had been guilty of some form of stealing, and 59 per cent of burglary or breaking and entering, 16 per cent were said to be guilty of 'stubbornness', 17 per cent of 'running away' and 32 per cent of offences against the public order, these last including such a miscellaneous collection as 'malicious injury to property, destruction to property, trespassing, evading fare, stealing rides, violating licence laws, false alarms, delaying cars, throwing missiles, violating parking rules, stoning train, breaking glass, breaking windows'.[2] Again, although it is clear from the figures that nearly 90 per cent of these delinquents had been convicted more than once (and over 40 per cent more than three times), it is still not possible to discover from the published particulars what was the distribution of these varied delinquencies among the individuals concerned—in how many cases, for instance, three convictions meant, say, two offences of trespassing and one of stubbornness, as against one assault, one burglary and one robbery with violence. And even with this information it would still be true that, official titles of offences being what they are, we should have no guarantee that the subjects did not differ in the degree of their iniquity (as well as in much else) to an extent which made it grossly misleading to lump them all together in a single category of delinquents; though the Gluecks make it clear that they themselves were not worried on this score. Certainly the fact that all the subjects of this investigation had been committed to correctional schools is at least evidence that they must have been regarded as serious cases by the judges who sentenced them; but, equally, the fact that all were drawn from only two of these schools may well raise a question as to how far they constituted a representative selection.

A few other American investigators have made attempts, on much the same lines as the Gluecks, to restrict their category of 'delinquent' at least to those whose anti-sociality is both persistent and pronounced. Thus Healy confined himself to the 'repeated offender', defined as 'that individual who in spite of reprimands, warnings, probation or punishment proceeds to further anti-social deeds', though he included some who had 'managed through family protection to escape prior contact with the courts'.[3] Others, on the other hand, have cast their nets very much more widely. In the United States, Fernald aimed to produce a group which should contain 'representatives of all types and degrees of delinquency ordinarily found among women

[1] Glueck, S. and E. T. (1951), p. 13. [2] ibid., p. 295. [3] Healy (1929), p. 13.

offenders',[1] using for this purpose the inmates of five New York institutions, together with a sixth group of women who had been put on probation. In this country Sessions Hodge and his colleagues examined 100 consecutive admissions to a boys' Classifying Approved School, in order to make comparisons between the electro-encephalograms of a delinquent and a non-delinquent population; and on the strength of this they were led to speculate on the possibility of a 'physiological sociology, in which both the consistencies and the vagaries of human society may turn out to be definable, if not wholly explicable, in terms of the properties of the central nervous system'.[2] Bagot's[3] delinquents included all those who over a certain period had been found guilty of an offence, and upon whom a particular sentence, namely, a period of detention in a remand home, had been passed. The majority of Burt's subjects, on the other hand, had never been charged at all; though Burt himself was, apparently, satisfied that they had for the most part committed 'such breaches of the law as would be punishable in an adult by penal servitude or imprisonment—stealing, burglary, damage, common assault, indecent assault, and soliciting'.[4] Some, however, were guilty only of 'inordinate lying' or of 'sexual impropriety' or of truancy, or were beyond their parents' control. In the Carr-Saunders study, it appears from the instructions at the head of the questionnaire issued to investigators that the subjects had been 'found guilty of offences punishable in the case of an adult with imprisonment without the option of a fine;' yet in the text itself, it is stated that for London cases 'the procedure adopted was to record, through the medium of the Probation Office and the London County Council Education Department, information relating to the first 1,000 cases brought before the Juvenile Courts in London after October 1, 1938';[5] and that, after rejection of cases in which the 'desired information' was not obtainable, 989 cases were finally used. Actually, a random selection of cases brought before the juvenile courts would be extremely heterogeneous, and would go far beyond those guilty of offences for which an adult is liable to imprisonment. It might, for instance, even include some who were guilty of offences, such as railway frauds, which are not punishable by imprisonment; and it might even cover some cases in which the defendants were found not guilty and discharged, or in which they were not charged with criminal offences at all, but were the subjects of civil actions, as when children are brought before the courts as being beyond parental control. Presumably, in view of the instructions quoted above all these types of case were excluded; but the contradiction between the wording in the questionnaire and the description in the text is all too symptomatic of the prevalent looseness even of quite vital definitions. Finally, in the studies of Ferguson[6] and of Bagot (1941), delinquents were defined as all those juveniles who had been found guilty by a court, except that Bagot excluded those whose offences were non-indictable—a restriction, incidentally, which would result

[1] Fernald and others (1920), p. 14. [2] Hodge and others (1953), p. 167.
[3] Bagot (1944). [4] Burt (1952), p. 13.
[5] Carr-Saunders and others (1942), pp. 134 and 55.
[6] Ferguson (1952).

in the omission of a child who got drunk or who cheated the railway, and the inclusion of one who stole a twopenny packet of sweets.

When one considers the variety of the happenings, or of the circumstances, which may lead to the inclusion of an individual in any of the categories thus defined as delinquents, it does indeed seem unlikely that such a miscellaneous collection will constitute a fruitful field of study. The reasons for the paucity of relevant generalizations become in fact all too plain. The selection is far too haphazard and arbitrary: it is almost as though a zoologist were to look for common characteristics (other than the presence of a tail) in all animals that have tails. If delinquents are defined by court findings of guilt, they must first have committed one of an extremely miscellaneous collection of misdeeds; they must then have been apprehended; next they must have been actually brought before the magistrates (which does not happen to by any means all those whose offences become known to the police); and the magistrates before whom they happen to appear must have been satisfied of their guilt beyond any reasonable doubt. Apart from the serious bias introduced into this sample by the exclusion of those who do not get found out, the variety of activities covered itself ranges from the trivial to the thoroughly dangerous. Crime to-day covers everything from the 'housewife who shakes her door-mat in the street after 8 a.m., or a shopkeeper who fails to stamp a cash receipt, or a guest who fails to enter his name, nationality and date of arrival in the hotel register, or the proprie or of a milk bar who allows his customers to play a gramophone quietly, behind closed doors, but without an entertainment licence from the justices' to the 'robber who hits an old woman with a length of iron pipe'.[1] Even amongst juveniles the range is nearly as great—as witness the list, in Appendix I, of offences committed by a sample of the children and young persons who have appeared in the Metropolitan Juvenile Court in which I commonly sit as Chairman. In this list (which consists of every fifth case that I have heard in the period April 1955 to July 1957) the offences are briefly described, not only by their legal classification, but also in terms of what actually happened. The use of legal categories serves only to obscure the endless variety of delinquent behaviour: for instance, in one of the only two charges of robbery with violence which it has fallen to my lot to try in more than fifteen years' experience covering some 5,000 cases, a boy of nine knocked another child off a bicycle (no injury resulted) in order to take 10s off him, thus swelling the statistics of what is generally thought to be as grave a crime as it is happily also rare. Even the brief notes which I have added in the Appendix to the formal legal categories themselves fail to do justice to the multifarious quality of these acts of delinquency; but that would unfortunately be true of any description of reasonable compass.

Alternatively, if delinquency or criminality is identified with committal to some penal institution, the selection is hardly less arbitary. Once again, any one of a great variety of offences must have been committed: again the offender must have been apprehended, charged and found guilty; and the

[1] Glanville Williams in Keeton and Schwarzenberger eds. (1955), p. 112.

court before which he appears must have formed the opinion (on whatever grounds, and the possibilities are legion) that committal to this particular type of institution was the most suitable treatment available. Anyone who has observed the variety of sentencing practice as between one court and another will realize the bias introduced here by the attitudes of the particular judges or magistrates whose decision results in such committal.

It seems, therefore, time that we recognized that delinquency or criminality (even with its major motoring component left out) is not a rational field of discourse. It takes all sorts to make the criminal world. If research serves only to confirm the old truth that 'there but for the grace of God go I', that is just what is to be expected. Nevertheless, the contrary belief dies hard, and the sad thing is that all this has been said so often before. The inherent absurdity of treating criminals, delinquents or prisoners, even of a given sex and age group, as sufficiently homogeneous for rational study has been repeatedly demonstrated. It is now over twenty years since Robison[1] made short work of the experience of the New York courts as an index of delinquency in that city; and the warnings which she gave have been repeated many times since by other authorities. Yet money and brains are still misdirected into the search for the distinguishing peculiarities of miscellaneous offenders, and we still remain obstinately blind to the fact that the one distinctive factor in the offender's experience is the way in which he has been treated by an outraged community; and that this experience, no less than an inherent predisposition to delinquency, may well account for any peculiarities that he does manifest. If it is indeed true that the encephalograms of Approved School boys show significant differences from those of their contemporaries whose education has been more orthodox, the possibility that the encephalograms are themselves affected by experience deserves at least to be considered; for in view, as has been said, of the extremely haphazard process of selection for Approved Schools, and the degree to which this depends upon the personal attitudes of magistrates, it is almost impossible to believe that the inmates of these institutions are really distinguished by the constitutional properties of their nervous systems.

This faith in the overwhelming importance of criminality as a thing-in-itself has certainly had a stultifying effect upon the trend of research in this field. Ultimately it seems to have its roots in the implicit self-righteousness of those who range themselves, as it were, instinctively, on the side of authority. It expresses the characteristic, if unspoken, premises of what Marx would have called the ruling class, and what today has become known as the Establishment. To the Establishment-minded the mere fact of conviction for law-breaking (always with a tacit exception of the laws which they themselves are most disposed to break) is of such magnitude as to dwarf into insignificance any consideration of what is broken or when or how—the common factor of 'delinquency' or 'criminality' being supposed to swamp all individual differences. Such an attitude has, moreover, been further encouraged by the fact (for which it is itself largely responsible) that criminology

[1] Robison (1936).

has become one of the recognized academic disciplines. In this, as in other spheres, the influence of academic frontiers upon the shape of the body of our knowledge is a fascinating study; for undoubtedly these frontiers, when unfortunately drawn, can be as cramping to the growth of understanding as their political counterparts have sometimes been to the growth of international harmony.

Happily, however, there are signs that times are changing. The Gluecks' attempt to circumscribe the concept of delinquency, inadequate though it may be, is at least an indication of the growth of more critical, and therefore more hopeful, definitions of the field to be investigated. More encouraging still is the now considerable development of studies that deal only with one particular category of offences. To name only one or two recent British examples, we now have Dr Radzinowicz's study[1] of sexual offenders, and Dr Gibbens' investigations into car thieves[2] and into parents convicted of cruelty to their children.[3] Even these, however, are still quite crude categories. Selection by the fact of conviction, even for a specific type of offence, still brings together a miscellaneous collection of people linked by a miscellaneous series of events. Persons convicted of sexual offences, for instance, include both homosexual and heterosexual offenders. Still finer discriminations will be needed in such matters as the nature and the frequency of offences and their concomitant circumstances, before we have really homogeneous material for investigation. At the least, however, concentration upon a specific offence is a great advance upon the study of an undifferentiated mass of 'delinquents'.

Encouraging also is the tendency to focus attention upon persistent offenders as distinct from the whole body of convicted persons. On the face of it, one might well guess that it would be in the persistent offender that significant peculiarities would most likely be found; though, even so, one must not forget the possibility that his peculiarities may be due at least as much to what has been done to him as to what he has himself done. Occasional convictions may well be explained by a host of more or less accidental circumstances; but the chances against those accidents recurring repeatedly in the life of the same individual (especially when he is by definition forewarned) must surely be more formidable. It is, therefore, somewhat surprising to find that in several cases the few hypotheses which emerge in tolerably respectable shape from the study of heterogeneous groups of offenders actually threaten to collapse when tested against the records of the recidivists. Notably is this true of that old favourite the broken home. Thus Healy and Bronner found to their surprise hardly any difference in the incidence of broken homes as between those who did and those who did not persist in delinquency.[4] As we have seen, the Gluecks, also, in their study of *Juvenile Delinquents Grown Up* have recorded that the same proportion of those of their subjects who subsequently reformed and of those who 'continued to recidivate' had 'enjoyed the affectionate regard of their mothers',

[1] Cambridge Department of Criminal Science (1957). [2] Gibbens (1958).
[3] Gibbens and Walker (1956). [4] Healy and Bronner (1926), p. 123.

and that the 'two groups further resemble each other in being to an equal extent the products of homes which had been broken';[1] while the Mannheim and Wilkins enquiry found that 'although more boys entered Borstal from "broken homes" than would be expected if the Borstal entry was drawn equally from complete and "broken homes", those from "broken homes" after Borstal training did not appear to be worse risks than those from complete homes'. Indeed, 'no factors in home background afforded a useful prognosis before Borstal, so long as there was a home background of some kind'.[2] These findings are the more thought-provoking inasmuch as, to many of those who have practical experience of delinquents, the stereotype of the product of the broken home tends to be the recidivist with the unhappy childhood story who is always in and out of trouble.

In the matter of religious affiliation, likewise, the recidivist fraction does not always correspond to the total criminal population from which it is drawn. In the Mannheim and Wilkins enquiry the proportion of Roman Catholics was more than double the estimated figure for the community in general, while the proportion of Nonconformists was only about half that to be expected. Yet no significant difference appeared in the proportion of Catholics and of Nonconformists respectively who kept out of trouble after their discharge.[3]

The factors that contribute to initial criminality may thus be different from those which encourage its continuance; just as the factors which lead one man to steal a car may be different from those which induce another to behave indecently in a public lavatory. From these and similar pointers one can only infer that the complexity of the influences which contribute to law-breaking is easily underestimated, that simple hypotheses are unlikely to be fruitful, and that it is important in future to take, not only more trouble, but much more trouble, to ensure that material selected for study is genuinely homogeneous. At the least it is to be hoped that we are coming to the end of studies of large miscellaneous classes of offenders selected only by the fact of their appearance in court.

II

In other respects, also, besides the heterogeneity of the material selected for study, the poor quality of our data is an obstacle to progress. Some of the difficulties here are inherent in the nature of the material with which the social scientist is concerned, and may have to be accepted as among the facts of life; but even in such cases risks are likely to be less if they are recognized. For example, if only for reasons of economy, we are constantly obliged to use the material that happens to be available as distinct from that which would ideally have been both relevant and adequate. A common practice is to select a group of subjects, list the information which it is desired to obtain about them, and then discard those for whom the requisite particulars cannot

[1] Glueck, S. and E. T. (1940), p. 108. [2] Mannheim and Wilkins (1955), p. 87.
[3] ibid., p. 89.

be obtained. Burt, for instance, states that his delinquents were 'all . . . for which I could get complete information for the particular conditions reviewed'.[1] In the studies reviewed in Chapter III of this book, generalizations are repeatedly made on a limited selection only of the cases under investigation. In their latest enquiry, the Gluecks, it seems, originally intended to draw only upon one industrial school for their subjects; but they were subsequently obliged to include additional children from a second school, when it became evident that from the first alone they 'would not be able to obtain a working quota of 100 boys a year who met all the requirements of the project'.[2] Rose's subjects were made up of two groups, of which one was composed of ex-servicemen and one of civilians. Of these the second was a random selection but the first was chosen 'upon the basis of their being the ones upon which there was the fullest information from the Army record'.[3]

This limitation to cases in which full information is available may result in quite a high proportion of rejections; and there is a risk that this may bias the final selection. Thus Mannheim and Wilkins found that the files of those of their cases who had been in several prisons since release from Borstal were more difficult to trace than were those of the men who had not had a subsequent prison record. In fact, 'there was a direct correlation between the time it took the Home Office staffs to trace the Borstal files and the proportion of successes [i.e. cases not reconvicted] in any batch. In total the success rate was 45 per cent, but in the first 300 files received the success rate was nearly 70 per cent. In the end we were fifty-six files short of the complete sample, and a search by the Criminal Record Office revealed that forty-six of these fifty-six cases were failures—a rate of 82 per cent'.[4] In view of this experience, the widespread practice of using samples from which cases with incomplete particulars have been discarded is decidedly disquieting; and the disquiet is likely to be aggravated when it is not even clear how the final selection has been made.

As records improve, the problems posed by sheer insufficiency of factual information may reasonably be expected to diminish. More intractable are the difficulties inherent in the nature of the data upon which research into social pathology, as indeed practically any form of investigation into human behaviour, must rely. By a convenient, if not logically watertight, classification, these data may be graded as either 'hard' or 'soft'. Hard events are those which are directly discernible by our physical senses, soft ones those which are not: a broken home in the sense of a home from which one parent is physically absent falls into the one category, while an experience of maternal deprivation, in which the affection, but not the physical presence, of a mother is lacking, into the other. Insofar as it may be argued that events which are not perceptible to the senses are only inferences from those which are, the philosophical ice is rather thin here; and we may easily find ourselves plunged into discussions about the nature of mind, and about the propriety, or impropriety, of dualistic language. Nevertheless, whatever view we may ultimately

[1] Burt (1952), p. 12. [2] Glueck, S. and E. T. (1951), p. 21.
[3] Rose, A. G. (1954), p. 14. [4] Mannheim and Wilkins (1955), pp. 55–56.

reach as to the nature of mind-body relationship, at the contemporary stage of social research the distinction between hard and soft material has great *practical* significance. Observations that relate, on the one hand, to concrete events, such as the number of rooms in a house or the number of children born to two parents, are of a quite different order from those that are concerned, on the other hand, with such abstractions as parental discipline or social status. The difference is a matter of exactness—even though in the case of apparently simple physical phenomena, definition and measurement are not always as simple as they seem: if one is counting rooms, there can always be an argument about the coal cellar. In such cases, however, the margin of uncertainty is small, and it is at least possible to say with precision what has actually been done.

In the case of soft data, on the other hand, the subjective element in observations is clearly very large. It may indeed be true that, from one angle, such data must be regarded as the expression, in an essential shorthand, of a multiplicity of hard facts too varied and too numerous ever to be recorded individually. An 'unloved child' is a shorthand term for the child which is seldom kissed or talked to, or allowed to do what it likes or called pet names, and which lacks a hundred and one other similar experiences: the condition of unlovedness manifests itself, in fact, in a vast range of external events conveniently summarized by this abstraction. Yet, even if soft data are themselves only inferences from, or summaries of, external events, it is rare indeed for those events to be explicitly recorded: indeed, as often as not, we are likely to be quite incapable of recording them. Parental discipline is seldom precisely defined in terms of the number of times per week that a child is struck with a given degree of force, or of the number of occasions upon which his expressed wishes are gratified: such concrete details, even if their value were appreciated, would seldom be obtainable. Discipline, like deprivation, domestic friction and many other concepts in which the study of social pathology deals, is subjectively assessed—largely, no doubt, on observations of behaviour that is itself perceptible to the senses, but on observations which nevertheless are not systematically recorded, nor even perhaps consciously recognized, by the observer. One has only to look, for example, at the instructions given to interviewers in the Carr-Saunders enquiry, in order to appreciate the profoundly subjective character of the resulting data. In addition to other particulars, these investigators were required to record the subject's 'ambition or desire for change' as exemplified by anything 'strongly desired' such as change of job, locality or school; to classify a child's attitude towards his parents into the three categories, 'obedient', 'troublesome', 'resentful'; and to quote any evidence of 'unusual keenness' in relation to hobbies or modes of occupying leisure time.[1] Clearly, important quantitative judgments are implied here, with no guarantee that these will be governed by any consistent scale. For, to judge from examples quoted in another context by Grygier, even parents themselves may be unable to make consistent assessments of their own children in such matters—as witness the mother who is reported as

[1] Carr-Saunders and others (1942), p. 137.

saying in one week that her son 'has ambitions and is able to follow them', and in the next that he 'has no ambitions or aspirations at all'. Indeed, in matters of behaviour the risks of error in observations even of physically discernible events are alarmingly great: a boy who tells the psychiatrist that he likes swimming and often goes to the baths turns out unable to swim at all and not to have tried for a year; and the father who says he knows of no clubs in the neighbourhood proves to have already made arrangements for his son to join one.[1]

The difficulties are, moreover, aggravated by the fact that, the complexities of human behaviour being what they are, all too often it is the soft data which are valuable, and the hard which are relatively easy to get. Moreover, so long as we continue to use dualistic language, we have to recognize that even the external factors which are found to be significant in human behaviour operate only through their effect on the mental processes of the individuals concerned. If, for example, overcrowding is significantly associated with gang violence, the link lies in the ideas and emotions, stimulated by overcrowding, which occupy the minds of violent offenders.

In principle there are two well-recognized ways of grappling with the elusive quality of soft data. The first is to discover hard facts which can be relied upon to serve as good indices of soft ones. A not very satisfactory example, from the field of social pathology, is the use of the external fact of physical separation from the mother as an index of loss of mother-love, as in some of the studies of maternal separation that are intended to test hypotheses relating to maternal deprivation in an emotional sense. In a quite different sphere, records of the journals that people read have been taken as an indication of their political attitude or even of their intelligence. Nevertheless, correlates that are reliable for such purposes are by no means easy to find; and it is therefore often necessary to have recourse to the alternative method of setting one investigator to check the findings of another, and to accept only those in which the independent recordings of two or more observers are tolerably congruent.

Unfortunately the use of these safeguards is not yet by any means standard practice in social investigation. Highly subjective assessments are still too often treated with quite unwarrantable reverence. The intelligence of 'problem parents', for example, is too often assessed on the basis of the personal judgments of social workers; and in the Ferguson enquiry scholastic attainment seems to have been estimated by the judgment of head teachers alone[2]—a procedure which may well be regarded with misgiving by those who have experience of the reports furnished by teachers to juvenile courts; and of the intense hostility to delinquent children which these not infrequently reflect.[3] The Carr-Saunders study also, as we have seen, included equally vague assess-

[1] Grygier (1955), pp. 219 and 221. [2] Ferguson and Cunnison (1951), p. 69.

[3] This observation is based upon my personal experience of something approaching 5,000 juvenile court cases. But cf: also Morris' statement in his Croydon enquiry that 'some teachers, in writing their reports showed an open hostility to the offender which led one to suppose them to be unduly prejudiced' (Morris, T. P., 1958, p. 142).

ments of intimate domestic relations. The Gluecks certainly gave very careful and detailed instruction to the 'home investigators' who were required to collect 'data about the socio-economic status of the family and the atmosphere in which the boy had been reared, as well as a personal view of the physical home; to secure some details concerning the boy's developmental health history; to ascertain the parents' knowledge of the boy's habits and use of leisure time; to gather additional vital statistics concerning the family; and to derive any information as to alcoholism, physical diseases, emotional instability, and the economic and educational status of members of the immediate family and of grandparents and aunts and uncles'. Nevertheless, they report that 'generally one interview was sufficient to secure the data needed in a particular case', though at times 'additional interviews were necessary, especially if the boy's parents were separated or divorced'. Each interviewer was moreover 'urged to use the method that was the most natural to him', while 'note-taking was kept to a minimum'.[1] In spite of the assurance that the interviewers were 'highly skilled', and in spite of checking from such officials and official records as were available, this seems a surprisingly credulous attitude to critical evidence, the more so as *all the families could not be visited by the same investigator*. One cannot but be struck by the contrast between this casual treatment of 'soft data', and the scrupulous pains generally taken to ensure accuracy in the recording of such hard facts as anthropomorphic measurements or in the scoring of standardized psychological tests. It is true that in addition to the social histories derived from visits to the boys' families, a psychiatrist's report on each boy was also obtained; but any discrepancies that this incidental cross-check revealed might well have served only to increase disquiet as to the reliability of the large volume of material which rested upon the judgment of one psychiatrist or one interviewer alone.[2]

Many indeed of the measures currently used are of dubious reliability. In the course of these pages there have been many references to the inexplicable variations, as between one area and another, or even one institution and another, of the figures relating to such phenomena as mental deficiency, psychiatric disturbance or criminality. Inevitably such variations raise doubts as to whether these phenomena are being or can be accurately measured. It is true, of course, that beggars cannot be choosers, and that we must, as has been said, often make do with what we can get. But what we can avoid is the practice of giving more weight to material than it deserves, or of putting it to uses for which it is unsuitable. One of the many weaknesses of contemporary social research is that, in our enthusiasm for technical improvements, we have allowed ourselves to disregard the obvious commonplace that the best techniques are still at the mercy of the raw material to which they are applied. In the past twenty or thirty years great advances have been made in the statistical treatment of social data. Quantification is now the rule in

[1] Glueck, S. and E. T. (1951), pp. 45–46 and 48.

[2] See, for instance, the conflicting reports on 'family cohesiveness' quoted by the Gluecks themselves on p. 72.

nearly all social investigations, and it has become almost routine practice to test the significance of observed phenomena by calculations of the probability that they could be the result of chance. With cheerful impartiality modern statistical techniques are now applied alike to hard and to soft data, and the results are assembled in tables, all of which present an equally imposing appearance. Yet inaccurate observations remain inaccurate, no matter how sophisticated the statistical processing to which they are subjected: the only effect of such processing is to create a regrettably spurious appearance of accuracy. In those cases, therefore, in which we are not yet able to devise methods of guaranteeing the soundness of our raw data, we should be well advised to resist the temptation to elaborate manipulation; and to content ourselves with such humble methods as purely descriptive treatment. In this way we could at least underline the distinction between what is reliable and what is not; while the status of more elaborate statistical work would itself be greatly improved, if it were only employed in cases where there was no cause to be uneasy about its foundations.

Certainly the most pressing task in the immediate future is not so much to elaborate statistical techniques still further, as to improve the quality of our raw material, and to establish more rigorous standards as to what is, and what is not, admissible. At the very least we ought to be reaching the stage at which it is unthinkable to build generalizations upon the uncorroborated judgments of one person, unless that person is equipped with measuring instruments the reliability of which has been adequately demonstrated. If, as may well often be the case, expense precludes adequate cross-checking of subjective assessments, then the only defensible course is to regard these assessments as too insecurely founded to sustain generalizations or to be susceptible to statistical manipulation. Tables such as those in the Eugenics Society's five enquiries into problem families[1] which purport to show, on the strength of an individual's judgment, and without the application of any formal test, how many of the members of these families are of subnormal intelligence, can only serve to mislead.

Meanwhile, the inadequacy of the social scientist's data is too often matched by the clumsiness of his tools; though it is to be hoped that reference to this deficiency will not be construed as an illustration of the proverb about bad workmen. More than once in these pages has it been necessary to comment upon the lack of accepted definitions and common measures. The broken home, for example, normally means homes broken by death, desertion, separation or divorce, and often also by long absence on account of illness: but the author of one study includes cases where the father is (by his standards) 'unemployable'. Again, 'truancy' from school is sometimes defined as 'persistent', usually without any quantitative measurement of what is meant by 'persistence', whilst in other cases truancy is just truancy, again without any measure of the frequency of the absence necessary for a child to qualify as a truant. And, to make confusion worse confounded, in cases where alternatives are available, information is by no means always given as to

[1] Blacker, ed. (1952), pp. 59, 65 and 76–77.

which definition has in fact been used. In the case of the family, for example, it is bad enough to find step-children counted by one investigator and ignored by another, but worse still to be left in the dark as to whether they have been included or not. One might as well define the yard in terms of the length of the Queen's umbrella, and allow different investigators to take their standards from the umbrellas used by different Queens.

Similarly, in researches into the spread of the risk of criminality through life (as is indeed all too apparent from Chapter V of this book) the material used relates to a most miscellaneous assortment of ages; and even where the span covered is the same, the actual groupings used are only too likely to be different. One enquirer will divide his subjects into those between, say, the ages of fifteen and eighteen, another will use a 16–18 or 15–19 age-group, whilst a third will subdivide his cases into those aged from fifteen to seventeen and those between seventeen and nineteen; and in yet other cases large age ranges will all be combined in a single category. The few occasions on which trouble has been taken to ensure the use of comparable definitions or measures are as welcome as they are still rare. Such are the Gluecks' choice of an occupational classification for their delinquent women, which was modelled upon Fernald's earlier study in order that 'the findings of the two researches might be comparable';[1] Mannheim's decision to base his geographical classification of offenders on place of residence in preference to the area in which the offence occurred so as to keep 'in line with . . . most other studies of this kind';[2] and Rose's attempts to arrange his material in such a way as, wherever possible, to keep in step with one of the Glueck enquiries.[3]

Researches into social pathology afford, in short, abundant illustrations of the truth that 'the maturity of an area of knowledge is reflected in the degree of standardization of its nomenclature'.[4] As things are, the lack of common measures or standardized terms makes it extraordinarily difficult to use one piece of work as a check upon another; and the effect of that, in turn, is that, instead of building up a cumulative body of knowledge, we tend to amass a miscellany of isolated, non-comparable bits of information. This is indeed one of our greatest contemporary weaknesses. Nor can standardization become effective until, not only are precise definitions drafted, but conventions as to their use are observed. And of these two requirements the second is even harder than the first to satisfy; for most social scientists have been nurtured in a strongly individualist tradition.

The value even of the information that we have is, moreover, still further diminished by lack of criteria by which it can be assessed. Even the use of controls has only become common practice in surprisingly recent history. Elaborate studies of deviant behaviour have been, and still are, undertaken which make no attempt to establish the norms from which the subjects are presumed to be deviating. Fernald's observation that this deficiency 'is responsible, more than any other one thing, for a general want of con-

[1] Glueck, S. and E. T., *Five Hundred Delinquent Women* (1934), p. 81.
[2] Mannheim (1948), pp. 34–35. [3] Rose, A. G. (1954).
[4] Shera (1951), p. 85.

clusiveness about our findings'[1] is almost as true to-day as it was when it was made nearly forty years ago. Stott,[2] for instance, has given in great detail a picture of the psychological processes which he finds to be characteristic of a group of Approved School boys; but the question how far this may or may not be also a faithful picture of other boys raised in the same social environment who have never found their way to an Approved School remains unanswered—and indeed unasked. Yet the greater the resemblance, the smaller the contribution that his researches can make to the understanding of delinquency.

Particularly in the many studies of broken homes or of maternal separation is this lack of relevant norms acutely felt. After all that has been written about the lamentable consequences of the broken home we are still, it must be repeated, without information as to the frequency with which, or the ages at which, or the reasons for which, homes are broken in a 'normal' population. Yet, most regrettably, Bowlby and his colleagues have turned their backs upon the idea of making a 'population survey' which would establish the incidence of separation experiences in the general population and the extent to which these experiences have had damaging results—on the ground that to do the job thoroughly by means of clinical appraisals of personality would not be feasible, while to do it more superficially would be doubtfully worth while.[3]

Meanwhile, even in those cases in which controls have been used, the problem of establishing exact comparability seems in some instances (and those not always of relatively early vintage) to have been treated in a surprisingly rough and ready fashion. Thus Capwell speaks of groups 'roughly equated for urban-rural backgrounds'.[4] Other investigators are content to describe their subjects and controls as 'approximately' matched in respect of age distribution;[5] and, in the Carr-Saunders study, controls were chosen by the head teacher of each subject's school who supplied 'the name and address of another boy of about the same age who could reasonably be regarded as a "mate" to the case'.[6] Even in enquiries dealing with closely related topics, the variety of 'matching' practice is bewilderingly great.

III

At a more fundamental level, it seems that our investigations have often come to nothing, because we have still not wholly outgrown the habit of confusing words with the concepts which they describe. As a minor manifestation of this confusion, one might quote the undue significance sometimes attached to a mere change of nomenclature. In some contexts the reason for such changes is clearly, in the main, political—as when unemployment becomes 'redundancy', tramps become 'persons without a settled way of living', depressed areas become 'special' areas and the ruling class becomes 'the

[1] Fernald and others (1920), p. 524. [2] Stott (1950).
[3] Ainsworth and Bowlby (1954), pp. 21–22. See also p. 151. [4] Capwell (1945), p. 213.
[5] Reinhardt and Harper (1931), p. 271, and also Banister and Ravden (1945), p. 82.
[6] Carr-Saunders and others (1942), p. 55.

Establishment'. But in the world of the social investigator name-changing is also quite frequently practised; and when that happens, labels often masquerade as explanations, and tautologies as meaningful statements. It is, for example, not clear what has been gained by re-naming the mad 'psychotic' or the completely self-centred 'psychopathic'. No doubt even these changes contain what in a broad sense may be called a political element, inasmuch as they express the changing balance of power in the conflict of academic disciplines. But what matters more is that they sometimes result in whole theories being built upon what is really a verbal foundation. The maturation theory of delinquency, discussed on pp. 161 ff., is a case in point. In effect, this theory appears to amount to no more than the proposition that the reason why most young men give up crime as they get older is the fact that they are older. Somewhat analogous also are the Glueck investigations into the relation of neurosis with delinquency, designed to distinguish between neurotic and emotionally healthy delinquents; between neurotic delinquents and neurotic non-delinquents; and between neurotic and emotionally healthy non-delinquents. In this enquiry delinquent subjects and non-delinquent controls were analysed in respect of forty-seven 'social' factors, forty-two 'traits' revealed by Rorschach tests and eighteen traits of temperament diagnosed by psychiatric examination. Five of these characteristics were then selected for the purpose of distinguishing the neurotic delinquent from his non-neurotic but still delinquent counterpart, these being (1) commonsense, (2) feelings of insecurity and or anxiety, (3) feelings of helplessness and powerlessness, (4) fear of failure and defeat, and (5) defensiveness of attitude. Neurotic delinquents, it was suggested, could be detected by a low score for commonsense and a high one on the other four qualities.[1] But in this enquiry there is one omission that is vital for this particular comparison: the meaning of 'neurotic' is nowhere defined. If, however, definitions are sought elsewhere, these will be found to run remarkably close to the criteria which the Gluecks suggest for discriminating between neurotics and non-neurotics in their various categories. Such symptoms as a sense of defeat or of failure or of anxiety, or an attitude of extreme defensiveness, are commonly described by authorities on psychiatric matters as typical indications of neurotic tendencies. If, however, they are accepted as such, the results of much of the Gluecks' investigation are reduced to mere tautologies. For if persons who are unusually prone to feelings of anxiety or of insecurity, or who suffer from a sense of failure or of defensiveness, are by definition neurotics, then the statement that these characteristics serve as criteria for the detection of the neurotics in any population, delinquent or other, is simply a way of saying that neurotics exhibit the symptoms of neurotics or indeed that neurotics are neurotic. Presumably the Gluecks have in mind some definition of neurosis which avoids this difficulty; but so long as none is given the reader must draw upon what he can find in other authorities; and he can hardly be blamed if he dismisses the whole investigation as resulting merely in an elaborate tautology.

[1] Glueck, E. T. (1956).

Perhaps it is some comfort to the social scientist to know that the representatives of other disciplines also are prone to fall into similar errors. As Wilson has put it: 'If I gave as a reason for why the room was cold, the explanation that it was due to the low temperature, it would be objected that I had not explained anything at all: for "cold" and "low temperature" are simply two ways of describing the same thing. Yet a similar mistake was actually committed by the first doctors who attempted to investigate the properties of opium. Opium puts people to sleep: and they offered as an explanation of this the view that it had a *vis dormitiva* or "soporific quality". Of course we can see that this is no explanation: it is just saying that opium puts people to sleep because it puts people to sleep, which is not very helpful. In other words, no new facts are being described by the phrase *vis dormitiva*.'[1]

For 'vis dormitiva' in this passage read, say, psychopathy, and the analogy is remarkably close. For to say that a persistently anti-social person behaves as he does because he is a psychopath, when psychopathy is defined as persistently anti-social behaviour, is indeed on the same level as saying that what puts people to sleep puts people to sleep, or that the room is cold because the temperature is low.

IV

In social research generally, constant vigilance is necessary against the risks of prejudice. No elaborate argument is necessary to show that, in the investigation of human affairs, prejudice is likely to be a more dangerous threat to scientific integrity than it is in, say, the study of crystalline structures. In the natural sciences integrity may be threatened by love of one's own hypothesis, or by the desire to discredit a rival or to maintain an intellectual position which has in effect become a vested interest. In the social sciences we have all this to cope with and more beside; for the social scientist has constantly to extricate himself from a tangle of social and ethical value-judgments. In the field of social pathology in particular, there is a risk that such judgments may have an undesirable influence upon the choice of hypotheses, and that the latter will be derived from irrelevant moral and social attitudes rather than from careful scrutiny of the available evidence. Such theories as that delinquents come from broken homes or have mothers who go out to work, or that they are not members of clubs or do not go to church, have certainly *originated* in the value-judgments of those who put them forward, whether or no they subsequently prove to be well founded. They are simply expressions of popular attitudes or prejudices in favour of clubs, churches and family life, and against the employment of women outside the home. Even the maternal deprivation hypothesis, it has been whispered, may not be unconnected with the desire to see women safely confined to domestic occupations.

This practice of importing hypotheses from general philosophical principles into the study of social phenomena involves peculiar risks. Every investigator

[1] Wilson, J. (1956), pp. 43–4.

is inclined to fall in love with his hypothesis, but association with high moral principle is a powerful added charm. The social scientist's susceptibility to the appeal of socially, or morally, attractive hypotheses has been abundantly illustrated in the researches reviewed in this book. But more serious even than the risk that a loved hypothesis will be treated with excessive tenderness is the danger that it will prove unfruitful; for the fruitful hypothesis is likely to be the one suggested by study of the actual material, rather than any that is the product of extraneous moral or social principles; and no one should be surprised if what are really irrelevant hunches prove to be sterile.

Prejudice also can make us curiously blind to the obvious. Neglect of the sex difference in crime, already remarked upon,[1] is one example. One of the few established features of criminality, and one which is repeated right round the world is the fact that at all ages many more males than females are convicted. In scale and constancy, the sex difference far outweighs any other factor which we have yet been able to associate with delinquent behaviour. No one seems to have any idea why; but hardly anyone seems to have thought it worth while to try to find out. The opportunity to avail ourselves of what amounts almost to a ready-made control experiment has been consistently neglected. Presumably, since the number of children of each sex is much the same, such experiences as the break-up of their homes, or the loss of parental affection, must fall with roughly equal frequency upon boys and girls. Yet no one asks why one sex should be nearly eight times more resistant to these shocks than the other. While there have been a few studies of women offenders, investigators have generally looked upon the difference between masculine and feminine criminality merely as a reason for eliminating female subjects from their researches on the ground that they provide insufficient material. Whether this insufficiency reflects a genuine difference in feminine propensity to crime, or merely the superior skill with which female lawbreakers elude detection, and how this difference is related to factors in the training and education of girls which they do not share with their brothers—these questions remain unanswered and indeed unasked. Consequently the myth is perpetuated that, whereas 'boys seem to express their unhappiness by delinquent acts, girls seem to find an outlet for theirs in sex'[2]—a proposition palpably at variance both with what is known as to the relative frequency of male delinquency and female sexual aberration, and also with the simple biological fact that, in the sexual acts to which she is said to be prone, a girl normally requires the co-operation of a male partner.

Accident and fashion may also join with prejudice in concentrating attention on some aspects of a problem to the neglect of others: and the choice of hypotheses is constantly conditioned by some unspoken first premise which is itself determined by these factors. The dramatic growth of the influence of psychiatric concepts in the past thirty years has necessarily encouraged emphasis upon the individual, rather than upon the social, factors in anti-social behaviour. Typically, the Gluecks, for all their insistence upon the need for an 'eclectic approach to the study of the causal process in human motivation

[1] See pp. 30 ff. [2] Henriques (1955), p. 120.

and behavior', and for the co-operation of several disciplines in delinquency research, dismiss very cursorily the work of sociological or ecological investigators, with the observation that 'this kind of approach to the problem of delinquency, although of much aid in studying the phenomenon in the mass, is of relatively little help in exploring the mechanisms of causation'.[1]

Undoubtedly the roots of this somewhat lopsided concentration upon individual, rather than upon social, factors go deep. Some of their more profound ramifications are discussed elsewhere in these pages.[2] But here it may be relevant to add that this again is one of the points where some influence must be ascribed to what one can only call the accidents of academic discipline. In this country it has so happened that psychiatrists and psychologists managed to establish themselves well and early in the study of social pathology; and the disciplines which succeed in appropriating a field of investigation generally also succeed, though doubtless without conscious design, in keeping their rivals out. The point is well illustrated by the contrast between the theories currently invoked to explain social failure, and those which are concerned with outstanding social success. While the former are predominantly psychiatric, the latter are, no less predominantly, sociological. Whereas the misfit tends to be explained in terms of a personality damaged by unhappy infantile experiences, social mobility, in the upward sense, is explained rather in terms of such social factors as parental occupation or educational opportunity. One might have supposed that the correlative of the hypothesis that the child who becomes an anti-social misfit is the child who has (to quote the Gluecks' prediction table) suffered from overstrict or erratic home discipline, parental indifference or an 'unintegrated' family would be the hypothesis that the child who makes good is the one who has enjoyed 'firm but kindly discipline' and 'warm' affection in a cohesive family background. Since, however, social failure is mainly the preserve of psychological disciplines, while upward social mobility happens to belong to the sociologists, current theories of social failure are seldom thus turned upside down to explain social success. Anyone who compares, for example, the proceedings of the 1955 International Congress of Criminology with those of the 1956 World Congress of Sociology cannot but be struck by the radical difference in the explanations offered of success on the one hand, and of failure on the other. The latter, it seems, is primarily a matter of personality; the former a matter of situation or opportunity.

Conformity to standard academic patterns has, moreover, tended to confine the search for information within unduly narrow limits. In consequence, the picture of the typical delinquent that emerges from contemporary investigations is curiously flat. Such a delinquent is found to come from a particular kind of home in a particular locality, and his relations with his parents are recorded as being of such and such a nature. In due course he goes to school where he may do well or badly, and in due course again he leaves school, and goes to work. The nature and the number of his job or jobs are duly noted, as are also the ways in which he spends his leisure—

[1] Glueck, S. and E. T. (1951), pp. 7 and 5. [2] See pp. 291, 292 and 329 ff.

whether in the cinema or the pub, in bird-watching or in art classes; and details may be added as to his health, his bodily make-up and the way in which his personality strikes a psychiatrist.

But nothing ever happens to him. He never gets discouraged at school because the class is too large or the teacher idle or incompetent; he never gets a new view of life from spending his holidays on a farm or with a seafaring uncle, or suffers bitter loneliness by being cut off from all his school friends because his father's job has necessitated removal from Glasgow to Plymouth. Ideas are not put into his head by glamorously rebellious types with whom he rubs shoulders at work. He is never turned down by a girl, or made miserable by a bullying foreman; and he never enjoys a run of luck on the pools, or gets his head turned because everyone falls for his good looks.

Yet all these things and a million more, as everybody knows, do happen to people and do help to shape their lives and their behaviour. In the typical delinquency study such occurrences pass unrecorded; and what we get instead represents the framework of a life rather than a life itself.

In the United States a gallant attempt to redress this balance was made by the late Professor Sutherland in his theory of 'differential association', postulating that criminal behaviour may be traced to contacts with criminal patterns. 'When persons become criminal, they do so because of contacts with criminal patterns and also because of isolation from anti-criminal patterns. Any person inevitably assimilates the surrounding culture unless other patterns are in conflict; a Southerner does not pronounce 'r' because other Southerners do not pronounce "r".'[1] Similarly, Reckless also has argued that the companionship factor is 'unquestionably the most telling force in male delinquency and crime', and has even had the temerity to find support for this in the data of the Gluecks' latest work. According to his interpretation, 'of all factors in the entire study, the amount or degree of relationship between the presence or absence of delinquent companions and the condition of delinquency or non-delinquency was found to occupy first place'. Nevertheless, 'The Gluecks overlooked the importance of the companionship factor in their final interpretation of their entire findings'.[2]

In theory at any rate the Gluecks are prepared to admit a widening of the scope of research. Indeed, for balanced comprehensiveness, one could not wish to improve upon Sheldon Glueck's description of the causes of anti-social behaviour as the result of a balance between 'internal and external pressures and inhibitions', such that 'if the total weight of pressures to anti-social behaviour exceeds the total strength of inhibitory forces, the person commits crime'. 'It is not mesomorphic constitution, or strong instinctual impulse, or an hereditary aggressive tendency, or weak inhibitory mechanism, or low intelligence, or excessive emotional lability, or marked suggestibility, or an unresolved Oedipus situation, or residence in a poverty-stricken "delinquency area" or in a region with a tradition of delinquency, or "differential association" with those already criminal, or an excess of anti-social "definitions of the situation" or any other biological, social or cultural

[1] Sutherland (1955), p. 78. [2] Reckless (1955), p. 77.

factor that *inevitably* conduces to delinquent behaviour'.[1] In what immediately follows, however, overwhelming weight is assigned to the personal characteristics and domestic relationships which figure prominently in the Gluecks' own work, the design of which, it will be remembered, eliminates the influence of external events and of all but a narrow range of socio-cultural factors.

The differential association theory is admittedly oversimplified. It is certainly open to the charge of neglecting everything except a particular class of events, and it occupies only a minority position in the criminological world. Nevertheless this theory has its uses as a reminder of how easily the lines of research harden into conventional moulds, and of how easily, in consequence, large areas of possibly relevant experience may be lost to view; for the Gluecks' firm belief that 'the tendency toward delinquency and criminalism is deeply rooted',[2] and that delinquency is predominantly traceable to forces operating either in the subject's own personality or in the narrow circle of his family, has certainly acquired almost the status of an axiom.

Other forces also, as well as the persistent conviction that the factors which cause a deviant to deviate lie in himself and in his home, rather than in anything which may happen in his life, have contributed to narrow the range of material from which hypotheses are fashioned. Some responsibility must rest upon the compelling need for measurement. From the mass of experience we tend to select only those items which can be reduced to a common form, in order that measurement and comparison may be possible. Yet the factors that are easily measurable are not necessarily those that are most powerful; and limitation to what is measurable may lead to the measurement of an inappropriate or an inadequate collection of quantities.

Measurement, in other words, is sometimes premature. But, so long as we persist in the attempt to identify the factors which are responsible for the occurrence of anti-social behaviour in one individual and its non-occurrence in another, we cannot afford to throw away potentially valuable material merely because we are in a hurry to get something on which we can work. Individual conduct emerges from the richness of individual experience, and even amongst those whose lives would by any standard be judged amongst the poorest, this is rich indeed. Those of us who have been guilty of unrecorded crimes (and it would seem that this is no small or unrepresentative group)[3] might do well to reflect upon the circumstances in which these offences were committed, upon the complexity of their causes as these appear to the principal actors concerned, and upon the possible changes in our own subsequent history that would have occurred, had these lapses come to light and been the subject of official action. Psychoanalytic influences notwithstanding, it seems unlikely that we should be content to explain those offences solely in terms, either of the qualities of our personality or of our infantile experience, to the exclusion of such factors as the strength of temptation inherent in the situation, or the calculated risk of detection and the probable consequences that would follow should this risk prove to be a bad one. We have no reason to suppose that the causation of similar actions by others is less complex.

[1] Glueck, Sheldon (1956), p. 105. [2] Glueck, S. and E. T. (1951), p. 3. [3] See p. 70.

What is true of criminal behaviour is no less true of other forms of social pathology. The train of events which leads to the birth of an illegitimate child, or to the decline of a family to problem family status, must be immensely variable; and in these cases even less information is usually available about the subjects' background history than has been obtained in many of the investigations that are concerned with lawbreakers. Both the past and future of the problem family, for instance, remain generally shrouded in mystery. Yet external misfortune may wreak havoc in the domestic life of a seemingly stable and satisfactory family. To quote a recently reported example: a man who loses his job as a result of a row with a foreman gets into financial difficulties and has to give up his home, but presently finds a new job and is reunited with his family. He then suffers an accident; and from that point on, one disaster follows another until no less than nine people find themselves called into conference to wrestle with the problems of one unfortunate family.[1]

What all this points to is that hypotheses need to be drawn, not from judgments that come from outside the material to be studied, nor even from a narrow range of the material itself, but from a better balanced and more comprehensive view of the facts of social pathology. At the moment we are much too apt to apply much too crude hypotheses (such as maternal deprivation) to much too miscellaneous material (such as undifferentiated groups of thieves, sexual deviants and people who are too free with their fists). Both halves of the process are at fault, and both argue too simple a view of human nature.

One step, though a modest one, which might help to increase the range and variety of our data, and to break through the shackles of what is fast becoming a rigid pattern of research, might be to extend the still exiguous literature of criminal and other anti-social biographies. At present this literature mainly consists, on the one hand, of the autobiographies of a few deviant men and women whose very articulateness proves them unrepresentative; and, on the other hand, of rather slight sketches such as those of the late Sir Leo Page. Fuller and more penetrating studies, such as Jean Evans' *Three Men*,[2] are still rare indeed. It is true, of course, that good material of this kind is not easily come by. Life stories are never easily told, even when their authors are genuinely concerned more with accuracy than with self-exculpation; and the biographies of those who defy the standards of their own society are doubly difficult to get straight. But it is worth some effort to get evidence that is both better rounded and more extended than most of what we have hitherto had—in the sense that it both covers more facets of life and extends through a larger span of time. And, even if investigations that are prolonged over considerable periods are bound to prove expensive, and to raise difficult practical problems of continuity, the fact has to be faced that the short-term static picture seldom has much value.

The fact has also to be faced that we must be prepared to deal with a much wider range of variables than has been usual in the past. The formulation

[1] Alstrom (1957). [2] Evans (1954).

and testing of hypotheses which take adequate account of the complexity of human behaviour is necessarily a slow and complicated business; and it will be all the slower and more complicated if we are prepared to admit that what we are looking for is not some predetermined factor, but similarities of the very nature of which we are unaware. The profusion of variables may indeed well prove unmanageable, at least so long as we adhere to the relatively crude methods now generally used. Just because of this profusion, it would seem that it is in the study of social affairs that modern electronic devices should be particularly useful. In a hundred years' time the notion that highly complex and variable behaviour can be explained by broad simple hypotheses such as separation from the mother in childhood may come to be regarded as childishly simple; and it may well have become standard practice for social data to be handled by mechanisms capable of dealing with far more variables than is the unaided human brain.

Even with such assistance, however, it may be wiser to set our sights lower. Much of the research reviewed in these pages is inspired by the hope that the connections between various manifestations of social pathology and other specific phenomena may prove to be a cause-and-effect relationship; and that the elimination of causes will result in cure. It cannot, however, be said that this type of enquiry has been very successful. The generalizations that have been reached are shaky; few of them are consistently supported by the work of any considerable number of investigators; and, even in those that do recur, the quantitative variations are apt to be very large. Many of these generalizations, moreover, are quite untenable as causes. In the study of criminal convictions (as ordinarily interpreted), for example, the associations with sex and age, size of family and criminal records in the home, are about the only ones which have any serious claim to be regarded as constants. Yet it clearly does not make sense to argue that delinquency is *caused* by youth, or masculinity or by the size of the offender's family; and, although it can more plausibly be suggested that the presence of one criminal in a family is a cause of the appearance of another, inasmuch as the one leads the other astray, nevertheless even here more than one other interpretation is possible. The police, for example, are likely to look for suspects in families in which there has already been trouble, so that the presence of one offender in a family may have the effect, not of deterring others from following his example, but of increasing their risk of detection if they do so; or alternatively, if criminality runs in families, it is conceivable that the explanation is to be found in hereditary factors.

Indeed, far too many of the generalizations that have been regarded as even tolerably likely causes of delinquent behaviour can be turned upside down. If delinquent children are found to be truants from school, the truancy does not necessarily cause the delinquency: the child who has committed a theft may stay away from school for fear of being found out; and the child who steals on a day when he should be in school may either have stayed away for this purpose, or else have discovered that shoplifting is an agreeable pastime for periods in which he has made up his mind for quite other reasons to play truant. Similarly, in older age-groups, if frequent changes of employment are found to be associated with a criminal record, a choice of interpretations is open. Job-changing and law-breaking may both be symptoms of a certain restlessness of character or of hostility to authority in any shape or form. Alternatively, boys who are inclined to dishonesty may for obvious reasons be more than averagely liable to get dismissed; or, again, they may themselves think it prudent to change their employers fairly often, so as to reduce the risk of their misdeeds coming to light. Similarly, if children from Approved Schools show a high proportion of abnormal EEG's, how can we be sure whether this is because they are abnormal children, or because they have had abnormal experiences? If certain types of anti-social behaviour tend to be localized in particular areas, is the cause to be found in the corrupting effect of the physical or social conditions prevailing there, or in the tendency for birds of a feather to flock together? And may not the maternal separation hypothesis be open to the objection that unstable or difficult children are more likely than others to find their way into institutions?

One could amuse oneself indefinitely by seeing how many of the causal explanations of delinquency, or of the typical aberrations of problem families, or of illegitimacy or of other social deviations can thus be reversed. But after a time the exercise becomes unprofitable, except as a demonstration of how far we are from being able to speak with confidence of 'causes'. What we have to recognize is that the discovery of the causes of social phenomena is the most ambitious goal at which we can aim, and is therefore relatively unlikely to be attained. By contrast, the record of experiments in prediction is much more encouraging and is also rapidly improving. Yet, as has already been observed, the predictive factors used by some of the most successful enquiries are obviously far removed from 'causes' as we have defined them. The demonstrably reliable findings of the Mannheim and Wilkins enquiry, which show that previous experience of an approved school or of probation, together with frequent changes of job, augur badly for an offender's post-Borstal record, can hardly be interpreted to imply that the abolition of approved schools and of the probation system, or the enactment of a law forbidding employees to discharge themselves, would improve the outlook. And, although it is true that the factors used by the Gluecks in their predictive tables (such as inconsistent discipline in the home) could more credibly be regarded as causes of delinquency, the validation of these is still awaited.

The moral seems to be that it is in their rôle as the handmaidens of practical decision that the social sciences can shine most brightly. Prediction may be a less ambitious goal than causation, but it is certainly more often within the reach of our present capacities and techniques. Though still unable to say much about the why or the wherefore of any given social events, we may yet be in a position to indicate which of a limited range of decisions is most likely to produce desired results; and the reason for this is just the fact that the range of possible alternatives is so closely limited. The factors, for instance, which throw light upon the relative success of alternative methods of dealing with particular types of offender are much more manageable than are the multifarious observations necessary to establish why people commit the crimes that they do. Already in this field exact observation of past experience has proved itself to be an invaluable guide; and it is significant that success has been greatest where the range of variables is least—as in dealing with the relatively homogeneous population of a particular type of penal institution, or with such relatively restricted practical matters as the decision to release, or not to release, a particular offender on parole.

Hitherto far too many vital social decisions have, perforce, been made with neither foresight nor hindsight. Every day magistrates and judges are obliged to pass sentences, quite unaware whether similar decisions in the past have turned out well or badly: in more senses than one justice has been blind. That is why systematic analyses of sentencing policy such as those of Mannheim, Spencer and Lynch[1] are especially welcome. By means of these and of others like them, essential raw material is gathered for the later and more difficult stage in which the success of alternative policies is evaluated; and hopes are raised that justice need not, always, in all senses, be blind.

To say that causation is more intractable than prediction is almost equivalent to saying that cure is easier than prevention; almost, but not quite. Prevention is sometimes possible even where causation is not understood, just as in medicine also the onset of a disease may sometimes be foreseen, even though its origin remains obscure. Although predictive techniques have hitherto been most successfully used in forecasting the future prospects of those whose conduct has already made them the subjects of official action, it is quite possible that they may also be capable of detecting anti-social propensities not yet actually manifested. Preventive, as well as curative, action will then be possible in the case of subjects in whom such tendencies have been diagnosed. That, at any rate, is the hope of the Gluecks and of others who work on similar lines. Yet even so, the reliable predictors may turn out to have nothing to do with what are ordinarily called causative factors. If a fidgety child turns out to be likely to become a difficult child, no one would argue that the fidgets are the cause of the difficult behaviour; yet fidgetiness may be easier to detect, and therefore a more useful indication of the need for preventive treatment, than any of the factors which could plausibly be regarded as causative.

If we can speak with tempered optimism of the development of prediction skills, at least as much can be said for progress in classification. That young sciences should be much concerned with classification is normal enough; and the social sciences are no exception. In social pathology, as elsewhere in human experience, the same patterns recur, and one of the marks of increased understanding is the ability to recognize these. The proliferation of new categories such as 'maladjusted', 'educationally subnormal', 'mental defective', 'psychopath' is evidence both of increasing awareness of this recurrence of patterns, and of increasing ability to discriminate between them—in short, of improved skill in classification. In spite of certain dangers, both theoretical and practical[2], every refinement of classification brings us

[1] Mannheim and others (1957). [2] See pp. 332 ff.

one step nearer to reality, for no classification can be finely enough graded to match the continuum of human qualities. Nature knows nothing of a crude dichotomy between 'adjustment' and 'maladjustment', but only an infinite gradation of degrees of adaptation to the environment.

V

The positive achievements of the social sciences in the field of social pathology may not yet be spectacular; but achievement in a negative sense is far from negligible. Up till now the chief effect of precise investigation into questions of social pathology has been to undermine the credibility of virtually all the current myths. Solid evidence that irreligion, or lack of interest in boys' clubs, or life in the squalor of a problem family or a mother's absence at work have the corrupting effects that they are said to have, or that the younger one embarks on a career of crime, the longer one is likely to stick to it, or that the delinquencies of the young are 'all the fault of the parents', or that problem families repeat themselves generation after generation—solid evidence for any of this is conspicuously lacking; and any evidence that can be found has a way of falling to pieces on closer inspection.

Unfortunately, however, to undermine credibility is not the same thing as to undermine credulity. Habits of loose generalization take a great deal of eradicating; and in relation both to social questions generally, and to problems of social pathology in particular, such habits are well-established. As a typical example, Scott's analysis of a collection of 500 cuttings from the British press on the ever-popular subject of juvenile delinquency may be quoted. Well over half the authors of these were journalists and contributors to correspondence columns: the rest consisted of police officials, magistrates, clergy, teachers, politicians, probation officers and local councillors and a small proportion (about 1 per cent or 2 per cent in each case) of psychiatrists, psychologists, social workers, lawyers and prison officials. The variation and the contradictory nature of the opinions expressed are equally remarkable. Thus 2·4 per cent considered juvenile delinquency to be more or less a 'natural' phenomenon; 4 per cent thought it was due to inborn factors; 23 per cent found the cause in lack of basic necessities such as living space, while a rather smaller proportion fastened on other environmental factors outside the home. Parental failure in responsibility or affection was blamed by 49 per cent, broken homes by 11·2 per cent, while modern social trends as 'governmental coddling' or 'the reaction to Victorianism' were quoted by over 33 per cent, and more religious teaching was demanded by 12 per cent. As to treatment, 35 per cent wanted this to be more severe, while 1·2 per cent held the opposite view. More use of psychological methods was demanded by 12·5 per cent, and vehemently opposed by 5·8 per cent. Scott's own gentle comments are worth quoting. 'The majority of contributors seemed to be giving an honest opinion . . . The high suggestibility of some contributors, notably speakers at public meetings, was apparent. Thus, after the publication of an opinion by a prominent person (by no means always an authority), the same opinion would be borrowed by speakers all round the country for a short while. Bowdlerism was commonly observed. The outstanding finding was the astonishing variety of opinions given and the fact that, in the great majority of cases, each contributor seemed certain that his own was the correct answer. There was no hesitation in stating dogmatically not only the cause, but the cure. Facts, figures and scientific methods were very rarely used . . . With very few exceptions, and invariably in the case of popular opinions, a directly opposite view could be discovered amongst the material. For example, the clubs for young people were considered not only essential but also a menace, psychological methods were useful and dangerous, there was to be more use of the stick and less direct punishment. This, as in any other sphere, must necessarily imply lack of knowledge, wide variations in the material studied, or both.'[1]

Even amongst professional social scientists similar lapses into unsupported generalizations occasionally occur. Thus Stott, with a magnificent disregard for all the tangled evidence on this difficult subject, is reported to have expressed the sweeping opinion that 'we can assume that with nine-tenths of the young people found guilty, there is some family trouble to be cleared up';[2] and so careful a student as Morris has tossed off the observation that 'persistent adult criminality is almost invariably the successor to a history of juvenile crime'[3]—although, as is shown by the data assembled in Chapter V of this book, this is a subject on which we are in no position to generalize at all. Such occasional blemishes are, however, usually incidental, and do not, as a rule, distort the main findings of serious works of research. While not important in themselves, they are quoted here as reminders that scientific discipline is not yet fully established in social investigation.

The establishment of such discipline is, moreover, itself hampered by the inheritance of an unfortunate academic tradition. In every branch of human studies the passage from the speculative to the scientific has been difficult and slow. In every branch the features of our philosophical ancestry are still traceable; Herbert Spencer's conception of a tragedy as 'a deduction killed by a fact' is not quite dead yet.[4] Anthropological studies were born, not amongst African tribesmen, or in the Australian bush, but in the Reading Room of the British Museum, where the late Sir James Frazer's monumental *Golden Bough* was compiled by one who had no first-hand contact with any civilization less sophisticated than that of the peoples of Western Europe. Psychology, likewise, originally rested upon no better an empirical base than the introspections of academic philosophers, and has only gradually broken away from its philosophical foundations; while the economists were long notorious for their habit of spinning elaborate deductive theories in complete seclusion from the hard realities of the market place.

Even to-day the gulf which separates those who expect generalizations to be supported by verifiable factual observations selected, when selection is necessary, in such a way as to safeguard against bias, from those who are

[1] Scott (1950), pp. 56–59. [2] Stott (December 1954), p. 218.
[3] Morris, T. P. (1958), p. 190. [4] Quoted by Simey (1957), p. 123.

content to rely upon the judgment of wise and experienced personages (or even upon that of the foolish and inexperienced) is wide indeed—so wide that communication across it at times seems almost impossible. Nor is it a gulf only between the educated and the uneducated. The fact has to be faced that there are some even among the educated and influential public who find the whole idea of the scientific study of social problems repugnant, and for whom communication with social scientists is impossible, because ears are deaf and sets switched off. In a *Letter to Posterity* broadcast in 1952, the Warden of Merton College, Oxford, referred to the invasion of Oxford by 'studies which by their titles suggested a humane subject-matter, but claimed, ominously, to use the methods of natural science. This invasion', he remarked, 'was no rude assault; it was a flattering influx of strangers more eager to share the prestige of the university than to reform it . . . Given peace', he thinks, 'they might have been quite happily absorbed.'[1] That these strangers might have some significant contribution to make to learning in their own right was not even contemplated: the best that could be hoped for was that they should be absorbed as decorously as possible by older and more reputable disciplines.

Inevitably, the first result of a demand for evidence which will stand up to rigorous scientific examination is the destruction of myths, and such destructive activity is likely for some time to come to be the main preoccupation of the social sciences. We do not hold the same beliefs after scientific investigation as we did before; and that goes for sciences which have a much better-established reputation than any of those which are concerned with human behaviour. Occasionally, also, it must be admitted, we run a risk of creating new myths of our own which linger on even after their creators have modified or renounced their claims: we must, for instance, expect much time to pass, before the extensive public which finds in maternal separation an easy explanation of problem behaviour becomes aware of the second thoughts voiced by Bowlby and his colleagues.[2] Even so, the quality of the evidence which the social sciences demand, even at their present stage, is unquestionably of a different order from that which has traditionally been regarded as adequate in the discussion of social problems; and probably the most important achievement that yet stands to the credit of those sciences, and one which far outweighs any of their positive findings except in a few still exceptional spheres, is just this insistence on a new standard of evidence. In the encouraging words of the Presidential Address to the British Association by one of the most distinguished natural scientists now living . . . 'In spite of our hesitations, we can see that there are facts to be found out about our usefulness in society and about our relations with one another and with the group to which we belong. It is too early to be cautious in encouraging these unfamiliar lines of research.'[3]

[1] Mure (1952). [2] Bowlby and others (1956). [3] Adrian (1954), p. 351.

CHAPTER XI

Conclusions—Practical

I

THROUGHOUT these pages the choice between what may be called the environmental and the individualistic approach to social problems has been a recurring theme; and, in spite of the outstanding exception afforded by a few ecological studies, psychiatric influences are steadily tipping the balance in research in favour of the latter. We prefer to-day to analyse the infected individual rather than to eliminate the infection from the environment; and it is typical that the Gluecks, by the simple device of choosing *both* their subjects *and* their controls from 'underprivileged' neighbourhoods, successfully eliminated practically all social factors from their monumental enquiry.

This preference involves both an intellectual and a practical simplification; and its practical consequences are potentially very far-reaching. By tracing the springs of anti-social behaviour to the individual rather than to his social environment, we are, after all, only following what has long proved itself to be the path of least resistance; for, difficult as it is to cope with the mishaps of individual men and women, the institutions in which they enchain themselves are even more obdurate still. Conditions which favour pathological developments, either in the medical or in the social sense, are notoriously awkward to deal with. In medical research, as Logan has, with exceptional candour, pointed out, 'The cynic may ask what, having shown that a disease is closely correlated with adverse living conditions, we propose to do about it, for it is admittedly beyond the ordinary powers of doctors to transfer their patients from Social Class V to Social Class I and so to relieve them of some of their bronchitis, tuberculosis, and myocardial degeneration (though increasing thereby their risk of coronary thrombosis).'[1] So also in social affairs, to treat an individual is a very different matter from converting the underprivileged into the privileged. Always it is easier to put up a clinic than to pull down a slum, and always it is tempting to treat the unequal opportunities of the slum and of the privileged neighbourhoods as part of the order of nature. If only for these reasons, theories which direct attention away from social conditions towards the deficiencies of individual personality are bound to enjoy a considerable practical advantage. They are very comfortable.

Such theories, as we have seen, can wear many different dresses; and in the contemporary fashion one can indeed recognize the familiar features of now outmoded attitudes. As we have seen, it is not so long ago that poverty, crime

[1] Logan (1954), p. 136.

and other social evils were explained as the product of the shiftlessness, the extravagance and the indolence of the lower orders—not so long ago that it was the moral delinquencies of individuals (especially among the working classes) which were held responsible for problems of social disorientation. To-day culpability is out of fashion: the vogue is for traumatic experience. But their essentially *personal* emphasis is a common feature of both these styles. Awareness of social factors, such as the tinsel glamour of an acquisitive society which offers glaringly unequal opportunities for acquisition, has left no mark on either. To-day the delinquent's misdeeds may no longer be his fault, but at least they are still traced to failings of his own, not to those of the society in which he finds himself, and for which we might all feel bound to take a measure of responsibility. In short, with the powerful support of psychiatry, we still prefer our social problems 'to the consequences of deliberate and heroic efforts so drastically to change the culture that man could live in uncomplicated adjustment to an uncomplicated world'.[1]

This reluctance to examine the imperfections of our institutions as thoroughly as we examine the faults, failings or misfortunes of individuals has also other, and curious, consequences. Among them is the fact that, in cases where individuals cannot adjust themselves to what exists, it is often found easier to invent new institutions than to improve the old—with the the result that Pelion is piled on Ossa, and that formidable administrative complexities, as well as, on occasion, strange contradictions follow.

This process is well illustrated by developments in the field of education and child training. One might reasonably suppose that the primary function of the school was to train the child in the business of adapting himself to the culture in which he has to live, and to help him to make the best contribution of which he is capable to that culture. In a society as tolerant and variable as our own, the schools are required to produce at least a minimal conformity to prevailing notions of what is right and proper in children whose parents may be burglars, alcoholics, republicans, nudists or pacifists, sexually promiscuous, resolutely idle, dirty or spendthrift. Notoriously, however, a certain number of children fail to adjust themselves to the educational institution which is thus intended to adjust them to life. Indeed it now appears that the ordinary school, far from achieving the adjustment which is its normal aim, sometimes actually has an exactly opposite effect. According to a recent official enquiry into maladjusted children, 'the school is probably seldom the direct or chief cause of maladjustment, but it may quite often be a precipitating or contributory factor'; and, to illustrate these risks of exposure to the educational system, the Committee from whose report these words are taken gives a graphic picture of the nervous child going to the school for the first time. If 'not handled successfully',[2] such a child, it is said, may develop a permanent attitude of resistance to the whole business; or he may break down under the stress of the eleven-plus re-assortment, or of a change of school consequent upon his parents' migration to a new district.

[1] Tappan (1952), p. 684.
[2] Ministry of Education, Committee on Maladjusted Children (1955), p. 32.

An obvious way of avoiding these catastrophes would seem to be to modify the régime in the ordinary school so that it might succeed better in what it is intended to do. But that is too difficult. On the principle that it is easier to create a new institution than to modify an existing one, child guidance clinics and schools for maladjusted children have to be invented to deal with the misfits of the normal educational system. At these clinics, we are told, 'as the psychiatrist comes to be accepted as an ally . . . the child is helped to bring his problems to the surface and face them, and through his relationship with the psychiatrist he gains the confidence needed to go forward to meet whatever the future has in store for him'.[1] Yet 'going forward with confidence to meet whatever the future has in store' is, surely, just what schools of every kind might be expected to help their pupils to achieve; and the teacher, no less than the psychiatrist, might be expected to be the child's ally, not his enemy. If in practice schools and teachers fail in these rôles, commonsense and economy alike would suggest that whatever is wrong with them should be put right, rather than that a whole fresh layer of institutions should be created to make good the deficiencies of those that we already have. Yet the latter is, apparently, the easier course. So we end with schools designed to supplement and to correct what is done in homes, and clinics or special educational institutions designed to supplement and to correct what is done in schools.

One cannot but wonder how the child's mind copes with the contradictions inherent in this situation. Conflicts between home and school are doubtless often inevitable, though certainly distressing or puzzling to many children. But conflicts between school and child-guidance clinics must add still further complications, thus providing yet another example of the incomprehensible inconsistencies of the adult world. Though schools differ greatly from one another, it is probably fair to say that those which are included in the public educational system (and a high proportion of those outside it) are on the whole imbued with authoritarian values and employ authoritarian methods.[2] The virtues which they inculcate are those of discipline and hard work, of respect for, and obedience to, properly constituted authority. Children are at least expected to behave politely and respectfully towards their teachers.

But not towards their psychiatrists. Typically, the climate of the clinic is permissive rather than authoritarian: the rôle of the adults is to help, indeed to serve, not to command, the children. Since most children are astonishingly quick to sense and to adapt themselves to differences in social climate, the child who attends both school and clinic (and there are many such) doubtless evolves patterns of behaviour appropriate to whichever situation he finds himself in; but his conception of adult values can hardly fail to become confused; and one cannot but wonder how he is to acquire the integrated personality and outlook which is generally regarded as so vital an element in mental health.

Other practical complications, of a somewhat similar nature, are caused

[1] Ministry of Education, Committee on Maladjusted Children (1955), p. 165.

[2] I have discussed this subject further in an article in *Highway* (March 1956) part of which is reproduced above.

by the very improvements in classification which have already been noticed as one of the more encouraging achievements of students of social pathology. While it is true that every refinement in classification means a closer approximation to the infinite variety of reality, nevertheless increased complexity of classification necessarily means also increased risks of error. If the world is divided into those who are raving mad and those who are sane, the number of cases in which the classification of a particular individual is likely to be called in question will not be very numerous. But if the mad are subdivided into the schizophrenics (of various brands), manic-depressives, senile psychotics and so on, and if in addition to the whole class of the demonstrably mad, we have 'psychoneurotics', 'psychopaths', 'maladjusted', 'intellectually or emotionally handicapped persons', the potential occasions of dispute are vastly multiplied.

Once again this would not matter so much if these classifications were purely theoretical exercises. But once again they are not. For refinements of classification tend to become incorporated into social practice with a speed quite disproportionate to the interest generally evoked by other advances in the social sciences: complication is always dear to administration. Hence we are constantly in the position of giving statutory or administrative recognition to new categories, and of providing new forms of specialized provision. The psychopath, the maladjusted, the educationally retarded, the mental defective and the normal delinquent, each must have his appropriate place in an ever more complex system of treatment.

Premature hardening of these categories into rigid administrative structures is, however, liable to produce unfortunate practical consequences, in spite of the theoretical virtues of finer discriminations. Particularly where specialized institutions (as distinct from specialized treatment within the same institution) are provided, classifications which do not deserve all the respect that they receive may well defeat their own ends. For the greater the number of categories requiring to be separately dealt with, the more complicated becomes the process of matching demand and supply, and the greater in consequence is the risk that a shortage of facilities for one category will coincide with a surplus in the case of another. In the case of unchangeable classifications, such as those based on sex or age, such a result may be accepted with resignation as the inevitable outcome of mistaken forecasting. If, for example, there are vacancies in the schools for boys, but a queue for admission to those for girls, one cannot get out of the difficulty by considering whether after all some of the girls might not be re-classified as boys; or if, in prisons, it is desired to keep first offenders apart from recidivists, one cannot rectify any miscalculation in the accommodation provided for each category, by pretending that some of the recidivists have a blameless record, or that some of the first offenders are old lags. Segregation might conceivably be abandoned, but the categories remain inevitably distinct. But, in the case of a child who is classified as 'maladjusted', it may well be questionable whether the diagnosis is firmly enough grounded to be maintained at all costs—especially since this may merely result in his being deprived of any special attention whatever, for want of vacancies in the particular type of institution which is deemed appropriate for him. One cannot help wondering whether without the label, and with sympathetic handling in some other environment, his problems might not still have been solved. Certainly it seems unfortunate that, as often in fact happens, children should wait months for admission to schools for the maladjusted at times when approved schools have plenty of vacancies. The only consolation is that many—perhaps even most—children prove in the end to be capable of resolving their own difficulties in their own way without special treatment of any kind.

In any event, it is a mistake to confuse specialized with segregated treatment. In the present context such confusion has probably been encouraged by the influence of medical analogies, and by the contemporary habit of conceiving social failure in medical terms. In physical illnesses, institutions offering specialized treatment have a place: the conditions suitable for tubercular patients may not be appropriate for those dying of cancer. Even in the treatment of physical complaints, however, the trend of opinion seems to be in favour of mixed institutions except where there are specially compelling reasons to the contrary; and, in cases of social maladjustment, the arguments against segregation are much stronger. Maladjustment is, after all, by definition an expression of failure to make a success of living in a mixed community. Segregation of tubercular patients may not matter, because inability to get on with other people is not a primary symptom of tuberculosis; whereas inability to get on with, or to conform to the standards acknowledged by, other people is the characteristic quality of those who make themselves, in one way or another, social nuisances. Just because it relieves them of that responsibility (and incidentally relieves others also of the converse obligation) segregation of misfits may have the effect of ruling out what should be a most—if not the most—desirable element in their treatment.

That is not to say, of course, that there are not occasions—indeed numerous occasions—when it is necessary to isolate anti-social persons from the rest of the community for their own good or for that of others. But if the emotionally unstable are to be shut up in one place, and the mentally retarded in another, this hardly promotes the process of their mutual adjustment, or of the adjustment of either to the normal world, and *vice versa*. Nor can we afford to ignore the damaging influence of specialized labels upon those who carry them. Just as it is easy to underestimate the effect of appearances in court or of residence in approved schools, Borstals or prisons in creating a delinquent culture based on the link of this common experience, so, in our enthusiasm for specialized treatment for specialized categories, we can easily fail to make allowance for the fact that the more peculiarly one is treated, the more peculiar one is apt to become.

Undoubtedly there has been, in recent years, a decided trend towards increased subtlety both in theoretical classifications and in practical policies in the field of social pathology. This trend is responsible, among other things, for the splintering of professional social work described in Appendix II; and it is reflected also in the recommendation of the recent Royal Commission on the Law relating to Mental Illness and Mental Deficiency that 'psychopaths' should be recognized as a new category for whom specialized training in adolescence and early life should be compulsory. Happily, however, there are already welcome signs of recognition that theoretical discrimination and practical segregation are not at all the same thing, and that the one does not necessarily imply the other is beginning to be appreciated. In the field of social work, for instance, the reaction in favour of 'generic' training courses has already been noticed. Recently, also, the Chief Medical Officer of the Ministry of Education has put forward a strong plea for the education of handicapped children in ordinary schools. Of the educationally subnormal, who constitute by far the largest group of those formally recognized as handicapped, he has written: 'Like other children, they should have, if possible, a normal environment in which to progress within their limitations. Their out-of-school activities can be fully shared with normal children; they can join in school gatherings, and they can participate in non-academic pursuits, thus gaining a sense of normality which helps to increase their well-being and happiness.'[1] Similarly, in the report of the Royal Commission just mentioned, recognition of new classes of mentally disordered persons is accompanied by a thoroughgoing attack upon segregated methods of treatment. After suggesting the classification of mental patients into three main groups (the mentally ill, the psychopathic and those with severely subnormal personality), the Commissioners proceed to recommend that there should be no 'rigid legal designation of hospitals for any one of these groups of patients only. The extent to which particular hospitals specialize in treating particular types of disorder should be a matter for medical and administrative arrangement, in the psychiatric field as in other branches of medicine. The arrangements should be capable of adaptation as medical developments may require, and there should be no legal barrier preventing the admission of any patient to any hospital which provides the sort of treatment he is thought to need.'[2]

II

Whatever may be thought of the scientific pretensions of psychiatry, there can be no question as to its humanizing effect upon the treatment of socially refractory persons and particularly of offenders against the criminal law. For those who, like the author of these pages, abhor all forms of violence and regard the use of force at best as a lamentable last resort, this humanizing influence is a good in itself, never to be discounted even if it should prove to be accompanied by awkward 'side-effects'.

As to the effectiveness, however, of the comparatively humane methods now in use, surprisingly little evidence is available. Perhaps for the very reason that reformative measures are themselves morally admirable, their effective-

[1] Ministry of Education, The Health of the School Child, Report for 1952 and 1953 (1954), p. 73.

[2] Royal Commission on the Law Relating to Mental Illness and Mental Deficiency, 1954–57, Report (1957), p. 6. Since the above was written, this distinction has been embodied in the Mental Health Bill.

ness tends to be taken for granted. The scraps of evidence that we have are indeed encouraging: as between the more and the less repressive institution, the latter has been found to have the better record of successes. The 'open' is more successful than the 'closed' Borstal,[1] even when allowance is made for difference in the quality of the material with which these institutions are respectively required to deal; and, in the United States also, occasional investigations into the records of different types of school point to similar conclusions.[2] At least we can say that, so far as offenders themselves are concerned, nothing has yet transpired which should discourage anyone, whether psychiatrically-minded or not, from urging the further development of humane methods of treatment. But if that is the least that can be said, it is also the most. Clear evidence that reformative measures do in fact reform would be very welcome.

And some attention does need to be given to possible side-effects. Of these, two only will be mentioned here. First is the fact that the attempt to make the punishment fit the criminal rather than the crime introduces new elements both of delay and of uncertainty into the judicial process. This delay is, at the time of writing, under investigation by an Interdepartmental Committee which will, it is to be hoped, in due course make suggestions for keeping it to a minimum. Nothing, however, can alter the fact that psychiatric assessments take time, and that the more carefully the disposal of an offender is decided in the light of all relevant factors (psychiatric or other) in his background, the longer, in general, is the time that must elapse between conviction and sentence—at least so long as extensive investigations before conviction are regarded, as they properly may be, as unjustifiable violations of privacy. Sentencing on the other hand which is based on the traditional 'tariff' system, in which degrees of severity are adjusted with reference only to the gravity of the offence and the number of the defendant's previous convictions, requires no elaborate investigations, and can obviously follow swiftly upon the finding of guilt. Moreover, of necessity, such sentencing follows a pattern, the consistency of which is plain for all to see; so that an offender should be able to form a fairly accurate forecast, immediately after his conviction, as to what his fate is likely to be.[3]

Both delay and uncertainty are likely to be distressing to the person most immediately concerned. Uncertainty, moreover, may well outrage the sense of justice, not only of the offender himself, but also of the wider community; and in that risk is inherent one of the most awkward of all the issues to be faced in the present transition from a system of dealing with anti-social behaviour which is concerned primarily with the past to one which looks rather to the future. Modern reformative methods of penal treatment, whether based upon psychiatric diagnoses or upon statistical prediction tables, demand that similar offences should entail very dissimilar consequences. Where two men are found guilty of the same offence, perhaps even on a joint charge, differences

[1] Mannheim and Wilkins (1955), pp. 110–113. [2] McCord (1953).

[3] Although even under a 'tariff' system considerable allowance must be made for the individual vagaries of judges and magistrates.

in personality may indicate that one is likely to respond favourably to lenient treatment and sympathetic understanding, whilst the other is a bad risk for whom prolonged detention is the only safe course; and in the case of children and young persons, totally different methods of handling may be indicated, not only by their own personalities, but by the quality of the homes from which they come. To a public conditioned to the belief that the punishment should fit the crime, such inequalities of treatment can only appear as monstrous injustices.

Such reactions cannot simply be ignored. The courts must function in the setting of the community which it is their business to serve; and they cannot afford wholly to ignore the attitudes, or even always to override the prejudices, of that community. Some concessions to popular values must be made, no matter how ardently one may believe that the treatment of anti-social persons should be scientific, in the sense that it should be based on a calculation of probable success derived from the most accurate available observation of experience. But how far those concessions should go is one of the most difficult questions that face every advocate of reformative treatment who finds himself in a position where he is called upon to pass sentence.

The problem is, moreover, made more difficult still by the second of the potentially unfortunate side-effects of reformative penal treatment, namely, the sharpening of the age-old conflict between deterrence and reform that has been brought about by contemporary attitudes. Every sentence has a two-fold reaction—upon the offender sentenced and upon his potential imitators, either of which it is perilous to ignore. Yet both psychiatric methods and predictive researches of the Mannheim-and-Wilkins type concentrate attention solely upon the future convicted person himself, as though no-one else in the world existed. Both are concerned only to make sure that the offender will mend his ways, no matter what happens to anybody else. The psychiatrists particularly who write on penal reform seem quite astonishingly unconcerned with the possible repercussions of their proposals upon a wider community, perhaps for the very reason that it is the doctor's duty to prescribe for his patient and for him alone.[1]

As has been said already,[2] this dual aspect of penal policy seems to have been generally ignored even in the traditional arguments about the rival claims of deterrence and reform—under cover of an assumption that psychological reactions in both spheres would follow similar patterns. Stern measures are presumed simultaneously to teach the offender not to repeat his offence and to teach other people not to copy him. Recently, when the Lord Chief Justice unequivocally declared the proper function of the criminal law to be deterrent, the context suggested no distinction between those who had actually offended and those who might offend but had not yet done so, and no recognition of the—surely very obvious possibility—that deterrent policies might have at once a disastrous effect upon the person subjected to them and a most wholesome effect on everybody else. For it may all too well be true that there

[1] As one typical example in a fairly extensive body of literature, reference may be made to Biggs (1955). [2] See pp. 252, 253.

is nothing like experience of harsh treatment for hardening a man's character in an anti-social mould; and at the same time that there is nothing like the fear of such treatment for deterring those who have not had this experience from running the risk of exposing themselves to it. That is the fundamental dilemma of penal reform which the currently fashionable psychiatric methods of dealing with criminals refuse to acknowledge.

Actually this dilemma raises a question in which again surprisingly little interest seems as yet to have been shown. Since 1955, the date to which the material in Chapter I of this book relates, a significant increase has been recorded in the number of convictions for many types of crime, which is widely (though not, it should be added, conclusively) believed to indicate a corresponding increase in criminality. What, however, has not yet been explored is the degree to which this increase is due to increased activity on the part of recidivists, or to the addition of fresh recruits to the army of the convicted. Although records are kept of the relative numbers of first offenders and recidivists in the total of convicted persons, we are still in the dark about the contribution which each of these classes makes to the total number of proved offences or to the recent increase in these. Yet clearly the social significance of increasingly extensive differs profoundly from that of increasingly intensive criminality; and the implications for practical policy are no less fundamentally diverse in the one case from what they would be in the other.

III

In part, the prevailing emphasis upon the medical element in anti-social behaviour must be seen as an expression of the unique prestige enjoyed to-day by the medical profession. This materialistic age, unable to look with confidence beyond the grave and believing the doctor to hold the keys of life and death, has invested him with the respect and awe once associated with the priesthood. The doctor, like father, knows best; and his prestige is expressed in many ways. The doctor, unlike the teacher or lawyer, is customarily addressed reverentially by the title of his profession. In the courts the doctor's time, unlike that of most other witnesses or of jurors, is assumed to be so valuable, that procedure must be adjusted to take account of this: his evidence must be taken early, and he must if possible be released immediately that it has been given. And, although even now doctors do not automatically get all the pay that they ask for, it is significant that since the war and in defiance of a long-standing tradition of equality, the salaries of medical staffs in universities are now always higher than, and sometimes more than twice as high as, those of their colleagues in other faculties.

Students of what is coming to be known as the sociology of knowledge will see nothing to wonder at in the fact that this high prestige has coloured contemporary attitudes towards, and influenced the direction of, research into problems of social pathology; for it is well known that research accommodates itself to the values and attitudes that prevail in the society in which it is conducted. Nor is this true of the social sciences alone, though in their case the pressure may be unusually compelling. In the contemporary climate, therefore, it is only to be expected that research workers in medicine should rival even their colleagues in atomic physics in their success in attracting funds; or that the hypotheses which they explore should pass into the current coin of the community. Nor is it remarkable that doctors have not, on the whole, neglected to avail themselves of this unprecedented opportunity to enlarge their empire. They would indeed have been less than human had they not.

In the context of the present study a significant—probably in the long run the most significant—result of the growing prestige associated with the practice of medicine in general and of psychiatry in particular, has been a shifting of the boundary between medical and moral problems. In Chapter VIII of this book I have examined one aspect of this development, namely, its effect upon traditional conceptions of criminal responsibility, and have sought to show that these conceptions have already been modified to a point at which they can no longer logically be defended; that they have, in fact, been effectively undermined by the advance of medicine into what used to be the sphere of morality. They may, it is true, linger for a long while yet: there are plenty of precedents for the survival of illogical practices and institutions. But we must certainly expect an increasing number of cases of extreme difficulty to arise, in which the decisions that have to be made as to responsibility bring into sharp focus the contradictions inherent in the present situation; and in the long run there will probably be more fundamental changes. If the argument in Chapter VIII is sound, no logical resting place can be found on the slippery slope that leads from a definition of irresponsibility at least as narrow as the McNaghten formula down to the complete abandonment, for legal purposes, of the very conception of responsibility itself. Illogical halts (such as that afforded by the present Homicide Act) may serve for a time; but the illogical is apt to become the temporary. And already in one small corner of Europe, the end of the road has apparently been reached: the abdication of morality is complete. In Luxembourg 'every person sentenced to a term of not less than three months' imprisonment and every juvenile offender is examined and observed in the Institute of Social Defence [where he is kept under continuous observation] by biological, medical, psychopathological and sociological methods'; and those who operate this system officially claim that '*We do not pass moral judgment, but we try to see only the man as he is. If he is incorrigible, no longer rehabilitable, or his prognosis is bad, we still pass no moral judgment*'.[1]

This intrusion of medicine into what has traditionally been the sphere of morality is sometimes accompanied by very extravagant claims. According to Dr Stafford-Clark it should be possible for a psychiatrist '*within the first few interviews* .. to gain an understanding of his patient in some ways more comprehensive and detailed than perhaps has ever been gained by any other single person, including, of course, the patient himself'[2]—and including also,

[1] From the Duchy of Luxembourg National Statement, quoted by Biggs (1955), p. 194, italics not original. [2] Stafford-Clark (1955), p. 11, italics not original.

one must suppose, the patient's spouse. Armed with this knowledge, the doctor constitutes himself an authority not merely on health but also on morals. 'The guardians of the nation's health may well be concerned with the moral climate of the country.'[1] This 'privileged and learned profession has a duty to the people in advising, and if necessary endeavouring to mould, public opinion'. Dr Curran's plea that psychiatry should restrict its claims, recognizing that 'many individuals present social rather than medical problems', and that 'social questions can only be answered in social terms'[2] strikes an unusual note; for, as has been shown at length in Chapter VII of this book, current concepts of mental health and mental illness are heavily flavoured with 'morals and ethics, religious fervor, personal investment, unvalidated psychological concepts',[3] and are, in fact, largely composed of pure judgments of value.

Such a confusion of medicine and morals, it could well be argued, does no service to science itself; for the success of scientific investigation always has depended, and always must depend, upon the complete exclusion of elements of value. But be that as it may, it is clear that medicine is ousting morality in two quarters simultaneously, and that in consequence large issues are raised as to the nature and the origin of moral judgments. For, on the one hand, as in the Luxembourg statement just quoted, moral judgments are beginning to be excluded from what has hitherto been the area of their most unchallengable rule; while, on the other hand, with the invention of what has been aptly called 'mental healthmanship', medicine takes upon itself the business of defining the Good Life. Indeed, the struggle between the rival empires of medicine and morality seems to have become the contemporary equivalent of the nineteenth-century battle between scientific and religious explanations of cosmic events or of terrestrial evolution. True, the modern battle is much more decorously conducted than was that which agitated the Victorians—so decorously indeed that it is not generally recognized as being a battle at all. But the issues are akin, and the victory seems likely to go the same way. Psychiatrists since Freud have been busy doing for man's morals what Darwin and Huxley did for his pedigree, and with not much less success.

[1] From letters in the *British Medical Journal* (21st January, 1956) p. 171.
[2] Curran (1952), pp. 376 and 378. [3] *Evaluation in Mental Health* (1955), p. 4.

APPENDICES

APPENDIX I

SAMPLE[1] OF CASES FOUND GUILTY AT A LONDON JUVENILE COURT FROM APRIL 1955 TO JULY 1957

Case	*Sex*	*Age*	*Offence*	*Alone or with others*	*Date*	*Previous Court finding, if any*
1	M	11	**Larceny.** Took watch from multiple stores; took another five days later.	Alone	July, '57	February, 1955: trespass on railway
2	M	16	**Larceny.** French boy on holiday, took gramophone record from shop.	Alone	July, '57	Not known
3	F	16	**Rail fraud.**	Alone	July, '57	None
4	F	15	**Insulting behaviour.** Having absconded from approved school, was found soliciting, with known prostitute, in Hyde Park: had already acquired two 'convictions' in adult court for soliciting.	Alone	July, '57	None, probably, except 'convictions' in adult court
5	M	16	**Rail fraud.**	Alone	July, '57	None
6	M	16	**Larceny.** French boy on holiday, took three gramophone records from shop.	With another	July, '57	Not known
7	M	16	**Larceny.** Stole £7 from workmate's wallet, and a suit and suitcase from hostel: tried to use Post Office savings book found in suitcase.	Alone	July, '57	About 1953, stole cycle lamp
8	M	10	**Larceny.** Stole seven bottles of lemonade from a warehouse.	With others	July, '57	None
9	M	9	**Larceny.** Stole seven postcards from a shop.	With others	July, '57	None
10	M	10	**Larceny.** Stole tools from bomb-site store.	With others	July, '57	(1) Sept., 1953, larceny (2) Sept., 1954, larceny (3) Nov., 1954, larceny and receiving (4) June, 1955, found on enclosed premises

[1] This sample includes every fifth new case in which there was a finding of guilt during the periods when Barbara Wootton was presiding between April 1955 and July 1957.

Case	*Sex*	*Age*	*Offence*	*Alone or with others*	*Date*	*Previous Court finding, if any*
11	M	16	**Take and drive.** After domestic upset and drinking, took motor-cycle, drove it a few days, abandoned it, then gave himself up to police.	Alone	July, '57	None
12	M	16	**Rail fraud.**	Alone	June, '57	None.
13	M	15	**Take and drive.** Whilst disqualified, took and drove a car.	With another	June, '57	(1) March, 1955, shopbreaking (2) Dec., 1955, took and drove scooter
14	M	16	**Rail fraud.**	Alone	June, '57	None
15	M	16	**Rail fraud.**	Alone	June, '57	None
16	M	15	**Rail fraud.**	Alone	June, '57	None
17	M	14	**Take and drive.**	Not known	June, '57	(1) June, 1956, took and drove motorcycle (2) June, 1957, found on enclosed premises
18	M	14	**Larceny.** Stole 14 bottles of pop from bomb-site snack bar.	With others	June, '57	1955, stole cycle
19	M	16	**Take and drive.**	With others	June, '57	None
20	M	15	**Rail fraud.**	Alone	May, '57	None
21	M	10	**Larceny.** Tried to get into a house to steal, with others who had previously stolen from the same house.	With others	May, '57	None
22	M	15	**Rail fraud.**	Alone	May, '57	None
23	M	16	**Rail fraud.**	Alone	May, '57	None
24	F	15	**Larceny.** Stole shoes from her shoe-shop employers.	Alone	May, '57	None
25	M	11	**Larceny.** Stole purse containing £1 from handbag left on public hall chair.	With others	May, '57	March, 1955, larceny
26	M	15	**Larceny.** Stole book from shop.	Alone	May, '57	None
27	M	16	**Suspected person.** Loitered in public lavatories during his lunch hour and attempted to steal.	Alone	May, '57	(1) April, 1955, larceny (2) Nov., 1955, larceny (3) March, 1957, stole lead

28	M	16	**Rail fraud.**	Alone	May, '57	None
29	M	14	**Larceny.** Stole watch, key, 10*s.*, etc., from football changing rooms	With others	May, '57	Dec., 1956, take and drive
30	M	16	**Break and enter.** Organized burglary, breaking into shops on various occasions, and stealing various articles.	With others	May, '57	None
31	M	11	**Break and enter.** Organized burglary, breaking into a shop on two occasions and stealing various articles.	With others	May, '57	None
32	F	14	**Larceny.** Stole two pairs of shorts, and two jumpers, from a West End Store.	With another	May, '57	May, 1955, larceny
33	M	11	**Larceny.** On leaving cinema, roamed on to roof, into room, and stole £6. Also took hand-drill which he saw after climbing over a wall into a yard.	With another	May, '57	Feb., 1955, trespass on railway
34	M	16	**Take and drive.** Was a passenger, with another, in a car driven by a third whilst disqualified.	With others	May, '57	(1) May, 1953, larceny (2) Feb., 1956, insulting words and behaviour (3) Oct., 1956, assault causing grievous bodily harm (but took a minor part)
35	F	15	**Rail fraud.**	Alone	April, '57	None
36	M	13	**Larceny.** Stole purse with 7*s.* 9*d.* from hotel, after running away from home (following alleged expulsion from school) and taking rat poison.	Alone	April, '57	Oct., 1956, stole £5 from father, and small articles from school
37	M	8	**Break and enter.** Broke into transport depot on two occasions, stealing sweets and cigarettes.	With others	April, '57	Not known
38	M	13	**Larceny.** Stole gramophone record from shop.	Alone	April, '57	Jan., 1955, attempted larceny
39	M	12	**False pretences.** Collected 15*s.*, ostensibly for Boy Scouts' movement.	With another	April, '57	None
40	M	9	**Wanton discharge of missile.** Fired catapult from moving bus at another bus, cracking window.	With another	April, '57	None
41	F	15	**Rail fraud.**	Alone	April, '57	None

Case	*Sex*	*Age*	*Offence*	*Alone or with others*	*Date*	*Previous Court finding, if any*
42	M	16	**Larceny.** Stole £2,500 (and £200 previous day) from employers, from unlocked safe when left alone. Had been gambling heavily, winning and losing thousands of pounds.	Alone	April, '57	Not known
43	M	13	**Take and drive.** Took and drove a scooter for several days.	With another	April, '57	April, 1956, larceny
44	M	16	**Larceny.** Stole a cycle	Alone	April, '57	March, 1953, stole biscuits
45	M	16	**Rail fraud.**	Alone	Mar., '57	None
46	F	15	**Larceny.** Stole a cardigan from a West End store.	With another	Mar., '57	Not known
47	F	13	**Larceny.** Stole ear-rings from a multiple store.	With others	Mar., '57	None
48	M	16	**Rail fraud.**	Alone	Mar., '57	None
49	F	16	**Larceny.** Stole pair of slacks from a West End store.	Alone	Mar., '57	None
50	M	14	**Larceny.** Stole gramophone records from two West End stores.	Alone	Mar., '57	Not known
51	M	14	**Larceny.** Stole ¾ cwt. lead from a roof.	With others	Mar., '57	Feb., 1957, larceny
52	M	16	**Larceny.** Stole 17 gramophone records from a shop.	With another	Mar., '57	(1) July, 1948, beyond control (2) Mar., 1953, larceny (3) Oct., 1956, rail fraud
53	M	16	**Rail fraud.**	Alone	Nov., '56	
54	M	10	**Larceny.** Stole necklaces and bracelets from multiple stores.	With others	Nov., '56	None
55	M	14	**Assault policeman.** 'Went for' policeman in anger after allegedly being knocked down by officer who was clearing people from a public place on Guy Fawkes night.	Alone	Nov., '56	Nov., 1948, beyond control
56	M	16	**Insulting behaviour.** Threw firework into a crowd of people on Guy Fawkes night.	Alone	Nov., '56	None

57	M	15	**Insulting behaviour.** Threw fireworks, and generally behaved roughly, on Guy Fawkes night.	Alone	Nov., '56	None
58	F	15	**Larceny.** Stole £1 by a ruse from a girl in hostel where she was staying.	Alone	Oct., '56	Not known
59	M	15	**Take and drive.** A scooter.	With others	Oct., '56	None
60	M	16	**Traffic—fail to stop.** When driving loaned motor cycle, not insured or licensed, failed to stop when signalled by policeman.	Alone	Oct., '56	None
61	M	16	**Rail fraud.**	Alone	Oct., '56	None
62	M	15	**Larceny.** Stole £1 from shop till where he worked; *very underpaid*.	Alone	Oct., '56	Not known
63	M	16	**Importuning.** Frequented a public lavatory, smiling at and trying to converse with men.	Alone	Oct., '56	Oct., 1955, fraud: got meat pies and cigarettes by false pretences
64	F	15	**Larceny.** Stole three pairs of shoes left by customer at place of employment.	Alone	Oct., '56	None
65	F	15	**Larceny.** Stole coat from residential club where she worked.	Alone	Oct., '56	None
66	M	14	**Rail fraud.**	Alone	Oct., '56	None
67	F	16	**Embezzle.** Entered on cash register 4*s.* less than a customer gave her in the shop where she worked.	Alone	Oct., '56	None
68	M	16	**Rail fraud.**	Alone	Sept., '56	May, 1956, rail fraud
69	M	14	**Larceny.** Stole £5; also took £107 over a period from aunt's loan club box.	Alone	Sept., '56	None
70	M	9	**Larceny.** Stole money from shops, people, houses, etc., on some 20 occasions.	With others	Sept., '56	None
71	M	15	**Larceny.** Stole a cycle.	Alone	Sept., '56	None
72	M	15	**Rail fraud.**	Alone	Sept., '55	None
73	F	16	**Larceny.** Stole a blouse from a West End store, and had a meal and shampoo without paying.	With another	Sept., '56	None
74	M	Not known	**Rail fraud.**	Alone	Sept., '56	None

Case	*Sex*	*Age*	*Offence*	*Alone or with others*	*Date*	*Previous Court finding, if any*
75	F	15	**Rail fraud.**	Alone	July, '56	None
76	M	12	**Rail fraud.**	Alone	July, '56	None
77	M	14	**Larceny.** Stole 3*s.* 6*d.* from a newspaper stand, and stole from stands on two other occasions.	Alone	July, '56	None
78	M	13	**Larceny.** Stole two books from bookstall, and ran away from home.	Alone	June, '56	Sept., 1953, larceny
79	F	16	**Rail fraud.**	Alone	June, '56	None
80	M	14	**Larceny.** With a friend, stole £28 from a friend's mother's room during two visits.	With another	June, '56	(1) Sept., 1950, larceny (2) March, 1954, larceny
81	M	14	**Take and drive.** Took and drove a motor-cycle, and partly dismantled it.	With others	June, '56	None
82	M	16	**Larceny.** Stole two milk bottles in West End, 5.30 a.m.: also stole 4*s.* in postage stamps from youth club.	With another	June, '56	June, 1955, larceny
83	M	15	**Larceny.** Climbed into shop area and stole cases and soda syphons, value £2.	With others	June, '56	March, 1951, stole 15*s.* in savings stamps
84	M	12	**Larceny.** Stole four bottles of orange juice from warehouse yard.	With another	June, '56	None
85	M	16	**Receiving.** Went into a yard with others, ate biscuits they had stolen, and drove a van which he saw in the yard.	With others	June, '56	None
86	M	Not known	**Insulting behaviour.** After a couple of drinks, tried to fight another youth, banged on shop door, played football in street, etc.	Alone	June, '56	Not known
87	M	16	**Rail fraud.**	Alone	June, '56	Dec., 1955, wrote slogans on transport property
88	M	14	**Larceny.** Stole chocolates, clock and cigarette case from theatre office.	With others	June, '56	None
89	M	16	**Rail fraud.**	Alone	June, '56	Oct., 1955, take and drive
90	F	16	**Rail fraud.**	Alone	June, '56	None

91	M	15	**Larceny.** Stole 56 lb. lead from derelict building.	With another	June, '56	(1) Feb., 1955, insulting behaviour on railway (2) Aug., 1955, stole torch from a car
92	F	16	**Rail fraud.**	Alone	May, '56	None
93	M	16	**Rail fraud.**	Alone	May, '56	None
94	M	16	**Rail fraud.**	Alone	May, '56	None
95	M	15	**Assault, bodily harm.** Had a scuffle with bus conductor, after conductor had accidentally kicked boy when bus lurched.	Alone	May, '56	None
96	M	14	**Take and drive.** Shortly after cleaning cars (pocket-money job), he was seen driving one of them. Apparently he intended to return it after a drive around.	Alone	May, '56	None
97	M	16	**Rail fraud.**	Alone	May, '56	None
98	M	15	**Larceny.** Took money and tickets from an unattended bus.	With another	May, '56	None
99	M	13	**Larceny.** Stole bottles of milk and juice, and damaged a caravan.	With others	May, '56	None
100	F	16	**Rail fraud.**	Alone	May, '56	None
101	F	16	**Larceny.** Stole a jumper from a West End store.	Alone	May, '56	None
102	M	15	**Rail fraud.**	Alone	May, '56	None
103	M	11	**Larceny.** Stole £1 from an unattended bus locker.	With others	May, '56	May, 1956, stole cycles
104	M	10	**Larceny.** Stole 30 purses and 25 gross press-studs, by getting through a window into store.	With others	May, '56	None
105	M	15	**Rail fraud.**	Alone	April, '56	None
106	M	15	**Rail fraud.**	Alone	April, '56	None
107	M	11	**Larceny.** Stole knives, torch, battery, etc., on two occasions, from multiple stores.	With another	April, '56	None
108	M	15	**Take and drive.** Drove and abandoned a car, and stole coat and gloves from it.	With others	April, '56	(1) Sept., 1949, stole cycle (2) July, 1955, stole lead
109	F	13	**Rail fraud.**	Alone	April, '56	None
110	M	8	**Larceny.** Stole 4*s.* 6*d.* worth of articles from two multiple stores.	With others	April, '56	None

Case	*Sex*	*Age*	*Offence*	*Alone or with others*	*Date*	*Previous Court finding, if any*
111	M	13	**Larceny.** Stole articles value £9 from several floors of a West End store on two days.	With another	April, '56	None
112	M	13	**Larceny.** Stole bottles of mineral water from back of club premises	With others	April, '56	Nov., 1955, stole pistol, pellets, goggles and diary from a shop
113	M	14	**Larceny.** Stole 8 lb. grapes from a market.	Alone	April, '56	None
114	F	15	**Rail fraud.**	Alone	April, '56	None
115	M	16	**Drunk.** After 'only a few pints' was drunk in Piccadilly on a Saturday night.	Alone	April, '56	(1) Nov., 1953, broke into warehouse (2) Dec., 1954, larceny
116	M	15	**Break and enter.** Broke into garage where he worked, stole motor-cycle and abandoned it when he couldn't make it work.	Alone	April, '56	Details incomplete, but stole two cycles at different times and was sent to an approved school
117	M	15	**Rail fraud.**	Alone	April, '56	None
118	M	12	**Larceny.** Stole shears, brushes, etc., to furnish a 'den'.	With another	April, '56	Sept., 1955, stole keys from a church
119	M	16	**Larceny.** Stole motor-cycle and began dismantling it in a shed at his home.	With others	Mar., '56	None
120	M	14	**Take and drive.** Went with two adults with criminal records to Brighton, spending three nights with them.	With others	Mar., '56	None
121	M	16	**Rail fraud.**	Alone	Mar., '56	None
122	M	13	**Larceny.** Stole several articles from exhibition buildings.	With others	Mar., '56	(1) Sept., 1954, damaged bus seat (2) Nov., 1955, stole 15*s*. from unattended bus
123	F	16	**Rail fraud.**	Alone	Dec., '55	None
124	F	16	**Rail fraud.**	Alone	Dec., '55	None
125	M	12	**Larceny.** Stole £6 of goods from multiple store, and guilty also of two similar occurrences.	With others	Dec., '55	June, 1955, stole 30*s*. from gas meters
126	M	16	**Firework.** Threw a firework in a public place on Guy Fawkes night	Alone	Dec., '55	None
127	M	16	**Rail fraud.**	Alone	Dec., '55	None

128	M	15	**Rail fraud.**	Alone	Dec., '55	None
129	M	16	**Larceny.** Stole watch from house whose owner he knows.	Alone	Dec., '55	None
130	M	16	**Rail fraud.**	Alone	Nov., '55	None
131	M	15	**Rail fraud.**	Alone	Nov., '55	None
132	M	12	**Larceny.** Stole 15*s*. from an unattended bus.	With others	Nov., '55	Aug., 1953, stole toys from a multiple store
133	M	15	**Take and drive.** Took and drove car, collided with a bus, which was slightly damaged, and struck a passer-by, who was uninjured.	Alone	Nov., '55	(1) Nov., 1948, larceny (2) Oct., 1949, breach of probation (3) Aug., 1951, larceny (4) Sept., 1951, larceny (5) June, 1952, storebreaking and larceny
134	M	14	**Larceny.** Stole six books from a stall.	With others	Nov., '55	None
135	F	16	**Rail fraud.**	Alone	Nov., '55	None
136	M	8	**Break and enter.** Broke into day nursery and stole two toys.	With another	Nov., '55	None
137	M	13	**Break and enter.** Broke shop window and stole hairbrush, pepperpots and draughts.	With another	Nov., '55	None
138	M	13	**Larceny.** Stole pistol, pellets, diary and goggles from shop.	With others	Nov., '55	None
139	M	16	**Insulting behaviour.** Threw firework into street on Guy Fawkes night.	Alone	Nov., '55	Dec., 1952, stole bottle of milk
140	F	15	**Rail fraud.**	Alone	Nov., '55	None
141	F	16	**Rail fraud.**	Alone	Nov., '55	None
142	M	13	**Larceny.** Stole balloon, windmill and fireworks from two shops.	Alone	Nov., '55	None
143	F	16	**Rail fraud.**	Alone	Oct., '55	None
144	F	13	**Larceny.** Stole shopping bag, etc., from West End shop, also perfume, etc., from multiple store.	With others	Oct., '55	None
145	F	16	**Rail fraud.**	Alone	Oct., '55	None
146	M	12	**Larceny.** Stole orange juice from unattended milk cart.	With another	Oct., '55	Not known

Case	Sex	Age	Offence	Alone or with others	Date	Previous Court finding, if any
147	M	14	**Larceny.** Stole five bottles of lemonade from kiosk.	With others	Oct., '55	Not known
148	M	16	**Rail fraud.**	Alone	Oct., '55	(1) Feb., 1955, larceny (2) Date unknown, attempted larceny
149	M	14	**Break and enter.** After absconding from an approved school, broke into 13 houses and stole.	With another	Oct., '55	No details, but had previously been sent to an approved school
150	F	16	**Rail fraud.**	Alone	Sept., '55	None
151	F	12	**Larceny.** Stole two wallets containing £40, also various articles. Wallets belonged to coalman in whose stable she and companion kept rabbits, and hoarded stolen articles.	With another	Sept., '55	None
152	M	9	**Larceny.** Stole two bicycles on which to run away from home.	With another	Sept., '55	Not known
153	M	15	**Larceny.** Stole two bicycles.	With others	Sept., '55	None
154	M	9	**Larceny.** Stole a packet of cigarettes from a car.	With another	Sept., '55	None
155	F	16	**Rail fraud.**	Alone	Sept., '55	None
156	M	12	**Larceny.** Went into office and took 10*s*. 8*d*. from desk.	With others	Sept., '55	None
157	M	16	**Indecency.** Annoyed people by urinating against a wall.	Alone	Sept., '55	No details, but said to have appeared in court previously
158	M	14	**Larceny.** Stole nine gramophone records from one shop and sold them to another.	With others	Sept., '55	Sept., 1951, stole a bottle of milk
159	M	16	**Larceny.** Stole a dress whilst delivering for his firm.	Alone	Sept., '55	(1) March, 1951, shopbreaking (2) Nov., 1953, larceny (3) Jan., 1954, suspected person (4) April, 1954, larceny and receiving
160	M	16	**Rail fraud.**	Alone	Aug., '55	None

161	M	16	**Larceny.** Stole a bicycle pump.	Alone	Aug., '55	Not known
162	M	14	**Rail fraud.**	Alone	Aug., '55	None
163	M	13	**Larceny.** Stole orange juice from door when delivering newspapers.	Alone	Aug., '55	None
164	F	16	**Rail fraud.**	Alone	Aug., '55	None
165	M	13	**Larceny.** Stole £4 from money boxes and handbags in a private house.	With another	Aug., '55	May, 1952, trespass on railway
166	M	16	**Rail fraud.**	Alone	Aug., '55	None
167	F	16	**Rail fraud.**	Alone	Aug., '55	None
168	M	16	**Rail fraud.**	Alone	July, '55	None
169	M	14	**Larceny.** Stole £8 of lead from a house in good repair.	With others	July, '55	None
170	F	15	**Rail fraud.**	Alone	July, '55	None
171	M	15	**Rail fraud.**	Alone	July, '55	None
172	M	12	**Break and enter.** Broke into a store and stole tubes of plastic balloon.	With others	July, '55	(1) Jan., 1954, larceny (2) March, 1954, larceny
173	F	15	**Rail fraud.**	Alone	June, '55	None
174	M	12	**Found in a shop.** After shop hours, presumably there to steal; a companion was in yard outside.	With another	June, '55	(1) Sept., 1953, stole a cycle (2) Sept., 1954, break and enter, and stealing
175	M	13	**Receiving.** Received £2 from a wallet which, with its contents of £151, was stolen by companions.	With others	June, '55	Not known
176	M	16	**Rail fraud.**	Alone	June, '55	None
177	M	15	**Larceny.** Stole £4 and cigarette lighter from manager's jacket, at employers' premises.	Alone	June, '55	None
178	M	12	**Trespass.** In railway goods depot.	Alone	June, '55	None
179	F	15	**Rail fraud.**	Alone	June, '55	None
180	M	14	**Larceny.** Stole brake and handlebars from a bicycle.	With others	June, '55	None
181	M	15	**Unlawful possession.** Found in possession of stolen binoculars; later failed to answer bail and was arrested at Dover, after hitch-hiking through France, Belgium, Luxembourg and Germany.	Alone	June, '55	Oct., 1953, shop-breaking
182	F	16	**Rail fraud.**	Alone	June, '55	None

Case	*Sex*	*Age*	*Offence*	*Alone or with others*	*Date*	*Previous Court finding, if any*
183	M	15	**Larceny.** Stole purse containing £7 from handbag in doctor's waiting-room.	Alone	June, '55	May, 1955, stole £1 from a shop
184	M	16	**Rail fraud.**	Alone	June, '55	May, 1954, rail fraud
185	M	11	**Larceny.** Stole 10*s.* from gas meter in own home.	Alone	May, '55	None
186	F	15	**Rail fraud.**	Alone	May, '55	None
187	F	15	**Rail fraud.**	Alone	May, '55	None
188	M	13	**Larceny.** Stole knives, sheaths and toy pistols, from two shops.	With others	May, '55	None
189	M	15	**Robbery.** Accosted man and demanded money, with threats.	With others	May, '55	None
190	M	15	**Rail fraud.**	Alone	May, '55	None
191	F	16	**Larceny.** Stole a skirt from a shop.	Alone	May, '55	None
192	M	16	**Insulting behaviour.** Was one of a crowd shouting, swearing and pushing one another around on the pavement.	With others	May, '55	(1) Jan., 1952, larceny (2) April, 1955, traffic offence
193	M	16	**Assault: bodily harm.** In a dance hall, threw a chair at a man during a general scuffle.	Alone	May, '55	None
194	F	16	**Rail fraud.**	Alone	May, '55	None
195	M	16	**Larceny.** During a theatre performance, stole a bottle of sherry from the bar.	Alone	May, '55	(1) April, 1952, stole from lorry (2) Aug., 1952, damaged haystack during play
196	M	15	**Rail fraud.**	Alone	April, '55	None
197	M	15	**Larceny.** Stole £1 from a shop whilst making a purchase.	Alone	April, '55	None
198	M	13	**Larceny.** Stole a purse containing 7*s.* 6*d.*	Alone	April, '55	None
199	M	16	**Rail fraud.**	Alone	April, '55	Sept., 1954, larceny
200	M	11	**Rail fraud.**	Alone	April, '55	None

APPENDIX II

Professionalism in Social Work

BY ROSALIND CHAMBERS

Introduction

ALTHOUGH there is no final and universally accepted definition of what constitutes a profession, certain attributes are generally accepted as essential; e.g. the acquisition of particular knowledge and skill, shown by the passing of recognized examinations or tests, acquired through accepted methods of education or training. Membership of a professional association may be necessary to professional status; a relationship of confidence must exist between the professor and the client; and finally, a profession is a calling of higher status and prestige than a trade or occupation with less exacting standards.

Social work has shared in the demand for professional status which has grown in Great Britain in recent years. From the early stages, more than sixty years ago, efforts were made to formulate and reach specific standards, and also to restrict entry to those with recognized qualifications. These efforts were at first closely linked with education for social work in general, but became more specialized as new forms of work developed, and consequently new professional associations evolved. In recent years some change has taken place, for while yearnings for professional status have not diminished, leaders in the field have deprecated the proliferation of more and more specialized branches, each demanding a particular form of training. The development of a general profession of social work is contemplated, with similar qualifications obtained through a uniform basic training which will be recognized and accepted by specific branches.

Apart from the development of basic training, there are signs that the frontiers of specialization are being crossed—for example Psychiatric Social Workers are now working as Children's Officers, Almoners, and in other posts than the purely psychological field of Child Guidance and Mental Hospitals.

One great difficulty remains in determining the status of social work as a profession—or as various professions. In most professions a decisive factor in the status of individuals or groups is that there are established and definite criteria of competence, required not only by the profession, but also by the community. In social work such definitions are less commonly accepted, and the position has become more obscure since the emphasis in case work shifted from the relief of various forms of need to the vague regions of maladjustment and personal relationships. Formerly, as the welfare state with its volume of social legislation impinged increasingly upon the life of the citizen, it was necessary for the social worker to possess full and accurate knowledge if satisfactory advice were to be given to the client, and her capacity and qualifications could be assessed by the result of her activity. But now that the emphasis is predominantly on social relationships, diagnosis and cure are more vague and questionable, although the apparatus of 'know how' and the professional vocabulary are more elaborate than ever before. 'Partly trained' or even 'untrained' social workers are thick on the ground, and in such far-reaching and indefinite fields of operation as 'personal difficulties', 'maladjustment' or 'unsatisfactory human relationships', it is not easy to assess results. Trained and untrained workers may not be equally efficient, but the difference, in many instances, will not be obvious to the general public who will regard all those concerned as 'social workers'. All this increases the difficulty of determining the content of the profession of social work—does the definition depend on the type and extent of training or the kind of work done? And within the many forms of training, what constitutes professional training? Professional status in social work is thus different from that in callings where recognized technical skill is required which renders its possessor fit to perform a particular task and is so recognized by the community.

Case Work as a Profession

Case work was the foundation of professional social work, and its founder institution was the Charity Organization Society (now the Family Welfare Association) which dates from 1869. By that year, Una Cormack says 'the stage was set for a new institution in social case work to appear'.[1] The principle of paid secretaries was accepted by 1883, and, in the Annual Report of the Society for 1897, it is noted that the training and education of voluntary workers has becomes a recognized function of many Committees. 'Such training is mainly intended to enable workers to understand the methods of charity and to accept its principles'. In 1899, the Committee on Training, which had been functioning for several years, reported; but it is significant that 'training' is still given inverted commas, as though it were not quite the real thing, and it is remarked that it may be carried out 'by conversation, by reading, or by practical illustration on cases or otherwise'.[2]

By 1900, the beginnings of social work as a 'profession' are clearly visible, though it was not of course established. It is asserted that the opinion is steadily gaining ground that there is definite knowledge and experience to be acquired in regard to theories and methods and resources of charity.[3] In 1903, a School of Sociology and Social Economics, under the direction of Professor Urwick, was established for training social workers, covering:

Sociology, based on Professor Hobhouse's theories, Social Theory, including administration, history and economic theory.

A specialized department of practical instruction in Poor Law administration.

Each of these was intended for a separate class of students—the first for the more systematic, the second for those specially interested in social betterment, and the third for Poor Law Officers and those wishing to enter that field. Some lectures were open to the general public, and it was also stressed that the education given was the general basic training of social workers, and was not to be confused with special vocational training for a specific job. This point is interesting in view of the developments of the past few years, and explains why some 'generic' enthusiasts believe that the next step in training and professionalization should be backwards—to 1903.

In 1914, the School of Sociology was merged with the Social Science Department of the London School of Economics. The reasons leading to this are obscure but it is obvious that grave misgivings were felt as to how far and how faithfully the COS tradition would be carried on. 'By a strange perversity as it seems sociologists and

[1] A. F. C. Bourdillon (ed.), *Voluntary Social Services*, Methuen, 1945.

[2] COS Annual Report, 1899. [3] ibid., 1901.

economists are frequently allowed to deal with questions of social science without acquiring at first hand any careful and consistent knowledge of the facts and conditions of personal and social life in the daily competition and struggle of the common people—the poor and the very poor who form the bulk of the population.'[1] 'With the transfer of what had begun as a professional educational plan for social workers to an academic institution without a clear idea of the differences involved, only one result could obtain. The professional aspects would become less important and the academic and theoretical more important.'[2]

The evolution of social work outside the COS and outside London altogether had also been taking place; by 1890 the Women's University Settlement, founded in Southwark rather earlier, saw the need for a regular course of training to improve the knowledge and quality of its residents, and arranged various courses of lectures, chiefly on the Poor Law (there was little else in the field of public social services to cover); and these led to more organized training, comprising detailed and guided reading, and writing papers as well as practical work. A little later, the Settlement, the COS and the National Union of Women Workers formed a Committee to arrange lecture courses for social workers, which were carried out between 1897 and 1901.[3] In 1904, through the joint efforts of the University of Manchester, the Victoria Settlement for Women and the COS, a School of Social Science was established in that city, while Birmingham instituted a Social Science Diploma in 1908, followed shortly afterwards by Bristol, Leeds and Liverpool, also Edinburgh and Glasgow, all these schemes being connected with the Universities. But as Macadam[4] remarks, until a stimulus to all types of training was given by the 1914–18 War, progress was slow, standards and methods variable and uncertain, and the numbers of students small, although workers were in increasing demand. Despite this slow development, it seems clear that by 1914, social work was well differentiated from the charity which produced it, and a body of workers qualified by recognized and fairly uniform types of training was appearing, who, though they may not have regarded themselves as belonging to a profession in its own right, did possess some of the characteristics of professionalism. By 1914 also, new branches of social work deriving principally from the parent stem of the COS were emerging, and 'social work' was intruding into fields of service, which, whatever they actually did, were regarded by themselves and the world as religious or philanthropic; and the developments in training and education, which were among the most important factors in furthering professionalism, were stimulated and coloured by this.

In 1916, the COS, still the dominant body in the field, saw 'the necessity for drafting a scheme of training extending over twelve months and for which a Certificate would be awarded'.[5] The Society already trained its own workers—sometimes after they had taken a Social Science qualification—and gave its own certificate, and workers in some of the newer branches could qualify for their jobs by taking this certificate. But many unorganized, specialized schemes of training were being launched—by the School Care Committees, the Royal College of St. Katherine's at Poplar (for Health Visitors), the London and Southwark Diocesan Boards of Women's Work, the YWCA, the Church Army and the Mildmay Deaconesses, all including a period in COS offices as an essential part. The COS was stimulated to establish a more organized scheme, and arrangements were made for a co-operative scheme with

[1] COS Annual Report, 1914.
[2] M. Smith, *Professional Education for Social Work in Great Britain*, FWA, 1955.
[3] E. Macadam, *The Equipment of the Social Worker*, Allen and Unwin, 1926.
[4] ibid. [5] COS Annual Report, 1916.

Bedford College, which proved very successful. On all these developments up to the end of the 1914–18 War, Dr M. Smith remarks, 'The movement begun in 1903 and brought to a culmination in 1912 to introduce social work training into the Universities resulted in two things: an increasing emphasis through the years upon academic and theoretical education on the one hand, and new and greater numbers of training schemes outside the Universities on the other.'[1]

The fortunes of case work in the inter-war period were strongly affected by two developments: first, the arrival from America of psychological methods and ideas as applied to social work, and second, the progress at home of the welfare state. The permeation of case work by ideas stressing the importance of human relationships and emphasizing the psychological approach came first, but, insofar as public action appeared to cut the ground from under the social worker's feet, the expansion into new fields of activity offered by American ideas and methods came in very handy. The development of public social services was important in another way, for a new species of social worker appeared. Before the Second World War, Health Visitors and Unemployment Assistance Board Officers were employed in activities, which to the uninitiated, including the consumer, seemed very like social work. As some of the Public Health Authorities took over the former Poor Law Hospitals, they sometimes appointed Almoners—sometimes untrained Almoners, and the difference between these and the orthodox trained worker was not always apparent to the patient or the public. After the war, the first two of these groups intensified their social work activities and were joined by the Local Authorities Welfare Officers under the Education Act, the National Assistance Act and the National Health Service Act, and by some workers in the Rehabilitation Services and the Insurance and Pension Offices. These interviewed, visited, assessed the extent of the needs submitted to them and were required to find a remedy. All this looked very like the kind of work done by highly trained social workers; the difference lay, and still lies, in the quality and type of service rendered. The workers in the public services were at first in no sense trained social workers, but civil and local authority servants generally in the lower grades. In later years, some professional social workers have been appointed—Psychiatric Social Workers, some Almoners, and many Children's Officers (appointed under the Children Act, 1948). But even these work alongside untrained people often doing the same jobs, and it is not always easy to discern the difference between them.

The trade depression of the nineteen-thirties followed by the 1939–45 War prevented the full impact of the new forces being felt in the more important agencies until the later years of the war. Psychiatric Social Workers were a fairly small group working mainly in a rather narrow field, and the welfare state was still in its early stages. A study of the Annual Reports of the COS does not show any marked change of attitude, except a growing tendency to make terms with the social services and accept the inevitability of public aid.

An indication of the new ways of thought is however shown in the Report for 1943, where it is noted that the Society had arranged for a Refresher Course on 'Marriage Problems' to be given; an advanced experimental course in 'Personal Relationships' had already been provided, and it was hoped that this and other projected courses might prove a useful link between the theoretical and practical aspects of the work. In 1944 an important step was taken when the Society announced its intention of changing its name to the Family Welfare Association, for it was

[1] M. Smith, *Professional Education for Social Work in Britain*, FWA, 1955.

agreed that, as the Society was likely to be increasingly concerned with family problems and welfare, the new name was a suitable one. The large amount of family case work involved in work with the Forces was mentioned in the Report for 1944.

In the Annual Report, 1945–46, new developments were noted; first, post-war forms of case work showed more concern with psychological aspects, as it became necessary to deal with war-time neurosis and the difficulties of marital and family adjustment experienced by ex-service personnel; secondly, the interest in social security and social reform aroused by the Beveridge Report and subsequent legislation stimulated the supply and training of social workers. The emphasis on family case work led the Association to a re-affirmation of its belief that future work would be chiefly concerned with family adjustment, marital disharmony and broken homes. The Association was therefore embarking upon an experiment in conjunction with the Marriage Guidance Council and was opening six centres in the Metropolitan area each in charge of a fully trained social worker. This prognosis of the future type of work does not seem to have been completely fulfilled; most FWA offices appear to deal still with a large number of cases concerned with material need, housing difficulties, etc.; and, although family disintegration and bad family relationships certainly appear, they seem often to be the results rather than the causes of more concrete troubles.

The work of Marriage Welfare was strengthened in 1947 when a grant from the Goldsmiths' Company made it possible to set up two full-time Marriage Welfare Centres with their own staff, the organization being assisted by advice from the Peckham Health Centre and the Tavistock Clinic. These centres carried on their work among those whose family and marital relationships were 'deeply disturbed', and also served as consultation centres in less extreme cases, working in close liaison with the Tavistock Clinic (later the Institute of Human Relations). Only one of these centres now exists—the Family Discussion Bureau, and the bulk of their work is carried out by social workers (with some participation from professional psychiatrists) who in addition to their ordinary case work qualifications take a special in-training under skilled supervision.

It would appear from a book dealing with these activities (*Social Case Work in Marital Problems*, Bannister and others, Tavistock Publications, 1955) that they do not cover very many people; the majority of those who come receive, it seems, only short term treatment—two or three interviews. The workers who contribute to the volume have fully absorbed the theories, technique and phraseology of psycho-analysis, but the small number of cases discussed and the rather exiguous treatment given make it difficult to draw any definite conclusions as to the value of the work.

Two developments which have taken place recently have affected the attitude of case workers towards their profession and its functions in the future. The first was the institution of the so-called basic or generic course in applied social studies, the first of which began at the London School of Economics with the assistance of a Carnegie Grant in 1954; other similar courses are now being held at the Universities of Birmingham and Southampton. The purpose of this is to give a picked group of students who already possess a Social Science qualification, a year's course combining a good deal of practical work with theory, the latter being strongly oriented towards case work. Three different specialisms have agreed to accept these students as having followed an adequate course of training—these are family case work, medical social work, and the probation service; any student who embarks on the 'Carnegie' course need not have been accepted by the authorities of his particular option. The best organized and perhaps most specialized body—the

Association of Psychiatric Social Workers—have not accepted this course as an adequate training for their field. The 'generic' training has aroused conflicting feelings; some fear is felt that it may take off the cream of the aspirants to social work and leave the skim milk to other forms. Others seem to welcome the possible reduction in specialized training.

The second development which has stirred professional social workers was the establishment in 1955 by the Ministry of Health of a Working Party under the chairmanship of Miss Eileen Younghusband to enquire into the place and functions of social workers in the health and welfare services and to make recommendations. A great deal of evidence has been offered to this body from social workers and their associations and many articles and letters have been written. By the time this Appendix appears, the Committee will have made its report, and perhaps its recommendations, whatever they may be, will have been adopted. The apologia produced in this connection has naturally stressed the importance of case work as a particular and specialized form of work. One writer defines it as 'a professional service offered to those who desire help with their personal and family problems. Its aim is to relieve stress and to help the client to achieve a better personal and social adjustment.'[1] The difference between the caseworker and the intrained or untrained worker lies in the skill required in assessing the effect of environment and the emphasis on family, social and cultural background—also the knowledge of personality development and functioning. Another writer in the same periodical[2] accepts this definition and stresses the importance of the co-operative relationship, which demands a high degree of skill and integrity used within the discipline of a high professional training: it is suggested that there should be three grades of social workers—caseworkers in the usual sense, who should form part of the staff of all welfare departments, then another grade of welfare workers, dealing with cases which do not require the help of a skilled professional worker, and below these a grade of assistants, who might be promoted to at least the second class. These views are typical of a great deal more, most of which is devoted to stressing the professional and highly skilled nature of case work.

In the view of its original sponsor, casework has become a family rather than an individual concern; in practice of course both are dealt with by the Family Welfare Association and its associated societies. But as the essence of the professional craft is now 'relationship', and it is necessary for a client to have a relationship—usually a maladjusted one—with at least one other person, who will probably be a member of the family, the emphasis naturally tends to be on the family group.

Casework technique as the distinguishing mark of a professional exponent is not restricted to the FWA, but is an integral part of other forms of social work—almoning, psychiatric social work and child care (where a trained worker is appointed); but with these callings, it is an essential method rather than a prime object. It is not synonymous with social work; Assistance Board officers, welfare officers, youth leaders, church workers are regarded as social workers. But they are not in the eyes of the élite, caseworkers, and until recently the gates of the heaven of professionalism were closed to them by those safely inside. A professional status outside the case worker élite is now being demanded by many groups of people who are quite sure that social work is a profession and that they belong to it, although they are not always clear as to the grounds of their claims. These two groups are represented by two Associations—the Association of Family Case-

[1] E. H. Davison, *Case Conference*, June 1956.

[2] K. McDougall, *Case Conference*, June 1956.

workers, membership of which is restricted to a rather narrow field of workers who have received training of a particular and specialized kind, approved by the Committee of the Association; and the Association of Social Workers, a much more amorphous body, which is trying to gain professional status by demanding some sort of training for its members, but which covers a much wider variety of work and worker. But its hankering after professional status is symptomatic of what is happening in the world of social work.

Moral Welfare Work

The origins of moral welfare are sometimes identified with Josephine Butler, but in fact she liberalized, enlightened and began to modernize a service that had long existed; its motives and views are reflected in the titles of its institutions—Magdalen Homes, Penitentiaries, etc.

The two branches of work—dealing with unmarried mothers and with the results of their sin, were for long kept entirely separate, and still are, to some extent. The Foundling Hospital (1745) was one of the first serious attempts to provide for illegitimate children; the first Magdalen Hospital for Prostitutes was opened in 1758, and was the only one for more than half a century. Early in the nineteenth century small religious groups made sporadic attempts to help 'fallen' girls, and in 1841 a society for the 'Protection of Young Females' was founded—the first recognition that the sinner might be more sinned against than sinning. The revival of Convents in the English Church also favoured the development of rescue work in the middle of the nineteenth century. The 'self-devoted' women, as they are described, who entered sisterhoods soon included this work among their activities; and penitentiaries were founded in 1849 at two convents and at others later; the Church Penitentiary Association, an organization for promoting interest in and prayer for the cause, was established in 1852. A privately printed and anonymous little book called *Work among the Lost* describes a Home at Brighton in the 1860s, and, except that the attitude shown towards the clientele is less condemnatory than was probably usual at that time, gives what would seem to be a faithful and certainly a vivid description of the life led by the penitents, where hard work was combined with a great deal of religious activity—but also with plenty of good food. This Home was very popular with the fallen; accounts are given of women making great efforts and waiting long and patiently to gain admission. One repentant prostitute walked all the way from London to Brighton, dressed in the 'shabby finery' of her profession. When she arrived, exhausted, hungry and dirty, instead of being given a meal, a bath and a bed, she was taken to the chapel for prayers and displayed not only to the other inmates, but to the chaplain and a group of ladies and gentlemen visiting the home.

In none of the work done during most of the nineteenth century was any effort made to keep the mother and child together—rather the reverse, for it was believed that the only way to give the penitent a fresh start was to remove all evidence of her sin. 'The unmarried mother in Victorian times had to choose between surrendering her child or remaining with him in the Workhouse.'[1]

Josephine Butler, the pioneer of moral welfare in the most modern sense, was less interested in 'sin' than in attacking the double standard of morals as between men and women, securing the repeal of the Contagious Diseases Act and fighting the White Slave Traffic. Her attitude was much less that of a benefactress towards a

[1] Cherry Morris (Ed.), *Social Case Work in Great Britain: Moral Welfare*. Faber and Faber, 1950.

sinner than that of many of the workers, who were very slow in adopting her ideas. But her views and methods set the standard for the future and, when the first and still the most important centre for training Moral Welfare Workers was opened in 1920, it was called after her.

By the end of the nineteenth century some rather sketchy statistics had appeared. In 1897 it was estimated that there were about 140,000 fallen women and prostitutes; there were 300 Magdalen Homes with roughly four workers for each, and the great majority of these were run by the Church Penitentiary Association, and carried on in convents by nuns. But the non-conventual work was also on a religious basis and was apparently supervised by the Female Aid Society. In the specific field of rescue work the unsatisfied need for suitable workers is emphasized, but this is hardly surprising in view of the qualifications demanded, the insistence on 'suitable dress' and the very arduous nature of the duties, which were chiefly residential; it was complained that people tended to take up the work owing to lack of private means and without a sense of vocation. 'Educated women—the more education the better' —were required; they should be able to impart both secular and religious knowledge to the girls in their care, must be hopeful, free from jealousy, loyal, winning in manner, and dressed in a way which must be scrupulously clean, but not observable, preferably black, but not unbecoming. It seems from a contemporary report of the Church Penitentiary Association that the only training given was a form of probationary experience, consisting of one year's work in the kitchen or workroom of a home, with some theoretical instruction from the superintendent or other officer. Outside work was recommended for a second year, under supervision, but there was not much outside work done, so that this part of the training was not generally undertaken. Before a worker was permanently appointed, it was recommended that she spent a few months doing locum work.

By the end of the nineteenth century, therefore, Rescue and Preventive Work was an established form of religious activity containing elements of social work; the authorities were becoming aware that certain qualifications were useful, but there was no accepted or established training and no professional standards; a 'vocation' was the prime necessity.

Little change took place till after the First World War, which showed up new and greater problems, particularly in connection with venereal disease, and rescue workers were involved with people who were different from the prostitutes and 'fallen' women, who had formerly been their main concern. During and just after the War, most of the social and follow-up work for VD patients, later taken over by Almoners, was done by Rescue Workers.[1]

Partly because of these new demands, and because standards of social work were changing, a searching enquiry was made by the Church Assembly of the Anglican Church into the extent and adequacy and characteristics of Rescue Work during the period 1917–19. The report was published in 1919 (Church Assembly Publications) and in the introduction, the Chairman, Lord Henry Cavendish Bentinck, remarked, 'Our attempts at preventive and rescue work have been inadequate and poorly supported: a new spirit is needed'. The enquiry covered 100 Rescue Homes, with about 2,000 residents, varying in age from six to twenty-six. All the Homes were under the direction of religious bodies. The 'Rescue' idea was weakening, but strong vestiges remained—many of the Homes are criticized for their policy of segregation and punishment. The report concludes by saying that 'Rescue work

[1] Cherry Morris (Ed.), *Social Case Work in Great Britain: Moral Welfare*. Faber and Faber, 1950.

should be placed on a more scientific basis. It is without doubt the most difficult department of social service, and calls for the aid of experienced and professional men and women'.

Seven training centres were open, all run by the Churches; there was a tendency to believe that a vocation was so important that any hint of 'professionalism' should be deprecated. All the schemes combined some theoretical with a great deal of practical work; two included University lectures. The lack of any psychology in any of these schemes was criticized; the development of psychological methods which later became marked in all branches of social work was beginning to show itself.

These criticisms and the change in public opinion which they reflected were not the only factors leading Rescue work to examine its role and field. From 1911 onwards the National Health Insurance, inadequate though its benefits seem now, had improved the unmarried mother's financial position and made her less dependent upon charity. The need for residential homes became less acute and outdoor work became more prominent. It is difficult to discover how far the criticisms of the 1919 Report were carried into effect. To some extent they were; the Josephine Butler Training Home for Moral Welfare Workers was founded in 1920 and particularly in recent years has set a high standard of work and inspired and fostered a liberal and humane outlook without losing sight of the religious basis.

During the inter-war period the emphasis was placed increasingly on outdoor work, especially on the preventive side. Special children's workers were appointed and, before the general appointment of Probation Officers under the Children and Young Persons Act, 1933, much of what is now probation work was done by Moral Welfare Workers. The activities in Public Health after the establishment of the Ministry of Health and the reduction of the work of the Poor Law after 1930 also made an impact on moral welfare; in some cases the work for unmarried mothers and their children was grant-aided and supported by the Local Authorities; in some the Moral Welfare Committees were looked upon as purely religious institutions, no financial help was given, and Health Visitors arranged for the care of the unmarried mothers during confinement but were not concerned with social casework.

The Second World War brought new problems of venereal disease, deserted mothers and illegitimate children and careless and promiscuous young women. But by this time other people were in the field; Almoners and medical social workers dealt with the follow-up work connected with venereal disease, Health Visitors assisted with maternity provisions, the Youth Service played some part in preventive work, and thus Moral Welfare Workers found their rôle more strictly defined than ever before. Just after the war also the duties of Moral Welfare Workers finally ceased to be combined with those of Probation Officers, in the few places where this still existed.

Moral Welfare shared in the general movement for analysing the functions, raising the status and improving the standards of training of social workers which has been apparent since 1945. Unlike Almoners and Psychiatric Social Workers, Moral Welfare Workers did not become public servants. A strong, but by no means universal, urge towards professional status was shown, but it is difficult to say how widespread or how justified this is, for the variations in work and standards are great, and there is no close controlling organization.

In 1955, as nearly as can be ascertained, there were about 165 Moral Welfare Workers who trained at Josephine Butler House working in Great Britain with the Church of England, and about thirty-five to forty working with other bodies or abroad. Of these twenty held a Social Science Certificate; but a further twenty-seven old students who had this qualification had left moral welfare for other employment. Of the students who had taken the shorter London Course of whom track had been kept, ninety-three were working in Moral Welfare work, four being employed as Diocesan Secretaries, the rest in indoor or outdoor work of different kinds. All but six of the County Councils gave grants in aid of Moral Welfare.

The present organization and control of these workers presents a rather confused picture. The most important controlling body is the Church of England Moral Welfare Council, which supervises and trains Anglican Moral Welfare Workers and many Free Church Workers, as these churches possess no comparable organization. The Council also does social and educational work on sex and family relationships through publications and lectures; this work is of a high quality but it would appear that there is rather a gulf between the educationists and some of the local Committees and workers, who tend to regard the former as dangerously advanced.

The Central Council lays down standards of efficiency and training and scales of salaries[1] which it tries to get generally adopted, but it has no powers of enforcement and has not been universally successful. There is a Council in each Diocese and a Committee in each Rural Deanery, the latter being finally responsible for the appointment of field workers. The Diocesan Councils, nearly all of which have an organizing secretary, have advisory and persuasive powers only, and can ultimately be ignored by the local Committees, who may exclude the Organizing Secretary from their meetings if they so wish. As the workers are mainly paid from Diocesan funds, local action is seldom carried to these lengths as a long-term policy, but in local crises of temporary significance, some Committees have thus acted. Indoor workers appear to be, generally, though not invariably, appointed by the Diocese.

Training is carried out at the Josephine Butler House in Liverpool where there is a two-year residential course for younger candidates; women over forty generally take a shorter non-residential London course, lasting six months. The Josephine Butler course includes practical and theoretical work; most students educationally qualified to do so take the Social Science course at Liverpool University, others have lectures at the House, some of which are given by members of the University social science department. Both groups have instruction in theology and Christian doctrine from the staff of the House, and all take an examination based on theoretical and practical work, after which the successful ones receive a certificate. The practical work follows the usual lines of social science training, including some actual moral welfare experience, and the whole course is comparable with other forms of professional education for social work; it is shortened for students who already possess social science or similar qualifications. In the course for older women, the practical side is more stressed and there is less social science; some good 'relevant experience' is demanded before a student can be accepted, but there is no hard and fast rule as to what this should be. Practical work occupies up to four months, and this is followed by a two months' theoretical course including some social administration. The students from either of these courses can rise to any post in the moral welfare field, and some of the older women who have taken the short course are now employed in the more highly paid and responsible posts. Status does not therefore necessarily depend on the period of training undertaken.

There is a professional association of Moral Welfare Workers, and since 1945

[1] 1956 salary scales; Organizers £450–£550 p.a. Outdoor workers £400–£450 p.a. Indoor workers £150–£250 p.a.

membership has been restricted to people who have either taken a moral welfare training or hold social or church work qualifications recognized by the Central Council for Women's Church Work, and who are sponsored by two existing association members. There is thus an attempt being made by the in-group to restrict membership and to uphold professional standards; the rôle of the association is entirely social and educational, and it tries through activities of this kind to improve the intellectual quality of the workers, promote 'neighbourliness' and friendly relations between them and to raise the general status of the work. It does not attempt to regulate conditions or determine salaries; according to one of its members 'it has no Trade Union functions'.

The Church of England is not the only religious body, of course, in Great Britain, nor the only one which engages in Moral Welfare work. But in so far as this has become a profession it is almost entirely carried on by the Church of England. The secular workers who are employed by some Local Authorities are nearly always Health Visitors; they do little in the way of case work, and, insofar as their work is of professional standard, it is a side-line of the nursing profession, not one in its own right, as many Moral Welfare Workers belonging to the Central Council would like theirs to be.

If a random sample of Moral Welfare Workers were taken, they would certainly present such a variety of education, qualifications and perhaps social background, and also such diverse attitudes to their work, that it would be difficult indeed to realize that they all followed the same profession or, in the ordinary sense of the phrase, to ascribe professional status to some of them. The gulf between the more modern workers and Committees and some of the really old-fashioned ones is wide, as is that between the best and the least qualified people. The policy pursued by the Moral Welfare Council is steadily directed towards improving the educational qualifications of the workers, to raising the standards of the work and to working for professional status. But a considerable body of supporters and some workers still hold the old ideas of rescue work, and almost regard profession and vocation as contradictory terms. The leaders can promote their policy by education and persuasion, but they cannot enforce it. The two groups are not, it would seem, looking for similar results; the more modern are at least as much concerned with rehabilitation as with repentance, and, while they certainly do not ignore the ideas of sin committed, they do not put them in the forefront; the traditionalists take an opposite view. With so great a divergence of ideas and standards, it is difficult to say that Moral Welfare work has become a profession.

The majority of Moral Welfare Workers, both those who have taken the longer training and those who have entered the field on easier terms, do not generally appear to belong to so high a social class as some other groups of social workers—for example, the Almoners and perhaps the Family Case Workers. If they have taken a University course, it is generally at a provincial University or perhaps a course for an External Diploma. The situation of Josephine Butler House is of course favourable for students to take a course in Social Science at Liverpool, and the number of these is increasing relatively to the untrained or 'intrained' women, many of whom started work with the Church Army or the Salvation Army, or are older and entered the field before training was really organized. The comparatively untrained groups are generally, but not always, lower in the social scale than those who have taken the regular training—though the woman of real industrial working-class origin is seldom found in moral welfare work at all, at all events in outdoor work. The better trained are those who are most anxious to obtain professional status for their work; they would like to equate it with case work, almoning, etc. and for this reason are anxious to restrict membership of the Moral Welfare Association. The continued existence of a substantial number of workers who have not had much training is a hindrance to these aspirations, because to the uninitiated they do the same kind of work and have the same qualifications as the superior product. And these older and less theoretically qualified women do not, it seems, in many cases care much whether they are regarded as professional or not.

The contention that the clientele of social work is no longer confined to the under-privileged, and that the roles of worker and applicant could be reversed, is not conspicuously true of moral welfare. The consequences of irregular sex relationships which form the main field for the work are regarded as more shocking among the middle and upper class than among the poor, and are if possible kept quiet. Also the better-off, or those who still have better-off standards, can deal with the unmarried mother and the illegitimate child more easily; they often, though not invariably, have more money with which to tackle the situation, they can more easily make arrangements to remove the erring girl during the awkward period, or, if they are ready to face the neighbourhood, their housing conditions enable them more easily to cope with the mother and child. However, many Moral Welfare Workers assert that their clientele is changing, and they are no doubt right. There is a large and increasing marginal class of clerical workers, shop assistants, waitresses, hospital workers, etc., many of whom live away from home, and who, if they 'get into trouble' cannot, at any rate immediately, return there. These form a considerable proportion of the worker's cases; but although, through social mobility and educational opportunity these women have obtained posts higher in social status than their parents had, their home background is not very different from that of the industrial worker; that is, one where supervision or interference in private life is a commonplace and where people are continually visiting about something. The School Attendance Officer, the Health Visitor, the Care Committee Worker, the Insurance man, the Rent Collector and the numerous representatives of commercial interests persuading the householder to buy something or calling for the payments—all these form part of the daily living pattern of the 'under-privileged'. Naturally, when another crisis arises they are disposed to find yet another agency to help—unlike the middle or professional classes, who not being accustomed to all these aids to the good life, will, especially where 'getting into trouble' is involved, try to deal with the situation, at first anyhow, themselves. Even though society continues to change in the direction of social equality, it will be many years before these very different attitudes towards social services are approximated to one another—if they ever are.

Medical Social Work

Almoning was one of the specialisms proliferating from the Charity Organization Society, and, in the first years of their existence, Almoners worked almost entirely with COS Committees and Provident Medical Associations. When Almoners were first appointed, hospital services were either provided free as charitable activities in voluntary hospitals, or were functions of the Poor Law; and the work for which Almoners were required was for many years that of preventing abuse and overcrowding of out-patients' departments by people, who, it was considered, were able to pay for treatment. This led on to Almoners becoming a connecting link between hospital departments and outside charities, whose help they enlisted in order to assist the patient to obtain the full benefit of treatment—perhaps so that he would not stay too long. The first appointment was to the Royal Free Hospital in 1895; more Almoners were appointed to other hospitals shortly afterwards, and after 1906 the trickle widened and there was a slow, though steady, increase. An important influence on the work and wider use of Almoners was the appointment in 1906 to St. Thomas's Hospital of Miss Anne Cummins, who may almost be called the patron saint of Almoners, and who became a legendary figure in her work, not only at her own hospital but also in publicising the merits and necessity for medical social work, and in promoting the training of Almoners. In spite of this, however, the numbers spread very slowly, for the hospitals were conservative bodies and their opposition was difficult to overcome; the authorities only gradually began to realize that Almoners had their uses in saving hospital funds and beds, by preventing their occupation by people who did not need free treatment—at any rate in the Almoner's eyes. But the social work which Miss Cummins and her successors wanted to see included as the most important of the Almoners' functions roused no enthusiasm. The extreme departmentalism which characterises administrators and Almoners to-day is a persistent hangover from the caution and conservatism which marked the early days of the Almoning profession.

A Hospital Almoners' Association was established in 1903, and a professional group of some form or other has continued ever since. The first Association was entirely a social body in which Almoners pooled their ideas and discussed their problems and difficulties; it had no functions relating to pay, hours or conditions of work. A Hospital Almoners' Council was set up in 1907 to be responsible for choosing, appointing and training Almoners; it originally consisted of leading members of the COS together with three doctors and two Almoners, and as the years went on the membership of the two latter groups was increased, Almoners being more strongly represented. The early training was carried on in close co-operation with the COS, six months' practical work being done in a COS office and six months in an Almoner's office, a certificate being awarded to successful students at the end. For a short time after 1912, two certificates were available, one for full and one for assistant Almoners, and apparently these represented parallel grades rather than steps on a ladder. Much the same selectiveness seems to have been displayed in early as in later times, for 50 per cent of all applicants were rejected by the Council.

As in other forms of social work, the 1914–18 War marked an important milestone. By 1914, Almoners' duties were generally recognized as the prevention of abuse of hospital services, and also as securing the patients' co-operation in treatment and the formation of a link between the patients' needs and various outside benevolent agencies. In some hospitals, notably St. Thomas's where thanks to Miss Cummins, Almoners had become an accepted part of the set-up, their activities covered a wider field and they did a certain amount of case work. The Hospital Almoners' Association had become a Committee, a more formal body with rules about membership and function, all Almoners being eligible to join it; but only two votes per hospital were allowed.

During the First World War, the demand for Almoners grew, but the number of students declined, and officers and prominent Almoners undertook missionary journeys to provincial cities, particularly University centres to publicize the work and to seek recruits. Some new training centres were also established, and these tactics proved successful; the number of students and subsequently of Almoners considerably increased.

After the war, the Almoners' Committee came more fully into the stream of social work and affiliated to the Federation of Professional Social Workers; the Committee (representing the professional Almoners) and the Council (representing administrative authority) also drew closer together, and the Committee appointed their own representatives to the Council. In 1920 a formal constitution was drawn up, and the Hospital Almoners Association was established apparently as a successor to the Committee.

From 1920 the scope of Almoners' work widened and the Association increased the emphasis on social work, and impressed on public opinion the fact that this side of their activities was more important than the collection of money. But concurrently with this the financial side of their work also increased; the voluntary hospitals began to charge fees graded according to the patients' income, and it was the Almoner's task to assess the liability. In many people's minds, therefore, and certainly in the group from which most patients were drawn, the Almoner was regarded as the person who decided how much you must pay, and any other work was considered subordinate to this.

Another development affecting the profession was the passing of the Local Government Act of 1929, and the Poor Law Act of 1930, which transferred the functions of the Poor Law to the Local Authorities, and handed over the hospitals to the Health Departments. This transfer was very slow in operation, and was not nearly complete by the outbreak of the 1939–45 War; but these Acts marked the gradual entrance of Almoners into Local Authority Hospitals. It does not appear that their introduction greatly raised the prestige of the profession, for they were chiefly engaged in routine administrative duties and had little opportunity of social casework. The Local Authorities were not so particular as to the qualifications of Almoners, and in some cases appointed untrained women or promoted clerks, who were not members of the Institute (this title had been assumed by the combined Council and Committee).

By 1939 the profession of Hospital Almoners was strongly established; the representation of workers on the Council of the Institute had been strengthened so that Almoners had acquired more responsibility for training and selection of candidates and for general policy. The Council recorded in 1939 that the work of Almoners fell into three sections: (1) Co-operation with the medical staff; (2) co-operation with outside bodies and agencies concerned; (3) administrative work, including the assessment of payments and collection of additional benefits from Approved Societies.

The Second World War and the social developments which followed it brought changes to the Almoners' profession. After the first chaotic period of evacuation and dislocation of hospital work, when thousands of beds were empty waiting for non-existent casualties and patients were discharged wholesale, apparently without any reference to the social workers interested in them, an official change of heart took place, the demand for Almoners increased, and in the later stages of the war their position was considerably strengthened.

In 1942 the Hospital Almoners' Association was invited to prepare a memorandum on the contribution which might be made by Almoners to the teaching of social medicine to medical students, a development which seemed to indicate a wider field and greater recognition for Almoners, although this expectation has not perhaps been fully realized.

In 1945 the administrative machinery of the profession was altered; the Institute of Hospital Almoners and the Hospital Almoners Association were liquidated and superseded by the Institute of Almoners, which took over the functions previously carried out by the other two bodies. Three years later, in July, 1948, the National

Health Service came into being, and Almoners became public servants; a memorandum issued in the same year by the Ministry of Health 'emphasized that the Almoner's place in the National Health Service was that of a medical social worker in the medical team'.[1] It went on to outline her functions as including: '1. Social investigation and interviews to provide personal understanding of the social and personal background of the patient and in particular to give the Doctor information which is relevant to diagnosis and treatment. 2. The making of arrangements with the Local Health Authority concerned for the home visiting of patients who may for a time and in some instances for a long period need help to ensure that the value of the treatment is not lost.'[2]

Since 1948 the position and functions of Almoners have in theory not changed very much. Their place is securely established and their numbers have increased, though the demand is still in excess of the supply. The virtual abolition of fees for treatment in hospital has finally removed money collection or assessment from the Almoner's duties, and she is free to concentrate on social work. The exact nature of her functions and status and her relationship to other forms of medical social work give rise to some interesting and debatable points, but these are contemporary problems, and the actual history of almoning may be left here.

Almoning has always been regarded as one of the more aristocratic forms of social work, demanding not only (so it is said) a high social and educational standard for its students, but also requiring them to undertake a long and extensive training. In the early days, when the profession was closely associated with the COS, that body was largely responsible for preparing the students. The preparation was chiefly 'in-training', though the students attended the School of Sociology for lectures during the years of its existence. As almoning became more established and Almoners increased in number, the training was extended and a theoretical basis was added. Students now undergo searching selection tests, including discussion groups, interviews, a selection board or boards, and sometimes a tea-party. A Social Science Certificate or Diploma is necessary, and this of course includes a period of practical work usually in a case work agency; this is followed by some months' training specially arranged by the Institute of Almoners, consisting of courses of study under the Institute's Director of Studies and work in different Almoners' offices, in all, nine months.

At the end of the war, when the demand for Almoners was increasing and was expected to increase more, the Council of the Institute made the experiment of organizing what they termed an Emergency Course of Training; six courses of this kind were held over a period of three years, giving each student a bare twelve months' course of theory and practice (not including of course a social science diploma) but a course which qualified them as Almoners. The majority of those attending these were older women, with a very few men; many of the students had been demobilized from some form of war service. Of the 320 who were accepted for training, 272 qualified successfully—very few proved unsuitable during the course, though a few withdrew before starting. Some have risen to the higher posts in the profession, and all seem to have been equally successful with those who took the long training usually required by the Institute. However, this experiment, successful as it seems to have been, was regarded as an emergency measure and the ordinary machinery of selection and training was reverted to in 1949.

In 1955, ninety Almoners qualified for the profession, and at that time there were

[1] *The Almoner*, Golden Jubilee Number, November 1953.

[2] HMC (48) BG 48 (57). (Ministry of Health.)

1,007 working in Hospitals in Great Britain as Almoners, two in Rehabilitation, and fifteen in Mental Hospitals (qualified Psychiatric Social Workers), sixty-one in Local Authority Health Clinics, and thirty-four overseas; with four qualified Almoners on the staff of the Institute, the total actually working was then 1,130.[1] The figures given in the Younghusband Report on Social Work, dated 1951, state that the total of working almoners is 906; the number qualifying in 1949 was 115.[2] The actual number of members of the Institute (including retired Almoners) was 1,543 in 1955 as compared with 1,308 in 1949, so that expansion is not taking place very quickly.

The Institute of Almoners is the professional association for the work, and membership is open to all qualified Almoners; this body is not only the recognized medium for discussion and action in regard to conditions of work and other subjects of general interest to the profession, but through its Council is the authority for the selection and training of students. A Quarterly Magazine, *The Almoner*, is issued, and this together with the Register of Appointments which is kept at Headquarters is the means by which nearly all vacancies are filled. The demand is still far in excess of the supply, and the August, 1957, number of *The Almoner* contains sixty-nine advertisements for Almoners of all grades. Salaries are fixed for all Almoners in accordance with the Whitley Council scale for the Professional and Technical 'A' Council, of which the Almoners form a part. At present salaries range from £435 p.a. starting salary minimum to £815 p.a. maximum, with a few higher paid posts; London weighting applies to all grades in addition.

Certain questions of function attaching to Almoners do not affect other social workers to the same extent: for example, some problems arise from the changes made by the National Health Service Act. Although, after the first few years of their existence, Almoners themselves ascribed increasing importance to case work, the general public regarded them as primarily concerned with the assessment of fees and contributions. But with the abolition of hospital payments in 1948 the financial duties of Almoners completely disappeared and they became public servants. Since then, although the necessity for Almoners—or Medical Social Workers as they are now often called—has been officially recognized, what their duties are and ought to be does not seem to be universally agreed.

Questions of supply and demand, training and qualifications were considered by a group of Committees appointed by the Ministry of Health and the Department of Health for Scotland shortly after the NHS Act was passed, being known as the Committees on Medical Auxiliaries (the 'Cope' Committees), and including Almoners in the subjects of their deliberations. Their reports were issued as a White Paper (CMD. 8188) in 1951; this made various recommendations, one being a suggestion for a Central Council for Medical Auxiliaries, on which the various callings included in the term—Almoners among them—should be represented, and which should control training, qualifications and appointments; all Almoners should be registered with this Council, thereby gaining 'recognition'. Two serving Almoners had been members of the Committee considering their field of work, and they, with a few other members of parallel Committees, produced a Minority Report disagreeing with the proposed machinery on the grounds that their callings were professions, and that, if the proposals were made effective, the sense of responsibility within the professions would be undermined, because it would no longer

[1] Figures supplied by Miss Steel, Secretary of the Institute of Almoners.

[2] E. Younghusband. *Social Work in Britain*, A Supplementary Report on the Employment and Training of Social Workers. Carnegie U.K. Trust, 1951.

be their function to maintain and establish standards of qualifications, ethics and practice. This attitude was supported by the Institute and nothing more has happened.

These Committees dealt with organization rather than function; the latter is complicated by the fact that the Almoner is not like most other social workers, the person who is consulted as it were entirely in her own right. The sick person who is her client is first of all concerned with the doctor and with the hospital's administrative authorities; and it is the relationships between the doctors and the Almoner, and between the latter and the administration which present difficulties in determining functions. This situation as it affects the medical staff is fully discussed in the recently published book *Ten Patients and an Almoner*,[1] which consists of a series of case studies, and concludes with a discussion between two doctors and two Almoners, who are said to form a 'team'. The summing up of the professor who heads the medical unit may be quoted: . . . 'I must finally underline the question of medical responsibility. It must never be forgotten that medical social work is quite different from an independent branch like family case work where the client consults the worker in the first place, and that worker has I presume the right and duty to direct the social treatment. Where social work is an adjunct to medicine, the medical view comes first. An almoner's work must always keep step with that of her medical colleagues, and in the last resort it is they who have the casting vote'. This is accepted without question by the Almoners, and it is no doubt inevitable in this work—but it seems severely to restrict the Almoner's scope. The things that most worry the majority of sick people who enter hospital are those connected with diagnosis and prognosis—how long the illness is likely to last, whether their job will be kept open, the likelihood of complete or partial recovery, the effect of the sickness upon their family—and this must vary with the nature and duration of illness. But these seem to be the very problems with which the Almoner can deal only within strict limits and with the doctor's permission. There remain of course many questions upon which advice and assistance can usefully be given. But the advent of the Welfare State and higher wages and full employment have made some of these less urgent and worrying than was the case ten years ago. Moreover, in the new model of social case work, problems of economic need, information about social services and provision of material help are becoming out-of-date; the chief role of the caseworker is seen in the somewhat undefined field of personal relationships and social maladjustment. The difficulties connected with sickness, particularly sudden and unforeseen sickness, certainly affect personal relationships, but it appears that the Almoner's powers here are limited. What is left? One may assume that the examples given in the book quoted above (except where they are clearly out of date owing to the developments in social legislation) are valid for to-day; but, though they show the usefulness of a friendly trustworthy and intelligent worker, they do not often seem to require more than this. Tactful persuasion about applying for statutory help, arrangements for convalescence, friendly and sensible conversations, enquiries into work relationships are typical forms of help; and it is difficult to feel entirely convinced that the long and varied training demanded for an Almoner is really necessary for some of the activities described.

The relationship between the Almoner and the administrative authorities is another point upon which little information is available; situations involving difficult social and family problems sometimes arise through what appear un-

[1] F. Beck, *Ten Patients and an Almoner*. Allen & Unwin, 1956.

imaginative arrangements for admission to or discharge from hospital, and here the Almoner has apparently little power to intervene or assist. This too is perhaps inevitable, and a regrettable feature of the hospital system, but it seems to limit the usefulness of the Almoner in dealing with emotional difficulties arising from sickness.

A third point which is obscure is the place and function of Almoners in relation to the Health Visitors. The latter were originally concerned with health education—information and propaganda on hygiene, feeding, cleanliness, etc. and their clientèle was almost entirely mothers and babies. But they have in recent years been more active in other fields, and, while their primary function is still educational, they actually do a certain amount of social work and some social science is included in their training, in addition to the ordinary nursing training which is of course required. The report of the recent Working Party[1] regards the primary functions of Health Visitors as health education and social advice, and envisages them playing a prominent part in 'hospital after-care as a whole'. Although it is not expected that Health Visitors will supersede Almoners, the report states that the relationship between Health Visitor and general practitioner 'will be more like that between Almoner and Consultant in hospital than the relationship of Doctor to Nurse'; and it is rather implied that the type of social work done by the Health Visitor will be not unlike that performed by the Almoner in her field. But the Health Visitor is not of course a trained social caseworker; the question arises again from a different angle as to how far the work actually done by the Almoner really requires the extensive qualifications which she possesses. Further, when the National Health Service came into being and even before, it was thought by the Institute that their members' functions would be considerably extended in the future, undertaking work for Local Authorities and work in connection with Tuberculosis and Venereal disease. But it is precisely in these fields that the social activities of Health Visitors should, according to the report of the Working Party, develop. Many Health Visitors now regard themselves as social workers and believe that they would do better social work with more training in social science. If the educational background of Health Visitors improves, as it will now that more of them stay at school till seventeen or eighteen and take GCE, they will be able to profit better by such training and cease to be at a disadvantage as they often are now, in comparison with Almoners.

It would seem therefore that Almoners are severely limited in their field owing to the necessary primacy of the doctors, the independence of the administrative authorities; and in some respects they seem to overlap with Health Visitors, doing much the same work. What are the exclusive, delicate and highly skilled duties for which only these carefully selected, extensively trained people are suitable?

Psychiatric Social Work

Psychiatric social work has a much shorter history than most forms of social work, having really made its début in 1927 in this country; and in the thirty years of its existence it has passed through fewer vicissitudes and faced fewer difficulties than family casework. From their early days Psychiatric Social Workers knew where they were; they had a clearly defined field of operations, a firmly established and widely recognized training; and almost, if not quite, simultaneously with the qualification of the first Psychiatric Social Workers trained in Great Britain, a pro-

[1] *An Enquiry into Health Visiting*, 1956, HMSO.

fessional association was set up, which has continued ever since, growing in membership and influence over the years. From the beginning also the demand for Psychiatric Social Workers has greatly exceeded the supply—a fact which has probably both strengthened the profession, and also perhaps threatened the regular trained workers with infiltration from outside, where local authorities or other employing bodies were unable to meet their requirements from orthodox sources.

Interest in the behaviour problems and personality difficulties of children particularly in relation to delinquency had been shown before the 1914–18 War, and was stimulated by the publication in 1925 of Professor Cyril Burt's *Young Delinquent*. In 1926, the Tavistock Square Clinic established in Central London for the treatment of adult patients opened a special department for children, and in the following year the Jewish Health Organization of Great Britain established the East London Child Guidance Clinic. There were at that time no specifically trained social workers in their field but, very shortly afterwards, training was offered in the USA, financed by the Commonwealth Fund, to a group of workers, including some social workers, to prepare them to forward the development of mental health work in Great Britain. In 1929, the London Mental Health Course, offering the first recognized training for Psychiatric Social Workers, was established at the London School of Economics, and the London Child Guidance Clinic, designed to be also a centre for practical training, was set up in the same year; both these developments received financial assistance from the Commonwealth Fund, which continued to help in this way for many years. At a later period courses on the same lines as the London one were established in Manchester and Edinburgh.

The first groups of students were employed, when qualified, mostly in Child Guidance Clinics, and work among children has continued to absorb the majority of workers coming into the field.

Psychiatric Social Workers present several interesting points of difference from other social workers, even when they are starting on their careers. They are generally only accepted for training after they have successfully completed a social science course, or have taken a relevant degree, and have also spent some time in actual social work.Thus they come to psychiatric social work as qualified and experienced people, and should enter their first jobs in the field with more *savoir faire* and status than does the newly fledged social worker in other spheres who in spite of a sometimes lengthy training is often very young and rather uncertain. Secondly, their status in relation to their colleagues in other kinds of work is high—higher apparently than that of, for example, Almoners. In the child guidance movement which has always been the most generally followed branch of work for Psychiatric Social Workers, the pattern of activity is that of a team—'medicine, psychology, and social work in the persons of psychiatrist, clinical psychologist and psychiatric social worker are all intent upon a common aim'.[1] This team work has to a great extent been reproduced in the other forms of social work, in which Psychiatric Social Workers are employed, including mental hospitals; and they are consequently much more on equal terms with other members of the team than Almoners are with the doctors with whom they work.

The third point to be noted, is that from the beginning, Psychiatric Social Workers have possessed a strong and well organized professional association; the Association of Psychiatric Social Workers was established in 1929, and obtained its first constitution in 1936. Its objects are to make a general contribution to the progress

[1] Ashdown and Brown, *Social Service and Mental Health*. Routledge, Kegan Paul, 1953.

of mental health and to raise and maintain the professional standards of psychiatric social work; any person who has successfully completed a year's recognized training in this field is eligible for membership of the association, although each applicant has to be elected by a two-thirds majority of those present at a general meeting. From its early days the Association was an energetic body with many educational and other activities, giving evidence as a group before Government Committees, such as the Feversham Committee on Voluntary Mental Health Services, and others. In 1936 one of the officers of the Association was co-opted on to the Selection Committee of the London School of Economics Mental Health Course, and ever since then the Association has co-operated in the choice of future workers. In the years just before the last war, a Policy Committee was established, and it is shown from the Annual Reports of this period that Psychiatric Social Workers were obtaining a wider recognition, and that their Association was working hard to obtain a permanent and established scale of salaries. During the war adaptation to emergency conditions was required, the demand for psychiatric Social Workers increased, and so did their range of activities. In 1944 a new Constitution came into effect, rather widening the basis of membership of the Association. By this time the contributions made by the Commonwealth Fund towards the cost of training at the London School of Economics had ceased, but the number of Psychiatric Social Workers was still increasing and the work could stand on its own feet, having more demands than workers to meet them. The Association became incorporated in 1948. By this year Psychiatric Social Workers had broadened their geographical field of operations and several of them were employed overseas. A glance at the literature of the Association of Psychiatric Social Workers shows that responsibility has always been well distributed among its members—it has a large number of sub-Committees involving a great many workers.

The year 1948 also marked the establishment of the National Health Service, which had considerable effects on the position of Psychiatric Social Workers, many of whom were employed by public authorities—though they were less affected than were Almoners. One of the most important developments was the establishment of a Whitley Council[1] to be responsible for salaries and conditions of work, and on this the Association of Psychiatric Social Workers was of course represented, and has since that time been periodically concerned with questions both of salary and status. Psychiatric Social Workers associated themselves with the Almoners in their disapproval of the Cope[2] Committee's proposal that they in common with other 'medical auxiliaries' should be included in a general register. They achieved a decision from the Ministry of Health which was conveyed to local Health Authorities that the title of Psychiatric Social Worker should be restricted to persons who had completed the recognized training in Mental Health and received a Certificate of Qualification.

The Association of Psychiatric Social Workers has thus played an important role in the evolution of this branch of social work, and it ends its story up to 1955 with a membership of 625 out of a total of 786 qualified Psychiatric Social Workers,[3] the majority of the non-members being people who are no longer working in the field of mental health, or who have retired from work altogether.

At the present time, Psychiatric Social Work holds a strong position, in spite of its comparative youth; throughout its existence, the demand for workers has

[1] Association of Psychiatric Social Workers Annual Report, 1950.
[2] CMD 8188, HMSO, 1951.
[3] Association of Psychiatric Social Workers Annual Report, 1955.

exceeded the supply, and this is probably even more true to-day than at earlier dates. But the profession is facing some of the problems with which social work in general has to deal, though perhaps to a lesser extent. The development of social work in the public services employing men and women who have had no generally recognized training does not represent any grave threat to Psychiatric Social Workers. It has always been recognized that they possess specific qualifications, and, as Ashdown and Brown point out, there has been a tendency to invest them with something akin to magical powers, owing to their alleged familiarity with the mysteries of psychiatry. Other social workers, both trained and untrained, have found Psychiatric Social workers arrogant, peculiar and irritating—as indeed have laymen—and they have been accused of regarding themselves as 'super people with a clue to some inner mystery which others lack'.[1] This has not prevented them from gaining and keeping a high status among social workers. They have also succeeded in restricting their title to men and women who have obtained a certificate from one of the recognized training centres; persons who are not qualified in this way may be and are found working in the same field, but they are not entitled to use the name of Psychiatric Social Worker.

The Association of Psychiatric Social Workers has not accepted the 'generic' or 'basic' course in Applied Social Studies as offering a suitable alternative to their normal scheme of training; they still require applicants for their work to undertake the established course. This condition might lead to the top group of social work trainees entering one of the fields of work where the 'Basic' course is regarded as adequate, and where the student could change relatively easily from one form of work to another. The supporters of the 'basic' training indeed urge as one of the points in its favour that its wider acceptance will reduce the rigid specialization, which has been increasingly characteristic of social work.

A second problem which might confront Psychiatric Social Work is that, both in this country and in the USA, it is suggested that the particular skills and knowledge which are sometimes regarded as the prerogatives of these specialists are not only applicable to the mentally abnormal or maladjusted, but are appropriate in other forms of social work—certainly in all case work, because, in the new model, relationships are the foundation of the 'helping process'. Therefore all training and education for social work ought to include a great deal of practical case work and much more psychology in its various aspects than is now the case, and, if this general training were properly organized, there would be no need for a specialized course in Psychiatric Social Work. The leaders in the latter field naturally do not look with favour on this suggestion, maintaining that their discipline is specific and ought to remain so.

It is, however, true that Psychiatric Social Workers appear to be more securely established as professional workers than those in most other branches of social work; Ashdown and Brown consider that, as far as their training and education go, they conform to the requirements of professionalism, but that in two other respects—the responsibility for increasing the body of relevant knowledge within their own sphere and for making available to those in training or outside their ranks the knowledge they already have—their claim to professional status is not so firmly established. Few workers engage in serious research, and there is little information available as to how far Psychiatric Social Workers engage in missionary activity regarding their discipline.

[1] Ashdown and Brown, *Social Service and Mental Health*. Routledge, Kegan Paul, 1953.

In the four branches of social work considered above, it would appear that as far as a clearly identifiable field of work is concerned, Moral Welfare Work and Psychiatric Social Work have the best claim to be considered as 'professions'; but the former has such varying standards, and is so loosely co-ordinated, that it is difficult to give it professional status, and it is uncertain whether many of its workers want this. The Almoners have a long and extensive training from carefully chosen applicants, but as pointed out, there is some uncertainty as to their actual field of work and some competitors in the field. Family Case Workers are again less easy to identify as professional workers; to the layman it sometimes appears that the work they do is being attempted perhaps successfully by those outside the field of trained workers. What is certain is that all these groups and many who are outside them, but included in 'social work', are struggling, along with other aspirants in other fields, to improve their status in a competitive world by gaining the cachet of 'Professional Workers'.

REFERENCES

Adrian, Lord, 'Science and Human Nature', a shortened, broadcast version of his Presidential Address to the 1954 meeting of the British Association for the Advancement of Science, *Lancet* (September 2, 1954).

Adrian, Lord, 'Organizers of Health', *British Medical Journal* (May 26, 1956).

Ahnsjö, Sven, 'Delinquency in Girls and its Prognosis', *Acta Paediatrica*, Vol. XXVIII, supplementum 3 (1941).

Ainsworth, Mary D., and Bowlby, John, 'Research Strategy in the Study of Mother-Child Separation', *Courrier* (March 1954).

Allardt, Erik, 'The Influence of Different Systems of Social Norms on Divorce Rates in Finland', *Marriage and Family Living* (November 1955).

Alstrom, Pat, 'Bureaucrats—that was the trouble with Harry . . .', *Forward* (February 15, 1957).

Andenaes, Johs, 'Recent Trends in the Criminal Law and Penal System in Norway', *British Journal of Delinquency* (July 1954).

Andry, R. G., *A Comparative Psychological Study of Parent/Child Relationships as associated with Delinquency* (Ph.D. thesis, London, 1955). Unpublished typescript.

Asher, Richard, 'Straight and Crooked Thinking in Medicine', *British Medical Journal* (August 21, 1954).

Aubry, Jenny, *La Carence de Soins Maternels* (Paris, Centre International de l'Enfance, 1955).

Bagot, J. H., *Juvenile Delinquency* (London, Cape, 1941).

Bagot, J. H., *Punitive Detention* (London, Cape, 1944).

Banister, H. and Ravden, M., 'The Environment and the Child', *British Journal of Psychology* (May 1945).

Bannister, Kathleen and others, *Social Casework in Marital Problems* (London, Tavistock Publications, 1955).

Bell, L. H. and others, 'Social and Economic Background of Children Attending L.C.C. Nutrition Clinics', *Medical Officer* (March 29, 1956).

Benson, Sir George, 'A Note on the Habitual Criminal', *British Journal of Delinquency* (January 1953).

Beres, David and Obers, Samuel J., 'The Effects of Extreme Deprivation in Infancy on Psychic Structure in Adolescence: A Study in Ego Development', *Psychoanalytic Study of the Child* (1950).

Berwick, Roxburgh and Selkirk Constabulary, *Report of the Chief Constable for the Year 1954* (Jedburgh, Chief Constable's Office, 1955).

Biggs, Jr., John, *The Guilty Mind* (New York, Harcourt, Brace, 1955).

Blacker, C. P., ed. *Problem Families: Five Inquiries* (London, Eugenics Society, 1952).

Board, Richard G., 'An Operational Conception of Criminal Responsibility', *American Journal of Psychiatry* (October 1956).

Bobroff, Allen, 'Economic Adjustment of 121 Adults, Formerly Students in Classes for Mental Retardates', *American Journal of Mental Deficiency* (January 1956).

Bodman, Frank and others, 'The Social Adaptation of Institution Children', *Lancet* (January 28, 1950).

Bosanquet, Helen, *Social Work in London, 1869 to 1912* (London, Murray, 1914).

Bourne, Harold, 'Protophrenia: A Study of Perverted Rearing and Mental Dwarfism', *Lancet* (December 3, 1955).

Bovet, Lucien, *Psychiatric Aspects of Juvenile Delinquency* (Geneva, World Health Organization, 1951).

Bowerbank, Mary W., 'Living on a State-maintained Income—II', *Case Conference* (April 1958).

Bowlby, John, *Forty-four Juvenile Thieves* (London, Baillière, Tindall and Cox, 1946).

Bowlby, John, *Maternal Care and Mental Health*, 2nd ed. (Geneva, World Health Organization, 1952).

Bowlby, John and others, 'The Effects of Mother-Child Separation: A Follow-up Study', *British Journal of Medical Psychology* (September 1956).

Britton, Clare, 'Casework Techniques in the Child Care Services', *Case Conference* (January 1955).

[Brock Report] Departmental Committee on Sterilization, *Report* (London, HMSO, 1934) (Cmd. 4485).

Bromberg, Walter, *The Mind of Man* (London, Hamish Hamilton, 1937).

Brown, Esther Lucile, *Social Work as a Profession*, 4th ed. (New York, Russell Sage Foundation, 1942).

Brown, Fred, 'Neuroticism of Institution Versus Non-Institution Children', *Journal of Applied Psychology* (1937).

Bruno, Frank J., *Trends in Social Work, 1874–1956*, 2nd ed. (New York, Columbia University, 1957).

Bunce, John Thackray, *Josiah Mason* (London and Edinburgh, Chambers, 1890).

Burgess, E. W. and Cottrell, L. S., Jr., *Predicting Success or Failure in Marriage* (New York, Prentice-Hall, 1939).

Burt, Sir Cyril, 'The Causal Factors of Juvenile Crime', *British Journal of Medical Psychology* (January 1923).

Burt, Sir Cyril, *The Young Delinquent*. 4th ed. (University of London Press, 1944, re-issued 1952).

Cambridge Department of Criminal Science, *Sexual Offences* (London, Macmillan, 1957), Vol. IX of English Studies in Criminal Science edited by Radzinowicz, Leon.

Capwell, Dora F., 'Personality Patterns of Adolescent Girls: I. Girls Who Show Improvement in IQ', *Journal of Applied Psychology* (1945).

Carr-Saunders, Sir A. M. and Wilson, P. A., *The Professions* (Oxford, Clarendon Press, 1933).

Carr-Saunders, Sir A. M. and others, *Young Offenders* (Cambridge University Press, 1942).

Carswell, Donald, ed., *Trial of Ronald True*, new ed. (Edinburgh, Hodge, 1950).

Castle, I. M. and Gittus, E., 'The Distribution of Social Defects in Liverpool', *Sociological Review* (July 1957).

Church of Scotland Youth Committee, *Youth at Leisure* (Edinburgh, the Committee, 1956).

Commissioners of Prisons, *Report* (London, HMSO, annual).

Conference on the Scientific Study of Juvenile Delinquency, London, 1949, *Why Delinquency? . . . Report . . .* (London, National Association for Mental Health, 1949).

Craig, R. N. and others, *Mental Abnormality and Crime* (London, Macmillan,

1944), Vol. II of English Studies in Criminal Science edited by Radzinowicz, Leon, and Turner, J. W. C.

Cressey, Donald R., 'The Differential Association Theory and Compulsive Crimes', *Journal of Criminal Law, Criminology and Police Science* (May–June 1954)

Criminal Statistics for England and Wales (London, HMSO, annual).

Critchley, Macdonald, ed., *The Trial of Neville George Clevely Heath* (London, Hodge, 1951).

Cunliffe, Muriel, addressing a conference held by the Association of General and Family Caseworkers, as reported in *Social Work* (London, July 1955).

Curran, Desmond, 'Psychiatry, Ltd', *Journal of Mental Science* (July 1952).

Darling, Harry F., 'Definition of Psychopathic Personality', *Journal of Nervous and Mental Disease* (February 1945).

Davidson, Henry A., 'Psychiatrists in Administration of Criminal Justice', *Journal of Criminal Law, Criminology and Police Science* (May–June 1954).

Davies, D. Seaborne and others, *The Modern Approach to Criminal Law* (London, Macmillan, 1945), Vol. IV of English Studies in Criminal Science, edited by Radzinowicz, Leon, and Turner, J. W. C.

Davis, Kingsley, 'Mental Hygiene and the Class Structure', *Psychiatry* (February, 1938).

Davis, Kingsley, 'Statistical Perspective on Marriage and Divorce', *Annals of the American Academy of Political and Social Science*, Vol. 272 (November 1950).

Davison, Evelyn H., 'Therapy in Casework', *Social Work* (London, July 1955).

Dawson, E. C., 'The Duties of a Doctor as a Citizen', *British Medical Journal* (December 18, 1954).

Departmental Committee on Persistent Offenders, *Report* (London, HMSO, 1932) (Cmd. 4090).

Donnison, David, *The Neglected Child and the Social Services* (Manchester University Press, 1954).

Donnison, David, 'Observations on University Training for Social Work in Great Britain and North America', *Social Service Review* (December 1955).

Douglas, J. W. B., 'Social Class Differences in Health and Survival during the First Two Years of Life; the Results of a National Survey', *Population Studies* (July, 1951).

Douglas, J. W. B. and Blomfield, J. M., *Children under Five* (London, Allen and Unwin, 1958).

Dunham, H. Warren, and Knauer, Mary E., 'The Juvenile Court in its Relationship to Adult Criminality', *Social Forces* (March 1954).

East, Sir W. Norwood, *An Introduction to Forensic Psychiatry in the Criminal Courts* (London, Churchill, 1927).

East, Sir W. Norwood, *Medical Aspects of Crime* (London, Churchill, 1936).

East, Sir W. Norwood, *The Adolescent Criminal* (London, Churchill, 1942).

East, Sir W. Norwood, ed., *The Roots of Crime* (London, Butterworth, 1954).

East, Sir W. Norwood and Hubert, W. H. de B., *Report on the Psychological Treatment of Crime* (London, HMSO, 1939).

Eaton, Joseph W., 'The Assessment of Mental Health', *American Journal of Psychiatry* (August 1951).

Eaton, Joseph W. and Weil, Robert J., *Culture and Mental Disorders* (Glencoe, Ill., Free Press, 1955).

Edelston, Harry, *The Earliest Stages of Delinquency* (Edinburgh, London, Livingstone, 1952).

Evaluation in Mental Health, Report of the Sub-Committee on Evaluation of Mental Health Activities, Community Services Committee, National Advisory Mental Health Council (Washington, US Department of Health, Education, and Welfare, 1955). (Public Health Service Publication, No. 413.)

Evans, Jean, *Three Men* (London, Gollancz, 1954).

Exner, Franz, *Kriminologie*, 3rd ed. (Berlin, Springer-Verlag, 1949).

Faatz, Anita J., *The Nature of Choice in Casework Process* (Chapel Hill, University of North Carolina, 1953).

Favez-Boutonier, Juliette, in address of May 18, 1954, to the Semaine Internationale de Strasbourg, May 18 to 22, 1954, *Les Orientations Nouvelles des Sciences Criminelles et Pénitentiaires* (Paris, Librairie Dalloz, 1955).

Fenichel, Otto, *The Psycho-analytic Theory of Neurosis* (London, Kegan Paul, Trench, Trubner, 1945).

Ferguson, Thomas, *The Young Delinquent in his Social Setting* (London, Oxford University Press for the Nuffield Foundation, 1952).

Ferguson, Thomas and Cunnison, James, *The Young Wage-earner* (London, Oxford University Press for the Nuffield Foundation, 1951).

Ferguson, Thomas and Cunnison, James, *In their Early Twenties* (London, Oxford University Press for the Nuffield Foundation, 1956).

Ferguson, Thomas and Pettigrew, Mary G., 'A Study of 718 Slum Families Rehoused for Upwards of Ten Years', *Glasgow Medical Journal* (August 1954).

Fernald, Mabel Ruth and others, *A Study of Women Delinquents in New York State* (New York, Century, 1920).

Feuer, Lewis Samuel, *Psychoanalysis and Ethics* (Springfield, Ill., Thomas, 1955).

Flexner, Abraham, 'Is Social Work a Profession?' *Proceedings of the National Conference of Charities and Correction*, 42nd annual session, 1915 (Chicago, Hildmann Printing, 1915).

Flugel, J. C., *A Hundred Years of Psychology, 1833–1933* (London, Duckworth, 1933, reprinted 1948).

Ford, Percy, and others, *Problem Families: Fourth Report of the Southampton Survey* (Oxford, Blackwell, 1955).

Fox, Sir Lionel, *The English Prison and Borstal Systems* (London, Routledge and Kegan Paul, 1952).

Frank, Lawrence K., 'The promotion of mental health', *Annals of the American Academy of Political and Social Science*, Vol. 286 (March 1953).

Frey, Erwin, *Der Frühkriminelle Rückfallsverbrecher* (Basel, Verlag für Recht und Gesellschaft, 1951).

Fuld, H. and Robinson, K. V., 'Malnutrition in the Elderly', *Lancet* (October 24, 1953).

Gibbens, T. C. N., 'Car Thieves', *British Journal of Delinquency* (April, 1958).

Gibbens, T. C. N. and Walker, A., 'Violent Cruelty to Children', *British Journa of Delinquency* (April, 1956).

Gibbs, D. N., *Some Differentiating Characteristics of Delinquent and Non-Delinquent National Servicemen in the British Army* (Ph. D. thesis, London, 1955) Unpublished typescript.

Gillin, J. L., 'Predicting Outcome of Adult Probationers in Wisconsin', *American Sociological Review* (August 1950).

Gittins, John, *Approved School Boys* (London, HMSO, 1952).

Glover, Edward, 'Medico-psychological Aspects of Normality', *British Journal of Psychology* (October 1932).

Glover, Edward, 'Research Methods in Psycho-analysis', *International Journal of Psychoanalysis* (1952).

Glueck, Bernard C., Jr., 'Changing Concepts in Forensic Psychiatry', *Journal of Criminal Law, Criminology and Police Science* (July–August 1954).

Glueck, Eleanor T., 'Identifying Juvenile Delinquents and Neurotics', *Mental Hygiene* (January 1956).

Glueck, Sheldon, 'Theory and Fact in Criminology', *British Journal of Delinquency* (October 1956).

Glueck, Sheldon and Eleanor T., *500 Criminal Careers* (New York, Knopf, 1930).

Glueck, Sheldon and Eleanor T., *One Thousand Juvenile Delinquents* (Cambridge, Mass., Harvard University Press, 1934).

Glueck, Sheldon and Eleanor T., *Five Hundred Delinquent Women* (New York, Knopf, 1934).

Glueck, Sheldon and Eleanor T., *Juvenile Delinquents Grown Up* (New York, The Commonwealth Fund, 1940).

Glueck, Sheldon and Eleanor T., *Criminal Careers in Retrospect* (New York, Commonwealth Fund, 1943).

Glueck, Sheldon and Eleanor T., *After-conduct of Discharged Offenders* (London, Macmillan, 1945), Vol. V of English Studies in Criminal Science, edited by Radzinowicz, Leon and Turner, J. W. C.

Glueck, Sheldon and Eleanor T., *Unraveling Juvenile Delinquency* (Cambridge, Mass., Harvard University Press for the Commonwealth Fund, 1950, re-issued 1951).

Glueck, Sheldon and Eleanor T., *Physique and Delinquency* (New York, Harper, 1956).

Goldfarb, William, 'The Effects of Early Institutional Care on Adolescent Personality', *Journal of Experimental Education* (December 1943).

Goldfarb, William, 'Effects of Psychological Deprivation in Infancy and Subsequent Stimulation', *American Journal of Psychiatry* (July 1945).

Gomberg, M. Robert, 'Criteria for Casework Helpfulness', in *Social Work in the Current Scene, 1950*, selected papers, National Conference of Social Work, 77th annual meeting, 1950 (New York, Columbia University Press for the National Conference of Social Work, 1950).

Goode, William J., *After Divorce* (Glencoe, Ill., Free Press, 1956).

Goodman, Leo A., 'The Use and Validity of a Prediction Instrument. I. A Reformulation of the Use of a Prediction Instrument', *American Journal of Sociology* (March 1953).

Greenland, Cyril, 'Unmarried Parenthood', *Lancet* (January 19, 1957).

Group for the Advancement of Psychiatry, *Criminal Responsibility and Psychiatric Expert Testimony*, Report No. 26 formulated by the Committee on Psychiatry and Law (Topeka, Kansas, Group for the Advancement of Psychiatry, 1954).

Grünhut, Max, *Juvenile Offenders Before the Courts* (Oxford, Clarendon Press, 1956).

Grygier, Tadeusz, 'Leisure Pursuits of Juvenile Delinquents: A Study of Methodology', *British Journal of Delinquency* (January 1955).

Guttmacher, Manfred S. and Weihofen, Henry, *Psychiatry and the Law* (New York, Norton, 1952).

Hadfield, J. A., *Psychology and Mental Health* (London, Allen and Unwin, 1950).

Hall, M. Penelope, *The Social Services of Modern England* (London, Routledge and Kegan Paul, 1952).

Hallas, W. A., 'A Probation Officer's Viewpoint', in a symposium 'Towards the Eradication of the Problem Family', *Journal of the Royal Sanitary Institute Transactions* (March 1953).

Hamilton, Gordon, *Theory and Practice of Social Case Work*, 2nd ed. (New York, Columbia University Press for the New York School of Social Work, 1952).

Hargrove, Aphra L., *The Social Adaptation of Educationally Subnormal School Leavers* (London, National Association for Mental Health, 1954). Mimeographed.

Hartmann, Heinz, 'Psycho-analysis and the Concept of Health', *International Journal of Psycho-analysis* (July–October 1939).

Hathaway, Starke R. and Monachesi, Elio D., 'The Minnesota Multiphasic Personality Inventory in the Study of Juvenile Delinquents', *American Sociological Review* (December 1952).

Hathaway, Starke R. and Monachesi, Elio D., *Analysing and Predicting Juvenile Delinquency with the MMPI* (Minneapolis, University of Minnesota Press, 1953).

Healy, William, *The Individual Delinquent* (Boston, Mass., Little, Brown, 1915, re-issued 1929).

Healy, William, and Bronner, Augusta F., *Delinquents and Criminals: Their Making and Unmaking* (New York, Macmillan, 1926).

Healy, William and Bronner, Augusta F., *New Light on Delinquency and its Treatment* (New Haven, Yale University for The Institute of Human Relations, 1936).

Henderson, D. K. and Gillespie, R. D., *A Text-book of Psychiatry*, 6th ed. (London, Oxford University Press, 1946).

Henriques, Sir Basil, *The Home-menders* (London, Harrap, 1955).

Hilliard, L. T. and Mundy, Lydia, 'Diagnostic Problems in the Feeble-minded', *Lancet* (September 25, 1954).

Hobson, William and Pemberton, John, *The Health of the Elderly at Home* (London, Butterworth, 1955).

Hoch, Paul H. and Zubin, Joseph, *Psychiatry and the Law* (New York, Grune and Stratton, 1955).

Hodge, R. Sessions and others, 'Juvenile Delinquency: An Electro-physiological, Psychological and Social Study', *British Journal of Delinquency* (January 1953).

Hollis, Florence, *Social Case Work in Practice* (New York, Family Service Association of America, 1939, reprinted 1948).

Hollis, Florence, 'Principles and Assumptions Underlying Casework Practice', *Social Work* (London, April 1955).

Holman, Portia, 'Some Factors in the Aetiology of Maladjustment in Children', *Journal of Mental Science* (October 1953).

Horst, Paul, and others, *The Prediction of Personal Adjustment*, Social Science Research Council Bulletin No. 48 (New York, The Council, 1941).

Housden, L. G., *The Prevention of Cruelty to Children* (London, Cape, 1955).

Howarth, Elizabeth, 'The Scope of Social Casework in Helping the Maladjusted', *Social Work* (London, July 1949).

Howarth, Elizabeth, 'The Present Dilemma of Social Casework', *Social Work* (London, April 1951).

Hudson, Anne, 'Mrs X and Her Rent Arrears', *Social Work* (London, July 1955).

Hunt, J. McV. and Kogan, Leonard S., *Measuring Results in Social Casework* (New York, Family Service Association of America, 1950, revised 1952).

Hunt, J. McV., and others, *Testing Results in Social Casework* (New York, Family Service Association of America, 1950).

Hurwitz, Stephan, *Criminology* (London, Allen and Unwin, 1952).

Institute for the Study and Treatment of Delinquency, and the Portman Clinic, Joint Committee. *Memorandum* presented to the Departmental Committee on Homosexuality and Prostitution (October 20, 1955). Mimeographed.

Irvine, Elizabeth E., 'Research into Problem Families: Theoretical Questions arising from Dr. Blacker's Investigations', *British Journal of Psychiatric Social Work* (May 1954).

Jefferys, Margot, *Mobility in the Labour Market* (London, Routledge and Kegan Paul, 1954).

Jephcott, Pearl, compiler, *Some Young People* (London, Allen and Unwin, 1954).

Jones, D. Caradog, ed., *The Social Survey of Merseyside* (University Press of Liverpool; London, Hodder and Stoughton, 1934).

Joseph, Betty, 'Psychoanalysis and Social Casework', *Social Work* (London, October 1951).

Juvenile Offences, memorandum of a Joint Committee of the Home Office (circular 807624) and the Board of Education (circular 1554) (London, HMSO, June 1941).

Kanner, Leo, *Child Psychiatry*, 2nd ed. (Oxford, Blackwell, 1948).

Kasius, Cora, ed., *Principles and Techniques in Social Casework* (New York, Family Service Association of America, 1950).

Kasius, Cora, ed., *New Directions in Social Work* (New York, Harper, 1954).

Keeton, George W. and Schwarzenberger, Georg, eds., *Current Legal Problems*, 1955 (London, Stevens, 1955).

Keith-Lucas, Alan, 'The Political Theory Implicit in Social Casework Theory', *American Political Science Review* (December 1953).

Kephart, William M., 'Occupational Level and Marital Disruption', *American Sociological Review* (August, 1955).

Kirman, Brian H., 'Research and Mental Deficiency', *Lancet* (December 14, 1957).

Kitchin, Mary, 'The Social Worker and the Social Conscience', report of a conference organized by the Association of Social Workers, *Social Work* (London, July 1952).

Kogan, Leonard S., and others, *A Follow-up Study of the Results of Social Casework* (New York, Family Service Association of America, 1953).

Kotinsky, Ruth and Witmer, Helen L., eds. *Community Programs for Mental Health* (Cambridge, Mass., Harvard University for The Commonwealth Fund, 1955).

Krapf, E. E., 'The Education of the International Sense in Children and Mental Health', *International Child Welfare Review* (1955).

Lander, Bernard, *Towards an Understanding of Juvenile Delinquency* (New York, Columbia University Press, 1954).

League of Nations, Advisory Committee on Social Questions, *Enquiry into measures of rehabilitation of prostitutes*, 4 parts (Geneva, 1938–39). Sales nos. (1938, IV. 1/2, 1939, IV. 4).

Lee, T. R., 'An Apparent Incidence of Maternal Deprivation under Normal School Conditions', a paper read at the Annual Conference of the British Psychological Society, St Andrews, 1957, quoted from an abstract in *Bulletin of the British Psychological Society* (May, 1957), Inset p. 10.

Leff, Samuel, *Social Medicine* (London, Routledge and Kegan Paul, 1953).

Lemert, Edwin M., *Social Pathology* (New York, McGraw-Hill, 1951).

Lemkau, Paul V., *Mental Hygiene in Public Health*, 2nd ed. (New York, McGraw-Hill, 1955).

Lemkau, Paul V., and others, 'The Implications of the Psychogenetic Hypothesis for Mental Hygiene', *American Journal of Psychiatry* (December 1953).

Lewis, Aubrey, 'Letter from Britain', *American Journal of Psychiatry* (December 1953).

Lewis, Aubrey, 'Health as a Social Concept', *British Journal of Sociology* (June 1953).

Lewis, Hilda, *Deprived Children* (London, Oxford University Press for the Nuffield Foundation, 1954).

Lidbetter, E. J., 'The Social Problem Group', *Eugenics Review* (April 1932).

Lidbetter, E. J., *Heredity and the Social Problem Group*, Vol. I (London, Arnold, 1933).

Liverpool City Police, *The Police and Children* (Liverpool City Police, 1956).

Logan, W. P. D., 'Social Class Variations in Mortality', *British Journal of Preventive and Social Medicine* (July 1954).

Lorenz, Konrad Z., *Man Meets Dog* (London, Methuen, 1954).

Lyons, J. F. and Heaton-Ward, W. A., compilers, *Notes on Mental Deficiency* (Bristol, Wright, 1953).

McCord, William and Joan, 'Two Approaches to the Cure of Delinquents', *Journal of Criminal Law, Criminology and Police Science* (November–December 1953).

McDonagh, Vincent P., 'A Review of the Problem, Procedure and Therapeutic Measures' in a symposium 'Towards the Eradication of the Problem Family', *Journal of the Royal Sanitary Institute Transactions* (March 1953).

Macdonald, E. K., 'Follow-up of Illegitimate Children', *Medical Officer* (December 14, 1956).

Macdonald, J. E., 'The Concept of Responsibility', *Journal of Mental Science* (July 1955).

McGregor, O. R., *Divorce in England* (London, Heinemann, 1957).

Mannheim, Hermann, *Social Aspects of Crime in England Between the Wars* (London, Allen and Unwin, 1940).

Mannheim, Hermann, *Juvenile Delinquency in an English Middletown* (London, Kegan Paul, Trench, Trubner, 1948).

Mannheim, Hermann, a review of two books by Frey, Erwin, *British Journal of Delinquency* (October 1952).

Mannheim, Hermann, *Group Problems in Crime and Punishment* (London, Routledge and Kegan Paul, 1955).

Mannheim, Hermann and others, 'Magisterial Policy in the London Juvenile Courts', *British Journal of Delinquency* (July and October 1957).

Mannheim, Hermann and Wilkins, Leslie T., *Prediction Methods in Relation to Borstal Training* (London, HMSO, 1955).

Markowe, Morris, 'Occupational Psychiatry: An Historical Survey and Some Recent Researches', *Journal of Mental Science* (January 1953).

Marzolf, Stanley S., 'The Disease Concept in Psychology', *Psychological Review* (July 1947).

Mays, John Barron, *Growing up in the City* (University Press of Liverpool, 1954).

Metfessel, Milton and Lovell, Constance, 'Recent Literature on Individual Correlates of Crime', *Psychological Bulletin* (March 1942).

Meyer, Henry J. and others, 'The Decision by Unmarried Mothers to Keep or Surrender Their Babies', *Social Work* (New York, April 1956).

Miles, Arthur P., *American Social Work Theory* (New York, Harper, 1954).

Ministry of Education, Committee on Maladjusted Children, *Report* (London, HMSO, 1955).

Ministry of Education, *The Health of the School Child*: Report of the Chief Medical Officer for the years 1952 and 1953 (London, HMSO, 1954).

Ministry of Health, *Report* for the year 1953, Part I (London, HMSO, 1954) (Cmd. 9321).

Moloney, James Clark, *Understanding the Japanese Mind* (New York, Philosophical Library, 1954).

Monachesi, Elio D., 'American Studies in the Prediction of Recidivism', *Journal of Criminal Law, Criminology and Police Science* (September–October 1950).

Monahan, Thomas P., 'Divorce by Occupational Level', *Marriage and Family Living* (November 1955).

Morris, Cherry, ed., *Social Case-work in Great Britain*, 2nd ed. (London, Faber, 1955).

Morris, J. N. and Heady, J. A., 'Social and Biological Factors in Infant Mortality: V. Mortality in Relation to the Father's Occupation, 1911–50', *Lancet* (March 12, 1955).

Morris, Norval, *The Habitual Criminal* (London, Longmans, Green, for the London School of Economics and Political Science, 1951).

Morris, T. P., *The Criminal Area* (London, Routledge and Kegan Paul, 1958).

Mure, Geoffrey, 'A Letter to Posterity, IV; An Oxford Warden to his Successor', *Listener* (January 24, 1952).

Myrdal, Gunnar, 'The Relation between Social Theory and Social Policy', *British Journal of Sociology* (September 1953).

National Assistance Board, *Report* (London, HMSO, annual).

National Assistance Board, *Reception Centres for Persons without a Settled Way of Living*, Report . . . to the Minister of National Insurance (London, HMSO, 1952).

National Commission on Law Observance and Enforcement, *Report on the Causes of Crime*, Vol. II, 'Social Factors in Juvenile Delinquency', by Shaw, Clifford, R. and McKay, Henry D. (Washington, U.S. Government Printing Office, 1931).

National Old People's Welfare Committee, *Over Seventy* (London, National Council of Social Service for the Sir Halley Stewart Trust and the National Old People's Welfare Committee, 1954).

National Society for the Study of Education, *Thirty-ninth Yearbook*, Part II (Bloomington, Ill., Public School Publishing Co., 1940).

National Society for the Study of Education, *Fifty-fourth Yearbook*, Part II (Chicago, Ill., National Society for the Study of Education, 1955).

New Trends in European Social Work: the Impact of Casework, Vienna, Astoria-Druck [1954].

New York City Youth Board, *Validation of Glueck Table for Identification of Juvenile Delinquents Based on Five Intra-family Factors* (New York, The Youth Board, Research Dept., December, 1953). Mimeographed.

O'Connor, N., 'Defectives Working in the Community', *American Journal of Mental Deficiency* (October, 1954).

O'Connor, N. and Tizard, J., *The Social Problem of Mental Deficiency* (London, Pergamon Press, 1956).

Offences Relating to Motor Vehicles, Return for 1955 (London, HMSO, 1956). House of Commons Papers (Session 1956–57) no. 5.

Ohlin, Lloyd E., *Selection for Parole* (New York, Russell Sage Foundation, 1951).

Ohlin, Lloyd E. and Duncan, Otis Dudley, 'The Efficiency of Prediction in Criminology', *American Journal of Sociology* (March 1949).

O'Kelly, Elizabeth, 'Some Observations on Relationships Between Delinquent Girls and their Parents', *British Journal of Medical Psychology* (March 1955).

Orlansky, Harold, 'Infant Care and Personality', *Psychological Bulletin* (January 1949).

Otterström, Edith, 'Delinquency and Children from Bad Homes', *Acta Paediatrica*, Vol. XXXIII, supplementum 5 (1946).

Page, Sir Leo, *The Young Lag* (London, Faber, 1950).

Pakenham, Lord, *Causes of Crime* (London, Weidenfeld and Nicolson, 1958).

Penrose, Lionel S., *The Biology of Mental Defect* (London, Sidgwick and Jackson, 1949).

Philp, A. F. and Timms, Noel, *The Problem of 'The Problem Family'* (London, Family Service Units, 1957).

Pinatel, J., *Le Pronostic du Récidivisme*, unpublished paper, prepared for the Third International Congress on Criminology, London, 1955.

Pinneau, Samuel R., 'The Infantile Disorders of Hospitalism and Anaclitic Depression', *Psychological Bulletin* (September 1955).

Pollak, Otto, *The Criminality of Women* (Philadelphia, University of Pennsylvania Press, 1950).

Porterfield, Austin L., *Youth in Trouble* (Fort Worth, Tex., Leo Potishman Foundation, 1946).

Pratt, Dallas, 'Making the Environment Respond to Basic Emotional Needs', *Psychiatry* (May 1952).

Pray, Kenneth L. M., *Social Work in a Revolutionary Age* (University of Pennsylvania, 1949).

Psychoanalysis and the Social Sciences, Vol. IV (New York, International Universities Press, 1955).

[Radnor Report] Royal Commission on the Care and Control of the Feeble-Minded, *Report* (London, HMSO, 1908) (Cd. 4202).

Rankin, T. G., 'Problem Families', *Case Conference* (September 1956).

Rapoport, Lydia, 'Towards a Definition of Social Case-work', *Social Work* (London, April 1954).

Reckless, Walter C., *The Crime Problem*, 2nd ed. (New York, Appleton-Century-Crofts, 1955).

Rees, J. Tudor and Usill, Harley V., eds. *They Stand Apart* (London, Heinemann, 1955).

Reinhardt, James M. and Harper, Fowler Vincent, 'Comparison of Environmental Factors of Delinquent and Non-delinquent Boys', *Journal of Juvenile Research* (October 1931).

Reiss, Albert J., Jr., 'Unraveling Juvenile Delinquency. II. An Appraisal of the Research Methods', *American Journal of Sociology* (September 1951).

Rich, John, 'Types of Stealing', *Lancet* (April 21, 1956).

Rich, Margaret E., 'Current Trends in Social Adjustment through Individualized Treatment', in *Report of the Third International Conference on Social Work: London, 1936* (London, Le Play House, 1938).

Richmond, Mary E., *Social Diagnosis* (New York, Russell Sage Foundation, 1917, reprinted 1925).

Richmond, Mary E., *The Long View* (New York, Russell Sage Foundation, 1930).

Robinson, Virginia P., *A Changing Psychology in Social Casework* (Chapel Hill, University of North Carolina, 1930).

Robison, Sophia Moses, *Can Delinquency Be Measured*? (New York, Columbia University Press for the Welfare Council of New York City, 1936).

Rolph, C. H., ed., *Women of the Streets* (London, Secker and Warburg, 1955).

Roper, W. F., 'A Comparative Survey of the Wakefield Prison Population in 1948', Part 1, *British Journal of Delinquency* (July 1950).

Roper, W. F., 'A Comparative Survey of the Wakefield Prison Population in 1948 and 1949', Part 2, *British Journal of Delinquency* (April 1951).

Rose, A. G., *Five Hundred Borstal Boys* (Oxford, Blackwell, 1954).

Rose, Arnold M., ed., *Mental Health and Mental Disorder* (New York, Norton, 1955).

Roudinesco, J. and Appell, Geneviève, 'De Certaines Répercussions de la Carence de Soins Maternels et de la Vie en Collectivité sur les Enfants de l à 4 ans', *Bulletins et Memoires de la Société Medicale des Hôpitaux de Paris*, Nos. 3–4 (Séance January 26 and February 2, 1951).

Rowntree, B. Seebohm and Lavers, G. R., *Poverty and the Welfare State* (London, Longmans, Green, 1951).

Rowntree, Griselda, 'Early Childhood in Broken Families', *Population Studies* (March 1955).

Rowntree, Griselda and Carrier, Norman H., 'The Resort to Divorce in England and Wales, 1858–1957', *Population Studies* (March 1958).

Royal Commission on Capital Punishment, 1949–53, *Report* (London, HMSO, 1953) (Cmd. 8932).

Royal Commission on the Law Relating to Mental Illness and Mental Deficiency, 1954–57, *Report* (London, HMSO, 1957) (Cmnd. 169).

Royal Commission on the Law Relating to Mental Illness and Mental Deficiency, 1954–57, *Minutes of Evidence* (London, HMSO, 1954–57).

Royal Commission on Lunacy and Mental Disorder, *Report* (London, HMSO, 1926) (Cmd. 2700).

Royal Commission on Marriage and Divorce, 1951–55, *Report* (London, HMSO, 1956) (Cmd. 9678).

Royal Commission on Marriage and Divorce, 1951–55, *Minutes of Evidence* (London, HMSO, 1952–56).

Ruggles-Brise, Sir Evelyn, *The English Prison System* (London, Macmillan, 1921).

Rumney, Jay and Murphy, Joseph P., *Probation and Social Adjustment* (New Brunswick, New Jersey, Rutgers University Press for Essex County Probation Office, 1952).

Schmidt, Bernardine G., 'Development of Social Competencies in Adolescents Originally Classified as Feebleminded', *American Journal of Orthopsychiatry* (January 1949).

Schneider, Alexander J. N., and others, 'Prediction of Behavior of Civilian Delinquents in the Armed Forces', *Mental Hygiene* (July 1944).

Schuessler, Karl F. and Cressey, Donald R., 'Personality Characteristics of Criminals', *American Journal of Sociology* (March 1950).

Schulz, T., 'The Means of Subsistence: Income from Earnings and from Assistance: 1935–53', *Bulletin of the Oxford University Institute of Statistics* (May, 1955).

Scott, P. D., 'Public Opinion and Juvenile Delinquency', *British Journal of Delinquency* (July 1950).

Scottish Council for Research in Education, Mental Survey Committee, *Social Implications of the 1947 Scottish Mental Survey* (University of London Press, 1953).

Scoville, Mildred C., 'An Inquiry into the Status of Psychiatric Social Work', *American Journal of Orthopsychiatry* (January 1931).

Sellin, Thorsten, *The Criminality of Youth* (Philadelphia, Pa., The American Law Institute, 1940).

Shaw, Clifford R. and McKay, Henry D., *Juvenile Delinquency and Urban Areas* (University of Chicago Press, 1942).

Shaw, L. A., 'Living on a State-maintained Income', *Case Conference* (March 1958).

Sheps, Cecil G. and Taylor, Eugene E., *Needed Research in Health and Medical Care* (Chapel Hill, University of North Carolina Press, 1954).

Shera, Jesse H., 'Classification as the basis of bibliographic organization' in Shera, Jesse H. and Egan, Margaret E., eds., *Bibliographic Organization* (University of Chicago Press, 1951).

Sheridan, Mary D., 'The Rehabilitation of Unsatisfactory Families in the Netherlands', *Public Health* (December 1955 and January 1956).

Shields, James, 'Personality Differences and Neurotic Traits in Normal Twin Schoolchildren', *Eugenics Review* (January 1954).

Simey, T. S., *Family Breakdown and Social Disorganization*, address to the Association of Children's Officers Annual Conference, 1955 (Unpublished, mimeographed).

Simey, T. S., 'Social Investigation: Past Achievements and Present Difficulties', *British Journal of Sociology* (June 1957).

Skeels, Harold M. and others, *A Study of Environmental Stimulation* (University of Iowa, 1938).

Slater, Eliot, 'The M'Naghten Rules and Modern Concepts of Responsibility', *British Medical Journal* (September 25, 1954).

Slater, Eliot and Woodside, Moya, *Patterns of Marriage* (London, Cassell, 1951).

Slawson, John, *The Delinquent Boy* (Boston, Badger, 1926).

Smith, M. Hamblin, *The Psychology of the Criminal*, 2nd ed. (London, Methuen, 1933).

Soddy, Kenneth, 'The Prevention of Juvenile Delinquency', *World Mental Health* (August 1955).

Soddy, Kenneth, ed., *Mental Health and Infant Development* (London, Routledge and Kegan Paul, 1955).

Spence, Sir James and others, *A Thousand Families in Newcastle upon Tyne* (London, Oxford University Press for the Nuffield Foundation and the Nuffield Provincial Hospitals Trust, 1954).

Spencer, John C., 'The Planning of a Social Project in Bristol', *Case Conference* (July 1954).

Spencer, John C., *Crime and the Services* (London, Routledge and Kegan Paul, 1954).

Spinley, B. M., *The Deprived and the Privileged* (London, Routledge and Kegan Paul, 1953).

Spitz, René A., 'Hospitalism: An Inquiry into the Genesis of Psychiatric Conditions in Early Childhood', *Psychoanalytic Study of the Child* (1945).

Spitz, René A., 'Hospitalism: A Follow-up Report on Investigation Described in Volume 1, 1945', *Psychoanalytic Study of the Child* (1946).

Spitz, René A., 'Anaclitic Depression: An Inquiry into the Genesis of Psychiatric Conditions in Early Childhood, II', *Psychoanalytic Study of the Child* (1946).

Spitz, René A., 'Autoerotism. Some Empirical Findings and Hypotheses on Three of its Manifestations in the First Year of Life', *Psychoanalytic Study of the Child* (1949).

Sprott, W. J. H., *The Social Background of Delinquency* (University of Nottingham, 1954) (Mimeographed, privately circulated).

Stafford-Clark, D., 'Principles and Practice in Psychiatric Treatment, II: Psychotherapy', *Case Conference* (March 1955).

Stephens, Tom, ed., *Problem Families* (London, Pacifist Service Units, 1945).

Stott, D. H., *Delinquency and Human Nature* (Dunfermline, Fife, Carnegie United Kingdom Trust, 1950).

Stott, D. H., 'Diagnosing Family Situations', *Social Work* (London, July 1954).

Stott, D. H., 'Young Offenders: A National Policy', *The Magistrate* (December, 1954).

Stycos, J. Mayone, 'A Consideration on Methodology in Research on Mental Disorder', *Psychiatry* (August 1949).

Sullenger, Thomas Earl, *Social Determinants in Juvenile Delinquency*. (Submitted . . . in the Graduate School of the University of Missouri, 1929.)

Sutherland, Edwin H., 'White-Collar Criminality', *American Sociological Review* (February, 1940).

Sutherland, Edwin H., *Principles of Criminology*, 5th ed. revised by Donald R. Cressey (Chicago, Lippincott, 1955).

Szasz, Thomas S., 'Malingering: "Diagnosis" or Social Condemnation?', *American Medical Association Archives of Neurology and Psychiatry*, 1956, Vol. LXXVI.

Tanner, J. M., 'Physique and Choice of Career', *Eugenics Review* (October 1954).

Tappan, Paul W., 'Sociological Motivations of Delinquency', *American Journal of Psychiatry* (March 1952).

The Registrar General's Decennial Supplement, England and Wales, 1951. *Occupational Mortality*, Part 2, Vol. I (London, HMSO, 1958).

The Registrar General's *Statistical Review of England and Wales, for the five years, 1946–50*. Text, Civil (London, HMSO, 1954).

The Registrar General's *Statistical Review of England and Wales for the year 1949. Supplement on Hospital In-patient Statistics* (London, HMSO, 1954).

Theis, Sophie van Senden, *How Foster Children Turn Out* (New York, State Charities Aid Association, 1924).

Thibaut, John W., 'The Concept of Normality in Clinical Psychology', *Psychological Review* (May 1943).

Thompson, Barbara, 'Social Study of Illegitimate Maternities', *British Journal of Preventive and Social Medicine* (April 1956).

Thompson, Richard E., 'A Validation of Glueck Social Prediction Scale for Proneness to Delinquency', *British Journal of Delinquency* (April 1953).

Thorpe, Louis P. and Katz, Barney, *The Psychology of Abnormal Behaviour: A Dynamic Approach* (New York, Ronald Press, 1948).

Titmuss, Richard M., 'Social Administration in a Changing Society', *British Journal of Sociology* (September 1951).

Tizard, J., 'The Prevalence of Mental Subnormality', *Bulletin of the World Health Organization* (1953).

Tizard, J., 'Institutional Defectives', *American Journal of Mental Deficiency* (October, 1954).

Tizard, J. and O'Connor, N., 'The Employability of High-grade Mental Defectives. II', *American Journal of Mental Deficiency* (July 1950).

Tómasson, Helgi, in a paper on 'Psychiatric Observation', read to the Icelandic Association of Criminalists, 1953, as reported in *Nordisk Kriminalistisk Arsbok* 1954, Introduction.

Towle, Charlotte, 'New Developments in Social Casework in the United States', *British Journal of Psychiatric Social Work* (1955, No. 2).

Tredgold, A. F., *A Text-book of Mental Deficiency* (*Amentia*), 8th ed. (London, Baillière, Tindall and Cox, 1952).

Trenaman, Joseph, *Out of Step* (London, Methuen, 1952).

United Nations, Department of Economic and Social Affairs, Bureau of Social Affairs, *The Prevention of Juvenile Delinquency in Selected European Countries* (New York, U.N., 1955). Sales no. (1955. IV. 129).

van Bemmelen, J. M., *Recidivism and the Constancy of Crime*, unpublished paper, prepared for the Third International Congress on Criminology, London, 1955.

Verkko, Veli, 'Finland's reversion to peacetime conditions with regard to criminality', address to the Association of Criminologists, Finland, 1952, as reported in *De Nordiska Kriminalist Föreningarnas Arsbok* (1951–52).

Vickers, Sir Geoffrey, 'Mental Health and Spiritual Values', *Lancet* (March 12, 1955).

Vincent, Clark E., 'The Unwed Mother and Sampling Bias', *American Sociological Review* (October 1954).

Vold, George B., *Prediction Methods and Parole* (Minneapolis, The Sociological Press, 1931).

Wall, W. D., *Education and Mental Health* (Paris, Unesco; London, Harrap, 1955).

Wallin, J. E. Wallace, *Personality Maladjustments and Mental Hygiene*, 2nd ed. (New York, McGraw-Hill, 1949).

Wattenberg, William W. and Balistrieri, James J., 'Gang Membership and Juvenile Misconduct', *American Sociological Review* (December 1950).

Wattenberg, William W. and Balistrieri, James J., 'Automobile Theft: A "Favored-Group" Delinquency', *American Journal of Sociology* (May 1952).

Whale, Margaret, 'Problem Families: The Case for Social Casework', *Social Work* (London, January 1954).

Whelan, Ralph W., 'An Experiment in Predicting Delinquency', *Journal of Criminal Law, Criminology and Police Science* (November–December 1954).

Whelan, Ralph W., *New York City Serves its Youth*, a report on the work of the Youth Board (New York City Youth Board, 1956). Mimeographed, privately circulated.

White, Robert W., *The Abnormal Personality* (New York, Ronald Press, 1956).

Williams, H. C. Maurice, 'Coping with "submerged" families', *Municipal Journal* (May 22, 1953).

Williams, H. C. Maurice, 'Laziness, low moral values: roots of "growing social menace" ', *Municipal Journal* (May 29, 1953).

Wilson, Harriett, 'Juvenile Delinquency in Problem Families in Cardiff' (unpublished typescript, 1957).

Wilson, John, *Language and the Pursuit of Truth* (Cambridge University Press, 1956).

Wofinden, R. C., 'Problem Families', *Eugenics Review* (October 1946).

Wofinden, R. C., *Problem Families in Bristol* (London, Eugenics Society and Cassell, 1950).

[Wolfenden Report] Home Office and Scottish Home Department, Committee on Homosexual Offences and Prostitution, *Report* (London, HMSO, 1957) (Cmnd. 247).

Wolff, Werner, *Contemporary Psychotherapists Examine Themselves* (Springfield, Ill., Thomas, 1956).

[Wood Report] Board of Education and Board of Control, Mental Deficiency Committee, *Report*. 3 pts. (London, HMSO, 1929, reprinted 1931).

Woodward, Mary, *Low Intelligence and Delinquency* (London, Institute for the Study and Treatment of Delinquency, 1955).

Wootton, Barbara, *Testament for Social Science* (London, Allen and Unwin, 1950).

Wootton, Barbara, 'The Ethics of the Wage Structure: Retrospect and Prospect', *Hibbert Journal* (January 1956).

Wootton, Barbara, 'Why Not Change the Schools?' *Highway* (March 1956).

Wootton, Barbara, 'Sickness or Sin?' *Twentieth Century* (May 1956).

World Federation for Mental Health, *Annual Report*, 1954 (London, WFMH., 1955).

World Health Organization, *Expert Committee on Mental Health, Report on the Second Session*, (Geneva, WHO, April, 1951) Technical Report Series No. 31.

Wright, Catherine, 'Problem Families: A Review and Some Observations', *Medical Officer* (December 30, 1955).

Wright, Catherine, in a symposium on 'Problem Families', *Eugenics Review* (April 1958).

Young, A. F. and Ashton, E. T., *British Social Work in the Nineteenth Century* (London, Routledge and Kegan Paul, 1956).

Younghusband, Eileen, 'The Past and Future of Social Work', *Social Work* (London, October, 1952).

Youth Board News (New York City Youth Board).

Zweig, Ferdynand, *The British Worker* (Harmondsworth, Middlesex, Penguin Books, 1952).

INDEX